Espenshade

# CULTURAL DIVIDES

# CULTURAL DIVIDES

## Understanding and Overcoming Group Conflict

*Deborah A. Prentice*
*and*
*Dale T. Miller*

*Editors*

RUSSELL SAGE FOUNDATION / NEW YORK

**The Russell Sage Foundation**

The Russell Sage Foundation, one of the oldest of America's general purpose foundations, was established in 1907 by Mrs. Margaret Olivia Sage for "the improvement of social and living conditions in the United States." The Foundation seeks to fulfill this mandate by fostering the development and dissemination of knowledge about the country's political, social, and economic problems. While the Foundation endeavors to assure the accuracy and objectivity of each book it publishes, the conclusions and interpretations in Russell Sage Foundation publications are those of the authors and not of the Foundation, its Trustees, or its staff. Publication by Russell Sage, therefore, does not imply Foundation endorsement.



**Library of Congress Cataloging-in-Publication Data**

Cultural divides : understanding and overcoming group conflict /
Deborah A. Prentice and Dale T. Miller, editors
p. cm.
Includes bibliographic references and index
ISBN 0-87154-690-6
1. Ethnic relations. 2. Cultural conflict—United States.
3. Intergroup relations—United States. 4. Multiculturalism—United States
5. Ethnopsychology—United States. 6. United States—Ethnic relations
I. Prentice, Deborah A. II. Miller, Dale T.
GN496.C8 1999
305.8—dc21
99-19380
CIP



The paper used in this publication meets the minimum requirements of American National Standard for Information Sciences—Permanence of Paper for Printed Library Materials. ANSI Z39.48–1992.

RUSSELL SAGE FOUNDATION
112 East 64th Street, New York, New York 10021
10 9 8 7 6 5 4 3 2 1

# Contents

# Contributors

DEBORAH A. PRENTICE is associate professor of psychology at Princeton University.

DALE T. MILLER is professor of psychology at Princeton University.

ROBERT P. ABELSON is Eugene Higgins Professor Emeritus of Psychology at Yale University.

BRENDA S. BANKER is doctoral candidate in the Psychology Department at the University of Delaware.

MARILYNN B. BREWER is professor of psychology and Ohio State Eminent Scholar in Social Psychology at Ohio State University.

SHARMAINE VIDANAGE CHELEDEN is doctoral candidate in political science at the University of California, Los Angeles.

INCHEOL CHOI is assistant professor in the Department of Psychology at the University of Illinois, Urbana-Champaign.

JACK CITRIN is professor of political science at the University of California, Berkeley.

JENNIFER CROCKER is professor of psychology at the University of Michigan, and faculty associate at the Research Center for Group Dynamics at the Institute for Social Research.

JOHN F. DOVIDIO is professor of psychology at Colgate University.

CHRISTOPHER M. FREDERICO is doctoral candidate in the Psychology Department at the University of California, Los Angeles.

GEORGE M. FREDRICKSON is Edgar E. Robinson Professor of United States History at Stanford University and codirector of the Stanford Research Institute for the Comparative Study of Race and Ethnicity.

SAMUEL L. GAERTNER is professor of psychology at the University of Delaware.

MARGARET GARNETT is doctoral candidate in political science at Yale University.

MARTIN P. GOODEN received his doctorate in psychology from Ohio State University in 1997 and is currently a research analyst at Nationwide Insurance in Columbus, Ohio.

DONALD P. GREEN is professor of political science and director of the Institution for Social and Policy Studies at Yale University.

PATRICIA GURIN is professor of psychology and women's studies at the University of Michigan, Ann Arbor.

SHEENA S. IYENGAR is assistant professor at the Columbia University Business School.

JAMES M. JONES is professor of psychology at the University of Delaware and director of the Minority Fellowship Program at the American Psychological Association.

JASON S. LAWRENCE is doctoral candidate in the Psychology Department at the University of Michigan.

MARK R. LEPPER is professor of psychology and, by courtesy, education at Stanford University.

SHANA LEVIN is assistant professor of psychology at Claremont McKenna College.

LEAH R. LIN is doctoral candidate in social psychology at Stanford University.

GRETCHEN LOPEZ is assistant professor of psychology at Syracuse University.

HAZEL ROSE MARKUS is Davis-Brack Professor in the Behavioral Sciences at Stanford University.

BIREN (RATNESH) A. NAGDA is assistant professor of social work at the University of Washington, Seattle. He is also affiliated with the Center for Multicultural Education and the Center for Environment, Education and Design Studies (CEEDS) at the University of Washington.

JASON A. NIER is doctoral candidate in the Psychology Department at the University of Delaware.

RICHARD E. NISBETT is the Theodore Newcomb Professor in the Department of Psychology at the University of Michigan.

ARA NORENZAYAN is doctoral candidate in the Department of Psychology at the University of Michigan.

TIMOTHY PENG is research associate at the Center for Home Care Policy and Research in New York, New York.

JOSHUA L. RABINOWITZ is doctoral candidate in the Psychology Department at the University of California, Los Angeles.

LEE ROSS is professor of psychology at Stanford University.

DAVID O. SEARS is professor of psychology and political science and director of the Institute for Social Science Research at the University of California, Los Angeles.

DAVID A. SHERMAN is doctoral candidate in social psychology at Stanford University.

JIM SIDANIUS is professor of psychology at the University of California, Los Angeles.

CLAUDE STEELE is Lucie Stern Professor of Psychology and chair of the Psychology Department at Stanford University.

COLETTE VAN LAAR is a postdoctoral fellow in educational studies and social psychology at Leiden University.

WILLIAM VON HIPPEL is associate professor of psychology at Ohio State University.

CHRISTINE M. WARD is doctoral candidate in the Psychology Department at the University of Delaware.

# Preface

In the spring of 1992, the president of the Russell Sage Foundation invited a group of social psychologists to a discussion about the implications of contemporary psychological research on culture and identity for predicting, understanding, and ultimately improving intergroup relations. That group, expanded and formalized somewhat as the Working Group on the Social Psychology of Cultural Contact continued to meet, with the foundation's support, for the next six years. This volume is one fruit of the group's collective efforts.

The original purpose of the working group was to use what social psychologists know about intergroup differences, perceptions, and relations to improve the outcomes of cultural contact in institutional settings. It brought together a collection of social and political psychologists with substantive interests in processes of social categorization, stereotyping, and group identification; strategies for coping with stigmatization and stereotype threat; the antecedents and consequences of cultural differences; and theories of intergroup relations. The working group gave us an opportunity to consider the implications of our work for ameliorating conflicts that arise in schools, communities, and especially workplaces. For most of us, this was a new and exciting endeavor—a chance to learn how the theories and phenomena we have investigated in the laboratory map onto real-world circumstances. The hope was that by learning more about problems of cultural contact and conflict in particular settings, we could develop new strategies for reducing intergroup conflict and improving cultural understanding.

To that end, we held a series of meetings, one at each of our home institutions in which we invited outside researchers and practitioners to educate us about the nature and outcomes of cultural contact in particular real-world contexts. One meeting, held at the University of Michigan, focused on cultural contact in the university setting and, in particular, on programs designed to reduce drop-out rates and improve academic performance among students of color. A second meeting, held at Yale University, explored the phenomenon of hate crime using evidence and observations from anti-hate-crime activists and law enforcement officers, as well as social science researchers. Several of our meetings focused on cultural contact in the workplace. We invited diversity management consultants to tell us about the problems that lead organizations to request their services and the strategies they use to address these problems. We also invited academic researchers in sociology, anthropology, and organizational behavior to tell us about their own work and about research in their disciplines on the topic of diversity in the workplace. This set of meetings was both stimulating and sobering: The problems of cultural contact in the workplace are intriguingly but unpredictably related to psychological theory and explanation. Each case is so context-bound, so particular, that it must be analyzed and addressed in its own terms. Psychological theory is certainly relevant—indeed, in some instances, critical—to understanding the outcomes of cultural contact, but the chances that any particular theory will provide insight into any particular case are quite small. These points may be common knowledge to anyone who has conducted problem-focused research in field settings, but to us, as relative newcomers to the enterprise, they were eye-opening.

In parallel with these meetings, the working group pursued an intellectual agenda, exchanging ideas, methods, and data from our own research on cultural contact and related topics. This exchange proved to be extremely valuable. As a group, we had considerable common ground. Most of us were trained as social psychologists, and thus we tended to share a similar set of assumptions and operate at a similar level of analysis. Yet we disagreed in interesting and productive ways. Nowhere was this disagreement more apparent than on the issue of when (and why) acknowledging and teaching about cultural and group differences promotes understanding, and when it increases stereotyping and intergroup differentiation. On the one hand, researchers who study the nature and consequences of cultural differences see ignorance about difference as the problem and cultural education as the solution. Their prototypical case of contact involves members of sharply different cultures (for example, Asians and European Americans), who have little history of interaction. The best strategy for improving the outcomes of cultural contact in these cases is to make both parties more knowledgeable about and therefore more tolerant of each other. On the other hand, researchers who study processes of social categorization and identity see stereotyping as the problem and establishing a common identity across groups as the solution. Their prototypical case of contact involves members of different racial or ethnic groups (for example, African- and European Americans) who have a substantial (and usually negative) history of interaction. The best strategy for improving the outcomes of cultural contact in these cases is to obscure divisive group boundaries in favor of a strong, superordinate identity. We had both the culture and identity perspectives well-represented in the working group, and the tension between these two views of cultural contact emerged quite often in our group meetings.

Our discussions gave rise to this volume. It represents our attempts to understand, explain, and predict the outcomes of increasing cultural diversity and cultural contact within American institutions. The volume reflects our history as a working group in at least two respects. First, its approach is convergent, bringing research on identity, stigmatization, culture, and politics to bear on a common set of issues and problems. The connections we are able to make across these diverse and typically separate literatures highlight the fact that we have been talking to each other for many years, attempting to bridge these conceptual boundaries. Second, the volume reflects a genuine concern with understanding cultural contact as it occurs with real groups and in real contexts. Some of the contributions make this concern explicit, analyzing contact as it occurs in particular groups and settings; others simply take particular cases of cultural contact as their starting points. Throughout, the authors maintain a very close connection between their research questions and the real-world phenomena they seek to understand.

We are indebted to many people for their assistance with this project. First and foremost, we would like to thank the Russell Sage Foundation and its president, Eric Wanner, for bringing us together and providing us with financial support. Although most of us were acquainted previously, it is safe to say that we never would have had the opportunity to profit so much from that acquaintance without the foundation's generosity. We would also like to thank the members of the foundation's Advisory Committee to the Working Group: Jennifer Crocker (whom we recruited as an author in this volume), Roy D'Andrade, Peggy Davis, and Phoebe Ellsworth. These individuals took a real interest in our activities and gave us good advice at a number of critical junctures.

Each of our home institutions hosted one meeting of the working group and provided a warm, collegial atmosphere for our activities. We are grateful to the Psychology Departments at the University of Michigan, Yale University, Princeton University, the Ohio State University, the University of California at Los Angeles, Stanford University, and the University of Delaware for their hospitality. Here at Princeton, we have been fortunate to have a succession of wonderfully talented research and administrative assistants. We thank Mary Ann Opperman, Marian Kowalewski, Jessica Haile, Carolyn Oates, Diana Usas, Jill Blettner, and

Allison Baer for their help with the book and with the group's other endeavors.

Our own chapters benefited from the comments of the members of the Race, Culture, and Inequality workshop. In addition, we are grateful to colleagues in the politics and sociology departments, especially Paul DiMaggio, Michèle Lamont, Jennifer Hochschild and Tali Mendelberg, who discussed this project with us. Finally, we thank the graduate students in the social psychology program here at Princeton, who read and commented on earlier drafts of all of the chapters. They and their colleagues hold the future of research on cultural contact, and we have written this book for them.

DEBORAH A. PRENTICE
DALE T. MILLER

# 1

# THE PSYCHOLOGY OF CULTURAL CONTACT

*Deborah A. Prentice and Dale T. Miller*

ETHNIC diversity currently preoccupies a sizable segment of U.S. society, from employers and school administrators, who must manage diversity within institutional settings, to politicians and social scientists, who must formulate policies for addressing the competing claims of different ethnic groups. The issue of diversity is fraught with anxiety. Ethnic conflicts in many countries around the world attest to the potential for relations across cultural boundaries to go seriously and destructively awry. Moreover, Americans' own struggles with race have left many pessimistic about the prospects for achieving positive, stable relations between ethnic groups. With new waves of immigrants coming from Asia and Latin America and higher birth rates among minority than majority groups, the U.S. population is becoming, and will continue to become, ethnically and culturally more diverse. Thus, how to promote positive relations across group boundaries is a question of paramount importance.

Thirty or forty years ago, psychologists thought they had an answer to this question. The contact hypothesis posited that if members of different ethnic groups interact with each other on an equal-status basis in pursuit of common goals, positive intergroup relations will result (Allport 1954). This hypothesis was so appealing that it spawned hundreds of studies designed to test and refine its claims. The results have been less than encouraging. Yes, equal-status contact can have positive results, but only if many conditions obtain: the contact should be meaningful and have the potential to extend beyond the immediate situation; the individuals should be as similar as possible on all dimensions besides group membership; the contact should be voluntary, extended in duration, and varied across contexts; and so on (for a more complete list, see Stephan 1985). In short, the main conclusion to draw from this literature is that contact between members of different ethnic or cultural groups has positive consequences if the conditions of contact are ideal. Needless to say, practitioners of positive intergroup relations have not found that conclusion terribly helpful.

From a theoretical point of view, what is striking about research on the contact hypothesis, in retrospect, is its lack of attention to the psychological processes underlying the effects of contact. Investigators have directed their work toward the more pragmatic question of how we should structure society's organizations and institutions to foster positive intergroup attitudes. In line with this pragmatic emphasis, they have sought to identify social, situational, and structural factors that moderate the effects of intergroup contact. The psychological processes that are triggered by contact and, in turn, shape the outcomes of contact have not been a central focus of the research.

Those psychological processes are the central focus here. This book explores the psychology of cultural contact. It is dedicated to the premise that what is in people's heads—how they think and feel about themselves and others, how they view changes in society, how they understand culture and diversity, and how they react to difference—plays a critical role in determining the outcomes of contact across group boundaries. This analysis certainly does not deny the importance of economic, political, and social structural factors, nor does it give causal primacy to the psychological. Indeed, several of the chapters in this volume describe ways in which structural factors, such as majority-minority status, place in the social hierarchy, and relative social power, shape individual psychology. Our claim is simply that the psychological level of analysis is also important for understanding cultural contact. What individuals think and feel matters and cannot be subsumed by these other factors.

This volume represents the attempts of a group of social psychologists to grapple with issues arising from increasing cultural diversity and cultural contact within American institutions. The individual chapters differ along many dimensions. Some make theoretical contributions; others have an empirical focus. Some describe initial results from new lines of investigation; others represent the fruits of decades of research. They vary in their scope, their theoretical orientation, and their methodology. And perhaps most strikingly, they reveal the authors' sharply different views on both the magnitude of racial and cultural problems in this country and the nature of their solutions. Despite these differences, all of the chapters reflect the conviction that psychology can help us in understanding and improving the outcomes of contact between racial and cultural groups.

## NORMATIVE ASSUMPTIONS

Before we can evaluate the implications of psychological theory and research for the improvement of intergroup contact, we need to specify the normative assumptions that guide our notions of improvement. How should members of different ethnic and cultural groups relate to one another? History provides us with four models of American ethnic relations that together serve as a useful framework for thinking about the various forms that a multicultural society might take (see Fredrickson, this volume). One is the ethnic hierarchy model, in which a dominant group claims rights and privileges not to be shared with other, subordinate groups. A second is the one-way assimilation model, in which minority groups are expected to conform to the mainstream culture to achieve full citizenship. A third is the cultural pluralism model, in which groups retain their distinctive cultures while adhering to a set of rules and understandings that enable them to live together. Finally, fourth is the group separatism model, in which culturally distinct groups withdraw from mainstream society and form autonomous, self-governing communities. Recent academic discussions of diversity have tended to favor the cultural pluralism model, although the United States is a long way from any kind of societal consensus on the matter.

Of course even if the country could agree on the desirability of cultural pluralism, numerous questions would remain. Most focus on how precisely to strike a balance between the claims of ethnic identity and the formulation and application of society-wide rules and understandings. Answers to these questions require contributions from many sources—demographers, economists, historians, sociologists, legal scholars, and political scientists all have much to offer. But for the individual level of analysis—for an understanding of how individuals function in a culturally plural context—we turn to psychologists.

## THEORETICAL CONSTRUCTS

Psychological analyses of cultural contact focus on theoretical constructs that are presumed to mediate between objective features of the environment and the individual's reaction to them. The three constructs that have been most prominent in analyses of contact and of intergroup relations more generally are social identities, collective representations, and intergroup attitudes. These constructs inform all of the contributions to this volume. We briefly describe the properties of each of them in turn.

## Social Identities

Social identities are conceptions of self and others that are derived from membership in social groups. Theories of social identity begin with the observation that people categorize themselves and others, just as they categorize other animate and inanimate objects, on the basis of salient perceptual dimensions. Distinctions of race and gender serve as obvious bases for categorization and therefore are prominent among people's social identities. Categorization is a primitive, inevitable, and, by most accounts, necessary feature of human cognition, though it is also flexible. The categorization of any particular individual depends not just on his or her characteristics but also on properties of the perceiver and the social context (see Gaertner et al., this volume).

Most theories of social identity go on to posit that people have a need to feel good about themselves and, by extension, about the social groups into which they categorize themselves. This combination of self-esteem enhancement and group identification produces a tendency to favor one's own group at the expense of other groups—so-called ingroup favoritism. Like categorization, self-esteem enhancement is viewed as primitive and inevitable, though its role in producing ingroup favoritism has been questioned (for a critique of this aspect of social identity theory, see Sidanius et al., this volume). Nevertheless, most theories agree that some ingroup-outgroup boundary is central to how people think about their social worlds and that individuals on either side of the boundary are evaluated quite differently.

A few theories of social identity take the fact of social categorization in a different direction, positing processes other than self-esteem enhancement that combine with categorization to influence intergroup relations. For example, recent work in cultural psychology and anthropology has documented the human tendency to essentialize some group differences. People believe that certain groups (such as, in the United States, racial and ethnic groups) have essences that differentiate them from each other and that make their members who they are. This tendency to see certain groups as composed of different kinds of people may contribute to the perception that differences that occur across these group boundaries are both fundamental and immutable (Miller and Prentice, this volume). It may therefore encourage participants in such disputes to adopt a strategy of withdrawal and self-segregation rather than attempt to resolve their differences by achieving common ground.

Finally, still other theories argue for the importance of the power differences that accompany social categorization. These theories assume that status hierarchies are an inevitable feature of social systems and that contact across group boundaries functions primarily to sustain status hierarchies. The most psychological of these theories traces social hierarchy to a psychological construct known as social dominance orientation: the extent to which an individual believes in the legitimacy and desirability of group-based hierarchy (Sidanius et al., this volume). Social dominance orientation contributes to the working of hierarchy-enhancing forces and hierarchy-attenuating forces within a society. These forces act in opposition, resulting in a hierarchical equilibrium that reflects a degree of group-based social hierarchy that is neither morally offensive nor structurally destabilizing.

Theories of social identity offer a psychological account for many of the observed outcomes of cultural contact. They trace these consequences to psychological processes that are inevitable and, in most cases, not subject to conscious control. Different versions of the theory hold different forms of ethnic relations to be most stable: self-esteem enhancement theories, with their focus on the divisive effects of an ingroup-outgroup boundary, suggest that harmony requires one-way (or possibly two-way) assimilation; essentialist theories suggest that pluralism produces a pull toward some degree of group separatism; and power theories argue for the inevitability of ethnic hierarchy. As regards cultural pluralism, all of the theories agree on one feature of the categorization process that makes pluralism possible: its flexibility. Although some form of categorization is inevitable, the basis of that categorization depends on many factors that are subject to modification: the perceiver's goals and expectations, the salience of particular categories, and the structure of the social context. Moreover, categorization can occur at multiple levels simultaneously, such that individuals can categorize themselves both as members of distinct ethnic groups and as members of the superordinate group, Americans (Gaertner et al., this volume; for limits on this flexibility, however, see Brewer, von Hippel, and Gooden, this volume). The flexibility of categorization is at once a source of optimism and pessimism for cultural pluralism: it suggests that this form of ethnic relations is certainly possible, but that it is inherently unstable and therefore is likely to require substantial structural support to be viable in the long run.

Virtually all of the chapters in this volume draw on these ideas about categorization and group identification, though the particular version of the theory to which they subscribe and the use they make of it differ from chapter to chapter.

## Collective Representations

Collective representations are beliefs, values, interpretive attitudes, and other habits of mind that are socially shared within a particular group, society, or culture. They include beliefs about groups and about the appropriate relation between groups; implicit theories of human nature and the causes of human behavior; and representations of self, other, and the boundary between the two. Collective representations are best conceived as properties of the group rather than of the individual members of the group. That is, individuals need not personally subscribe to the group's collective representations; they simply need to know that those representations reflect what "we" think, feel, and do.

Collective representations exert a powerful influence on the meanings and consequences of cultural contact. Perhaps the most obvious example is the deleterious effect that discriminatory stereotypes against African Americans have had on race relations in the United States. But stereotypes are not the only collective representations that play such a role. Another example is the belief in essential differences between racial and ethnic groups, which, as we already noted, influences the strategies used to deal with group conflict and the optimism with which those strategies are employed (Miller and Prentice, this volume). Still other examples are the legitimizing myths that provide moral and intellectual justification for systems of group-based social hierarchy (Sidanius et al., this volume). Relations across ethnic and racial group boundaries are regulated to a considerable extent by these collective representations of how they are and should be conducted.

Collective representations of the relative standing of different ethnic groups also have a powerful effect on the individual members of those groups, though that effect is not always simple or predictable. Consider, for example, the consequences of membership in devalued or stigmatized groups. One might expect, as many researchers initially did, that the collective representations of one's group are internalized—that is, that members of devalued groups incorporate that devaluation into their self-concepts. In fact, reactions to stigmatizing collective representations are much more complex than that. Although some groups do show a tendency to internalize disadvantage, others disengage or disidentify from the society that devalues them (see Crocker and Lawrence, this volume). Indeed, in the face of devaluation in one context, individuals show a remarkable ability to find their way to another context that affords them a more positive identity (Steele and Sherman, this volume).

Collective representations can also influence the outcome of cultural contact when that contact brings into conflict differing cultural views. For example, consider collective representations of self and other. In the United States, a highly individualistic culture, the distinction between self and other is critical. Individuals are viewed as separate and autonomous entities, free agents, whose behavior is guided by their own thoughts, feelings, and preferences. By contrast, in Japan, a more collectivistic culture, the distinction between self and other is blurred. Individuals are viewed not as bounded wholes but as fundamentally connected to one another, with behavior guided by others' thoughts, feelings, and preferences more than their own. These differences in collective representations of self and other produce striking differences in how members of these two cultures analyze the causes of an individual's behavior (Norenzayan, Choi, and Nisbett, this volume), evaluate the actions of friends and strangers (Iyengar, Lepper, and Ross, this volume), and react to choices made by self and others (Iyengar et al., this volume). It is easy to imagine how these profoundly different worldviews can generate cultural misunderstandings in contact situations.

Cultural differences have particular relevance to contact situations that involve collective representations of conflict. Cultures hold sharply different views of the meanings of conflict, the conditions under which it occurs, and the appropriate way to treat it. In European American cultures, for example, conflict is seen as arising when there is interference between the activities, beliefs, or preferences of two self-determined individuals. It is a negative state, to be avoided if possible and resolved quickly if not. The goal of that resolution is to eliminate the conflict with minimal infringement on the ideas, interests, and rights of the two conflicting parties. By contrast, in Asian and Asian American cultures, conflict is seen as a natural and inevitable outgrowth of long-term relationships. It is therefore to be managed, not avoided. Conflict management is oriented toward minimizing the negative consequences of the disagreement before it escalates to confrontation. The goal is to maintain the relationship rather than to satisfy the interests of the two conflicting parties (Markus and Lin, this volume). Again, it is easy to imagine how these different understandings of conflict can clash when they come into direct contact with each other.

As for the implications of collective representations for the viability of cultural pluralism in this country, they are equivocal. We have, in our cultural repertoire, collective representations that support this form of ethnic relations, though most Americans view the importance these representations accord to ethnic group membership with some misgivings (see Sears, Citrin, Cheleden, and van Laar, this volume). Moreover, work on cultural differences suggests that considerable cultural education is essential if we expect members of different groups to live and work together under conditions of mutual understanding and respect.

## Attitudes

Intergroup attitudes, and especially prejudice, have traditionally been the central construct in social psychological research on racial and cultural contact, both as determinants of the valence of intergroup relations and as targets of interventions. That attitudes play a critical role in intergroup relations is beyond dispute, but how much they matter, especially relative to other psychological and nonpsychological constructs, is currently a subject of considerable debate (see Green, Abelson, and Garnett, this volume).

The most well-developed account of the origins and consequences of intergroup attitudes is symbolic politics theory (Sears et al., this volume). According to this theory, people respond to ethnic groups in light of long-standing attitudes acquired through the socialization process. There is nothing inherently special about ingroup identity, nor about the distinction between ingroup and outgroup within this framework. Rather, individuals are expected to manifest a strong ethnic identity or outgroup prejudices only if the conditions of their socialization have fostered these predispositions. Socialization can as easily lead to a weak ethnic identity as a strong one; it can produce tolerance as well as prejudice.

Symbolic politics theory argues that the socialization histories of different ethnic groups have produced radically different attitudes among the members of those groups. For example, whites have been socialized to have a very weak ingroup identity, since their ethnicity has been of little significance in most regions of the country. Societal stereotypes and other collective representations have left them with generally benign outgroup attitudes, with one exception: whites have been socialized to hold strongly negative views of blacks. For blacks, by contrast, the conditions of their socialization have produced a highly crystallized ingroup identity. Their low status in society, combined with the impermeable boundaries, strict inclusion criteria (such as the "one drop" rule), and high political profile of their group, have left them with strong group consciousness and perceptions of group interest. They think and behave very much as social identity theories would predict: their relations with other groups and their politics more generally are informed—indeed, shaped—by their strong ethnic identity.

The implications of symbolic politics theory for our notions of the form that ethnic relations should take are twofold. First, the theory places no constraints on the types of political and social arrangements of which humans are capable. Its central psychological mechanism—socialization—privileges no particular arrangements over others. At the same time, the theory points to the fact that current socialization practices tend to favor some forms of ethnic relations over others. In particular, because political norms in the United States have traditionally emphasized individual over group rights, conventional socialization practices have left most Americans only modestly supportive of claims for ethnic group recognition and accommodation. As a result, cultural pluralism, American style, is likely to have a distinctly individualistic flavor.

## THE CHAPTERS

Now we turn to a more specific consideration of the chapters in this volume. They are organized into three sections, reflecting the three major questions that have animated research in this general area:

1. How important is ethnic identity to people's thoughts and feelings about themselves and others?
2. How do members of different ethnic and cultural groups differ?
3. How does the particular history of race relations in the United States shape the outcomes of cultural contact today?

### The Claims of Ethnic Identity

Our first perspective on the importance of ethnic identity is a historical one. George Fredrickson, in chapter 2, describes the varying forms that ethnic relations have taken in U.S. history. He organizes his description around the four models of ethnic relations we cited earlier: ethnic hierarchy, one-way assimilation, cultural pluralism, and group separatism models. In his analysis, these models have both descriptive and normative significance: each represents the form that relations between ethnic groups have taken at some time and place in the United States and also serves as an ideal-type model of the form these relations might take in the future. Fredrickson ends the chapter with an expression of the prevailing view, at least in the academy, that cultural pluralism is indeed the most promising alternative.

In chapter 3, David Sears and his colleagues evaluate the claim that increasing ethnic diversity in this country will inevitably lead to ethnic balkanization. This claim rests on the assumption that increasing diversity produces more ethnic tension and more negative attitudes toward members of other ethnic groups. In addition, it heightens the salience of one's own ethnicity and increases support for group-rights systems of political representation. Do we see this pattern occurring in the United States? Sears and his colleagues bring data from public opinion surveys to bear on this question. They find that increasing diversity is producing more tension and polarization around political issues particularly relevant to minorities. But they do not find any increase in outgroup antagonism, ethnic self-identification, or support for political systems organized around group rights. Instead, they find an older pattern of anti-black sentiment among a sizable proportion of the white population, a prejudice that dictates these people's attitudes toward policies affecting any minority group.

In chapter 4, Jim Sidanius and his colleagues provide an overview of social dominance theory, a far-reaching account of ingroup favoritism and outgroup derogation. As we described earlier, social dominance theory analyzes status hierarchies as an inevitable feature of social systems and argues that contact across group boundaries functions primarily to sustain these hierarchies. At the individual level, hierarchies are controlled by social dominance orientation. The most provocative and controversial claim of this theory is that differences in the degree of hierarchy within any institution, organization, or society can be traced to differences in the social dominance orientation of its members. In their contribution, Sidanius and his colleagues provide an overview of their theory and contrast it to its two most prominent competitors: social identity theory and symbolic politics theory.

The final chapter in this section, by Patricia Gurin, Timothy Peng, Gretchen Lopez, and Ratnesh Nagda, offers a sharply different and much more optimistic view of pluralism than do Sidanius and his colleagues. These investigators contend that diversity and group identity can, under certain circumstances, be congenial to democracy and community. They report on the Intergroup Relations, Conflict, and Community Program, a curricular and living-learning program aimed at helping students understand the relationship between groups and democracy. The program incorporates elements of many psychological approaches to improving intergroup relations (for example, many of the conditions identified in investigations of the contact hypothesis) but also focuses more heavily than most approaches on difference and on making group boundaries salient. The chapter examines the impact of this program on intergroup perceptions, attitudes, and behaviors. It also examines the role of preexisting power differentials, hypothesizing that group identity is threatening for members of dominant but not of subordinate groups.The results Gurin and her colleagues report attest to the importance of both of these factors. Their research serves as an experiment in cultural pluralism. Can we acknowledge and celebrate group differences and still have unity?

## Cultural Differences: Real and Imagined

The next set of chapters is concerned with cultural differences. Psychological research on the perception of differences between groups has tended to focus on error—either the overestimation of differences that are in fact trivial or nonexistent, or the underestimation (or failure to appreciate) of differences that are significant. And consistent with the liberal politics and pragmatism that have characterized research in this area, both theory and data have focused either on real differences that are benign in content or on imagined differences that are invidious in content. We begin the section with two chapters on the overperception of difference.

In chapter 6, Samuel Gaertner and his colleagues review their program of research on the Common Ingroup Identity Model. The goal of this model is to explore how we can utilize the cognitive processes that usually produce intergroup bias—especially the processes of categorization—to produce an intergroup structure that reduces the perception of invidious differences between groups. In particular, these researchers show that inducing members of different groups to think of themselves in terms of a superordinate group identity—one that they share—leads them to think about, feel, and act more positively toward each other. Moreover, invoking this superordinate identity does not require individuals to forsake their subgroup identities. Indeed, for some outcomes (such as generalization of positive attitudes and behaviors beyond the immediate situation), recognizing both connection (superordinate group identity) and difference (original subgroup identity) is optimal.

In chapter 7, Dale Miller and Deborah Prentice present the category divide hypothesis: the claim that a difference will seem wider, more pervasive, and more difficult to resolve when it occurs between members of different social groups than between members of the same social group. The logic of this hypothesis is as follows: People's perceptions of the magnitude, pervasiveness, and mutability of a difference between two individuals depend on what they see as the source of that difference. When they encounter a difference between members of different social groups, group membership provides one obvious answer to the question, why do these two people differ? And when the groups in question are seen as differing in their essences—as defining different social kinds—then the difference is seen as a chasm, across which no bridge can be built. So the category divide hypothesis does not apply to differences between all social groups, only those that people essentialize. It provides a psychological account for the pessimism people have about the possibility of resolving differences across group boundaries.

The remaining three chapters in this section document real, psychological differences between members of different cultures. In chapter 8, Ara Norenzayan, Incheol Choi, and Richard Nisbett seek to uncover the true nature of cultural differences in social inference. Previous studies have shown that members of East Asian cultures are much less likely to commit the "fundamental attribution error"—that is, to overestimate the extent to which an individual's behavior reflects his or her dispositions, beliefs, or preferences rather than something about the situation or context in which the behavior occurred—than are members of Western cultures (see Miller 1984). In this chapter, the authors probe more specifically the locus of the difference. Is it that people engaged in European American cultural contexts think less dispositionally than people engaged in East Asian cultural contexts? That Westerners are less sensitive to situational information than are Easterners? They find that both Easterners and Westerners think dispositionally; the two cultures converge on the extent to which dispositional information is used to explain and predict the behavior of others. Where they diverge is in the extent to which they consider situational information as well. Westerners simply do not, regardless of how salient or predictive the situational information might be. Easterners, on the other hand, take situational factors into account when information about those factors is available (and especially when it is salient).

In chapter 9, Sheena Iyengar, Mark Lepper, and Lee Ross document cultural differences in how individuals represent the social world. Their primary claim is that in European American cultures contexts the boundary between the self and another person (any other person) is primary, whereas in East Asian cultures the boundary between the ingroup (the self and other members of important groups) and the outgroup is primary. To test this claim, the authors adapted a number of research paradigms that have been used to demonstrate self-other differences among members of Western cultures and added a distinction between ingroup and outgroup others. For example, their first study was concerned with trait ascription. Previous research has shown that Westerners assign more traits to others than to self. The authors asked students of Caucasian and Asian descent to assign traits to self, an ingroup member, and an outgroup member. The results showed that Caucasian students assigned fewer traits to self than to ingroup or outgroup members, but that Asian students assigned fewer traits to self and ingroup members than to outgroup members. A similar pattern was shown for attributional charity (Asian students show charity to ingroup members as well as self) and for intrinsic motivation (Asian students are intrinsically motivated by ingroup member choices as well as their own).

Finally, in chapter 10, Hazel Markus and Leah Lin suggest that most models of contact and conflict among groups are rooted in European American and particularly Anglo-American collective representations of conflict and are tied to specific European American understandings of the source, nature, and consequences of conflict. In an effort to reveal that contact and conflict can be understood and modeled in a diversity of ways, they stitch together a widely scattered set of observations and findings to describe some practices and meanings of conflict in four different cultural contexts: European American, Asian American, Mexican American, and African American. The European and Asian cases follow directly from the differences in conceptions of self and other documented by Iyengar and her colleagues in chapter 9 and also by Markus and her colleagues in earlier work (see Markus and Kitayama 1991). But the other two cases are more complex and not as well captured by the familiar distinctions between individualistic and collectivistic psychologies. In Mexican American culture, conflict is defined as a loss of harmony between individuals. Status differences are critical, as is *simpatía:* the ability to respect and understand another's feelings. Conflict occurs in a context in which people are striving to maintain harmonious, unequal relationships, and as a result, Mexicans try to avoid conflict if at all possible. When avoidance strategies fail, confrontational discussions do occur. However, these confrontations maximize the possibility of reestablishing harmony. The final goal in the Mexican American context is a mutual coordination of feelings rather than the resolution of an issue. By contrast, in African American culture, the meaning of conflict is simultaneously individual and relational. It is conceived as individuals having differing points of view, but the focus is on the discrepancy, rather than on the consequences of the discrepancy. In African American cultural contexts, people tend to confront others about points of disagreement in an attempt to resolve the problem that initially caused the disagreement. But unlike in European American contexts, resolution depends on the compelling presentation of arguments rather than on attempts to appeal to some objective truth.

Taken together, the five chapters in this section offer strikingly different answers to the question of what drives cultural groups apart. Chapter 6 by Gaertner and his colleagues, and especially our own contribution (chapter 7), suggest that by overgeneralizing differences between ourselves and particular members of other cultural groups, or by failing to recognize the superficiality of these differences, we frequently forego opportunities for productive engagement and reconciliation. By contrast, the three chapters on cultural differences suggest that by failing to recognize that an interpersonal difference is cultural or by misinterpreting its cultural meaning, we frequently create occasions of miscommunication and alienation. It is easy to say that individuals should strive to avoid both of these errors, but the inherent tension between them makes this goal difficult to achieve. Indeed, the higher the threshold one sets for avoiding one error, the lower the threshold necessarily becomes for making the other. This tension also exists for researchers who study the real and perceived bases of cultural differences, for by choosing to study one error over the other, they run the risk of either overlooking real cultural differences or reifying superficial or illusory ones.

## The Psychology of Race in the United States

The final section of the book contains a diverse set of chapters that deal with the psychology of race in the United States. It begins, in chapter 11, with Marilynn Brewer and her colleagues addressing the question of how newcomers to an organization—in this case, students entering college—are incorporated into the organizational structure and culture. The authors are especially interested in how the outcomes and processes underlying this incorporation vary depending on whether the newcomers are Caucasian or members of a non-Asian ethnic minority group. Thus, they examine whether the relation between identification with one's ethnic group and identification with the university differs for members of majority and minority groups. The results from two studies, one conducted at the University of Michigan and the other at UCLA, indicate that it does. For whites, the relation between ethnic identification and institutional identification is zero; for ethnic minorities, the relation is negative. These findings call into question the optimism that Gaertner and his colleagues have about dual identities. In many contexts, ethnic minorities may find (or at least perceive) that their ethnic identities conflict with superordinate institutional or organizational identities. In these cases, they may not be able to adopt a dual identity and thereby receive the benefits of both connection and difference.

In chapter 12, Jennifer Crocker and Jason Lawrence attempt to account for a puzzle: Why is it that members of stigmatized groups—especially African Americans—do not have low self-esteem? Surveys show that blacks have levels of self-esteem comparable to those of whites, even though the feedback about themselves they get through interactions with others has to be considerably more negative. Do these results indicate that the prevailing theories of self-esteem, which point to the importance of reflected appraisal, are misguided? And how can these theories account for the fact that Asian Americans—a successful minority group, by many standards—have significantly lower self-esteem than members of other groups? The solution to this puzzle, according to the authors, is that whites, blacks, and Asians base their self-esteem on different sources of information. In particular, whites and Asians base their self-esteem on others' approval to a much greater extent than do blacks. Blacks show a pattern of more internal and less contingent sources of self-esteem. As a result, they are better insulated against the effects of devaluation and discrimination.

Chapter 13 addresses a similar theme from a very different perspective. Claude Steele and David Sherman present what they term the "afforded psychology" of welfare mothers, afforded in the sense that it is a response to a life situation that enables the development of some psychological characteristics more than others. This afforded psychology has two major features: a strong commitment to self-sufficiency and independence (in the sense of not being economically dependent on other people in their lives), and a lack of trust in the available opportunity structure. Steele and Sherman present the results of interviews with twenty women at a homeless shelter in the Bronx. They use these interviews to substantiate their psychological model and to explore more broadly the bases of these women's sense of identity and self-esteem. In the latter connection, their results complement those of Crocker and Lawrence: the factors they identify as important to participants' identity and sense of self-worth are very different from those identified in previous studies using college-student populations. More generally, their analysis serves as an excellent example of how social psychologists approach social problems, a contribution that is most evident in the section that compares their theory with other social science theories of welfare dependency.

We turn, in chapter 14, from welfare mothers to white supremacists and hate-crime perpetrators. Donald Green, Robert Abelson, and Margaret Garnett report the results of a survey designed to compare systematically the views of hate-crime perpetrators, white supremacists, and the general public. Respondents were people known to have participated in hate-crime activity in North Carolina between 1986 and 1995, and a comparison sample drawn from the general population in North Carolina. Results show that white supremacists and hate-crime perpetrators are not notably more frustrated economically or more pessimistic about the financial futures of their communities than are ordinary people. But, they fear diversity: the specter of race-mixing, immigration, and the blurring of gender roles looms much larger in their minds than in the minds of the general public. It is their discomfort with social change, rather than heightened feelings of economic resentment, that sets these individuals apart.

Finally, in chapter 15, James Jones offers a theoretical perspective on race, culture, and intergroup relations that unites many of the ideas in the foregoing chapters. He argues that most analyses of racism have defined it as a belief in the biological inferiority of others (most commonly, African Americans) compared to the self (most commonly, European Americans). In so doing, they have ignored what Jones terms "cultural racism": the belief that another's culture is inferior to one's own. Jones argues that recent attempts to combat biological racism have left cultural racism relatively intact. He describes the nature of cultural racism and examines its consequences for African Americans and for race relations in this country.

## PARTICULARISM IN SOCIAL PSYCHOLOGY

The chapters in this volume have significance beyond their substantive contributions; they also reflect a paradigm shift that has occurred in social psychology over the last two decades. Traditionally (and somewhat stereotypically), social psychologists have seen themselves as engaged in the discovery of the universal principles and invariant processes underlying social behavior. Their goal has been to identify psychological laws that hold across all people in all times and all places. They have viewed individual differences, including those arising from social group membership, as a nuisance—a threat to the universality of the process in question. When confronted with such differences, their typical strategy has been to identify a psychological variable that can explain the difference as yet another manifestation of the underlying (and invariant) process. Thus, gender differences have been traced to differences in influenceability, interpersonal sensitivity, or emotionality; race differences to differences in liberalism, anxiety, or reactions to a white experimenter; cultural differences to differences in individualism or collectivism; and so on. To the extent that researchers have examined individual differences, it has been as a way of studying a common, underlying psychology.

In recent years, there has been a fundamental change in how social psychologists think about individual and group differences. Instead of seeing them as a nuisance to be explained away, researchers increasingly view them as the heart of the matter, the substantive findings of interest. The most extreme advocates of this point of view argue that at least some differences between social groups provide us with evidence of separate psychologies. These researchers (including several represented in this volume) have moved away from the pursuit of universal processes that operate for all people; they maintain that at least some observed group differences demarcate qualitatively different ways of thinking. A more moderate position holds that these differences may or may not define separate psychologies, but they certainly are interesting. In this view, evidence for differences across well-defined social boundaries indicates, at the very least, that a study is capturing something important and meaningful about people's real-life experiences.

This shift in how social psychologists interpret difference is, in large part, a result of increasing cultural diversity, both in the worlds that researchers inhabit and in the populations from which they draw their research participants. Studies that have included men and women, blacks and whites, Japanese and Americans, have turned up evidence for psychological differences between these groups that cannot be easily reconciled with universalist notions. As a result, social psychological theories are becoming more particularistic, and gender, racial, and cultural differences are becoming topics worthy of study in their own right.

The chapters in this volume reflect this growing particularism. In them, we learn that members of different ethnic groups have sharply different political dispositions (Sears et al.); that the determinants of their academic achievement and self-esteem differ (Brewer et al.; Crocker and Lawrence); and that their experiences of a college campus differ (Gurin et al.). We learn that not all social categories are perceived similarly—some are essentialized (Miller and Prentice). We learn that different cultures offer strikingly different analyses of the causes of human behavior (Norenzayan et al.), see themselves in different relations to their ingroups (Iyengar et al.), and approach conflict in different ways (Markus and Lin). And we learn about the distinctive psychologies of white supremacists (Green et al.) and welfare mothers (Steele and Sherman).

Another aspect of this paradigm shift has been an increasing eclecticism on the methodological side. This change, too, is reflected in the research presented in this volume. Although some of the chapters describe the results of traditional laboratory experiments, these are the minority. Most use survey methods to tap into individuals' thoughts and experiences in context. Some use cultural comparisons, both to identify cultural differences that might arise in multicultural contact settings and to provide insight into our own culture through comparison with another. Some provide in-depth analyses of particular groups using survey and interview techniques. And a number use multiple methodologies to test the various predictions of their theoretical frameworks.

Of course, not all social psychologists have embraced this new particularism. Many of them still orient their research toward the discovery of universal psychological processes; many still seek out psychological variables that can explain away individual and group differences; and many, perhaps most, still conduct the majority of their research in the laboratory. But there is no question that the field is more tolerant of particularism now than in the past, and that tolerance has opened the way to new theories of cultural contact, more eclectic methodological approaches, and stronger connections to research in anthropology, sociology, and other social sciences.

## PRESCRIPTIONS FOR AMELIORATING GROUP CONFLICT

Finally, the chapters in this volume have important implications for ameliorating group conflict. Conventional wisdom in social psychology has emphasized the inherent divisiveness of group boundaries. In the best-known demonstration of this point, Muzafer Sherif and his colleagues found that simply dividing twenty-two previously unacquainted boys into two groups of eleven and placing the groups in competition resulted in the bitterest kind of intergroup conflict and hostility (Sherif et al. 1961). Subsequent research has demonstrated that competition is not necessary to produce antagonism between groups: even dividing people according to a meaningless criterion leads them to favor members of their own group at the expense of other groups (Tajfel and Turner 1986). These and many similar findings have led social psychologists to a very pessimistic position on intergroup relations. As Roger Brown (1986) summarized: "Conflict between groups is like a sturdy three-legged stool. It is sturdy because two legs are universal ineradicable psychological processes, ethnocentrism and stereotyping, and the third leg is a state of society, unfair distribution of resources, which has always existed everywhere" (533).

The recommendations for improving intergroup relations that have emerged from this literature focus on obscuring group boundaries and emphasizing commonalities. These recommendations are grounded in strong empirical evidence: numerous studies have demonstrated that groups get along better to the extent that they are similar—in status, attitudes, goals, procedures, friends, enemies, and so on. The best example of this approach in the present volume is the work of Gaertner and his colleagues, which has demonstrated quite convincingly the positive consequences of a common ingroup identity. Several of the other chapters take a similar perspective on promoting intergroup harmony.

But most of the chapters challenge the idea that we can or should deemphasize group differences. They offer evidence for the inevitability of group differentiation, the psychological importance of ethnic identity, and the reality and ubiquity of cultural differences. They suggest that attempts to emphasize common ground will often fail (a fact to which many practitioners of positive intergroup relations can attest). And some even call into question the morality of obscuring, rather than celebrating, group differences. In short, the message that emerges from this volume is that any strategy for ameliorating group conflict and promoting intergroup harmony will have to embrace cultural pluralism and acknowledge diversity.

We are left, then, with the question of how to recognize and appreciate ethnic and cultural differences without reifying divisive group boundaries. This question is considerably more complex and difficult to answer than the one with which social psychologists began research on cultural contact almost a half-century ago. But we believe that this formulation represents real progress in the field's efforts to understand and overcome group conflict. We hope that our volume will contribute to this ongoing project.

## REFERENCES

Allport, Gordon. (1954). *The nature of prejudice.* Cambridge, Mass.: Addison-Wesley.

Brown, Roger. (1986). *Social psychology.* 2nd ed. New York: Free Press.

Markus, Hazel, and Kitayama, Shinobu. (1991). Culture and self: Implications for cognition, emotion, and motivation. *Psychological Review, 98,* 224–53.

Miller, Joan. (1984). Culture and the development of everyday social explanation. *Journal of Personality and Social Psychology, 46,* 961–78.

Sherif, Muzafer., Harvey, O. J. , White, B. Jack, Hood, William, and Sherif, Carolyn. (1961). *Intergroup Conflict and Cooperation: The Robbers Cave Experiment.* Norman: University of Oklahoma Book Exchange.

Stephan, Walter. (1985). Intergroup Relations. In Gardner Lindzey and Elliot Aronson (eds.), *The handbook of social psychology* (3rd ed., vol. 2, pp. 599–658). New York: Random House.

Tajfel, Henri, and Turner, John. (1986). The social identity theory of intergroup behavior. In Stephen Worchel and William Austin (Eds.), *Psychology of intergroup relations* (2nd ed., pp. 7–25). Chicago: Nelson-Hall.

# Part I

## THE CLAIMS OF ETHNIC IDENTITY

# 2

# MODELS OF AMERICAN ETHNIC RELATIONS: A HISTORICAL PERSPECTIVE

*George M. Fredrickson*

THROUGHOUT its history, the United States has been inhabited by a variety of interacting racial or ethnic groups. In addition to the obvious "color line" structuring relationships between dominant whites and lower-status blacks, Indians, and Asians, there have at times been important social distinctions among those of white or European ancestry. Today we think of the differences between white Anglo-Saxon Protestants and Irish, Italian, Polish, and Jewish Americans as purely cultural or religious, but in earlier times these groups were sometimes thought of as "races" or "subraces"—people possessing innate or inborn characteristics and capabilities that affected their fitness for American citizenship. Moreover, differences apparently defined as cultural have sometimes been so reified as to serve as the functional equivalent of physical distinctions. Indians, for example, were viewed by most nineteenth-century missionaries and humanitarians as potentially equal and similar to whites. Their status as noncitizens was not attributed to skin color or physical appearance; it was only their obdurate adherence to "savage ways" that allegedly stood in the way of their possessing equal rights and being fully assimilated. Analogously, conservative opponents of affirmative action and other antiracist policies in the 1990s may provide a "rational" basis for prejudice and discrimination by attributing the disadvantages and alleged shortcomings of African Americans to persistent cultural "pathology" rather than to genetic deficiencies (D'Souza 1995).

It can therefore be misleading to make a sharp distinction between race and ethnicity when considering intergroup relations in American history. As I have argued extensively elsewhere, ethnicity is "racialized" whenever distinctive group characteristics, however defined or explained, are used as the basis for a status hierarchy of groups who are thought to differ in ancestry or descent (Fredrickson 1997, ch. 5).

Four basic conceptions of how ethnic or racial groups should relate to each other have been predominant in the history of American thought about group relations—ethnic hierarchy, one-way assimilation, cultural pluralism, and group separatism. This chapter provides a broad outline of the historical career of each of these models of intergroup relations, noting some of the changes in how various groups have defined themselves or been defined by others.

## ETHNIC HIERARCHY

Looking at the entire span of American history, we find that the most influential and durable conception of the relations among those American racial or ethnic groups viewed as significantly dissimilar has been hierarchical. A dominant group—conceiving of itself as society's charter membership—has claimed rights and privileges not to be fully shared with outsiders or "others," who have been characterized as unfit or unready for equal rights and full citizenship. The hierarchical model has its deepest roots and most enduring consequences in the conquest of Indians and the enslavement of blacks during the colonial period (Axtell 1981; Jordan 1968). But it was also applied in the nineteenth century to Asian immigrants and in a less severe and more open-ended way to European immigrants who differed in culture and religion from old-stock Americans of British origin (Higham 1968; Miller 1969). The sharpest and most consequential distinction was always between "white" and "nonwhite." The first immigration law passed by Congress in 1790 specified that only white immigrants were eligible for naturalization. This provision would create a crucial difference in the mid-nineteenth century between Chinese "sojourners," who could not become citizens and voters, and Irish immigrants, who could.

Nevertheless, the Irish who fled the potato famine of the 1840s by emigrating to the United States also encountered discrimination. Besides being Catholic and poor, the refugees from the Emerald Isle were Celts rather than Anglo-Saxons, and a racialized discourse, drawing on British precedents, developed as an explanation for Irish inferiority to Americans of English ancestry (Knobel 1986). The dominant group during the nineteenth and early twentieth centuries was not simply white but also Protestant and Anglo-Saxon. Nevertheless, the Irish were able to use their right to vote and the patronage they received from the Democratic Party to improve their status, an option not open to the Chinese. Hence, they gradually gained the leverage and respectability necessary to win admission to the dominant caste, a process that culminated in Al

Smith's nomination for the presidency in 1928 and John F. Kennedy's election in 1960.

The mass immigration of Europeans from eastern and southern Europe in the late nineteenth and early twentieth centuries inspired new concerns about the quality of the American stock. In an age of eugenics, scientific racism, and social Darwinism, the notion that northwestern Europeans were innately superior to those from the southern and eastern parts of the continent—to say nothing of those light-skinned people of actual or presumed west Asian origin (such as Jews, Syrians, and Armenians)—gained wide currency. A determined group of nativists, encouraged by the latest racial "science," fought for restrictive immigration policies that discriminated against those who were not of "Nordic" or "Aryan" descent (Higham 1968). In the 1920s the immigration laws were changed to reflect these prejudices. Low quotas were established for white people from nations or areas outside of those that had supplied the bulk of the American population before 1890. In the minds of many, true Americans were not merely white but also northern European. In fact, some harbored doubts about the full claim to "whiteness" of swarthy immigrants from southern Italy.

After immigration restriction had relieved ethnic and racial anxieties, the status of the new immigrants gradually improved as a result of their political involvement, their economic and professional achievement, and a decline in the respectability of the kind of scientific racism that had ranked some European groups below others. World War II brought revulsion against the genocidal anti-Semitism and eugenic experiments of the Nazis, dealing a coup de grâce to the de facto hierarchy that had placed Anglo-Saxons, Nordics, or Aryans at the apex of American society. All Americans of European origin were now unambiguously white and, for most purposes, ethnically equal to old-stock Americans of Anglo-Saxon, Celtic, and Germanic ancestry. Hierarchy was now based exclusively on color. Paradoxically, it might be argued, the removal of the burden of "otherness" from virtually all whites made more striking and salient than ever the otherness of people of color, especially African Americans.

The civil rights movement of the 1960s was directed primarily at the legalized racial hierarchy of the southern states. The Civil Rights Acts of 1964 and 1965 brought an end to government-enforced racial segregation and the denial of voting rights to blacks in that region. But the legacy of four centuries of white supremacy survives in the disadvantaged social and economic position of blacks and other people of color in the United States. The impoverished, socially deprived, and physically unsafe ghettos, barrios, and Indian reservations of this nation are evidence that ethnic hierarchy in a clearly racialized form persists in practice if not in law.

## ONE-WAY ASSIMILATION

Policies aimed at the assimilation of ethnic groups have usually assumed that there is a single and stable American culture of European, and especially English, origin to which minorities are expected to conform as the price of admission to full and equal participation in the society and polity of the United States (Gordon 1964, ch. 4). Assimilationist thinking is not racist in the classic sense: it does not deem the outgroups in question to be innately or biologically inferior to the ingroup. The professed goal is equality—but on terms that presume the superiority, purity, and unchanging character of the dominant culture. Little or nothing in the cultures of the groups being invited to join the America mainstream is presumed worthy of preserving. When carried to its logical conclusion, the assimilationist project demands what its critics have described—especially in reference to the coercive efforts to "civilize" Native Americans—as "cultural genocide."

Estimates of group potential and the resulting decisions as to which groups are eligible for assimilation have varied in response to changing definitions of race. If an ethnic group is definitely racialized, the door is closed because its members are thought to possess ineradicable traits (biologically or culturally determined) that make them unfit for inclusion. At times there have been serious disagreements within the dominant group about the eligibility of particular minorities for initiation into the American club.

Although one-way assimilationism was mainly a twentieth-century ideology, it was anticipated in strains of nineteenth-century thinking about Irish immigrants, Native Americans, and even blacks. Radical white abolitionists and even some black antislavery activists argued that prejudice against African Americans was purely and simply a result of their peculiarly degraded and disadvantaged circumstances and that emancipation from slavery would make skin color irrelevant and open the way to their full equality and social acceptability (Fredrickson 1987, ch. 1). These abolitionists had little or no conception that there was a rich and distinctive black culture that could become the source of a positive group identity, and that African modes of thought and behavior had been adapted to the challenge of surviving under slavery.

If the hope of fully assimilating blacks into a color-blind society was held by only a small minority of whites, a majority probably supposed that the Irish immigrants of the 1840s and 1850s could become full-fledged Americans, if they chose to do so, simply by changing their behavior and beliefs. The doctrine of the innate inferiority of Celts to Anglo-Saxons was not even shared by all of the nativists who sought to slow down the process of Irish naturalization (Knobel 1986). A more serious problem for many of them was the fervent Catholicism of the Irish; Anglo-Protestant missionaries hoped to convert them en masse. The defenders of unrestricted Irish immigration came mostly from the ranks of the Democratic Party, which relied heavily on Irish votes. Among them were strong believers in religious toleration and a high wall of separation between church and state. They saw religious diversity as no obstacle to the full and rapid Americanization of all white-skinned immigrants.

The most sustained and serious nineteenth-century effort to assimilate people who differed both culturally and phenotypically from the majority was aimed at American Indians. Frontier settlers, military men who fought Indians, and many other whites had no doubts that Indians were members of an inherently inferior race that was probably doomed to total extinction as a result of the conquest of the West. Their views were graphically expressed by General Philip Sheridan when he opined that "the only good Indian is a dead Indian." But an influential group of eastern philanthropists, humanitarian reformers, and government officials thought of the Indians as having been "noble savages" whose innate capacities were not inferior to those of whites. Thomas Jefferson, who had a much dimmer view of black potentialities, was one of the first to voice this opinion (Koch and Peden 1944, 210–11). For these ethnocentric humanitarians, the "Indian problem" was primarily cultural rather than racial, and its solution lay in civilizing the "savages" rather than exterminating them. Late in the century, the assimilationists adopted policies designed to force Indians to conform to Euro-American cultural norms; these included breaking up communally held reservations into privately owned family farms and sending Indian children to boarding schools where they were forbidden to speak their own languages and made to dress, cut their hair, and in every possible way act and look like white people. The policy was a colossal failure; most Native Americans refused to abandon key aspects of their traditional cultures, and venal whites took advantage of the land reforms to strip Indians of much of their remaining patrimony (Berkhofer 1978; Hoxie 1984; Mardock 1971).

In the early twentieth century, the one-way assimilation model was applied to the southern and eastern European immigrants who had arrived in massive numbers before the discriminatory quota system of the 1920s was implemented. While some nativists called for their exclusion on the grounds of their innate deficiencies, other champions of Anglo-American cultural homogeneity hoped to assimilate those who had already arrived through education and indoctrination. The massive "Americanization" campaigns of the period just prior to World War I produced the concept of America as a "melting pot" in which cultural differences would be obliterated. The metaphor might have suggested that a new mixture would result—and occasionally it did have this meaning—but a more prevalent interpretation was that non-Anglo-American cultural traits and inclinations would simply disappear, making the final brew identical to the original one (Gordon 1964, ch. 5).

Before the 1940s, people of color, and especially African Americans, were generally deemed ineligible for assimilation because of their innate inferiority to white ethnics, who were now thought capable of being culturally reborn as Anglo-Americans. Such factors as the war-inspired reaction against scientific racism and the gain in black political power resulting from mass migration from the South (where blacks could not vote) to the urban North (where the franchise was again open to them) led to a significant reconsideration of the social position of African Americans and threw a spotlight on the flagrant denial in the southern states of the basic constitutional rights of African Americans. The struggle for black civil rights that emerged in the 1950s and came to fruition in the early 1960s was premised on a conviction that white supremacist laws and policies violated an egalitarian "American Creed"—as Gunnar Myrdal had argued in his influential wartime study *An American Dilemma* (1944). The war against Jim Crow was fought under the banner of "integration," which, in the minds of white liberals at least, generally meant one-way assimilation. Blacks, deemed by Myrdal and others as having no culture worth saving, would achieve equal status by becoming just like white Americans in every respect except pigmentation.

When it became clear that the civil rights legislation of the 1960s had failed to improve significantly the social and economic position of blacks in the urban ghettos of the North, large numbers of African Americans rejected the integrationist ideal on the grounds that it had been not only a false promise but an insult to the culture of African Americans for ignoring or devaluing their distinctive experience as a people. The new emphasis on "black power" and "black consciousness" conveyed to those whites who were listening that integration had to mean something other than one-way assimilation to white middle-class norms if it was to be a solution to the problem of racial inequality in America (Marable 1991; Van Deburg 1992).

It should be obvious by now that the one-way assimilation model has not proved to be a viable or generally acceptable way of adjusting group differences in American society. It is based on an ethnocentric ideal of cultural homogeneity that has been rejected by Indians, blacks, Asians, Mexican Americans, and even many white ethnics. It reifies and privileges one cultural strain in what is in fact a multicultural society. It should be possible to advocate the incorporation of all ethnic or racial groups into a common civic society without requiring the sacrifice of cultural distinctiveness and diversity.

## CULTURAL PLURALISM

Unlike assimilationists, cultural pluralists celebrate differences among groups rather than seek to obliterate them. They argue that cultural diversity is a healthy and normal condition that does not preclude equal rights and the mutual understandings about civic responsibilities needed to sustain a democratic nation-state. This model for American ethnic relations is a twentieth-century invention that would have been virtually inconceivable at an earlier time. The eighteenth and nineteenth centuries lacked the essential concept of the relativity of cultures. The model of cultural development during this period was evolutionary, progressive, and universalistic. People were either civilized or they were not. Mankind was seen as evolving from a state of "savagery" to "barbarism" to "civilization," and all cultures at a particular level were similar in every way that mattered. What differentiated nations and ethnic groups was their ranking on the scale of social evolution. Modern Western civilization stood at the apex of this universal historical process. Even nineteenth-century black nationalists accepted the notion that there were universal standards of civilization to which people of African descent should aspire. They differed from white supremacists in believing that blacks had the natural capability to reach the same heights as Caucasians if they were given a chance (Moses 1978).

The concept of cultural pluralism drew on the new cultural anthropology of the early twentieth century, as pioneered by Franz Boas. Boas and his disciples attempted to look at each culture they studied on its own terms and as an integrated whole. They rejected theories of social evolution that ranked cultures in relation to a universalist conception of "civilization." But relativistic cultural anthropologists were not necessarily cultural pluralists in their attitude toward group relations within American society. Since they generally believed that a given society or community functioned best with a single, integrated culture, they could favor greater autonomy for Indians on reservations but also call for the full assimilation of new immigrants or even African Americans. Boas himself was an early supporter of the National Association for the Advancement of Colored People (NAACP) and a pioneering advocate of what would later be called racial integration.

An effort to use the new concept of culture to validate ethnic diversity within the United States arose from the negative reaction of some intellectuals to the campaign to "Americanize" the new immigrants from eastern and southern Europe in the period just before and after World War I. The inventors of cultural pluralism were cosmopolitan critics of American provincialism or representatives of immigrant communities, especially Jews, who valued their cultural distinctiveness and did not want to be melted down in an Americanizing crucible. The Greenwich Village intellectual Randolph Bourne described his ideal as a "transnational America" in which various ethnic cultures would interact in a tolerant atmosphere to create an enriching variety of ideas, values, and lifestyles (Bourne 1964, ch. 8). The Jewish philosopher Horace Kallen, who coined the phrase "cultural pluralism," compared the result to a symphony, with each immigrant group represented as a section of the orchestra (Higham 1984, ch. 9; Kallen 1924). From a different perspective, W. E. B. DuBois celebrated a distinctive black culture rooted in the African and slave experiences and heralded its unacknowledged contributions to American culture in general (Lewis 1993). But the dominant version advocated by Kallen and Bourne stopped, for all practical purposes, at the color line. Its focus was on making America safe for a variety of European cultures. As a Zionist, Kallen was especially concerned with the preservation of Jewish distinctiveness and identity.

Since it was mainly the viewpoint of ethnic intellectuals who resisted the assimilationism of the melting pot, cultural pluralism was a minority persuasion in the twenties, thirties, and forties. A modified version reemerged in the 1950s in Will Herberg's (1960) conception of a "triple melting pot" of Protestants, Catholics, and Jews. The revulsion against Nazi anti-Semitism and the upward mobility of American Jews and Catholics inspired a synthesis of cultural pluralism and assimilationism that made religious persuasion the only significant source of diversity among white Americans. Herberg conceded, however, that black Protestants constituted a separate group that was not likely to be included in the Protestant melting point. He therefore sharpened the distinction between race or color and ethnicity that was central to postwar thinking about group differences. Nevertheless, Herberg's view that significant differences between, say, Irish and Italian Catholics were disappearing was challenged in the 1960s and later, especially in the "ethnic revival" of the 1970s, which proclaimed that differing national origins among Euro-Americans remained significant and a valuable source of cultural variations.

The "multiculturalism" of the 1980s operated on assumptions that were similar to those of the cultural pluralist tradition, except that the color line was breached and the focus was shifted from the cultures and contributions of diverse European ethnic groups to those of African Americans, Mexican Americans, Asian Americans, and Native Americans. Abandonment of the earlier term "multiracialism" signified a desire to escape from the legacy of biological or genetic determinism and to affirm that the differences among people who happened to differ in skin color or phenotype were the result of their varying cultural and historical experiences. Under attack was the doctrine, shared by assimilationists and most earlier proponents of cultural pluralism, that the cultural norm in the United States was inevitably European in origin and character. Parity was now sought for groups of Asian, African, and American Indian ancestry. This ideal of cultural diversity and democracy was viewed by some of its critics as an invitation to national disunity and ethnic conflict (Schlesinger 1992). But its most thoughtful proponents argued that it was simply a consistent application of American democratic values and did not preclude the interaction and cooperation of groups within a common civic society (Hollinger 1995). Nevertheless, the mutual understandings upon which national unity and cohesion could be based needed to be negotiated rather than simply imposed by a Euro-American majority.

## GROUP SEPARATISM

Sometimes confused with the broadened cultural pluralism described here is the advocacy of group separatism. It originates in the desire of a culturally distinctive or racialized group to withdraw as much as possible from American society and interaction with other groups. Its logical outcome, autonomy in a separate, self-governing community, might conceivably be achieved either in an ethnic confederation like Switzerland or in the dissolution of the United States into several ethnic nations. But such a general theory is a logical construction rather than a program that has been explicitly advocated. Group separatism emanates from ethnocentric concerns about the status and destiny of particular groups, and its advocates rarely if ever theorize about what is going to happen to other groups. Precedents for group separatism based on cultural differences can be found in American history in the toleration of virtually autonomous religious communities like the Amish and the Hutterites and in the modicum of self-government and immunity from general laws accorded to Indian tribes and reservations since the 1930s.

The most significant and persistent assertion of group separatism in American history has come from African Americans disillusioned with the prospects for equality within American society. In the nineteenth century, several black leaders and intellectuals called on African Americans to emigrate from the United States in order to establish an independent black republic elsewhere; Africa was the most favored destination. In the 1920s, Marcus Garvey created a mass movement based on the presumption that blacks had no future in the United States and should identify with the independence and future greatness of Africa, ultimately by emigrating there. More recently, the Nation of Islam has proposed that several American states be set aside for an autonomous black nation (Fredrickson 1995, chs. 2, 4, 7). At the height of the black power movement of the 1960s and early 1970s, a few black nationalists even called for the establishment of a noncontiguous federation of black urban ghettos—a nation of islands like Indonesia or the Philippines, but surrounded by white populations rather than the Pacific Ocean.

The current version of black separatism—"Afrocentrism"—has not as yet produced a plan for political separation. Its aim is a cultural and spiritual secession from American society rather than the literal establishment of a black nation. Advocates of total separation could be found among other disadvantaged groups. In the late 1960s and 1970s: Mexican American militants called for the establishment of the independent Chicano nation of Atzlan in the American Southwest (Gutierrez 1995, 184–85) and some Native American radicals sought the reestablishment of truly independent tribal nations.

Group separatism might be viewed as a utopian vision or rhetorical device expressing the depths of alienation felt by the most disadvantaged racial or ethnic groups in American society. The extreme unlikelihood of realizing such visions has made their promulgation more cathartic than politically efficacious. Most members of groups exposed to such separatist appeals have recognized their impracticality, and the clash between the fixed and essentialist view of identity that such projects entail and the fluid and hybrid quality of group cultures in the United States has become increasingly evident to many people of color, as shown most dramatically by the recent movement among those of mixed parentage to affirm a biracial identity. Few African Americans want to celebrate the greater or lesser degree of white ancestry most of them possess, but many have acknowledged not only their ancestral ties to Africa but their debt to Euro-American culture (and its debt to them). Most Mexican Americans value their cultural heritage but do not have the expectation or even the desire to establish an independent Chicano nation in the Southwest. Native Americans have authentic historical and legal claims to a high degree of autonomy but generally recognize that total independence on their current land base is impossible and would worsen rather than improve their circumstances. Asian Americans are proud of their various cultures and seek to preserve some of their traditions but have shown little or no inclination to separate themselves from other Americans in the civic, professional, and economic life of the nation. Afrocentrism raises troubling issues for American educational and cultural life but hardly represents a serious threat to national unity.

Ethnic separatism, in conclusion, is a symptom of racial injustice and a call to action against it, but there is little reason to believe that it portends "the disuniting of America." It is currently a source of great anxiety to many Euro-Americans primarily because covert defenders of ethnic hierarchy or one-way assimilation have tried to confuse the broad-based ideal of democratic multiculturalism with the demands of a relatively few militant ethnocentrists for thoroughgoing self-segregation and isolation from the rest of American society.

Of the four models of American ethnic relations, the one that I believe offers the best hope for a just and cohesive society is a cultural pluralism that is fully inclusive and based on the free choices of individuals to construct or reconstruct their own ethnic identities. We are still far from achieving the degree of racial and ethnic tolerance that realization of such an ideal requires. But with the demographic shift that is transforming the overwhelmingly Euro-American population of thirty or forty years ago into one that is much more culturally and phenotypically heterogeneous, a more democratic form of intergroup relations is a likely prospect, unless there is a desperate reversion to overt ethnic hierarchicalism by the shrinking Euro-American majority. If that were to happen, national unity and cohesion would indeed be hard to maintain. If current trends continue, minorities of non-European ancestry will constitute a new majority sometime in the next century. Well before that point is reached, they will have the numbers and the provocation to make the country virtually ungovernable if a resurgent racism brings serious efforts to revive the blatantly hierarchical policies that have prevailed in the past.

## REFERENCES

Axtell, James. (1981). *The European and the Indian: Essays in the ethnohistory of colonial North America.* New York: Oxford University Press.

Berkhofer, Robert F., Jr. (1978). *The white man's Indian: Image of the American Indian from Columbus to the present.* New York: Alfred A. Knopf.

Bourne, Randolph S. (1964). *War and the intellectuals: Collected essays, 1915–1919.* New York: Harper Torch.

D'Souza, Dinesh. (1995). *The end of racism: Principles for a multiracial society.* New York: Free Press.

Fredrickson, George M. (1987). *The black image in the white mind: The debate on Afro-American character and destiny, 1817–1914.* Middletown, Conn.: Wesleyan University Press.

———. (1995). *Black liberation: A comparative history of black ideologies in the United States and South Africa.* New York: Oxford University Press.

———. (1997). *The comparative imagination: On the history of racism, nationalism, and social movements.* Berkeley: University of California Press.

Gordon, Milton M. (1964). *Assimilation in American life: The role of race, religion, and national origins.* New York: Oxford University Press.

Gutierrez, David. (1995). *Walls and mirrors: Mexican Americans, Mexican immigrants, and the politics of ethnicity.* Berkeley: University of California Press.

Herberg, Will. (1960). *Protestant-Catholic-Jew: An essay in American religious sociology.* Garden City, N.Y.: Anchor Books.

Higham, John. (1968). *Strangers in the land: Patterns of American nativism, 1860–1925.* New York: Atheneum.

———. (1984). *Send these to me: Jews and other immigrants in urban America.* Baltimore: Johns Hopkins University Press.

Hollinger, David. (1995). *Postethnic America: Beyond multiculturalism.* New York: Basic Books.

Hoxie, Frederick E. (1984). *A final promise: The campaign to assimilate the Indians, 1880–1920.* Lincoln, Neb.: University of Nebraska Press.

Jordan, Winthrop D. (1968). *White over black: American attitudes toward the Negro, 1550–1812.* New York: University of North Carolina Press.

Kallen, Horace. (1924). *Culture and democracy in the United States: Studies in the group psychology of American peoples.* New York: Boni & Liveright.

Koch, Adrienne, and Peden, William. (Eds.). (1944). *The life and selected writings of Thomas Jefferson.* New York: Modern Library.

Knobel, Dale T. (1986). *Paddy and the republic: Ethnicity and nationality in antebellum America.* Middletown, Conn.: Wesleyan University Press.

Lewis, David Levering. (1993). *W. E. B. DuBois: Biography of a race, 1868–1919.* New York: Henry Holt.

Marable, Manning. (1991). *Race, reform, and rebellion: The second reconstruction in black America.* Jackson, Miss.: University of Mississippi Press.

Mardock, Robert W. (1971). *The reformers and the American Indian.* Columbia, Mo.: University of Missouri Press.

Miller, Stuart Creighton. (1969). *The unwelcome immigrant: The American image of the Chinese, 1785–1882.* Berkeley: University of California Press.

Moses, Wilson Jeremiah. (1978). *The golden age of black nationalism, 1850–1925.* Hamden, Conn.: Archon Books.

Myrdal, Gunnar. (1944). *An American dilemma.* New York: Harper and Row.

Schlesinger, Arthur M., Jr. (1992). *The disuniting of America.* New York: Norton.

Van Deburg, William L. (1992). *New day in Babylon: The black power movement and American culture, 1965–1975.* Chicago: University of Chicago Press.

# 3

# CULTURAL DIVERSITY AND MULTICULTURAL POLITICS: IS ETHNIC BALKANIZATION PSYCHOLOGICALLY INEVITABLE?

*David O. Sears, Jack Citrin, Sharmaine V. Cheleden, and Colette van Laar*

> The Yugoslav experience showed that cultural and geopolitical divides turned out to be decisive. . . . The current fault line overlaps with those of the Roman Empire [Theodosian line] between Rome, Byzantium, and Islam, as well as with the border between the Ottoman and Hapsburg Empires.
>
> —President Franjo Tudjman, Croatia

> You can't keep a dog and a cat in a box together. Either they would always be quarreling and fighting or they would have to stop being what they are.
>
> —General Radovan Karadzic, Bosnian Serb

THE ETHNIC diversity of the American people has substantially increased in recent years, owing both to increased immigration from Latin America and Asia and to differential birth rates across groups. Political conflict has intensified about issues that are intimately tied to diversity, such as immigration control, language policy, and affirmative action. The United States is hardly unique in this regard, since ethnic and nationality groups all over the globe seem to be engaged in intensified domestic conflict, often threatening the integrity of nation-states.

President Tudjman and General Karadzic offer a clear sociopsychological theory to explain these political developments: ethnic identity, outgroup antagonism, and intergroup conflict are as central to human psychology as dog-ness or cat-ness and as their age-old conflicts are to those two species. Historically different ethnic groups cannot live together in harmony. "Ethnic balkanization" is the term often used to describe the pervasive and entrenched hostility between ethnic groups that has seemed so emblematic of the Balkans throughout much of this century. American history has to this point not shown that ethnic balkanization is inevitable here. But many fear that it is overtaking American society, perhaps driven by inherent psychological tendencies toward group identity and group conflict. "Multiculturalism" as a political ideology is often seen as intimately involved with these issues; offered by some as a political solution to the problems posed by diversity, while being described by others as itself an exacerbating cause of ethnic balkanization.

How well in fact does a theory that interethnic relations will inevitably evolve to balkanization hold up in the context of contemporary American society? We approach this question in three ways. First, what kind of society do Americans really want, given the nation's increasing cultural diversity? Do they prefer a nativist "cleansing" in which alien cultural influences disappear over time? A "melting pot" whose evolving mainstream reflects the influences of a wide variety of cultural origins? A "salad bowl" in which each ingredient retains its distinctive taste in a harmonious overall dish? Or a multicultural "mosaic" whose pieces remain deliberately separate but form a pleasing mixture, at least when viewed from a distance? Second, is the increase in cultural diversity actually producing greater ethnic balkanization, in terms of heightened ethnic consciousness and antagonism toward other groups, and increased intergroup conflict? And finally, are both African Americans and today's waves of new immigrants fated to be perpetually disadvantaged minority groups, or are they likely to assimilate into the society's mainstream?

To anticipate our argument, we do find signs of ethnic tension among Americans. Many believe that increasing ethnic diversity has caused a deterioration in the quality of life, and there is sharp ethnic polarization about political issues relevant to minorities. However, we do not find that ethnicity is becoming a dominant ingroup political identity, nor do we find any simple pattern of ingroup favoritism in evaluations of ethnic and racial groups. There is little public support for a group-rights system of communal representation, even among ethnic minorities. The waves of new immigrants, as they flood into our metropolitan areas, could potentially stimulate a politically defensive response from both whites and blacks, but heavily immigrant social contexts seem not to have that effect. Ethnic polarization about political issues relevant to minority groups' interests derives more from the residues of earlier socialization than from a sense of threat from growing ethnic competition.

Rather than a general pattern of ethnic balkanization, we find evidence of an older and more intractable form of group conflict: the pervasive influence of anti-black attitudes on whites' preferences about minority-related policy issues, even those, like multilingualism, that scarcely involve blacks at all. The political trajectory of the "new" immigrant groups seems to parallel the assimilationist paths of earlier European newcomers more closely than the continuing stigmatization and incomplete assimilation of the African American population. A multiculturalist "mosaic" of politically separate ethnic groups is neither psychologically inevitable nor desired by ordinary Americans, whether whites or blacks or Latinos. Its advocacy seems more likely to stimulate a nativist response from whites and further isolate the African American population.

## WAVES OF IMMIGRATION

To set the stage, it might be helpful to look back to previous waves of immigration in American history. The United States has often been described as "a nation of immigrants" and prides itself on a long history of absorbing very diverse peoples into a common political culture. The reality is, of course, a bit more complicated. The first wave of immigrants came primarily from the British Isles in the seventeenth and eighteenth centuries. They largely imported an intact political culture and so left an indelible stamp on the language, the legal and political institutions, and many other features of what is often described as "Anglo-American" society (Wood 1991).

The second great wave of immigrants came with the African slave trade from the mid-seventeenth century to the early nineteenth century. From the beginning, almost all black Africans were treated as property rather than as citizens and not permitted to become a part of the political culture. They have ever since constituted a large, widely stigmatized, and poorly assimilated minority group, though in recent years they have finally been accorded equal formal rights. The third wave consisted of large numbers of other Europeans—especially from Ireland, eastern and southern Europe, and Scandinavia—who arrived in the period from the beginnings of American industrialization to the passage of highly restrictive immigration legislation shortly after World War I. That wave left a wide variety of hyphenated Americans who are now largely assimilated socially and politically. It is mainly the trajectory of these latter groups that gives rise to America's self-image as a "melting pot" (see, for example, Lieberson 1980).

The current wave, which began with liberalized immigration legislation in the mid-1960s, has come disproportionately from Latin America and Asia. Unlike the African slaves, but like the later Europeans, they have been voluntary and self-selected immigrants, they did not arrive in the degraded role of chattel slaves, and from the beginning the United States has promised them full citizenship.[1] Culturally, of course, they arrive as "foreigners," but on average they seem closer to the relatively mild level of strangeness of the turn-of-the-century Europeans than to the near-species-level chasm that colonial whites felt separated them from the Africans. On the other hand, like the Africans, they are often viewed as physically dissimilar enough from the original, mainly Anglo-Saxon settlers to be described on occasion as from different "races" (though the Anglo-Saxon "natives" sometimes described the later Europeans as of a different race in the nineteenth century as well).

The receiving American society has also changed. General principles of group equality along racial, gender, religious, and ethnic lines are now more institutionalized and more broadly accepted by the American public than they were even in the mid-twentieth century (see, for example, Schuman et al. 1997). Today's immigrants do not bear the brunt of prejudice as heavily as did those in the nineteenth century, though they are still vulnerable to it. And the black civil rights movement, together with a host of successor movements, legitimated and provided visible models for political action by disadvantaged social groups. Analogies with earlier waves of immigrants are evocative, then, but necessarily imprecise.

## NORMATIVE THEORY

This rapidly increasing ethnic diversity has opened a new round in the enduring American debate over how to balance unity and diversity. Four normative alternatives are often presented, although, of course, here we oversimplify to make the contrast. First, the "nativist" model treats cultural differences as temporary or deviant, favoring homogeneity over diversity. In the nineteenth century, a nativist response to the influx of non-English and non-Protestant immigrants was to maintain that only Anglo-Saxons possessed the moral and intellectual qualities required for American citizenship. If members of other groups were to be admitted to the polity, they first had to undergo a deliberate program of Americanization to produce close conformity to the cultural majority. For the nativist, then, the proper activity within the melting pot is cleansing, not blending (Higham 1985; Smith 1993).

Second, a nation might aspire to a "cosmopolitan liberal" society in which diverse groups comfortably coexist, tolerating each other's modest differences but sharing a strong bond of loyalty to the superordinate nation (Citrin et al. 1994). This universalistic traditional ideal of American integration is perhaps most often captured in the idea of the "melting pot." To its adherents, the melting pot means the intermingling of varied cultural streams in the crucible of American life. Immigrants enrich popular culture without threatening the distinctive core of national identity, a Lockean commitment to individual rights shared by all citizens. In principle, though less fully in practice, this conception of American identity is ethnically inclusive, its adherents believing that American society could assimilate all newcomers.

Today a "multiculturalist" model offers an alternative vision in which the differences between groups are not only appreciated but institutionalized, in formal power-sharing coalitions. The term "multiculturalism" was first advanced in Canada. There the intent was to ensure that the integration of immigrant groups did not imply the loss of their original cultures, both because the maintenance of that heritage was seen as necessary for the psychological well-being of individual citizens and because cultural diversity was seen as a valuable resource for society as a whole (Berry, Kalin, and Taylor 1977). The guiding political principles of multiculturalism are the recognition of and respect for individuals' cultural identity, the primacy of ethnic identity in defining political interests, the idea of communal representation, and the importance of public policies that respond to the claims of subordinate cultural groups. In that sense, multiculturalism is a redistributive ideology that justifies the claims of subordinate groups to a greater share of society's goods. It does so by invoking the notion of group rather than individual rights (Glazer 1997; Merelman 1994; Ravitch 1990; Schlesinger 1998; Taylor, 1992).

Multiculturalism is a contested and emotionally loaded concept (Ravitch 1990). Its varied definitions all approve of the benefits of *pluribus* and criticize the concept of *unum.* "Soft," pluralistic versions of multiculturalism emphasize the need for mutual recognition, respect, and tolerance among diverse ethnic groups, as in the "melting pot" or "salad bowl" metaphors, and no longer evoke much controversy. Thus, we focus our attention here on the "hard," particularistic version, which asserts the viability and merit of multiple cultures within a society and advocates government action to maintain these equally worthy cultures. As an ideal image of society, multiculturalism rejects the assimilationist ethos of the melting pot in favor of the mosaic, which typically consists of differently colored tiles isolated from each other by impenetrable grout. It construes racial or ethnic identity as the preferred choice of self-definition.

One additional aspect of multiculturalism is peculiar to the United States but is central to our story. The rise of multiculturalism was inspired by the civil rights movement of the 1950s and 1960s. Its roots, therefore, are in the distinctively African American struggle, including groups with histories and status fundamentally different from those of African Americans. Yet it extends the model of blacks' struggle for equality in two senses. First, it regards all the distinct cultures within the country as morally and intellectually equal, most notably including the new immigrants from Latin America and Asia. Indeed, what might be called "identity politics" goes beyond ethnicity to include such groups as women, gays, and the disabled. Second, it advocates official action to achieve equality for all groups.

## THEORIES OF GROUP IDENTITY AND CONFLICT

Any normative debate ultimately implicates psychological assumptions, though it usually cannot be entirely reduced to them. This chapter focuses on the psychological processes that generate public responses to ethnic diversity. We would suggest that underlying both the ethnic balkanization perspective advanced by President Tudjman and General Karadzic and a hard multiculturalism is a fairly clear psychological theory. It shares some elements with a number of currently prominent theories in social psychology, though it mirrors none of them exactly.

Contemporary social psychology has increasingly turned to theories that focus on group categories as powerful determinants of behavior and are therefore in particular harmony with the psychological assumptions undergirding the multicultural model. The simplest are cognitive categorization theories, which suggest that people automatically and even unconsciously categorize individuals (themselves as well as others) into social groups, particularly on the basis of salient perceptual dimensions such as race, gender, and age (Fiske and Neuberg 1990).

Social identity theory (Tajfel 1978) takes a further step, suggesting that we have a basic need for a specifically *social* identity and thus tend universally to form solidary groups and allocate resources along group lines, even in the absence of any especially self-interested reason to do so. This produces categorization specifically into ingroups and outgroups, and generates systematic "ingroup favoritism" or "group-serving biases" that favor the ingroup at the expense of outgroups. While social identity theory assumes that humans are innately predisposed to define themselves in terms of group identity, it does not claim that any particular identity is inherently preferred or psychologically required. Indeed, people can have multiple group identities, given the existence of different levels of self-representation—"subtyping" can differentiate global categories in subtle ways, and superordinate categories can unite quite disparate groups (Brewer, Dull, and Lui 1981; Brewer and Gardner 1996; Dovidio et al. 1995). Presumably, social context has much to say about the salience of any particular identity. Political mobilization is often a key player in that process, as the recent cases of Bosnia and Kosovo illustrate.

Social-structural theories of group competition, such as realistic group conflict theory (Bobo 1983), sense of group position theory (Blumer 1958; Bobo and Hutchings 1996), and social dominance theory (Sidanius 1993), also assume the ubiquity of group formation. But they go further by assuming more stable hierarchies of status and power as well as the inevitability of intergroup competition. Exactly which group divisions display the sharpest conflicts presumably depends on the particular historical and social context. "Power theory" takes this reasoning yet another step further, predicting that social contexts with many members of subordinate groups are politically threatening to members of the dominant group, motivating them to make political choices that protect its power (Blalock 1967; Giles and Hertz 1994; Key 1949; Taylor 1998). By this theory, increasing ethnic diversity in America will threaten the hegemonic whites, hardening their ethnic identity, increasing outgroup antagonism, and generating conservative political preferences.

Some more anthropologically oriented theorists go still further and privilege race and ethnicity as essentialist dimensions of categorization, such as in the notion of "primordial attachments" or the competition between national identity and "communal," "tribal," or other subnational groupings (Geertz 1964; Horowitz 1985). Even if these categories are only socially constructed, they may nonetheless be taken by ordinary people to be psychologically essential or genotypic (Appiah and Gutmann 1996; Medin and Ortony 1989; Miller and Prentice, this volume). This perceived essentialism of racial categories may stem from a natural tendency for children to form categories about kinds of humans (Hirschfeld 1996).[2] Still, such essentialist assumptions are not required in order to view ethnicity and race as central dimensions of group categorization in contemporary American society, since the prevailing sociopolitical context has long given them ample attention.

There are, of course, important differences between these several group-centered theories. For example, social identity theory does not give the prominence to distinctions between dominant and subordinate groups that social-structural theories do, or to the distinctions between majority and minority groups that categorization theories do. Most social psychologists assume that the role of ethnicity depends heavily on the cultural context in question. Nevertheless, these theories generally share the view that group categories, ingroup identity, antagonism toward outgroups, and intergroup competition are central elements of human psychology.

In the contemporary United States, the most important application of these theories is to ethnic and racial cleavages. They would generally lead us to expect that greater diversity will strengthen ethnic group boundaries, provoking the dominant whites to protect their own privileges and ethnic minority groups to demand more resources in their group's interests. Diversity would in this sense generate ethnic polarization over resource allocations. Organizing a society along "multiculturalist" lines might then be a natural political solution: ethnic groups would be treated as if they were subnations with their own group rights; the peace would be kept by binding treaties that ensured equitable allocations of resources among groups, as in Belgium and Lebanon.

## SYMBOLIC POLITICS THEORY

The psychological centrality of group categories and identity is not seen as so inevitable in symbolic politics theory (Sears 1993). The core assumption of this approach is that long-standing predispositions, based in earlier socialization, are strong and enduring influences over the public's politics. The most salient symbols in a political controversy determine its "symbolic meaning," and therefore which predispositions are evoked. To take a simple example, affirmative action targeted explicitly for blacks is likely to evoke attitudes toward African Americans, whereas debates about abortion centered on God-given rights to life are more likely to evoke religious attitudes. The political environment therefore plays a key role both in nurturing the original socialization process and in determining which predispositions are evoked by political stimuli later on in life.

Principally for reasons of parsimony, symbolic politics theory assumes that essentially the same process explains the acquisition of attitudes toward social groups and attitudes toward any other political objects. To be sure, groups can be stereotyped and thus rendered cognitively simpler attitude objects than other political objects, such as policy outcomes, complex regulations, or political systems. So strong attitudes toward groups might be especially easily acquired for that reason. But neither ingroup identity nor the distinction between ingroup and outgroup is inherently privileged in this process. Rather, each of us has attitudes toward numerous social groupings that depend on our own social and political contexts. Ethnic identity is sometimes strongly socialized, as in the Nazi movement's glorification of the "Aryan race," but in other cases it may have only minor significance, as in the declining political role of the various European ethnic identities in the United States. Outgroup prejudices can be strongly socialized, as in the antiblack prejudice of the old South, but they are not inevitable either. Indeed, most groups of ordinary people are generally regarded favorably by most nonmembers.[3]

If outgroup antagonism depends mainly on prior socialization of stigmatizing attitudes toward specific groups, increasing diversity need not produce a more threatened and defensive political stance among whites. Symbolic politics theory assumes that direct personal experience outside the political realm usually does not have much influence on adults' political attitudes, and there is much empirical evidence to back up that assumption (Sears and Funk 1991). Nor is group conflict, including conflict among ethnic groups, viewed as inherently likely. Since attitudes toward both ingroups and outgroups are derivative of other processes, outgroups do not inevitably pose a threat to the ingroup. Moreover, not only outgroup antagonisms but tolerance can be socialized.

By this view, then, responses to the great social changes and political events of any era depend on the individual's own history, and particularly on the groundwork laid down in earlier socialization. They also depend on the symbolic nature of contemporary political contention, and which specific predispositions are evoked. As a result, people will respond to ethnic diversification according to long-standing political predispositions that may or may not involve any given ingroup (of which there are potentially many) or any given outgroup (of which there are still more). The centrality of any given group depends on the particular symbolism of the political controversy in question, and on the particular prior socialization pattern that is relevant to it.

These psychological theories raise several empirical questions about Americans' political responses to cultural diversity. First of all, theories that assert the power of group identity might persuade us that increasing diversity is leading to increased ethnic balkanization, the "cultural divides" this book addresses. This expectation might be reflected in perceptions of a deteriorating quality of life, strengthened ingroup identity, ingroup favoritism in group evaluations, and ethnic polarization over policies relevant to ethnic and racial minorities. Extensive ethnic balkanization might be accompanied by increased acceptance of a group basis for political rights. Ethnic minorities in particular might support group rights as being in their own interest. And the political responses to diversity shown by the increasingly displaced prior groups, both whites and blacks, might be strongly influenced by both their ingroup identity and the realistic threats posed by the incoming immigrant minorities.

A symbolic politics theory would assume, in contrast, that whites' own ingroup identity is not likely to be a major political force, since their "whiteness" has generally been of secondary political significance outside of the Jim Crow South.[4] Outgroup evaluations would tend to reflect society-wide and consensual traditional stereotypes. Nor should living in an ethnically diverse context be likely to produce a more threatened and defensive political stance, given the usual modest influence of direct personal experience. And since American political norms have historically emphasized individual rather than group rights (Lipset 1996), conventional socialization is likely to have left most Americans unreceptive to the "hard" version of multiculturalism. Even immigrant minorities might well reflect these conventional norms.

The symbolic politics framework focuses on the most strongly socialized attitudes in a culture. Accordingly, a "black exceptionalism" hypothesis suggests that, in the United States, African Americans are especially likely to have been the focus of prior stigmatizing socialization. They have been negatively stereotyped by whites since the earliest days of slavery. They have had a high political profile ever since, as witness their centrality in debates about slavery when the Declaration of Independence and the Constitution were written, in the Civil War era, through nearly a century of the southern Jim Crow system, and more recently in the debates over busing, affirmative action, welfare, crime, and drugs. In contrast, relatively few white (or black) Americans have had long and strong socialization histories that would influence their attitudes about Hispanics, except in some areas of the Southwest, or about Asians, except for a few locales in the Far West at certain historical junctures. We suggest therefore that whites' attitudes toward blacks will be especially negative and strongly crystallized and so will have a disproportionate influence over their attitudes toward any minority-related issues, even those involving other groups (Sears and van Laar 1999).[5]

The black exceptionalism hypothesis would also imply that African Americans' own ingroup identity is especially highly crystallized. Their history includes three centuries of being dealt with as a unitary group with impermeable boundaries. The "one drop" rule for group categorization, by which any African ancestry at all classified a person as "colored," was uniquely applied to African Americans (Davis 1991). And they have long been the defining lower-caste group in American society. As a result, we might expect group consciousness and a perception of group interest to play a stronger role for blacks than for whites (also see Dawson 1994).

Most new immigrant groups, in contrast, encounter some prejudice as they enter American society, but without the long stigmatizing history experienced by blacks. Under such conditions, both ethnics' own distinctive social identity and others' prejudice against them should tend to erode over time and generations. So for the "new immigrants," as for the earlier European immigrants, acculturation should depend on the primacy, length, and intensity of their experience with the new socializing environment. Here we examine political acculturation, in terms of adopting conventional American attitudes and values, rather than structural acculturation, as would be reflected in socioeconomic terms.

In this chapter, we address these conflicts with public opinion data of three kinds. We begin with attitudes that could reflect "ethnic balkanization": perceptions of the quality of life and preferences about policies targeted for minority groups. Then we turn to its presumed underlying psychological dynamics: hardened ingroup identities, ingroup favoritism in group evaluations, and preferences for a multicultural solution to political conflict. We next test whether whites' attitudes about the policies most relevant to diversity—immigration and language—are based in the threats posed by a strongly ethnic context or in early-socialized outgroup evaluations, especially anti-black prejudices. Finally, we examine whether blacks' and Latinos' views of immigration are based in realistic intergroup competition or acculturation to conventional American values.

## DATA

The data presented in this chapter are drawn from face-to-face interviews administered to a nationally representative sample of adults in the 1994 General Social Survey (GSS) and two random-digit-dial, computer-assisted telephone surveys representing adults living in Los Angeles County in the 1994 and 1995 Los Angeles County Social Surveys (LACSS). The GSS had an overall sample of 2,992, but the data we present come principally from the multiculturalism module administered to half that sample. This was 81 percent white, 13 percent black, 4 percent Hispanic (both sufficient for aggregate estimates but insufficient for individual-level analysis), and 2 percent Asian (insufficient for either purpose). The 1994 LACSS had a sample of 821 respondents and oversampled telephone exchanges containing 65 percent or more African American telephone households, yielding 37 percent white, 30 percent black, 25 percent Hispanic, and 7 percent Asian. The 1995 LACSS had 595 respondents, of whom 44 percent were white, 12 percent black (whom we use at the aggregate level only), 30 percent Hispanic, and 8 percent Asian. We pooled the Asian respondents in the 1994 and the 1995 LACSS for aggregate level purposes only. In general, the attitude measures are described when they are introduced. Scale construction is described in this chapter's appendix.

## LIFE IN THE ETHNIC CAULDRON

We begin by examining ethnic diversity in the proximal social environment. Los Angeles County, with a population of about nine million, has in recent years undergone a swift process of ethnic diversification, with a particularly rapid increase in the Latino population.[6] In 1970, 71 percent were non-Hispanic whites; in 1990 only 41 percent were. The Hispanic population has increased the most, from 18 percent in 1970 to 38 percent in 1990 (Clark 1996). Los Angeles has also been the site of some serious ethnic conflicts in recent decades, including large-scale urban riots in 1965 in Watts and in South Central Los Angeles in 1992 (following the acquittal of four Los Angeles Police Department officers involved in the videotaped beating of the black motorist Rodney King). Several heated and successful statewide campaigns have also been waged in recent years on ballot measures relevant to minorities—eliminating fair housing laws in 1964 (Proposition 14), declaring English to be the state's "official language" in 1986 (Proposition 63), restricting public services for illegal immigrants in 1994 (Proposition 187), abolishing official affirmative action programs in 1996 (Proposition 209), and restricting bilingual education in 1998 (Proposition 227).

We measured ethnic context in two ways: objectively, in terms of the percentage from each ethnic group living within the respondent's zip code at the time of the 1990 census; and subjectively, with perceptions measured in the 1994 LACSS (for more detail, see Sears, Cheleden, and Henry 1997).[7] In general, the rapidly changing ethnic composition of Los Angeles County has markedly decreased whites' isolation in recent years: the number of census tracts that were at least 80 percent white dropped from 60 percent in 1970 to 20 percent by 1990 (Clark 1996). And indeed, by both our indicators, whites in the 1994 LACSS were on average surrounded by considerable diversity. The median white respondent lived in a zip code that was 68 percent white, and just 60 percent felt that whites were the main ethnic or racial group in their neighborhood. About half said the ethnic or racial makeup of their neighborhood was changing, virtually all of them saying it was becoming less white. And quite aside from their residences, most reported that they "very often" or "often" had contact in their daily lives with people who did not speak English very well.

This pattern of increasing diversity, and considerable interethnic contact, held for blacks as well for whites. The median black respondent lived in a zip code that was 60 percent black, and only about half (46 percent) felt they now lived in predominantly black neighborhoods. Most (63 percent) felt that their neighborhoods were becoming less black, principally owing to the very rapid movement of Hispanic immigrants into the portions of South Central Los Angeles that had long been primarily African American. And most (57 percent) felt that they at least "often" had extensive daily contact with people who did not speak English very well. So both whites and blacks were living in a substantially more ethnically mixed world than they had even a decade earlier.[8]

Whites seemed to link increased diversity with a worsening quality of life in the metropolitan area. The vast majority thought that Los Angeles had become a worse place to live, and relatively few felt that ethnic groups were getting along these days, as shown in table 3.1. Considerably more thought racial and ethnic relations would continue to get worse than thought they would improve. These baleful views apparently reflect a meaningful cluster of beliefs linking diversity to perceptions of the deteriorating quality of life, since they cohere reasonably well statistically (Cronbach's alpha = .65 for a "quality of life" scale). Ethnic minorities shared many of the same concerns about the community as a whole and also overwhelmingly felt that Los Angeles had become a worse place to live. But they were less likely to feel that ethnic groups were in severe conflict and were more optimistic about the future. The general perception of conflict and sagging quality of life may have been influenced by the 1992 rioting, which most whites and Asians, the principal targets of the rioting, attributed to "criminal elements." Blacks and Latinos were much more likely to believe that it was caused by a "protest." All these data are shown in table 3.1.

This widespread perception that the quality of life is deteriorating, along with group polarization and perceived ethnic conflict, seems to reflect growing ethnic balkanization. Perhaps surging immigration does threaten whites even if it does not threaten ethnic minorities themselves. But two other findings qualify that conclusion. First, these are negative perceptions about the distal community; whites seemed to feel much less threatened at a personal level. Although many perceived that the ethnic makeup of their own neighborhoods was changing, relatively few reported great distress about the change. As shown in table 3.1, only 20 percent felt that change was bad for the neighborhood, and only 13 percent reported feeling uneasy around people of different ethnicities. So we might speculate that whites' pessimistic views about ethnic diversity reflect symbolic perceptions of the larger community more than they do realistic anxieties about their personal well-being.[9] Second, blacks appeared to feel economically threatened by the influx of new immigrants, even if whites did not. Not surprisingly, Latinos and Asians, many of whom were immigrants, were less likely than either whites or blacks to

TABLE 3.1 *Perceived Effects of Ethnic Diversity on Quality of Life, by Respondent Ethnicity*

| | Whites (%) | | Blacks (%) | | Hispanics (%) | | Asians (%) |
|---|---|---|---|---|---|---|---|
| | 1994 | 1995 | 1994 | 1995 | 1994 | 1995 | |
| Collective Quality of Life | | | | | | | |
| In the last five years, Los Angeles has become:[a] | | | | | | | |
| A worse place to live | 78 | 67 | 65 | 62 | 57 | 64 | 62 |
| A better place to live | 2 | 4 | 6 | 7 | 11 | 10 | 8 |
| Are ethnic groups in Los Angeles in conflict? | | | | | | | |
| A lot | 50 | 38 | 35 | 25 | 36 | 34 | 22 |
| Some | 29 | 39 | 26 | 35 | 31 | 37 | 33 |
| Getting along | 21 | 23 | 39 | 39 | 33 | 29 | 44 |
| The main cause of the 1992 Los Angeles riots: | | | | | | | |
| Criminal elements | 58 | — | 15 | — | 36 | — | 52 |
| Protest | 42 | — | 85 | — | 64 | — | 48 |
| The wide variety of ethnic groups in Los Angeles hurt quality of life | 48 | 41 | 48 | 35 | 48 | 53 | 29 |
| Ethnic relations in the next five to ten years will:[a] | | | | | | | |
| Get worse | 42 | 42 | 35 | 53 | 42 | 44 | 20 |
| Improve | 30 | 28 | 41 | 28 | 41 | 38 | 45 |
| The wide variety of ethnic groups in Los Angeles hurts the local economy (yes)[a] | 50 | — | 65 | — | 48 | — | 29 |
| Personal Impact of Diversity | | | | | | | |
| Ethnic/racial makeup of my neighborhood is: | | | | | | | |
| Changing, bad for neighborhood | 20 | — | 20 | — | 11 | — | 11 |
| Not changing | 52 | — | 37 | — | 59 | — | 63 |
| Changing, good for neighborhood | 28 | — | 43 | — | 30 | — | 26 |
| I generally feel uneasy with different ethnicities[a] | 13 | — | 23 | — | 12 | — | 26 |

*Sources:* 1994 and 1995 Los Angeles County Social Surveys. Entries for Asians pool both surveys.

[a]Some response options are not shown.

feel that immigration will have negative consequences. These data are also shown in table 3.1. Overall, these perceptions of the quality of life are consistent with a balkanization story.

## Policy Preferences

Major political battles have been fought in recent years, especially in California, over policies bearing on the well-being of ethnic minorities. The most contentious issues have involved immigration, language, and affirmative action. In general, there are sharp aggregate differences between ethnic groups in attitudes toward these policy issues. The differences are those that would be expected from theories that emphasize group identity, group interest, and group conflict.

To begin with, the largely nonimmigrant whites and blacks were considerably more opposed to liberal immigration policies than were Latinos and Asians. As table 3.2 shows, most would have preferred to decrease the number of legal immigrants and to spend more to tighten border security and deport illegal aliens. Many even raised questions about the "give me your tired, your poor" ideal; almost half felt that it was too easy for political refugees to be admitted to this country. Both whites and blacks wanted to tighten entitlements for immigrants, such as delaying legal immigrants' access to government social services and refusing work permits to illegal immigrants. A large minority were even prepared to reverse the constitutional provision granting automatic citizenship to children born in the United States of illegal immigrant parents.

On all these questions, Latinos were considerably more favorable to immigration than were either whites or blacks. On the nine immigration items in the 1994 LACSS, an average of 60 percent of the whites and 63 percent of the blacks chose the most restrictive alternative, as against 35 percent of the Latinos. Similarly, Proposition 187, the 1994 statewide ballot measure intended to eliminate the access of illegal immigrants to many public services, was supported by most whites, almost half of the blacks, but only 18 percent of the Latinos. Table 3.2 shows that similar ethnic differences emerged in the 1995 LACSS and 1994 GSS.

Asians show a somewhat different, but also seemingly group-interested, pattern of preferences. Like the Latinos, they show considerable support for liberal policies concerning legal immigration; for example, in terms of numbers of legal immigrants and their eligibility for social services. However Asians are generally more negative to illegal immigration, more closely resembling whites and blacks. For example, they tend to support more spending for deporting illegals and tightening border

TABLE 3.2 *Support for Multicultural Policy Preferences, by Respondent Ethnicity*

| | Whites (%) | | | Blacks (%) | | | Hispanics (%) | | | Asians (%) |
|---|---|---|---|---|---|---|---|---|---|---|
| | 1994 | 1995 | GSS | 1994 | 1995 | GSS | 1994 | 1995 | GSS | |
| Immigration Control | | | | | | | | | | |
| Total number of legal immigrants: | | | | | | | | | | |
| Increase | 8 | 9 | 5 | 10 | 3 | 11 | 22 | 17 | 13 | 21 |
| Decrease | 58 | 59 | 66 | 65 | 68 | 66 | 48 | 46 | 44 | 34 |
| Spend more to deport illegals? (no) | 24 | 33 | — | 30 | 36 | — | 60 | 64 | — | 49 |
| Spend more for border security? (no) | 15 | — | — | 15 | — | — | 48 | — | — | 17 |
| Too difficult to be admitted as refugees? (yes) | 9 | — | — | 19 | — | — | 10 | — | — | 11 |
| Entitlements for Immigrants | | | | | | | | | | |
| Legals eligible for social services immediately? (yes) | 42 | 34 | 33 | 36 | 43 | 29 | 62 | 45 | 42 | 56 |
| Illegals entitled to work permits? (yes) | 20 | — | 12 | 26 | — | 18 | 75 | — | 32 | 30 |
| Illegals' children entitled to be citizens? (yes) | 49 | — | 50 | 56 | — | 56 | 92 | — | 76 | 50 |
| Proposition 187 (oppose) | — | 45 | — | — | 58 | — | — | 82 | — | 52 |
| Too difficult to attain U.S. citizenship? (yes) | 3 | — | — | 31 | — | — | 6 | — | — | 11 |

| | | | | | | | | | | |
|---|---|---|---|---|---|---|---|---|---|---|
| Language Policy | | | | | | | | | | |
| English as official language of the United States (oppose) | 24 | 23 | 25 | 28 | 21 | 37 | 66 | 65 | 55 | 31 |
| Bilingual education (favor) | 49 | — | 64 | 60 | — | 85 | 87 | — | 86 | 59 |
| Classes in native languages for children not speaking English? (yes) | | | | | | | | | | |
| Through high school | 6 | 2 | 14 | 14 | 7 | 22 | 19 | 9 | 18 | 5 |
| Only for a year or two | 57 | 54 | 49 | 60 | 62 | 49 | 59 | 68 | 54 | 45 |
| All classes only in English | 37 | 44 | 37 | 26 | 31 | 29 | 22 | 23 | 28 | 50 |
| Print ballots in languages other than English? (favor) | 47 | — | 60 | 65 | — | 76 | 83 | — | 86 | 68 |
| Special Treatment of Minority Groups | | | | | | | | | | |
| Should government help improve the position of blacks and other minorities? (yes) | 20 | 34 | — | 35 | 56 | — | 47 | 50 | — | — |
| Preferential hiring and promotion of blacks due to past discrimination (favor) | 10 | 15 | 8 | — | 46 | 61 | 19 | 32 | 16 | 28 |
| Preferential hiring and promotion of Hispanics due to past discrimination (favor) | 12 | 12 | — | 36 | 45 | — | — | 53 | — | 24 |

*Sources:* 1994 and 1995 Los Angeles County Social Surveys, 1994 General Social Survey. Entries for Asians pool the first two surveys.

security, restricting their work permits, and supporting Proposition 187. Presumably this reflects the fact that illegal immigration is considerably more common among Latinos than among Asians.

Ethnic differences in attitudes toward language policies followed a similar pattern, as also shown in table 3.2, though the differences were less marked than in the case of immigration. Only Latinos opposed English as the official language or the insistence that children make the transition more quickly to English. Still, both whites and blacks exhibited some support for a more empathic, "soft" multiculturalism: about half supported the general concept of bilingual education, most favored a gradual rather than sudden transition to English for children, and at least half favored printing ballots in non-English native languages.[10]

Questions of special treatment for minority groups yielded similar patterns of ethnic polarization that seemed to be congruent with each group's own interests. Most whites were opposed to special treatment for minorities in general, and they specifically opposed giving preferences to either blacks or Hispanics.[11] Blacks and Hispanics were more supportive of special treatment for minorities in general, but considerably more inclined to support preferential treatment for members of their own group than for members of the other minority group. Asians supported preferential treatment for neither of those other groups. These data are also shown in table 3.2.

Such clear ethnic differences are consistent with the view that increased ethnic diversity is leading to narrowly group-interested politics. The heavily immigrant Latinos were more favorable to policies benefiting immigrants than were the largely nonimmigrant blacks and whites. Asians supported legal immigration, and both blacks and Latinos supported policies that benefited their own group more than they did policies that benefited the other minority group.

But caution is again in order, for two reasons. First, Latinos departed from a narrow definition of their own group's interests in several ways: they consistently supported decreasing legal immigration, and many wanted to delay access to government services for legal immigrants and force children to make the transition into English-language instruction. Also they had decidedly mixed feelings about preferential treatment, even for Latinos. Second, such aggregate-level differences are descriptively consistent with group-interested responses, to be sure; however, to infer that these ethnic differences are motivated by the respondents' senses of their own group interests requires more direct evidence than these aggregate-level data provide—ideally evidence of motives to benefit the ingroup (perhaps at the expense of the outgroup) (Sears and Kinder 1985).

## INGROUP IDENTITY AND OUTGROUP ANTAGONISM?

A group-centered view would lead us to expect heightened ethnic identity, antagonism toward ethnic outgroups, and ingroup favoritism (in terms of more favorable evaluations of the ingroup than of ethnic outgroups). A symbolic politics approach, on the other hand, would lead us to expect little ingroup identification among whites and outgroup evaluations that followed long-established, conventional, and consensual patterns of cultural socialization—in particular, unusually high levels of antagonism toward blacks.

Do we indeed find whites "circling the wagons" around their own ethnic group? One test was to ask whether they tended to identify politically more with their own white subgroup, as white supremacist groups do, or with a superordinate national identity. In answer to the question, "When you think of social and political issues, do you think of yourself mainly as a member of a particular ethnic, racial, or nationality group, or do you think of yourself mainly as just an American?" over 90 percent of the Los Angeles whites chose the inclusive "just an American." Few saw themselves as "white." Similarly, over 80 percent thought of themselves as "just an American" "on all or most issues." In both respects, the national GSS data are remarkably parallel to those from the two Los Angeles surveys. Nor did many whites express the sense that their white ingroup was being disadvantaged because of special treatment for minorities. Almost none thought that they or whites in general had borne much of the brunt of discrimination. All these findings are shown in table 3.3. So increasing diversity seems not to have stimulated much ingroup consciousness among whites.

More interesting is that most respondents in each ethnic minority group also tended to identify themselves politically with a superordinate national identity than with their own ethnic subgroup. About two-thirds of each minority group, in each survey, thought of themselves as "just an American." A follow-up question asked what identity they adopted on "all" or "most issues." All minority groups were about twice as likely to say "just an American" as to cite their own ethnic or racial group.

However, this does not mean that these ethnic and racial groups completely ignore their own ingroups as sources of political identity. This can be seen in two ways. First, many viewed themselves as having a dual identity. In the 1995 Los Angeles survey, those who said they thought of themselves as "just an American" were then asked, "Which of the following is most true for you: just an American or both American and [white, black, Hispanic, or Asian, depending on earlier self-

TABLE 3.3 *Sociopolitical Identity, by Respondent Ethnicity*

| | Whites (%) | | | Blacks (%) | | | Hispanics (%) | | | Asians (%) |
|---|---|---|---|---|---|---|---|---|---|---|
| | 1994 | 1995 | GSS | 1994 | 1995 | GSS | 1994 | 1995 | GSS | |
| Political Identity[a] | | | | | | | | | | |
| On social/political issues, do you think of yourself as: | | | | | | | | | | |
| Just an American | 93 | 94 | 96 | 68 | 70 | 66 | 72 | 67 | 80 | 71 |
| Just an American, but also as a member of a group | — | 16 | — | — | 55 | — | — | 56 | — | 59 |
| Member of an ethnic/racial/nationality group | 4 | 5 | 3 | 30 | 30 | 29 | 26 | 29 | 17 | 27 |
| On all, most, some, or just a few issues | | | | | | | | | | |
| Just an American on all/most issues | 81 | 82 | 89 | 50 | 46 | 51 | 37 | 36 | 69 | 46 |
| Member of ethnic/racial/nationality group on all/most issues | 2 | 9 | 2 | 22 | 42 | 21 | 16 | 54 | 6 | 13 |
| Ethnic Group Consciousness | | | | | | | | | | |
| Discrimination against self (always/frequently) | 4 | — | — | 19 | — | — | 29 | — | — | 11 |
| Discrimination against fellow group members (always/frequently) | 9 | — | — | 45 | — | — | 46 | — | — | 15 |
| America owes my group a better chance (agree) | 17 | — | — | 67 | — | — | 72 | — | — | 37 |
| America has given my group a fair opportunity (disagree) | 10 | — | — | 56 | — | — | 26 | — | — | 28 |

*Sources:* 1994 and 1995 Los Angeles County Social Surveys, 1994 General Social Survey. Entries for Asians pool the first two surveys.
[a]In all cases, the base for percentaging is the total number of respondents in the specified ethnic group interviewed in that survey, excluding only those failing to respond to the original question.

identification]?" As shown in table 3.3, over half the putative "just Americans" among each ethnic minority group viewed themselves as both an American and a member of their own group. Second, their overall preference for American identity coexisted with widespread perceptions of being discriminated against: almost half believed that "other members of my ethnic group are discriminated against at least frequently," most felt that "America owes my group a better chance," and most blacks at least did not feel that "America has given my group a fair opportunity." Note that Asians were consistently less likely than blacks or Hispanics to feel badly treated.

Is there evidence of either blanket antagonism toward outgroups or systematic ingroup favoritism in group evaluations? One test used measures of stereotypes in which various groups were rated as "lazy" or "hardworking," "violent" or "peaceful," and "unintelligent" or "intelligent."[12] First, there is no evidence of blanket derogation of outgroups; indeed, most people evaluated most groups favorably. Instead, respondents from all four ethnic groups largely shared the same conventional and long-established group stereotypes. For example, all groups tended to see Asians as hardworking, intelligent, and law-abiding, and they tended to evaluate blacks less favorably on all three dimensions. Immigrants were generally viewed as quite hardworking. To illustrate these points, the data for the lazy-hardworking stereotype are presented in table 3.4. Moreover, there was little evidence of systematic ingroup favoritism. Overall, respondents evaluated their own ingroups more favorably than outgroups in just over half (55 percent) of the sixty-two available comparisons. On balance, group evaluations reflected the conventional and long-established group stereotypes of the broader American society more than they did ingroup favoritism.

The bottom line here is threefold. The predominant political identity, in all three ethnic groups, was allegiance to the superordinate American identity rather than to their own ethnic group, contrary to the notion of widespread ethnic balkanization. To be sure, there was a substantial sense of grievance among blacks and Latinos about discrimination and lack of fair treatment. But overall, Americans' views of outgroups did not reflect a simple ingroup favoritism pattern of strong ingroup loyalty and general antagonism toward outgroups. Instead, they seemed mainly to reflect a quite traditional and consensual pattern of cultural prejudices.

## THE NORMS REGARDING MULTICULTURALISM

What kind of a society would contemporary Americans prefer? Not surprisingly, whites strongly opposed "hard" multiculturalism. First, the

TABLE 3.4 *Stereotypes of Groups as Hardworking/Lazy, by Respondent Ethnicity*

| | Whites (%) | | | Blacks (%) | | | Hispanics (%) | | | Asians (%) |
|---|---|---|---|---|---|---|---|---|---|---|
| | 1994 | 1995 | GSS | 1994 | 1995 | GSS | 1994 | 1995 | GSS | |
| Target Group | | | | | | | | | | |
| Whites | 39 | 29 | 45 | 23 | 39 | 20 | 8 | 19 | 29 | 4 |
| Blacks | −18 | −11 | −29 | 2 | 16 | 43 | −53 | −26 | −9 | −40 |
| Hispanics | 14 | 25 | −13 | 27 | 48 | 7 | 43 | 50 | 46 | 12 |
| Asians | 55 | 68 | 41 | 46 | 53 | 67 | 37 | 41 | 67 | 72 |
| Legal immigrants | 35 | — | 23 | 28 | — | 44 | 47 | — | 61 | 49 |
| Illegal immigrants | 19 | — | −1 | 28 | — | 29 | 50 | — | 51 | 32 |

*Sources:* 1994 and 1995 Los Angeles County Social Surveys, 1994 General Social Survey. Entries for Asians pool the first two surveys.
*Note:* Each entry is the percentage perceiving target group members as hardworking (points 1 to 3 on a 7-point scale) minus the percentage perceiving them as lazy (points 5 to 7).

vast majority of whites thought people should assimilate to the broader culture, and that government should not encourage ethnic separateness. A plurality in each survey preferred "the melting pot" to ethnic distinctiveness, as shown in table 3.5 (those who chose the midpoint on the seven-point scale are not shown). Those who opted for "distinct cultures" were then asked if it was "up to the government to help racial and ethnic groups maintain their distinct cultures"; only 2 percent agreed. Similarly, virtually no whites thought that "people should think of themselves first and foremost as a member of a racial, religious, or ethnic group" (9 percent). Second, whites strongly opposed a group basis for representation: almost none (8 percent or fewer) wanted to tie congressional or educational representation to the size of various ethnic communities, adhering instead to the individualistic norm that "they should be considered purely on the basis of their ability without regard to their racial or ethnic background." Third, whites were almost unanimously opposed to ethnic or racial segregation. Only 12 percent agreed that "we would have less social problems if people of the same ethnic background lived and worked with people like themselves," and only 14 percent disagreed with the statement that "political organizations based on race or ethnicity promote separatism and make it hard for all of us to live together."

Since ethnic minorities are the presumed beneficiaries of multiculturalism, one might think they would support it out of group interest. But even they preferred a system of individually based rights over "hard" multiculturalism. Only about one-third in each minority group

TABLE 3.5 *Support for Norms of Multiculturalism, by Respondent Ethnicity*

| | Whites (%) | | | Blacks (%) | | | Hispanics (%) | | | Asians (%) |
|---|---|---|---|---|---|---|---|---|---|---|
| | 1994 | 1995 | GSS | 1994 | 1995 | GSS | 1994 | 1995 | GSS | |
| Social Multiculturalism | | | | | | | | | | |
| Should ethnic/racial groups: | | | | | | | | | | |
| Maintain distinct cultures? | 26 | 27 | 30 | 27 | 34 | 41 | 27 | 35 | 31 | 29 |
| Blend in, as in a melting pot? | 50 | 46 | 39 | 53 | 41 | 37 | 60 | 56 | 47 | 53 |
| People should think of themselves as individual Americans, not as members of racial/ethnic/nationality groups (disagree) | 9 | 9 | — | 22 | 24 | — | 24 | 25 | — | 19 |
| People of the same ethnic background should live/work with their own (agree) | 13 | 12 | — | 21 | 14 | — | 52 | 54 | — | 26 |
| Political Multiculturalism | | | | | | | | | | |
| Should congressmen match constituent ethnicity? (yes) | 8 | — | 6 | 18 | — | 27 | 23 | — | 15 | 9 |
| Should teachers match student ethnicity? (yes) | 6 | — | 6 | 13 | — | 18 | 10 | — | 18 | 11 |
| Are people best represented politically by their own? (yes) | 35 | — | 33 | 41 | — | 43 | 37 | — | 47 | 43 |
| Political organizations based on race/ethnicity promote separatism/conflict (disagree) | 14 | — | 13 | 30 | — | 28 | 28 | — | 47 | 30 |
| Racial/ethnic experience should be taught by a teacher from that group (agree) | 33 | — | 22 | 46 | — | 46 | 47 | — | 26 | 38 |
| Is too little attention given to racial/ethnic history? (yes) | 28 | — | 16 | 60 | — | 60 | 44 | — | 48 | 44 |

*Sources:* 1994 and 1995 Los Angeles County Social Surveys, 1994 General Social Survey. Entries for Asians pool the first two surveys.

supported maintaining distinct cultural groups, and even fewer thought government should help support the distinctiveness of ethnic groups (for example, 6 percent of the blacks and 8 percent of the Latinos). Over 40 percent "agreed strongly" that people should first and foremost think of themselves as individual Americans, while fewer than one-quarter felt that people should think of themselves primarily as members of ethnic or racial groups.[13] Blacks and Asians, like whites, also overwhelmingly opposed voluntary separatism, defined as "living and working among your own kind."[14]

This heavy opposition to a multiculturalist society does not mean that support for it was totally absent in minority communities. Among both blacks and Latinos, a visible minority supported some form of ethnic representation, and the size of that minority increased as the proposal moved away from the strict reliance on ethnicity characteristic of "hard" multiculturalism. About 20 percent supported basing political representation directly on ethnic quotas; about 30 percent endorsed ethnically based interest organizations; about 40 percent believed that "people are best represented by leaders of their own racial or ethnic background"; and about half believed that racial and ethnic history has received too little attention and that it should be taught by an individual from that ethnic group. But this sympathetic response to education about minority history and culture represented the high-water mark of support for multiculturalism and emerged only for the softer version that emphasized recognition and respect for diverse peoples.

In sum, there was little normative support for an ethnically divided society in any ethnic group. Most members of all three minority groups, as well as whites, preferred that individuals identify primarily with the culture as a whole rather than with their own ethnic groups; all four groups supported the norm of a superordinate national culture rather than a society organized according to ethnic subdivisions. Americans seem not to favor a "hard" multiculturalism as a political solution to whatever problems are posed by growing ethnic diversity.

## THE "ETHNIC CAULDRON" AS A THREAT TO WHITES

Does ethnic diversification threaten whites by heightening ingroup identity, outgroup antagonism, perceived deterioration in the quality of collective life, and resistance to minority-targeted policies? A power theory would suggest that a social context heavily populated by new immigrants will have all these effects. On the other hand, a symbolic politics theory would suggest that personal exposure to diversity will have less influence than long-standing predispositions based in cultural socialization, of which anti-black prejudices would seem to be the strongest.

Our test of exposure to diversity compared the attitudes of whites living in ethnically mixed neighborhoods with those of whites living in almost all-white neighborhoods. Because the heaviest immigration flows to Los Angeles have involved Latinos, our specific context predictors included: (1) Hispanic percentage in the respondent's zip code; (2) perception that whites are not the main group in the respondent's neighborhood; (3) perception that the white percentage in the neighborhood is dropping; and (4) perception of frequent contact with people who do not speak English very well. We also included as controls (5) the black percentage in the respondent's zip code and (6) respondent's fear of walking alone around his or her own block at night. In hierarchical regression analyses, four standard demographic variables (age, sex, education, and income) were entered in a second stage as controls.

Contrary to the threat hypothesis, a more ethnic context heightened neither whites' perceptions that they were being unfairly treated as a group nor their outgroup antagonism (defined in terms of symbolic racism targeted at blacks).[15] As shown in table 3.6 (columns 1 and 2), context explains less than 2 percent of the variance in each variable. Indeed, the only significant effect is that whites with the *fewest* blacks in their zip codes were the highest in symbolic racism (though that figure is probably not meaningful since in practice whites and blacks are so highly segregated that the median percentage of blacks in whites' zip codes is only 3 percent).

Instead, the residues of earlier socialization seem to be the key to both ingroup attachment and outgroup antagonism. Older whites were more likely to express pride in America and to feel that whites were being treated fairly, suggesting a generational difference in socialization rather than a threat-based response to ethnic diversity. Similarly, as a socialization theory might expect, older and less educated whites were highest in symbolic racism.[16]

Were whites' perceptions linking diversity to a deteriorating quality of community life driven by the realities of that diversification, as if increasing numbers of immigrants were displacing whites from their privileged positions? Or were such perceptions more symbolic in nature, stemming from long-standing racial and ethnic prejudices? Table 3.6 (column 3) presents the same regression analysis on the quality of life scale mentioned earlier. The five ethnic context terms again explained almost no variance, while symbolic racism against blacks had a strong effect. Whites' perceptions that diversity causes a deterioration of the community seemed to be based more in racial prejudices than in realistic ethnic threats.

TABLE 3.6 *Origins of Whites' Attitudes Toward Ethnic Diversity*

| | Unfair Treatment of Whites | Symbolic Racism | Declining Quality of Life | Opposition to Immigration | Opposition to Multilingualism |
|---|---|---|---|---|---|
| Context | | | | | |
| Hispanic percentage | −.03 | −.11 | −.03 | −.11 | −.11 |
| Outgroup main | .11 | .08 | .01 | −.02 | .00 |
| Change to outgroup | .09 | −.04 | −.02 | .00 | .02 |
| Foreign contact | −.02 | −.06 | .01 | .16** | .01 |
| Black percentage | −.03 | −.17* | .00 | −.02 | −.01 |
| Fear on block | .07 | .11 | .12 | .04 | .00 |
| Demographics | | | | | |
| Sex | −.10 | .00 | .00 | −.10 | .00 |
| Age | −.21** | .14* | .01 | −.03 | .11 |
| Education | −.04 | −.18* | −.14 | −.06 | .06 |
| Income | −.15* | .05 | −.04 | −.07 | .06 |
| Symbolic predispositions | | | | | |
| American identity | | | −.05 | .19** | .19** |
| Unfair treatment of whites | | | −.06 | .03 | .01 |
| Symbolic racism | | | .23*** | .34*** | .22*** |
| Poor quality of life | | | | .21*** | .21** |
| Adjusted $R^2$ | | | | | |
| Context only | 1.6% | 0.6% | 0.0% | 1.7% | 0.0% |
| Total | 6.2 | 4.4 | 5.2 | 28.1 | 15.9 |

*Sources:* 1994 Los Angeles County Social Survey.
*Note:* Each column is a separate regression equation. Entries are standardized regression coefficients (betas), and $n = 225$ to 239.
$^{*}p < .05$ $^{**}p < .01$ $^{***}p < .0001$

We saw earlier that whites were markedly more opposed than blacks or Latinos to policies that would benefit those minorities. However, this opposition also proves to stem more from long-standing racial and ethnic prejudices than from an increasing ethnic diversity that displaces whites from their privileged position. As a set, the context variables explained very little variance in opposition to these liberal immigration and language policies (1.7 percent and 0.0 percent, respectively). Perceptions that whites were discriminated against had no effect either. Instead, the presumed main products of earlier socialization—symbolic racism toward blacks and a sense of American identity—both had strong effects. The apparently more symbolic perceptions of a deteriorating quality of life, which were linked to unfavorable racial attitudes, as just indicated, also had a significant effect. It might be noted that the amount of variance accounted for in attitudes toward immigration was unusually high by the standards of such research ($r$ squared = 28.1 percent).[17]

In sum, the ethnic diversity of whites' residential contexts had very little effect on any of these political attitudes. However, it might be argued that ethnic diversification has been so pervasive in the Los Angeles basin that even whites living in nearly all-white neighborhoods experienced it at very high levels. This possibility could be checked, at least at the aggregate level, by comparing the attitudes of whites living in Los Angeles (as reflected in the LACSS) with the national sample interviewed in the GSS. If this context-driven hypothesis were correct, Los Angeles whites would seem more ethnically threatened and politically defensive than whites in the nation at large, given that Los Angeles far exceeds the average level of ethnic diversity elsewhere. However, Los Angeles whites, as reflected in the LACSS, had strikingly similar attitudes to those held by whites elsewhere, as reflected in the GSS, in terms of policy preferences (table 3.2), political identity (table 3.3), group stereotypes (table 3.4), and norms about multiculturalism (table 3.5). Further evidence on the same point comes from a study that tested the effects of ethnic context on whites' immigration and language policy preferences within the 1994 GSS (Sears, Cheleden, and Henry 1997). In that case, context could be measured only at the city or county level, not at the neighborhood level. But, there too, context had no effect: whites living in highly diverse communities had very similar attitudes to those living in largely all-white areas. So the lack of effect of ethnic context appears to be a reasonably robust finding. Either growing ethnic diversity is not personally threatening to whites or such threats do not have much political effect.[18]

Thus, these findings are contrary to the ethnic balkanization viewpoint in two ways. Living in the midst of rapid ethnic diversification seemed not to generate a politically defensive response among whites, whether in terms of ingroup solidarity, outgroup antagonism, perceived quality of life, or opposition to policies benefiting ethnic minorities. Rather, in all these cases the presumed products of earlier cultural socialization (symbolic racism and American identity) were considerably more central. Linked to them as well were more symbolic perceptions that the quality of collective life was going downhill. Second, whites' perceptions of being discriminated against as a group were not generally a central factor; such perceptions were neither stimulated by heavily ethnic contexts nor very powerful in generating anti-minority policy preferences. This finding parallels the results of a number of earlier studies, which found that whites' ingroup identity and ingroup consciousness were considerably less powerful factors in their political thinking than were their outgroup antagonisms (see Jessor 1988; Sears and Jessor 1996; Sears, van Laar, et al. 1997).

## BLACK EXCEPTIONALISM

The "black exceptionalism" hypothesis proposes that whites' attitudes toward ethnic minorities are more complex than the simple ingroup-outgroup divide would suggest. African Americans are especially likely to be the object of negative and highly crystallized predispositions because they have been both especially stigmatized and at the center of political controversy for over three centuries. In contrast, Latinos and Asians, the main contemporary immigrant groups, have had a much lower political profile over the years; as a result, relatively few white Americans have had such long and strong socialization histories about them.

### The Centrality of Anti-Black Attitudes

One implication of this theory is that whites' attitudes toward blacks will be more negative than their attitudes toward the large, newer immigrant groups. Table 3.4 has already shown that whites in our study regarded blacks as "lazier" than they did Asians, Latinos, or immigrants. Data presented elsewhere show that whites display more symbolic racism toward blacks as well (Sears and van Laar 1999). A second implication is that whites' attitudes toward blacks will be more crystallized than their attitudes toward more recent immigrant groups. Data presented elsewhere show that different racial attitudes (symbolic racism and stereotypes) are more consistent with each other when targeted for blacks than when targeted for either Hispanics or Asians (Sears and van Laar 1999). Also, racial policy attitudes are more stable over time than most other policy attitudes (Converse and Markus 1979; Kinder and Sanders 1996; Sears 1983b).

A third implication is that attitudes toward blacks will have more influence over preferences about minority-relevant policies than will attitudes toward other minority groups. Anti-black attitudes will, of course, dominate preferences about policies that have explicitly to do with African Americans. But according to this hypothesis, they will also intrude to an unusual degree into preferences about policies primarily relevant to other minority groups.

The results of the empirical test of this "black exceptionalism" proposition are presented in figure 3.1. Issues relevant to minorities are classified into three groups: those explicitly targeted for blacks (such as preferences for blacks in hiring and promotion), those implicitly targeted for blacks (such as welfare), and those primarily targeted for other minority groups (such as bilingual education).[19] A regression equation is estimated for each issue in which the predictors were both symbolic racism and stereotypes toward each of the three minority groups. In general, only symbolic racism had significant effects. As a result, figure 3.1 displays the mean regression coefficient for each form of symbolic racism, averaging across all issues in each category.

Not surprisingly, symbolic racism toward blacks had by far the strongest effect on preferences about policies targeted explicitly for blacks. Attitudes toward other minorities played essentially no role. It still had the dominant influence over attitudes about policies targeted implicitly for blacks, though the effects were not as strong.[20] But anti-black attitudes intruded even into whites' responses to policies targeted implicitly or explicitly for Latinos and Asians, such as immigration, language, and affirmative action for them, generally matching even the effects of attitudes toward the target groups themselves. In brief, white Americans do not treat all outgroups equally. Specifically, anti-black attitudes have a disproportionate influence over whites' preferences about policies relevant to any minority groups.

## African Americans in a Diversifying Society

Blacks have been the largest and most visible minority group throughout America for many years. In areas such as Los Angeles, however, they are beginning to be displaced by both Hispanics and Asians. In 1970 Los Angeles County was 18 percent Hispanic and 11 percent black; in 1990 it was 38 percent Hispanic and 10 percent black. In 1980 blacks outnumbered Asians two to one in Los Angeles County, but by 1990 the two groups were about equal in number (Clark 1996). Blacks are being politically displaced as well: in the 1993 Los Angeles mayoralty race, black voters outnumbered Hispanic voters by two to one, but in the 1997 race, Hispanic voters outnumbered black voters.

Does an increasingly immigrant context therefore threaten blacks as well as whites, perhaps generating strong anti-immigrant attitudes? Or do the residues of earlier socialization dominate current personal threats for blacks as well as whites? In fact, ethnic context again does not seem to have a significant political effect. Blacks do not seem to find the increasing ethnic diversity of their neighborhoods threatening per se; indeed, they find the change to be for the better, if anything (see table 3.1). Nor does the increasingly Hispanic proximal context fuel a defen-

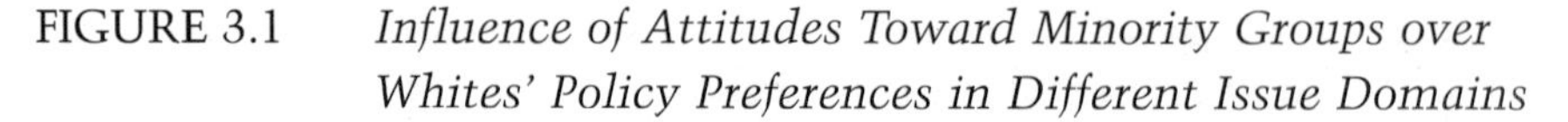

FIGURE 3.1 *Influence of Attitudes Toward Minority Groups over Whites' Policy Preferences in Different Issue Domains*

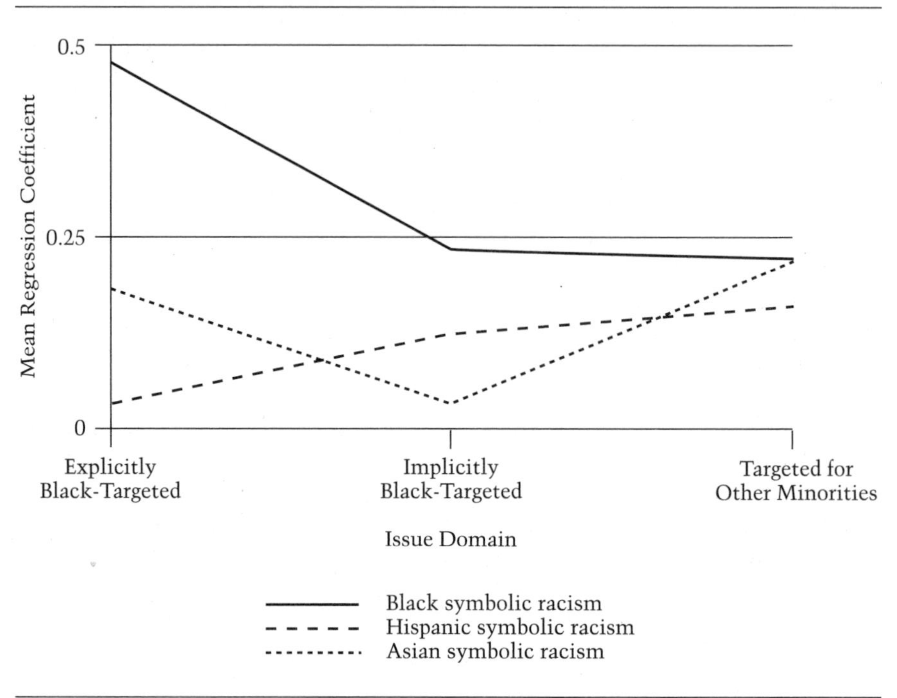


*Note:* Entries are mean standardized regression coefficients (betas).

sive political response. To test this, we carried out regression equations on blacks similar to those on whites presented in table 3.6 (see Sears, Cheleden, and Henry 1997). The context variables explained almost none of the variance in attitudes toward the ingroup, outgroups, or policy preferences (only one of the fifteen context terms was statistically significant). In contrast, socialization variables had consistent effects.[21] Better educated, younger blacks were considerably more likely to perceive racial discrimination and more likely to identify with their own racial subgroup than were less educated or older blacks.

As suggested earlier, there is good reason to expect that blacks' own ingroup identity might be especially highly crystallized and thus that perceived group interest might play an especially prominent political role for blacks. We did indeed find evidence of a group-interested response to increased immigration, based particularly in a sense of economic competition with Hispanics. Blacks were especially likely to predict negative economic consequences of immigration (table 3.1) and to be opposed to liberal immigration and language policies (table 3.2). And as shown in table 3.7, their attitudes toward immigration policy seemed

TABLE 3.7 *Regression Analyses of Opposition to Immigration Policy: Black Respondents*

| | Correlation Coefficients | Regression Coefficients |
|---|---|---|
| Perceived impact of Hispanic immigration on blacks | .32** | .22** (.07) |
| American identity | .20** | .10 (.07) |
| Symbolic racism against Hispanics | .09** | .01 (.08) |
| Political identity | | |
| Party identification | .10 | .03 (.04) |
| Ideology | .07 | .03 (.03) |
| $R^2$ | — | 14% |

*Notes:* Regression coefficients are unstandardized (Bs) with their corresponding standard errors. High scores on party identification and ideology refer to greater Republicanism and conservatism.
*Source:* 1994 Los Angeles County Social Survey.
$^*p < .05$
$^{**}p < .01$

to stem in part from perceptions that Hispanic immigration will have negative consequences for blacks (also see Vidanage and Sears 1995). However, ingroup identity did not play a large role in this group-interested response to immigration. Both black identity (the inverse of American identity) and perceived discrimination were actually slightly negatively correlated with opposition to immigration ($r$ = -.20, -.07).

In sum, whites had more negative and more crystallized attitudes toward blacks than they did toward other minority groups, presumably because of longer and more negative socialization. Those anti-black attitudes also had a broader influence over whites' policy preferences, even affecting their preferences about policies that had almost nothing to do with blacks. Blacks' opposition to liberal immigration policies apparently stemmed in part from group interest. However, this group interest seemed to originate more in generational and educational experiences than in factors emphasized in group-centered theories, such as a highly ethnic immediate context or black political identity.

## LATINOS: OLD OR NEW PATTERNS OF POLITICAL ADAPTATION?

Are Latinos, the largest body of new immigrants, likely to follow a multicultural model, involving the persistence of Latin language and culture, a Latino political identity, continuing support for immigration, and perhaps ethnic separatism? Or are they more likely to assimilate into the "melting pot," as more of them are socialized within the American culture? According to a symbolic politics theory, longer residence in American culture, especially beginning in youth, will erode Latinos' own distinctive social identity, produce more identification with the larger society, and reduce support for policies that contribute to a multicultural "mosaic," such as liberal immigration policies and widespread acceptance of Spanish as an alternative to English.

We have already noted some findings that suggest this more assimilationist trajectory. Latinos preferred a political identity of "just an American" over a more ethnic designation and generally opposed "hard" multiculturalist norms. They had a more positive view of collective life in Los Angeles than whites did, suggesting more satisfaction with the community.

But the cultural socialization model could be tested more systematically using the 1994 LACSS. Data on attitudes toward immigration are shown in figure 3.2 (analagous data on attitudes toward multilingualism are not shown; see Vidanage, van Laar, and Sears 1996). Indicators of socialization to the American culture included having parents born in the United States (19 percent had at least one born in the United States), having been born in the United States oneself (25 percent were), years lived in the United States, and age (alpha = .69).[22] Available indicators of behavioral assimilation included preferring to be interviewed in English rather than Spanish (38 percent preferred English), having American citizenship (44 percent did), and living in a non-entry neighborhood (alpha = .51).

This simple model was quite successful, explaining 34 percent of the variance in Latinos' attitudes toward immigration policy, and 27 percent of the variance in their attitudes toward language policy.[23] It showed that longer and earlier exposure to American culture promoted both a sense of American identity and assimilationist behavior, and that they in turn promoted more conservative, less group-interested preferences about immigration and multilingualism.[24] Put another way, second-generation Latinos, who had mastered English and lived in the United States for most of their lives, identified themselves more as Americans than as Latinos and did not take such sharply group-interested positions on these issues.[25]

How then can we understand the apparently group-interested attitudes described earlier, such as Latinos' perceptions of discrimination and relatively high levels of support for liberal immigration, language, and affirmative action policies? These attitudes are not necessarily inconsistent with the view that a broad process of acculturation of Latinos to American society is under way, since most Latinos in Los Angeles are comparative newcomers from Mexico, and so they dominated the overall response of Latinos in our sample. According to this view, the group-

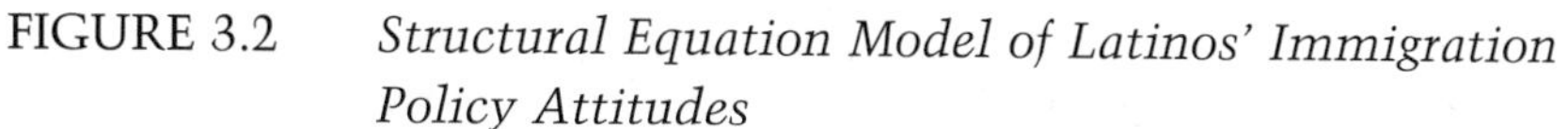
FIGURE 3.2 *Structural Equation Model of Latinos' Immigration Policy Attitudes*

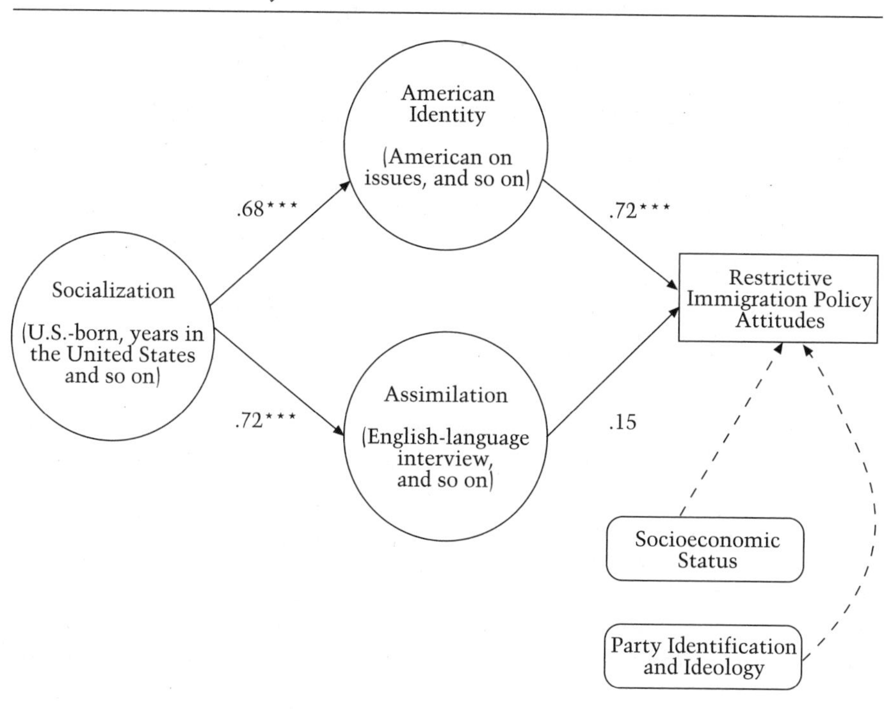


$^{***}p < .001$

interested response would be transitional, since such policy preferences are more typical of the less assimilated newcomers than of those more fully socialized in the United States, whose numbers will grow as time goes on. In this sense, Latinos seem to resemble turn-of-the-century European immigrants more than they do African Americans.

## SUMMARY

This chapter presents the preliminary findings from a larger project on Americans' attitudes toward both ethnic diversity and multiculturalist policy proposals. It is based on data from representative samples of adults in both the large and diverse Los Angeles metropolitan area and the nation as a whole. In two respects, we see clear evidence of the political tensions created by America's growing cultural diversity. Many people in all ethnic groups perceived a deterioration in the quality of collective life, and they seemed to connect growing ethnic diversity to that. Moreover, there was a sharp and seemingly group-interested ethnic polarization about policies that have a direct impact on minority groups, such as immigration policy, multilingualism, and affirmative action. These phenomena would seem at first glance to be symptoms of a growing ethnic balkanization.

On the other hand, a "hard" multiculturalism did not have much popular resonance, even among the racial, ethnic, and immigrant groups intended to receive its benefits. Neither the majority whites nor ethnic minorities wished to privilege race and ethnicity as a primary basis for social identity, political representation, or resource allocation.[26] These findings suggest that the vast majority of Americans in all ethnic groups remain committed to a system of individual rights rather than one of group rights.

These normative preferences also open up questions about underlying psychological processes. Contemporary social psychological theories often emphasize the ubiquity of group identities, outgroup antagonisms, and intergroup competition. In their extreme forms, such perspectives tend to depict a simple Hobbesian "we versus them" universe in which the arrival of new immigrants inevitably breeds a resentful defensive reaction from the dominant white majority. Such perspectives would certainly seem to be apt ones for understanding contemporary American life given the widespread ethnic diversification of our society and the sharp political conflicts it has generated.

However, the data were generally more consistent with a symbolic politics interpretation, which focuses instead on socialization experiences through the life course, the ensuing predispositions, and the political symbols that become most salient in adults' information environments. In this latter framework, psychological necessity does not privilege groups in the formation, crystallization, and accessibility of fundamental predispositions. Nor are group objects necessarily destined to become the most politically salient political symbols.

In a number of respects, whites' political identifications in the face of increased diversity did not seem to portend severe ethnic balkanization in the future. Almost all identified themselves as "just an American" rather than as white people, and they expressed few complaints about being mistreated because they were white.[27] As a group, they showed neither blanket rejection of ethnic outgroups nor any simple pattern of ingroup favoritism in group evaluations. Their only consistent outgroup antagonism focused on blacks. Nor did their responses to contemporary policy debates seem much influenced by the threats posed by an increasingly diverse ethnic context. Their preferences on minority-related policy issues were less influenced by any sense that diversity is working to the disadvantage of whites as a group than by long-standing attitudes toward blacks, reflecting the continuing impact of the oldest and most difficult of America's ethnic and racial tensions.

These relatively impervious white responses to diversity are perhaps not too surprising, given their historically dominant role in American society. But even though ethnic minorities would presumably be the beneficiaries of a group-based multiculturalist political system, we do not see much ethnic balkanization in their attitudes either. Relatively few supported tying political rights and entitlements to ethnicity, preferring a traditional American individualism instead. Relatively few identified politically primarily with their own ethnic group, most describing themselves principally as "just an American." If pressed further, about half indicated a bicultural identity, but even they did not reject the superordinate national identity. Their evaluations of outgroups were not generally antagonistic; indeed, the group stereotypes held by all three minority groups tended to follow a society-wide pattern of some derogation of blacks and much respect for immigrants. As a result, they did not show any simple ingroup favoritism in evaluations of the various ethnic and racial groups. Blacks' political attitudes did not seem much influenced by a context-driven sense of threat from new waves of immigrants. Latinos as a whole did show a pattern of group-interested policy preferences, but this seemed transitional since those preferences eroded with longer residence in the United States.

To be sure, our data do show some signs of ethnic conflict. Most notably there is sharp ethnic polarization in the main areas of minority-targeted policy. But as just indicated, this seemed to be driven by old anti-black prejudices among whites, and among Latinos it tended to hold only for the new arrivals (of whom there are many in Los Angeles today). A considerable percentage in each minority group identified themselves as hyphenated Americans (also see Huo et al. 1996). However, ethnicity was a secondary political identity for most, and it, too, was more common among recent immigrants, suggesting that with time it will become a less prominent feature of those populations. Blacks and Latinos perceived considerable continuing discrimination against their own groups (also see Hochschild 1995). However, such perceptions did not seem to be centrally driving ethnic polarization over policy issues. And we see evidence that blacks felt considerable economic competition with Latinos; such feelings do seem to heighten their opposition to further immigration and, in that sense, contribute to ethnic divisions.

In short, there was little mass support among either the white majority or the racial and ethnic minority groups for official recognition of these ethnic differences or for special entitlements attached to them. And the reality is that the "new immigrants" are in the process of politically assimilating to mainstream American society. It may therefore be that the conventional wisdom about ethnic balkanization, reputedly responsible for the so-called cultural divides in American society and politics, has been somewhat exaggerated, at least as far as the new immigrant groups are concerned.

## CONCLUSIONS

The multiculturalist movement grew out of the black civil rights movement. In an important sense, it is an ideological response to the persistence of racial inequalities and the failure to achieve Martin Luther King Jr.'s dream of a color-blind society. But it has gone considerably further, by extending its principles from blacks to a host of other disadvantaged groups. It proposes that all "people of color," whether black, brown, or yellow, share the common history of having been victims of prejudice and discrimination, and all should be redressed accordingly.

One can raise questions about this extension of the distinctively African American struggle to other groups. The greatest enduring exception to the generally upward trajectory of American immigrant groups after entry has been the chronically disadvantaged position of African Americans. They continue to face obstacles considerably greater than those faced by the newer immigrant groups. We have seen just one piece of that picture in our findings that whites' attitudes toward blacks are both more negative and more powerful than their attitudes toward either Latinos or Asians. Others have documented the persistent disadvantages of blacks in education, income, and wealth and the continuing housing segregation they experience (Farley 1996; Massey and Denton 1993; Oliver and Shapiro 1995; also see Glazer 1997).

To be sure, new immigrant groups have historically suffered systematic discrimination and other forms of disadvantage. However, such disadvantages have typically endured for relatively short periods of time. It would be difficult to argue that serious prejudice against Irish immigrants lasted much more than a century after the great potato famine; by contrast, prejudice against African Americans remains a vital force today, more than three centuries after the start of the slave trade. Today's Latino and Asian immigrants often suffer great economic and other structural disadvantages. But already they are considerably less residentially segregated than are blacks (Clark 1996), and from our data they appear to be politically assimilating as well. In that sense, their experience seems to resemble that of earlier European immigrant groups more closely than that of African Americans. One can therefore question the multicultural extension of the African American analogy to groups that have fundamentally different histories and status.

A particularistic multiculturalism proposes a fundamental structural reorganization of traditional principles of communal representation. It would presumably empower minority groups by making ethnicity more central in allocation decisions. Greater power ought, in principle, to produce more equality, but one can see a number of hazards of the multicultural approach. Most obviously, advocacy of the multiculturalist agenda has generated—and presumably will continue to do so—a strong conservative counterreaction. It advocates a far-reaching change in American society that is distasteful to most of the general public. This in turn may exacerbate nativist reactions to all issues relevant to ethnic minorities. Also, most white Americans tend to equate the term "minorities" with "blacks." As a result, issues that may be specific to the needs of new immigrant groups, such as immigration and language policies, may become absorbed in the older, more difficult American struggle over race rather than dealt with in their own terms.

The other side of that coin is that debates over multiculturalism may distract attention from the more basic problems of our society, such as the reality of continuing black disadvantage, especially the persisting black underclass, and economic inequality more generally. The age-old dream of a race-blind society may be only a dream, at least in its most literal form. Nevertheless, this nation has made impressive progress toward that goal in this century (see, for example, Schuman, Steeh, Bobo, and Krysan 1997). As we have emphasized, it still has far to go. But we agree with those who believe that a further and substantial obstacle will be set if ethnic and racial groups privilege their own group identities (Kennedy 1997).

The lack of mass support for "hard" multiculturalism observed in all ethnic groups holds despite much supportive elite rhetoric and official policy both in California and in the nation more generally. This gap between elite and mass creates a dynamic that might have a number of long-term outcomes. It could conceivably lead to acceptance of institutionalized multiculturalism by the mass public, in the event that liberal elites are sufficiently persuasive and official policy sufficiently pervasive. At this time that seems unlikely, since multiculturalism clearly has already generated strong elite opposition, which has recruited considerable popular support. The successes in California of Proposition 187 in 1994, Proposition 209 in 1996, and Proposition 227 in 1998 are concrete indicators of this resistance. Finally, elite contention over the multicultural agenda could spread ethnic polarization beyond the policy issues we have examined to the very principles of communal representation, replacing what we see now as a rather consensual rejection of multiculturalism.

The tensions between official policy and mass attitude have yet to fully play themselves out, in our view. But they are likely to do so in the next few years as the effects of massive immigration increasingly make themselves felt, not just in California but in the numerous other areas that have also experienced major demographic change. Whether the nation then begins to polarize along ethnic lines, as so many other nations have, and/or between the defenders of traditional Americanism and the proponents of some new multiculturalism, remains to be seen.

In general, a symbolic politics account assumes that people respond to ongoing political issues according to their long-standing political predispositions. Our data show the staying power of a traditional American ethos, one that emphasizes a common national identity and cultural assimilation. But the particular symbols dominating the current political debate are also crucial in that they determine which predispositions are elicited. Proposals that challenge deep-seated and long-standing values are unlikely to succeed. Much therefore depends on elites' political response to increasing diversity. In this regard, it is striking that President Clinton, despite his well-publicized commitment to "recognizing" and "representing" America's diversity, repeatedly emphasizes the priority of finding "common ground" and achieving racial reconciliation in a more integrated society.

The relative salience of various political symbols is typically not completely arbitrary, of course. Ethnic diversity is a salient issue in today's politics in part because of the realities of massive immigration, and in part because of both the demands made by ethnic minorities and the political responses to them. But elites also make political choices: they emphasize some of the many political issues offered up by a complex society and remain silent on others. If elites on either side choose to make ethnicity salient, they can stimulate ingroup identities or outgroup antagonisms by "playing the race card" (or the "racism card"), the "meritocratic" or "equality" card, or the "illegal alien" card. Proposition 187, for example, seems to have won in part by stimulating outgroup antagonism among whites. But it created considerable bitterness in minority communities. In our data, blacks' and Hispanics' ethnic identities (in terms of the question about "all" or "most issues") were considerably stronger in the 1995 survey, conducted shortly after the passage of Proposition 187, than they had been in 1994 (see table 3.3). This increased group consciousness closely resembles findings from surveys done following the Watts rioting in 1965 (see Sears and McConahay 1973). Ingroup favoritism *can* be created by a polarizing political environment, then, even if it is not inherent in the beast.

It could be argued that the contemporary debate among elites about diversity has to a significant degree been structured as one between nativism and "hard" multiculturalism, both of which make ethnicity the centerpiece of their stories. The advocacy of multiculturalism, by stimulating nativism (and racism), may therefore have ironically set into motion political events that make even the softer versions of multiculturalism more difficult to achieve. That is perhaps one of the lessons of the politics of the last decade, with California's plebiscitary democracy at the head of the class.

## APPENDIX

The following describes the scales used in tables 3.6 and 3.7, and in figure 3.2, based on the 1994 LACSS. All scales were composed by standardizing the constituent items and then adding them together.

*Quality of Life* Five items: those shown in table 3.1 on conflict between ethnic groups, effects of ethnicity on the quality of life, future of ethnic relations, and effects of ethnic groups on the economy, plus one on the effects of ethnic groups on government effectiveness. Cronbach's alpha for whites = .55.

*American Identity* Three items: one shown in table 3.3 on being "just an American" on issues, plus items on pride in being American and willingness to move outside the United States to improve one's work or living conditions. For whites, alpha = .38; for blacks, alpha = .43; for Hispanics, alpha = .63.

*Symbolic Racism* Three items: do blacks get more attention from the government than they deserve; should they work their ways up without special favors; and are they too demanding in their push for equal rights. For whites, alpha = .73. For blacks the same items were used except using Hispanics rather than blacks as the target group; alpha = .51.

*Unfair Treatment of Whites* The four items in the "ethnic group conciousness" panel of table 3.3; for whites, alpha = .59.

*Immigration policy* Nine items: Those shown in the "immigration" panels of table 3.2 except for the Proposition 187 item, plus one on requiring national identity cards. For whites, alpha = .66; for blacks, alpha = .69; for Hispanics, alpha = .74.

*Language Policy* Four items shown in table 3.2. For whites, alpha = .56; for Hispanics, alpha = .70.

*Impact of Hispanic Immigration* Two items on perceived increases in crime and higher taxes. For blacks, alpha = .47.

---

This chapter is a summary of results that have been presented elsewhere separately (Sears et al. 1994a, 1994b; Citrin et al. 1995; Sears, Cheleden, and Henry 1997; Sears and van Laar 1999; Sears et al. 1997; Vidanage and Sears 1995; Vidanage, van Laar, and Sears 1996). We wish to express our particular thanks to Michael Greenwell and Nicholas Valentino for their help with data collection and analysis, and to Marilynn Brewer, P. J. Henry, and Jim Sidanius for their helpful comments.

## NOTES

1. We wish neither to oversimplify the conditions under which immigrants of all groups have arrived in the United States nor to say that there have not been cases of at least quasi-slavery and indentured servitude in other groups. Our point is that the ancestors of the vast majority of today's African Americans arrived as slaves, whereas relatively few of the ancestors of today's hyphenated Americans of other groups did.
2. Although see Eberhardt and Randall 1997.
3. This is the aggregate-level consequence of the individual-level "person-positivity bias" (see Sears 1983a).
4. One reason, as categorization theories would suggest, is that whites have historically been so numerically dominant in most of the United States that "whiteness" has been of as little note as the air they breathe. But that does not change the fact that in general white group identity has had relatively low political salience.
5. This would, of course, be expected for any sizable and visible minority group that has been stigmatized for centuries.
6. The city of Los Angeles is a separate political entity and contains approximately one-third of the population of Los Angeles County.
7. An interesting sidelight of this two-pronged strategy is that most respondents proved quite accurate in describing the ethnicity of their own neighborhoods.
8. This increasing ethnic mixing holds in most other major metropolitan areas of the United States, though usually to a lesser degree (Clark 1996). But it must be qualified in three important ways. The mixing more often involves Hispanics, African Americans, and Asians than whites; it is greater at the city or community level than at the neighborhood or block level; and it is likely that residential segregation is greater than that in other spheres of life (Clark 1996). To be sure, Los Angeles, like all large American cities, exhibits very high levels of black-white housing segregation (Massey and Denton 1993).
9. This, of course, does not rule out their responding to a sense that their group hegemony is being threatened (that is, that there is a threat to their sense of group position; see Bobo and Hutchings 1996; Blumer 1958).
10. It should be remembered that many whites and blacks do not have a clear understanding of the term "bilingual education," often confusing it with foreign language instruction (Huddy and Sears 1995).
11. As opposed to: "The government should not make any special effort to help minorities because they should help themselves." The sharp change from

1994 to 1995 probably mainly reflects a change in item wording in which a middle option ("somewhere in between") was dropped. Whites were strongly opposed to preferential treatment even when the memory of past injustice was invoked: in the 1994 LACSS, 85 percent disagreed that "because of the history of slavery, blacks are more deserving of special treatment from the government than are other groups in our society."

12. Questions about the lazy-hardworking stereotype were asked in all three surveys; questions about the other two appeared only in the 1995 LACSS. Similar findings hold for the other measure of outgroup antagonism we have relied on here, symbolic racism (see Sears and van Laar 1999).

13. This may underestimate support for ethnically based political identities to the extent that blacks and Latinos were thinking about whites' racial identity, rather than their own, when they responded to this item.

14. Latinos were more sympathetic to such separatism, but this is the only case in which a norm of social multiculturalism was supported by a majority within any minority group.

15. Our primary index of outgroup antagonism is symbolic racism targeted at blacks. Symbolic racism has substantially stronger effects on whites' political attitudes than do older versions of anti-black antagonism, such as old-fashioned racism, group affect, or stereotypes (Sears, van Laar, et al. 1997). Second, as seen later in the chapter, symbolic racism against Hispanics or Asians has substantially weaker effects (also see Sears and van Laar 1999).

16. Symbolic racism is not explained very well by this model ($r$ squared = 4.4 percent), but we would not expect it to be very helpful since our theoretical assumption is that most symbolic racism can be traced to quite stable, long-standing racial attitudes and nonracial values (see Miller and Sears 1986; Sears 1983). With those measured, it is explained much better, with $r$-squares over 30 percent (see Sears, van Laar, et al. 1997).

17. Both immigration and language policy have been the subject of considerable political debate in California, so it is not surprising that whites' attitudes are rather well crystallized (the alphas are .72 and .62).

18. Most tests of ethnic context are vulnerable to a "white flight" artifact: the threatened whites flee to all-white areas, leaving only the tolerant behind (Voss 1996). This might lead us to expect that residents of far-flung, all-white suburbs will have more anti-minority policy preferences than those living in more ethnically diverse neighborhoods. However, this does not occur in our data either (see table 3.6). It is logically possible, though an empirical long shot, that a threat-driven conservatism in diverse neighborhoods and the "white flight" conservatism in distant suburbs have exactly offsetting effects, yielding overall null effects of context.

19. These analyze only the white respondents in the 1994 GSS and the 1994 and 1995 LACSS. There were twelve, eighteen, and thirty-two issues in these three categories, respectively. For details, see Sears and van Laar (1999).

20. These are simplified, underspecified models. More fully specified models show that the variables omitted in figure 3.1 do not play a large role in these policy preferences (Sears and van Laar 1999, 1997).

21. In the symbolic politics framework, generational and education effects are usually treated as indicators of earlier socialization (see Miller and Sears 1986; Sears and McConahay 1973).
22. In the 1994 LACSS, 70 percent of the foreign-born Latinos were of Mexican origin.
23. Both scale reliabilities were quite similar for Latinos (.74 and .64) and whites (.72 and .62).
24. Interestingly enough, symbolic racism against blacks was not the issue for Latinos that it was for whites. The reliability of the scale was much lower among Latinos (.44 to .72), and it did not play a strong role in Latinos' policy preferences.
25. A standard alternative model focuses instead on social class (see, for example, Cain, Kiewiet, and Uhlaner 1991). In this view, working-class Latinos would identify with the Democratic Party and its more liberal policies, and middle-class Latinos would gravitate toward the Republican Party and its conservative politics. However, this alternative received little support. By themselves, social class, party identification, and ideology explained 7 percent of the variance in immigration policy attitudes, and 11 percent of the variance in language policy attitudes. In both cases, only social class was statistically significant.
26. Nor do we see evidence that multiculturalism is "the wave of the future," in the sense of being especially popular among the young and better-educated (for these analyses, see Sears et al. 1994a; Citrin et al. 1995).
27. It might be argued that whites consider American identity to be the same as white identity. We cannot test this. However, note the null results for perceived white discrimination. And we can say that here, as elsewhere, there is little mass appeal to white supremacist politics.

## REFERENCES

Appiah, K. Anthony, and Gutmann, Amy. (1996). *Color conscious: The Political morality of race.* Princeton, N.J.: Princeton University Press.

Berry, John W., Kalin, Rudolf, and Taylor, Donald M. (1977). *Multiculturalism and ethnic attitudes in Canada.* Ottawa: Minister of Supply and Services.

Blalock, Hubert M., Jr. (1967). *Toward a theory of minority-group relations.* New York: Wiley.

Blumer, Herbert (1958). Race prejudice as a sense of group position. *Pacific Sociological Review, 1,* 3–7.

Bobo, Lawrence. (1983). Whites' opposition to busing: Symbolic racism or realistic group conflict? *Journal of Personality and Social Psychology, 45,* 1196–1210.

Bobo, Lawrence, and Hutchings, Vincent L. (1996). Perceptions of racial group competition: Extending Blumer's theory of group position to a multiracial social context. *American Sociological Review, 61,* 951–73.

Brewer, Marilynn B., Dull, Valerie, and Lui, L. (1981). Perceptions of the elderly: Stereotypes as prototypes. *Journal of Personality and Social Psychology, 41,* 656–70.

Brewer, Marilynn B., and Gardner, Wendi. (1996). Who is this "we"?: Levels of collective identity and self representations. *Journal of Personality and Social Psychology, 71,* 83–93.

Cain, Bruce E., Kiewiet, D. Roderick, and Uhlaner, Carole J. (1991). The acquisition of partisanship by Latinos and Asian Americans. *American Journal of Political Science, 35,* 390–422.

Citrin, Jack, Haas, Ernest B., Muste, Christopher, and Reingold, Beth. (1994). Is American nationalism changing?: Implications for foreign policy. *International Studies Quarterly, 38,* 1–31.

Citrin, Jack, Sears, David O., Muste, Christopher, and Wong, Cara. (1995). Liberalism and multiculturalism: The new ethnic agenda in mass opinion. Paper presented at the annual meeting of the American Political Science Association, Chicago (1995).

Clark, William A. V. (1996). Residential patterns: Avoidance, assimilation, and succession. In Roger Waldinger and Mehdi Bozorgmehr (Eds.), *Ethnic Los Angeles* (pp. 109–38). New York: Russell Sage Foundation.

Converse, Philip E., and Markus, Gregory B. (1979). *Plus ça change . . :* The new CPS election study panel. *American Political Science Review, 73,* 32–49.

Davis, F. James. (1991). *Who is black? One nation's definition.* University Park: Pennsylvania State University Press.

Dawson, Michael. (1994). *Behind the mule: Race and class in African American politics.* Princeton, N.J.: Princeton University Press.

Dovidio, John F., Gaertner, Samuel L., Isen, Alice M., and Lowrance, Robert. (1995). Group representations and intergroup bias: Positive affect, similarity, and group size. *Personality and Social Psychology Bulletin, 21,* 856–65.

Eberhardt, Jennifer L., and Randall, Jennifer L. (1997). The essential notion of race. *Psychological Science, 8,* 198–203.

Farley, Reynolds. (1996). *The new American reality: Who we are, how we got here, where we are going.* New York: Russell Sage Foundation.

Fiske, Susan T., and Neuberg, Steven L. (1990). A continuum of impression formation, from category-based to individuating processes: Influences of information and motivation on attention and interpretation. *Advances in Experimental Social Psychology, 23,* 1–74.

Geertz, Clifford. (1964). Ideology as a cultural system. In David E. Apter (Ed.), *Ideology and discontent* (pp. 47–76). New York: Free Press.

Giles, Michael W., and Hertz, Kaenan. (1994). Racial threat and partisan identification. *American Political Science Review, 88,* 317–26.

Glazer, Nathan. (1997). *We are all multiculturalists now.* Cambridge: Harvard University Press.

Higham, John. (1985). *Strangers in the land: Patterns of American nativism 1860–1925.* 2nd ed. New York: Atheneum.

Hirschfeld, Lawrence A. (1996). *Race in the making: Cognition, culture, and the child's construction of human kinds.* Cambridge, Mass.: MIT Press.

Hochschild, Jennifer L. (1995). *Facing up to the American dream.* Princeton, N.J.: Princeton University Press.

Horowitz, Donald L. (1985). *Ethnic groups in conflict.* Berkeley: University of California Press.

Huddy, Leonie, and Sears, David O. (1995). Opposition to bilingual education: Prejudice or the defense of realistic interests? *Social Psychology Quarterly, 58,* 133–43.

Hughes, Michael. (1997). Symbolic racism, old-fashioned racism, and whites' opposition to affirmative action. In Steven A. Tuch and Jack K. Martin (Eds.),

*Racial attitudes in the 1990s: Continuity and change* (pp. 45–75). Westport, Conn.: Praeger.
Huo, Yuen J., Smith, Heather J., Tyler, Tom R., and Lind, E. Allen. (1996). Superordinate identification, subgroup identification, and justice concerns: Is separatism the problem? Is assimilation the answer? *Psychological Science, 7*(1), 40–45.
Jessor, Tom. (1988). Personal interest, group conflict, and symbolic group affect: Explanations for whites' opposition to racial equality. Ph.D. dissertation, Department of Psychology, University of California, Los Angeles.
Kennedy, Randall. (1997). My race problem—and ours. *Atlantic Monthly* (May), 55–66.
Key, V. O., Jr. (1949). *Southern politics in state and nation.* New York: Vintage Books.
Kinder, Donald R., and Sanders, Lynn M. (1996). *Divided by color: Racial politics and democratic ideals.* Chicago: University of Chicago Press.
Lieberson, Stanley. (1980). *A piece of the pie: Black and white immigrants since 1880.* Berkeley: University of California Press.
Lipset, Seymour M. (1996). *American exceptionalism: A double-edged sword.* New York: Norton.
Massey, Douglas S., and Denton, Nancy A. (1993). *American apartheid: Segregation and the making of the underclass.* Cambridge, Mass.: Harvard University Press.
Medin, Douglas L., and Ortony, Andrew. (1989). Psychological essentialism. In Stella Vosnaidou and Andrew Ortony (Eds.), *Similarity and analogical reasoning* (pp. 179–95). Cambridge: Cambridge University Press.
Merelman, Richard M. (1994). Racial conflict and cultural politics in the United States. *Journal of Politics, 56,* 1–20.
Miller, Steven, and Sears, David O. (1986). Stability and change in social tolerance: A test of the persistence hypothesis. *American Journal of Political Science, 30,* 214–36.
Oliver, Melvin L., and Shapiro, Thomas M. (1995). *Black wealth/White wealth: A new perspective on racial inequality.* New York: Routledge.
Ravitch, Diane. (1990). Multiculturalism: E Pluribus Plures. *American Scholar, 59,* 337–54.
Schlesinger, Arthur M., Jr. (1998). *The disuniting of America: Reflections on a multicultural society.* Revised edition. New York: W. W. Norton.
Schuman, Howard., Steeh, Charlotte, Bobo, Lawrence, and Krysan, Maria. (1997). *Racial attitudes in America: Trends and interpretations.* Revised edition. Cambridge, Mass.: Harvard University Press.
Sears, David O. (1983a). The person-positive bias. *Journal of Personality and Social Psychology, 44,* 233–50.
———. (1983b). The persistence of early political predispositions: The roles of attitude object and life stage. In Ladd Wheeler and Philip Shaver (Eds.), *Review of personality and social psychology* (vol. 4, pp. 79–116). Beverly Hills, Calif.: Sage.
———. (1993). Symbolic politics: A sociopsychological theory. In Shante Iyengar and William J. McGuire (Eds.), *Explorations in political psychology* (pp. 113–49). Durham, N.C.: Duke University Press.
Sears, David O., Citrin, Jack, Vidanage, Sharmaine, and Valentino, Nicholas. (1994a). Americans' attitudes toward multiculturalism: Ethnic conflict in the midst of diversity. Paper presented at the annual meeting of the International Society of Political Psychology, Santiago, Spain (July 13, 1994).

———. (1994b). What ordinary Americans think about multiculturalism. Paper presented at the annual meeting of the American Political Science Association, New York City (September 1, 1994).
Sears, David O., Cheleden, Sharmaine V., and Henry, P. J. (1997). Living in the ethnic cauldron: Ethnic context, social identity, and symbolic politics. Unpublished paper, University of California, Los Angeles.
Sears, David O., and Funk, Carolyn L. (1991). The role of self-interest in social and political attitudes. In Mark Zanna (Ed.), *Advances in experimental social psychology* (vol. 24, pp. 1–91). Orlando, Fla.: Academic Press.
Sears, David O., and Jessor, Tom. (1996). Whites' racial policy attitudes: The role of white racism. *Social Science Quarterly, 77*(4), 751–59.
Sears, David O., and Kinder, Donald R. (1985). Whites' opposition to busing: On conceptualizing and operationalizing group conflict. *Journal of Personality and Social Psychology, 48,* 1141–47.
Sears, David O., and McConahay, John. B. (1973). *The politics of violence: The new urban blacks and the Watts riot.* Boston: Houghton Mifflin.
Sears, David O., and van Laar, Colette. (1999). Black exceptionalism in a multicultural society. Unpublished manuscript, University of California, Los Angeles.
Sears, David O., van Laar, Colette, Carrillo, Mary, and Kosterman, Rick. (1997). Is it really racism?: The origins of white Americans' opposition to race-targeted policies. *Public Opinion Quarterly, 61,* 16–53.
Sidanius, Jim. (1993). The psychology of group conflict and the dynamics of oppression: A social dominance perspective. In Shanto Iyengar and William J. McGuire (Eds.), *Explorations in political psychology* (pp. 183–224). Durham, N.C.: Duke University Press.
Smith, Rogers M. (1993). Beyond Tocqueville, Myrdal, and Hartz: The multiple traditions in America. *American Political Science Review, 87,* 549–67.
Tajfel, Henri. (1978). *Differentiation between social groups: Studies in the social psychology of intergroup relations.* London: Academic Press.
Taylor, Charles. (1992). *Multiculturalism and "the politics of recognition."* Princeton, N.J.: Princeton University Press.
Taylor, Marylee C. (1998). How white attitudes vary with the racial composition of local populations: Numbers count. *American Sociological Review, 63,* 512–35.
Vidanage, Sharmaine, and Sears, David O. (1995). The foundations of public opinion toward immigration policy: Group conflict or symbolic politics? Paper presented at the annual meeting of the Midwest Political Science Association, Chicago (April 6–8, 1995).
Vidanage, Sharmaine, van Laar, Colette, and Sears, David O. (1996). Becoming an American: The political socialization of Latinos. Paper presented at the annual meeting of the American Political Science Association, San Francisco (August 29–September 1).
Voss, Stephen D. (1996). Beyond racial threat: Failure of an old hypothesis in the New South. *Journal of Politics, 58,* 1156–70.
Wood, Gordon S. (1991). *The radicalism of the American revolution.* New York: Knopf.

4

# PEERING INTO THE JAWS OF THE BEAST: THE INTEGRATIVE DYNAMICS OF SOCIAL IDENTITY, SYMBOLIC RACISM, AND SOCIAL DOMINANCE

*Jim Sidanius, Shana Levin, Joshua L. Rabinowitz, and Christopher M. Federico*

QUESTION: What's the difference between capitalism and communism?
ANSWER: Under capitalism you have the exploitation of man by man. Under communism it's the other way around.

—Russian saying

WE DON'T need to look very far in either time or space to witness groups in conflict. Examples of group conflict abound, ranging from mild forms of ingroup favoritism—such as a preference for friends of the same ethnicity—to the most destructive forms of intergroup aggression, including the massacre of Armenians in Turkey,[1] the Holocaust in central Europe, "ethnic cleansing" in Bosnia, and mass genocide of Tutsis in Rwanda in 1994. In some sense, all of these horrific events can be taken as signs of "the beast within," illustrating people's pervasive tendency to show not only favoritism toward members of their ingroup but also a more disturbing enthusiasm for the denigration, humiliation, and subjugation of "the other." That people tend to favor ingroups over outgroups has been noted since the dawn of modern social science (see, for example, Sumner 1906) and continues to be documented across a range of populations and a vast array of judgment and allocation tasks (for reviews, see Brewer 1979; Hinkle and Schopler 1979, 1986; Messick and Mackie 1989; Mullen, Brown, and Smith 1992; Tajfel 1982). A variety of theoretical accounts have been offered to explain this remarkably robust finding. Despite differences in emphasis, these accounts all share the assumption that, in intergroup situations, people often act in terms of their membership in social groups rather than in terms of their individual identities. That is, as group members, people find themselves under the influence of a variety of unique cognitive and motivational processes with serious implications for intergroup relations. Three of these theoretical perspectives have received particular attention. Social identity theory (Tajfel and Turner 1979, 1986) emphasizes a drive for positive group distinctiveness; symbolic racism (SR) theory (Sears 1988)[2] focuses on the interactive role of anti-black affect and support for traditional American values in the formation of whites' political attitudes; and lastly, social dominance (SD) theory (Pratto, in press; Sidanius 1993; Sidanius and Pratto, in press) emphasizes the tendency for human social systems to form group-based social hierarchies and attempts to identify the primary mechanisms responsible for establishing and maintaining these hierarchies.

Over the last decade, social identity theory has become the dominant paradigm in research on intergroup relations, and symbolic racism theory has become one of the most influential approaches to the study of racial conflict between European and African Americans in the United States. While acknowledging the important contributions made by both of these theories, we believe that social dominance theory offers a more comprehensive and generalizable perspective on group conflict and the social and psychological dynamics of group domination.

A more recent model of intergroup conflict, social dominance theory addresses the shortcomings of earlier social psychological approaches, integrating sociological, institutional, psychological, and evolutionary forms of analysis. Social dominance theory builds on earlier research in four ways: it recognizes and incorporates the notion of individual differences, usually the domain of the more typically "psychological" approaches to intergroup relations (see, for example, Adorno et al. 1950; Altemeyer 1981; Eysenck and Wilson 1978; Rokeach 1960; Wilson 1973); it integrates its analysis of group conflict into a larger analysis of the ways in which groups cooperate in the maintenance of group-based social hierarchies, in the production of broad social ideologies, and in the operations of social institutions; it explains a variety of forms of intergroup conflict, both among artificial, lab-based groups and among real-world groups with different social, economic, and political agendas; and it tries to situate this understanding of group structure and intergroup relations within the larger framework of our understanding of the evolved mechanisms and predispositions common to humans and other species of hominoids. While the basic contours of the theory have been outlined in much more detail elsewhere (see Pratto, in press; Sidanius 1993; see especially Sidanius and Pratto, in press), recent studies have brought the distinctions between social dominance theory and its predecessors into even sharper relief.

As a point of departure for the present discussion, the first part of this chapter is devoted to a brief overview of social dominance theory, detailing its basic assumptions, relevant empirical findings, and the broader implications of the perspective. In the second half of the chapter, we highlight the theoretical and empirical distinctions between social dominance theory, on the one hand, and the social identity and symbolic racism approaches, on the other.

## SOCIAL DOMINANCE THEORY

Social dominance theory begins with the observation that human societies tend to be structured as *group-based social hierarchies,* with one or a small number of dominant groups at the top of the social structure and at least one subordinate group at the bottom. In general, members of dominant groups enjoy a disproportionate share of positive social value (such as wealth, status, and power), and members of subordinate groups are forced to endure a disproportionate share of negative social value (for example, poverty, lack of prestige, and relative powerlessness).

By the term "group-based social hierarchy" we refer to something quite distinct from an individual-based social hierarchy. Individual-based social hierarchies may come very close to embodying what might be called "pure meritocracy": an individual's relative station in life is primarily the result of his or her own effort, talent, intelligence, virtue, ruthlessness, or cunning. In contrast, in a group-based social hierarchy, the individual's relative station in life is largely (or at least substantially) a function of his or her membership in an ascribed and socially constructed group such as a "race," gender, age cohort, religion, clan, tribe, lineage, or social class. This is not to argue that the power, prestige, and privilege of individuals in most group-based social hierarchies are completely independent of the individual's personal characteristics and qualities. Rather, we are merely suggesting that the social status of individuals is not completely independent of the status and power of the groups to which they belong. Access to the *means of individual achievement* (for example, education or social connections) is differentially distributed across social groups. Thus, even in modern, "democratic" societies, the "achieved" component of social status is substantially dependent on the social status and power of one's ascribed group.

It is useful to think of group-based and individual-based social hierarchies as defining "ideal types" on opposite ends of a single social porosity continuum. *Strictly* group-based social hierarchies are absolutely nonporous and allow for no social mobility based on individual merit. On the opposite end, *strictly* individual-based social hierarchies are completely porous: one's position in the social system is determined only by individual characteristics unrelated to ascribed group membership. While individual-based, completely porous social systems in many ways define the modern "democratic" ideal, the empirical evidence indicates that such social systems have in fact never actually existed. Social dominance theory is an attempt to understand the mechanisms preventing the realization of such systems.

While there are any number of ways of organizing social stratification systems, social dominance theory categorizes human stratification systems into three types: an age system, in which "adults"—within the limits of decrepitude—command greater political, social, and military power than "children"; a gender system, in which males command more political, social, and military power than females[3]; and an arbitrary-set system, in which individuals within certain socially constructed and essentially arbitrarily defined categories enjoy a disproportionate degree of status and power over individuals in other socially constructed categories (for example, "races," social classes, nationalities). While recognizing the age system of social hierarchy, social dominance theory devotes most of its time to exploring the implications of the gender and arbitrary-set systems of group-based hierarchy.

## Patriarchy as a Human Universal

While women have made essential contributions to the economic subsistence of the group within both hunter-gatherer and post-hunter-gatherer societies, there is no known society in which women, as a group, have had control over the political life of the community, the community's interaction with outgroups, or the technology and practice of warfare, arguably the ultimate arbiter of political power. Despite the claim that matriarchy is the foundation of human society (see, for example, Bachofen 1861; Gimbutas 1989), the best anthropological and historical evidence available finds very little empirical support for this claim. There are several examples of matrilineal societies (descent is traced through the family of the mother), matrilocal or uxorilocal societies (newly married couples reside with the wife's kin), and societies in which women have near economic parity with men (Murdock 1949), but there are no known examples of matriarchal societies—that is, societies in which women, as a group, control the political and military authority (see Collier and Yanagisako 1987; Keegan 1993). Furthermore, the fact that even hunter-gatherer societies are stratified by gender has been widely recognized for some time. For example, in his now-classic analysis of social hierarchies, Lenski (1984) remarks that in hunter-gatherer societies "women invariably occupy a position inferior to men, though in some societies the differential is not great. Women are almost always excluded from the role of headman and usually are ineligible to become shamans or participate in council meetings" (111).

Furthermore, patriarchy is not simply restricted to human societies but appears to be relatively widespread across hominoid species in general (for example, among chimpanzees, gorillas, and baboons as well as humans). The only known exception to this generalized patriarchy among hominoids is found among bonobos. Bonobo society is more accurately described as matriarchical: the females tend to form long-lasting political alliances with one another, while bonobo males do not. This alliance formation allows groups of females to dominate individual males both "politically" and "economically"—that is, in gaining access to food (see de Waal 1997).

## Making Something out of Nothing: Arbitrary-Set Hierarchies

While age and gender systems of group-based social hierarchy appear to be completely universal across all human and almost all hominoid social systems, arbitrary-set systems are largely restricted to those societies that produce sustainable economic surplus. Marxists have traditionally thought of these group-based systems within surplus-producing economies exclusively in terms of divisions of social class (see Marx and Engels 1846/1970; see also Cohen 1978; Habermas 1978; Lenski 1984; Ng 1980). In addition, Marxist scholars have defined other group distinctions (for example, "race" and ethnicity) almost exclusively in terms of the dynamics and exigencies of social class. To the extent that Marxist scholars have recognized issues of race, tribalism, nationalism, or generalized ethnocentrism, they have regarded these conflicts as largely epiphenomenal and derivable from the dynamics of what they consider *the* basic social division in society, namely, class conflict.

Within social dominance theory, the Marxist argument is turned almost on its head. Rather than regarding class conflict as the "fundamental" conflict from which all other social divisions are derived, social dominance theory assumes that class conflict is a special case of a much more general tendency of human societies to form arbitrarily defined ingroup/outgroup boundaries and subsequently to engage in various acts of ingroup favoritism and outgroup denigration on the basis of these constructed group distinctions. Such socially constructed group distinctions include those based on caste, estate, clan, lineage, region, "race," religion, ethnicity, and minimal groups, as well as just about any other essentially arbitrary, situationally contingent division one can think of.

According to social dominance theory, arbitrary-set hierarchies differ from age- and gender-based systems of group hierarchy in terms of their definitional fluidity; the role of economic surplus in their emergence; their dynastic character; and the greater level of violence associated with maintaining them.

*Definitional Fluidity* Unlike the age and gender systems, the arbitrary-set system tends to display a remarkable degree of definitional plasticity and situational sensitivity. For example, it appears that the conceptual categories of "child" and "adult" are cultural universals, even though the precise definitional criteria for membership in each category show a certain degree of cross-cultural variation. Similarly, the conceptual distinctions between "male" and "female" also tend to be cultural universals: the criteria for membership in each category are highly, although not absolutely, predictable from culture to culture. In contrast, arbitrary-set distinctions tend to display a very high degree of contextual and historical fluidity. Within the arbitrary-set system, the process by which groups are defined and certain ones become salient is deeply embedded in specific cultural and historical contexts. For example, the arbitrary-set distinction of "race"—that is, who was considered "white" and who was considered "black"—was quite clear and self-evident to Americans in the early nineteenth century. During this period, membership in the "black" race was defined by the "one-drop" or "octoroon" rule: a person was "black" if he or she had at least one-eighth African heritage. The same degree of African ancestry, however, would not classify one as "black" in America in the late 1990s. Similarly, virtually the same degree of "Africanness" would have clearly classified one as "mulatto" in the Caribbean or in South Africa in the 1850s, and as "white" in late-twentieth-century Sweden. Furthermore, the popular understanding of the concept of "race" itself did not come into widespread usage until the late nineteenth century (see especially Gobineau 1915).

The most extreme example of the great plasticity of arbitrary-set distinctions can be found in the "minimal-group" studies that laid the groundwork for social identity theory (see Tajfel and Turner 1986). This influential body of research has demonstrated that it is quite easy to get people to discriminate against artificial, lab-generated outgroups that exist only in the minds of experimental subjects (for classic examples, see Billig and Tajfel 1973; Tajfel 1970; Tajfel et al. 1971; see also Tajfel 1978). Similarly, in a national survey conducted by the American Jewish Committee (see Smith 1991), a large random sample of Americans were found to have relatively low regard for "Wisians," even though there is no such ethnic group! It is because of this great definitional plasticity, as well as the fact that humans seem quite capable of discriminating even against nonexistent outgroups, that we have labeled social distinctions of this third type *arbitrary*-set systems.

However, despite the high degree of cross-cultural variation in the conceptualization of arbitrary-set dimensions and the precise definitional criteria for membership within each arbitrary-set group, the *existence* of arbitrary-set systems appears to be culturally universal. Regardless of how ingroups are defined, the "us" is always perceived to be quite distinct from the generalized "them." Furthermore, the ingroup, or generalized "us," is almost always better liked and judged to be morally superior to the generalized "them" (see, for example, Murdock 1949; Sumner 1906). Moreover, this universal tendency toward ethnocentrism seems to imply that the distinction between "us" and "them" —however it is defined—is an integral part of the architecture of the human mind. While both the exact dimensions along which the categories of "us" and "them" are socially constructed and the exact criteria for membership in each category are highly sensitive to situational and historical circumstances, the categories themselves appear to be a constant of social life.

*The Role of Economic Surplus* The second major distinction between the age- and gender-based systems of group hierarchy, on the one hand, and arbitrary-set systems, on the other, is that age and gender systems are found in all societies, including hunter-gatherer societies, but arbitrary-set systems are rarely, if ever, found in hunter-gatherer societies. However, this does not imply that hunter-gatherer societies are completely without status distinctions other than those engendered by the gender and age systems. On the contrary, most hunter-gatherer societies recognize a number of "traditional" status distinctions, embodied, for example, in the relatively high-status roles of chief, shaman, elder, and so on. However, since hunter-gatherer societies generally cannot afford to tolerate fools and incompetents in leadership roles, elevation to such positions tends to be based almost exclusively on individual merit rather than ascribed group membership. In other words, within hunter-gatherer societies social status outside of the gender and age systems is generally individualistic, not dynastic, hereditary, or *group-based* in character. In addition, the political and spiritual leaders of hunter-gatherer societies do not enjoy any substantial economic privilege over other members of the social group (see Lenski 1984).

Hunter-gatherer societies do not tend to have group-based, arbitrary-set systems of social hierarchy apparently because they do not have the technology to produce sustained economic surplus. Within hunter-gatherer societies, every able-bodied male usually devotes most of his waking time to procuring food and nourishment and has precious little time left to specialize in the arts of war or intellectual sophistry. Because every adult male essentially possesses the same military tools and skills as every other adult male, there is also a rough military equilibrium among males. However, as soon as social systems develop the technologies that enable them to produce economic surplus, role specialization and arbitrary-set social hierarchies begin to develop and are ultimately enforced by legitimizing ideologies and military force. These arbitrary-set systems are found in all societies capable of producing an economic surplus, including agrarian, horticultural, industrial, and post-industrial societies (see Giddens 1971; Godelier 1976; Habermas 1978; Lenski 1984; Marx 1973; Marx and Engels 1846/1970; Ng 1980).

Not only are there few if any documented societies with arbitrary-set systems that do not produce a surplus, but there are also no known societies that *do* produce an economic surplus and have failed to develop arbitrary-set social hierarchies. Furthermore, every attempt to abolish arbitrary-set hierarchies within surplus-producing societies has, without exception, failed. These failed attempts range from very large-scale efforts, in the form of major revolutions (for example, the French, Russian, Mexican, and Chinese Revolutions), to very small-scale attempts, in the form of utopian communities (such as New Harmony, Indiana; New Lanark, Scotland; the Oneida Community, New York; for other examples, see Erasmus 1977). This apparently perfect correlation between the production of sustainable economic surplus and the emergence of arbitrary-set social hierarchies would seem to imply that arbitrary-set-based systems of oppression emerge *as soon as economic conditions allow.* This fact comes as close to demonstrating the presence of a "predisposition" toward the establishment and maintenance of arbitrary-set hierarchies as we can imagine.

*Dynastic Character* A third way in which arbitrary-set hierarchies differ from age and gender hierarchies is that positions of power and status associated with arbitrary-set distinctions tend to be dynastic and hereditary while, of course, those associated with gender and age systems do not. That is, within arbitrary-set systems one's social status tends more or less to be passed on to one's offspring. This dynastic quality is found even in social systems with democratic and individualistic pretensions; for example, the adult offspring of members of low-status groups have a greater than even chance of remaining in positions of low status, while the adult offspring of members of high-status groups have a greater than even chance of remaining in positions of high status, *all other things being equal* (including individual talent and drive).

*Violence* The fourth and final way in which arbitrary-set systems differ from age and gender systems is reflected in the relatively greater level of violence and brutality associated with the maintenance of arbitrary-set systems. While violence—sometimes of a lethal intensity—is certainly involved in the enforcement of age and gender systems of hierarchy, the level of violence and brutality associated with arbitrary-set distinctions often achieves a scope and magnitude rarely found in the age and gender systems. At its most extreme, such violence takes the form of mass slaughter, sometimes ending in genocide. Any society employing this level of horror within its age and gender systems would, of course, quickly pass into extinction.

## The Stability and Ubiquity of Group-Based Hierarchies

One of the most impressive features of group-based social hierarchies is the remarkable degree of stability they exhibit. The dominance of adults over children is an obvious instance of the stability of group-based hierarchy. Perhaps less well known is the evidence indicating that the dominance of males over females stretches far back into prehistory. As we discussed earlier, patriarchy appears to be a human universal (see Keegan 1993; Collier and Yanagisako 1987). The evidence suggests that certain arbitrary-set systems, while not as stable as gender hierarchies, are also relatively stable. For example, the Indian caste system has remained relatively intact for at least three thousand years. While caste is no longer part of the legal order of Indian society, and "untouchable" status was outlawed after Indian independence in 1947, caste still remains an extremely important aspect of Indian social and political life: most people still marry within-caste, politicians rely on the "caste vote," castes continue to act as economic and political pressure groups, intercaste violence continues, and castes are still informally ranked in terms of "purity" and "pollution" (see Standing and Stirrat 1996).

Although the United States is a much younger nation than India, the American version of the caste system also shows signs of impressive stability. Despite concerted efforts to eliminate racism from American life, the dominance of European Americans over African Americans has persisted for nearly four hundred years. While perhaps not as impressive as the Indian example, an illustration of the stability of the American system of ethnic hierarchy can be found in public opinion data recently analyzed by Tom Smith (1991). Using national probability samples of Americans, Smith tabulated the perceived social standing of thirty-six American ethnic groups, first with 1964 data and then once again with data collected in 1989 (see figure 4.1). The data indicate that the correlation between the perceived social status of American ethnic groups across a quarter-century of American history was as high as 0.93. This correlation is even more impressive when one considers the intense and

FIGURE 4.1 *Perceived Social Status of American Ethnic Groups in 1989 as a Function of Perceived Social Status in 1964*

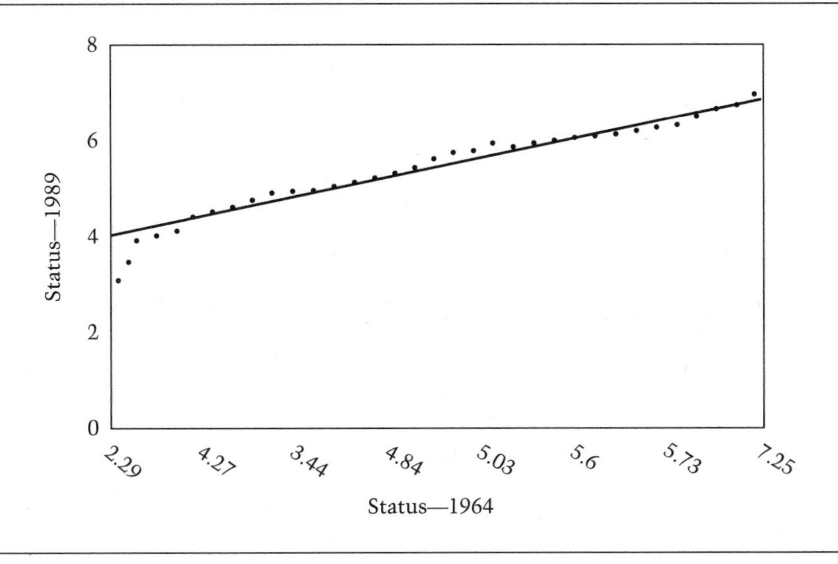


*Source:* Smith 1991.

often violent efforts during this period to achieve a more egalitarian and democratic society.

Not only do group-based hierarchies tend to be highly stable, but research shows a very high degree of consensus as to which groups are "dominant" and which groups are "subordinate." For example, in a recent study of this *status consensuality effect,* a random sample of 823 UCLA undergraduates were asked to rate the social status of American whites, blacks, Latinos, and Asians on a scale ranging from 1 ("very low status") to 7 ("very high status") (Sidanius and Pratto, in press). Not surprisingly, the data showed that European Americans were rated the highest in social status, followed by Asian Americans, with African Americans and Latinos essentially tied for last place (see, for example, Sidanius and Pratto, in press). More important, these ratings also showed a very high degree of consensuality across individuals and ethnic groups. For example, use of an indicator of inter-rater agreement (the intraclass correlation) revealed an impressive level of agreement across both individuals and different ethnic groups ($r$ = .9995 and $r$ = .9948, respectively; see figure 4.2). This high degree of consensuality in group-status ratings is by no means restricted to the United States; it has been found in other multi-ethnic nations as well (see, for example, Hraba, Hagendoorn, and Hagendoorn 1989).

FIGURE 4.2 *The Social Status of Four American Ethnic Groups as Perceived by Members of Four American Ethnic Groups (UCLA Sample)*

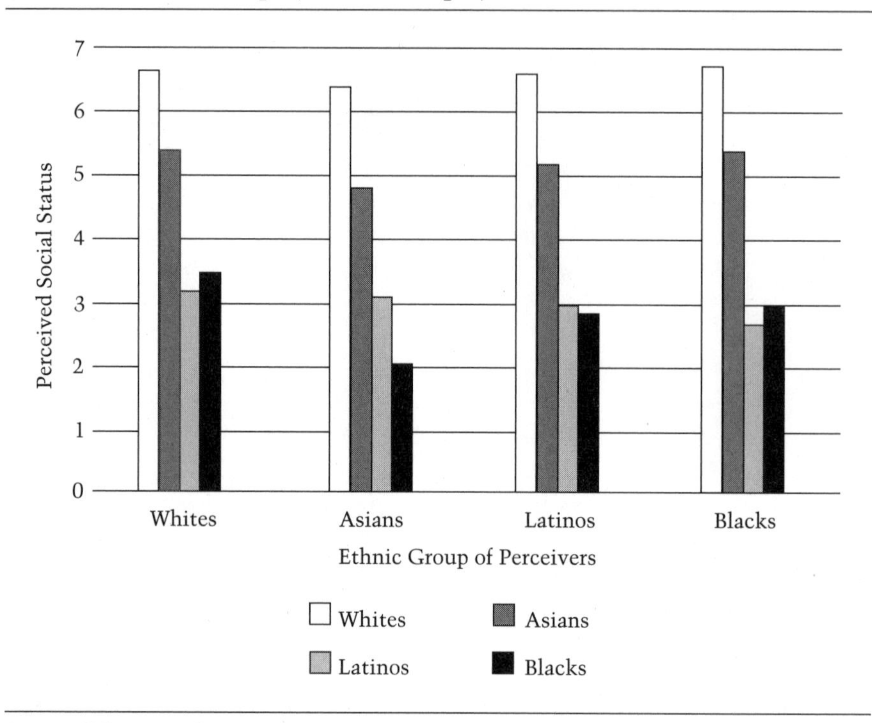


*Source:* Sidanius and Pratto, in press.

## Evidence from Other Primate Species

The phenomenon of group-based social hierarchy is not limited to human societies but can also be found in most primate groups closely related to humans (see, for example, Bercovitch 1991; Leonard 1979; Mazur 1985; Rowell 1974; Sapolsky 1993, 1995; Wade 1978). All primates within the *hominoid clade* (chimpanzees, bonobos, gorillas, baboons, and humans), for example, have group-based systems of social dominance. Anthropological research suggests that, among primates, social status is a function of: (1) age, with older animals dominating younger animals (see, for example, Kawanaka 1989); (2) sex, with males dominating females (Kawanaka 1982; Nadler 1987; Strier 1994)[4]; and (3) a very rudimentary arbitrary-set system (Rowell 1974). Among primates, this rudimentary arbitrary-set system most often consists of mother-offspring lineage bonds: the social rank of the offspring is influenced by the social rank of the mother (Alberts and Altmann 1995; Hausfater, Altmann, and Altmann 1982; Lee and Oliver 1979). Another common type of arbitrary-set system among primates involves the formation of "political" coalitions and alliances among dominant males (Harcourt 1988; Harcourt and Stewart 1987; Leigh and Shea 1995; Noe and Sluijter 1995; Riss and Goodall 1977; also see de Waal 1997).

A number of other features of primate social organization are relevant to the present discussion: the existence of closed social networks, or what might be called "ingroups"; communal territoriality; and the dominant male role in maintaining hostile relations between groups, including the stalking, attacking, and killing of outgroup males (Ghiglieri 1989; Wrangham 1987). One of several conclusions suggested by this list of common social characteristics is that the entire hominoid clade appears to be predisposed toward an "ethnocentric" orientation, with boundary maintenance vis-à-vis outgroups enforced largely by males.

## Basic Assumptions of Social Dominance Theory

Building on the preceding observations about the stability and ubiquity of group-based social hierarchy, social dominance theory posits three assumptions:

1. Most forms of group conflict and oppression (such as racism, ethnocentrism, sexism, nationalism, classism, and regionalism) can be regarded as different manifestations of the same basic human predisposition toward the formation of group-based social hierarchy.
2. Human social systems are subject to *hierarchy-enhancing* (HE) forces, which push them toward greater levels of group-based social inequality, and to the contradictory effects of *hierarchy-attenuating* (HA) forces, which push them toward greater levels of social equality.
3. The conflict between hierarchy-enhancing and hierarchy-attenuating forces ultimately yields relatively stable social systems that have tended to bestow adaptive benefits on humans. Although the precise balance created by this regulatory mechanism is subject to situational, ecological, and social influences, it always entails some sort of group-based hierarchical arrangement.

## Mechanisms of Hierarchy Production and Maintenance

Given these three basic assumptions, the main corpus of social dominance theory concerns itself with the specific psychological, social, institutional, and ideological mechanisms that contribute to group-based social hierarchy, and in turn, with how systems of hierarchy themselves

FIGURE 4.3 *Schematic Overview of Social Dominance Theory*

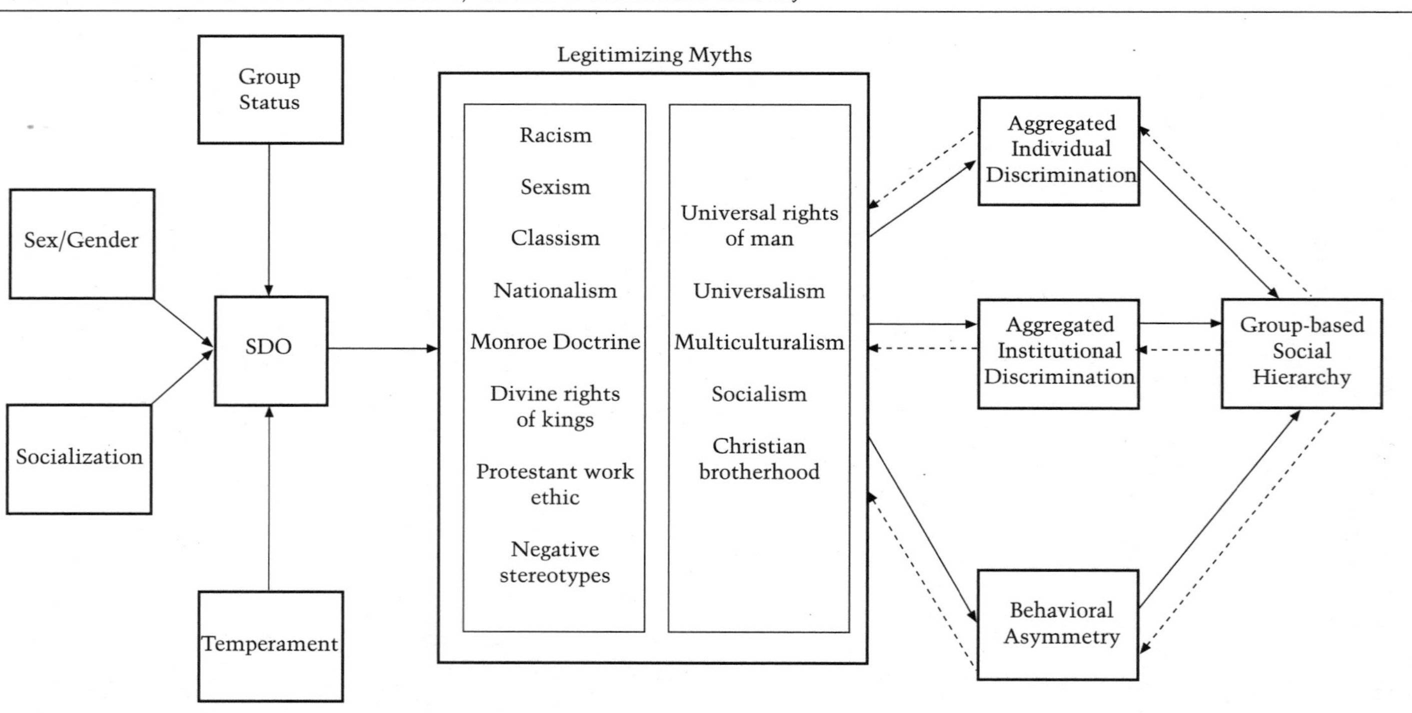

affect these contributing mechanisms. Figure 4.3 provides a general sketch of the set of processes by which group-based social hierarchy is created and maintained. The right-hand side of the figure shows the three proximal processes believed to drive group-based social hierarchy: aggregated individual discrimination, aggregated institutional discrimination, and behavioral asymmetry.

*Individual Discrimination* Individual discrimination is any event in which an individual from group A allocates fewer positive and more negative resources to an individual from group B, based on the second individual's membership in group B. When such acts of individual discrimination are aggregated over many thousands of interpersonal interactions over time, the dominance of group A over group B tends to be enhanced.

*Institutional Discrimination* Institutional discrimination can be said to occur when the formal and informal rules and procedures of various social institutions result in the disproportionate allocation of positive and negative social value to dominant and subordinate groups, respectively. For our purposes, it is sufficient to distinguish between two types of institutional discrimination: overt institutional discrimination and covert institutional discrimination.[5] Overt discrimination consists of institutional rules and decisions that explicitly and openly target subordinates for negative and harmful treatment. The Jim Crow laws that characterized much of life in the American South are examples of this type of institutional discrimination. With covert discrimination, however, institutions do not explicitly and openly target subordinate groups. Rather, covert discrimination can be said to occur when institutional rules and procedures, which may even have the appearance of fairness and evenhandedness, systematically have a deleterious effect on members of subordinate groups. Because covert institutional discrimination allows dominant groups to allocate negative outcomes disproportionately to subordinate groups while maintaining a veneer of fairness and equity, it should not be surprising that, in the latter half of the twentieth century, most societies with democratic pretensions practiced covert rather than overt institutional discrimination.

A rather clear and unambiguous example of covert institutional discrimination is found in the anti-drug legislation passed by Congress in the middle and late 1980s. The Anti-Drug Abuse Acts of 1986 and 1988 specified a mandatory five-year minimum federal prison sentence for anyone found in possession of five grams or more of crack cocaine, and a ten-year mandatory minimum sentence for anyone possessing fifty grams or more of crack cocaine. However, in order to be sentenced to a five-year mandatory minimum federal prison sentence for possession of *powder* cocaine, one would have to possess five hundred grams of cocaine; in order to be sentenced to a ten-year mandatory minimum sentence, one would have to possess five thousand grams of powder cocaine. In other words, despite the fact that crack and powder cocaine have been shown to have the same pharmacological and behavioral effects (see U.S. Sentencing Commission 1995), one must possess one hundred times more powder cocaine in order to receive the same punishment meted out for possession of crack cocaine.

This legislation makes no explicit mention of race or ethnicity and therefore gives the impression of evenhandedness across the arbitrary-set continuum. However, when one looks beyond these "evenhanded" rules to certain facts, the very dramatic differences in imprisonment rates by ethnicity begin to make sense. Drug surveillance tends to be much more active and widespread within subordinate (that is, black and Hispanic) communities than within dominant (white) communities, and powder cocaine is disproportionately used by whites, whereas crack cocaine is disproportionately used by blacks and Hispanics.[6] In figure 4.4, we have plotted levels of relative crack cocaine usage and relative federal conviction rates for crack cocaine possession as a function of ethnicity. We see that, although 52 percent of those using crack cocaine were white, only 10.3 percent of those convicted for simple possession of crack cocaine were white. On the other hand, although only 38 percent of crack users were black, fully 84.5 percent of those facing harsh federal convictions for crack possession were black (U.S. Sentencing Commission 1995). Even more dramatically, although African Americans constituted only 12 percent of illicit drug users in 1991, they represented 74 percent of those serving state prison sentences for drug use in 1992 (see Mauer and Huling 1995).

Close examination of institutional behavior reveals that covert discrimination is not restricted to the criminal justice system but is also found across a wide variety of domains, including the educational system, the labor market, the housing market, the health care system, and even the retail market. Furthermore, this widespread institutional discrimination against subordinates is not restricted to the United States but has been found in every nation and culture in which the question has been seriously explored, including Canada, Australia, Great Britain, New Zealand, Holland, France, Israel, Germany, Brazil, and Sweden (see Sidanius and Pratto, in press).

*Behavioral Asymmetry* Behavioral asymmetry implies that, on average, there are systematic differences in the behavioral repertoires of individuals belonging to dominant and subordinate groups—differences

FIGURE 4.4 *Use and Conviction Rates for Crack Cocaine Usage by Race*

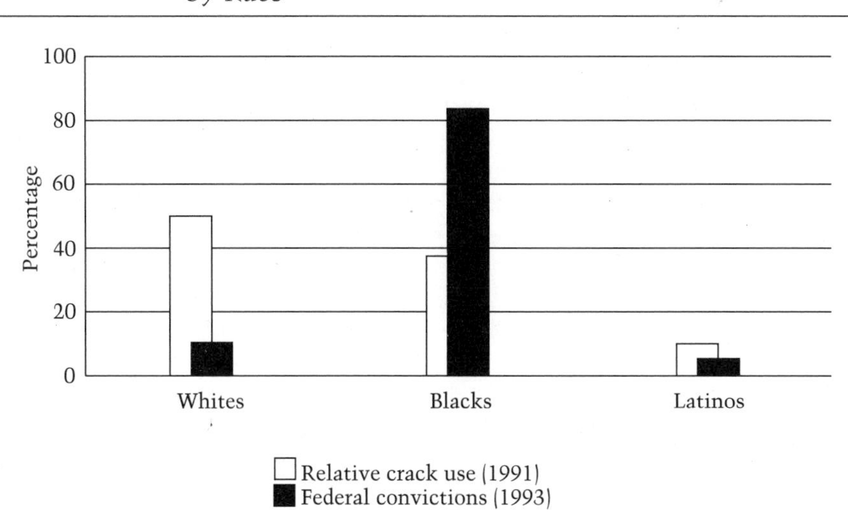


*Source:* U.S. Sentencing Commission (1995), pp. xi, 156.

that contribute to the establishment and maintenance of the hierarchical relationships among these groups. Four types of behavioral asymmetry have been identified: asymmetrical ingroup bias, systematic outgroup favoritism or deference, self-debilitating behavior, and ideological asymmetry.

As we discuss in more detail later, both the general ethnocentrism hypothesis (see Sumner 1906) and social identity theory have argued that people tend to favor the ingroup over the outgroup. However, the asymmetrical ingroup bias hypothesis suggests that the apparently universal tendency to favor ingroups over outgroups is asymmetrical across the social power continuum. Everything else being equal, dominants tend to show greater ingroup bias than subordinates do, especially with respect to important, power-relevant dimensions. The net result of this asymmetrical ingroup bias is the reinforcement of the hegemonic group's dominance over the subordinate group.

Deference, or outgroup favoritism, can be seen as a more extreme case of asymmetrical ingroup bias and occurs when members of subordinate groups actually discriminate in favor of dominant outgroups. One of the best-known examples of outgroup favoritism or deference is found in Clark and Clark's (1947) classic doll studies, in which black children were found to prefer white dolls over black dolls. This finding has been replicated many times since the 1940s, and in nations other than the United States (see, for example, Gopaul-McNichol 1988, 1995; Powell-Hopson and Hopson 1988, 1992).[7]

Self-debilitation occurs when subordinates engage in greater amounts of self-destructive, self-defeating behavior than dominants. One of the most dramatic examples of disproportionately high levels of self-defeating behavior can be found among African American males. Data from the National Crime Victimization Survey shows that, between 1987 and 1992, the average annual rate of handgun victimization among young black males was three to four times that of young white males. In 1992 alone, black males between the ages of twelve and twenty-four were almost ten times more likely to be victims of homicide than were white males in the same age range (114.9 per 100,000 and 11.7 per 100,000, respectively; see Bastian and Taylor 1994). More to the point, however, the data also show that the extremely high level of victimization among black males was largely inflicted by other black males, with 82 percent of the violence inflicted on black males within this age range committed by other black males.[8]

Ideological asymmetry is the most subtle form of behavioral asymmetry. Social dominance theory suggests that, all other things being equal, one's endorsement of social policies and ideologies that promote greater levels of group-based inequality (that is, hierarchy-enhancing policies and ideologies) is strongly driven by anti-egalitarian values. The ideological asymmetry hypothesis maintains that the strength of this association between support for hierarchy-enhancing policies and ideologies, on the one hand, and anti-egalitarian values, on the other, varies systematically as a function of the social power of one's primary reference group. For dominants, for whom maintenance of the status quo is very important, these relationships are expected to be substantially more positive than those within subordinate groups. Research conducted by both social dominance theorists and those working outside of the social dominance paradigm offers consistent evidence for the ideological asymmetry hypothesis. For example, using an adult probability sample from Los Angeles County, Mitchell and Sidanius (1993) found that the relationship between support for the death penalty (a hierarchy-enhancing social policy) and group-based anti-egalitarianism was significantly more positive among dominants than among subordinates. Similarly, Sidanius, Levin, and Pratto (1996) found that a long array of hierarchy-enhancing social policies and ideologies was more positively related to basic anti-egalitarian values among European Americans than among African Americans (see also Combs and Comer 1982; Federico, in press; Rabinowitz, in press; Young 1993).

## Legitimizing Myths

At a more distal level, the degree of group-based social inequality is also thought to be influenced by levels of support for various legitimizing ideologies (see figure 4.3). Legitimizing myths (LMs) are defined as those attitudes, values, beliefs, stereotypes, attributions, and ideologies that provide moral and intellectual justification for systems of group-based social hierarchy within all three hierarchical systems (age, gender, and arbitrary-set). The notion that social ideologies serve to justify and rationalize the exercise of political power is a very old idea indeed and has been discussed by a wide variety of theorists, including Marx ("ideology"; Marx and Engels 1846/1970), Mosca (the "political formula"; 1896/1939), Pareto ("derivations"; 1935/1963), Gramsci ("cultural hegemony"; 1971), Moscovici ("social representations"; 1981, 1988), and Durkheim ("collective representations"; 1893/1933). However, in contrast to Marxian thinking, within social dominance theory the use of the term "legitimizing myth" does not suggest that these ideologies are "false" in any epistemological sense. An analysis of the relative "truth" or "falsity" of these beliefs is not the aim of SD theory, which instead concerns itself with the functional role of these beliefs in systems of social hierarchy. More specifically, the theory focuses on whether these beliefs are motivated by anti-egalitarian values and whether they help to enhance or attenuate the degree of group-based social inequality within any given society.

In addition, social dominance theory argues that LMs can be distinguished by two independent characteristics: functional type and potency. The *functional type* of a particular LM is what facilitates either group-based social *inequality* or its exact opposite, social *equality.* LMs that facilitate increased levels of group-based social inequality are hierarchy-enhancing (HE-LM), and LMs that facilitate increased levels of group-based social equality are hierarchy-attenuating (HA-LM). Examples of HE-LMs include ideologies such as racism, sexism, classism, Confucianism, the "white man's burden," manifest destiny, the divine rights of kings, meritorious karma, and internal attributions for the plight of the poor. These HE-LMs are counterbalanced by the beliefs, values, ideologies, and attitudes of hierarchy-attenuating LMs. Whereas HE-LMs serve to sharpen and maintain group-based social inequality, HA-LMs have the opposite effect and serve to promote greater levels of group-based social egalitarianism. Examples of HA-LMs are doctrines such as feminism, socialism, communism, the universal rights of man, liberation theology, themes in the American Declaration of Independence, and thematic elements of the New Testament.[9]

LMs are potent to the degree to which they promote or contradict a given group-based hierarchy. A given LM's potency is affected by at least four factors: consensuality, embeddedness, certainty, and mediational strength.

By the term *consensuality* we refer to the degree to which the LM is shared and endorsed by the population across the continuum of social power. For example, for most of American history the belief that blacks are inherently inferior to whites was held not simply by most whites but by a substantial number of blacks as well. The more both blacks and whites endorse the ideology of white superiority, the less the system of racial dominance needs to be enforced by the use of raw force and terror. It was this very widespread and *shared* belief in white superiority, along with several other factors, that gave the racial caste system in the United States such power and stability over more than three centuries.

*Embeddedness* refers to the degree to which a given LM is anchored to other beliefs within the social system. For example, within American and Western culture, the color white is associated with purity, innocence, and righteousness, and the color black with evil, depravity, and filth. Because these color labels are also associated with the dominant and subordinate groups, the relative ranking of these social groups appears to be all the more legitimate and correct.

*Certainty* refers to the degree to which given LMs appear to be "correct" and "true" in a moral, metaphysical, or scientific sense. For example, the ideology of white superiority was a potent belief in the midnineteenth century in part because it appeared to be so consistent with the emerging "scientific" literature of the time, including the new evolutionary thinking and its social Darwinist offshoots (see, for example, Gobineau 1915).

Finally, *mediational strength* refers to the degree to which a given LM mediates between the endorsement of group-based social hierarchy and dominance, on the one hand, and the endorsement of hierarchy-enhancing or hierarchy-attenuating social policies, on the other hand. For SD theory to designate a social ideology as a legitimizing myth, the ideology must be shown to mediate between the generalized endorsement of group-based inequality and support for policy issues concerning the distribution of social resources between dominant and subordinate groups. The more strongly an LM mediates the relationship between the desire for group-based hierarchy and a given social policy, the more potent the LM is said to be.

## Social Dominance Orientation

Perhaps the most "psychological" aspect of social dominance theory centers on the construct known as social dominance orientation (SDO). SDO is defined as the degree to which an individual desires and supports

TABLE 4.1 *The* $SDO_6$ *Scale*

INSTRUCTIONS

Below are a series of statements with which you may either agree or disagree. For each statement, please indicate the degree of your agreement/disagreement by *circling* the appropriate number from 1 to 7. Remember that your first responses are usually the most accurate.

| | Strongly Disagree/ Disapprove | | | | | | Strongly Agree/ Favor |
|---|---|---|---|---|---|---|---|
| 1. Some groups of people are just more worthy than others | 1 | 2 | 3 | 4 | 5 | 6 | 7 |
| 2. In getting what your group wants, it is sometimes necessary to use force against other groups. | 1 | 2 | 3 | 4 | 5 | 6 | 7 |
| 3. Superior groups should dominate inferior groups | 1 | 2 | 3 | 4 | 5 | 6 | 7 |
| 4. To get ahead in life, it is sometimes necessary to step on other groups | 1 | 2 | 3 | 4 | 5 | 6 | 7 |
| 5. If certain groups of people stayed in their place, we would have fewer problems | 1 | 2 | 3 | 4 | 5 | 6 | 7 |
| 6. It's probably a good thing that certain groups are at the top and other groups are at the bottom | 1 | 2 | 3 | 4 | 5 | 6 | 7 |
| 7. Inferior groups should stay in their place | 1 | 2 | 3 | 4 | 5 | 6 | 7 |
| 8. Sometimes other groups must be kept in their place | 1 | 2 | 3 | 4 | 5 | 6 | 7 |
| 9. It would be good if all groups could be equal | 1 | 2 | 3 | 4 | 5 | 6 | 7 |
| 10. Group equality should be our ideal | 1 | 2 | 3 | 4 | 5 | 6 | 7 |
| 11. All groups should be given an equal chance in life | 1 | 2 | 3 | 4 | 5 | 6 | 7 |
| 12. We should do what we can to equalize conditions for different groups | 1 | 2 | 3 | 4 | 5 | 6 | 7 |
| 13. Increased social equality | 1 | 2 | 3 | 4 | 5 | 6 | 7 |
| 14. We would have fewer problems if we treated different groups more equally | 1 | 2 | 3 | 4 | 5 | 6 | 7 |
| 15. We should strive to make incomes more equal | 1 | 2 | 3 | 4 | 5 | 6 | 7 |
| 16. No one group should dominate in society | 1 | 2 | 3 | 4 | 5 | 6 | 7 |

*Note:* Items 9–16 should be reverse-coded. The use of $_6$ refers to the sixth version of the scale.

group-based social hierarchy and, by extension, the domination of "inferior" groups by "superior" groups. The groups that people have in mind when completing the SDO measure can be quite arbitrary, embracing whatever socially constructed group distinctions happen to be salient within a given social or situational context (see table 4.1).

Quite consistent with the expectations of social dominance theory,

SDO has been found to relate to a wide variety of policy attitudes, legitimizing ideologies, group evaluations, and social attributions. For example, the evidence shows that SDO is related to political conservatism, nationalism, patriotism, hierarchy-enhancing/hierarchy-attenuating career choices, racism, sexism, belief in fate, and internal attributions for the fate of the poor (see Mitchell and Sidanius 1993; Pratto et al. 1994; Sidanius et al. 1997; Sidanius and Liu 1992; Sidanius, Liu, et al. 1994; Sidanius and Pratto 1993a, in press; Sidanius, Pratto, and Bobo 1996; Sidanius, Pratto, and Mitchell 1994; Sidanius, Pratto, and Rabinowitz 1994; Sidanius, Pratto, Sinclair, and van Laar 1996).

In addition, SDO has shown itself to be conceptually and empirically distinct from an array of related constructs, such as: interpersonal dominance (Pratto et al. 1994); authoritarianism (Altemeyer 1996, 1998; McFarland and Adelson 1996; Pratto et al. 1994); political conservatism (Pratto et al. 1994); and racism (Sidanius, Pratto, and Bobo 1996). Furthermore, the finding that SDO is associated with legitimizing ideologies and social policies is not restricted to the United States (where most of this research has been conducted) but has been found across a wide range of cultures, including Israel, Taiwan, Canada, New Zealand, Mexico, Sweden, and the People's Republic of China (Sidanius and Pratto, in press; Pratto et al. 1998). For example, SDO has been found to relate to: the belief that Jews have the right to all of the land in Israel; the belief that the gods and fate determine economic inequality in Taiwan; racial prejudice in Mexico; sexism in the People's Republic of China (see Pratto et al. 1998); and political conservatism in Canada, New Zealand, and Sweden (Sidanius and Pratto 1993a).

Finally, the construct of SDO has also been helpful in explaining poorly understood empirical relationships among variables that, in principle, should have little to do with one another. For example, a great deal of research across several different countries has shown political conservatism to be consistently and positively related to racism and ethnocentrism (see Dator 1969; Eysenck 1951, 1971, 1976; Eysenck and Coulter 1972; Jackson and Kirby 1991; Nias 1972; Sidanius 1987; Sidanius and Ekehammar 1979; Sidanius, Ekehammar, and Ross 1979; Stone and Russ 1976; Wilson 1973; Wilson and Bagley 1973; Wilson and Lee 1974; Wilson and Patterson 1968). Recent analyses have shown that the relationship between political conservatism and racism can be completely accounted for in terms of their mutual dependence on SDO (Sidanius and Pratto 1993a; Sidanius, Pratto, and Bobo 1996). In other words, conservatives tend to be ethnocentric because both conservatism and ethnocentrism are driven by the same value, namely, group-based anti-egalitarianism.

SDO is thought to be driven by four factors: group status, gender/

sex, socialization experiences, and temperament. First, everything else being equal, the greater the social status of one's ingroup, the higher one's level of SDO should be. Members of dominant groups are expected to be more supportive of ideologies that justify the unequal distribution of social value, since these ideologies serve to maintain the privileges conferred on them by their group's superior position. For example, consistent with these expectations, European Americans are found to have higher SDO scores than African Americans, and Ashkenazi Jews are found to have higher SDO scores than Sephardic Jews and Israeli Arabs (see Sidanius and Pratto, in press; Levin, Sidanius, and Pratto 1998).

Second, it is expected that, everything else being equal, males have, on average, higher levels of SDO than females. We refer to this thesis as the *gender invariance hypothesis* (Sidanus, Pratto, and Bobo 1994). The higher level of SDO among males is perhaps the best-documented empirical finding generated by SD theory. Thus far, social dominance theorists have examined forty-five independent samples across ten nations, including more than nineteen thousand respondents.[10] Of these forty-five independent tests, males had significantly higher SDO than females in thirty-nine cases, there were no significant gender differences in six cases, and females had significantly higher SDO scores than males in no cases at all. The probability that all thirty-nine significant differences would show males having higher SDO scores than females, if these results were actually due to chance, is on the order of $10^{-11}$. Furthermore, these male-female differences in SDO remain essentially constant over factors such as: nationality and culture, education, income, age, gender-role norms, religiosity, ethnicity and "race," political ideology, levels of racism, occupational role, employment status, degree of American acculturation, and child-rearing practices (see Sidanius and Pratto, in press; Sidanius, Pratto, and Bobo 1994; see also Altemeyer 1998).

Third, aside from the effects of one's gender and the status of one's group, a number of socialization experiences should also affect one's level of SDO. Among the most important of these is general level of education. Work with both student and adult samples has shown that, even after controlling for other factors such as gender, ethnicity, and social class, higher levels of education appear to be associated with lower levels of social dominance orientation (Sidanius, Pratto, and Bobo 1996). These findings, in turn, are consistent with the large body of literature showing that ethnic and racial prejudice tend to be negatively related to formal education (Sidanius et al. 1991). Nevertheless, the question of why both SDO and general ethnocentrism appear to decline with increasing formal education has yet to be definitively answered.

Besides formal education and membership in broadly stigmatized social groups (for example, being black or poor), other stigmatization experiences are expected to affect one's level of SDO. These experiences might include being disabled, unattractive, or just "odd" according to prevailing social norms. We have reason to believe that the experience of stigmatization affects both generalized identification with the "underdog" and generalized empathy (see Wurst and Wolford 1994) and, by extension, one's level of SDO (see, for example, Pratto et al. 1994).

Finally, there is reason to believe that temperament factors may also contribute to SDO. Out of the long array of partially heritable personality predispositions, two temperament factors seem particularly relevant: empathy and aggressivity. A consistent body of twin studies has shown that empathy and aggressivity have high levels of heritability (see, for example, Cates et al. 1993; Coccaro, Bergeman, and McClearn 1993; Davis, Luce, and Kraus 1994; Emde et al. 1992; Ghodsian-Carpey and Baker 1987; Matthews et al. 1981). As suggested earlier, previous research in the social dominance tradition has shown that greater levels of SDO are correlated with lower levels of empathy and greater levels of aggressivity (Pratto et al. 1994).

## Reining in the Beast: Hierarchical Constraints and Equilibrium

Given the historical and anthropological record, it seems reasonable to assume that hominoid social systems are predisposed to organize themselves as group-based hierarchies. Furthermore, all other things being equal, the degree of group-based social hierarchy in any social system should tend to stabilize around a given level, which we can refer to as the *point of hierarchical equilibrium.* We would suggest that this equilibrium can be thought of as a result of the combined effects of hierarchy-enhancing (HE) forces and hierarchy-attenuating (HA) forces.

Hierarchy-enhancing forces are the complete set of social ideologies, beliefs, attitudes, traditions, social institutions, and social roles that tend to promote and maintain group-based hierarchy within social systems. Besides the HE-LMs mentioned earlier, these HE forces also consist of institutions and social roles, such as internal security forces (such as local and secret police), major elements and actors within the criminal justice system (such as prosecutors), and major institutions within the business community (for example, banks and insurance companies). Hierarchy-attenuating forces are those social institutions, traditions, and ideologies that tend to promote a greater degree of group-based social equality. Besides HA-LMs, other examples of HA forces include social institutions such as civil rights and social welfare organizations, charities, the public defender's office, and certain religious bodies, such as the Society of Friends.

Because HE and HA institutions are hypothesized to serve competing functions in the maintenance of group-based social hierarchy, it is reasoned that they are staffed by personnel with group-relevant attitudes that are consistent with the nature of their social roles. Specifically, we would expect personnel within HE institutions and roles to have relatively high SDO levels, and personnel within HA institutions and roles to have relatively low SDO levels. Thus far, research has offered consistent support for these expectations. Sidanius, Liu, Pratto, and Shaw (1994), for example, compared SDO levels of Los Angeles police officers (HE roles), Los Angeles County public defenders (HA roles), and a random sample of adults called to jury duty. As expected, the police officers were found to have significantly higher SDO scores than the average citizen (that is, the jurors), and the public defenders were found to have significantly lower SDO scores than the average citizen. Furthermore, these comparisons held even after controlling for demographic factors such as ethnicity, age, social class, and gender. Follow-up studies have also revealed that these HE-HA differences in SDO are not simply a function of the socialization experiences associated with social roles but are also a function of self-selection processes. For example, Sidanius, Pratto, Sinclair, and van Laar (1996) examined the relationship between SDO and the perceived attractiveness of HA and HE career paths among a large sample of UCLA students, who, of course, had not yet embarked on professional careers. Consistent with expectations, the greater the perceived attractiveness of HA careers, the lower the SDO level. Similarly, the greater the perceived attractiveness of HE careers, the higher the SDO level. Finally, a canonical correlation analysis revealed that an array of HE and HA career paths cast a unidimensional, bipolar shadow within SDO attitude space, with HE careers at one end of the continuum and HA careers at the other end (see also van Laar et al. 1999).

The counterbalancing and mutually constraining effects of hierarchy-enhancing and hierarchy-attenuating forces are thought to be among the factors that help to maintain the hierarchical equilibrium in a given society over time. Furthermore, we would posit that, within relatively stable social systems, hierarchical equilibrium is found at the point that simultaneously organizes the social system in a hierarchical fashion and does not allow the degree of group-based social hierarchy to become either too morally offensive or structurally destabilizing.

Lastly, social dominance theory also suggests that the major components of the model found in figure 4.3 are endogenous to one another. Thus, for example, while individual discrimination, institutional discrimination, and behavioral asymmetry all tend to affect the degree of group-based social hierarchy within a given society, this degree of hierarchy, in turn, also affects the nature and intensity of individual discrimination, institutional discrimination, and behavioral asymmetry, as well as the nature and power of legitimizing myths.

## THE RELATIONSHIP BETWEEN SOCIAL DOMINANCE THEORY AND OTHER THEORIES OF INTERGROUP CONFLICT

Now that we have provided a general overview of the social dominance approach, we can turn our attention to its relationship with other lines of research and theory. Social identity theory (Hogg and Abrams 1988; Tajfel and Turner 1986), of course, has been the dominant paradigm in intergroup research over the last decade. We review the theory here and contrast its predictions with those of social dominance theory. Theoretical and empirical contrasts highlight the differences between the theories in the emphasis they place on the roles of self-esteem, ingroup identification, social dominance orientation, group status, and group power in the genesis of intergroup discrimination. Differences between the theories in how they explain (or fail to explain) outgroup favoritism effects, and in the emphasis they place on ingroup favoritism versus outgroup derogation as sources of intergroup bias, are also discussed.

Moreover, the relationship between social dominance theory and yet another approach to intergroup attitudes and behavior, Sears's (1988) symbolic racism theory, is also discussed. We suggest that the effects of symbolic racism on whites' opposition to redistributive racial policies in the United States are perhaps best explained in terms of the role of symbolic racism as a legitimizing myth within the framework of social dominance theory.

### Social Identity Theory

In its original form, social identity theory explained intergroup behavior in terms of the interplay between two separate processes: the cognitive process of categorization, which assigns individuals to social categories, thereby simplifying the complex social world in contextually meaningful ways; and the motivational process of self-esteem enhancement, which drives individuals to enhance their self-image as group members (Abrams and Hogg 1988; Hogg and Abrams 1990). While the categorization process has been well documented, the self-esteem process lacks consistent empirical support (see discussion later in the chapter). In fact, self-categorization theory (Turner 1985; Turner et al. 1987), a recent extension of social identity theory, focuses entirely on categorization and never directly addresses self-esteem. Although categorization processes are undoubtedly fundamental to our ability to make intergroup distinctions, categorization alone cannot explain the human motivation to engage in more extreme forms of intergroup discrimination and oppression (such as mass murder and genocide).

As noted earlier, the motivational component of social identity theory suggests that ingroup favoritism results from attempts to achieve positive group distinctiveness, or a favorable evaluation of the individual's own group relative to other groups. This process is thought to be driven by the individual's social identity needs, or, in other words, the desire to enhance those aspects of the self-image that relate to group membership. As such, a positive social identity is achieved when intergroup comparisons favor the ingroup. A negative social identity, in contrast, results from unfavorable comparisons with the outgroup and can pose a threat to self-esteem.

*Self-Esteem* As Abrams and Hogg (1988; Hogg and Abrams 1990) note, two self-esteem hypotheses may actually be derived from social identity theory: the hypothesis that successful intergroup discrimination enhances social identity and thus elevates self-esteem; and the hypothesis that low or threatened self-esteem promotes intergroup discrimination. The second hypothesis is of particular relevance to the present discussion. Given its suggested role as an antecedent of intergroup discrimination, low self-esteem should operate in much the same way as high social dominance orientation. In light of this functional similarity, one might be tempted to speculate that the effects of SDO on intergroup discrimination stem from an overlap between low self-esteem and high SDO. However, no empirical support has been found for this suggestion. Using nine different samples, Pratto and her colleagues (1994) found that SDO tended to be uncorrelated with scores on Rosenberg's (1965) self-esteem measure; Rabinowitz and Sidanius (1995) reached similar conclusions. Furthermore, McFarland and Adelson (1996) found that SDO was uncorrelated with both the Rosenberg measure of personal self-esteem and Luhtanen and Crocker's (1992) measure of collective self-esteem. Lastly, Sidanius, Pratto, and Mitchell (1994) found that, even after controlling for the effects of self-esteem, greater SDO levels were associated with greater ingroup bias.

More broadly, however, evidence for the role of self-esteem as either a cause or a consequence of intergroup discrimination is mixed (Abrams and Hogg 1988; Hogg and Abrams 1990; Rubin and Hewstone 1998). Tests of the self-esteem hypothesis have yielded mixed results in part because self-esteem is often measured at a global level. It may be that self-esteem is more affected by intergroup comparisons at the level of a specific social identity. Furthermore, because individuals are members of many different social groups, it may be more appropriate to consider self-esteem in terms of multiple social identities (see van Knippenberg and Ellemers 1990, 1993). Whatever the case may be, it appears that social identity theory's original self-esteem hypothesis falls short as an explanation for intergroup discrimination.

*Ingroup Identification* As noted, social identity theory suggests that the mere categorization of individuals into social groups engages social identity needs. The more one identifies with the ingroup, the more relevant group membership should be to one's self-image, and the stronger these social identity needs should be. In turn, group members should meet these enhanced social identity needs through increased ingroup bias. On this basis, then, social identity theory would expect higher levels of ingroup identification to be associated with stronger ingroup favoritism among all groups. Contrary to these predictions, however, previous research has not consistently demonstrated strong positive relationships between ingroup identification and ingroup bias (Hinkle and Brown 1990). Hinkle and Brown's review of this literature suggests that consistent and robust positive correlations between identification and bias occur only when group members feel both connected with their ingroup and concerned about how their group is faring relative to other groups. Recent research by Hinkle, Brown, and their colleagues has offered support for these theoretical suggestions (see Brown et al. 1992).

Social dominance theory suggests that other factors—ones that, as far as we know, have not been considered by social identity theorists—may also moderate the relationship between ingroup identification and ingroup bias. SDO, for example, may interact with ingroup identification to affect ingroup bias. For example, Sidanius, Pratto, and Mitchell (1994) found that individuals with high SDO and strong ingroup identification exhibited the most ingroup bias, and Levin (1992) found that subordinate group members with high SDO and low ingroup identification maximally favored the outgroup. Thus, high ingroup identification among high SDO members of dominant groups may promote ingroup favoritism, and low ingroup identification among high SDO members of subordinate groups may drive outgroup favoritism. This pattern of relationships is, of course, the sort that would tend to lead to the maintenance of systems of social dominance.

As these findings suggest, social dominance orientation has very different implications for the ingroup identification of members of dominant and subordinate groups. Individuals who favor group-based inequality should tend to identify more strongly with dominant ingroups because their members have greater access to resources (such as political power) that can be used to maintain the social hierarchy. However, the situation of high SDO individuals within subordinate groups is more problematic. Because desires for group-based inequality emphasize the inferiority of subordinate groups, high SDO individuals should *disidentify* with these inferior ingroups. High levels of SDO should thus be associated with increased ingroup identification among dominants and decreased ingroup identification among subordinates (but see Rabinowitz, in press). Consistent with these predictions, Sidanius, Pratto, and Rabinowitz (1994) found that SDO was positively correlated with measures of ingroup salience and ingroup closeness among whites, and negatively correlated with measures of ingroup salience and ingroup closeness among Latinos and African Americans. Additionally, in a study comparing whites and Latinos in the United States, Ashkenazi and Sephardic Jews in Israel, and Israeli Jews and Arabs, Levin and Sidanius (in press) found that SDO was positively related to ingroup identification among all dominant groups (whites, Ashkenazi Jews, and Jews as a superordinate group), and that SDO was negatively related to ingroup identification among the subordinate groups of Latinos and Arabs.

Another interesting question regarding ingroup identification involves the relation between social identifications at different levels of inclusiveness, such as the relation between identification with a subgroup like African Americans and a superordinate group like Americans. Social dominance theory suggests that, in a given social system, the relationship between identification at the subgroup and superordinate levels of social identity varies with the position of one's ethnic group in the social hierarchy. National identity, or the perception of belonging to the nation as a whole, is expected to be more strongly and positively associated with ethnic identity among dominant groups and less strongly associated with ethnic identity among subordinate groups. This asymmetry in the interface between ethnic and national identity is expected to occur in all societies organized as group-based hierarchies. Because groups in power want to stay in power, they tend to regard themselves as having preeminent rights to citizenship and ownership of their nation and its domains. There is therefore a strong, positive relationship between ethnic and national identity among dominant groups. However, identification with subordinate ingroups highlights differences between ethnic groups, thereby enhancing perceptions of group inequality and reducing identification with a nation in which the subordinate ingroup is oppressed. There is therefore a negative relationship between ethnic and national identity among subordinate groups. Consistent with these expectations, in a cross-national study of intergroup relations in the United States and Israel, Sidanius, Feshbach, Levin, and Pratto (1997) found that identification with dominant ethnic ingroups (European Americans and Israeli Jews, respectively) was *positively* related to patriotic sentiment, and that identification with subordinate ethnic ingroups (African Americans and Israeli Arabs, respectively) was *negatively* related to patriotism (see also Sinclair, Sidanius, and Levin, in press).

*Ingroup Favoritism or Outgroup Derogation?* Previous research in the social identity tradition has found that ingroup identification is more strongly associated with ingroup favoritism than with intergroup differentiation (Hinkle, Taylor, Fox-Cardamone, and Crook 1989). Because social identity theory assumes that intergroup biases are primarily expressed through ingroup preference rather than through outgroup derogation (Brewer 1979; Mummendey and Schreiber 1983, 1984; Mummendey and Simon 1989; Spears and Manstead 1989), the model implies that ingroup identification should have little or no effect on outgroup affect or outgroup denigration.

So what, then, are the forces driving outgroup affect and outgroup denigration? Social dominance theory provides one answer to this question. Although desires for positive social identity should indeed manifest themselves in more positive ingroup affect, regardless of one's group membership, desires for social dominance should manifest themselves in a combination of more positive affect toward the dominant group and more negative affect toward the subordinate group (also regardless of one's group membership). With regard to outgroup affect, then, high levels of SDO should be associated with more negative outgroup affect among dominants and more positive outgroup affect among subordinates. Outgroup denigration among dominants and outgroup favoritism among subordinates can fuel discriminatory attitudes and behaviors that reinforce the inferior position of the subordinate group, thus facilitating the group-based hierarchy.

To tease apart the effects of SDO and ingroup identification on ingroup favoritism and outgroup derogation, Levin and Sidanius (in press) examined the relationships between SDO, ingroup identification, and ingroup and outgroup affect among dominant and subordinate groups in three intergroup contexts: whites (dominants) and Latinos (subordinates) in the United States; Ashkenazi (dominants) and Sephardic Jews (subordinates) in Israel; and Jews (dominants) and Arabs (subordinates) in Israel. Results supported the social identity prediction that group members with stronger ingroup identification would exhibit more positive ingroup affect. Furthermore, in line with social dominance predictions, SDO was negatively related to the *outgroup* affect of all dominant groups, and negatively related to the *ingroup* affect of the subordinate Latinos and Arabs. The net result of SDO driving more negative outgroup affect among dominants and more negative ingroup affect among subordinates is an increase in derogation of the subordinate group among individuals at all levels of the social hierarchy. Ingroup bias, then, may always be more a function of ingroup preference than of outgroup hostility (as suggested, for example, by Brewer 1979); rather, when such bias stems from one's desire for group-based dominance, it may be expressed more through derogation of subordinate groups than through favoritism of dominant groups, regardless of one's group membership.

As suggested earlier, increased negative affect toward the subordinate outgroup and increased identification with the dominant ingroup may enable dominants to simultaneously meet social dominance and social identity needs. However, given the threat to positive social identity posed by unfavorable intergroup comparisons, subordinates cannot simultaneously meet social dominance and social identity needs by exhibiting more negative ingroup affect. The research that shows a negative relationship between ingroup identification and SDO among subordinate groups (Levin and Sidanius, in press; Sidanius, Pratto, and Rabinowitz 1994) suggests that one way in which high SDO individuals express more negative feelings toward the subordinate ingroup while at the same time maintaining a positive identity is by identifying less with their inferior ingroup.

*Outgroup Favoritism* As mentioned previously, social identity theory expects ingroup favoritism to be exhibited in biased group evaluations on all dimensions that are not tied to actual differences in group status (Sachdev and Bourhis 1987, 1991; Schwarzwald, Amir, and Crain 1992). However, because the theory assumes that the same needs for positive social identity drive ingroup bias across the status continuum, the theory has difficulty explaining the occurrence of outgroup favoritism among subordinate group members on dimensions not directly related to the intergroup status differential (for examples, see Clark and Clark 1939, 1947; Gopaul-McNichol 1988; Powell-Hopson and Hopson 1988; see also Yee and Brown 1988).

Social dominance theory, in contrast, clearly emphasizes the conditions under which outgroup favoritism should occur among subordinate group members. Specifically, as SDO increases, there should be more affective ingroup bias among dominant group members and less affective ingroup bias among subordinate group members (asymmetrical ingroup bias). The more favorably individuals are disposed toward dominant ingroups, and the less favorably they are disposed toward subordinate ingroups, the more likely they are to support discriminatory attitudes and policy preferences that serve to maintain group-based social inequality (but see Rabinowitz, in press).

In contrast to social identity theory, social dominance theory expects affective asymmetry to occur: as SDO increases, affective bias in favor of the ingroup is expected to *increase* among dominants and to *decrease* among subordinates. Although both theories predict that affective ingroup bias will occur for all dominant group members, only SD theory predicts that affective ingroup bias will decrease for those subordinate group members who have high SDO. Consistent with these predictions, Sidanius and his colleagues (Levin, Sidanius, and Pratto 1998) found that SDO was *positively* correlated with ingroup bias (defined as the difference between ingroup and outgroup affect) among dominant American whites, and *negatively* correlated with ingroup bias among subordinate American Latinos. Similarly, Levin (1996) found that SDO increased affective ingroup bias among dominants and tended to decrease affective ingroup bias among subordinates in both the United States and Israel.

*Status Versus Power Concerns* A final distinction between social identity theory and social dominance theory can be made with regard to the roles they assign to status and power in intergroup relations. Though power and status are closely related concepts in both classical sociology (such as Weber 1946) and contemporary social and political psychology (for example, French and Raven 1959; Tajfel 1978; Tajfel and Turner 1986), a clear distinction can be drawn between the two constructs. Power, following the classical usage, refers to the ability of an individual or group to enforce its own will over others, despite resistance (see French and Raven 1959; Gerth and Mills 1953; Jones 1972; Ng 1980; Parkin 1971; Raven 1992; Sachdev and Bourhis 1985, 1991; Weber 1946, 1947). Status, on the other hand, refers simply to prestige along some evaluative dimension (see Berger et al. 1977; Ng 1982a; Sachdev and Bourhis 1987; Tajfel 1978; Tajfel and Turner 1986; Weber 1946).

This distinction is the focus of a key point of divergence between social identity theory and social dominance theory. As noted earlier, social identity theory explains intergroup behavior primarily in terms of a supposed motive for identity enhancement. In other words, we engage in ingroup favoritism so as to guarantee the positive distinctiveness of our group vis-à-vis other groups. This emphasis on the implications of relative group standing has generally led social identity theorists to focus on the role of status differences in intergroup relations; both the existence of and desire for positive ingroup distinctiveness have been suggested as primary antecedents of ingroup bias (see earlier discussion, as well as Abrams and Hogg 1988; Tajfel 1978; Tajfel and Turner 1986). On the other hand, social identity theory has directed far less attention to the role of power. Group status has clear implications for the evaluative standing of the groups to which we belong—and by extension, for the identities we derive from them as individuals—but the effects of power on social identity are not as easily understood. In fact, social identity theory has tended to look at power as just another dimension of social comparison contributing to overall status differences between groups (see Tajfel and Turner 1986; for a critique, see Sachdev and Bourhis, 1991).

Perhaps most troubling for the social identity perspective on status and power is the research suggesting that the two constructs have very distinct effects, even in minimal-group contexts (for a review, see Hogg and Abrams 1988). Although both group power (see, for example, Ng 1982b; Sachdev and Bourhis 1985, 1991) and group status (for example, Caddick 1982; Commins and Lockwood 1979; Mullen, Brown, and Smith 1992; Sachdev and Bourhis 1987, 1991; Skevington 1981; Turner 1978; Turner and Brown 1978; van Knippenberg 1984; van Knippenberg and van Oers 1984) have been shown to enhance various manifestations of ingroup favoritism, they appear to do so in different ways. Two lines of research provide evidence for this contention. First, although increased status may in fact lead to enhanced ingroup favoritism, it appears that power is what makes discrimination possible in the first place (Ng 1982b, 1984; Sachdev and Bourhis 1985, 1991). Research on the effects of power and status insecurity demonstrates this principle: groups with insecure high power show *less* ingroup favoritism (see Ng 1982a, 1984), and groups with insecure high status show *more* ingroup favoritism (see Brewer and Kramer 1985; see also Hogg and Abrams 1988). Results like these suggest that, although threats to the status of one's group may indeed encourage compensatory ingroup favoritism, such acts of favoritism are not attempted when the group's ability to impose its will on others is in doubt.

Second, it appears that status and power affect different group-relevant variables: status differentials explain most of the variance in ingroup identification and intergroup perceptions (that is, the variables more directly related to the social identity needs posited by social identity theory), while power differentials explain most of the variance in actual discrimination (that is, intergroup behavior; see Ng 1984; Sachdev and Bourhis 1991). Thus, while consideration of the status differentials emphasized by those in the social identity tradition may very well help us explain certain patterns of beliefs about groups, a complete understanding of the actual oppressive behaviors underlying group-based systems of hierarchy also requires that we more thoroughly examine the role of power in intergroup relations.

In line with these observations, social dominance theory focuses chiefly on the role of power differentials in intergroup conflict (see Pratto, in press; Sidanius 1993; Sidanius and Pratto, in press). Like classical sociological perspectives on the role of power in class relations (for example, Marx and Engels, 1846/1970; Mosca 1939; Weber 1947) and ethnic relations (Barth and Noel 1972; Marger 1985; Schermerhorn 1970), SD theory suggests a very different relationship between status and power than that posited by social identity theory: group-based status differentials, according to SD theory, derive from power differentials, rather than the other way around.

Moreover, unlike social identity theory, social dominance theory is directly concerned with the dynamics of group-based forms of dominance and oppression. Rather than focusing on the role of identity needs in intergroup behavior, SD theory focuses directly on the motives underlying the establishment and preservation of group-based power hierarchies. Because hierarchy enhancement, rather than identity or esteem enhancement, is the motive of primary significance, it logically follows that status should be of only secondary importance in SD theory. This has in fact been the guiding assumption behind much of the work in SD theory on the attitudinal and behavioral asymmetries prevalent among groups at different levels of the social hierarchy (see Mitchell and Sidanius 1993; Sidanius 1993; Sidanius et al. 1997; Sidanius and Pratto, in press, 1993b; Sidanius, Pratto, and Mitchell 1994; Sidanius, Pratto, and Rabinowitz 1994; Sinclair, Sidanius, and Levin, in press).

*Summary: Social Identity or Social Dominance?* The theoretical and empirical distinctions between social identity theory and social dominance theory can be categorized into three broad areas: social identity theory's emphasis on identity-maintaining processes as antecedents of intergroup behavior, versus SD theory's emphasis on group hierarchy-maintaining processes as the determinants of such behavior; social identity theory's assumption that intergroup bias is more a function of ingroup preference than outgroup denigration, versus SD theory's assumption that desires for group-based dominance are expressed both through derogation of subordinate groups *and* through favoritism of dominant groups; and social identity theory's failure to explain instances of outgroup favoritism, versus SD theory's basic expectation that outgroup favoritism occurs among high SDO members of subordinate groups, thereby reinforcing the system of hierarchy. Many empirical studies have highlighted the need to take both social identity and social dominance motives into account when attempting to explain the various forms of intergroup conflict we both witness in the real world and create in the laboratory.

## Symbolic Racism Theory

Another leading approach to the understanding of intergroup relations is symbolic racism (SR) theory. Unlike social dominance theory and social identity theory, symbolic racism theory has a somewhat narrower focus and has primarily been developed to explain American whites' continued antagonism toward blacks, despite the assumed demise of "old-fashioned" Jim Crow racism (Sears 1988, 1993; Sears, Citrin, Cheleden, and van Laar, this volume; Sears et al. 1997; see also Kinder and Sanders 1996). According to SR theorists, classical American racism, centered on the notion of black inferiority and a demand for racial segregation, has given way to a subtler form of racism. This new form of racial antipathy is essentially a combination of generalized anti-black affect and traditional American values—a powerful blend that is thought to drive attitudes toward racially targeted social policies (Sears 1988; see also Kinder and Sanders 1996; McConahay 1986; McConahay, Hardee, and Batts 1981).

The narrower focus of symbolic racism theory is both its strength and its weakness. The strength of the approach is reflected in the ability of the various SR scales to predict a variety of attitudinal and behavioral outcomes, even when controlling for political ideology, partisan identification, and classical racism (Sears 1988; Sears et al. 1997). For example, Sears and his colleagues (1997) present a number of studies indicating that symbolic racism contributes both uniquely and strongly to the stances whites take on a range of racial issues, including opposition to federal assistance to blacks, opposition to equal opportunity for blacks, and even to political candidate preference.

At the same time, however, it is difficult to generalize the theory to other instances of ethnocentrism and group conflict. The theory does not consider racial attitudes in the context of issues of social structure, it does not incorporate basic anti-egalitarian or group dominance motives into its conceptual schema, and it does not easily generalize to instances of group conflict outside of the American context (such as in Bosnia, Rwanda, Somalia, and so forth).[11] Both social identity theory and social dominance theory, in contrast, are far less culturally specific and attempt to provide relatively consistent and parsimonious explanations across a wide variety of cultures and historical epochs.

Besides the issue of the cultural and historical specificity of symbolic racism theory, another major difference between SR and SD theories is their focus. SR theory, like many traditional theories of prejudice, concentrates almost exclusively on the racial attitudes of European Americans. However, since SD theory focuses on the manner in which social ideology intersects with and is dependent on overall social structure, SD theorists do not exclusively concern themselves with the social attitudes of dominants alone, but with subordinates as well. More important, the SD approach tries to illuminate the manner in which the social beliefs and behavioral repertoires of both dominants *and* subordinates intersect and collaborate in the maintenance of group-based social hierarchy.

Unlike social identity theory, however, both the symbolic racism and social dominance approaches emphasize the impact of stable individual differences: SR theory emphasizes the role of symbolic racial values, and SD theory emphasizes the role of generalized group-based anti-egalitarianism (that is, SDO). Although both the SR and SD approaches tend to be oriented toward individual differences and deal with many of the same kinds of variables, these variables are structured and conceptualized in very different ways. For example, the SR model does not accept the idea, central to SD theory, that anti-egalitarianism is a central motive driving European Americans' attitudes toward social and political policy. This, however, does not imply that SR theorists are unaware of the power of anti-egalitarian motives. For example, in reviewing the empirical literature on the relative power of anti-egalitarianism versus individualism (so central to SR theory) in predicting whites' reactions to issues of racial policy, David Sears (1988) writes:

> It seems most appropriate then, to conclude, at least provisionally, that anti-egalitarianism does have stronger effects than individualism. If this conclusion proves to be correct, it would alter our view of symbolic racism. It would imply that resistance to racial change is more rooted in genuine resistance to equality than is implied by our original emphasis on perceptions that blacks violate nonracial individualistic values such as ambition, hard work, and delayed gratification. It would be a more pessimistic view of race relations. (73)

We suggest that the cumulative evidence is now quite strong that anti-egalitarianism and the closely related construct of SDO really are more powerful determinants of whites' reactions to issues of racial policy compared to "traditional American values" (see, for example, Feldman 1983; Kluegel and Smith 1983; Pratto et al. 1994; Sears, Huddy, and Schaffer 1984; Sidanius, Devereux, and Pratto 1992; Sidanius and Pratto 1993a; Sidanius, Pratto, and Bobo 1996). Despite this consistent and strong evidence, SR theorists have yet to come to terms with the enduring power of anti-egalitarian motives, have made no fundamental changes to the SR model, and have failed to incorporate the central importance of the anti-egalitarian motive into their thinking in any theoretically coherent fashion. Because SR theorists continue to resist conceiving of American race relations in terms of the general forces producing and maintaining group-based, hierarchical social relations, they have been unable to deal with the even more pernicious construct of SDO or to place this construct into a larger theoretical context.

While the SR theorists continue to ignore the construct of SDO, SD theorists have not ignored the important role that symbolic racism plays in the determination of whites' racial policy attitudes. One important, but not exclusive, reason for this theoretical asymmetry is the fact that SD theory was originally designed to integrate the valid positions of several extant models of intergroup relations, including social identity theory and symbolic racism theory (among several others). Because SR theory was developed before either social identity theory or SD theory hit the scene in any serious manner, it is not surprising that SR theorists have had some difficulty in incorporating and adjusting to these later theoretical developments. Within SD theory, SR attitudes are largely seen as legitimizing ideologies, working together with a plethora of other legitimizing ideologies (for example, political conservatism and denial of racial discrimination) to both protect and maintain the integrity of arbitrary-set systems of group-based social hierarchy.

Furthermore, because the items used to measure symbolic racism almost always refer to specific groups (usually blacks) and often indirectly refer to specific policies, the measures of symbolic racism often show an uncomfortably high overlap with measures of the policy attitudes they are designed to explain. As a matter of fact, some critics have claimed that this proximity is so close that the SR measures and the social policy attitudes they are designed to predict almost collapse into the same thing (see Sniderman and Tetlock 1986). In contrast, the measures of SDO are always conceptually distinct from specific policy outcomes within any specific country or historical period. As can be seen in table 4.1, the SDO scale refers to neither particular social groups nor particular social policies. While this level of generality has the advantage of enabling the SDO scale to be used in many different cultural, historical, political, and social contexts (see, for example, Pratto et al. 1998), it also implies that, on average, the scale is not as strongly related to a specific set of policy attitudes as a scale directly designed to measure attitudes toward specific policies within specific political and social contexts. On the whole, however, given the overall purpose of social dominance theory, this level of generality is considered a definite advantage.

The manner in which social dominance theory conceives of the relationship between social dominance orientation, endorsement of legitimizing ideologies (for example, symbolic racism, classical racism, and political conservatism), and policy attitudes is depicted in figure 4.5. Concentrating first on the portion of the figure labeled "Symbolic Racism Theory," we see a schematic version of how SR theorists conceive of the relationships between political conservatism, classical racism, symbolic racism, and whites' racial policy preferences across a range of

FIGURE 4.5 *Symbolic Racism Theory as Nested Within Social Dominance Theory*

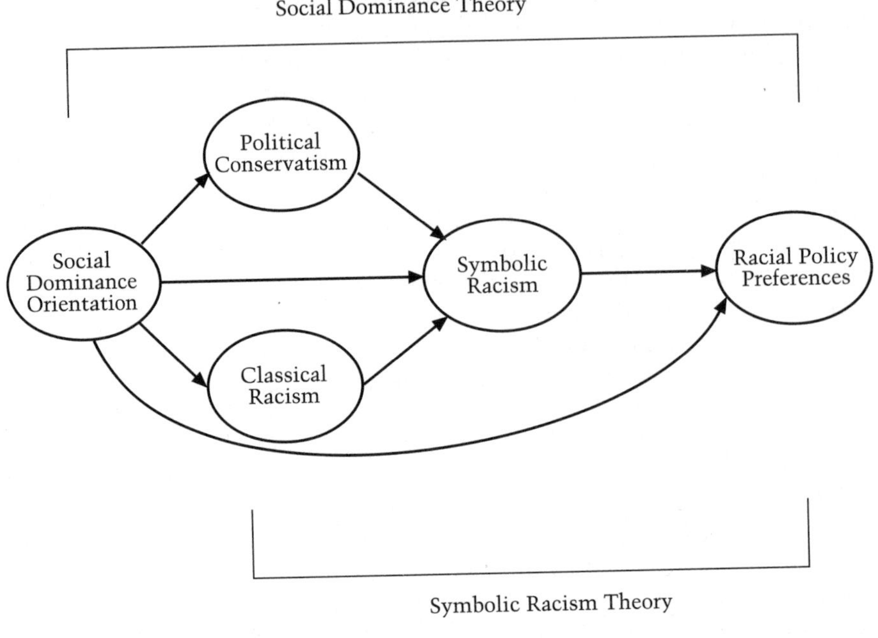


issues (such as busing, fair housing laws, and affirmative action). SR theorists would picture racial policy preferences as being most proximally driven by symbolic racism, which is, in turn, affected by both political conservatism and classical racism.

Social dominance theorists would not essentially dispute this picture, but they would argue that it is missing some rather essential components. Specifically, SD theorists would argue that, among dominants (for example, European Americans), a recognition of their desire to maintain their dominant position within society (their SDO) is critical to understanding the logic of their racial policy choices and political preferences. This logic is not restricted to dominants within the United States but is seamlessly extendable to other hierarchically organized social systems as well. SDO should have both direct effects on racial policy attitudes and indirect effects on racial policy attitudes through legitimizing ideologies. In the model presented in figure 4.5, these legitimizing ideologies are political conservatism, classical racism, and symbolic racism.

Although we have provided examples of legitimizing myths throughout this chapter, we can now be more precise in our definition of a "legitimizing myth." If the social dominance model is correct, three conditions must be met in order for a given social belief or attitude to qualify as an LM. First, the potential LM must be shown to have a particular type of correlation with SDO. All hierarchy-attenuating LMs must be shown to be *negatively* related to SDO, and all hierarchy-enhancing LMs must be shown to be *positively* related to SDO. Second, all ideologies regarded as HA-LMs must be *negatively* related to opposition to redistributive policies favoring subordinates, and all ideologies regarded as HE-LMs must be *positively* related to opposition to redistribution policies favoring subordinates. Third and finally, SDO must have a significant indirect relationship to redistributive social policy attitudes through the LMs. More precisely, SDO must be shown to have a *negative* indirect effect on support for HA policies and a *positive* indirect effect on support for HE policies.

To illustrate the empirical support for this position, we tested two LISREL structural equation models using a random sample of 173 European American adults from Los Angeles County in 1996. The social policy of interest was opposition to affirmative action.[12] In one model, the set of causal relationships suggested by symbolic racism theory (see figure 4.5) was tested, and in the second model, the set of causal relationships suggested by social dominance theory (a more complete model including the SDO component) was tested.

Use of LISREL showed the data to be quite consistent with the assumptions of the symbolic racism part of the model in figure 4.5. The measure of symbolic racism was significantly related to both political conservatism ($\gamma = .49, p < .01$) and classical racism ($\gamma = .16, p < .05$). In turn, symbolic racism was found to be strongly and significantly related to opposition to affirmative action ($\beta = .49, p < .01$). In addition, this simple model was found to fit the data quite nicely: $\chi^2(2) = 3.98$, $p = .14$, Goodness of Fit Index (GFI) = .99, Adjusted Goodness of Fit Index (AGFI) = .94. Finally, and most importantly for SR theorists, releasing the path from political conservatism directly to opposition to affirmative action did not significantly increase the fit of the model, $\chi$ $2(1) = 2.02$, $p = .15$. In other words, while political conservatism had a statistically significant indirect effect on opposition to affirmation action through symbolic racism (indirect effect = .22, $p < .01$), it had no substantial direct effect on affirmative action opposition once the direct effects of symbolic racism were taken into account.[13]

In figure 4.6, we examined a model congruent with social dominance theory. In examining the results of this larger model, there are four points of interest. First, the overall fit of the model was at least as

FIGURE 4.6 *Test of Symbolic Racism Theory as Nested Within Social Dominance Theory*

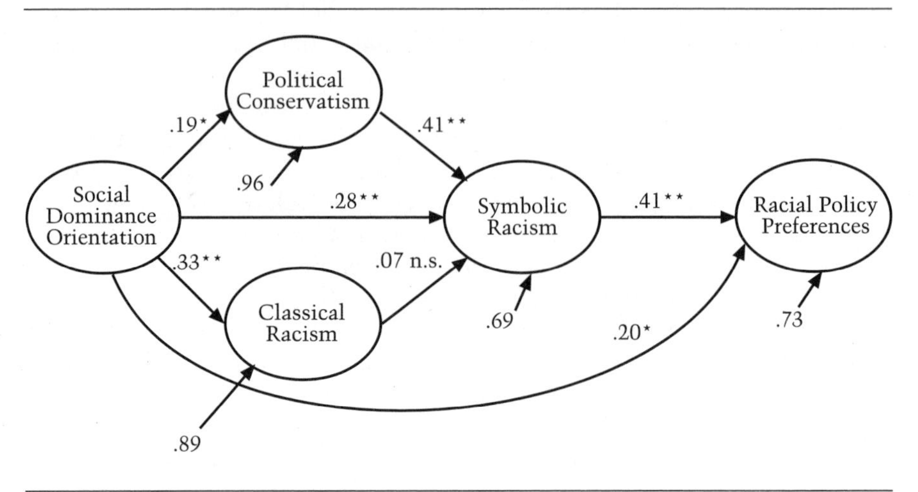


*Source:* Los Angeles County Social Survey, 1996.

good as, if not better than, the fit of the smaller symbolic racism model: $\chi^2(3) = 2.56$ $p = .46$, GFI = .99, AGFI = .97. Second, as expected, SDO was found to have statistically significant relationships with all of the variables considered to be LMs, including political conservatism ($\gamma = .19$, $p < .05$), classical racism ($\gamma = .33$, $p < .01$), and symbolic racism ($\gamma = .28$, $p < .01$). Furthermore, and somewhat at odds with the basic spirit of SR theory, if we include both the hypothesized direct and indirect effects of SDO on symbolic racism (that is, the total effect), we see that this total effect is as high as 0.38.[14] In other words, consistent with the claims of social dominance theorists and with previous findings (see Sidanius, Devereaux, and Pratto 1992), there is a substantial relationship between SDO and symbolic racism. Third, SDO was found to have a *direct* relationship with affirmative action opposition, even independent of the direct effect of symbolic racism ($\gamma = .20$, $p < .05$). Fourth, and very importantly, we recall that SD theory asserts that much of the effect of SDO on public policy choice is indirect, and mediated by a series of legitimizing ideologies. If this assumption is true, then we must be able to find a *statistically significant, positive,* and *indirect* effect of SDO on affirmative action opposition through the legitimizing ideologies. The results of the LISREL analysis supported this expectation. There was indeed a positive and statistically significant indirect effect of SDO on affirmative action opposition with political conservatism, classical racism, and symbolic racism as the mediators (indirect effect = .16, $p < .01$).

In sum, as with all other legitimizing ideologies, symbolic racism certainly has effects on racial policy attitudes that are quite independent of the desire to establish and maintain hierarchical relationships among socially constructed groups. However, in order to more fully understand the dynamics of intergroup conflict, we must take into account the powerful manner in which these symbolic attitudes serve to provide intellectual and moral legitimacy to the domination of "inferior" groups by "superior" groups and to the overall hierarchical structure of intergroup relations.

## Conclusions

Where does all this leave us with respect to Martin Luther King's noble dream that people be judged by the content of their character rather than by the color of their skin? Historical experience and present theory suggest that relative intergroup peace is certainly possible, even in complex societies. Furthermore, historical experience and theory suggest that the absence of arbitrary-set, group-based hierarchy is also possible, at least within social systems that produce no economic surplus. Unfortunately, however, there is nothing in either the five thousand years of recorded human history[15] or in any well-reasoned and empirically supported scientific theory that would lead us to believe that the absence of arbitrary-set discrimination and oppression is possible within societies that do produce an economic surplus. Major efforts to eliminate oppression and structural privilege often entail great social conflict. Once some measure of group-based social equality and relative intergroup peace is temporarily achieved, history has confronted us with either the quick reemergence of the ancien régime or the emergence of some alternative arbitrary-set hierarchy defined on the basis of newly constructed group distinctions (such as the Soviet Union's *nomenklatura*). Although one can cite a number of historical examples of relatively stable and peaceful multicultural societies in human history (for example, the Egyptian, Benin, Mayan, Shang, Russian, and British empires), all of these societies were examples of highly inegalitarian arbitrary-set hierarchies. In other words, despite certain temporary setbacks, the forces of discrimination, oppression, and hierarchical domination—the Beast—appear always to be with us. While the Beast is extremely adept at changing both its form and expression from one situation to another, it is never entirely defeated and appears never to go away.

Within the context of American race relations in the late 1990s, we are witnessing the reemerging forces of hierarchical domination in a series of court rulings, executive decisions, and political referenda.[16] The cumulative effects of these rulings and decisions make it rather clear that the United States is now well on its way to what might be called "the end of the Second Reconstruction." Despite the rhetoric of fairness and inclusiveness used to defend these legal and political decisions, there is every sign that their ultimate impact, rather than helping to open up opportunities for members of subordinate groups, will instead precipitate the further closing of opportunities for subordinates and the reaffirmation of racial and ethnic hegemony in the United States.

Therefore, if our basic conclusion is sound and Martin Luther King's noble dream is essentially unattainable within economies of surplus, the pertinent questions then become: Just how close to this noble ideal can societies actually come? What are the precise social, economic, and contextual conditions that will allow us to approach and sustain this level of social justice and reduction of group-based oppression? Unfortunately, neither historical precedent nor well-grounded social science theory are yet able to provide us with good answers to these questions. However, if we begin to look honestly and directly into the jaws of the Beast and recognize the powerful forces that animate it, an assiduous, fierce, and intellectually rigorous scientific approach to these questions may generate some valid answers in the not-too-distant future.

## NOTES

1. The Turkish government massacred thousands of Armenians between 1894 and 1896. During the First World War, the Turkish government's mass deportation of Armenians from Anatolia resulted in the massacre and death of somewhere between 600,000 and 1,000,000 Armenians in what has been called the "first genocide of modern times" (see *Grolier Multimedia Encyclopedia* 1996).
2. See also the very closely related work of Kinder and Sanders (1996).
3. For a cognitively oriented discussion of the importance and primacy of age and gender categories as the basis for social categorization, see Brewer and Liu (1989); see also Brewer (1988).
4. With the exception of bonobos (de Waal 1997).
5. For a more complex classification scheme of institutional discrimination, see Feagin and Feagin (1978).
6. For example, the 1991 National Household Survey on Drug Abuse found that of those who used powder cocaine, 75 percent were white, 15 percent were black, and 10 percent were Latino. On the other hand, of those who used crack cocaine, 52 percent were white, 38 percent were black, and 10 percent were Latino.
7. Other examples of outgroup favoritism in psychological research have been outlined by Jost (1995).

8. For other examples of self-debilitating behavior among subordinate groups, see Steele and Aronson 1995.
9. "And, behold, there are last which shall be first, and there are first which shall be last" (Luke 13:30, King James Version).
10. These nations include the United States, Australia, Canada, Israel, the Palestinian territories of the West Bank and Gaza Strip, Mexico, New Zealand, Sweden, the former Soviet Union, and the People's Republic of China.
11. This is not to say that generalizing SR theory to other domains is impossible. It seems feasible to claim that prejudice (wherever and however it manifests itself) is driven by, in part, the combination of anti-outgroup affect and the feeling that the outgroup is violating major, consensually held value ideologies (see Crandall 1994; Swim et al. 1995). However, this is a hypothesis that has been neither put forward by most SR theorists nor, to our knowledge, empirically tested in cultures outside the United States.
12. This survey was part of an annual computer-assisted telephone interview survey of Los Angeles residents conducted by the Institute for Social Science Research at UCLA. General *opposition to affirmative action* was measured by this item: "In general, do you support or oppose affirmative action? Please tell me if you strongly support, somewhat support, somewhat oppose, strongly oppose, or have never heard of affirmative action." The higher the score, the stronger the degree of opposition to affirmative action. *Symbolic racism* was measured by four items commonly used by Sears:

    1. "If blacks work hard, they almost always get what they want."
    2. "Hard work offers little guarantee of success for blacks."
    3. "Blacks are getting too demanding in their push for equal rights."
    4. "The Irish, Italians, Jews, and many other minorities overcame prejudice and worked their way up. Blacks should do the same without any special favors."

    All items were answered on a four-point scale ranging from "strongly agree" to "strongly disagree" ($\alpha = .65$).

    *Political conservatism* was measured by asking the respondents to classify themselves as: very liberal, somewhat liberal, neither conservative nor liberal, somewhat conservative, or very conservative. *Classical racism* was indexed by a single item asking respondents to indicate the degree to which they felt that blacks were worse off in America "because most blacks have less in-born ability to learn." The responses were given on a four-point scale ranging from "strongly agree" to "strongly disagree." *Social dominance orientation* was measured by use of the standard sixteen-item $SDO_6$ scale (see table 4.1). The reliability of the SDO scale in this sample was quite satisfactory ($\alpha = .82$).
13. It is worth noting that classical racism also had a small indirect effect on affirmative action opposition (indirect effect = .08, $p < .05$).
14. Note that in the context of the proposed model, this total effect is the same as the overall, product-moment correlation between SDO and SR, namely $r = .38$.
15. A full-blown writing system was first invented by the Sumerians five thousand years ago in approximately 3100 B.C. (see Gelb and Whiting 1996).

16. We are referring to the U.S. Supreme Court decisions in *San Antonio v. Rodriguez, Milliken v. Bradley,* and *Shaw v. Reno;* the U.S. Fifth Circuit Court's ruling in *Hopwood v. Texas;* the decision of the Board of Regents of the University of California to ban affirmative action in hiring and student admissions while, at the same time, refusing to end VIP admissions for the children of wealthy donors; and the passage of California's Propositions 187 and 209.

## REFERENCES


Abrams, Dominic, and Hogg, Michael A. (1988). Comments on the motivational status of self-esteem in social identity and intergroup discrimination. *European Journal of Social Psychology, 18,* 317–34.

Adorno, Tthodor W., Frenkel-Brunswik, Else, Levinson, Daniel J., and Sanford, R. Nevitte. (1950). *The authoritarian personality.* New York: Harper.

Alberts, Susan C., and Altmann, Jeanne. (1995). Preparation and activation: Determinants of age at reproductive maturity in male baboons. *Behavioral Ecology and Sociobiology, 36,* 397–406.

Altemeyer, Bob. (1981). *Right-wing authoritarianism.* Manitoba: University of Manitoba Press.

———. (1996). *The authoritarian specter.* Cambridge, Mass.: Harvard University Press.

———. (1998). The other "authoritarian personality." In Mark P. Zanna (Ed.), *Advances in experimental social psychology* (vol. 30, pp. 48–92). New York: Academic Press.

Bachofen, Johann J. (1969). *Das Mutterrecht: Eine Untersuchung uber die Gynaikokratie der altern Welt nach ihrer religiosen und rechlichen Natur.* Bruxelles: Culture et Civilisation. (Originally published in 1861)

Barth, Ernest, and Noel, Donald. (1972). Conceptual frameworks for the analysis of race relations. *Social Forces, 50,* 333–48.

Bastian, Lisa D., and Taylor, Bruce M. (1994). *Young black male victims.* Crime Data Brief NCJ–147004. Washington, D.C.: U.S. Department of Justice.

Bercovitch, Fred B. (1991). Social stratification, social strategies, and reproductive success in primates. *Ethology and Sociobiology, 12,* 315–33.

Berger, Joseph, Fisek, Mustafa H., Norman, Robert Z., and Zelditch, Morris, Jr. (1977). *Status characteristics and social interaction.* New York: Elsevier.

Billig, Michael., and Tajfel, Henri. (1973). Social categorization and similarity in intergroup behavior. *European Journal of Social Psychology, 3,* 27–52.

Brewer, Marilynn B. (1979). Ingroup bias in the minimal intergroup situation: A cognitive-motivational analysis. *Psychological Bulletin, 86,* 307–24.

———. (1988). A dual process model of impression formation. In Thomas K. Srull and Robert S. Wyer Jr. (Eds.), *Advances in social cognition: Vol. 1. A dual process model of impression formation* (pp. 1–36). Hillsdale, N.J.: Erlbaum.

Brewer, Marilynn B., and Kramer, Roderick M. (1985). The psychology of intergroup attitudes and behavior. *Annual Review of Psychology, 36,* 219–43.

Brewer, Marilynn B., and Lui, Layton N. (1989). The primacy of age and sex in the structure of person categories. *Social Cognition, 7,* 262–74.

Brown, Rupert, Hinkle, Steve, Ely, Pamela G., Fox-Cardamone, Lee. (1992). Recognizing group diversity: Individualist-collectivist and autonomous-relational social orientations and their implications for intergroup processes. *British Journal of Social Psychology, 31,* 327–42.

Caddick, Brian. (1982). Perceived illegitimacy and intergroup relations. In H. Tajfel (Ed.), *Social identity and intergroup relations: Studies in the social psychology of intergroup relations* (pp. 137–54). Cambridge: Cambridge University Press.

Cates, David S., Houston, B. Kent, Vavak, Chrisitne R., and Crawford, Michael H. (1993). Heritability of hostility-related emotions, attitudes, and behaviors. *Journal of Behavioral Medicine, 16,* 237–56.

Chomsky, Noam. (1973). *For reasons of state.* New York: Vintage.

Clark, Kenneth B., and Clark, Mamie K. (1939). The development of consciousness of self and the emergence of racial identification in Negro preschool children. *Journal of Social Psychology, 10,* 591–99.

———. (1947). Racial identification and preference in Negro children. In Theodore M. Newcomb and Eugene L. Hartley (Eds.), *Readings in social psychology* (pp. 169–78). New York: Holt, Rinehart and Winston.

Coccaro, Emil F., Bergeman, Cindy S., and McClearn, Gérald E. (1993). Heritability of irritable impulsiveness: A study of twins reared together and apart. *Psychiatry Research, 48,* 229–42.

Cohen, Gerald Allan. (1978). *Karl Marx's theory of history: A defense.* New York: Oxford University Press.

Collier, Jane F., and Yanagisako, Sylvia J. (1987). *Gender and kinship: Essays toward a unified analysis.* Stanford, Calif.: Stanford University Press.

Combs, Michael W., and Comer, John C. (1982). Race and capital punishment: A longitudinal analysis. *Phylon, 12,* 350–59.

Commins, Barry, and Lockwood, John. (1979). The effects of status differences, favoured treatment, and equity on intergroup comparisons. *European Journal of Social Psychology, 9,* 281–89.

Crandall, Christian S. (1994). Prejudice against fat people: Ideology and self-interest. *Journal of Personality and Social Psychology, 66,* 882–94.

Dator, James A. (1969). Measuring attitudes across cultures: A factor analysis of the replies of Japanese judges to Eysenck's inventory of conservative-progressive ideology. In Glendon Shubert and David J. Danelski (Eds.), *Comparative judicial behavior* (pp. 71–102). New York: Oxford University Press.

Davis, Mark H., Luce, Carol, and Kraus, Stephen J. (1994). The heritability of characteristics associated with dispositional empathy. *Journal of Personality, 62,* 369–91.

De Waal, Frans B. M. (1997). *Bonobo: The forgotten ape.* Berkeley: University of California Press.

Durkheim, Émile. (1933). *The division of labor in society.* Translated by G. Simpson. New York: Macmillan. (Originally published in 1893)

Emde, Robert N., Plomin, Robert, Robinson, JoAnn, and Corley, Robin. (1992). Temperament, emotion, and cognition at fourteen months: The MacArthur Longitudinal Twin Study. *Child Development, 63,* 1437–55.

Erasmus, Charles J. (1977). *In search of the common good: Utopian experiments past and future.* New York: Free Press.

Eysenck, Hans J. (1951). Primary social attitudes as related to social class and political party. *British Journal of Sociology, 11,* 198–209.

———. (1971). Social attitudes and social class. *British Journal of Social Psychology, 10,* 201–12.

———. (1976). Structure of social attitudes. *Psychological Reports, 39,* 463–66.

Eysenck, Hans J., and Coulter, Thelma T. (1972). The personality and attitudes of working-class British communists and fascists. *Journal of Social Psychology, 87,* 59–73.
Eysenck, Hans J., and Wilson, Glenn D. (1978). *The psychological basis of ideology.* Baltimore: University Park Press.
Feagin, Joe R., and Feagin, Clarice B. (1978). *Discrimination American style: Institutional racism and sexism.* Englewood Cliffs, N.J.: Prentice-Hall.
Federico, Christopher M. (in press). The interactive effects of social dominance orientation, group status, and perceived stability on favoritism for high-status groups. *Group Processes and Intergroup Relations.*
Feldman, Stanley. (1983). Economic individualism and American public opinion. *American Politics Quarterly, 11,* 3–30.
French, John R. P., Jr., and Raven, Bertram H. (1959). The bases of social power. In Darwin Cartwright (Ed.), *Studies in social power* (pp. 150–67). Ann Arbor: University of Michigan.
Gelb, Ignance J., and Whiting, Robert M. (1996). The evolution of writing systems. *Grolier Multimedia Encyclopedia.* New York: Grolier's Electronic Publishing Co.
Gerth, Hans, and Mills, C. Wright. (1953). *Character and social structure.* New York: Harcourt, Brace and World.
Ghiglieri, Michael P. (1989). Hominoid sociobiology and hominid social evolution. In Paul G. Heltne and Linda A. Marquardt (Eds.), *Understanding chimpanzees* (pp. 370–79). Cambridge, Mass.: Harvard University Press.
Ghodsian-Carpey, Jilla, and Baker, Laura A. (1987). Genetic and environmental influences on aggression in four- to seven-year-old twins. *Aggressive Behavior, 13,* 173–86.
Giddens, Anthony. (1971). *Capitalism and modern social theory.* Cambridge: Cambridge University Press.
Gimbutas, Marija A. (1989). *The language of the goddess: Unearthing the hidden symbols of Western civilization.* New York: Harper and Row.
Gobineau, Arthur. (1915). *The inequality of human races.* New York: Putnam's.
Godelier, Maurice. (1976). *Perspectives in Marxist anthropology.* Cambridge: Cambridge University Press.
Gopaul-McNichol, Sharon-Ann. (1988). Racial identification and racial preference of black preschool children in New York and Trinidad. *Journal of Black Psychology, 14*(2), 65–68.
———. (1995). A cross-cultural examination of racial identity and racial preference of preschool children in the West Indies. *Journal of Cross-cultural Psychology, 26,* 141–52.
Gramsci, Antonio. (1971). *Selections from the prison notebooks.* London: Wishart.
*Grolier Multimedia Encyclopedia.* (1996). Computer software. Danbury, Conn.: Grolier Electronic Publishing.
Habermas, Jurgen. (1978). *Communication and the evolution of society.* Translated by Thomas McCarthy. Boston: Beacon Press.
Harcourt, Alexandria H. (1988). Alliances in contests and social intelligence. In Richard W. Byrne and Andrew Whiten (Eds.), *Machiavellian intelligence: Social expertise and the evolution of intellect in monkeys, apes, and humans* (pp. 132–52). Oxford: Clarendon Press/Oxford University Press.
Harcourt, Alexander H., and Stewart, Kelly J. (1987). The influence of help in contests on dominance rank in primates: Hints from gorillas. *Animal Behaviour, 35,* 182–90.

Hausfater, Glenn, Altmann, Jeanne, and Altmann, Stuart. (1982). Long-term consistency of dominance relations among female baboons (*Papio cynocephalus*). *Science, 217,* 752–55.

Hinkle, Steve, and Brown, Rupert. (1990). Intergroup comparisons and social identity: Some links and lacunae. In Dominic Abrams and Michael A. Hogg (Eds.), *Social identity theory: Constructive and critical advances* (pp. 48–70). New York: Harvester Wheatsheaf.

Hinkle, Steve, and Schopler, John. (1979). Ethnocentrism in the evaluation of group products. In William G. Austin and Stephen Worchel (Eds.), *The social psychology of intergroup relations.* Monterey, Calif.: Brooks/Cole.

———. (1986). Bias in the evaluation of ingroup and outgroup performance. In Stephen Worchel and William G. Austin (Eds.), *Psychology of intergroup relations* (pp. 196–212). Chicago: Nelson-Hall.

Hinkle, Steve, Taylor, Laurie A., Fox-Cardamone, Lee, and Crook, Kimberly F. (1989). Intragroup identification and intergroup differentiation: A multicomponent approach. *British Journal of Social Psychology, 28,* 305–17.

Hogg, Michael A., and Abrams, Dominic. (1988). *Social identifications: A social psychology of intergroup relations and group processes.* London: Routledge.

———. (1990). Social motivation, self-esteem and social identity. In Dominic Abrams and Michael A. Hogg (Eds.), *Social identity theory: Constructive and critical advances* (pp. 28–47). London: Harvester Wheatsheaf.

Hraba, Joseph, Hagendoorn, Lauk, and Hagendoorn, Roeland. (1989). The ethnic hierarchy in the Netherlands: Social distance and social representation. *British Journal of Social Psychology, 28,* 57–69.

Jackson, James S., and Kirby, Darie. (1991). Models of individual outgroup rejection: Cross-national western Europe–United States comparisons. Paper presented at the Symposium on the Social Psychology of Intergroup Relations, American Sociological Association annual meeting, Cincinnati, Ohio (August).

Jones, James M. (1972). *Prejudice and racism.* Reading, Mass.: Addison-Wesley.

Jost, John T. (1995). Negative illusions: Conceptual clarification and psychological evidence concerning false consciousness. *Political Psychology, 16,* 397–424.

Kawanaka, Kenji.(1982). Further studies on predation by chimpanzees of the Mahale Mountains. *Primates, 23,* 364–84.

———. (1989). Age differences in social interactions of young males in a chimpanzee unit-group at the Mahale Mountains National Park, Tanzania. *Primates, 30,* 285–305.

Keegan, John. (1993). *The history of warfare.* New York: Alfred A. Knopf.

Kinder, Donald R., and Sanders, Lynn M. (1996). *Divided by color: Racial politics and democratic ideals.* Chicago: University of Chicago Press.

Kluegel, James R., and Smith, Eliot R. (1983). Affirmative action attitudes: Effects of self-interest, racial effect, and stratification beliefs on whites' views. *Social Forces, 61,* 797–824.

Lee, Phyllis C., and Oliver, J. I. (1979). Competition, dominance, and the acquisition of rank in juvenile yellow baboons (*Papio cynocephalus*). *Animal Behaviour, 27,* 576–85.

Leigh, Steven R., and Shea, Brian T. (1995). Ontogeny and the evolution of adult body size dimorphism in apes. *American Journal of Primatology, 36,* 37–60.

Lenski, Gerhard E. (1984). *Power and privilege: A theory of social stratification.* Chapel Hill: University of North Carolina Press.

Leonard, June W. (1979). A strategy approach to the study of primate dominance behavior. *Behavioural Processes, 4,* 155–72.
Levin, Shana. (1992). Intergroup biases as a function of social dominance orientation, ingroup status, and ingroup identification. Master's thesis, University of California, Los Angeles.
———. (1996). A social psychological approach to understanding intergroup attitudes in the United States and Israel. Ph.D. diss., University of California, Los Angeles.
Levin, Shana, and Sidanius, Jim. (in press). Social dominance and social identity in the United States and Israel: Ingroup favoritism or outgroup derogation? *Political Psychology.*
Levin, Shana, Sidanius, Jim, and Pratto, Felicia. (1998). Social dominance orientation, ingroup favoritism, and ethnic status: Beyond the asymmetrical ingroup bias effect. Manuscript in preparation.
Luhtanen, Riia, and Crocker, Jennifer. (1992). A collective self-esteem scale: Self-evaluation of one's social identity. *Personality and Social Psychology Bulletin, 18,* 302–18.
Marger, M. N. (1985). *Race and ethnic relations: American and global perspectives.* Belmont, Calif.: Wadsworth.
Marx, Karl. (1973). *Grundrisse.* Harmondsworth, Eng.: Penguin.
Marx, Karl, and Engels, Friedrich. (1970). *The German ideology.* London: Lawrence and Wishart. (Originally published in 1846)
Matthews, Karen A., Batson, C. Daniel, Horn, Joseph, and Rosenman, Ray H. (1981). "Principles in his nature which interest him in the fortune of others . . .": The heritability of empathic concern for others. *Journal of Personality, 49,* 237–47.
Mauer, Marc, and Huling, Tracy. (1995). *Young black Americans and the criminal justice system: Five years later.* Washington, D.C.: The Sentencing Project.
Mazur, Allan. (1985). A biosocial model of status in face-to-face primate groups. *Social Forces, 64,* 377–402.
McConahay, John B. (1986). Modern racism, ambivalence, and the Modern Racism Scale. In John F. Dovidio and Samuel Gaertner (Eds.), *Prejudice, discrimination, and racism* (pp. 91–125). Orlando, Fla.: Academic Press.
McConahay, John B., Hardee, Betty B., and Batts, Valerie. (1981). Has racism declined in America? It depends on who is asking and what is asked. *Journal of Conflict Resolution, 25,* 563–79.
McFarland, Sam G., and Adelson, Sherman. (1996). An omnibus study of personality, values, and prejudice. Paper presented at the annual meeting of the International Society of Political Psychology, Vancouver, Canada (July).
Messick, David M., and Mackie, Diane. (1989). Intergroup relations. *Annual Review of Psychology, 40,* 45–81.
Mitchell, Michael, and Sidanius, Jim. (1993). Group status and asymmetry in the relationship between ideology and death penalty support: A social dominance perspective. *National Journal of Sociology, 7,* 67–93.
Mosca, Gaetano. (1939). *The ruling class: Elements of political science.* New York: McGraw-Hill. (Originally published in 1896)
Moscovici, Serge. (1981). On social representation. In Joseph P. Forgas (Ed.), *Social cognition: Perspectives on everyday understanding.* London: Academic Press.
———. (1988). Notes towards a description of social representations. *European Journal of Social Psychology, 18,* 211–50.

Mullen, Brian, Brown, Rupert, and Smith, Colleen. (1992). Ingroup bias as a function of salience, relevance, and status: An integration. *European Journal of Psychology, 22,* 103–22.
Mummendey, Amilie, and Schreiber, Hans-Joachim. (1983). Better or just different? Positive social identity by discrimination against or by differentiation from outgroups. *European Journal of Social Psychology, 13,* 389–97.
———. (1984). Different just means better: Some obvious and some hidden pathways to ingroup favoritism. *British Journal of Social Psychology, 23,* 363–67.
Mummendey, Amelie, and Simon, Bernd. (1989). Better or just different?: III. The impact of importance of comparison dimension and relative ingroup size upon intergroup discrimination. *British Journal of Social Psychology, 28,* 1–16.
Murdock, George P. (1949). *Social structure.* New York: Macmillan.
Nadler, Ronald D. (1987). Sexual aggression in the great apes. Conference of the New York Academy of Sciences: Human sexual aggression: Current perspectives. *Annals of the New York Academy of Sciences, 528,* 154–62.
Ng, Sik H. (1980). *The social psychology of power.* New York: Academic Press.
———. (1982a). Power and appeasement in intergroup discrimination. *Australian Journal of Psychology, 34,* 37–44.
———. (1982b). Power and intergroup discrimination. In Henri Tajfel (Ed.), *Social identity and intergroup relations: Studies in the social psychology of intergroup relations* (pp. 179–206). Cambridge: Cambridge University Press.
———. (1984). Social psychology and political economy. In Henri Tajfel (Ed.), *The social dimension: European developments in social psychology* (pp. 624–45). Cambridge: Cambridge University Press.
Nias, David K. B. (1972). The structuring of social attitudes in children. *Child Development, 43,* 211–19.
Noe, Ronald, and Sluijter, Albertha A. (1995). Which adult male savanna baboons form coalitions? *International Journal of Primatology, 16,* 77–105.
Pareto, Vilfreo. (1935/1963). *The mind and society: A treatise on general society.* New York: Dover.
Parkin, Frank. (1971). *Class inequality and political order: Social stratification in capitalist and communist societies.* London: MacGibbon and Kee.
Powell-Hopson, Darlene, and Hopson, Derek S. (1988). Implications of doll color preferences among black preschool children and white preschool children. *Journal of Black Psychology, 14*(2), 57–63.
———. (1992). Implications of doll color preferences among black preschool children and white preschool children. In A. Kathleen Hoard Burlew, W. Curtis Banks, Harriette P. McAdoo, and Daudi Ajani ya Azibo (Eds.), *African American psychology: Theory, research, and practice* (pp. 183–89). Newbury Park, Calif.: Sage.
Pratto, Felicia. (in press). The puzzle of continuing group inequality: Piecing together psychological, social, and cultural forces in social dominance theory. In Mark P. Zanna (Ed.), *Advances in experimental social psychology* (vol. 31, pp. 191–263). San Diego: Academic Press.
Pratto, Felicia, Liu, James., Levin, Shana, Sidanius, Jim, Shih, Margaret, and Bachrach, Hagit. (1998). Social dominance orientation and the legitimization of inequality across cultures. Manuscript in preparation.
Pratto, Felicia, Sidanius, Jim, Stallworth, Lisa M., and Malle, Bertram F. (1994). Social dominance orientation: A personality variable predicting social and political attitudes. *Journal of Personality and Social Psychology, 67,* 741–63.
Rabinowitz, Joshua L. (in press). Go with the flow or fight the power? The inter-

active effects of social dominance orientation and perceived injustice on support for the status quo. *Political Psychology.*

Rabinowitz, Joshua L., and Sidanius, Jim. (1995). Social dominance orientation, ethnic status, and intergroup evaluation: Consequences for self-esteem. Paper presented at the seventy-fifth annual meeting of the Western Psychological Association, Los Angeles (March).

Raven, Bertram H. (1992). A power/interaction model of interpersonal influence: French and Raven thirty years later. *Journal of Social Behavior and Personality, 7,* 217–44.

Riss, David C., and Goodall, Jane. (1977). The recent rise to the alpha-rank in a population of free-living chimpanzees. *Folia Primatologica, 27,* 134–51.

Rokeach, Milton. (1960). *The open and closed mind.* New York: Basic Books.

Rosenberg, Morris. (1965). *Society and the adolescent self-image.* Princeton, N.J.: Princeton University Press.

Rowell, Thelma E. (1974). The concept of social dominance. *Behavioral Biology, 11,* 131–54.

Rubin, Mark, and Hewstone, Miles. (1998). Social identity theory's self-esteem hypothesis: A review and some suggestions for clarification. *Personality and Social Psychological Review, 2,* 40–62.

Sachdev, Itesh, and Bourhis, Richard Y. (1985). Social categorization and power differentials in group relations. *European Journal of Social Psychology, 15,* 415–34.

———. (1987). Status differentials and intergroup behavior. *European Journal of Social Psychology, 17,* 277–93.

———. (1991). Power and status differentials in minority and majority group relations. *European Journal of Social Psychology, 21,* 1–24.

Sapolsky, Robert M. (1993). The physiology of dominance in stable versus unstable social hierarchies. In William A. Mason and Sally P. Mendoza (Eds.), *Primate social conflict* (pp. 171–204). Albany: State University of New York Press.

———. (1995). Social subordinance as a marker of hypercortisolism: Some unexpected subtleties. In George P. Chrousos, Richard McCarty, Karel Pacak, Giovanni Cizza, Esther Sternberg, P. W. Gold, and Richard Kvetnansky (Eds.), *Stress: Basic mechanisms and clinical implications.* Annals of the New York Academy of Sciences (vol. 771, pp. 626–39). New York: New York Academy of Sciences.

Schermerhorn, Richard A. (1970). *Comparative ethnic relations: A framework for theory and research.* New York: Random House.

Schwarzwald, Joseph, Amir, Yigal, and Crain, Robert L. (1992). Long-term effects of school desegregation experiences on interpersonal relations in the Israeli Defense Forces. *Personality and Social Psychology Bulletin, 18,* 357–68.

Sears, David O. (1988). Symbolic racism. In P. A. Katz and D. A. Taylor (Eds.), *Eliminating racism: Profiles in controversy* (pp. 53–84). New York: Plenum Press.

———. (1993). Symbolic politics: A socio-psychological theory. In Shanto Iyengar and William McGuire (Eds.), *Explorations in political psychology* (pp. 113–49). Durham, N.C.: Duke University Press.

Sears, David O., Huddy, Leonie, and Schaffer, L. G. (1984). Schemas and symbolic politics: The case of racial and gender equality. In Richard R. Lau and David O. Sears (Eds.), *Political cognition* (pp. 159–202). Hillsdale, N.J.: Erlbaum.

Sears, David O., van Laar, Colette, Carrillo, Mary, and Kosterman, Rick. (1997). Is it really racism? The origins of white Americans' opposition to race-targeted policies. *Public Opinion Quarterly, 61,* 16–53.
Sidanius, Jim. (1987). Social attitudes and political party preferences among Swedish youth. *Scandinavian Political Studies, 10,* 111–24.
———. (1993). The psychology of group conflict and the dynamics of oppression: A social dominance perspective. In Shanto Iyengar and William McGuire (Eds.), *Explorations in political psychology* (pp. 183–219). Durham, N.C.: Duke University Press.
Sidanius, Jim, Devereux, Erik, and Pratto, Felicia. (1992). A comparison of symbolic racism theory and social dominance theory: Explanations for racial policy attitudes. *Journal of Social Psychology, 132,* 377–95.
Sidanius, Jim, and Ekehammar, B. O. (1979). Political socialization: A multivariate analysis of Swedish political attitude and preference data. *European Journal of Social Psychology, 9,* 265–79.
Sidanius, Jim, Ekehammar, B. O., and Ross, Michael. (1979). Comparisons of socio-political attitudes between two democratic societies. *International Journal of Psychology, 14,* 225–40.
Sidanius, Jim, Feshbach, Seymour, Levin, Shana, and Pratto, Felicia. (1997). The interface between ethnic and national attachment: Ethnic pluralism or ethnic dominance? *Public Opinion Quarterly, 61,* 102–33.
Sidanius, Jim, Levin, Shana, and Pratto, Felicia. (1996). Consensual social dominance orientation and its correlates within the hierarchical structure of American society. *International Journal of Intercultural Relations, 20,* 385–408.
Sidanius, Jim, and Liu, James H. (1992). Racism, support for the Persian Gulf War, and the police beating of Rodney King: A social dominance perspective. *Journal of Social Psychology, 132,* 685–700.
Sidanius, Jim, Liu, James H., Pratto, Felicia, and Shaw, John S. (1994). Social dominance orientation, hierarchy-attenuators and hierarchy-enhancers: Social dominance theory and the criminal justice system. *Journal of Applied Social Psychology, 24,* 338–66.
Sidanius, Jim, and Pratto, Felicia. (1993a). Racism and support of free-market capitalism: A cross-cultural analysis. *Political Psychology, 14,* 383–403.
———. (1993b). The inevitability of oppression and the dynamics of social dominance. In Paul M. Sniderman and Philip Tetlock (Eds.), *Prejudice, politics, and the American dilemma* (pp. 173–211). Stanford, Calif.: Stanford University Press.
———. (in press). *Social dominance: An intergroup theory of social hierarchy and oppression.* New York: Cambridge University Press.
Sidanius, Jim, Pratto, Felicia, and Bobo, Lawrence. (1994). Social dominance orientation and the political psychology of gender: A case of invariance? *Journal of Personality and Social Psychology, 67,* 998–1011.
———. (1996). Racism, conservatism, affirmative action, and intellectual sophistication: A matter of principled conservatism or group dominance? *Journal of Personality and Social Psychology, 70,* 476–90.
Sidanius, Jim, Pratto, Felicia, and Brief, Diana. (1995). Group dominance and the political psychology of gender: A cross-cultural comparison. *Political Psychology, 16,* 381–96.
Sidanius, Jim, Pratto, Felicia, Martin, Michael, and Stallworth, Lisa M. (1991). Consensual racism and career track: Some implications of social dominance theory. *Political Psychology, 12,* 691–721.

Sidanius, Jim, Pratto, Felicia, and Mitchell, Michael. (1994). Ingroup identification, social dominance orientation, and differential intergroup social allocation. *Journal of Social Psychology, 134,* 151–67.

Sidanius, Jim, Pratto, Felicia, and Rabinowitz, Joshua L. (1994). Gender, ethnic status, ingroup attachment, and social dominance orientation. *Journal of Cross-cultural Psychology, 25,* 194–216.

Sidanius, Jim, Pratto, Felicia, Sinclair, Stacey, and van Laar, Colette. (1996). Mother Teresa meets Genghis Khan: The dialectics of hierarchy-enhancing and hierarchy-attenuating career choices. *Social Justice Research, 9,* 145–70.

Sinclair, Stacey, Sidanius, Jim, and Levin, Shana. (in press). The interface between ethnic and social system attachment: The differential effects of hierarchy-enhancing and hierarchy-attenuating environments. *Journal of Social Issues.*

Skevington, Suzanne. (1981). Intergroup relations and nursing. *European Journal of Social Psychology, 11,* 43–59.

Smith, Tom W. (1991). *What do Americans think about Jews?* Working Paper on Contemporary Anti-Semitism. New York: American Jewish Committee, Institute of Human Relations.

Sniderman, Paul M., and Tetlock, Philip E. (1986). Symbolic racism: Problems of motive attribution in political analysis. *Journal of Social Issues, 42,* 129–50.

Spears, Russell, and Manstead, Anthony S. R. (1989). The social context of stereotyping and differentiation. *European Journal of Social Psychology, 19,* 101–21.

Standing, Hilary, and Stirrat, R. L. (1996). Castes in India. In *Grolier's Multimedia Encyclopedia.* CD-ROM. Danbury, Conn.: Grolier Electronic Publishing Co.

Steele, Claude M., and Aronson, Joshua. (1995). Stereotype threat and the intellectual test performance of African Americans. *Journal of Personality and Social Psychology, 69,* 797–811.

Stone, William F., and Russ, Raymond C. (1976). Machiavellianism as tough-mindedness. *Journal of Social Psychology, 98,* 213–20.

Strier, Karen B. (1994). Brotherhoods among atelins: Kinship, affiliation, and competition. *Behaviour, 130,* 151–67.

Sumner, William G. (1906). *Folkways: A study of the sociological importance of usages, manners, customs, mores, and morals.* Boston: Ginn.

Swim, Janet K., Aikin, Kathryn J., Hall, Wayne S., and Hunter, Barbara A. (1995). Sexism and racism: Old-fashioned and modern prejudices. *Journal of Personality and Social Psychology, 68,* 199–214.

Tajfel, Henri. (1970). Experiments in intergroup discrimination. *Scientific American, 223,* 96–102.

———. (1978). Social categorization, social identity, and social comparison. In Henri Tafjel (Ed.), *Differentiation between social groups* (pp. 61–76). London: Academic Press.

———. (1982). Social psychology of intergroup relations. *Annual Review of Psychology, 33,* 1–30.

Tajfel, Henri, Flament, Claude, Billig, Michael, and Bundy, R. (1971). Social categorization and intergroup behavior. *European Journal of Social Psychology, 1,* 149–78.

Tajfel, Henri, and Turner, John C. (1979). An integrative theory of intergroup conflict. In William G. Austin and Stephen Worchel (Eds.), *The social psychology of intergroup relations* (pp. 33–47). Monterey, Calif.: Brooks/Cole.

———. (1986). The social identity theory of intergroup behavior. In Stephen Worchel and William G. Austin (Eds.), *Psychology of intergroup relations* (pp. 7–24). Chicago: Nelson-Hall.

Turner, John C. (1978). Social comparison, similarity, and ingroup favoritism. In Henri Tajfel (Ed.), *Differentiation between social groups: Studies in the social psychology of intergroup relations* (pp. 235–50). San Diego: Academic Press.

———. (1985). Social categorization and the self-concept: A social-cognitive theory of group behavior. In Edward J. Lawler (Ed.), *Advances in group processes,* vol. 2, *Theory and research* (pp. 77–121). Greenwich, Conn.: JAI Press.

Turner, John C., and Brown, Rupert J. (1978). Social status, cognitive alternatives, and intergroup relations. In Henri Tajfel (Ed.), *Differentiation between social groups: Studies in the social psychology of intergroup relations* (pp. 201–34). London: Academic Press.

Turner, John C., Hogg, Michael A., Oakes, Penelope J., Reicher, Stephen D., and Wetherell, Margaret. (1987). *Rediscovering the social group: A self-categorization theory.* Oxford: Blackwell.

U.S. Sentencing Commission. (1995). *Special Report to the Congress: Cocaine and Federal Sentencing Policy.* Washington, D.C.: U.S. Sentencing Commission (February).

Van Knippenberg, Ad. (1984). Intergroup differences in group perceptions. In Henri Tajfel (Ed.), *The social dimension: European developments in social psychology* (vol. 2, pp. 560–78). Cambridge: Cambridge University Press.

Van Knippenberg, Ad, and Ellemers, Naomi. (1990). Social identity and intergroup differentiation processes. In Wolfgang Stroebe and Miles Hewstone (Eds.), *European review of social psychology* (vol. 1, pp. 137–69). Chichester, Eng.: Wiley.

———. (1993). Strategies in intergroup relations. In Michael A. Hogg and Dominic Abrams (Eds.), *Group motivation: Social psychological perspectives* (pp. 17–32). New York: Harvester Wheatsheaf.

Van Knippenberg, Ad, and van Oers, Hub. (1984). Social identity and equity concerns in intergroup perceptions. *British Journal of Social Psychology, 23,* 351–61.

Van Laar, Colette, Sidanius, Jim, Rabinowitz, Joshua, and Sinclair, Stacey. (1999). The three R's of academic achievement: Reading, 'riting, and racism. *Personality and Social Psychology Bulletin, 25,* 139–51.

Wade, Ted D. (1978). Status and hierarchy in nonhuman primate societies. In Paul P. G. Bateson and Peter H. Klopfer (Eds.), *Perspectives in ethology: II. Social behavior* (pp. 109–34). New York: Plenum.

Weber, Max. (1946). Class, status, party. In Hans Gerth and C. Wright Mills (Eds.), *From Max Weber: Essays in sociology* (pp. 180–95). New York: Oxford University Press.

———. (1947). *The theory of social and economic organization.* Translated by A. M. Henderson and Talcott Parsons. New York: Oxford University Press.

Wilson, Glenn D. (1973). *The psychology of conservatism.* San Diego: Academic Press.

Wilson, Glenn D., and Bagley, Christopher. (1973). Religion, racialism, and conservatism. In Glenn D. Wilson (Ed.), *The psychology of conservatism* (pp. 117–28). London: Academic Press.

Wilson, Glenn D., and Lee, Hyun S. (1974). Social attitude patterns in Korea. *Journal of Social Psychology, 94,* 27–30.
Wilson, Glenn D., and Patterson, John R. (1968). A new measure of conservatism. *British Journal of Social and Clinical Psychology, 7,* 264–69.
Wrangham, Richard W. (1987). The significance of African apes for reconstructing human social evolution. In W. G. Kinsey (Ed.), *The evolution of human behavior: Primate models* (pp. 51–71). Albany: State University of New York Press.
Wurst, Stephen A., and Wolford, Karen. (1994). Integrating disability awareness into psychology courses: Applications in abnormal psychology and perception. *Teaching of Psychology, 21,* 233–35.
Yee, Mia D., and Brown, Rupert J. (1988). *Children and social comparisons.* Final report to Economic and Social Research Council (England).
Young, Thomas J. (1993). Alcohol misuse and criminal violence among Native Americans. *Psychiatric Forum, 16,* 20–26.

# 5

# CONTEXT, IDENTITY, AND INTERGROUP RELATIONS

*Patricia Gurin, Timothy Peng, Gretchen Lopez, and Biren A. Nagda*

CAN PLURAL groups whose members strongly identify with their own groups live together in reasonable harmony, forge an American identity, and commit themselves to democratic citizenship, or will they inevitably be splintered, exist in unresolvable conflict, and threaten democracy? These are questions that have perplexed political analysts of democracy from the ancient Greeks to contemporary times. They lie behind the critique of multicultural education by those who worry that identities based on race, ethnicity, gender, class, or other categorizations are inevitably divisive. It is thought that these identities privilege group rights over individual rights, which are the bedrock of American democracy, and that they will tear the United States apart in a manner similar to the upheavals in Eastern Europe of the 1990s (for a review of the major criticisms, see Sleeter 1995). Arthur Schlesinger (1991), one of the more prolific of these critics, writes that when multicultural education means "the assumption that ethnicity is the defining experience for every American . . . that we must discard the idea of a common culture and celebrate, reinforce, and perpetuate separate ethnic and racial communities, then multiculturalism not only betrays history but undermines the theory of America as one people" (13–14).

In this chapter, we set the issue of unity and diversity in a historical context, arguing that there is nothing new about the tensions between them. The major theories of intergroup relations within social psychology generally support a picture of an inevitable divisiveness in the interplay of group identities, even though the empirical literature in social psychology does not always support that picture. We suggest that a contextualized approach that emphasizes power and particular circumstances in intergroup contact is needed to explain when group identity is divisive and inimical to democracy and when it is congenial to a particular conception of democracy, one that draws more from Aristotle than from the Enlightenment figures who provided the rationale for liberal democracies. We present a field experiment in intergroup relations that is predicated on the assumption that under certain conditions, diversity and group identity are congenial to rather than a threat to democracy and community. We analyze the relationship between group identity and a variety of intergroup perceptions, attitudes, and behaviors among students four years after they participated in this experiment, and among a matched sample of students who did not.

## UNITY AND DIVERSITY

### The Long History

Current controversies about unity and diversity take us back to the struggles that the early Greeks had with the same issues. Arlene Saxonhouse in *Fear of Diversity* (1992) describes how the pre-Socratic playwrights, Plato, and Aristotle dealt with the fear that "differences bring on chaos and thus demand that the world be put into an orderly pattern" (x). Saxonhouse contends that the fear of diversity that their senses told them existed led the pre-Socratic playwrights to dismiss what is seen—the senses—in favor of what is not seen—the mind and its capacity to create unity through language, reason, and decrees that difference was to be ignored. As she shows, however, the characters in their plays—Eteocles, Creon, Antigone, Praxagora—suffer when they attempt to discard difference in their longing for unity and simplicity. Plato, too, struggled with the problem of unity and diversity, warning of the danger in striving for too much unity, at the same time that he defined a basis of unity in Socrates' beloved Callipolis by getting rid of male and female, the family, and sexuality. All citizens were to be the same, and the city was to be unified by similarity. Saxonhouse concludes that Plato was never entirely comfortable with this solution, and she points out that only Aristotle was able "to overcome the fear and welcome the diverse" (x). "Aristotle goes beyond the others who warned of the dangers and the tragedy of the excessive pursuit of unity. He embraces diversity as the others had not. . . . The typologies that fill almost every page of Aristotle's *Politics* show him uniting and separating, finding underlying unity and significant differences" (235). Aristotle struggled to construct a political theory in which unity could be achieved through difference and contended that democracy would thrive best through such a unity, not through one based on sameness. What makes democracy work, according to Aristotle, is equality among peers (admittedly only men, not women and slaves) who are also diverse and hold multiple perspectives, and whose relationships are governed by freedom and rules of civil discourse. It is discourse over conflict, not unanimity, that helps democracy thrive (Pitkin and Shumer 1982).

A theory of democracy more akin to that of the pre-Socratics and Plato than to Aristotle's has prevailed in the United States. It is the Republican tradition, represented by Rousseau on through Jefferson, in which democracy and citizenship are believed to require social homogeneity, simplicity, and an overarching common identity rather than heterogeneity, complexity, and multiple identities. The model is the town meeting, where people, interdependent through their similarity and familiarity, come together to debate the common good. Guided by this concept of democracy, the founding fathers faced a critical dilemma: Needing homogeneity, what were they to do with the obvious heterogeneity (Native Americans, slaves of African ancestry, and Europeans not of Anglo-Saxon descent) of the new nation's people? Although it was not clear how they were to accomplish it, the goal was quite clear to the founding fathers: American democracy required a common identity that was to be formed according to Anglo-American conformity (Levine 1996). Thus, for most of our history the major models of intergroup life and democratic unity have been ethnic hierarchy or one-way assimilation, both of which call for the muting of differences and cultural identities (Fredrickson, this volume).

There were always some dissenting voices. Lawrence Levine in *The Opening of the American Mind* (1996) points to Ralph Waldo Emerson, who in 1845 wrote of a more dynamic, progressive conception of American identity that would be constructed out of the energy of Irish, Germans, Poles, Cossacks, and all the European tribes, and out of the energy of the Africans and Polynesians as well. Fredrickson (this volume) outlines the intellectual basis of cultural pluralism, a twentieth-century model of intergroup life offered by Randolph Bourne and Horace Kallen. Fredrickson defines the common argument among cultural pluralists, then and now, as a belief that "cultural diversity is a healthy and normal condition that does not preclude equal rights and the mutual understandings about civic responsibilities needed to sustain a democratic nation-state." The early advocates, in contrast to current advocates of multiculturalism, stopped at the color line. There was a voice even at the turn of the century, however, that presaged the multiculturalism of the 1980s: W. E. B. Du Bois explicitly raised the question of national identity for non-European groups. He argued that Americans of Negro descent were to maintain their racial identity because only as a group could "they fulfill themselves as well as continue their essential contributions to the nation in which they lived" (Levine 1996, 117). Contemporary advocates of multiculturalism, like Du Bois, argue that groups of color as well as ethnic groups of European descent contribute to a rich cultural complexity in the United States that is congenial to a common civic society.

## The Current Debate

With this long history and unresolved set of questions about unity and diversity, why are we now facing cultural, disciplinary, and political debates of great intensity over multiculturalism? Why the renewed and grave concern about the implications of group identity for national unity?

Sears, Citrin, Cheleden, and van Laar (this volume) suggest that elite rhetoric and the size and composition of current immigration are factors in the politics of multiculturalism. They suggest that elite rhetoric advancing a hard, particularistic multiculturalism, akin to ethnic separatism, engenders a negative political reaction. They further argue that whites tend to act defensively to protect their privileges as diversity increases through the now heavily Asian and Latin American character of immigration.

Glazer (1993) gives another answer. He argues that many of the critics of multiculturalism lack an appreciation of earlier battles over diversity because they grew up and experienced schooling in America between the 1920s and 1950s, a period during which educational institutions were largely free of contentious claims by different groups. In fact, Glazer points out, these were atypical years in our history; there were many "great school wars" before the current ones. The first school war, in the 1840s, was instigated by demands from Catholic leaders that something approaching equal treatment for Catholic students be provided in public schools, whose principal aim, they worried, was to inculcate Protestant moral values. Catholic leaders lost the battle, and private Catholic schools were formed. The second war, fought between the 1880s and 1890s, was over the rights of German immigrant children to receive instruction in German, a demand that was successful in some parts of the country until German-speaking public instruction was destroyed by the national chauvinism following World War I. Then, with the near ending of immigration in 1924, there ensued a period up to the 1960s of homogeneity, assimilation, and freedom from conflict over diversity in American schools and universities. It was this period that spawned the erroneous view, held by critics of multiculturalism, that claims generated from ethnic identities are entirely new, totally un-American, and completely illegitimate.

## The Standard View in Social Psychology

The long-standing tension over unity and diversity reverberates in discussions of group identity in contemporary social psychology. On the one hand, it is understood that groups—especially racial, ethnic, and nationality groups—are alive, well, and must be reckoned with. It is recognized that group membership and group identity are important resources for deprived groups as they try to redress group-based inequalities and mobilize for political influence with less money, less education, and fewer political positions than other groups have in the United States. On the other hand, the potential divisiveness of groups and of group identity, especially when groups are aroused and manipulated by political elites, is part of the worldwide phenomenon of intergroup conflict. By and large, the standard view in current social psychology, based largely on the influential work that has come from categorization and identity theories (Tajfel 1981; Turner and Oakes 1989), emphasizes the negative over the potentially positive effects of group identity.

From this predominant approach to group identity, the effects of categorization—exaggeration of group differences, homogenization of outgroup members, ingroup favoritism and outgroup discrimination, and stereotyping—are thought to be greater when group boundaries are made salient. Group identity is presumed to be one of the factors that increase the salience of group boundaries. Actually, there are few studies that assess whether people identified with a group are more prone to ingroup bias and outgroup discrimination. Crocker and Luhtanen (1990), who conducted one of the few relevant studies, found evidence of increased ingroup bias among students with stronger group identities (what they call private collective self-esteem).

The presence of ingroup bias does not necessarily entail outgroup discrimination, however, and generally the empirical literature in intergroup relations finds little evidence of the latter. Even the Tajfel minimal-group studies that established the ties between categorization, social comparison, and intergroup behavior found that subjects generally allocated rewards based on ingroup favoritism or fairness rather than on outgroup discrimination. Gaertner, Dovidio, Nier, Ward, and Banker (this volume) conclude that "whereas social categorization can initiate intergroup biases, the type of bias due largely to categorization primarily represents a pro-ingroup orientation (that is, a preference for ingroup members) rather than an anti-outgroup orientation usually associated with hostility or aggression." The motive is to "create positive social comparisons, a result which can be achieved by evaluating the ingroup positively without it being necessary to negatively evaluate the outgroup" (Stephan 1985, 615).

Our work on racial and ethnic identity among adult Americans likewise shows that there is no inevitable relationship between group identity and outgroup hostility. In a national survey of African Americans (Gurin, Hatchett, and Jackson 1989), we found that the most common kind of African American identity, one based on group membership being cognitively central and based on common fate, was related, as expected, to pro-black sentiments and group political consciousness, not based in anti-white sentiments. Moreover, this kind of group identity was associated with greater, not lesser, awareness of and sympathy for the power disadvantages faced by *other* groups of color in America. We found another kind of African American identity that was exclusivist, but it was extremely rare in the national African American population.

Moreover, analyses of the ethnic and racial conflict in various parts of the world suggest that there is nothing intrinsic about ingroup identity that precipitates these conflicts. Rather, it is the arousal and manipulation of group identities in particular political, economic, and historical circumstances that largely explain when racial, ethnic, and national identities are mobilized into overt conflict (Connor 1992; Eriksen 1993; Gonzalez and McCommon 1989; Olzak 1983).

## A Contextual Social Psychological Approach

The critical question, we believe, is: When is group identity divisive, and when is it congenial to democracy and positive intergroup relations? Several approaches in social psychology provide answers to this question. One approach suggests that positive intergroup relations are fostered by decreasing the salience of group boundaries and, by implication, the importance of group identity (for an overview of the major approaches, see Brewer 1997; Gaertner et al., this volume). This can be done through several decategorization strategies, for example, by helping ingroup members individuate and personalize outgroup members (Brewer and Kramer 1985), by altering group composition (Mullen 1991), and by deemphasizing difference (Mullen 1991; Mullen, Brown, and Smith 1992). Another approach, more consonant with individuals maintaining group identities, focuses on the efforts of groups to work together and get along despite their differences. An example is a cooperative learning group in which students of different backgrounds are deliberately put together to learn and to solve problems. Slavin (1996) reviews the extensive literature on cooperative learning strategies and concludes that "the experimental evidence on cooperative learning has generally supported the main tenets of contact theory . . . when the conditions outlined by Allport are met in the classroom, students are more likely to have friends outside their own racial groups than they would in traditional classrooms" (631). Yet another approach to achieving positive intergroup relations is to find common ground (Gaertner et al. 1989). It involves creating a common or superordinate group representation that does not necessarily require that subgroups forsake their earlier categorizations, and in fact it allows people to hold a dual identity. Gaertner and his colleagues (this volume) conclude that this perspective differs from strategies that recommend that people first perceive members of outgroups as individuals rather than as group members. Instead, they argue that ingroup formation and functioning do not necessarily push outgroup members or undifferentiated others further away and in fact can be used productively to bring former outgroup members closer to the self and to generalize positive intergroup learnings beyond the particular intergroup setting in which they were attained.

*The Importance of Power* Social psychologists have paid far more attention to the immediate context in intergroup relations than to long-lasting contexts defined by power, societal norms, or features of institutions (Stephan 1985). Psychological studies of social identity have been conducted most often in experimental settings that either establish groups of equal power and status or create ad hoc, unstable power divisions between groups. Societal-level power differences represent a very different type of power relationship among social groups in that such differences are remarkably stable and long-lasting (Sidanius et al., this volume), providing an enduring social context within which identities are formed and interact.

We hypothesize that power plays an important role in explaining when group identity is more likely to have divisive consequences. High-power groups that are able to establish a dominant relationship over other groups are apt, at least in individualistic cultures such as the United States, to deny that groups exist or that they shape the life chances of individuals. Fiske (1993), Snodgrass (1992), and Miller (1976) argue that the structure of power relationships results in the more powerful or dominant paying little attention to members of other groups. They can afford to ignore other groups, and ingroup identity is generally rather weak and unimportant in such dominant groups. In a meta-analysis of ingroup bias studies, Mullen, Brown, and Smith (1992) conclude that, at least in "real groups" (those in natural settings rather than in the laboratory), ingroup bias is weaker among high-status groups than among low-status ones (see Jost and Banaji [1994] for a different perspective). In today's universities, white students, far more than students of color, express a longing for individuals to just be individuals and argue that groups are not, or at least should not, be important in students' lives (Gurin 1992). Still, when members of high-power groups are threatened by the demands of other groups or by policies that make groups highly salient, their ingroup identification increases and they generally react defensively to protect their privileges. Moreover, they become especially aware of group boundaries, favor their own group, and discriminate against outgroups, all in the name of doing what is good for America, not just for their own group. Why is this? Sidanius and his colleagues (this volume) suggest that when members of dominant groups are threatened, perhaps especially those members with strong social dominance orientations (SDOs), they engage in various hierarchy-enhancing (HE) behaviors in order to preserve or restore their dominance. We also argue that along with their new recognition and acceptance of groups, those who identify with dominant groups find themselves with little preparation for dealing with outgroups. Their lack of experience with groups and the likelihood that they have rather simple stereotypes of outgroups are factors that also foster outgroup discrimination (Fiske 1993). Moreover, holding the privileged position of having institutions generally function in their behalf has kept members of dominant groups from learning how to negotiate conflicts based on the claims of different groups.

Members of low-power groups, in contrast, know that groups often do shape personal fortunes and that group membership is a critical feature of the American stratification system. They are likely to have stronger group identities than members of dominant groups. Members of subordinate groups—both those identified as subordinate and those less identified as such—have more experience in dealing with other groups. Except in conditions of utter segregation, members of subordinate groups have to interact frequently with members of dominant groups (and often with members of other subordinate groups as well). They have to negotiate differences and group-based conflicts in their daily lives. They are exposed through the media and mainstream institutions to the cultures of the dominant groups. Since they have learned to pay attention to people in dominant groups, they are more likely to have developed relatively complex and less stereotypic views of those groups (Fiske 1993). For all of these reasons, members of subordinate groups are apt to have less negative attitudes and to discriminate less toward outgroups. Because they have accepted the importance of groups, their own and others, identified subordinate group members may hold even less divisive attitudes than other members of these groups. They are also likely to have thought more about intergroup life and to have struggled cognitively and emotionally with the possibilities of both conflict and harmony between groups.

*The Importance of the Immediate Context* Particular features of intergroup relations—especially whether they are competitive or cooperative, involve groups of equal or unequal size and status, allow or hinder the development of personal relationships, and reflect strong or weak categorization—have received considerable attention from social psychologists. We, too, are interested in the impact of a particular context, one that for various theoretical reasons should decrease group polarization in attitudes and allow identity groups to discern commonalities as well as differences between groups.

The Intergroup Relations, Conflict, and Community (IGRC) program is a curricular and living-learning program aimed at helping students understand the relationship between groups and a particular conception of democracy. This kind of democracy is defined by Pitkin and Shumer (1982) as an

> encounter among people with differing interests, perspectives, and opinions—an encounter in which they reconsider and mutually revise opinions and interests, both individual and common. It happens always in a context of conflict, imperfect knowledge, and uncertainty, but where community action is necessary. The resolutions achieved are always more or less temporary, subject to reconsideration, and rarely unanimous. What matters is not unanimity but discourse. The substantive common interest is only discovered or created in democratic political struggle, and it remains contested as much as shared. (47)

The IGRC program places students from diverse groups together, presents materials and lectures that analyze the histories of ethnic and racial groups in the United States, covers theories of group conflict and strategies of conflict management, and asks students to participate in ten-week dialogue groups based on their group identities (Asian Americans and African Americans, Arab Americans and Jewish Americans, and so on). The dialogue groups include equal numbers of members of two groups that historically have held or currently hold conflicting interests or points of view. The dialogue groups have two goals: to explore these conflicting perspectives, and by the end of the group sessions, to discover specific issues or particular areas of commonality that the two groups could use as a basis for at least a temporary coalition.

This program includes elements of many approaches to intergroup relations—achieving equal status through equal numbers of students in the two groups dialoguing with each other; lending authority to intergroup discourse by insisting that all students in the course participate in such groups; stating an explicit goal of discovering some bases for a "we"; designing the dialogues to last over time and to include explicit exercises for individuals to get to know and personalize each other across group lines.

It differs from some approaches, however, by more dramatically emphasizing difference (see Fine, Weis, and Powell 1997). Group boundaries are made salient, certainly at the outset of the dialogue groups and usually throughout the semester, as members of the two identity groups attempt to discover commonalities as well as differences.

## HYPOTHESES

We predicted that:

1. Group identity is stronger among members of subordinate than dominant groups.
2. The implications of group identity for intergroup relations differs for subordinate and dominant groups.
   a. Given the saliency of the university's official diversity program (the "Michigan Mandate"), which may threaten dominant groups, we predicted that group identity among dominant groups is associated with perception of intergroup divisiveness and little perception of intergroup commonality; negative views of group-based conflicts; fewer overall interactions with outgroup members; more negative interactions; more anxiety and fewer positive feelings in interethnic/racial situations; and more negative attitudes toward diversity policies.
   b. In contrast, we predicted that group identity among subordinate groups is either unrelated to these negative intergroup perceptions, interactions, and attitudes or related to more positive intergroup outcomes.
3. The IGRC program has a major effect, resulting in more positive intergroup outcomes.
4. Participation in the IGRC program mutes negative effects and/or enhances positive effects of group identity that might be found for both dominant and subordinate groups.

## PARTICIPANTS AND DESIGN

In 1990 through 1991 a study was designed to compare and follow 174 students; half were enrolled in the IGRC program, and half were selected to provide a matched control sample. The control students were drawn from a larger, comprehensive study of the class entering the university in 1990 (known as the Michigan Student Study, or MSS; see Gurin 1992). They were matched to the program participants on the following demographic dimesions: gender, race/ethnicity (white, African

American, Asian American, Latina, and Latino), precollege residency (in-state, out-of-state), and college residence hall.

These students were surveyed at entrance, at the end of the first year (when the program participants had completed their first course), at the end of their sophomore year, and again by two mail questionnaires at the end of their senior year. One senior questionnaire was sent by the MSS, and the second by the Psychology Department. The measures used in this chapter come primarily from the two senior questionnaires. (Selectivity is checked using the baseline, entrance questionnaire.)

Overall, 74 percent of the original sample were successfully reached in the senior year ($n = 128$). Approximately 70 percent of both the original and follow-up groups were white students, and the remainder students of color.

## MEASURES

### Group Identity

Group identity, following Tajfel (1981), is defined as the individual's subjective awareness and acceptance of belonging to a social group. Virtually all people who are categorized as belonging to a group have some awareness of their group membership and thus have some level of group identity. Yet group identity is clearly stronger and more influential for some group members than for others. A critical question, then, is what properties of the internal representation of group membership give identity its psychological significance.

Tajfel (1978) suggested that identity is more influential when the individual is clear about his or her membership, feels positively about being a member, and is emotionally invested in membership. In general, however, the studies spawned by Tajfel's seminal work have not attempted to measure various dimensions of identity—or for that matter to measure identity directly at all. Usually identity is inferred from subjects' responses to manipulations intended to arouse it.

Recently, more attention has been given in the identity literature to measuring multiple dimensions of group identity and to studying their motivational and behavioral implications. One dimension emphasized by several scholars is the centrality or importance of the identity in the person's self-concept (the term "importance" is used by Luhtanen and Crocker 1992; the term "centrality" by Sellers et al. 1997, Gurin and Markus 1988, and Gurin, Hatchett, and Jackson 1989; and the term "identity achievement" by Phinney 1992).

In this research, we measured both centrality and importance. Following Converse's (1964) conceptual definition of centrality as the amount of thought an individual devotes to an object or to an aspect of the self, we asked students, "How often do you think about being a member of your group and what you have in common with others in your group?" Students responded on a scale ranging from 1 ("hardly ever") to 4 ("a lot"). Importance was measured by asking students to "rate how important your [group] identity is to the way you think about yourself"—again on a scale ranging from 1 ("not very important") to 4 ("extremely important").

Another dimension of identity that has been studied of late is the individual's feelings about the group and about being a group member. Phinney (1992) calls this "affirmation," Luhtanen and Crocker (1992) "private collective self-esteem," and Sellers and his colleagues (1997) "private racial regard." We think of it as group pride. We wanted to capture the emotion that African Americans may have, for example, about the achievements of a Tiger Woods, a Malcolm X, or a Thurgood Marshall, or that women (probably only politically liberal women) had when Geraldine Ferraro was nominated as the first woman to run for vice president. We asked students, "How proud do you feel when a member of your group accomplishes something outstanding?" They responded on a scale ranging from 1 ("not at all") to 4 ("a great deal").

Guided by Lewin's (1948) emphasis on member interdependence as a signifier of groupness, and by our previous work showing that interdependence is the most politically relevant dimension of group identity (Gurin and Markus 1989; Gurin et al. 1989), we attempted to measure respondents' sense of common fate with other group members. We asked students to "indicate the extent to which something that happens in your life is affected by what happens to other people in your group." They judged this on a scale ranging from 1 ("not at all") to 4 ("a great deal").

To obtain measures of these dimensions, we first asked each student to "put down how you identify yourself in the following categories" (race or ethnicity, gender, socioeconomic class, religion, and sexual orientation), and then to judge the four dimensions (importance, centrality, pride, and common fate) for each of these group identities. In this chapter, we are using the responses only for the racial or ethnic and gender categories.

Because our hypotheses concern differences between dominant and subordinate groups, we assessed the internal reliability of the racial or ethnic identity dimensions separately for white students and students of color, and the internal reliability of the gender identity dimensions separately for men and women. The alpha for the racial or ethnic identity measure for white students is 0.68, and for students of color 0.88. The alpha for the gender identity measure for men is 0.69, and for women

0.64. With only four items for each scale, these are respectable alphas, although clearly the internal coherence of identity is strongest for racial or ethnic identity of students of color.

Despite the evidence of reasonable internal reliability, item analyses show that for both of the dominant groups (whites and men) the measure of centrality sometimes bears a relationship to measures of intergroup relations quite different from those of the other three dimensions of identity. For that reason, in the analyses here of results for whites and for men, we use one index of pride, importance, and common fate and separately summarize results using the measure of centrality. There was no evidence that centrality (or any other dimension) operates differently from other dimensions of identity for the two subordinate groups (students of color and women).

## Intergroup Relations

*Intergroup Perceptions* Following the goals of the IGRC program, we developed measures of perceived intergroup divisiveness and commonality in interests and values with members of other groups, positive views of conflict, and negative views of conflict.

Perceived divisiveness was measured by responses to five questions on a scale ranging from 1 ("strongly agree") to 4 ("strongly disagree"):

1. The university's commitment to diversity fosters more division among racial or ethnic groups than intergroup understanding.
2. The current focus on multiculturalism in our schools undermines the common ties that bind us as a nation.
3. I have learned that thinking about groups is largely divisive.
4. The university's focus on diversity puts too much emphasis on differences between racial or ethnic groups.
5. The university's emphasis on diversity means I can't talk honestly about racial, ethnic, and gender issues.

The alphas for students of color, whites, women, and men for the divisiveness scale range from 0.78 to 0.86.

Commonality in interests and values was measured as the other side of the coin. The MSS developed a measure of commonality by first asking students to check racial or ethnic labels that applied to them, and then requesting that they indicate the name of the one that they would be thinking about in answering the commonality questions. Commonality of interests was defined as following:

> People often feel that some groups in our society share many common political and economic interests, while other groups have few common interests or are even competing politically and economically. For each of the groups listed below (African Americans, Asian Americans, Hispanics/Latinos, Native Americans, and white Americans), please indicate, on a scale ranging from 1 ("much more similar than different") to 4 ("much more different than similar") how much their interests and your group's interests are similar or different.

Commonality of values was defined thus: "How about important values in life—like values about work and family. How similar or different are your group's values and those of the following [same list] groups?" For white students, we report results here using an averaged response across commonality judgments for African Americans, Asian Americans, Hispanic/Latinos, and Native Americans. For students of color, results are presented for commonality of interests and values with whites.

Positive and negative views of conflict were each measured by agree/disagree responses (the same four-point scale) to four statements. Positive views were represented by statements such as: "I believe that intergroup conflict can have positive consequences," and, "I believe that conflict is healthy in a democracy." Examples of negative views were: "I am afraid of conflicts when discussing social issues," and, "Conflict rarely has constructive consequences." Factor analysis confirmed separate factors for the positive and negative statements. Alphas for the positive scale range from 0.67 to 0.72 for students of color, whites, women, and men; alphas for the negative scale range from 0.61 to 0.71.

*Interethnic or Racial Interaction* Two sets of questions were asked about intergroup and intragroup interaction. (We did not ask many questions about interaction across gender, and thus a fuller analysis is provided for white students and students of color.) One set measured the amount of interaction the student had had in college with students of five groups (African Americans, Asian Americans, Hispanic or Latino students, Native Americans, and white students). For each of these groups, students were asked to indicate on a scale ranging from 1 ("no interaction") to 5 ("the most interaction"). For white students, a scale of outgroup interaction is formed using an average of the responses to interaction with African American, Asian American, Hispanic or Latino, and Native American students, while ingroup interaction is presented as reported interaction with other white students. For students of color, outgroup interaction is presented as the amount of interaction reported with whites, while ingroup interaction is given as the amount of interaction with the student's own ethnic or racial group.

The other set assessed the quality of interactions with a particular ethnic or racial outgroup. Each student was asked how much he or she had participated in potentially positive and negative activities with a particular outgroup, defined as following in the questionnaire: "Which of these groups [same list], other than your own, have you had the most interaction with over your four years at Michigan?" The student was then asked to write down the name of the group and to respond, on a scale ranging from 1 ("not at all") to 5 ("a great deal"), to eight questions about his or her interactions with that group. Factor analysis confirmed a positive distinction between positive and negative in these responses. Positive interaction was represented by having frequently "studied together," "attended social events together," "had intellectual discussions outside of class," "shared personal feelings and problems," "participated in extracurricular activities together," or "had meaningful and honest relations about race and/or ethnic relations outside of class." The alpha for this scale for white students is 0.85, and 0.92 for students of color. Negative interaction was represented by having frequently had "tense, somewhat hostile interactions" or "guarded, cautious interactions." The alpha for this scale for white students is 0.64, and for students of color 0.71.

*Emotions in Interracial or Ethnic Interactions* Using a modified version of the Stephan and Stephan (1985) measure of general intergroup anxiety, we asked each student to indicate how often, on a scale ranging from 1("always") to 5 ("never"), he or she had had twelve different feelings when "interacting with people from a different race or ethnicity than your own." Factor analyses revealed that a measure of intergroup anxiety (and of intragroup anxiety) comprised frequently feeling "anxious," "not able to understand them," or "frustrated," and that a measure of positive intergroup (and intragroup) feelings comprised frequently feeling "hopeful," "proud," "excited," or "happy." Alphas for the *inter*ethnic or racial anxiety scale are 0.69 for white students and 0.68 for students of color, and for the positive feeling scale alphas are 0.72 for white students and 0.79 for students of color. Alphas for the *intra*ethnic or racial anxiety scale are 0.59 for whites and 0.80 for students of color, and alphas for the positive intraethnic or racial feelings scale are 0.81 for whites and 0.85 for students of color.

*Approval or Disapproval of University Policies* The students who were enrolled at the university during the course of the study were made quite aware of the university's positive stance toward greater inclusion of students, staff, and faculty of color and toward policies intended to foster multicultural understanding. Orientation for incoming students included diversity workshops. The president issued the Michigan Mandate, a call for university support of inclusion and multiculturalism. There was good reason to believe, therefore, that students would have had ample time to develop real attitudes toward these policies. Factor analyses of responses to ten attitude measures revealed two dimensions, attitudes toward traditional affirmative action policies and attitudes toward multicultural policies. Four items represented the former, including: "Students of color are given advantages that discriminate against other students at colleges and universities," and, "Different admissions criteria with respect to the SAT and ACT scores may be justified for some students of color." Students responded to these items on a scale ranging from 1 ("strongly agree") to 4 ("strongly disagree"). Alphas for this measure range from .67 to .80 for students of color, whites, women, and men. Seven items measured attitude toward multiculturalism, again judged on a four-point scale. Some examples are: "Colleges and universities should have a requirement for graduation that students take at least one course covering the role of ethnicity in society," "An understanding of the roots of the American experience requires studying African American, Hispanic or Latino, Native American, and Asian American as well as European American history," and, "Attempts to bring multiculturalism into the curriculum come at the expense of other topics students need to learn." Alphas for the traditional affirmative action scale range from 0.67 to 0.80, and for the multiculturalism scale from 0.76 to 0.81, for the four groups.

## Control Measures

Given the emphasis in this study on intergroup perceptions and behavior, we tested to see whether the participants and nonparticipants in the IGRC program differed on measures of psychological openness to other people. The parent first-year baseline survey conducted by the Office of Academic and Multicultural Initiatives included two measures that seemed pertinent to this concern. One was the perspective-taking subscale of Davis's (1983) measure of empathy. Davis defines this subscale as capturing the ability to step outside the self and to shift perspectives in dealing with other people. The second is a modified version of the attributional complexity scale developed by Fletcher, Danilovics, Fernandez, Peterson, and Reeder (1986). This measure captures the individual's enjoyment in causal thinking and especially the tendency to think about a variety of different causes for human behavior. We reasoned that students who have stronger perspective-taking skills and are more prone to think in complex ways about human behavior might be more likely to participate in the IGRC program and to be more open to people who present a variety of social differences. If this were true, program effects might result from selectivity rather than from the program itself, and our analyses would benefit from controlling for empathy and attributional complexity. The analysis of sample self-selection bias shows, however, that the participants and nonparticipants do not differ significantly on either of these measures, which were collected when they were first-year students.[1]

## ANALYSES

Participants' responses were examined by means of ordinary multiple regression, testing for the main effects of identity and course participation on each scale, with the inclusion of a single interaction term (identity × program participation). The analyses were performed separately for white students and for students of color (as a group). The analyses were also performed separately for men and women. For the interaction analyses, we present tables using median splits for the identity measures; these are provided to assist in the interpretation of the nature of the regression interaction. While the tables do not directly represent the actual regression interaction, we did perform analyses of variance that correspond directly to the tables, using a median split for the identity measures. The interaction effects from these analyses are presented within their respective tables.

## RESULTS

### Level of Identity Among Dominant and Subordinate Groups

As predicted (hypothesis 1), group identity is stronger among members of subordinate groups than among members of dominant groups (see table 5.1). With or without the inclusion of the measure of cognitive centrality, the average racial or ethnic identity scores of students of color are about one standard deviation higher than the scores of white students ($t = 7.10$, $p < 0.001$). The average gender identity scores of women are approximately one and a half standard deviations higher than those of men ($t = 7.08$, $p < 0.001$).

### Intergroup Implications of Identity Among Dominant and Subordinate Groups

We predicted (hypothesis 2) that group identity would be associated with negative intergroup perceptions, attitudes, and behaviors among

TABLE 5.1 *Mean Levels of Identity for Dominant and Subordinate Groups*

| | Students of color Mean (σ) | $t$ | White Students Mean (σ) |
|---|---|---|---|
| Racial/ethnic ID | 3.12 (0.72) | 7.10*** | 2.17 (0.59) |
| Racial/ethnic ID 2[a] | 3.17 (0.71) | 7.05*** | 2.21 (0.63) |
| | Women Mean (σ) | $t$ | Men Mean (σ) |
| Gender ID | 2.96 (0.52) | 7.08*** | 2.21 (0.57) |
| Gender ID 2[a] | 3.04 (0.54) | 8.28*** | 2.18 (0.56) |

[a]These measures do not include the cognitive centrality component for identity.
***$p < 0.001$

members of dominant groups, but either unrelated to these negative outcomes or associated with positive outcomes among members of subordinate groups. We present the results for two dominant groups, white students and men, and then the results for two subordinate groups, students of color and women.

*Dominant: White Students* As predicted, racial identity among whites (as measured by an index of the importance of being white, pride in the group, and sense of common fate) is consistently associated with intergroup cleavage in perceptions and attitudes (see table 5.2). More highly identified white students, compared to those less identified, perceive more intergroup divisiveness. They have more negative views of intergroup conflict and tend to have less positive views of conflict as well. As we will see later, however, program participation mutes this relationship. Identified whites also more often believe that whites as a group share few common interests and values with various groups of color. They are considerably more negative than other white students toward university policies that encourage multiculturalism and toward traditional affirmative action policies. There is in fact no intergroup measure that is unrelated to white identity.

The intergroup behavioral and emotional implications of a white identity are also well supported in these results (see table 5.3). The identified white students have fewer contacts than less identified whites with members of various groups of color, and the contacts they have are also more negative—"tense, somewhat hostile interactions," and "guarded, cautious interactions." They also report more anxiety than do less identified whites when interacting with students of different racial or ethnic backgrounds. Ingroup interaction, in contrast, is not related to

TABLE 5.2 *Relationship of Identity to Perceptions of Campus Intergroup Relations and Educational Equity*

| | White Students | | | | Students of Color | | | |
|---|---|---|---|---|---|---|---|---|
| | Main Effects | | Interactions | | Main Effects | | Interactions | |
| | ID β | Course β | ID × Course | *F*[a] | ID β | Course β | ID × Course | *F*[b] |
| Intergroup conflict | | | | | | | | |
| Divisiveness | 0.214* | −0.107 | −0.044 | 2.426* | −0.317* | −0.277* | 0.248 | 3.481* |
| Positive views of conflict | −0.152 + | 0.228* | 0.200 + | 3.130* | 0.121 | 0.414* | 0.169 | 3.729* |
| Negative views of conflict | 0.181* | −0.146 | −0.269** | 4.121** | 0.072 | −0.158 | 0.087 | 0.519 |
| Intergroup commonality | | | | | | | | |
| Interests: Outgroup[c] | −0.193* | 0.202* | −0.125 | 2.926* | −0.288* | 0.042 | 0.567*** | 8.493*** |
| Values: Outgroup[d] | −0.201* | 0.310** | 0.002 | 5.185** | −0.479** | 0.075 | 0.211 | 4.020* |
| Educational equity | | | | | | | | |
| Traditional affirmative action | −0.229* | 0.209* | 0.072 | 3.975* | 0.488** | 0.293* | 0.065 | 6.808** |
| Multiculturalism | −0.383*** | 0.200* | 0.087 | 8.676*** | 0.600*** | 0.332* | −0.226 | 12.004*** |

[a] *F* values for (72,3) d.f. where an interaction exists, (74,2) where one does not.
[b] *F* values for (25,3) d.f. where an interaction exists, (26,2) where one does not.
[c] For white students, average common interests with African American, Asian American, Latino/Latina, and Native American groups; for students of color, common interests with whites.
[d] For white students, average common values with African American, Asian American, Latino/Latina, and Native American groups; for students of color, common values with whites.
$+ p < 0.10$, $^{*}p < 0.05$, $^{**}p < 0.01$, $^{***}p < 0.001$

TABLE 5.3 *Relationship of Identity to Campus Intergroup Interactions*

| | White Students | | | | Students of Color | | | |
|---|---|---|---|---|---|---|---|---|
| | Main Effects | | Interactions | | Main Effects | | Interactions | |
| | ID β | Course β | ID × Course | $F^a$ | ID β | Course β | ID × Course | $F^b$ |
| Quality of interactions with outgroup | | | | | | | | |
| Positive interactions | −0.003 | 0.047 | 0.127 | 0.093 | −0.228 + | 0.496*** | 0.489*** | 13.631*** |
| Negative interactions | 0.207* | −0.106 | −0.100 | 2.157 + | 0.208 | 0.000 | −0.203 | 0.655 |
| Amount of interactions with outgroup | | | | | | | | |
| With outgroup[c] | −0.248* | 0.034 | 0.030 | 2.694* | −0.494** | −0.008 | 0.220 | 4.673* |
| With ingroup | −0.114 | 0.139 + | 0.224* | 2.187* | 0.560*** | −0.041 | −0.226 | 6.195** |
| Feelings generated during outgroup interactions | | | | | | | | |
| Anxiety | 0.232* | −0.094 | −0.034 | 2.611* | 0.351* | −0.134 | −0.065 | 2.674* |
| Positive feelings | −0.075 | −0.057 | 0.021 | 0.404 | 0.158 | 0.230 + | 0.154 | 1.286 |
| Feelings generated during ingroup interactions | | | | | | | | |
| Anxiety | 0.123 | −0.068 | 0.030 | 0.779 | 0.040 | −0.018 | 0.180 | 0.031 |
| Positive feelings | 0.130 | −0.181* | −0.044 | 2.965* | 0.393** | 0.074 | 0.110 | 3.022* |

[a]$F$ values for (72,3) d.f. where an interaction exists, (74,2) where one does not.
[b]$F$ values for (25,3) d.f. where an interaction exists, (26,2) where one does not.
[c]Average self-reported interactions with African American, Asian American, Latino/Latina, and Native American students for white students; average of interactions with white students for students of color.
$+ p < 0.10$, $*p < 0.05$, $**p < 0.01$, $***p < 0.001$

identity among white students. This is true of both the number of interactions and the feelings with which they are associated.

*Dominant: Men Students* The study included only five identical intergroup measures, and two policy measures, for male students. Of these, men's gender identity is significantly related to two: negative attitudes toward policies that encourage multiculturalism, and negative interactions with the outgroup, in this case with women (see tables 5.4 and 5.5). However, the nonsignificant associations between identity and the other intergroup measures (perception of intergroup divisiveness, negative views of conflict, negative attitude toward traditional affirmative action, and fewer positive interactions with the outgroup) are all in the expected direction as well.

*A Cognitively Central Identity: Thinking About Group Membership* As already noted in the section on measures, one dimension of group identity—its cognitive centrality based on thinking a lot of being white (or a man)—operates somewhat differently from the other dimensions that formed the index of identity for these dominant groups. We found in a separate analysis, summarized here, that cognitive centrality often has a different meaning from other bases of identity for whites and men. This is true even though the measure of cognitive centrality is positively and fairly equally related to the other dimensions of identity.

First of all, a white identity that is cognitively central is unimportant in explaining several dimensions of intergroup cleavage to which the other three bases of white identity consistently relate: thinking about being white is unrelated to perception of intergroup divisiveness, degree of common interests with groups of color, positive views of conflict, and opposition to traditional affirmative action policies. Second, and more dramatic, cognitive centrality sometimes has opposite relationships to those of the other three dimensions of white identity. White students who think a lot about being white, and about what they have in common with other white students, actually have fewer, not more, negative views of conflict ($p < 0.05$). They support, rather than oppose, multicultural policies of the university ($p < 0.05$). They also tend ($p < 0.10$) to have more positive interactions with various groups of color.

Men's gender identity based on cognitive centrality—thinking about being a man and what one has in common with other men—also has a different meaning from identity based in pride, importance, or common fate. An identity based in cognitive centrality is associated with more positive views of conflict ($p < 0.10$) as well as less negative views

TABLE 5.4 *Relationship of Identity to Perceptions of Campus Intergroup Relations and Educational Equity*

| | Men | | | | Women | | | |
|---|---|---|---|---|---|---|---|---|
| | Main Effects | | Interactions | | Main Effects | | Interactions | |
| | ID β | Course β | ID × Course | $F^a$ | ID β | Course β | ID × Course | $F^b$ |
| Intergroup conflict | | | | | | | | |
| Divisiveness | 0.147 | −0.330* | −0.108 | 2.801* | −0.288** | −0.008 | −0.020 | 3.899* |
| Positive views of conflict | −0.059 | 0.138 | 0.330* | 1.932 + | 0.173* | 0.335** | 0.119 | 6.969*** |
| Negative views of conflict | 0.191 | −0.261 + | −0.158 | 2.131 + | −0.171 + | −0.078 | −0.109 | 1.541 |
| Educational equity | | | | | | | | |
| Traditional affirmative action | −0.191 | 0.266 + | 0.272 | 2.007 + | 0.375*** | 0.122 | 0.013 | 7.502*** |
| Multiculturalism | −0.294* | 0.299* | 0.026 | 3.572* | 0.167 + | 0.222* | −0.038 | 3.369* |

[a] $F$ values for (35,3) d.f. where an interaction exists, (36,2) where one does not.
[b] $F$ values for (80,3) d.f. where an interaction exists, (81,2) where one does not.
+ $p < 0.10$, * $p < 0.05$, ** $p < 0.01$, *** $p < 0.001$

TABLE 5.5 *Relationship of Identity to Intergroup Interactions*

| | Men | | | | Women | | | |
|---|---|---|---|---|---|---|---|---|
| | Main Effects | | Interactions | | Main Effects | | Interactions | |
| | ID β | Course β | ID × Course | $F^a$ | ID β | Course β | ID × Course | $F^b$ |
| Quality of interactions with outgroup | | | | | | | | |
| Positive interactions | −0.156 | 0.160 | −0.012 | 0.882 | 0.072 | 0.052 | 0.286* | 2.429* |
| Negative interactions | 0.386* | −0.034 | −0.262 | 2.922* | 0.156 + | −0.097 | 0.180 + | 1.419 |

[a] $F$ values for (35,3) d.f. where an interaction exists, (36,2) where one does not.
[b] $F$ values for (80,3) d.f. where an interaction exists, (81,2) where one does not.
+ $p < 0.10$, * $p < 0.05$

($p < 0.05$). Moreover, for men, this kind of gender identity is not related to opposition to multiculturalism or affirmative action policies, while the other bases of identity are consistently associated with opposition to those policies.

*Subordinate: Students of Color* In general, consistent with the emphasis we give to the importance of power as a long-lasting social context, the results show that identity has different implications for students of color than for white students. For students of color, identity sometimes proves irrelevant to intergroup outcomes; sometimes it is associated with positive rather than negative intergroup perceptions and attitudes; sometimes the effect of identity depends on whether the student of color had participated in the IGRC; sometimes it operates as ethnic or racial identity does for white students.

In general, the intergroup perception implications of a racial or ethnic identity among students of color either depend on IGRC participation or are the opposite of the identity results for white students. We see this in several results presented in table 5.2. The relationship between the racial or ethnic identity of students of color and their perception of commonality in interests with whites depends very much on program participation (discussed later). The results further show, contrary to the usual expectations, that racial identity among students of color is related to perception of less, not more, intergroup divisiveness. Moreover, in contrast to identified white students, identified students of color do not hold negative views of conflict. The one exception to these findings that challenge the standard view about identity shows that identity has a negative effect on perception of common values with whites. Regardless of program participation, identified students of color perceive less value commonality than other students of color. Finally, not surprisingly, identified students of color are much more positive about the multicultural and affirmative action policies of the university.

With respect to intergroup and intragroup behavior, the results consistently support the standard view that identity is associated with more frequent and positive ingroup than outgroup relationships. The more identified students of color, compared to other students of color, have more contact with members of their own group of color, and they feel more positively when interacting with their own group (see table 5.3). They also have significantly fewer interactions with white students, and they feel greater anxiety when they do interact with the outgroup (see table 5.3). We see later in the chapter, however, that identified students of color who participated in the IGRC, compared to other students of color, have much more positive relations with white students.

*Subordinate: Women Students* The results for women consistently show that gender identity has positive, not negative, intergroup implications. Identified women, compared to those less identified, perceive less intergroup divisiveness and hold more positive, as well as less negative, views of intergroup conflict. They express much greater support for multicultural and affirmative action policies (see table 5.3.) The one exception is that identified women tend to have more negative interactions with the outgroup (see table 5.4), although, as we see later, participation in the IGRC program affects the quality of interaction that identified women have with men.

## IGRC Program Participation and Intergroup Outcomes

We predicted that participation in the IGRC in the first year of college would be associated, even four years later, with positive intergroup outcomes for both dominant and subordinate groups. The results for intergroup perceptions and attitudes in general support this prediction. In contrast, participation has less consistent effects on intergroup and intragroup contact patterns four years later.

We look first at dominant groups. White students who participated in the IGRC program are more able than other students to see positive effects of group conflict; they perceive greater commonality in both interests and values with various groups of color; and they more frequently support multicultural and affirmative action policies (see table 5.2). The program has similar implications for male students; in addition, male participants less often believe that groups are inevitably divisive (see table 5.4). The program also has effects on subordinate groups. Students of color who participated perceive less intergroup divisiveness and hold more positive views about intergroup conflict (as do women participants); they also support group-relevant university policies more frequently (as do women participants with respect to multiculturalism) (see tables 5.2 and 5.4).

The IGRC has few effects on outgroup and ingroup interaction, but one outgroup effect is important. Students of color who participated in IGRC report having more positive interactions with white students four years later. Moreover, though not significant, the relationships between program participation and feeling less anxious and more positive in outgroup interactions supports this positive outcome for students of color. There is also an ingroup effect for white students. White participants in IGRC report less positive feelings in their interactions with other whites.

FIGURE 5.1 *Identity × Course Interactions: Dominant Groups*

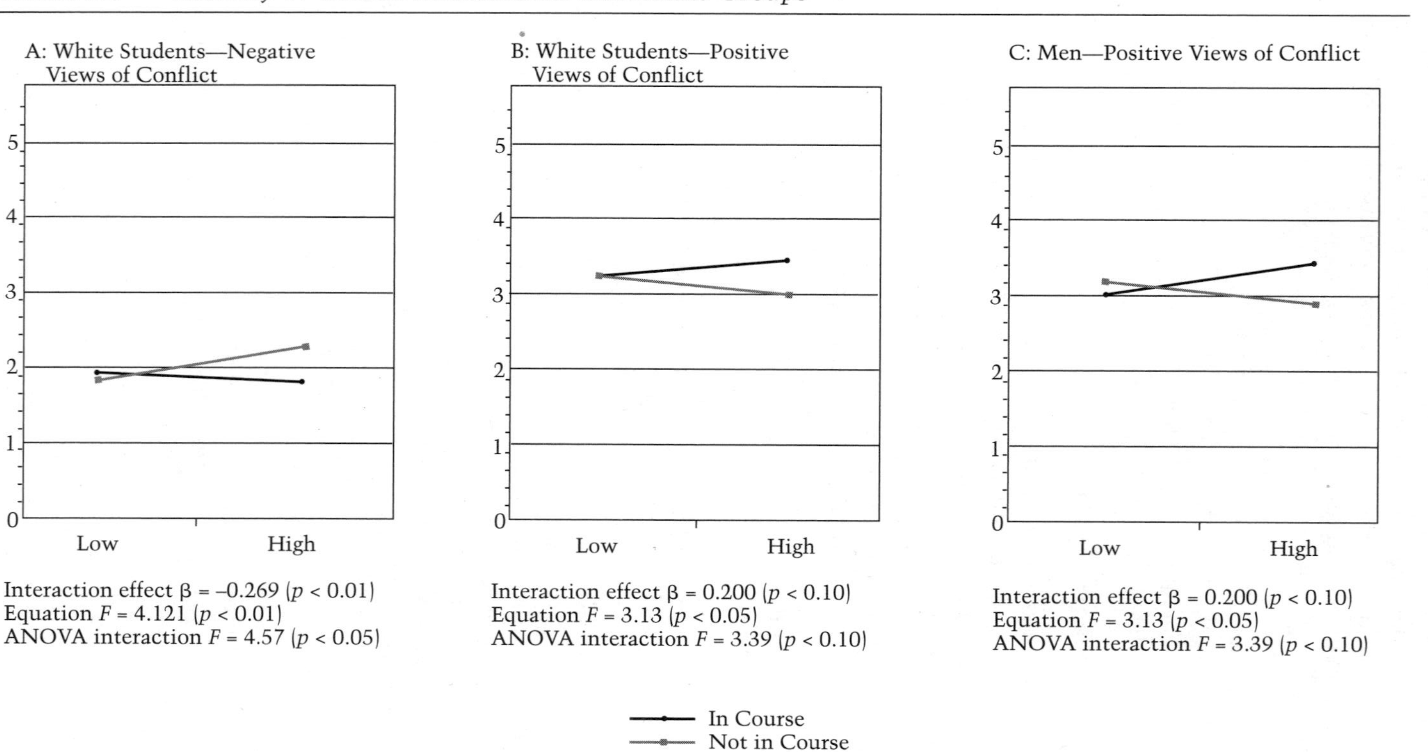

## Program Participation and Identity Interactions

In general, there are only a few significant participation identity interactions, but those we find all support the prediction that participation would mute negative intergroup implications or enhance positive intergroup implications of group identity.

With members of dominant groups, participation mutes three negative effects of group identity on intergroup perceptions (see table 5.2). Identified white students who participated in the program as first-year students have less negative views of conflict (figure 5.1, panel A), and a tendency as well toward more positive views of conflict (figure 5.1, panel B). In contrast, the identified white students who did not participate in IGRC have more negative and less positive views. Among men, there is a similar interaction between participation and identity with perception of conflict as positive. Identified men who participated in IGRC as first-year students see conflict four years later as more positive, while identified men who did not participate see conflict as less positive than other men (see table 5.4 and figure 5.1, panel C).

With members of subordinate groups, program participation dramatically affects the relationship between identity and how positive outgroup contacts are as seniors. With students of color, we find that the identified who participated in IGRC as first-year students actually have more positive interactions with whites as seniors, while the identified who did not participate earlier have fewer positive interactions with whites (see table 5.3 and figure 5.2, panel A). These differences are quite marked and show that the implications of group identity depend greatly on social context. Likewise, program participation alters the implication of gender identity for the quality of outgroup interaction for women. Gender-identified women who participated in the program as first-year students report more positive interactions with men as seniors, while identity is unrelated to how positive such interactions are for nonparticipants (see table 5.5 and figure 5.2, panel B).

For students of color, another significant interaction shows that the relationship between identity and perception of commonality with whites depends greatly on whether they had participated in IGRC as first-year students (see table 5.2 and figure 5.2, panel C). The main (negative) effect of racial or ethnic identity on perception of common interests with whites is altered when we test for interaction. The identified students of color who participated in the program not only do not perceive less commonality in interests with whites but actually perceive greater commonality with them.

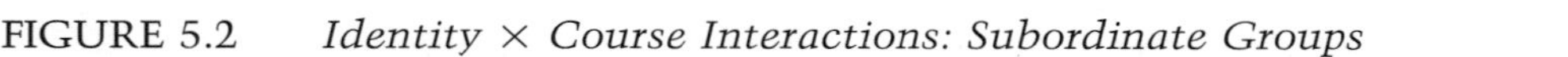

FIGURE 5.2 *Identity × Course Interactions: Subordinate Groups*

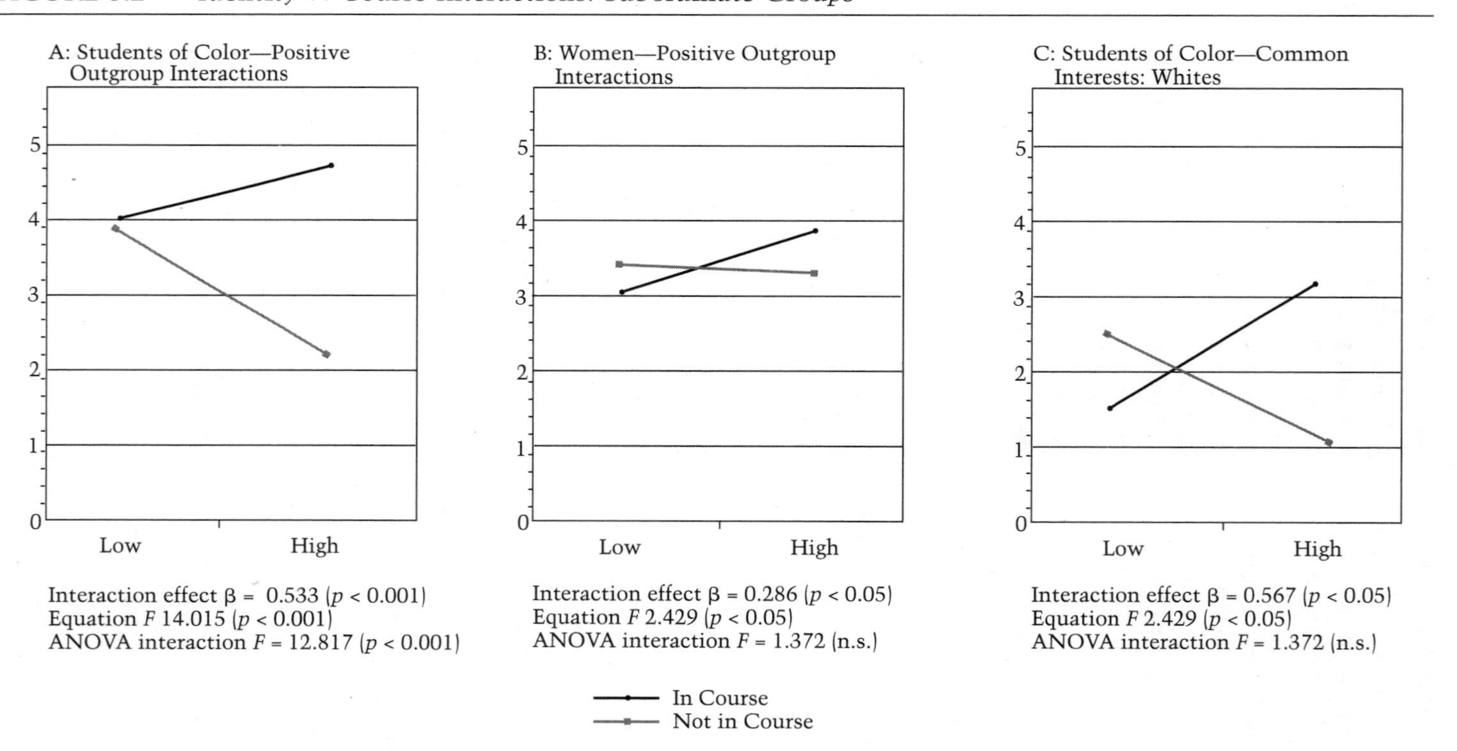

# DISCUSSION

## The Importance of Context

In this study, we examined two aspects of social context: the long-standing power divisions between natural groups, and the particular immediate context provided by the IGRC program at the University of Michigan. In general, the results support the importance of a contextual approach to the question of when group identity is divisive and when it is not.

The power division is consistently influential. Hypothesis 1 (that identity is stronger among members of subordinate than of dominant groups) is supported on both racial or ethnic and gender power lines. We also find that attitudes toward traditional affirmative action and multicultural policies of the university reflect the power positions of the dominant and subordinate groups. White students and men disapprove of these policies the most; students of color and women approve of them the most.

Results testing hypothesis 2 (that the implications of identity for intergroup life differ for dominants and subordinates) also validate the importance of the power division. Overall, the results show, as predicted, that group identity is associated with considerably more intergroup cleavage for members of dominant than subordinate groups. With both dominant groups, identity is associated with negative intergroup perceptions, attitudes, and behaviors. With both subordinate groups, identity is associated with more positive perceptions of intergroup life, especially if identified students in these groups were involved in the IGRC program. Power also conditions the association between identity and intragroup contacts. Among white students, it is essentially irrelevant to the amount and quality of ingroup contact, but among students of color, identity is related both to more ingroup contact and to positive feelings in those interactions. Outgroup interaction is the one dimension of intergroup life that has similar (negative) associations with group identity across power lines. With both groups, identity appears to be at an early stage of development, one characterized by avoidance, anxiety, or anger toward outgroups (Cross 1971; Helms 1990; Parham and Parham 1989; Tatum 1992). But even here, program participation affects the conclusions that should be drawn about outgroup contact. Finally, power is also evident in the association of group identity with policies toward affirmative action and multiculturalism. Identified members of dominant groups especially oppose these policies; identified members of subordinate groups especially approve of them.

The effects of participation in the IGRC program (hypothesis 3) provide a second perspective on context, which, in the context of the IGRC program, proves to be important in four ways. First, for both dominant and subordinate groups, program participation is related to positive intergroup perceptions and attitudes. Conclusions about unity and disunity should not be drawn, therefore, without considering the particular circumstances in which potentially conflicting groups relate to each other. Second, while the IGRC program does not obliterate hierarchy, it does shift power-related viewpoints in a meaningful way. White students and men who had participated do not subscribe to a dominant perspective as much as their nonparticipant peers. Of course, since the program also has effects on the viewpoints of students of color and women, there is still a dominant-subordinate division, although a somewhat smaller one, among participants. Third, the IGRC program appears to offer different opportunities for identity development for students of color and whites. For students of color, it affords the development of a later-stage identity that allows a comfortable inclusion of others. For white students, the program has no impact on outgroup interactions or feelings but is associated with marginally more numerous but significantly less positive ingroup interactions. This fits with an intermediate stage of identity development among whites (Tatum 1992). Fourth, this particular context has a different relationship to identity for dominant and subordinate groups. For members of subordinate groups, identity and participation generally are mutually reinforcing. For members of dominant groups, identity and participation generally operate in opposite ways.

The intergroup perception and policy effects of participating in the IGRC program are seen four years after these students participated as entering college students. What might account for these long-term effects? One explanation is that the program had an immediate effect of fostering an interest in multiculturalism that resulted in the participants becoming more involved than nonparticipants in intergroup curricular and extracurricular activities in the intervening four years. Indeed, we find (see table 5.6) that as seniors the participants more than the nonparticipants report having taken more courses that focused on culture, diversity, and inequality during their college years. They report having read more about race and ethnicity, and they participated in more of the campus cultural events of various groups (for example, Native American Month, Martin Luther King Day, Asian American Awareness Month, and other activities). Finally, as expected in light of the IGRC program's goal of helping students gain skills in intergroup discourse and conflict management, the participants report more frequently than the nonparticipants that they had facilitated dialogue groups and other intergroup discussions during their four years in college.

TABLE 5.6 *Self-Reported Exposure to Multicultural Initiatives on Campus*

| University-Sponsored Events[a] | | | Dialogue Groups[b] | | | Courses and Readings[c] | | |
|---|---|---|---|---|---|---|---|---|
| In Course | $t$ | Control | In Course | $t$ | Control | In Course | $t$ | Control |
| 1.89 | 2.5* | 1.23 | 0.85 | 12.72*** | 0.10 | 3.85 | 3.57* | 3.20 |

[a]Participation ranges from 0 (no events listed) to 7 (seven events listed).
[b]Participation ranges from 0 (did not participate) to 1 (did participate).
[c]Participation ranges from 0 (not at all) to 5 (a great deal).
$^{*}p < 0.05$, $^{**}p < 0.001$

## Limited Behavioral and Emotional Effects

In contrast to this picture of long-standing effects on intergroup perceptions and group-based policies, participation in the IGRC program has few long-standing effects on intergroup behaviors or emotions. It is for students of color that IGRC participation is most associated with behavior and emotions: outgroup interactions are more positive, and positive feelings are generated, to some extent, in such interactions.

There is another way in which intergroup behavior proves to be different from intergroup perceptions and attitudes. While identity-perception relations depend greatly on power, this is not true of identity-intergroup behavior. The identified in both dominant and subordinate groups are less likely than other members to interact with members of outgroups, and when they do, they are more likely to feel anxious. Another way to highlight the distinction between perceptions and behavior concerns the pattern of identity relationships for members of subordinate groups. Although identity is not consistently associated with perception of division or divisive attitudes in these groups, it is associated with reduced intergroup contact, just as it is in dominant groups.

This distinction is nothing new in social psychological studies. We customarily expect a disjuncture between perception or attitude and behavior. We expect that factors correlated with perception and attitudes may not be correlated with behavior. Moreover, we expect that a host of opportunities and constraints affect behavior but influence perceptions and attitudes much less. Even so, the robust perception or attitude results should not be discounted simply because intergroup behavior is only weakly tied to the factors we have studied. Improving intergroup perceptions and broadening the base of support for group-based policies are important goals in themselves, and they are also likely to play an influential role in the politics of intergroup life (see Sears et al., this volume; Sidanius et al., this volume).

## Dominant Group Identity: Is It Inevitably Anti-Outgroup?

The results clearly substantiate that the strongest anti-outgroup perspectives are held by identified whites (and, though with fewer measures, by identified men). These results support the view offered by many theories (and by several authors in this volume) that dominant groups under threat become defensively and protectively identified with the group. For example, Sidanius and his colleagues (this volume) suggest that identity and social dominance orientation are positively correlated for dominant groups and uncorrelated for subordinate groups. We also suspect that identity and intergroup perceptions are reciprocally related. Perception of divisiveness may both create dominant group identity and become stronger as a consequence of identifying with a threatened group.

The dominant group identity can be altered by education, however, and thus there is nothing inevitable about its negative outgroup implications. We see this in two ways. First, the positive main effects of the IGRC program on intergroup perceptions and attitudes demonstrate that a particular educational curriculum can shift how members of dominant groups, both the identified and nonidentified, perceive intergroup life. Second, the significant interactions between program, identity, and views of conflict indicate that the IGRC program has targeted effects on the very students who have the strongest dominant group identities. For these identified students in particular (both whites and men), the program's explicit coverage of conflict and teaching of conflict management skills normalizes intergroup conflict. Thus, one condition that presumably fosters a defensive, protective identity among dominant groups—conflict over privilege and power—can be addressed in a program that directly challenges students to understand intergroup conflict.

Finally, there is evidence in the results on cognitive centrality for whites and men that a dominant group identity is not inevitably divisive. Through whichever process members of dominant groups come to think a lot about their membership in such groups (perhaps through classes, perhaps through workshops, perhaps through readings), that kind of cognitive activity can have a positive impact on their intergroup relations. We cannot know if the thinking alluded to in our measure of cognitive centrality includes reflection on power and privilege, although the direction of the relationships between cognitive centrality and intergroup perceptions and policy attitude suggests that it probably does. If members of dominant groups come to recognize and understand their privileged positions as part of thinking about themselves as members in these groups, their attachments to other members and their identities are transformed in critical ways. We are not arguing that their ingroup bonds or identities will be weaker, but as in multicultural coalition groups, whites and men can learn to think and feel about themselves so as to allow new conceptions of outgroup members and of their relations with them (Crowfoot and Chesler 1996). We found evidence for the distinctiveness of a cognitively central identity in earlier work as well (Gurin and Markus 1989). Despite finding a positive correlation between a cognitively central identity and one based in common fate, we found that these two bases of identity have very different implications for the gender-based political attitudes of women with traditional role orientations. The particular effects that cognitively central identities are likely to have depend, however, on the power position of the group, and thus the direction of its effects in the study of women is not the same as in this study.

## Unity and Disunity

The issue of unity and disunity is far too complicated to be accounted for by simple, universal, cross-situational theories of intergroup life. There is great fluidity in how groups relate to each other and how identified members conceptualize group issues and interact across cultural divides. Although the concerns of the critics of multiculturalism are not trivial, they miss the situational complexities and temporal fluidities of intergroup relations.

The major purpose of this chapter is to point out the importance of social context, both the long-standing context of power and the short-term, immediate context of the IGRC. The particular results of our study are less significant than the general point we are making about social context.

As already noted, many elements called for by contact theory are included in the IGRC program, especially in its dialogue groups. The program differs, however, from interventions guided by intergroup contact theory because it places more emphasis on group *differences*. The IGRC program is an effort to build a community in which common action and feeling do not deny the importance of differences.

Fine, Weis, and Powell (1997) discuss why a focus on difference is critical to building multicultural or multiracial communities. They point out that although research verifies that interracial relations, attitudes, and networks improve when equal status conditions are met, over time these contexts ultimately suffer from exclusion and interaction barriers. This happens, they believe, because the standard equal status contact approach to intergroup relations tends to overemphasize commonality. Generally, group members are asked to leave differences—especially differences in power and privilege—at the door. Failure to deal with the differences that most natural groups face in the world generally leads to the reproduction of privilege in the guise of neutrality or color-blindness.

The IGRC program insists that students bring their identities and differences in power and privilege into the open so that a pluralistic, multicultural, and democratic community can be envisioned. Five elements are thought to be critical to this goal: acknowledging and exploring group identities and differences; normalizing conflict by exploring its positive as well as negative impact on intergroup life; conducting this exploration of difference and conflict using clear rules for democratic discourse and explicitly taught skills in conflict management; doing this work both cognitively and emotionally; and through these intellectual and emotional steps, helping groups form temporary coalitions over issues on which they can agree to work together. Why are temporary intergroup coalitions so important? Crowfoot and Chesler (1996) argue that an effective settlement structure for both realistic and symbolic group conflicts is required by the increasing diversity of populations and workforces in the United States. If whites and members of various groups of color can learn how to form temporary and issue-focused coalitions, both assimilation and balkanization—"the Scylla and Charybdis of U.S. racial relations" (Crowfoot and Chesler 1996, 206)—can be avoided. The IGRC program is one of many educational interventions that attempts to build unity—usually temporary—without denying differences that are likely to continue to exist.

Of course, we cannot know what aspects of the IGRC program produced the results we have presented. The number of students who participated in the four-year longitudinal study examined here discourages efforts to detail the effects of separate aspects of the program or to demonstrate the interactive significance of combining them all. A serious limitation in our study is the necessity of combining all groups of color: doing so misses distinctive patterns of group identities and intergroup relationships. Process research needs to be conducted with large enough separate groups of color to capture the subtleties and complexities of dominant-subordinate group relations.

## NOTES

1. We also attempted to check selectivity on political ideology, since liberalism-conservatism has been found to be associated with attitudes toward different groups in American society (Kinder and Sears 1983). The parent survey included the traditional National Election Study seven-point self-identification as liberal or conservative in the first-year baseline study. Unfortunately, such a sizable proportion of the students chose the alternative "haven't thought much about it" that we were unable to check for selectivity on this measure.

## REFERENCES

Brewer, Marilynn B. (1997). The social psychology of intergroup relations: Can research inform practice? Paper presented at the Society for the Psychological Study of Social Issues sixtieth anniversary convention, Ann Arbor, Mich. (May 31).

Brewer, Marilynn B., and Kramer, Roderick M. (1985). The psychology of intergroup attitudes and behavior. *Annual Review of Psychology, 36,* 219–43.

Connor, Walker. (1992). The Nation and its Myth. *International Journal of Comparative Sociology, 33,* 47–57.
Converse, Philip E. (1964). The nature of belief systems in mass publics. In David E. Apter (Ed.), *Ideology and discontent* (pp. 206–61). New York: Free Press.
Crocker, Jennifer, and Luhtanen, Riia. (1990). Collective self-esteem and ingroup bias. *Journal of Personality and Social Psychology, 58,* 60–67.
Cross, Dolores E. (1971). The relationship bwtween individualization of instruction and teacher perception of pupil behavior. Ph. D. dissertation, University of Michigan, Ann Arbor.
Crowfoot, James E., and Chesler, Mark A. (1996). White men's roles in multicultural coalitions. In Benjamin P. Bowser (Ed.), *Impacts of racism on white Americans* (pp. 202–29). Thousand Oaks, Calif.: Sage.
Davis, Mark H. (1983). Measuring individual differences in empathy: Evidence for a multidimensional approach. *Journal of Personality and Social Psychology, 44*(1), 113–26.
Eriksen, Thomas H. (1993). *Ethnicity and nationalism: Anthropological perspectives.* London: Pluto Press.
Fine, Michelle, Weis, Lois, and Powell, Linda C. (1997). Communities of difference: A critical look at desegregated spaces created for and by youth. *Harvard Educational Review, 67*(2), 247–84.
Fiske, Susan T. (1993). Controlling other people: The impact of power on stereotyping. *American Psychologist, 48*(6), 621–28.
Fletcher, Garth J., Danilovics, Paula, Fernandez, Guadalupe, Peterson, Dena, and Reeder, Glenn D. (1986). Attributional complexity: An individual differences measure. *Journal of Personality and Social Psychology, 51*(4), 875–84.
Gaertner, Samuel L., Mann, Jeffrey, Murrell, Audrey, and Dovidio, John F. (1989). Reducing intergroup bias: The benefits of recategorization. *Journal of Personality and Social Psychology, 57,* 239–49.
Glazer, Nathan. (1993). School wars: A brief history of multiculturalism in America. *Brookings Review* (Fall), 16–19.
Gonzalez, Nancie L., and McCommon, Carolyn S. (Eds.). (1989). *Conflict, migration, and the expression of ethnicity.* Boulder, Colo.: Westview.
Gurin, Gerald. (1992). *The Michigan Study: Expectations and experiences of first-year students with diversity.* Ann Arbor: University of Michigan, Office of Academic Multicultural Initiatives.
Gurin, Patricia, Hatchett, Shirley, and Jackson, James S. (1989). *Hope and independence: Blacks' response to electoral and party politics.* New York: Russell Sage Foundation.
Gurin, Patricia, and Markus, Hazel. (1988). Group identity: The psychological mechanisms of durable salience. *Revue Internationale de Psychologie Sociale, 1*(2), 257–74.
———. (1989). Cognitive consequences of gender identity. In Suzanne Skevington and Deborah Baker (Eds.), *The social identity of women* (pp. 152–72). New York: Sage Publications.
Helms, J. E. (1990). *Black and white racial identity: Theory, reseach, and practice.* New York: Greenwood Press.
Jost, John T., and Banaji, Mahzarin R. (1994). The role of stereotyping in system-justification and the production of false consciousness. *British Journal of Social Psychology, 33,* 1–27.
Kinder, Donald R., and Sears, David O. (1983). Political opinion and political

action. In Gardner Lindzey and Elliot Aronson (Eds.), *The handbook of social psychology* (3rd ed., pp. 659–742). Reading, Mass.: Addison-Wesley.

Levine, Lawrence W. (1996). *The opening of the American mind: Canons, culture, and history*. Boston: Beacon Press.

Lewin, Kurt. (1948). *Resolving social conflict*. New York: Harper and Brothers.

Luhtanen, Riia, and Crocker, Jennifer. (1992). A collective self-esteem scale: Self-evaluation of one's social identity. *Personality and Social Psychology Bulletin, 18,* 302–18.

Miller, Jean B. (1976). *Toward a new psychology of women*. Boston: Beacon Press.

Mullen, Brian. (1991). Group composition, salience, and cognitive representations: The phenomenology of being in a group. *Journal of Experimental Social Psychology, 27,* 297–323.

Mullen, Brian, Brown, Rupert, and Smith, Colleen. (1992). Ingroup bias as a function of salience, relevance, and status: An integration. *European Journal of Social Psychology, 22,* 103–22.

Olzak, Susan. (1983). Contemporary ethnic mobilization. *Annual Review of Sociology, 9,* 355–74.

Parham, William D., and Parham, Thomas A. (1989). The community and academic achievement. In Gordon LaVern Berry (Ed.), Black students: Psychosocial issues and academic achievement (Vol. 109, pp. 120–37). Newbury Park, Calif.: Sage Publications.

Phinney, Jean S. (1992). The multigroup ethnic identity measure: A new scale for use with diverse groups. *Journal of Adolescent Research, 7*(2), 156–76.

Pitkin, Hanna F., and Shumer, Sara M. (1982). On participation. *Democracy, 2,* 43–54.

Saxonhouse, Arlene. (1992). *Fear of diversity: The birth of political science in ancient Greek thought*. Chicago: University of Chicago Press.

Schlesinger, Arthur M., Jr. (1991). Writing, and Rewriting, History. *The New Leader, 74*(14), 12–14.

Sellers, Robert M., Rowley, Stephanie A. J., Chavous, Tabbye, Shelton, J. Nicole, and Smith, Mia. (1997). Multidimensional inventory of black identity: Preliminary investigation of reliability and construct validity. *Journal of Personality and Social Psychology, 73,* 805–15.

Slavin, Robert E. (1996). Cooperative learning and intergroup relations. In James A. Banks and Cherry A. McGee Banks (Eds.), *Handbook of research on multicultural education* (pp. 628–34). New York: Simon & Schuster-Macmillan.

Sleeter, Christine E. (1995). An analysis of the critiques of multicultural education. In James A. Banks and Cherry A. McGee Banks (Eds.), *Handbook of research on multicultural education* (pp. 81–96). New York: Simon & Schuster-Macmillan.

Snodgrass, Sara E. (1992). Further effects of role versus gender on interpersonal sensitivity. *Journal of Personality and Social Psychology, 62*(1), 154–58.

Stephan, Walter G. (1985). Intergroup relations. In G. Lindzey and E. Aronson (Eds.), *The handbook of social psychology* (pp. 599–658). New York: Random House.

Stephan, Walter G., and Stephan, Cookie W. (1985). Intergroup anxiety. *Journal of Social Issues, 41,* 157–75.

Tajfel, Henri. (1978). Social categorization, social identity, and social comparison. In Henri Tajifel (Ed.), *Differentiation between social groups: Studies in the social psychology of intergroup relations* (pp. 61–76). New York: Academic Press.

———. (1981). *Human groups and social categories*. New York: Cambridge University Press.
Tatum, Beverly D. (1992). Talking about race, learning about racism: The application of racial identity development theory in the classroom. *Harvard Educational Review, 62*(1), 1–24.
Turner, John C., and Oakes, Penelope J. (1989). Self-categorization theory and social influence. In Paul B. Paulus (Ed.), *The psychology of group influence* (2nd ed., pp. 233–75). Hillsdale, N.J.: Erlbaum.

# Part II

## CULTURAL DIFFERENCES: REAL AND IMAGINED

# 6

# ACROSS CULTURAL DIVIDES: THE VALUE OF A SUPERORDINATE IDENTITY

*Samuel L. Gaertner, John F. Dovidio, Jason A. Nier, Christine M. Ward, and Brenda S. Banker*

Give me your tired, your poor,
Your huddled masses yearning to breathe free.
—Emma Lazarus

DESPITE this promising invitation, the relations among racial, ethnic, and religious groups in the United States have traditionally been tense and problematic. In a nation founded on principles of justice and equality, prejudice and discrimination pervade intergroup relations and are embedded in official policies (Feagin and Feagin 1996; Feagin and Sikes 1994). This contradiction between principle and practice, recognized over fifty years ago (Myrdal 1944), has been characterized as the "American Dilemma."

The contemporary social attitudes of *individuals,* particularly those in the majority group, reflect an analogous contradiction. Aversive racism (see Dovidio and Gaertner 1991, 1996, 1998; Dovidio, Mann, and Gaertner 1989; Gaertner and Dovidio 1986; Gaertner, Dovidio, and Banker et al. 1997; Kovel 1970), for instance, has been identified as a modern form of prejudice that characterizes the social attitudes of many whites who endorse egalitarian values and regard themselves as nonprejudiced, but harbor, perhaps unconsciously, negative attitudes toward minorities. These negative attitudes are expressed in subtle, rationalizable forms of discrimination. Whereas traditional forms of prejudice are direct and overt, aversive racism is indirect and subtle. Most of the work on aversive racism examines whites' attitudes toward blacks, but similar dynamics are also involved in attitudes toward Latinos (Dovidio et al. 1992) and women (Dovidio and Gaertner 1983; Swim et al. 1995).

Evidence of the American dilemma, at both the national and individual levels, is apparent today. On the one hand, the expressed social attitudes of whites are becoming consistently more positive, tolerant, and accepting. Negative stereotyping of blacks and Latinos has declined (Davis and Smith 1994; Devine and Elliot 1996; Dovidio and Gaertner 1986; Dovidio et al. 1992; Karlins, Coffman, and Walters 1969), and whites' acceptance of minority group members across a range of formal (for example, work) and informal (for example, social) settings is at an unprecedented high (Dovidio et al. 1996; Dovidio et al. 1992; Schuman, Steeh, and Bobo 1985). For example, in 1958 the majority of whites reported that they would not be willing to vote for a well-qualified black presidential candidate; in 1994 over 90 percent said that they would (Davis and Smith 1994). Social beliefs and attitudes have changed dramatically.

On the other hand, the United States is still "two nations" (Hacker 1995), with gaps between blacks and whites in social, economic, and personal well-being remaining large, and in some areas, growing. Minorities are increasingly underrepresented in industry, government, and the military in positions of higher status, prestige, and control (Dovidio, Gaertner, and Bachman, in press). The majority of blacks in America today have a profound distrust for the police and legal system, and about one-third are overtly distrustful of whites in general (Anderson 1996). Bias in the treatment of both Latinos and blacks in judicial, hiring, and promotion decisions is amply documented (Dovidio, Smith, et al. 1997; Stephan and Stephan 1986). These disparities are rooted in cultural biases—involving language and custom—as well as in individual and institutional biases (Jones 1997; see also Crocker and Lawrence, this volume; Ramirez 1988). Thus, despite the rapid improvement of expressed social attitudes, significant racial and ethnic disparities persist.

The United States is entering the next millennium in the midst of fundamental demographic change. Projections indicate that 50 percent of the children in U.S. schools will soon represent groups of color. These figures promise unprecedented opportunities for intergroup contact, whether out of necessity in a multicultural workforce or by choice. From different sectors, voices have been asking, "Is contact enough to ensure harmonious, equitable relations between members of different groups?" The answer is clearly no. Social psychologists have known for some time that contact between members of different groups is not sufficient to guarantee harmonious, nonbiased intergroup relations (see Allport 1954; Brewer and Miller 1984; Hewstone and Brown 1986). In fact, contact can often exacerbate intergroup bias and increase open conflict (Sherif and Sherif 1969). However, under certain conditions, intergroup contact can be one of the most effective strategies for combating and eliminating intergroup bias. This chapter explores the psychological processes underlying bias and examines how intergroup contact may be structured to reduce this bias. Specifically, we address three interrelated questions: What are the psychological processes that contribute to the development and maintenance of intergroup bias? Given these processes, how can intergroup contact effectively reduce bias? And how can the benefits of intergroup contact generalize and extend to other group members who are not present?

The purpose of this chapter is to address these questions from the perspective of social psychology and also to provide an overview of our own work on the Common Ingroup Identity Model and to illustrate how this model speaks to these issues (Gaertner et al. 1993; Gaertner, Rust, et al. 1994, 1996). We begin by considering some basic cognitive and motivational consequences of categorizing people into different groups and the contribution of this awareness to intergroup bias.

## THE PSYCHOLOGY OF BIAS: THE ROLE OF CATEGORIZATION

One universal and essential facet of human thinking is the individual's ability to sort quickly and effectively the many different objects, events, and people he or she encounters into a smaller number of meaningful categories (Hamilton and Trolier 1986; Hamilton and Sherman 1994). Categorization enables the individual to make quick decisions about incoming information: the instant an object is categorized, it is assigned the properties shared by other category members. Time-consuming consideration of each new experience is forfeited because it is usually wasteful and unnecessary. Categorization often occurs spontaneously on the basis of physical similarity, proximity, or shared fate (Campbell 1958). In this respect, people may be characterized as "cognitive misers": we compromise total accuracy for efficiency when confronted with the often overwhelming complexity of our social world (Fiske and Taylor 1991; Macrae, Milne, and Bodenhausen 1994).

The process of social categorization, however, is not completely uncontrollable and unalterable. Categories are hierarchically organized, and higher-level categories (such as animals) are more inclusive of lower-level ones (cats and dogs, for example). When a perceiver's goals, motives, past experiences, and expectations are modified, as well as factors within the perceptual field and the situational context more broadly, the level of category inclusiveness that will be primary in a given situation can be altered. Although the easiest and most common way of forming impressions is to perceive people in terms of a social category, appropriate goals, motivation, and effort can produce more individuated impressions of others (Brewer 1988; Fiske and Neuberg 1990). This malleability of the level at which impressions are formed—from broad to more specific categories to individuated responses—is important because of its implications for altering the way people think about members of other groups, and consequently about the nature of intergroup relations.

When people or objects are categorized into groups, actual differences between members of the same category tend to be perceptually minimized (Tajfel 1969) and often ignored in making decisions or forming impressions. Members of the same category seem to be more similar than they actually are, and more similar than they were before they were categorized together. In addition, although members of a social category may be different in some ways from members of other categories, these differences tend to become exaggerated and overgeneralized. Thus, categorization enhances perceptions of similarities within groups and differences between groups—emphasizing social difference and group distinctiveness. For social categorization, this process becomes more ominous because these within- and between-group distortions have a tendency to generalize to additional dimensions (such as character traits) beyond those that differentiated the categories originally (Allport 1954). Furthermore, as the salience of the categorization increases, the magnitude of these distortions also increases (Abrams 1985; Brewer 1979; Brewer and Miller 1996; Deschamps and Doise 1978; Dion 1974; Doise 1978; Skinner and Stephenson 1981; Turner 1981, 1985).

Moreover, in the process of categorizing people into groups, people typically classify themselves *into* one of the social categories (and *out of* the others). The insertion of the self into the social categorization process increases the emotional significance of group differences and thus leads to further perceptual distortion and to evaluative biases that reflect favorably on the ingroup (Sumner 1906), and consequently on the self (Tajfel and Turner 1979). Perhaps ethnocentrism is so prevalent in part because these biases operate even when the basis for the categorization is quite trivial, as when group identity is assigned randomly (Billig and Tajfel 1973).

Tajfel and Turner (1979) proposed that an individual's need for positive self-identity may be satisfied by membership in prestigious social groups. Thus, this need motivates social comparisons that favorably differentiate ingroup from outgroup members. According to this perspective, the individual also defines or categorizes the self along a continuum of social identity that ranges from the self as the embodiment of a social collective or group to the self as a separate individual with personal motives, goals, and achievements. At the latter extreme, the individual's personal welfare and goals are most salient and important. At the group level, the goals and achievements of the group are merged with those of the individual (see Brown and Turner 1981), and the group's welfare is paramount. At each extreme, self-interest is represented by the pronouns *I* and *we,* respectively. Intergroup relations begin when people think about themselves as a group member rather than as a distinct individual.

Although the categorization process may place the individual at either extreme of the continuum from social identity to personal identity, Brewer's (1991) Theory of Optimal Distinctiveness suggests that there is a point along the continuum that optimally satisfies the individual's identity needs. At some intermediate point, the individual's need to be different from others and need to belong and share a sense of similarity to others are balanced. Optimally, perceiving one's group as especially positive and distinctive relative to other groups satisfies both needs simultaneously. Unfortunately, one consequence of this process is intergroup bias. Thus, social categorization into ingroups and outgroups lays the foundation upon which intergroup bias or ethnocentrism develops.

Social categorization leads people to favor ingroup members in reward allocations (Tajfel et al. 1971), in esteem (Rabbie 1982), and in the evaluation of the products of their labor (Ferguson and Kelley 1964). Ingroup membership decreases psychological distance and facilitates the arousal of promotive tension or empathy (Hornstein 1976). Relatedly, prosocial behavior is offered more readily to ingroup than to outgroup members (Piliavin et al. 1981). In addition, people are more likely to be cooperative and to exercise more personal restraint when using endangered common resources when these are shared with ingroup members rather than with others (Kramer and Brewer 1984). People retain more information in a more detailed fashion for ingroup members than for outgroup members (Park and Rothbart 1982), have better memory for information about ways in which ingroup members are similar to the self and outgroup members are dissimilar (Wilder 1981), and remember less positive information about outgroup members (Howard and Rothbart 1980). Moreover, people are more generous and forgiving in their explanations for the behaviors of ingroup members relative to outgroup members. Positive behaviors and successful outcomes are more likely to be attributed to the internal, stable characteristics (the personality) of ingroup members, whereas negative outcomes are more likely to be ascribed to the personalities of outgroup members (Hewstone 1990; Pettigrew 1981). Relatedly, observed behaviors of ingroup and outgroup members are encoded in memory at different levels of abstraction (Maass et al. 1989). Undesirable actions of outgroup members are encoded at more abstract levels that presume intentionality and dispositional origin (for example, "she is hostile") than identical behaviors of ingroup members ("she slapped the girl"). Desirable actions of outgroup members, however, are encoded at more concrete levels ("she walked across the street holding the old man's hand") relative to the same behaviors of ingroup members ("she is helpful").

These cognitive biases help to perpetuate social biases and stereotypes even in the face of countervailing evidence. For example, because people encode positive behaviors of outgroup members at relatively concrete levels, they are less likely to generalize their counterstereotypic positive behaviors across situations or other outgroup members (see also Karpinski and Von Hippel 1996). People do not remember the "helpful" nature of an outgroup member, but only his or her concrete descriptive actions. Thus, people are not likely to let their outgroup stereotypes that contain information pertaining to traits, dispositions, or intentions be influenced by their observations of counterstereotypic outgroup behaviors.

Language also plays a role in intergroup bias through associations with collective pronouns. Collective pronouns, such as "we" or "they," that are used to define people's ingroup or outgroup status are frequently paired with stimuli that have strong affective connotations. As a consequence, these pronouns may acquire powerful evaluative properties of their own and can increase the availability of positive or negative associations and thereby influence beliefs about, evaluations of, and behaviors toward other people, often automatically and unconsciously (Perdue et al. 1990).

Whereas social categorization can initiate intergroup biases, the type of bias it initiates represents primarily a pro-ingroup orientation rather than an anti-outgroup orientation, usually associated with hostility or aggression. Nevertheless, disadvantaged status due to preferential treatment of one group over another can be as pernicious as discrimination based on anti-outgroup orientations (Murrell et al. 1994). Pro-ingroup biases can also provide a foundation for generating hostility and conflict that can result from intergroup competition for economic resources and political power.

Because categorization is fundamental to intergroup bias, social psychologists have targeted this basic process as a place to begin to improve intergroup relations. In the next section, we explore how the forces of categorization can be harnessed and redirected toward the elimination of intergroup bias.

## REDUCING INTERGROUP BIAS

Although it may be impossible to short-circuit the categorization process altogether, the levels of category inclusiveness people use when categorizing other people, including themselves, may be open to change. It may also be possible to alter whether people identify themselves as distinct individuals or as group members on the continuum proposed by Tajfel and Turner 1979; (see also Brewer 1988; Brewer and Miller 1984; Fiske and Neuberg 1990; Wilder 1978). From these perspectives, it is possible to engineer a *recategorization* or *decategorization* of perceived group boundaries in ways that reduce the original intergroup bias and conflict (see Wilder 1986).

In each case, reducing the salience of the original group boundaries is expected to decrease intergroup bias. With recategorization as proposed by the Common Ingroup Identity Model (Gaertner et al. 1993), if members of two different groups are induced to conceive of themselves as a single, more inclusive superordinate group, rather than as two separate groups, attitudes toward former outgroup members should become more positive through processes involving pro-ingroup bias. In terms of decategorization, if these memberships are induced to conceive of themselves and others as separate individuals (Wilder 1981) or to have more personalized interactions with one another, intergroup bias should also be reduced (Brewer and Miller 1984); more personalized contact should degrade pro-ingroup biases and undermine the validity of outgroup stereotypes (Miller, Brewer, and Edwards 1985).

Theoretically, the rationale for these changes in intergroup bias rests on two related conclusions from Brewer's (1979) analysis that fit nicely with social identity theory (Tajfel and Turner 1979; Turner 1975) and with self-categorization theory (Turner 1985). First, intergroup bias often takes the form of ingroup enhancement rather than outgroup devaluation. Second, the formation of a group brings ingroup members closer to the self, whereas the distance between the self and non-ingroup members remains relatively unchanged. Thus, when an ingroup forms, or when an individual assumes a group-level identification, the egocentric biases that favor the self are transferred to other ingroup members. Increasing the inclusiveness of group boundaries enables some of the cognitive and motivational processes that contributed initially to intergroup bias to be redirected or transferred to former outgroup members. If ingroup and outgroup members are induced to conceive of themselves as separate individuals rather than as group members, former ingroup members no longer benefit from the egocentric biases transferred to the group when they self-categorized as group members.

The recategorization and decategorization strategies and their respective means of reducing bias were directly examined in a laboratory study (Gaertner et al. 1989). In this experiment, members of two separate, laboratory-formed groups were induced through various structural interventions (for example, the seating arrangement) either to recategorize themselves as one superordinate group or to decategorize themselves and to conceive of themselves as separate individuals. These changes in the perceptions of intergroup boundaries supported the value of altering the level of category inclusiveness, thus reducing bias. Furthermore, as expected, these strategies reduced bias in different ways. Recategorizing ingroup and outgroup members as members of a more inclusive group reduced bias by increasing the attractiveness of the former outgroup members. Decategorizing members of the two groups by inducing conceptions of themselves as separate individuals decreased bias by decreasing the attractiveness of former ingroup members. Consistent with Turner's (1985) theory of self-categorization, "the attractiveness of an individual is not constant, but varies with the ingroup membership" (60).

These ideas about recategorization and decategorization have also been used to explain how the apparently loosely connected diverse features specified by the contact hypothesis may operate psychologically to reduce bias. Allport's (1954) revised contact hypothesis proposed that for contact between groups to be successful, certain features must be present, including: equal status between the groups; cooperative (rather than competitive) intergroup interaction; opportunities for personal acquaintance between the members, especially with those whose personal characteristics do not support stereotypic expectations; and supportive norms by authorities within and outside of the contact situation. Although this prescription has not been easy to implement, there is evidence to support its efficacy when these conditions are present, particularly for changing attitudes toward the people who happen to be in the contact setting (Cook 1984; Johnson, Johnson, and Maruyama 1983; Pettigrew 1998).

## Decategorization and Personalization

Offering a provocative, conceptually unifying theoretical framework, Brewer and Miller (1984) proposed that the features specified by the contact hypothesis (equal status, cooperative interaction, self-revealing interaction, and supportive norms) share the capacity to *decategorize* group boundaries and to promote more differentiated and personalized conceptions, particularly of outgroup members. When people have a more differentiated representation of outgroup members, they recognize that there are different types of outgroup members (for example, sensitive as well as tough professional hockey players), and thus the effects of categorization, and the tendency to minimize and ignore differences between category members, are weakened. When interactions are personalized, ingroup and outgroup members move toward the individual end of the individual-group social identity continuum. People "attend to information that replaces category identity as the most useful basis for classifying each other" (Brewer and Miller 1984, 288).

During personalized interactions, the individual focuses on information about an outgroup member that is relevant to the self (as an individual rather than as a group member). Repeated personalized interactions with a variety of outgroup members should over time undermine the value of the individual's category stereotype as a source of information about members of that group. Thus, he or she should be able to generalize the effects of personalization to new situations as well as to unfamiliar outgroup members. For the benefits of personalization to be generalized, however, it is, of course, necessary for outgroup members' group identity to be salient, although not primary, during the interaction to enable the group stereotype to be weakened.

A number of experimental studies provide evidence supporting this theoretical perspective (Bettencourt et al. 1992; Marcus-Newhall et al. 1993; Miller et al. 1985). In the study by Miller and his colleagues (1985), for example, contact that permitted more personalized interactions (for example, when interaction was person-focused rather than task-focused) resulted in more positive attitudes not only toward the outgroup members present but toward other outgroup members viewed on video. Thus, these conditions of intergroup contact reduced bias in both an immediate and generalizable fashion (see also Pettigrew 1997).

Although there are similarities between the perception of ingroup and outgroup members as "separate individuals" and "personalized interactions" with outgroup members, these are related but theoretically distinct concepts. Personalization involves receiving self-relevant, more intimate information about outgroup members that enables the individual to differentiate each outgroup member from the others when comparing them with his or her own self. In contrast, structurally perceiving either outgroup members alone (see Wilder 1986) or both ingroup and outgroup members as separate individuals is perceiving them as individuals, not as groups. Doing so is not necessarily based on information exchange. For example, strangers waiting for a bus may regard themselves as separate individuals, not a group. Thus, increasing the perception that outgroup members are separate individuals by revealing the variability in their opinions or having them respond as individuals rather than as a group renders each such member more distinctive and thus potentially blurs the prior categorization scheme (Wilder 1978). Another decategorization strategy is to criss-cross category memberships by repeatedly forming new subgroups, each composed of members from former subgroups; this changes the pattern of who's "in" and who's "out" (Brewer et al. 1987; Commins and Lockwood 1978; Deschamps and Doise 1978; Vanbeselaere 1987) and can also render the earlier categorization less salient (Brown and Turner 1981).

In addition to decategorization, we propose that the features specified by the contact hypothesis also reduce bias through recategorization, which increases rather than decreases the level of category inclusiveness (Gaertner et al. 1993, 1994; Gaertner, Rust, et al. 1996). That is, these contact conditions facilitate a reduction in bias in part because they share the capacity to transform members' representations of the memberships from separate groups to a more inclusive social entity. We do not necessarily, however, regard the decategorization and recategorization frameworks as mutually exclusive theoretically; we believe they are capable of working in parallel and complementary ways. Given the complexity of intergroup attitudes, it is plausible that these features of contact operate through several related as well as different pathways. In the next section, we present support for the Common Ingroup Identity Model and the effects of recategorization, and we discuss the value of a "dual identity": original group identities are maintained, but within the context of a superordinate identity.

## The Common Ingroup Identity Model

In contrast to decategorization approaches, recategorization is not designed to reduce or eliminate categorization but rather to define groups at a higher level of category inclusiveness so as to reduce intergroup bias and conflict. Specifically, we hypothesize that if members of different groups are induced to conceive of themselves within single groups rather than within completely separate groups, attitudes toward former outgroup members become more positive through processes involving pro-ingroup bias (Gaertner et al. 1993).

This model identifies potential antecedents and outcomes of recategorization, as well as mediating processes. Figure 6.1 summarizes the general framework and specifies the causes and consequences of a common ingroup identity. Specifically, we hypothesize that the different types of intergroup interdependence and cognitive, perceptual, linguistic, affective, and environmental factors can either independently or in concert alter individuals' cognitive representations of the aggregate (for example, Dovidio et al. 1995). The resulting cognitive representations (one group, two subgroups with one group, two groups, or separate individuals) then lead to the specific cognitive, affective, and overt behavioral consequences (listed on the right). Thus, the causal factors (listed on the left, they include features specified by the contact hypothesis) influence people's cognitive representations of the memberships (center) that, in turn, mediate the relationship, at least in part, between the causal factors and cognitive, affective, and behavioral consequences. In addition, we propose that common ingroup identity may be achieved by increasing the salience of existing common superordinate memberships (for example, in a school, a company, or a nation) or by introducing fac-

FIGURE 6.1 *The Common Ingroup Identity Model*

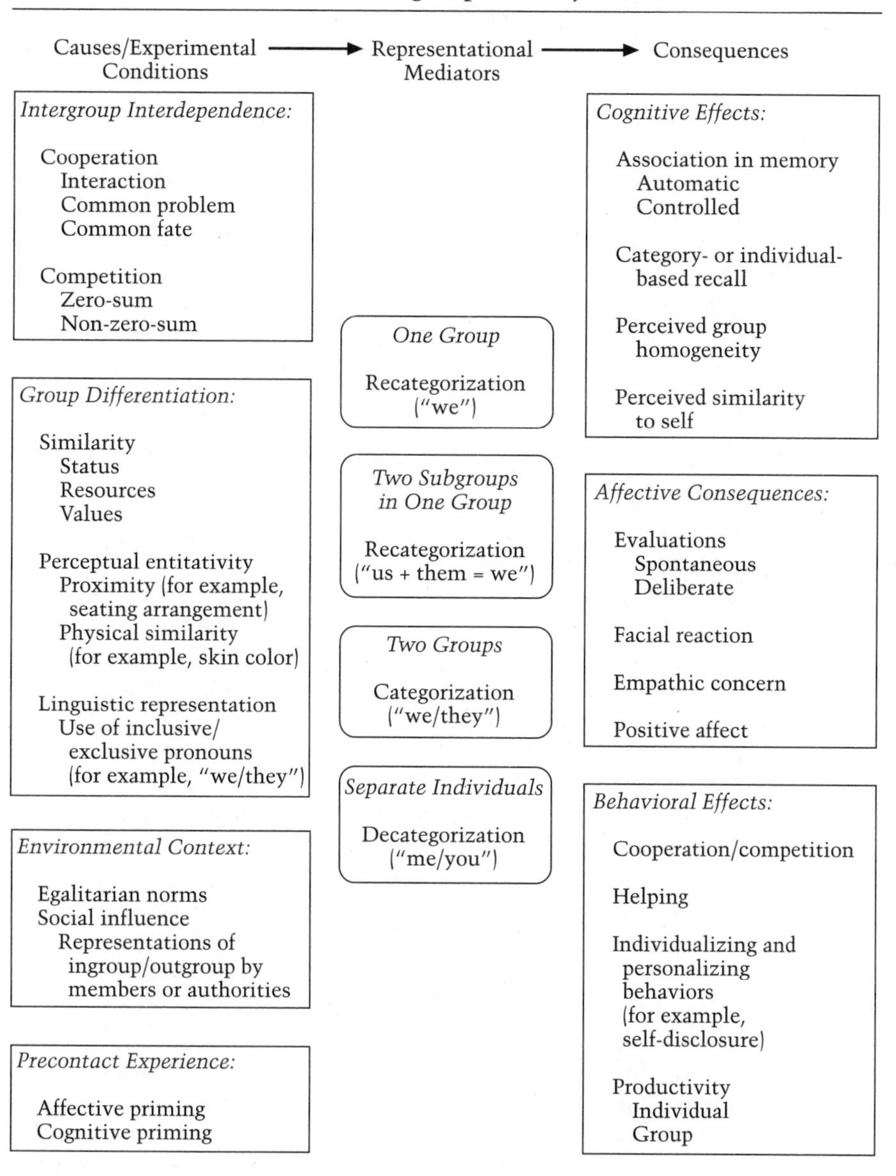


tors (for example, common goals or fate) that are perceived to be shared by the memberships.

Once outgroup members are perceived as ingroup members, they are accorded, we propose, the benefits of ingroup status heuristically and in stereotyped fashion. Ingroup members are likely to have more positive thoughts and feelings, and to engage in more positive behaviors (listed on the right), toward these former outgroup members after categorizing them as ingroup members. These more favorable impressions of outgroup members are not likely to be finely differentiated, at least initially (see Mullen and Hu 1989). Rather, we propose, more elaborated, personalized impressions can soon develop within the context of a common identity because the newly formed positivity bias is likely to encourage more open communication and greater self-disclosing interaction between former outgroup members. Over time a common identity encourages personalization of outgroup members and thereby initiates a second route to achieving reduced bias.

The development of a common ingroup identity does not necessarily require that each group forsake its less inclusive group identity completely. As Ferdman (1995) notes, every individual belongs to multiple groups. For example, Rodriguez-Scheel (1980) found that Chicanos in Detroit chose nonethnic categories, such as religion, occupation, and family, as often as ethnic labels to describe themselves. As depicted by the "subgroups within one group" (dual-identity) representation, people can conceive of two groups (for example, parents and children) as distinct units within the context of a superordinate (family) identity. When group identities and the associated cultural values are central to members' functioning, or when they are associated with high status or highly visible cues to group membership, it would be undesirable or impossible for members to relinquish their group identities or, as perceivers, to be "color-blind." Indeed, demands to forsake their group identities or to adopt a color-blind ideology would be likely to arouse strong reaction among members, resulting in especially poor intergroup relations (see Schofield 1986). If, however, people were to continue to regard themselves as members of different groups but all playing on the same team, or as part of the same superordinate entity, intergroup relations between these subgroups would be more positive than if people considered themselves members of separate groups only (see Brewer and Schneider 1990).

*Tests of the Model* Among the antecedent factors proposed by the Common Ingroup Identity Model (listed on the left) are the features of contact situations—such as interdependence between groups, equal status, and equalitarian norms (Allport 1954)—that are necessary for intergroup contact to be successful. From this perspective, cooperative interaction, for example, enhances positive evaluations of outgroup members (an affective consequence listed on the right) at least in part because cooperation transforms members' representations of the memberships from separate groups to one group.

From this recategorization perspective, cooperation among Sherif and Sherif's (1969) groups of summer campers increased positive attitudes toward outgroup members because it changed members' perceptions of one another from "us and them" to a more inclusive "we." To test this hypothesis directly, we conducted a laboratory experiment that brought two three-person laboratory groups together under conditions designed to vary independently the members' representations of the aggregate as one group or two groups (by varying factors such as seating arrangement), as well as the presence or absence of intergroup cooperative interaction. In the absence of cooperative interaction, participants induced to feel like one group relative to those whose separate-group identities were reinforced reported that the aggregate did feel more like one group. They also had lower degrees of intergroup bias in their evaluations (likable, cooperative, honest, trustworthy) of ingroup and outgroup members. We regard this as an important preliminary finding because it helps to establish the causal relation between the induction of a one-group representation and reduced bias, even in the absence of intergroup cooperation.

Supportive of the hypothesis that cooperation reduces bias, the results showed that among participants induced to feel like two groups, the introduction of cooperative interaction increased their perceptions of being one group and also reduced their bias in evaluative ratings relative to the bias of those who did not cooperate during the contact period. As predicted by the Common Ingroup Identity Model, bias was reduced after cooperation was introduced because evaluations of outgroup members became more favorable. Consistent with Brewer's (1979) analysis, cooperation appeared to move the new ingroup members closer to the self.

Consistent with our mediation hypothesis, cooperation induced formation among members of the two groups and also reduced bias. In addition, more direct support for the mediation hypothesis was revealed by the multiple regression mediation approach, a form of path analysis (see Baron and Kenny 1986). This analysis indicated that the influence of the introduction of cooperation on more positive evaluations of outgroup members was substantially reduced when the mediating effects of group representations and perceptions of cooperation and competition were considered. Furthermore, consistent with our model, only the one-group representation, among these potential mediators, related independently to evaluations of outgroup members.

The advantage of the experimental design is that we know that cooperation preceded the changes in participants' representations of the aggregate from two groups to one group, as well as the changes in intergroup bias. Also, when we manipulated only the representations of the aggregate (that is, we did not introduce cooperation), we know that the one-group representation preceded changes in intergroup bias. Such certainty regarding the direction of causality is not afforded by our correlational studies of the effects of contact hypothesis variables on intergroup bias that we conducted involving more natural contexts. However, we can rely on the results of the experimental study to at least support the plausibility of the direction of causality proposed by our model as it is applied to the study of the effects of cooperation and the other features specified by the contact hypothesis on intergroup harmony in more natural contexts.

Three survey studies conducted in natural settings across very different intergroup contexts offered converging support for the hypothesis that the features specified by the contact hypothesis increase intergroup harmony in part because they transform members' representations of the memberships from separate groups to one, more inclusive group. Participants in these studies included 1,353 students attending a multiethnic high school (Gaertner, Rust, et al. 1994, 1996); 229 banking executives who had experienced a corporate merger involving a wide variety of banks across the United States (Bachman 1993; Bachman and Gaertner 1999), and 86 college students who were members of blended families whose households were composed of two formerly separate families trying to unite into one (Banker 1997; Banker and Gaertner 1998).

To provide a conceptual replication of the laboratory study of cooperation, the surveys included items (specifically designed for each context) to measure participants' perceptions of the conditions of contact (equal status, self-revealing interaction, cooperation, equalitarian norms), their representations of the aggregate (one group, two subgroups within one group, two separate groups, and separate individuals), and a measure of intergroup harmony or bias. For example, contact hypothesis items measuring participants' perceptions of equal status between the groups included items such as "Teachers at this school are fair to all groups of students," "Employees from organization A [participants' company] and organization B are seen as equal members of the merged organization," and "My stepparent treats me, my siblings, and stepsiblings equally." Participants' cognitive representations of the aggregate as one group were measured by the items "Despite the different groups at school, there is frequently a sense that we are just one group," "Within the merged organization, it feels like one group," and "Living in my house, it feels like one family." Also, for each context, items were designed to measure the extent to which participants maintained a dual identity: "Although there are different groups at school, it feels like we are playing on the same team," "Within the merged organization, it

FIGURE 6.2 *The Contact Hypothesis and the Common Ingroup Identity Model*

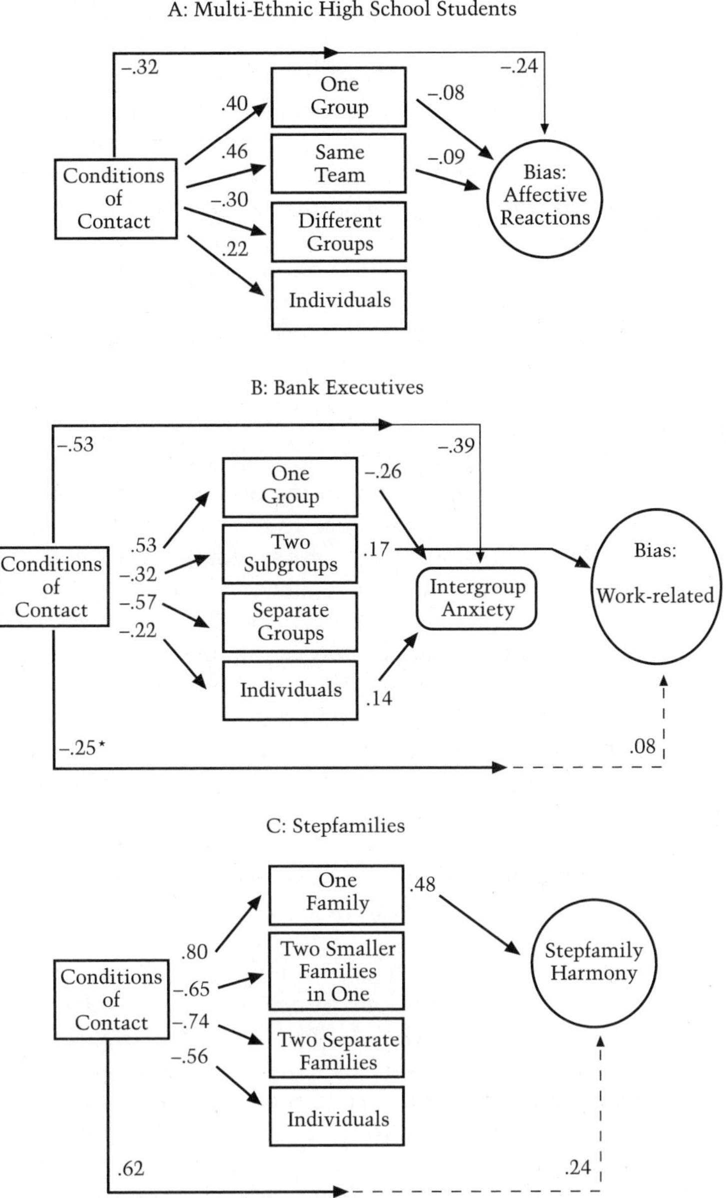


*Notes:* Thick bold lines depict reliable ($p < .05$) paths. Thick bold lines that become thinner depict reliable direct paths that become significantly less reliable when the mediators are considered. Thin dash lines indicate that the direct paths are no longer reliable after the mediators are considered.

feels like two subgroups within one group," and "Living in my house, it feels like two smaller families within one larger family."

Although the measures of intergroup bias or harmony were different across the three contexts, each study included some measure of affective reactions (such as feeling good, respectful, happy, awkward) to ingroup and outgroup members. For the high school study, the main outcome measure was bias in these affective reactions. For the corporate merger study, the main measure of bias was the extent to which the corporate executives perceived members of organizations A and B to have different work-related characteristics (intelligent, hardworking, organized, skilled, creative). In the stepfamily study, the major dependent measure involved stepfamily harmony (for example, "I would characterize the environment at my house as harmonious"). Within each setting, composite indices were created for each of the major components of our model—that is, the conditions of contact, the representations, and intergroup harmony or bias.

As in our laboratory study, the data from each survey study were examined with the multiple regression mediation analysis described by Baron and Kenny (1986). The results of these analyses support the predictions derived from the Common Ingroup Identity Model. The results depicted in figure 6.2a (high school students), figure 6.2b (bank executives) and figure 6.2c (stepfamilies) reveal that the conditions of contact reliably predict (indicated by thick bold arrows) each of the measures of intergroup harmony and bias before the mediators are considered. Also, the conditions of contact influence each of the participants' representations of the aggregate, as would be expected if one or more of these representations were a mediator. For example, the conditions of contact predict the extent to which participants rate the aggregate as one group ($\beta = .40$ among high school students; $\beta = .53$ among bank executives; and $\beta = .80$ among stepfamilies). In each case, the more favorably the conditions of contact are perceived, the more the aggregate feels like one group.

Moreover, consistent with the hypothesized mediating process, the relationships between the conditions of contact (on the left) and bias in affective reactions (figure 6.2a), intergroup anxiety (figure 6.2b), and stepfamily harmony (figure 6.2c) is substantially weaker after the mediators are considered than before (for example, $-.24$ versus $-.32$ in figure 6.2a). Furthermore, in each case the extent to which the aggregate felt like one group was a primary predictor of affective reactions. As predicted by the model, the more participants felt like one group, the lower the bias in affective reactions in the high school, the less the intergroup anxiety among the bank executives, and the greater the harmony in stepfamilies.

In contrast to the consistent, significant effect for the one-group representation, the role of the dual-identity measure functioned differently across the three intergroup settings. In the high school setting, the better the conditions of contact, the more students regarded the aggregate as "different groups on the same team." In contrast, in the bank executive and stepfamily settings, the more favorable the conditions of contact, the less participants indicated that the aggregate felt like two subgroups or two smaller families within a larger group. Also, in the bank executive context, the more the merged organization felt like two subgroups within one group, the greater the amount of ingroup bias these executives had in their perceptions of the work-related characteristics of the members of the two formerly separate organizations. Thus, in this context, the more strongly salient both subgroup and superordinate group identities were simultaneously, the greater the extent to which ingroup members were regarded as more intelligent, hardworking, skilled, and creative than outgroup members. In the multi-ethnic high school context, however, the more students reported that the aggregate felt like "different groups all playing on the same team" (the dual-identity item), the lower their bias in affective reactions.

We suspect that contextual differences between these intergroup settings may alter the relative desirability and utility of maintaining a dual identity in lieu of a more inclusive one-group representation (see Gaertner, Dovidio, and Bachman 1996). For example, maintaining strong identification with the earlier subgroup identities following a corporate merger may threaten the primary goal of the merger. Similarly, in stepfamilies the salience of the former family identities, even with the simultaneous recognition of a more inclusive family identity, may violate members' expectations about what their ideal family should be like. Consequently, the salience of these subgroup identities may be diagnostic of serious problems—reflected, in part, by the fact that these dual identities become stronger in the merger and stepfamily contexts as the conditions of contact become more unfavorable. Of course, the direction of causality could be reversed. That is, it is possible that the stronger the experience of a dual identity, the worse people perceive the contact conditions to be. In either case, the relationship is quite different than it is in the high school context, where the salience of subgroup and superordinate identities would not be incompatible with the goals of the superordinate organization. There the salience of the subgroup identities, within the context of a superordinate entity that provides connection between the subgroups, may signal the prospects for good intergroup relations without undermining the goals of the school or those of the different ethnic or racial groups.

In summary, the findings of our survey studies in natural settings converge with those of the laboratory study in offering support for the Common Ingroup Identity Model. Perceptions of more favorable conditions of contact predicted less differentiated, more superordinate representations of the memberships that, in part, seemed to contribute to reduced intergroup bias in affective reactions. These studies also offer evidence for the role of a dual identity in intergroup bias. In intergroup contexts in which the formation of a single, more inclusive superordinate group is a desired goal, the continued existence of the earlier subgroup identities (even simultaneously with a superordinate identity) may be perceived as a sign that the amalgamation process is failing. Corporate mergers and the formation of blended families seem, from our preliminary research, to represent such contexts. In contrast, in contexts in which the two subgroups are conceived as working constructively toward a common goal—such as being on the "same team" in the high school study—a dual identity predicts more positive intergroup relations.

These findings reflect upon enduring issues in intergroup relations in the United States. Several structural integration patterns (assimilation, pluralism, and separatism) have characterized American racial and ethnic relations (see Fredrickson, this volume). Assimilation comes closest to the "melting pot" metaphor: achieving homogeneity and integration. This pattern, however, in practice usually requires that minorities forsake their cultural distinctiveness as the price of acceptance into the mainstream or dominant culture. Pluralism's metaphor is the mosaic: the cultural distinctiveness of all groups is visible and accepted within an integrated society. Separatism is characterized by the mixture of oil and water: each group remains structurally apart (segregated) from the others, and each maintains its cultural distinctiveness.

Which pattern (assimilation, pluralism, or separatism) in any particular situational context would best encourage more positive beliefs, feelings, and behaviors toward members of other groups? To examine the impact of structural integration patterns on expectations regarding the likely contact conditions between two groups and members' commitment to a superordinate entity, we conducted an experiment involving a corporate merger simulation (Mottola et al. 1997). In this study, we manipulated the merger integration pattern utilized to bring two companies together in terms of whether the culture (policies and norms) of the merged organization reflected just one of the premerger companies (an absorb pattern, a type of assimilation in which one group is expected to forsake its cultural identity), aspects of both companies (a blend pattern, analogous to pluralism), or an entirely new culture (a combine pattern that reflected a more equalitarian form of assimilation). As we would have expected, perceptions of the conditions of contact, organizational unity, and commitment to the merged organization were most favorable when the combine pattern prevailed, followed in turn by the blend pattern and then the absorb pattern. Another finding in this laboratory study that was conceptually similar to those of our three survey studies in natural settings was that the relation between favorable conditions of contact and increased commitment to the merged organization was mediated by participants' perceptions of organizational unity (one group).

Beyond generating more positive intergroup attitudes, the degree of organizational unity experienced can have implications for the effectiveness and productivity of a merged organization. For example, in a military context, Manning and Ingraham (1983) obtained a correlation between battalion cohesion and measures of performance effectiveness, including operations readiness. Similarly, we have found that the extent to which members of two groups perceived of themselves as one superordinate group correlated with the actual effectiveness of their task solution ($r = .28$, $p < .02$). This relationship is also consistent with the meta-analytic conclusions of Mullen and Copper (1994), who found that group cohesiveness significantly predicts group productivity ($r = .246$). Moreover, Mullen and Copper suggest that the relationship between cohesiveness and productivity may be bidirectional and thus iterative: cohesiveness enhances productivity, and successful accomplishment, in turn, further increases cohesiveness. Indeed, the relationship between successful performance and subsequent cohesiveness is even stronger ($r = .505$) than the relationship between initial cohesiveness and productivity. Thus, the development of a common ingroup identity can help form a basis for more harmonious intergroup relations to develop through mutual success and achievement, which reinforce the common bond and identity between the groups.

Group representations also relate to cultural identity and thus can have very important and fundamental psychological consequences for individuals as well as groups. Patterns of integration involving assimilation, pluralism, and separatism represent structural and functional relations between groups that reflect separate-group or superordinate-group representations, or a combination of both (dual identity). Berry (1984), for example, presents four forms of cultural relations in pluralistic societies that represent the intersection of yes-no responses to two relevant questions: Are cultural identity and customs of value to be retained? Are positive relations with the larger society of value, and to be sought? When the answer to both questions is yes, subgroup and superordinate groups are both important. This represents the dual-identity representation within our model. Are the prospects for intergroup relations more positive relative to when a person answers "no" to one of Berry's questions—within the context of our model, when only superordinate identity or separate group identities are salient? We consider this issue in the context of the Common Ingroup Identity Model in the next section.

## More Evidence on the Role of a Dual Identity

The procedure of the multi-ethnic high school study permitted an additional test of the value of a dual identity in which both superordinate and subgroup identities are salient. When students first identified their group identities on the survey, some minority students checked both "American" (a superordinate identity) and their ethnic group identity (for example, "Vietnamese"), whereas others identified themselves only by their ethnic or racial group. As predicted by our hypothesis about the value of a dual identity, those minority students who used both a superordinate (American) identity and their ethnic or racial group identity had lower bias in affective reactions relative to those who used only their ethnic group identity. Whereas there may be many differences between these two groups of students (such as American citizenship), they did have different cognitive representations of the student body. Minority students who identified themselves as both an American and a member of a minority group endorsed the item "Although there are different groups at school, it feels like we are all playing on the same team" more strongly than did those students who identified themselves using only their minority group identity.

A field experiment (Nier et al. 1999) conducted at the University of Delaware football stadium prior to a game between the University of Delaware and Westchester State University demonstrates how simultaneously salient superordinate and subgroup identities can increase behavioral compliance with a request for assistance from a person of a different race. In this experiment, black and white male and female students approached fans of the same sex as themselves from both universities just before the fans entered the stadium. These fans were asked whether they would be willing to be interviewed about their food preferences. Our student interviewers wore either a University of Delaware or Westchester State University hat. By selecting fans who also wore clothing that identified their university affiliation, we systematically varied whether fans and our interviewers had a common or different university identity in a context in which we expected university identities to be particularly salient. Although we planned to oversample black fans, the sample was still too small to yield any informative findings.

Among white fans, however, sharing superordinate university identity with the black interviewers reliably increased their compliance (59.6 percent) compared to when they did not share a common identity with the black interviewer (37.8 percent). When the interviewers were white, they gained similar levels of compliance when they shared a common university identity with the fan (43 percent), and these levels were higher than when they appeared to be affiliated with the rival university (40 percent). These fans were not color-blind—only black interviewers who shared a common university affiliation with the fans were accorded especially high levels of compliance. Although there are a number of plausible explanations for this particular pattern of compliance, these findings offer support for the idea that outgroup members can be treated especially favorably when they are perceived to share a more inclusive, superordinate identity.

The value of a superordinate identity for increasing positive reactions to racial outgroup members was also revealed in a laboratory experiment (Nier et al. 1996). In this study, white subjects participating with a black or white confederate were induced to perceive themselves as separate individuals participating at the same time or as members of the same laboratory team. The results revealed a reliable interaction involving the other participant's race and the team manipulation. Whereas the evaluations of the white partner were virtually equivalent in both the team and individual conditions, the evaluations of the black partner were reliably more positive when they were teammates than when they were just individuals without a common group connection. In fact, for members of the same team, black partners were evaluated more favorably than white partners. Thus, in field and laboratory settings, racial outgroup members were accorded especially positive reactions when they shared common ingroup identity with white subjects compared to when the context did not emphasize their common group membership.

In another laboratory experiment, we obtained support for the prediction (see figure 6.1) that a common ingroup identity reduces intergroup bias in helping and self-disclosure (see Dovidio, Gaertner, et al. 1997). First, members of two three-person laboratory groups ("over- and under-estimators"; see Tajfel 1969) were induced to conceive of themselves as either one group or two groups (as in Gaertner et al. 1989, 1990). Then some participants were given an opportunity to help or to engage in a self-disclosing interaction with an ingroup or outgroup member. For helping, participants listened individually to an audio recording of another student (characterized in a previous session as either an over- or under-estimator) describe how illness had prevented her from completing an important survey of student life for a committee on which she served. Subsequently, participants received a note ostensibly from this person that contained an appeal to help her by placing posters recruiting volunteers to participate in the survey in various locations across campus. The other participants were engaged in a self-disclosure task in which they were asked to discuss the topic "What do I fear most?" During this task, subjects interacted with either an ingroup or outgroup member who had participated earlier in their session.

The results for the helping and self-disclosure measures converged to support predictions from our model. In each case, the bias favoring ingroup members that was present in the two-groups condition was reduced (and actually reversed) for those induced to regard the aggregate as one group. That is, in the one-group condition, more positive behaviors were directed toward outgroup members than toward ingroup members, albeit by an amount that was not statistically significant. These findings are important for at least two reasons. First, the finding that outgroup members in the one-group condition received especially positive reactions for both self-disclosure and helping parallels the amplified compliance accorded black interviewers who shared a common university affiliation in the football stadium study as well as the more positive evaluations of the black teammates in the laboratory study.

One important aspect of this pattern of change across these different studies is the suggestion that upon recognition of a superordinate group connection, newly regarded ingroup members are initially accorded especially positive reactions compared to when they were regarded only as outgroup members. Also, these reactions to newcomers are even more extreme compared to the reactions accorded original ingroup members. If indeed superordinate connection motivates initially amplified positive reactions to "newcomers," this emotional reaction can perhaps be leveraged to promote more harmonious long-term relationships.

A second important aspect of these findings is the demonstration that common ingroup membership can initiate more personalized interactions between former outgroup members. This consequence can thereby activate an additional, independent pathway for increasing intergroup harmony. Similarly, in another experiment (Gaertner, Rust, and Dovidio 1997), we observed that the capacity of personalized, self-disclosing interactions to bring ingroup and outgroup members psychologically closer also transformed their perceptions of the aggregate from being two groups to being one group. Thus, common ingroup identity and personalized interactions seem to share reciprocally the capacity to facilitate each other, supporting our view that these processes are not necessarily competitive but complementary.

We are encouraged by some recent independent evidence that, in addition to increasing positive evaluations, compliance, helping, self-revealing interactions, and cooperative behavior toward people who would otherwise be regarded as outgroup members, a common superordinate identity can also reduce subtle linguistic biases that serve to perpetuate stereotypes (Maass, Ceccarelli, and Rudin 1996; study 2). In this recent laboratory experiment, northern and southern Italians living in Switzerland received messages that emphasized the differentiation between northern and southern Italians (in a two-groups condition) or between Italians and the Swiss (in a superordinate "Italian" condition). These participants were then shown cartoons depicting northern and southern Italians performing positive and negative behaviors. Participants were asked to choose one of four response alternatives corresponding to the four levels of abstraction (see Semin and Fiedler 1988).

When the distinction between northern and southern Italians was emphasized, the results replicated the linguistic bias effect. Higher levels of abstraction were used to describe positive behaviors of ingroup members (for example, "she is helpful") than for outgroup members ("she walked with the old lady"). Also, higher levels of abstraction were used to describe undesirable behaviors of outgroup members compared to descriptions of the behaviors of ingroup members. This linguistic bias was not evident in the superordinate identity condition. Thus, a superordinate identity fundamentally changed how behavioral information about ingroup and outgroup members was processed, and importantly, in a way that reduced this subtle bias in information processing. In addition, recent research by Karpinski and Von Hippel (1996) reveals that this linguistic bias mediates the extent to which people maintain stereotypic expectancies in the face of disconfirming information. Thus, the development of a common ingroup identity can not only reduce general intergroup prejudice but also, by reducing intergroup linguistic bias, help to change intergroup stereotypes.

Other independent research supports the value of a dual racial or ethnic identity for reducing bias and improving intergroup relations. Earlier we discussed the possibility that acceptance of a superordinate identity does not require that members forsake their ethnic or racial group identity (Gaertner et al. 1989), and our own research on dual identity seems to support this idea. In addition, two recent studies further suggest that the intergroup benefits of a strong superordinate identity remain relatively stable even when the subordinate identity becomes just as strong (Huo et al. 1996; Smith and Tyler 1996). This suggests that social cohesion does not require that individuals deny their ethnic identity.

For example, in a survey study of white adults, Smith and Tyler (1996, study 1) measured the strength of respondents' superordinate identity as an American and also the strength of their identification as white. Following Berry's (1984) strategy of creating four groups on the basis of a median split on each measure, the investigators identified four groups of respondents who varied in terms of the relative strength of their superordinate and subgroup identities. The results revealed that regardless of whether they strongly identified with being white, respondents with a strong American identity were more likely to base their support for affirmative action policies that would benefit blacks and other minorities on relational concerns about the fairness of congressional representation than on whether these policies would increase or decrease their own well-being. However, members of the group who identified themselves more strongly with being white than with being American based their position on affirmative action more strongly on how they regarded the instrumental value of these policies for themselves.

This pattern of findings suggests that a strong superordinate identity allows individuals to support policies that would benefit members of other racial subgroups without giving primary consideration to their own instrumental needs. Furthermore, once people identify with the superordinate entity, the relative strength of their subgroup identity does not significantly change their bases for supporting policies that benefit other groups within the superordinate collective. This finding also provides evidence that superordinate identity more broadly influences attitudes toward members of other subgroups; it is not limited to the specific subgroup members encountered during intergroup contact. Recall, in our laboratory study (Dovidio, Gaertner, et al. 1997), that the helping measure also provided some evidence of the generalization of positive behaviors beyond those outgroup members actually present during intergroup contact. The person in need was presented as a participant from a previous session. In the next section, we address more directly and fully the issue of how the benefits of intergroup contact can generalize and extend to other group members who are not present.

## GENERALIZATION OF THE BENEFITS OF INTERGROUP CONTACT

Although research on the effects of intergroup contact has found support for the contact hypothesis for group members directly involved, these beneficial effects typically do not reliably generalize to the outgroup as a whole or to intergroup attitudes more generally (Stephan and Stephan 1996). Nevertheless, success in promoting harmony among the members of the different groups present in the contact situation is not a trivial accomplishment. In many intergroup contexts, this is precisely the major goal to be achieved.

One major reason generalization fails is that the now positively evaluated outgroup members are regarded as exceptions, that is, as not necessarily typical of outgroup members more generally (Allport 1954; Wilder 1984). In this respect, the dual identity (for example, African American) may be a particularly promising mechanism through which generalization may occur. In contrast to a separate-individuals or purely one-group representation, the dual identity maintains the associative link (see Rothbart and John 1985) to additional outgroup members. This dual-identity representation is also compatible with the Mutual Intergroup Differentiation Model (Hewstone and Brown 1986; Hewstone 1996), which proposes that introducing a cooperative relationship between groups without degrading the original ingroup-outgroup categorization scheme is an effective way to change intergroup attitudes and to have these attitudes generalize to additional outgroup members. The Trade-off Hypothesis (Gaertner et al. 1993), however, proposes that although attitudes toward outgroup members present during contact would be less favorable with a dual- than with a purely one-group identity, the modest change in attitude could more easily generalize to additional outgroup members.

Hewstone and Brown (1986) argue that generalization to the outgroup as a whole is more likely when group identities are more rather than less salient during intergroup contact. Findings that pleasant contact with more typical rather than less typical outgroup members is associated with more favorable attitudes toward the outgroup more generally supports Hewstone and Brown's position (Hewstone 1996; Wilder 1984; see also Desforges et al. 1991). More specifically, Hewstone and Brown would encourage groups working together to recognize their mutual superiorities and inferiorities and to value equally the dimensions favoring each group. From the perspective of the Common Ingroup Identity Model, the realization of Hewstone and Brown's recommendation would create ideal conditions for keeping earlier group identities salient while simultaneously providing a superordinate connection between the groups.

Although there is some evidence that inducing a superordinate identity without deliberately attempting to emphasize the outgroup members' subgroup identity can yield generalization in terms of the delivery of prosocial behavior (see Dovidio, Gaertner, et al. 1997), there is also reason to believe that a dual identity may have even stronger potential for generalization. This idea was examined directly in an experiment by Hornsey and Hogg (1996). Their instructions emphasized students' individual identities, their separate-group identities (as humanities or math-science students), their superordinate university identity, or both their separate-group identities and their superordinate university identities (that is, a dual-identity condition). These students were then asked a number of questions regarding how positive they would feel about working with students in each group (that is, the humanities and math-science subgroups).

Although students felt more positively overall about the prospects of working with students in their own group, the least amount of bias occurred in the dual-identity condition. Contrary to what we would have expected, however, the most bias did not occur in the separate-groups condition, but rather when the superordinate identity alone was emphasized (perhaps as a consequence of arousing needs to establish group distinctiveness). Nevertheless, these results offer support for the value of a dual identity in promoting positive attitudes toward the outgroup more generally. Indeed, with a dual identity, outgroup attitudes were more positive than those associated with a superordinate identity alone.

In addition to a dual identity in which subgroup composition is convergent with original ingroup and outgroup members, as we have been considering thus far, subgroup composition may also cross-cut these original group boundaries. With the convergent composition, the subgroups are composed homogeneously of members from the originally separate groups, but these subgroups are associated with the same superordinate group identity: [(AA)(BB)]. With cross-cut composition, each subgroup is heterogeneously composed of members from different original subgroups, and these subgroups are connected by an overarching superordinate identity: [(AB)(AB)].

Building on earlier research by Marcus-Newhall and her colleagues (1993), Rust (1996) varied the presence or absence of a superordinate group identity when freshmen (F) and sophomores (S) were assigned preliminary tasks on the basis of cross-cut (FS)(FS) or convergent (FF)(SS) patterns. Replicating the findings of Marcus-Newhall and her colleagues, Rust found that bias toward the ingroup and outgroup members present was lower in the cross-cut condition than in the convergent one. Whereas the manipulation of a superordinate identity did not directly influence evaluations of the outgroup members present, nor of outgroup members more generally, the more participants perceived themselves as "crossed subgroups within a superordinate entity" [(FS)(FS)], the more positive were their evaluations of the outgroup members present, and also of outgroup members more generally. The representation involving crossed groups without a superordinate connection (FS)(FS) did not relate to outgroup attitudes at all. Although the "convergent subgroups within a superordinate" representation [(FF)(SS)] did not relate directly to more general outgroup attitudes, it did relate marginally ($p < .06$) to the outgroup members who were present. Overall, attitudes toward outgroup members in the contact situation predicted generalized outgroup attitudes. Thus, the "convergent subgroups within a superordinate" representation may lead to more positive generalized outgroup attitudes indirectly through its capacity to influence attitudes toward the outgroup members present. The "convergent" representation without a superordinate boundary (FF)(SS), however, did not relate to outgroup attitudes more generally, or to those outgroup members who were present during contact. This finding suggests that a superordinate identity may be compatible with the acceptance of a hierarchical differentiation of the subgroups because members of these groups can see themselves as part of something larger they share in common. This may help explain why in many nonegalitarian societies that deal with ethnic and communal diversity by means of status hierarchies, members of different groups live together in relative peace, each group more or less accepting its assigned societal position. Thus, whether subgroups are constructed with a cross-cut or convergent configuration, the presence of a superordinate group connection seems to facilitate the development of more positive evaluations of outgroup members.

When tasks or roles can be assigned using either cross-cut or convergent subgroup configurations within a superordinate entity, the cross-cut pattern may offer more stable consequences for harmonious intergroup relations and for generalization, assuming original group identities are not completely degraded. The relative salience of the assigned subgroup and superordinate boundaries are likely to vary over time, as does the figure-ground relationship within ambiguous figures, but the variation in the relative strength of the group boundaries may have fewer negative consequences with a cross-cut than with a convergent subgroup configuration; to the extent that original ingroup and outgroup members regard themselves as members of the *same subgroup*, the benefits of a common group identity could be realizable when the subgroups are cross-cut despite changes in the relative salience of the additional superordinate boundary. That is, common subgroup identity may be sufficient to redirect pro-ingroup bias toward former outgroup members even when the superordinate identity is present but relatively weak. When the salience of the superordinate boundary is relatively weak among convergent subgroups, however, the salience of separate-group identities along the original intergroup boundaries may reemerge, reestablishing intergroup bias and conflict.

The value of the cross-cut relative to the convergent configuration within a superordinate entity is particularly evident in our study of stepfamilies (Banker and Gaertner 1998). Specifically, when participants perceived the coalition between themselves and their biological parent (a convergent subgroup within the stepfamily) as strong, their evaluations of the level of stepfamily harmony were relatively lower. On the other hand, participants who perceived the cross-cutting coalition between themselves and their stepparent as stronger reported greater levels of stepfamily harmony. Although the relationships between these particular coalitions and stepfamily harmony are well documented (Brown, Green, and Druckman 1990; Crosbie-Burnett 1984), our analyses additionally reveal that, consistent with our model, the relation between each coalition and stepfamily harmony is mediated by the extent to which participants perceived their family as being one group.

In summary, the results of a range of empirical studies offer supporting evidence that the benefits of an intergroup contact can, under appropriate conditions, generalize beyond that situation to improve more encompassing intergroup attitudes. Consistent with our model, recognizing both connection (superordinate group identity) and difference (original subgroup identity) facilitates generalization. The superordinate identity activates and redirects pro-ingroup biases to improve attitudes toward the original outgroup members present, whereas the simultaneous salience of original identities provides the associative links for these attitudes to generalize to other members of these groups.

## THE COMMON INGROUP IDENTITY MODEL IN PERSPECTIVE

We have reviewed some evidence suggesting that a common ingroup identity partially mediates the effects of contact hypothesis variables, increasing positive feelings and behaviors toward specific outgroup members. Also, it seems to have some potential to increase positive attitudes toward outgroup members more generally. Furthermore, we are encouraged by the finding that a superordinate identity can initiate more self-disclosing, personalized interactions as well as more cooperative, prosocial orientations toward outgroup members. Although the cognitive representation of a superordinate identity may itself often be fleeting and unstable, it seems to be capable of initiating behaviors that call forth reciprocity and can thus have more permanent intergroup consequences. Also, some of these behaviors can initiate processes that can reduce bias through additional, independent pathways. Thus, we regard the major strength of inducing a common identity to be its capacity to change temporarily the course of intergroup interactions and to initiate constructive intergroup processes and exchanges that produce longer-lasting positive relations between groups.

Whereas the development of a common ingroup identity does not necessarily require that each group forsake its earlier identity, we could anticipate that groups of higher status are more resistant to joining forces with lower-status groups in order to maintain their positive distinctiveness (Ellemers et al. 1992). Lower-status groups, however, may relish the idea of improving their standing by developing super-ordinate connections with higher-status groups. Rust's (1996) study of college freshmen and sophomores, for example, quite clearly revealed the greater reluctance of the sophomores, compared to the freshmen, to conceive of themselves as members of the same superordinate group.

A critical element in this process involves one of the fundamental functions of group identity—to maintain and enhance "positive distinctiveness" and esteem (Tajfel and Turner 1979). One of the conditions for successful intergroup contact, identified by the contact hypothesis, is that the groups must be of equal status in that context. As our earlier work on the conditions specified by the contact hypothesis suggests, equal status would be expected to facilitate the development of a common ingroup identity. However, bringing different groups together, particularly when they are similar on an important dimension (such as task-relevant status), might arouse motivations to achieve "positive distinctiveness," which could exacerbate rather than alleviate intergroup bias (Brown and Wade 1987). In this respect, establishing a common superordinate identity while simultaneously maintaining the salience of subgroup identities (that is, developing a dual identity as two subgroups within one group) would be particularly effective because it permits the benefits of a common ingroup identity to operate without arousing countervailing motivations to achieve positive distinctiveness. We conducted two experiments investigating this hypothesis.

In one study (Dovidio, Gaertner, and Validzic 1998), groups of three students were given feedback indicating that, based on their performance on an earlier task, their group was higher, lower, or equal in status than another group with which they were about to cooperate. This status manipulation was crossed factorially with whether the groups were assigned identical or different task perspectives in preparation for their cooperative interaction. The discussions involved the Winter Survival Problem (Johnson and Johnson 1975) and groups with different task perspectives: the members of one group were told to assume that they would hike to safety, while the members of the other group were asked to assume that they would stay put to await search parties. As predicted, the analyses revealed that when the groups were of equal status and task perspectives were different, intergroup bias was lower and the representation of the aggregate as one group was higher than in each of the other three conditions (equal status–same task, unequal status–different task, and equal status–same task). In addition, the one-group representation mediated the relation between the experimental manipulations of status and task perspective on intergroup bias. These findings are consistent with the proposed value of equal status—primarily, as Hewstone and Brown (1986) propose, when the distinctiveness between groups is maintained.

In another study, we varied relative group status among actual employees of many different companies by asking them to imagine that their current organization was about to merge with another (Mottola 1996). In one condition, their present company was described as higher in status than the other in terms of generating greater sales and greater profits. In another condition, their company was lower in status on both dimensions. In a third condition, both companies were described as having equal status in terms of both sales and profit. In a fourth condition, their company was described as higher in status on one dimension, but the other company was higher on the other dimension. Consistent with Hewstone and Brown's (1986) ideas about the benefits of maintaining the mutual distinctiveness of groups working together, participants in the fourth condition—one company had higher profits and the other higher sales—anticipated that they would more strongly identify with the merged organization than did participants in each of the other three conditions (which did not differ from one another). Thus, when each group can maintain positive distinctiveness, we can anticipate greater acceptance of a superordinate identity from the members of both groups. This would be particularly important in organizational settings when subgroups must be formed and only the convergent pattern is realistically possible. Furthermore, when the basis of group differentiation facilitates the merged group's effectiveness, the development of "unity" can be enhanced. For example, as in the study by Mottola (1996), when each subgroup contributes a different, but necessary component to the merged organization's effectiveness, group differentiation can enhance the acceptance of organizational identification.

The benefits of the development of a common ingroup identity are also consistent with the models of second-culture acquisition. For example, the assimilation model (Gordon 1978) describes how a member of a minority group is absorbed into the dominant culture. In general, research shows that minorities who are more assimilated experience less stress and anxiety and have lower levels of failure in school and of substance abuse (Burnam et al. 1987; Pasquali 1985). However, there may also be psychological costs associated with assimilation. For instance, academically successful African Americans may feel that they have to reject the values of the African American community to succeed (Fordham 1988). Thus, when the development of a common identity involves abandoning important racial or ethnic identities, the potential benefits may be compromised by other personal and psychological considerations.

Nevertheless, as we have proposed, the development of a common ingroup identity does not necessarily require that people forsake their separate-group identities. The consideration of a dual identity within the Common Ingroup Identity Model is, in fact, consistent with other models of cultural identity and well-being. For instance, the alternation model of second-culture acquisition (LaFromboise, Coleman, and Gerton 1993) suggests that it is possible for an individual to know two cultures, identify with both, and draw on both identities at different times. The multicultural model suggests that an individual can maintain a positive identity while simultaneously participating in and identifying with a larger entity composed of many other racial and ethnic groups (Berry 1986). Indeed, the development of a bicultural or multicultural identity not only is possible but can contribute to the social adjustment, psychological adaptation, and overall well-being of minority group members (LaFromboise et al. 1993; Ogbu and Matute-Bianchi 1986) in ways superior to full assimilation or acculturation.

Unlike strategies that seek to reduce bias by focusing primarily on the perpetrators rather than on their victims, the development of a common ingroup identity requires the participation of both memberships. Victims may assume, however, that only those responsible for bias and discrimination should actively participate in the necessary therapy. Also, victims may be so distrustful of their persecutors that they strongly resist the prospects of common ingroup membership. Unfortunately, when overtures to join together are resisted by one group, the prospects for developing more harmonious relations may become more tenuous than before. Also, majority group members, whose traditions usually dominate the cultural landscape, may resent minority group members' allegiance to their original heritage, even in the context of a dual identity. In particular, the loyalty or patriotism of these minorities may be suspect. Whites in the United States, for example, may assume that for African Americans their African identity is always stronger than their American identity, and consequently weaker than whites' own American identity. Although the utilization of the dual identity may reduce intergroup bias among minorities, the use of the dual identity by minorities may exacerbate intergroup tensions among majorities. For the dual identity to provide positive intergroup consequences for both groups, it may be critical therefore for minorities to demonstrate clearly their allegiance to the inclusive superordinate entity.

Although we are encouraged by the demonstrated value of inducing a common ingroup identity, its capacity to reduce bias has been examined only among groups that were not engaged in severe or mortal intergroup conflicts—that is, where bias usually takes a more pro-ingroup than anti-outgroup form. If the rash of recent armed conflicts among the various ethnic groups in Eastern Europe following the decentralization of the Warsaw Pact is to be any guide, it would appear that appeals to the national identities of these combatants would not be likely to decrease the ferocity of their fighting. At the same time, the perception of a common identity, albeit cemented by a totalitarian central regime, may have been the glue that kept these groups together before decentralization.

In terms of our future work, the capacity of a common identity to change the tone and direction of more hostile intergroup relations needs to be addressed. In addition, the correlational approach of our survey work in natural group settings, such as corporate mergers and stepfamilies, would benefit from a longitudinal approach that enables more careful assessment of the directions of causality between the constructs proposed in the model. In closing, we remind the reader that we do not regard a common ingroup identity as a panacea for the problematic relations between groups. Instead, it seems to have the capacity to activate cognitive and motivational processes that change the tone and direction of immediate intergroup relations, changes that can, in turn, initiate other, more stable processes and pathways toward the achievement of more productive, harmonious relations between groups.

---

This chapter is the winner of the 1998 Gordon Allport Intergroup Relations Prize awarded by the Society for the Psychological Study of Social Issues and the Gordon W. Allport Memorial Fund. Preparation of this chapter was facilitated by NIMH Grant MH 48721.

## REFERENCES

Abrams, D. (1985). Focus of attention in minimal intergroup discrimination. *British Journal of Social Psychology, 24,* 65–74.

Allport, Gordon W. (1954). *The nature of prejudice.* Cambridge, Mass.: Addison-Wesley.

Anastasio, P. A., Bachman, B. A., Gaertner, Samuel L., and Dovidio, John F. (1997). In R. Spears, Penelope J. Oakes, N. Ellemers, and S. Alexander Haslam (Eds.), *The social psychology of stereotyping and group life* (pp. 236–56). Oxford: Blackwell.

Anderson, J. (1996). Black and blue. *New Yorker* (April 29 and May 6), 62–64.

Bachman, Betty A. (1993). An intergroup model of organizational mergers. Ph.D. dissertation, University of Delaware.

Bachman, Betty, and Gaertner, Samuel (1999). An intergroup model of organizational mergers. Unpublished manuscript, Siena College.

Banker, Brenda S. (1997). The Common Ingroup Identity Model: Recategorization and its relation to stepfamily harmony. Master's thesis, University of Delaware.

Banker, Brenda S., and Gaertner, Samuel L. (1998). Achieving stepfamily harmony: An intergroup-relations approach. *Journal of Family Psychology, 12,* 310–25.

Baron, Ruben M., and Kenny, David A. (1986). The moderator-mediator variable distinction in social psychological research: Conceptual, strategic, and statistical considerations. *Journal of Personality and Social Psychology, 51,* 1173–82.

Berry, J. W. (1984). Cultural relations in plural societies. In Norman E. Miller and Marilynn B. Brewer (Eds.), *Groups in contact: The psychology of desegregation* (pp. 11–27). Orlando, Fla.: Academic Press.

———. (1986). Multiculturalism and psychology in plural societies. In L. H. Ekstrand (Ed.), *Ethnic minorities and immigrants in a cross-cultural perspective* (pp. 37–51). Lisse, The Netherlands: Swets and Zeitlinger.

Bettencourt, B. A., Brewer, Marilynn B., Croak, M. R., and Miller, Norman. (1992). Cooperation and the reduction of intergroup bias: The roles of reward structure and social orientation. *Journal of Experimental Social Psychology, 28,* 301–19.

Billig, M. G., and Tajfel, Henri. (1973). Social categorization and similarity in intergroup behavior. *European Journal of Social Psychology, 3,* 27–52.

Brewer, Marilynn B. (1979). Ingroup bias in the minimal intergroup situation: A cognitive-motivational analysis. *Psychological Bulletin, 86,* 307–24.

———. (1988). A dual process model of impression formation. In Srull, Thomas, Wyer, Robert (Eds), *Advances in social cognition,* Vol. 1. (pp. 1–36). Hillsdale, N.J.: Lawrence Erlbaum Associates.

———. (1991). The social self: On being the same and different at the same time. *Personality and Social Psychology Bulletin, 17,* 475–82.

Brewer, Marilynn B., Ho, H., Lee, J., and Miller, Norman. (1987). Social identity and social distance among Hong Kong school children. *Personality and Social Psychology Bulletin, 13,* 156–65.

Brewer, Marilynn B., and Miller, Norman. (1984). Beyond the contact hypothesis: Theoretical perspectives on desegregation. In Norman Miller and Marilynn B. Brewer (Eds.), *Groups in contact: The psychology of desegregation* (pp. 281–302). Orlando, Fla.: Academic Press.

———. (1996). *Intergroup relations.* Buckingham, Eng.: Open University Press.

Brewer, Marilynn B., and Schneider, S. (1990). Social identity and social dilemmas: A double-edged sword. In D. Abrams and M. Hogg (Eds.), *Social identity theory: Constructive and critical advances* (pp. 169–84). London: Harvester Wheatsheaf.

Brown, A. C., Green, R. J., and Druckman, J. (1990). A comparison of stepfamilies with and without child-focused problems. *American Orthopsychiatric Association, 60,* 556–66.

———. (1981). Interpersonal and intergroup behavior. In John C. Turner and H. Giles (Eds.), *Intergroup behavior* (pp. 33–64). Chicago: University of Chicago Press.

Brown, Rupert, and Turner, John (1979). The criss-cross categorization effect in intergroup discrimination. *British Journal of Social and Clinical Psychology, 18,* 371–83.

———. (1981). Superordinate goals and intergroup behavior: The effect of role ambiguity and status on intergroup attitudes and task performance. *European Journal of Social Psychology, 17,* 131–42.

Brown, R. J., and Wade, G. (1987). Superordinate goals and intergoup behavior. The effect of role ambiguity and status on intergroup attitudes and task performance. *European Journal of Social Psychology, 17,* 131–42.

Burnam, M. A., Telles, C. A., Karno, M., Hough, R. L., and Escobar, J. I. (1987). Measurement of acculturation in a community population of Mexican Americans. *Hispanic Journal of the Behavioral Sciences, 9,* 105–30.

Campbell, David T. (1958). Common fate, similarity, and other indices of the status of aggregates of persons as social entities. *Behavioral Science, 3,* 14–25.

Cook, Stuart W. (1984). Cooperative interaction in multi-ethnic contexts. In Norman Miller and Marilynn B. Brewer (Eds.), *Groups in contact: The psychology of desegregation* (pp. 291–302). Orlando, Fla.: Academic Press.

Commins, B., and Lockwood, J. (1978). The effects on intergroup relations of mixing Roman Catholics and Protestants: An experimental investigation. *European Journal of Social Psychology, 8,* 218–19.

Crosbie-Burnett, M. (1984). The centrality of the step relationship: A challenge to family theory and practice. *Family Relations, 33,* 459–63.

Davis, J. A., and Smith, T. W. (1994). *General social surveys, 1972–1994: Cumulative codebook.* Chicago: National Opinion Research Center.

Deschamps, J. C., and Doise, Willem. (1978). Crossed-category membership in intergroup relations. In Henri Tajfel (Ed.), *Differentiation between social groups* (pp. 141–58). London: Academic Press.

Desforges, D. M., Lord, Charles G., Ramsey, S. L., Mason, J. A., Van Leeuwen, M. D., and Lepper, Mark R. (1991). Effects of structured cooperative contact on changing negative attitudes toward stigmatized groups. *Journal of Personality and Social Psychology, 60,* 531–44.

Devine, Patricia, and Elliot, Andrew (1996). Are racial stereotypes really fading? The Princeton trilogy revisited. *Personality and Social Psychology Bulletin, 21,* 1139–50.

Dion, Kenneth L. (1974). A cognitive model of ingroup-outgroups bias. Paper presented at the American Psychological Association Meeting, New Orleans (September).

Doise, Willem. (1978). *Groups and individuals: Explanations in social psychology.* Cambridge: Cambridge University Press.

Dovidio, John F., Brigham, J., Johnson, B. T., and Gaertner, Samuel L. (1996). Stereotyping, prejudice, and discrimination. In N. Macrae, C. Stangor, and Miles Hewstone (Eds.), *Foundations of stereotypes and stereotyping* (pp. 276–319). New York: Guilford.

Dovidio, John F., and Gaertner, Samuel L. (1983). The effects of sex, status, and ability on helping behavior. *Journal of Applied Social Psychology, 13,* 191–205.

———. (1986). Prejudice, discrimination, and racism: Historical trends and contemporary approaches. In John F. Dovidio and Samuel L. Gaertner (Eds.), *Prejudice, discrimination, and racism* (pp. 1–34). Orlando, Fla.: Academic Press.

———. (1991). Changes in the nature and expression of racial prejudice. In H. Knopke, J. Norrell, and R. Rogers (Eds.), *Opening doors: An appraisal of race relations in contemporary America* (pp. 201–41). Tuscaloosa: University of Alabama Press.

———. (1996). Affirmative action, unintentional racial biases, and intergroup relations. *Journal of Social Issues, 52*(4), 51–76.

———. (1998). On the nature of contemporary prejudice: The causes, consequences, and challenges of aversive racism. In Jennifer Eberhardt and Susan T. Fiske (Eds.), *Racism: The problem and the response* (pp. 3–32). Newbury Park, Calif.: Sage.

Dovidio, John F., Gaertner, Samuel L., Anastasio, P. A., and Sanitioso, R. (1992).

Cognitive and motivational bases of bias: The implications of aversive racism for attitudes toward Hispanics. In S. Knouse, P. Rosenfeld, and A. Culbertson (Eds.), *Hispanics in the workplace* (pp. 75–106). Newbury Park, Calif.: Sage.

Dovidio, John F., Gaertner, Samuel L., and Bachman, B. A. (in press). Racial bias in organizations: The role of group processes in its causes and cures. In M. Turner (Ed.), *Groups at work: Advances in theory and research.* Hillsdale, N.J.: Erlbaum.

Dovidio, John F., Gaertner, Samuel L., Isen, A. M., and Lowrance, R. (1995). Group representations and intergroup bias: Positive affect, similarity, and group size. *Personality and Social Psychology Bulletin, 21,* 856–65.

Dovidio, John F., Gaertner, Samuel L., and Validzic, A. (1998). Intergroup bias: Status, differentiation, and a Common Ingroup Identity. *Journal of Personality and Social Psychology, 75,* 109–20.

Dovidio, John F., Gaertner, Samuel L., Validzic, A., Matoka, K., Johnson, B., and Frazier, S. (1997). Extending the benefits of recategorization: Evaluations, self-disclosure, and helping. *Journal of Experimental Social Psychology, 33,* 401–20.

Dovidio, John F., Mann, J. A., and Gaertner, Samuel L. (1989). Resistance to affirmative action: The implications of aversive racism. In F. A. Blanchard and F. J. Crosby (Eds.), *Affirmative action in perspective* (pp. 83–102). New York: Springer-Verlag.

Dovidio, John, Smith, Jennifer, Donnella, Amy, and Gaertner, Samuel (1997). Racial attitudes and the death penalty. *Journal of Applied Social Psychology, 27,* 1468–87.

Ellemers, N., Doosje, B., van Knippenberg, A., and Wilke, H. (1992). Status protection in high status minority groups. *European Journal of Social Psychology, 22,* 123–240.

Feagin, J. R., and Feagin, C. B. (1996). *Racial and ethnic relations.* 5th ed. Upper Saddle River, N.J.: Prentice-Hall.

Feagin, J. R., and Sikes, M. P. (1994). *Living with racism: The black middle-class experience.* Boston: Beacon Press.

Ferdman, Bernardo M. (1989). Affirmative action and the challenge of the color-blind perspective. In F. A. Blanchard and F. J. Crosby (Eds.), *Affirmative action in perspective* (pp. 169–76). New York: Springer-Verlag.

———. (1995). Cultural identity and diversity in organizations: Bridging the gap between group differences and individual uniqueness. In M. M. Chemers, S. Oskamp, and M. A. Costanzo (Eds.), *Diversity in organizations: New perspectives for a changing workplace* (pp. 37–61). Thousand Oaks, Calif.: Sage.

Ferguson, C. K., and Kelley, H. H. (1964). Significant factors in over-evaluation of own groups' products. *Journal of Abnormal and Social Psychology, 69,* 223–28.

Fiske, Susan T., and Neuberg, S. L. (1990). A continuum model of impression formation: From category-based to individuating processes as a function of information, motivation, and attention. In M. P. Zanna (Ed.), *Advances in experimental social psychology* (vol. 23, pp. 1–74). San Diego: Academic Press.

Fiske, Susan, and Taylor, Shelley. (1991). *Social cognition* (2nd ed.). New York: McGraw-Hill.

Fordham, S. (1988). Racelessness as a factor in black students' school success: Pragmatic strategy or pyrrhic victory? *Harvard Educational Review, 58,* 54–58.

Gaertner, Samuel L., and Dovidio, John F. (1986). The aversive form of racism. In John F. Dovidio and Samuel L. Gaertner (Eds.), *Prejudice, discrimination, and racism* (pp. 61–89). Orlando, Fla.: Academic Press.

Gaertner, Samuel L., Dovidio, John F., Anastasio, P. A., Bachman, B. A., and Rust, M. C. (1993). The Common Ingroup Identity Model: Recategorization and the reduction of intergroup bias. In W. Stroebe and Miles Hewstone (Eds.), *European review of social psychology* (vol. 4, pp. 1–26). London: Wiley.

Gaertner, Samuel L., Dovidio, John F., and Bachman, B. A. (1996). Revisiting the contact hypothesis: The induction of a common ingroup identity. *International Journal of Intercultural Relations, 20*(3, 4), 271–90.

Gaertner, Samuel L., Dovidio, John F., Banker, Brenda S., Rust, M. C., Nier, Jason A., and Ward, Christine M. (1997). Does pro-whiteness necessarily mean anti-blackness? In M. Fine, L. Powell, Lois Weis, and M. Wong (Eds.), *Off White* (pp. 167–78). New York: Routledge.

Gaertner, Samuel L., Mann, J. A., Dovidio, John F., Murrell, A. J., and Pomare, M. (1990). How does cooperation reduce intergroup bias? *Journal of Personality and Social Psychology, 59,* 692–704.

Gaertner, Samuel L., Mann, J. A., Murrell, A. J., and Dovidio, John F. (1989). Reduction of intergroup bias: The benefits of recategorization. *Journal of Personality and Social Psychology, 57,* 239–49.

Gaertner, Samuel L., Rust, M. C., and Dovidio, John F. (1997). The value of a superordinate identity for reducing intergroup bias. Unpublished paper, University of Delaware.

Gaertner, Samuel L., Rust, M. C., Dovidio, John F., Bachman, B. A., and Anastasio, P. A. (1994). The contact hypothesis: The role of a common ingroup identity on reducing intergroup bias. *Small Groups Research, 25*(2), 224–49.

———. (1996). The contact hypothesis: The role of a common ingroup identity in reducing intergroup bias among majority and minority group members. In J. L. Nye and A. M. Brower (Eds.), *What's social about social cognition?* (pp. 230–360). Newbury Park, Calif.: Sage.

Gordon, M. M. (1978). *Human nature, class, and ethnicity.* New York: Oxford University Press.

Hacker, A. (1995). *Two nations: Black and white, separate, hostile, unequal* (2nd Ed.). New York: Ballantine.

Hamilton, David L., and Sherman, J. W. (1994). Stereotypes. In R. S. Wyer and T. K. Srull (Eds.), *Handbook of social cognition* (2nd ed., vol. 2, pp. 1–68). Hillsdale, N.J.: Erlbaum.

Hamilton, D. L., and Trolier, T. K. Stereotypes and stereotyping: An overview of the cognitive approach (pp. 127–63). In J. F. Dividio and S. L. Gaertner (Eds.), *Prejudice, discrimination, and racism.* Orlando, Florida: Academic Press.

Hewstone, Miles. (1990). The "ultimate attribution error"? A review of the literature on intergroup causal attribution. *European Journal of Social Psychology, 20,* 311–35.

———. (1996). Contact and categorization: Social psychological interventions to change intergroup relations. In N. Macrae, C. Stangor, and Miles Hewstone (Eds.), *Foundations of stereotypes and stereotyping* (pp. 323–68). New York: Guilford.

Hewstone, Miles, and Brown, Rupert J. (1986). Contact is not enough: An intergroup perspective on the contact hypothesis. In Miles Hewstone and Rupert Brown (Eds.), *Contact and conflict in intergroup encounters* (pp. 1–44). Oxford: Blackwell.

Hornsey, M., and Hogg, Michael. (1996). Structural differentiation within groups: A test of three models of the effects of category salience on subgroup relations. Unpublished paper, University of Queensland, Australia.

Hornstein, H. A. (1976). *Cruelty and kindness: A new look at aggression and altruism.* Englewood Cliffs, N.J.: Prentice-Hall.

Howard, J. M., and Rothbart, Myron. (1980). Social categorization for ingroup and outgroup behavior. *Journal of Personality and Social Psychology, 38,* 301–10.

Huo, Y. J., Smith, H. H., Tyler, T. R., and Lind, A. E. (1996). Superordinate identification, subgroup identification, and justice concerns: Is separatism the problem? Is assimilation the answer? *Psychological Science, 7,* 40–45.

Johnson, David W., and Johnson, Frank P. (1975). *Joining together: Group theory and group skills.* Englewood Cliffs, N.J.: Prentice-Hall.

Johnson, David W., Johnson, Frank P., and Maruyama, G. (1983). Interdependence and interpersonal attraction among heterogeneous and homogeneous individuals: A theoretical formulation and a meta-analysis of the research. *Review of Educational Research, 52,* 5–54.

Jones, James M. (1997). *Prejudice and racism.* 2nd ed. New York: McGraw-Hill.

Karlins, Marvin, Coffman, Thomas, and Walters, Gary (1969). On the fading of social stereotypes: Studies in three generations of college students. *Journal of Personality and Social Psychology, 13,* 1–16.

Karpinski, A., and Von Hippel, William. (1996). The role of the linguistic intergroup bias in expectancy maintenance. *Social Cognition, 14,* 141–63.

Kovel, Joel. (1970). White racism: A psychohistory. New York: Pantheon.

Kramer, Roderick M., and Brewer, Marilynn B. (1984). Effects of group identity on resource utilization in a simulated commons dilemma. *Journal of Personality and Social Psychology, 46,* 1044–57.

LaFromboise, T., Coleman, H. L. K., and Gerton, J. (1993). Psychological impact of biculturalism: Evidence and theory. *Psychological Bulletin, 114,* 395–412.

Maas, A., Ceccarelli, R., and Rudin, S. (1996). Linguistic intergroup bias: Evidence for ingroup-protective motivation. *Journal of Personality and Social Psychology, 71,* 512–26.

Maass, A., Salvi, D., Arcuri, L., and Semin, G. R. (1989). Language use in intergroup contexts: The linguistic intergroup bias. *Journal of Personality and Social Psychology, 57,* 981–93.

Macrae, C. N., Milne, A. B., and Bodenhausen, Galen V. (1994). Stereotypes as energy-saving devices: A peek inside the cognitive toolbox. *Journal of Personality and Social Psychology, 66,* 37–47.

Manning, Frederick, and Ingraham, Larry (1983). Drug "overdoses" among U.S. soldiers in Europe. *International Journal of the Addictions, 18,* 89–98.

Marcus-Newhall, Amy, Miller, Norman, Holtz, R., and Brewer, Marilynn B. (1993). Cross-cutting category membership with role assignment: A means of reducing intergroup bias. *British Journal of Social Psychology, 322,* 125–46.

Miller, Norman, Brewer, Marilynn B., and Edwards, K. (1985). Cooperative interaction in desegregated settings: A laboratory analog. *Journal of Social Issues, 41*(3), 63–75.

Mottola, Gary. (1996). The effects of relative group status on expectations of merger success. Ph.D. dissertation, University of Delaware.

Mottola, Gary R., Bachman, Betty, Gaertner, Samuel L., and Dovidio, John F. (1997). How groups merge: The effects of merger integration patterns on expectations of organizational commitment. *Journal of Applied Social Psychology, 27,* 1335–58.

Mullen, Brian, and Copper, C. (1994). The relation between group cohesiveness and performance: An integration. *Psychological Bulletin, 115,* 210–27.

Mullen, Brian, and Hu, L. T. (1989). Perceptions of ingroup and outgroup variability: A meta-analytic integration. *Basic and Applied Social Psychology, 10,* 233–52.

Murrell, Audrey J., Dietz-Uhler, Beth L., Dovidio, John F., Gaertner, Samuel L., and Drout, C. E. (1994). Aversive racism and resistance to affirmative action: Perceptions of justice are not necessarily color-blind. *Basic and Applied Social Psychology, 5*(1, 2), 71–86.

Myrdal, Gunnar. (1944). *An American dilemma: The Negro problem and modern democracy.* New York: Harper.

Nier, Jason A., Gaertner, Samuel L., Banker, Brenda S., Ward, Christine M. (1999). *Changing interracial evaluations and behavior.* Unpublished manuscript, University of Delaware.

Nier, Jason, Rust, M. C., Ward, Christine M., and Gaertner, Samuel L. (1996). Changing interracial attitudes and behavior: The effects of a common ingroup identity. Poster presentation at the annual Eastern Psychological Association Convention, Philadelphia (March).

Ogbu, J. U., and Matute-Bianchi, M. A. (1986). Understanding sociocultural factors: Knowledge, identity, and social adjustment. In California State Department of Education, Bilingual Education Office, *Beyond language: Social and cultural factors in schooling* (pp. 73–142). Sacramento: California State University at Los Angeles, Evaluation, Dissemination, and Assessment Center.

Park, Bernadette, and, Rothbart, Myron. (1982). Perception of out-group homogeneity and levels of social categorization: Memory for the subordinate attributes of in-group and out-group members. *Journal of Personality and Social Psychology, 42(6),* 1051–68.

Pasquali, E. A. (1985). The impact of acculturation on the eating habits of elderly immigrants: A Cuban example. *Journal of Nutrition for the Elderly, 5,* 27–36.

Perdue, C. W., Dovidio, John F., Gurtman, M. B., and Tyler, R. B. (1990). "Us" and "them": Social categorization and the process of intergroup bias. *Journal of Personality and Social Psychology, 59,* 475–86.

Pettigrew, Thomas (1981). The ultimate attribution error: Extending Allport's cognitive analysis of prejudice. *Personality and Social Psychology Bulletin, 5,* 461–76.

———. (1997). Generalized intergroup contact effects on prejudice. *Personality and Social Psychology Bulletin, 23,* 173–85.

———. (1998). Intergroup contact theory. *Annual Review of Psychology, 49,* 65–85.

Piliavin, Jane A., Dovidio, John F., Gaertner, Samuel L., and Clark, Russell D., III. (1981). *Emergency intervention.* New York: Academic Press.

Rabbie, J. M. (1982). The effects of intergroup competition and cooperation on intragroup and intergroup relationships. In V. J. Derlega and J. Grzelak (Eds.), *Cooperation and helping behavior: Theories and research* (pp. 128–51). New York: Academic Press.

Ramirez, A. (1988). Racism toward Hispanics: A culturally monolithic society. In P. Katz and D. Taylor (Eds.), *Towards the elimination of racism: Profiles in controversy* (pp. 137–57). New York: Plenum.

Rodriguez-Scheel, J. (1980). An investigation of the components of social identity for a Detroit sample. Unpublished paper, Occidental College, Psychology Department.

Rothbart, Myron, and John, O. P. (1985). Social categorization and behavioral

episodes: A cognitive analysis of the effects of intergroup contact. *Journal of Social Issues, 41*(3), 81–104.
Rust, Mary C. (1996). Social identity and social categorization. Ph.D. dissertation, University of Delaware.
Schofield, Janet W. (1986). Causes and consequences of the color-blind perspective. In John F. Dovidio and Samuel L. Gaertner (Eds.), *Prejudice, discrimination, and racism* (pp. 231–53). Orlando, Fla.: Academic Press.
Schuman, H., Steeh, C., and Bobo, L. (1985). *Racial attitudes in America: Trends and interpretations.* Cambridge, Mass.: Harvard University Press.
Semin, G. R., and Fiedler, K. (1988). The cognitive function of linguistic categories in describing persons: Social cognition and language. *Journal of Personality and Social Pyshology, 54,* 558–68.
Sherif, M., and Sherif, C. W. (1969). *Social psychology.* New York: Harper and Row.
Skinner, M., and Stephenson, G. M. (1981). The effects of intergroup comparisons on the polarization of opinions. *Current Psychological Research, 1,* 49–61.
Smith, Heather J., and Tyler, T. R. (1996). Justice and power: When will justice concerns encourage the advantaged to support policies which redistribute economic resources and the disadvantaged to willingly obey the law? *European Journal of Social Psychology, 26,* 171–200.
Stephan, Walter G., and Stephan, C. W. (1986). Habla ingles?: The effects of language translation on simulated juror decisions. *Journal of Applied Social Psychology, 16,* 577–89.
———. (1996). *Intergroup relations.* Madison, Wisc.: Brown and Benchmark.
Sumner, W. G. (1906). *Folkways.* New York: Ginn.
Swim, Janet K., Aikin, K. J., Hall, W. S., and Hunter, B. A. (1995). Sexism and racism: Old-fashioned and modern prejudices. *Journal of Personality and Social Psychology, 68,* 119–214.
Tajfel, Henri. (1969). Cognitive aspects of prejudice. *Journal of Social Issues, 25*(4), 79–97.
Tajfel, Henri, Billig, M. G., Bundy, R. F., and Flament, C. (1971). Social categorization and intergroup behavior. *European Journal of Social Psychology, 1,* 149–77.
Tajfel, Henri, and Turner, John. (1979). An integrative theory of intergroup conflict. In W. G. Austin and S. Worchel (Eds.), *The social psychology of intergroup relations* (pp. 33–48). Monterey, Calif.: Brooks/Cole.
Turner, John C. (1975). Social comparison and social identity: Some prospects for intergroup behavior. *European Journal of Social Psychology, 5,* 5–34.
———. (1981). The experimental social psychology of intergroup behavior. In John C. Turner and H. Giles (Eds.), *Intergroup behavior* (pp. 66–101). Chicago: University of Chicago Press.
———. (1985). Social categorization and the self-concept: A social cognitive theory of group behavior. In E. J. Lawler (Ed.), *Advances in group processes* (vol. 2, pp. 77–122). Greenwich, Conn.: JAI Press.
Vanbeselaere, N. (1987). The effects of dichotomous and crossed social categorization upon intergroup discrimination. *European Journal of Social Psychology, 17,* 143–56.
Wilder, D. A. (1978). Reduction of intergroup discrimination through individuation of the outgroup. *Journal of Personality and Social Psychology, 36,* 1361–74.

———. (1981). Perceiving persons as a group: Categorization and intergroup relations. In David L. Hamilton (Ed.), *Cognitive processes in stereotyping and intergroup behavior* (pp. 213–57). Hillsdale, N.J.: Erlbaum.
———. (1984). Predictions of belief homogeneity and similarity following social categorization. *British Journal of Social Psychology, 23,* 323–33.
———. (1986). Social categorization: Implications for creation and reduction of intergroup bias. In L. Berkowitz (Ed.), *Advances in experimental social psychology* (vol. 1, pp. 291–355). Orlando, Fla.: Academic Press.

# 7

# SOME CONSEQUENCES OF A BELIEF IN GROUP ESSENCE: THE CATEGORY DIVIDE HYPOTHESIS

*Dale T. Miller and Deborah A. Prentice*

When two people discover that they have strongly opposing beliefs about an issue of great importance, they typically have one of two reactions: either they approach each other and initiate a dialogue in the hopes of better understanding and possibly persuading one another, or they actively withdraw from one another and, if forced to interact, scrupulously avoid discussing the source of their disagreement. These two reactions are so strikingly and significantly different in both their short- and long-term consequences that it becomes important to understand when one as opposed to the other will occur.[1] This chapter attempts to answer this question.

Our analysis begins by positing that an important determinant of whether disagreeing parties will approach or avoid one another is their explanation of the disagreement. When people find themselves at odds with someone, whether over beliefs and values, likes and dislikes, or reactions and feelings, they naturally wonder: Why do we differ? How deep is our difference? Is our difference resolvable? Their answers to these questions will determine to a considerable extent whether they choose to approach or avoid one another. But what determines how the two parties will answer these questions? One important determinant, we propose, is whether they see themselves as belonging to the same or a different social category. When they belong to different ethnic, religious, gender, or cultural categories, they have available an explanation for their disagreement—cultural difference—that is not available to same-group disputants. For example, a man and a woman who ask themselves the question "Why do we see it so differently?" have a compelling answer staring them in the face. They belong to different gender groups.

Because homogeneous and heterogeneous pairs are disposed to explain interpersonal disagreements differently, the same disagreement will provoke very different reactions in the two kinds of pairs. Members of a homogeneous pair are likely to react to the discovery of disagreement by approaching one another. The ultimate outcome of their disagreement may be a straining of their personal relationship, but this outcome will not occur without at least some dialogue. In a disagreement between members of a heterogeneous pair, the opposite dynamic will occur. Rather than approach and have a dialogue, the two are likely to react with avoidance and silence.

## CULTURAL DIFFERENCE AND ATTRIBUTIONAL AMBIGUITY

In a general vein, disagreements between members of different social categories produce attributional ambiguity. On the one hand, the disagreement may reflect a personal difference between the two individuals that is independent of group membership; on the other hand, it may reflect a broader difference between the cultures or perspectives of the groups to which the two individuals belong. This causal ambiguity creates the possibility of two attributional errors.

First, the disputants may fail to recognize when a difference between them reflects a general cultural difference, attributing it instead to personal idiosyncrasy. Every cultural anthropologist (and virtually every comedian) tells at least one amusing story about confusion arising from cultural misinterpretation. Indeed, the growing incidence of cultural contact worldwide has spawned a torrent of books on the problems (many of them far from humorous) wrought by cultural miscommunication (see, for example, Brislin 1990; Brislin and Yoshida 1994; Cohen 1991).

It is certainly true that people can be led astray when they interpret a difference between themselves and someone from a different culture as though its meaning were the same as it would be if it occurred between themselves and someone from their own culture. As an example, imagine an American businesswoman (call her Nancy) who finds herself in a serious conversation with a business associate who remains silent and impassive as she speaks. No matter how attentive and responsive Nancy is when her associate speaks, her associate continues to be silent and unresponsive when Nancy herself speaks. If Nancy is like most of us, this experience will frustrate her and lead her to wonder why the other person is behaving so differently from her: "Is he rude, or is he just not interested in me or what I have to say?" Witnesses to the interaction could be expected to react similarly. And this reaction would not be unreasonable if the other person were a fellow American. It would be unreasonable, however, if the other person were from a culture where the norms guiding conversational behavior are different from American norms. The inferences that Nancy (or any American observer) drew about the meaning of the differences could be seriously in error. This would be the case, for example, if the other person were a Finn, for Finns convey attention and encouragement to an interlocutor, not by active verbal or nonverbal acknowledgment that the message is being heard, but by remaining completely silent when he or she is speaking (Smith and Bond 1994).

Second, and of primary interest in this chapter, disputants can mistake a personal difference for a broader group or cultural difference. This error can be quite costly, for once we label a difference as group-based, we tend to assume that it is immutable—that the other person is unlikely ever to see things our way and that we are unlikely ever to see things his or her way. The presumption of immutability, in turn, will inhibit efforts to seek consensus or mutual understanding, leading us instead to find a way to live with the difference, possibly by fashioning a compromise or by disengaging from the relationship. Thus, if a disagreeing man and woman were to conclude that their difference of opinion is gendered, irrespective of whether this is true, they could be expected to be neither curious about one another's thinking nor optimistic that they could change it.

The message of the foregoing analysis is both clear and troubling: the attributional account that members of different social categories generate for any particular disagreement between themselves is much more likely to drive them apart than is the attributional account that members of the same social category generate for the same disagreement. The most serious consequence of this difference in accounts is that interpersonal differences will seem more immutable and more unbridgeable when they occur between members of different groups than between members of the same group. A difference between individuals from different groups will appear to be not just a difference but a divide.

We should note parenthetically here that the intergroup dynamic we have sketched, for all its undesirable aspects, does not include one of the most problematic aspects of intergroup relations: open conflict and hostility. Although long-standing enmity, hostility, and distrust are commonplace in many intergroup contexts, they are neither an inevitable nor a central component of the phenomenon we discuss. Our analysis is concerned with self-segregation, not with open conflict; it seeks to explain why members of different groups drift apart, agreeing to disagree as it were, not why they engage in open hostility. Multicultural contact may or may not be characterized by open conflict and hostility, but it is almost always characterized by self-segregation and avoidance.

Appearances to the contrary, these two errors—mistaking a group difference for a personal difference and mistaking a personal difference for a group difference—are neither oppositional nor contradictory in their implications; in fact, their thrust is quite different. In one case, the problem lies with the meaning imputed to another's actions—for example, inferring rudeness rather than politeness from an interlocutor's silence. In the other case, the problem lies with the cultural generality inferred from a self-other difference—that is, inferring a cultural difference rather than merely a personal difference from a disagreement between oneself and a member of another cultural group.

## PERCEIVING SOCIAL GROUPS AS SOCIAL KINDS

What we term the category divide hypothesis—that disagreeing parties from different social groups will be disposed to attribute their disagreement to group difference—raises two questions. First, why is a difference between members of different groups so readily attributed to a group difference? True, a between-group interpersonal difference, unlike a within-group difference, can be attributed to group membership, but it is not clear why this attribution should dominate the other possible attributions. Second, why does locating a between-group interpersonal difference in group membership render the difference less mutable? Answers to both of these questions, we propose, can be found in people's representations of social groups.

Recent work in psychology and related disciplines has documented the human tendency to see at least some groups of people as *kinds* of people (Appiah 1990; Atran 1990; Eberhardt and Randall 1997; Goldberg 1993; Hirschfeld 1996; Medin 1989; Medin and Ortony 1989; Rothbart and Taylor 1982; Yzerbyt, Rocher, and Schadron 1997). People believe that certain groups (for example, racial and gender categories) have essences that differentiate them from other groups and that make them who they are (Atran 1990; Medin 1989). Furthermore, people act as though a group's essence or underlying nature is "a part of the objective physical world waiting to be discovered" (Rothbart and Taylor 1982, 17).

Of course, the existence of a humankind-creating module does not mean that all human groups trigger its operation (Gelman and Hirschfeld, in press; Hirschfeld 1996). Not all human aggregates are viewed as social groups (Hogg and Abrams 1988), and not all social groups are viewed as social kinds. Specifying when a social group will or will not be a social kind is not easy. One criterion that has been proposed for the definition of a social kind is unalterability of group membership; members of groups with essences cannot cease being members of the group (Rothbart and Taylor 1982; Yzerbyt, Rocher, and Schadron 1997). By this criterion, ascribed categories, like race and gender, would clearly constitute social kinds; achieved categories would not. However, even this distinction sometimes blurs. For example, consider the fact that Japanese Americans were placed in internment camps during World War II, whereas German and Italian Americans were not: it appears that the perceived essential properties of the Germans and Italians could be lost when they became American citizens, whereas those of the Japanese could not.

The assumption that different social groups have different essences provides us with a ready-made explanation for any difference that we observe between members of those groups (Hoffman and Hurst 1990). When a difference occurs between people who belong to groups that we believe to have different essences, we infer that the observed difference signifies a deeper group difference (Hirschfeld 1996; Martin and Parker 1995). Of course, not all disagreements between individuals from groups perceived to have different essences are seen as reflecting those different essences. To the extent that individuals have evidence of intragroup variability on a particular dimension, they are less likely to locate a difference between themselves and a member of the other group in their respective group essences. For example, a man who prefers Coke and a woman who prefers Pepsi will not see their soda preferences as gendered to the extent that they know a number of Coke-preferring women and Pepsi-preferring men. Nevertheless, evidence that not all differences correlate with social category will not diminish the belief that the two groups have different essences (Martin and Parker 1995). Men and women know that there are many dimensions on which there is as much within-gender as between-gender variability, but this knowledge does not prevent them from assuming that a difference between themselves and a member of the opposite sex on a novel dimension reflects a difference in gender essence. Moreover, even when men and women know that there is variability within their sex on a particular dimension (for example, soda preference), they still may be disposed to see disagreement on that dimension differently when it involves a member of the opposite sex.

It is important to note that the belief that groups differ in their essences does not necessitate knowledge of what those differences are. The idea that there are intrinsic differences between groups of humans can exist independently of any specific content beliefs about those differences (Allport 1954; Appiah 1990; Goldberg 1993). Thus, one can believe that the essence of another group differs from that of one's own without having any preconceptions about how the difference manifests itself. The belief that two groups have different essences simply means that the belief holder displays a readiness to attribute any observed difference between members of the two groups to a more fundamental difference.

It is true, of course, that interpersonal differences frequently conform to preconceptions (for example, racial differences in reactions to the verdict in the O. J. Simpson case). Moreover, it is also true that behaviors that conform to expectations or stereotypes are more likely to be attributed to an underlying disposition of the actor (see Bodenhausen and Wyer 1985; Fiske 1997). But the tendency to view differences between members of different groups as less mutable than differences between members of the same group is not reducible to a difference in expectations. A difference that was expected may seem more immutable than one that was not, but even unexpected differences seem more immutable if they occur between members of different groups than between members of the same group. A difference between members of different groups, even if unpredicted, could still be interpreted as stemming from a difference in essence, whereas the same is not true for a difference between members of the same group, who are assumed to share the same essence.

In fact, stereotypes may follow from as often as they guide the tendency to essentialize between-group differences, for once the inference is made that a difference between two people stems from their being different kinds of people, it is difficult to resist the inference that the observed behaviors are typical of those kinds of people. Indeed, previous research has established that behavior is most likely to be taken as characteristic of a group (one's own included) when it contrasts with the behavior of another group (Hogg and Turner 1987). Thus, although beliefs about groups certainly influence the interpretation of a difference between representatives of those groups, the reverse is also true: interpretation of a difference between representatives of different groups influences beliefs about their respective groups.

## RELATED THEORETICAL PERSPECTIVES

Before considering empirical support for the category divide hypothesis, we will examine the relation of this hypothesis to others pertaining to intergroup relations. This examination is important because the category divide hypothesis, although it takes a novel perspective on intergroup relations, does share a number of assumptions, and even some predictions, with other theoretical accounts.

## The Contact Hypothesis

The hypothesis that contact between members of different racial, ethnic, or cultural groups fosters positive intergroup attitudes has been part of the received wisdom of social psychology for almost fifty years. Empirical tests of the hypothesis have specified a laundry list of conditions that must be true for it to hold (see Amir 1969; Stephan 1985): the contact must involve cooperative activities; the participants must have equal status; they must also be similar on nonstatus dimensions; they must hold no negative views of each other at the outset; the outcome of the interaction must be positive; and so on. The contact hypothesis thus provides a very broad, outcome-focused perspective on how contact can promote positive intergroup relations (Brewer and Miller 1984, 1988; Cook, 1984; Gaertner et al. 1993).

The category divide hypothesis, by contrast, is a much narrower theory, focusing on one particular psychological mechanism that determines whether contact has positive or negative consequences. Contact between members of distinct social categories is less easily sustained than contact between equally diverse individuals from the same social category because the inevitable disagreements or differences in perspective that arise are attributed, in the former case, to group membership—a highly immutable and deeply rooted source. Still, the two hypotheses converge on virtually all of their predictions: for example, the category divide hypothesis, like the contact hypothesis, argues that contact must involve cooperative activities so as to reduce the possibility that alienating disagreements will arise.

## Ultimate Attribution Error

Pettigrew (1979) proposed that an observer's explanations for the desirable and undesirable behaviors of an actor are influenced by whether the actor is a member of the ingroup or the outgroup. Specifically, Pettigrew posited that observers show the greatest readiness to make an internal attribution in the case of either an ingroup member performing a desirable behavior or an outgroup member performing an undesirable behavior, and that they show the greatest readiness to make an external attribution in either the case of an outgroup member performing a desirable behavior or an ingroup member performing an undesirable behavior. Pettigrew referred to this ingroup-enhancing attributional asymmetry as the "ultimate attribution error" (for a recent review, see Hewstone 1990).

The ultimate attribution error and the category divide hypothesis, although superficially similar, differ in two important respects. First, although both invoke attributional processes as a basis for intergroup conflict, they diverge in the targets of those attributions. The ultimate attribution error points to the different explanations people give for the similar (either desirable or undesirable) behaviors of ingroup and outgroup members (Islam and Hewstone 1993; Weber 1994); the category divide hypothesis points to the unitary (group-focused) explanation people give for the dissimilar behaviors of ingroup and outgroup members. The category divide hypothesis is silent on the attributional tendencies of people confronted with similarly acting individuals, speaking only to the attributional tendencies of people confronted with difference. Second, the category divide hypothesis does not restrict itself to situations involving ingroup-outgroup differences. It predicts that the tendency of observers to attribute dissimilar behavior to the dispositions of the actors will occur whenever the actors are members of two distinct groups, whether ingroup or outgroup. The ultimate attribution error formulation makes no predictions about the attributional tendencies of people confronting members from two distinct, neutrally evaluated outgroups.

## Belief Incongruence Theory

A theoretical perspective closer to our own is Rokeach's belief incongruence theory (Rokeach 1979; Rokeach and Mezei 1966). Its central tenet is that people do not reject others simply because they belong to different cultural groups; rather, they reject them because they believe that members of different cultural groups must have attitudes, values, and beliefs that are different from their own. The difference in Rokeach's case is assumed rather than actual—there is no need for members of different groups to disagree on anything for the assumption to be invoked. This, then, is the major difference between Rokeach's view and our own: Rokeach argues that a preexisting and enduring assumption of cultural difference impedes social contact between groups (for a review of the empirical evidence, see Insko, Nacoste, and Moe 1983); the category divide hypothesis argues that when groups have contact with each other, cultural differences serve as a ready-made explanation for any disagreement or discomfort that arises, whether expected or not.

Although the intergroup effects on which we and Rokeach focus are different, the underlying psychology may be the same. Both effects—the tendency to expect different beliefs from members of different groups and the tendency to interpret belief differences (whether expected or not) one way when they occur within groups and another way when they occur between groups—may reflect a belief in group essence. When racial categories are made salient, as they are when one has (or even anticipates having) an interaction with a member of a different race, people may be primed to think of group essence. Thinking of group essence may dispose them, in turn, to think of group difference. This chain of associations could lead them both to expect groups to differ and to interpret even unexpected differences as based in group essence. In brief, perception of intergroup difference leads people to think about group essence, and thinking about group essence leads people to predict intergroup difference.

Despite various points of divergence, then, the belief incongruence theory and the category divide hypothesis share a number of assumptions, including the assumption that the difficulty that arises between members of different groups is often found in superficial cognitive processing biases rather than in strongly entrenched feelings of racial antipathy.

## Self-Categorization Theory

A final perspective closely related to ours is self-categorization theory (Turner 1982; Turner et al. 1987). A central claim of this theory is that viewing individuals as belonging to a group or a social category greatly affects not only our own view of them but their view of themselves. The relevance of self-categorization theory to the category divide hypothesis becomes clear when we consider the means by which category membership or social identity is most commonly manipulated in empirical tests of the theory—as the instantiation of an outgroup. By making an outgroup salient, or simply by contrasting any outgroups, the social identity of the target groups is made salient.

According to self-categorization theory, one consequence of thinking about members of a group in terms of their social identity is a view of them as more similar to one another (see, for example, Doise et al. 1972; Haslam et al. 1995, 1996). For example, a man is seen as more typically male when he is characterized as a male, and he is more likely to be characterized as a male when women are also in the context. The reasoning behind the category divide hypothesis is similar. It, too, claims that a man is more likely to think of himself as male when women are present, and that he is more likely to attribute any divergence between his behavior and that of a woman to a more general male-female difference.

The major difference between self-categorization theory and the category divide hypothesis lies in their accounts of why disagreement with a person from another group not only makes one's own group and the other's seem more homogeneous but also makes oneself and the other seem more typical or representative of the respective groups. From the perspective of self-categorization theory, both of these phenomena result from a shift in the representation of the person, from an individual with a distinct personal identity to a member of a category sharing a social identity. According to the category divide hypothesis, these phenomena also result from a shift in the representation of the person, but in this case from an individual to a kind of person, one who shares an essence with other members of that kind. Self-categorization theory claims that group members share an identity; the category divide hypothesis claims that they share an essence.

This distinction between essence and identity leads the category divide hypothesis to make some novel predictions. In particular, the concept of group essence provides an account of why the discovery of a difference between members of different groups leads observers to see the individuals' respective positions, and hence the difference between them, as less mutable than the discovery of the same difference between members of the same group. Specifically, the difference is seen as less mutable because it is seen as reflecting something more deeply rooted. Self-categorization theory does not predict that between-group differences will seem especially immutable.

## EMPIRICAL SUPPORT FOR THE CATEGORY DIVIDE HYPOTHESIS

In our empirical work to date, we have sought support for several key predictions of the category divide hypothesis. Specifically, we have tested the claims that a difference between two individuals from different social categories will be perceived as (1) more diagnostic of the propensities of the groups in question (the *generalizability prediction*), (2) greater in magnitude (the *magnitude prediction*), and (3) more immutable (the *mutability prediction*), than the same difference between members of the same social category. The first two studies provided indirect tests of the generalization and mutability predictions, using gender as the category divide. The second two studies tested all three predictions more directly, using both gender and race as category divides.

### Studies 1 and 2

In our first two studies, we examined the inferences that people make regarding the generalizability and mutability of a characteristic that either is constant or varies across gender lines (Prentice and Miller 1996). Thus, the critical comparison in these studies was between a case of gender similarity and a case of gender difference. We expected people to infer from the observation of a target person with a particular propensity that that propensity would be more common in the person's gender category and more difficult to change if they also had evidence of an opposite propensity in a member of the opposite gender. In other words, we expected evidence for a between-group difference to trigger attributions to group essence.

In study 1, we tested the generalizability prediction by introducing a novel and somewhat mysterious difference between a male and a female participant. Specifically, we gave participants a test that allegedly assessed their perceptual style (for details, see Miller, Turnbull, and McFarland 1988). In this test, participants were shown a series of ten slides on which varying numbers of dots appeared and were asked to estimate the number of dots on each slide. The slides were presented extremely quickly, so that participants could only guess at the number of dots on each. In introducing the task, the experimenter explained to participants that the test provided a reliable and valid indication of perceptual style: people tended either to overestimate consistently or to underestimate consistently the number of dots on the slides, and these tendencies reflected "a characteristic way of perceiving the world that is related to a number of other psychological aspects of the person." Following the task, the experimenter scored participants' answers and informed them that the test revealed them to be either an overestimator or an underestimator. Participants were randomly assigned to one of three conditions: in the *gender similarity condition,* participants completed the task in mixed-gender pairs and were told that they had the same perceptual style; in the *gender difference condition,* they completed the task in mixed-gender pairs and were told that they had different perceptual styles; and in the *control condition,* they completed the task individually. After participants received their feedback, they completed a questionnaire on which they were asked to estimate the percentage of male and female students who shared their perceptual style.

The results supported our prediction (see figure 7.1). Participants in the gender difference condition assumed that their perceptual style was more common among their same-gender peers and less common among opposite-gender peers than did participants in either the gender similarity or control conditions. These students apparently inferred that their different perceptual styles were diagnostic of a more general gender difference.

One important aspect of these results is their demonstration that the tendency to infer a group difference from an interpersonal difference does not require that the difference in question fit with prior knowledge or preconceptions. Participants in this study came to the laboratory with no knowledge about perceptual style, and certainly no knowledge

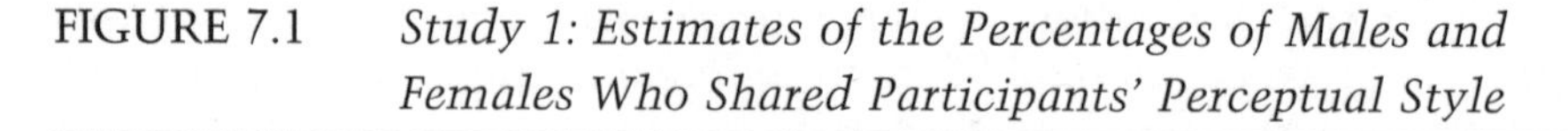

FIGURE 7.1 *Study 1: Estimates of the Percentages of Males and Females Who Shared Participants' Perceptual Style*

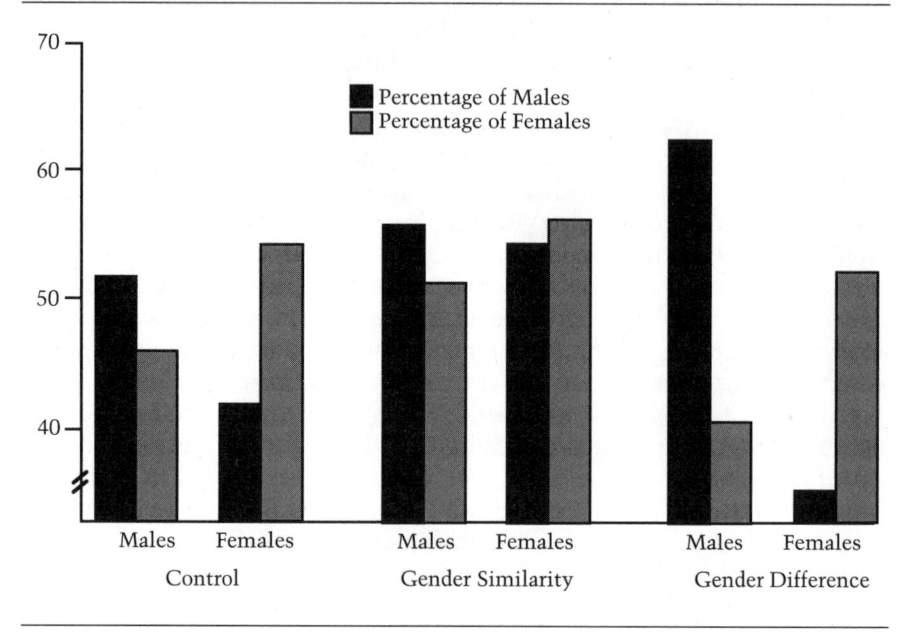


about how males and females might differ in this domain. Indeed, when we asked participants to predict their perceptual style prior to completing the task, their responses (and comments) indicated that they had no preconceptions whatsoever. What they did have, however, was a belief that males and females are fundamentally different (Fuss 1989; Martin and Parker 1995; Taylor 1996), and it was this belief that disposed them, when they encountered a male-female difference on a novel dimension, to infer that it was diagnostic of a more general gender difference. Moreover, they made this inference despite the fact that they surely came into the experiment knowing that there are many nongendered dimensions on which a difference between any particular male-female pair might emerge.

The finding that participants were more willing to generalize from individuals to their gender categories when they had evidence for a cross-gender difference has some interesting implications for stereotyping processes. Essence, it appears, reveals itself in difference. Indeed, the tendency to essentialize between-group differences may be one of the factors underlying the role of perceived covariation, illusory and otherwise, in the development and maintenance of stereotypes (for a review, see Hamilton and Sherman 1989).

Having obtained support for the generalizability prediction, we next sought evidence for the mutability prediction. In study 2, we examined the link between the covariation of a characteristic with category membership and the perceived mutability of that characteristic. Specifically, study 2 tested the prediction that a person's attitude, when consistent with the attitude held by the majority of his or her gender, will seem especially immutable when it also contrasts with the majority attitude held by members of the opposite gender. We based this prediction on the assumption that an attitude that is both widespread within a group and distinctive to that group is likely to be seen as stemming from that group's essence and thus as relatively immutable.

Study 2 presented participants with information about the voting preferences of the members of one particular work unit in a large insurance company that was made up primarily of men. Participants were asked simply to read the information and then to indicate how difficult they thought it would be to change the attitude of any one of the employees in the unit. Three different versions of the information were presented. In every version, the (predominantly male) target group was described identically: 80 percent of them were leaning toward voting for the incumbent. The three versions varied, however, in the additional information they provided. In one version, participants were told that 80 percent of the members of another department, made up primarily of women, also supported the incumbent (*gender similarity condition*). In a second version, participants were told that 80 percent of the members of another department, made up primarily of women, supported the challenger (*gender difference condition*). In a third version, no additional information was provided (*control condition*).

As predicted, participants indicated that it would be more difficult to change the candidate preference of a member of the target group when they were informed that the opposite preference was shared by most members of an opposite-sex group. The mean level of difficulty assigned by participants in the gender difference condition was 7 (on a scale from 1 ["not at all difficult"] to 9 ["very difficult"]), compared to a mean of 5.76 in the control condition. Thus, it appears that simply knowing that a preference is widely shared within a social category is not sufficient to induce the perception that it reflects an essential, immutable characteristic of the category members; that preference must also be distinctive to the category. Participants in the gender similarity condition also indicated that the preference would be more difficult to change ($M = 6.75$), but this perception of immutability was almost certainly driven by a stimulus attribution. That is, given the information that the majority of employees across two units preferred the incumbent, it was reasonable for these participants to infer that the incumbent was simply the superior candidate and that the majority preference was well founded.

In summary, studies 1 and 2 provided initial support for the category divide hypothesis. Participants showed the hypothesized tendency to infer that a difference between two individuals from different social categories reflects a more general group difference and that such group differences are resistant to modification. We contend that both of these inferences stem from people's naive belief in group essence. Observation of a difference between members of different social categories triggers an attribution to group essence, which, in turn, makes the difference seem deeply based and therefore immutable.

## Studies 3 and 4

In our next two studies, we sought more direct evidence for the predictions of the category divide hypothesis, using both gender and race as category divides (Carlsmith, Prentice, and Miller 1997). Both of these studies employed a common paradigm: participants acted as observers of several interpersonal disagreements, which they viewed on videotape. We developed this paradigm with several goals in mind. First, we wanted to move beyond a simple interpersonal difference to a case of real disagreement. Our predictions, and in particular the mutability prediction, are best tested under conditions in which the differing parties have the opportunity to engage with one another in an attempt to resolve their disagreement. Second, we wanted to disentangle, as best we could, the cognitive, inferential processes that are the focus of our analysis from the emotional and motivational processes that are engendered by interpersonal disagreements. Having participants serve as observers of, rather than as actors in, an interpersonal dispute enabled us to focus on these inferential processes. Finally, we wanted to generalize beyond gender categories to racial categories, but at the same time we did not want to alert participants either to our hypothesis or to any concerns they might have about appearing biased or racist. The paradigm we developed appears to have accomplished these goals.

In study 3, we sought evidence for the magnitude prediction: a difference between two people seems to be greater if it occurs between members of different social groups than if it occurs between members of the same social group. Participants viewed a series of videotaped discussions between pairs of students about familiar and contentious campus issues. In all the discussions, the two students disagreed. We varied the gender and racial composition of the disagreeing student pairs. In some of the discussions, the two stimulus persons were the same race (either African American or Caucasian) and gender; in others, they were the same race but different genders; in others, they were the same gender but different races; and in still others, they were different races and genders. All of the arguments were scripted, and the videotapes were edited so that each of the eight stimulus persons always made the same arguments but appeared to be making those arguments to different partners. Across videotapes, every stimulus person appeared in all four types of interactions. Each participant viewed one practice videotape and then four experimental videotapes that included one of each type of interaction (same-group, male-female, black-white, and double-difference). Each participant saw each stimulus person in only one interaction.

The question of principal interest was whether the disagreeing parties would be seen as further apart in their positions when the two stimulus persons were from different gender or racial groups. To assess this prediction, participants were asked after each video to indicate how far apart the positions of the two speakers were on the issue (from 1 ["identical"] to 9 ["extremely different"]); to rate how strongly they disagreed (from 1 ["mildly"] to 9 ["vehemently"]); and to locate the positions of the two speakers on a ten-centimeter line marked with opposing positions at the poles.

Their responses to these questions supported our prediction (see figure 7.2). Participants perceived that the two parties were further apart in their positions, and that they disagreed more strongly, when the two differed in their gender or race. This result is especially impressive given that the videotaped discussions of both homogeneous and heterogeneous pairs were created by splicing together the presentations of the same eight stimulus persons making the same arguments. The finding that cross-race and cross-gender disagreements were perceived to reflect a greater difference than within-race and within-gender disagreements adds an important component to our story, for it provides direct evidence that people's perception of a disagreement is affected by whether it occurs between individuals from the same or different groups. A disagreement that seems to be a minor difference of opinion when it takes place between individuals within the same group can seem to be an unbridgeable divide when it occurs between individuals from different groups.

Finally, in study 4, we sought to replicate and extend the results of study 3 to test some additional predictions of the category divide hypothesis. In particular, we wanted to examine the contention that between-group disagreements are perceived not simply as greater in magnitude than within-group disagreements but also as deeper, more fundamental, and more difficult to resolve. We used the same procedure

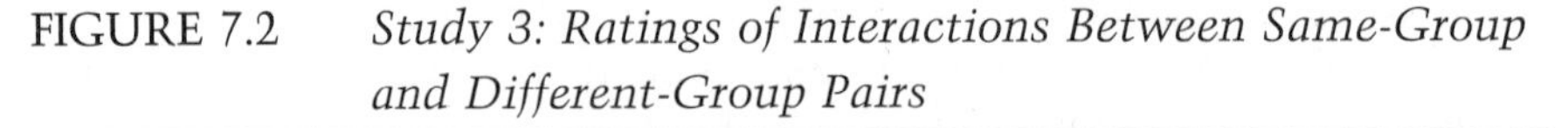

FIGURE 7.2 *Study 3: Ratings of Interactions Between Same-Group and Different-Group Pairs*

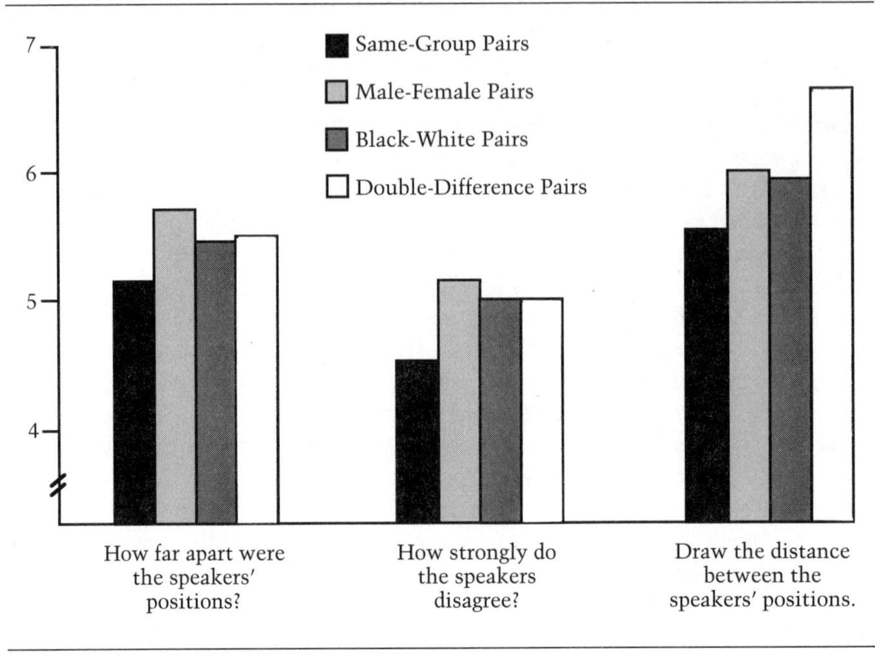


as in study 3, except that each participant saw only three experimental videotapes depicting one same-group, one male-female, and one black-white disagreement. After viewing each video, participants were asked to indicate how strongly the two people disagreed (this time on a scale of 1 to 7); to what extent their difference of opinion reflected a difference in their underlying values or attitudes (from 1 ["not at all"] to 7 ["completely"]); and how difficult it would be for them to resolve the issue (from 1 ["very easy"] to 7 ["very difficult"]). They were also asked to draw a Venn diagram with two identical circles that displayed the degree to which the speakers' opinions overlapped. (We scored this last question by measuring the distance between the centers of the circles minus the sum of their radii.)

Their responses again supported our predictions (see figure 7.3, which shows the results for the three new questions in this study). When the two parties differed in their gender or race, participants perceived that they were further apart in their positions, disagreed more strongly, and would have more difficulty resolving the issue. Moreover, they perceived that between-group disagreements were more strongly

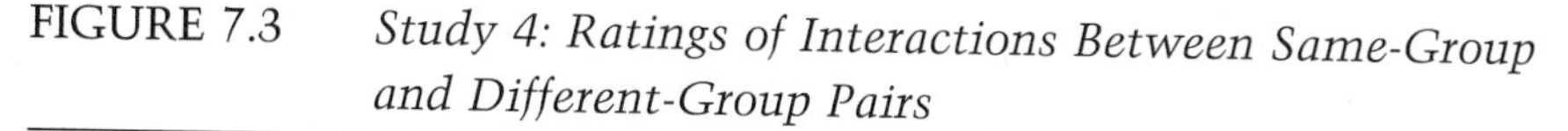

FIGURE 7.3 *Study 4: Ratings of Interactions Between Same-Group and Different-Group Pairs*

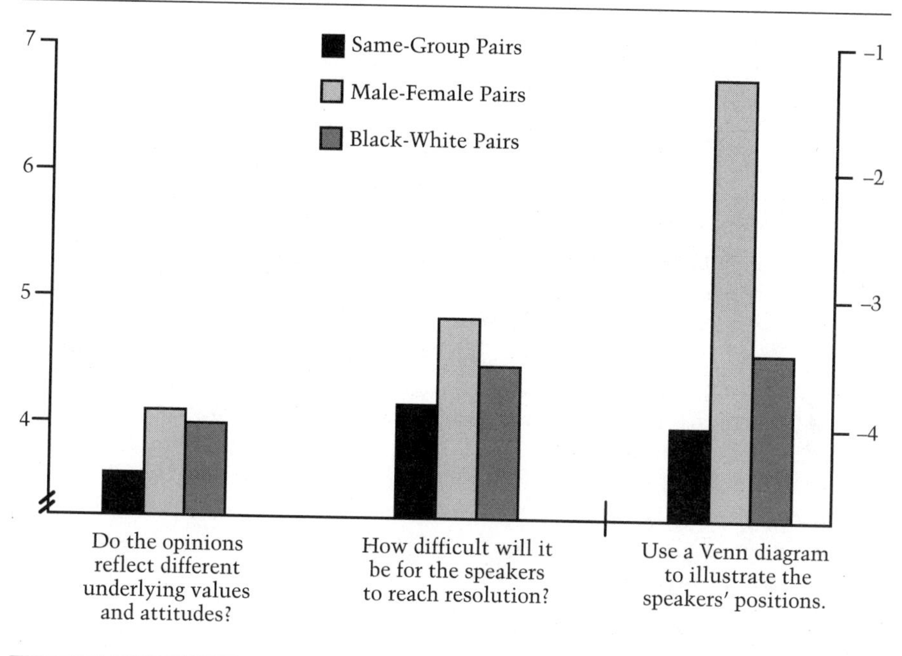


rooted in attitude and value differences than were within-group differences. (We should note that, unlike in study 3, the differences in study 4 were considerably stronger for the gender manipulation than for the race manipulation. We believe that this difference reflects a higher degree of concern among participants in study 4 about appearing racist, which resulted from a few time-saving modifications in the experimental procedure between studies 3 and 4.)

These results provide perhaps the strongest evidence we have obtained thus far for the category divide hypothesis, in that they demonstrate that disagreements in heterogeneous pairs are seen as wider, deeper, and more immutable than the same disagreements in homogeneous pairs. The most parsimonious account for this pattern of findings, in our view, invokes people's belief in group essence. Participants perceived disagreements across gender or racial lines as rooted in something basic and fundamental about the groups in question. This interpretation of the disagreements as group-based rather than individual-based made them seem greater in magnitude, more firmly entrenched in opposing attitudes and values, and more difficult to resolve.

## DISCUSSION

Multicultural social life inevitably yields encounters with difference. Many of the differences people experience with members of other ethnic, religious, or cultural groups are ones they would seldom, or never, experience with members of their own group. But the difference between multicultural and monocultural life is found not only in the differences experienced. It is also found in the experience of the differences, that is, in how individuals interpret and respond to them.

The thesis of this chapter is that a difference occurring between two people who belong to different groups is perceived differently than the same difference occurring between two people who belong to the same group. A difference between people from different groups tends to be *essentialized* (that is, seen as reflecting deep, immutable, group-based differences) and hence *universalized* (seen as reflecting a more widespread group difference). These differences in interpretation and inference, in turn, produce differences in reaction. People tend to be less optimistic that a difference can be resolved when it occurs between people from different groups, or at least between groups seen as different social kinds. This tendency to attribute differences between people to their being different kinds of people serves, of course, to reinforce the perception that social groups constitute social kinds.

### The Category Divide: More Than a Case of Discounting

One of the central propositions of attribution theory is the discounting principle (Kelley 1973), which states that the weight people attach to any one cause is reduced (discounted) to the extent that other plausible causes exist. At first blush, this principle would seem to offer a compelling account of why people are less likely to see an interpersonal difference as stemming from personal factors when it occurs between people from different groups as when it occurs between people from the same group. After all, a factor (group membership) that provides a plausible alternative account to personal factors in the former case does not exist in the latter case. But our analysis suggests that more than discounting is operating in the case of the category divide hypothesis. Group membership does not simply constitute an additional plausible cause, in our view; it constitutes an especially compelling cause.

We are not the first to make this claim. Other researchers have also noted that people are especially compelled by group-shared traits in the explanations they offer for individual behavior (see Rothbart and Mauro 1997; Yzerbyt et al. 1997). Furthermore, this attributional preference for group-shared traits is consistent with a number of other attributional tendencies—for example, the tendency to locate the cause of another's behavior in his or her dispositions rather than in equally plausible situational factors (Jones 1990; Norenzayan, Choi, and Nisbett, this volume; Ross 1977). Our findings suggest that people also exhibit an attributional preference in the case of interpersonal differences between people from different groups. Even when personal differences and group differences are equally plausible explanations for these differences, people prefer the latter.

We can only speculate as to why a group-based attribution might prevail over an individual-based attribution. One possibility is that people prefer the inference that yields the greatest induction-potential (Yzerbyt et al. 1997), believing that more information is generated by a group-based attribution than by an person-based attribution. An alternative possibility bears more directly on the concept of group essence. We noted earlier that theorists, speculating about the layperson's belief in group essence, frequently speak as though the identification of group essence is a powerful goal of the social perceiver. Not only do people believe in essence, but they believe it is important to discover it (Rothbart and Taylor 1982). And because of their desire to identify a group's essence, people might weight potential attributional errors differently. Misclassifying a group difference as merely a personal difference might seem a more serious error than misclassifying a personal difference as a group difference. Support for this possibility comes from Martin and Parker (1995), who found that college students believe that detecting biologically based sex differences is so important that it is "more important to err on the side of reporting sex differences (even if none exists) than to be conservative by not reporting sex differences" (54).

One final suggestion is that group-based attributions are preferred to individual-based attributions because the former serve to rationalize group differences in resources or treatment (Jost and Banaji 1994; Tajfel and Turner 1986; Yzerbyt et al. 1997). In this view, the tendency to essentialize differences between oneself and a member of another group might be motivated by the desire to enhance the ingroup at the expense of the outgroup, or perhaps by the desire to justify the power differential between ingroups and outgroups. We do not find this explanation compelling in the present context for two reasons. First, the tendency to make group-based attributions is not restricted to the explanation of differences between oneself and members of another group; it applies to the explanation of a difference between members of any two groups, including two outgroups. Second, even when one of the two groups is an ingroup, the belief in group difference need not be accompanied by a belief in ingroup superiority. One can see two groups as fundamentally different without seeing one as better than the other. Indeed, the category divide hypothesis suggests that merely believing in group difference can have a number of important implications that are independent of the valences attached to that difference. We now turn to those implications.

## Implications of the Category Divide Hypothesis

*For Interpersonal Relations* It should be clear from our analysis that the experience of difference per se need not inevitably be an impediment to the acquaintanceship process. It can even facilitate the process by providing the impetus for further contact and discussion, which, in turn, can lead to the development of stronger bonds, either through the discovery of all that is shared or through an increased understanding of what is different or contested. We believe that these positive effects will not be realized, however, when the difference experienced occurs between people who perceive their social categories to be distinct social kinds. In these cases, they will be inclined to attribute the difference to more general group differences and, in so doing, will freight the difference with greater significance. Because they will be seen as both deeper and broader, group-based differences will be insulated from the relationship-building scrutiny and exploration that individual-based differences receive. Note that we do not mean to imply that people are uninterested in other kinds of people. They often are extremely curious about others, but their interest simply takes a distinct form. Rather than seeking to find out what *this person* is like or why *this person* sees things differently, they are interested in finding out what *these people* are like or why *these people* see things differently.

Once again, we are not claiming that people are incapable of coexisting comfortably, or even happily, with different kinds of people. But it is a different kind of relationship, one characterized by different goals and different standards. What getting along means is different for two people who perceive themselves to be of the same kind compared to its meaning for people who perceive themselves to be of different kinds. The same is true of natural kind categories. To say that two pets get along means something quite different when the comment is about animals that belong to different natural kinds (such as a cat and a dog) rather than animals that belong to the same natural kind (two cats). Indeed, one of the criteria for getting along with those of a different kind is to be understanding and respectful of their essential otherness. Thus, when a woman describes a distinctive behavior of her male partner as a "guy thing," she is marking it as something she can accept and perhaps respect, but never understand or hope to change. The behavior so signified becomes one of those non-actionable aspects of male-female relations that must be respected, or at least tolerated, if the two are to get along.

*For Self-Examination* In addition to its implications for relationship development, the category divide hypothesis has implications for self-development, or perhaps the lack of it. To the extent that people see differences between themselves and others as group-based, they are disinclined to reevaluate either their own position or the issue at hand. The discovery that one sees or evaluates an issue differently than another is much more likely to raise the possibility that one's position is wrong or misguided when the other is a member of one's own group. Outgroup members typically have less social influence over us than ingroup members: we are less persuaded by them and conform less to their attitudes and behaviors (Turner 1991). Our resistance to outgroup influence presumably derives from our assumption that any difference between us on the attitude dimension is due to the difference between us on the group membership dimension. As a result, we are inclined to dismiss their views as irrelevant. Their outgroup status provides a ready attribution for why they differ from us and, hence, for why we do not need to reconsider the validity of our own position.

*For Object Evaluation* We have argued that people's commitment to psychological essentialism leads them to assume that they have learned something about social categories when they witness people from those categories differing on some issue or dimension. It is also possible that they assume they have learned something about the issue or dimension as well. Consider a study that investigated the relation between religion and university fields selected by American professors (Steinberg 1974). This study found that Catholics outnumber other religious groups in the humanities (art, philosophy, languages), that Protestants outnumber other religious groups in traditional scientific fields (chemistry, physics, biology), and that Jews are relatively more numerous in the behavioral sciences (economics, sociology, psychology). Observers, consistent with the category divide hypothesis, might well be inclined to attribute these differences in discipline preferences to differences in the essential qualities of the different religious groups. But it also seems likely that learning these facts might lead observers to see choice of academic discipline as more significant than they had previously assumed. After all, if choice of discipline reflects group essence, it must tap into something deep and meaningful in people, something more meaningful than a similar degree of variation within social kind would suggest. Thus, having come to the conclusion that variation on an issue or dimension reflects a deep difference between social kinds, people may well come to imbue any variation along this dimension with greater significance.

## Prospects for Bridging the Category Divide

Does the category divide hypothesis provide any insight into how intergroup relations can be improved? We think so. The key is information—in particular, information about the variability of opinions, behaviors, and perceptions both within one's own category and within the other's category. If we know that not everyone in our category sees the situation as we do, and that not everyone in the other's category sees the situation as he or she does, we are unlikely to perceive our difference with the other as group-based and therefore as immutable. Moreover, the more contact we have with members of other categories, the more likely we are to encounter within-category heterogeneity on any particular issue or in any particular respect.

Contact does not necessarily diminish the belief in group essence. Increased contact with members of the opposite gender, and hence with the diversity of opinions or preferences within their ranks, should diminish the likelihood that we will mistake a personal difference for a gender difference, but it will not necessarily diminish our belief that men and women have different essences. Indeed, because the belief in group essence takes a top-down rather than a bottom-up form, it is possible for us to believe that men and women have different essences without being able to identify a single instance of such a difference. The belief that members of different races and genders have different essences seems primitive and not easily modified. Nevertheless, its biasing impact can be reduced. The belief in group essence simply predisposes people to interpret interpersonal differences as group differences; it does not mandate that they do so. Through education, it is possible to teach people that not all the differences they experience with members of other categories are category differences.

Finally, we should note that conceptions of which social categories constitute social kinds are not hardwired. Perceptions vary considerably across time and cultures. For example, Yzerbyt and his colleagues (1997) point out that "the working class" appears to constitute a social kind in Europe (in that people retain this category membership even if they become rich and successful), but not in America. Similar differences occur across time. For example, Fredrickson (this volume) describes how the Irish who fled the potato famine for America were viewed as a distinct racial category (presumably with a distinct essence) but gradually came to lose their distinctive racialized status as they increasingly became viewed as white Americans. Rothbart and Taylor (1982) point to a similar historical shift in the conceptualization of Jews from the early Christian era to the Nazi period. Depending on the particular historical epoch, being a Jew was alternately perceived as something, like being a Protestant, that could be changed by voluntary actions (for example, conversion) or as something, like being black, with a seemingly distinct essence that could not be altered by voluntary or involuntary actions. Stereotypes, then, can change in two ways: the content of people's beliefs about a social category can change, but so, too, can their ontological classification of the social category.

## NOTE

1. This question parallels in important respects a question posed by the economist Albert Hirschman (1970): When does one respond to an unsatisfying relationship by exiting the situation, and when by giving voice to one's dissatisfaction?

## REFERENCES

Allport, Gordon. (1954). *The nature of prejudice.* Cambridge, Mass.: Addison-Wesley.

Amir, Yehuda. (1969). The contact hypothesis in ethnic relations. *Psychological Bulletin, 71,* 319–42.

Appiah, K. Anthony. (1990). Racisms. In David T. Goldberg (Ed.), *Anatomy of racism* (pp. 21–37). Minneapolis: University of Minnesota Press.

Atran, Scott. (1990). *Cognitive foundations of natural history.* New York: Cambridge University Press.

Bodenhausen, Galen, and Wyer, Robert. (1985). Effects of stereotypes on decision making and information processing strategies. *Journal of Personality and Social Psychology, 48,* 267–82.

Brewer, Marilynn B., and Miller, Norman E. (1984). Beyond the contact hypothesis: Theoretical perspectives on desegregation. In Norman E. Miller and Marilynn B. Brewer (Eds.), *Groups in contact: The psychology of desegregation* (pp. 281–303). New York: Academic Press.

———. (1988). Contact and cooperation: When do they work? In Phylis Katz and Dalmas Taylor (Eds.), *Eliminating racism: Profiles in controversy* (pp. 315–25). New York: Plenum Press.

Brislin, Richard W. (Ed.). (1990). *Applied cross-cultural psychology.* Newbury Park, Calif.: Sage.

Brislin, Richard W., and Yoshida, Tomoko. (1994). *Intercultural communication: An introduction.* Thousand Oaks, Calif.: Sage.

Carlsmith, Kevin M., Prentice, Deborah A., and Miller, Dale T. (1997). Perceptions of disagreement in a multicultural context: The category divide hypothesis. Paper presented at the annual meeting of the American Psychological Society, Washington, D.C. (May 21).

Cohen, Raymond. (1991). *Negotiating across cultures: Common obstacles in international diplomacy.* Washington, D.C.: U.S. Institute of Peace Press.
Cook, Stuart W. (1984). The social science statement and school desegregation: A reply to Gerard. *American Psychologist, 39,* 819–32.
Doise, Willem, Csepli, G., Dann, H., Gouge, C., Larsen, K., and Ostell, A. (1972). An experimental investigation into the formation of intergroup representations. *European Journal of Social Psychology, 2,* 202–4.
Eberhardt, Jennifer L., and Randall, Jennifer L. (1997). The essential notion of race. *Psychological Science, 8,* 198–203.
Fiske, Susan T. (1997). Stereotyping, prejudice, and discrimination. In Daniel T. Gilbert, Susan T. Fiske, and Gardner Lindzey (Eds.), *The handbook of social psychology* (4th ed., pp. 357–411). New York: McGraw-Hill.
Fuss, Diana. (1989). *Essentially speaking: Feminism, nature, and difference.* New York: Routledge.
Gaertner, Samuel L., Dovidio, John F., Anastasio, Phylis A., Bachman, Betty A., and Rust, Mary C. (1993). The Common Ingroup Identity Model: Recategorization and the reduction of intergroup bias. *European Review of Social Psychology, 4,* 1–26.
Gelman, Susan A., and Hirschfeld, Lawrence A. (in press). How biological is essentialism? In Douglas L. Medin and Scott Atran (Eds.), *Folk biology.* Cambridge, Mass.: MIT Press.
Goldberg, David T. (1993). *Racist culture: Philosophy and the politics of meaning.* London: Blackwell.
Hamilton, David L., and Sherman, Steven J. (1989). Illusory correlation: Implications for stereotype theory and research. In Daniel Bar-Tal, Carl F. Graumann, Arie W. Kruglanski, and Wolfgang Stroebe (Eds.), *Stereotyping and prejudice: Changing conceptions* (pp. 59–83). New York: Springer-Verlag.
Haslam, S. Alexander, Oakes, Penelope J., Turner, John C., and McGarty, Craig. (1995). Social categorization and group homogeneity: Changes in the perceived applicability of stereotype content as a function of comparative context and trait favorableness. *British Journal of Social Psychology, 34,* 139–60.
———. (1996). Social identity, self-categorization, and the perceived homogeneity of ingroups and outgroups. In Richard M. Sorrentino and E. Tory Higgins (Eds.), *Handbook of motivation and cognition* (vol. 3, pp. 182–222). New York: Guilford.
Hewstone, Miles. (1990). The ultimate attribution error?: A review of the literature on intergroup causal attribution. *European Journal of Social Psychology, 20,* 311–35.
Hirschfeld, Lawrence A. (1996). *Race in the making: Cognition, culture, and the child's construction of human kinds.* Cambridge, Mass.: MIT Press.
Hirschman, Albert O. (1970). *Exit, voice, and loyalty.* Cambridge, Mass.: Harvard University Press.
Hoffman, Curt, and Hurst, Nancy. (1990). Gender stereotypes: Perception or rationalization? *Journal of Personality and Social Psychology, 58,* 197–208.
Hogg, Michael A., and Abrams, Dominic. (1988). *Social identifications: A social psychology of intergroup relations and group processes.* London: Routledge.
Hogg, Michael A., and Turner, John C. (1987). Intergroup behavior, self-stereotyping and the salience of social categories. *British Journal of Social Psychology, 26,* 325–40.
Insko, Chester A., Nacoste, Rupert W., and Moe, Jeffrey L. (1983). Belief congruence and racial discrimination: Review of the evidence and critical evaluation. *European Journal of Social Psychology, 13,* 153–74.

Islam, Mir Rabiul, and Hewstone, Miles. (1993). Intergroup attributions and affective consequences in majority and minority groups. *Journal of Personality and Social Psychology, 64,* 936–50.
Jones, Edward E. (1990). *Interpersonal perception.* New York: Freeman.
Jost, John T., and Banaji, Mahzarin R. (1994). The role of stereotyping in system justification and the production of false consciousness. *British Journal of Social Psychology, 33,* 1–27.
Kelley, Harold H. (1973). The process of causal attribution. *American Psychologist, 28,* 107–28.
Martin, Carol L., and Parker, Sandra. (1995). Folk theories about sex and race differences. *Personality and Social Psychology Bulletin, 21,* 45–57.
Medin, Douglas L. (1989). Concepts and conceptual structure. *American Psychologist, 45,* 1469–81.
Medin, Douglas L., and Ortony, Andrew. (1989). Psychological essentialism. In Stella Vosnaidou and Andrew Ortony (Eds.), *Similarity and analogical reasoning* (pp. 179–95). Cambridge: Cambridge University Press.
Miller, Dale T., Turnbull, William, and McFarland, Cathy. (1988). Particularistic and universalistic evaluation in the social comparison process. *Journal of Personality and Social Psychology, 55,* 908–17.
Pettigrew, Thomas F. (1979). The ultimate attribution error: Extending Allport's cognitive analysis. *Personality and Social Psychology Bulletin, 5,* 461–76.
Prentice, Deborah A., and Miller, Dale T. (1996). Not all differences between members of different cultural groups are cultural differences. Paper presented at the annual meeting of the Society for Experimental Social Psychology, Sturbridge, Mass. (October 14).
Rokeach, Milton. (1979). Some unresolved issues in theories of beliefs, attitudes, and values. *Nebraska Symposium on Motivation, 27,* 261–304.
Rokeach, Milton, and Mezei, Louis. (1966). Race and shared belief as factors in social distance. *Science, 151,* 167–72.
Ross, Lee D. (1977). The intuitive psychologist and his shortcomings: Distortions in the attribution process. In Leonard Berkowitz (Ed.), *Advances in experimental social psychology* (vol. 10, pp. 174–222). New York: Academic Press.
Rothbart, Myron, and Mauro, Robert. (1997). Social categories and decision making: How much differentiation do we need? In David M. Messick and Anne E. Tenbrunsel (Eds.), *Codes of conduct: Behavioral research into business ethics* (pp. 143–60). New York: Russell Sage Foundation.
Rothbart, Myron, and Taylor, Marjorie. (1982). Category labels and social reality: Do we view social categories as natural kinds? In Gun R. Semin and Klaus Fiedler (Eds.), *Language, interaction, and social cognition* (pp. 11–36). Newbury Park, Calif.: Sage.
Smith, Peter B., and Bond, Michael H. (1994). *Social psychology across cultures.* Needham Heights, Mass.: Allyn and Bacon.
Steinberg, Stephen. (1974). *The academic melting pot.* New York: McGraw-Hill.
Stephan, Walter G. (1985). Intergroup relations. In Gardner Lindzey and Elliot Aronson (Eds.), *The handbook of social psychology* (3rd ed., vol. 2, pp. 599–659). New York: Random House.
Tajfel, Henri, and Turner, John C. (1986). The social identity theory of intergroup behavior. In Stephen Worchel and William G. Austin (Eds.), *Psychology of intergroup relations* (2nd ed., pp. 7–25). Chicago: Nelson-Hall.
Taylor, Marianne. (1996). The development of children's beliefs about social and biological aspects of gender differences. *Child Development, 67,* 1555–71.

Turner, John C. (1982). Toward a cognitive redefinition of the social group. In Henri Tajfel (Ed.), *Social identity and intergroup relations* (pp. 15–41). Cambridge: Cambridge University Press.

———. (1991). *Social influence.* Pacific Grove, Calif.: Brooks/Cole.

Turner, John C., Hogg, Michael A., Oakes, Penelope J., Reicher, Stephen D., and Wetherell, Margaret S. (1987). *Rediscovering the social group: A self-categorization theory.* Oxford: Blackwell.

Weber, Joseph G. (1994). The nature of ethnocentric attribution bias: Ingroup protection or enhancement? *Journal of Experimental Social Psychology, 30,* 482–504.

Yzerbyt, Vincent, Rocher, Steve, and Schadron, Georges. (1997). Stereotypes as explanations: A subjective essentialistic view of group perception. In Russell Spears, Penelope J. Oakes, Nicholas Ellemers, and S. Alexander Haslam (Eds.), *The social psychology of stereotyping and group life* (pp. 20–50). Oxford: Blackwell.

# 8

# EASTERN AND WESTERN PERCEPTIONS OF CAUSALITY FOR SOCIAL BEHAVIOR: LAY THEORIES ABOUT PERSONALITIES AND SITUATIONS

*Ara Norenzayan, Incheol Choi, and Richard E. Nisbett*

UNDERSTANDING others is a difficult and risky business, but if history is any guide, understanding others in intercultural encounters is truly a great challenge. When dealing with a person from a different culture, the lay psychologist is faced with the possibility of a radical divergence between his or her own everyday understanding of behavior and that of the other. To the extent that there is such a divergence, people of different cultures draw different conclusions from the same encounter, thus leading to cultural misunderstandings.

In this chapter, we focus on one likely source of such misunderstandings, namely, the fundamental attribution error (FAE) (Ross 1977), or the correspondence bias (Gilbert and Malone 1995). The FAE, a central finding of social psychology, describes a curious and pervasive aspect of folk psychology in Western culture. People make "correspondent inferences" from behaviors to attitudes, traits, or other presumed dispositions of an individual. Attributing the individual's behavior to a corresponding disposition is sometimes justified, and usually it cannot be shown to be mistaken, but often it constitutes an error, because people attribute situationally determined behavior to a disposition. This error in attribution appears to be linked to a very coherent and widespread theory about personality traits. Examinations of lay perceptions of individual differences show that there is substantial agreement about the dimensions of personality and the relations between the various dimensions (Goldberg 1990; McCrae, Costa, and Yik 1996). This consensus among lay observers is not accompanied, however, by anything like as much validity as the lay observer believes to exist. Since the time of Mischel's (1968) critique, it has been known that the observer cannot predict the actor's behavior in a novel situation as accurately as the observer believes he or she can. Such "validities" almost never exceed a correlation of .30, even when based on long acquaintance with the target (or a battery of personality tests) and typically are far lower. Predictions from one situation presumed to tap a given trait to another situation presumed to tap the same trait almost never exceed .10. Yet people believe they can do far better than this. When asked how well they could predict behavior in one situation from behavior in another that presumably measured the same trait, participants in a study by Kunda and Nisbett (1986) stated their belief that they could do so with accuracy corresponding to a correlation of $r = .70$ or more.

The FAE has been demonstrated so many times, in so many important and interesting contexts, that it has become a staple of modern social psychology. Despite several decades of intensive research, however, a complete theoretical account of the FAE continues to elude social psychologists and has led many theorists to see it as the central problem of social psychology. Recently researchers have come to realize that the FAE and the attribution process in general are affected by a multitude of factors, including perceptual, cognitive, pragmatic, and epistemic ones (for a recent review, see Gilbert and Malone 1995). During the last decade, growing cross-cultural research has brought culture to prominence as another crucial influence on the attribution process and the FAE.

Until very recently, social psychologists tacitly assumed that the FAE is cross-culturally universal. Various theorists have attributed the error to Heider's (1958) notion that "behavior engulfs the field" making it easy to see behavior as the product of attributes of the actor rather than of the field (the social situation) in which the behavior occurs. This essentially perceptual explanation for the error implies that everyone should be subject to it. And yet there have been reasons to suspect that the FAE might not be so universal, especially to the extent that the error rests on foundations of lay theory of social behavior. The modern West is unique in the extent to which it locates the responsibility for behavior exclusively in the individual. From the time of Aristotle onward, the locus of behavior has been seen to lie primarily in the attributes of the person—attitudes, preferences, and motives. This idea of the nature of the individual prompts the social observer to attend to, and when necessary to create imaginatively, internal reasons for action that make the actor an agentic figure.

But as many theorists have pointed out (Hirschfeld 1995; Hsu 1953,

1981; Markus and Kitayama 1991; Munro 1985; Triandis 1995), most of the rest of humanity does not share this highly individualist theory of behavior. Most people live in social worlds that are constrained by roles, by relationships within a broad network of extended family and community, and by a variety of deeply ingrained social traditions. Focusing on the contrast between China, a characteristically collectivist or interdependent society, and America, the prototypical individualist society, the psychologist L.-H. Chiu (1972) writes:

> Chinese are situation-centered. They are obliged to be sensitive to their environment. Americans are individual-centered. They expect their environment to be sensitive to them. Thus, Chinese tend to assume a passive attitude while Americans tend to possess an active and conquering attitude in dealing with their environment. . . . [The American] orientation may inhibit the development of a tendency to perceive objects in the environmental context in terms of relationships or interdependence. On the other hand, the Chinese child learns very early to view the world as based on a network of relationships; he is *socio-oriented,* or *situation-centered.* (236, 241)

In what follows, we first highlight some of the evidence regarding cross-cultural variation in causal attribution and the FAE, focusing mainly on the East Asian cultural area (consisting of China, Korea, and Japan) and the West (encompassing Western European and European American cultures). (For a more comprehensive review of this literature, see Choi, Nisbett, and Norenzayan 1999.) As we will see, the evidence for cultural differences in attribution is robust, emerging in diverse methodologies and research paradigms. We review evidence for a cross-culturally widespread dispositionism, examine the degree to which different cultures endorse different kinds of dispositionism, and argue that the cultural differences derive primarily from differential emphasis on the context of behavior rather than from differential emphasis on dispositionism.

The kind of evidence we consider in this chapter is diverse, including self- and other-description, social explanation, ethnographic accounts of everyday understanding of social behavior, studies of the cognitive organization of personality information, behavioral prediction, attitude attribution, ratings of lay theories of social behavior, and implicit theories of personality. Despite their apparent diversity, all these studies and approaches tap into some aspect of social inference—people's reasoning about social behavior, and their beliefs about how and to what extent social behavior is determined by situational versus dispositional factors. We do not address the question of how the group membership of the actor vis-à-vis the observer affects the attributions of members of different cultural groups. For an analysis of this important topic, see Iyengar, Lepper, and Ross (this volume). Finally, we speculate about the origins of the cross-cultural differences and regularities in attribution and discuss implications for intercultural contact.

## SOCIAL INFERENCE WEST AND EAST

If societal differences in attribution are truly accompanied by differences in theories of social behavior, we might find differences in person-perception in independent versus interdependent societies. And indeed, beginning with research by Shweder and Bourne (1982), evidence has been mounting that this is the case. Those investigators asked both Hindu Indian and American respondents to describe several close acquaintances. The descriptions were different in the degree to which they emphasized attributes of the individual. The American descriptions relied on traits and other presumed internal dispositions. The Indian descriptions emphasized the situation and broader context in which the person was located. Other studies comparing East Asians have found similar results, even when the person being described is the self (Cousins 1989; Ip and Bond 1995; Markus, Mullaly, and Kitayama 1997; Rhee et al. 1995; Trafimow, Triandis, and Goto 1991; Triandis 1989; Triandis, McCusker, and Hui 1990).

If people living in relatively interdependent cultures seem to be less likely to produce dispositional descriptions of people, this raises the possibility that they might not be as prone to causal analysis, which betrays a dispositionist bias. And indeed, Joan Miller (1984) set the field of social psychology back on its heels when she reported that, when asked to explain a person's behavior that had either good or bad consequences, Hindu Indians offered explanations in terms of social roles and other contextual factors whereas her American participants showed the usual tendency to explain the behaviors in terms of either good or bad traits. Indians made contextual attributions twice as often as Americans did; Americans made dispositional explanations twice as often as Indians did. Miller also showed that the different attributional preferences of the two cultures develop gradually. American and Indian adults were much more unlike each other in their modes of inference than were American and Indian children.

Miller's demonstration proved not to be an isolated one. Morris and Peng (Morris 1993; Morris, Nisbett, and Peng 1995; Morris and Peng 1994) took advantage of two tragedies that occurred at about the same time. A postal worker in Detroit who was angry about his treatment by his supervisor shot and killed the supervisor and several bystanders, and a Chinese Ph.D. candidate at a midwestern university who was angry about his treatment by his adviser shot and killed the adviser and several bystanders. Though accounts of both murders in American newspapers explained the behavior of the perpetrators in dispositional terms, focusing almost exclusively on the presumed mental instability and other negative dispositions of the two alleged murderers, accounts in Chinese newspapers speculated on situational, contextual, and even societal factors that might have been at work. Morris and Peng showed that the same attributions were obtained when Chinese and American university students were asked to explain the events: American participants preferred dispositional explanations and Chinese participants preferred situational ones. Lee, Hallahan, and Herzog (1996) have shown a comparable difference in the types of explanations for sports events given by American and Hong Kong journalists. American journalists were more likely to refer to dispositional factors, whereas Hong Kong journalists were more likely to refer to contextual ones. They found similar cultural differences in explanations for failure to attain a goal (Hallahan, Lee, and Herzog, in press).

But perhaps the Asians in these studies were simply expressing their theories about particular types of social behavior, which are in fact under more situational and role constraints than the comparable behaviors in the West. If this were the case, Asians might not be showing that they are less prone to the FAE but simply that they live in societies where situations and context are more important, and it might be that their social theories reflect this. This possibility cannot be ruled out even for the sports study by Lee and her colleagues (1996), since the particular sports being commented on were not the same in the two cultures. Another study by Morris and Peng (1994), however, makes this interpretation less likely. The authors created animated cartoon displays of fish moving in relation to one another in various ways. Each vignette displayed a single fish behaving in one way and a group of fish behaving in another. In one cartoon, for example, the single fish moved away from the group. In another, the single fish was joined by the group. Participants were asked whether the behavior of the single fish was best explained by external factors or internal ones. Anthropological observations have shown that lay theories of human behavior often "invade" explanations for animal behavior, and sometimes vice versa (see, for example, Hallowell 1976). Therefore it is possible that cultural differences in lay theories of human behavior would emerge in explanations for animal behavior. The results confirmed this hypothesis. Morris and Peng's Chinese participants emphasized external factors, whereas American participants focused on internal ones.

There are grounds for believing that meta-theories of behavior go beyond perception even of animal behavior. Kurt Lewin (1935) noted that people tend to see even the behavior of objects as being due exclusively to attributes of the object—a mistaken physical theory that he called "Aristotelian." In Aristotelian physics, a stone dropped into water falls because it has the property of "gravity." A piece of wood floats on water because it has the property of "levity." Lewin contrasted Aristotelian physics with "Galilean" physics, which recognized that the behavior of objects is the result of an interaction between the object and the environment.

But this fundamental principle had been understood in China fifteen hundred years earlier (Nakamura 1964/1985; Needham 1962). Consistent with the claim that Chinese understanding of physical reality is more sensitive to the field in which the object is located, Peng and Nisbett (in press) have shown that Chinese are more likely to refer to the field in their explanations for ambiguous physical events, whereas Americans are more likely to refer solely to factors internal to the object. They presented their participants with computer-generated physical events for which causality was transparent—for example, a schematic object resembling a ball appearing to hit another schematic ball, followed by the second ball moving away in the direction of the impact—as well as events for which causality was not so clear. The latter events included ones that appeared to be hydrodynamic—for example, a schematic ball was dropped into a schematic medium, and the ball either dropped to the bottom or remained on the surface. Aerodynamic-appearing events also were presented. Though the explanations of the "billiard ball" dynamics were identical for the two groups, the explanations for the more ambiguous ones diverged: Americans were more likely to give explanations that were purely internal to the object.

These cultural differences seem to be embedded in larger, coherent, culture-specific cognitive styles. In addition to a focus on the object and relative insensitivity to the field, Western thought relies on abstract categories in reasoning. In recent studies, for example, Choi, Nisbett, and Smith (1997) found that Koreans were less likely than Americans to rely spontaneously on categories in category-based induction, and Norenzayan, Nisbett, and Smith (1999) found that category learning based on formal application of rules was more difficult for East Asians than for Americans. So it appears that Asian and Western understandings of the causes of events are different in fundamental ways. Americans presume that events are produced by attributes or category memberships of the individual or object; Chinese presume that behavior is at least in part a consequence of factors operating in the field in which behavior occurs.

We may now ask two important questions about the divergent theories of social behavior in the East and the West, questions that have not been addressed in past cross-cultural studies:

1. What is the origin of this East-West cultural difference? Is it due to differences in dispositional theory, or to differences in situational theory, or to a combination of the two? Do East Asians have weak or nonexistent personality theories, and is this why a cultural difference is observed in explanations for behavior?
2. Can Western meta-theories about causality be shown to be literally mistaken such that they produce erroneous explanations where East Asian explanations would be correct? In other words, can one make a clear normative statement about cultural differences as opposed to a mere preferential bias statement?

A careful look at the psychological evidence across cultures, ethnographic studies, and recent experimental work—our own and that of others—suggest that the answer to the first question is that stronger situational attribution for Asians may be the primary source for the cultural difference, and that there is relatively little difference in the strength of dispositional theories across cultures. As to the second question, preliminary evidence supports the normative interpretation of cultural variation in causal attribution: it can be shown that East Asians are sometimes more accurate in their causal attributions than Americans. In what follows, we present evidence suggesting that dispositionism is a widespread mode of thinking across cultures, including East Asian cultures. Next, we review experimental evidence supporting the conclusion that the primary source of the East-West cultural difference lies in a stronger belief among East Asians in the power of the social situation to shape social behavior.

## PERSONALITY THEORIES WEST AND EAST

There is much support in the anthropological literature for the claim that Western theory of behavior is uniquely dispositional and that non-Western societies, both literate and preliterate, are less enamored of traits (Dumont 1985; Hsu 1953; Read 1955; Shweder and Bourne 1991). These views clearly fit with the data on descriptions of self and other and with the evidence on attributions that we have just discussed. Thus, it comes as a surprise to discover that personality theories are very much alive and well in the East.

## Ethnographic Accounts of Lay Dispositionism

In fact, the anthropological literature itself provides evidence of dispositional thinking in many non-Western cultures. Often, ethnopsychological reports that describe a situation-centered folk theory of behavior also report some degree of dispositionism in the same societies. For example, after describing a rich situation-centered folk psychology among the Ifaluk—an indigenous people of Micronesia—Lutz (1985) points out that "a final type of explanation for behavior is one made in terms of enduring personality traits such as 'hot temper' or 'calmness'" (58). Similarly, various ethnographers have reported dispositionist thinking in traditional societies in Africa (Abimbola 1973; La Fontaine 1985; Olivier de Sardan 1973; Whiting 1996) and in certain historical periods in China (Elvin 1985; Munro 1985; Nakamura 1964/1985).

In a study of the Brahman community in India—a people with a situation-centered theory of the person—Richard Shweder (cited in Shweder and Bourne 1991) gave his Indian informants a list of phrases describing concrete behaviors and asked them to categorize these behaviors in terms of underlying general personality characteristics. The informants successfully generated abstract trait and type terms, indicating that the informants were capable of inferring underlying general traits from concrete behaviors. Referring to words for personality traits in the Oriya language, Shweder and Bourne (1991) wrote that "a casual perusal of G. C. Praharaj's seven-volume lexicon of the Oriya language (1931–1940) should dissuade anyone who believes that the Oriya informants speak a language that lacks abstract personality trait and type concepts" (141).

## Cognitive Organization of Personality Structure Across Cultures

A growing body of research has found that, when English-language personality instruments are translated into other languages, the same five-factor model, or "Big Five" factors, of personality—extroversion, neuroticism, conscientiousness, agreeableness, and openness (Goldberg 1990)—are extracted from ratings of self and others by Dutch, German, Spanish, Italian, Finnish, and Polish participants (McCrae, Costa, and Yik 1996). There is also evidence that the Big Five emerge in East Asian cultures. The same five-factor structure was extracted in Hong Kong Chinese undergraduates using the Chinese translation of the NEO-PI-R, an instrument based on the Big Five and developed and standardized in the United States (McCrae et al. 1996). The five factors were also replicated in mainland China (Leung et al. in press), in Taiwan (Yang and Bond 1990) and in Korea (Piedmont and Chae 1997). Some replications in East Asia have produced fewer than five factors. For example, the first four of the five factors were clearly identified for Japanese (Bond, Nakazato, and Shiraishi 1975) and in the Philippines (Guthrie and Bennet 1971), but the same is often true in the West (Digman 1990; McCrae et al. 1996).

All of these studies used translated versions of personality assessment inventories developed in the United States. Recently Cheung and her colleagues launched a major effort in China to develop an indigenous Chinese personality inventory (Cheung et al. in press; Cheung et al. 1996). Based on a rich variety of indigenous material, as well as personality scales commonly found in English-language tests, the authors constructed the Chinese Personality Assessment Inventory (CPAI) and administered it to a large sample of participants from Hong Kong and other parts of mainland China. Their factor-analytic solution revealed four factors, three of which roughly corresponded to the conscientiousness, extroversion, and neuroticism of the Big Five. Interestingly, the researchers found an indigenous factor, which they described as the "Chinese tradition" factor, a construct that captures personality descriptions related to maintenance of interpersonal and inner harmony and *Ren Qin* (relationship orientation). Cheung et al. (1996) subsequently conducted a joint factor analysis of the CPAI items and the Chinese translation of the NEO-PI-R based on the same Chinese sample. The results revealed six factors, the five factors plus the Chinese tradition factor. It is worth noting that none of the NEO-PI-R scales loaded on the Chinese tradition factor, and none of the CPAI scales loaded on the openness factor. Thus, openness, the smallest and least reliable factor of the Big Five, although recognizable, seems not to be a culturally relevant personality dimension for the Chinese. Conversely, the Chinese tradition dimension is a major personality construct for the Chinese entirely missed by Western personality instruments (though it is an interesting question for further research to see whether the factor would emerge for Westerners responding to a translated CPAI).

In sum, the cross-cultural replications of the cognitive organization of personality structure—based on imported as well as indigenous instruments—clearly suggest that people in East Asia recognize and cognitively organize personality information in a manner rather similar to that in the West. Although the number of personality dimensions that emerge varies from study to study, and the salience of various personality constructs differs across cultures in interesting ways, implicit personality theory appears to coexist with situationist thought in the cultures of East Asia.

## Trait-Based Predictions of Social Behavior

Thus, there is good evidence for a substantial overlap between Western and East Asian perceptions of personality structure. Representing personality information, however, does not guarantee the *use* of that information in social judgment. But recent social psychological evidence shows that East Asians can indeed be shown to make dispositional inferences from behavioral data in much the same way that Westerners do. When Norenzayan, Choi, and Nisbett (1998) asked Chinese and American participants to make predictions about the behavior of an actor given knowledge of the actor's behavior in another situation, East Asian participants made predictions that were fully as disposition-based as those of Americans. Following a paradigm established by Kunda and Nisbett (1986), these investigators presented participants with items stating that two people had been observed in the same situation and person A had been found to be more helpful (or dishonest, talkative, and so on) than person B; participants were then asked to predict the likelihood that person A would behave in a more helpful fashion when observed in a later situation. American and Chinese participants gave the same, quite mistakenly high, estimates. Participants' probability estimates corresponded to correlation coefficients of .64 and .68 for Americans and Chinese, respectively. In a second condition, trait-implying behaviors were described concretely without mentioning any traits. For example, the concrete behavior scenario for "helpful" read:

> Suppose you observed two people, A and B, being asked to participate in a blood donation drive and saw that A volunteers to work more hours than B collecting blood. What do you suppose is the probability that, being approached by a homeless person asking for money to buy food, A gives more money to the homeless person than B?

For this variant, both American and Chinese participants predicted consistencies equivalent to a correlation of .66. Another manipulation draws on evidence by Reeder and Brewer (1979) and Gidron, Koehler, and Tversky (1993) showing that people implicitly quantify the consistency of traits in terms of their *scope.* Traits high in scope (for example, helpful, talkative) are perceived to require many behavioral instances to infer their existence, whereas traits low in scope (for example, dishonest, creative) are perceived to require very few behavioral instances. In other words, low-scope traits are believed to be more strongly disposition-based than high-scope traits. Gidron and his colleagues found that undesirable traits were perceived to have low scope whereas desirable ones have higher scope. Norenzayan and his colleagues extended this finding, demonstrating that trait scope, often measured using a frequency estimation method, also affects predictions of cross-situational consistency of behavior. Participants predicted higher cross-situational stability for low-scope behaviors compared to high-scope behaviors. Their Chinese participants proved to be fully as sensitive to the scope manipulation as were their American participants. This finding indicates that the two cultural groups share the same implicit beliefs about the relative dispositional strength of high-scope and low-scope behaviors.

In another study, Norenzayan et al. (1998) manipulated the apparent similarity of the situations about which participants were to make predictions. If Asians possess a strong personality theory, they might be expected to make trait-based predictions not only for similar situations but also from one situation to another, quite different one. And indeed, Chinese participants were not only as likely to make strong predictions about consistency as American participants for the similar situations, they were also as likely to do so for the different situations. Moreover, neither group of participants was significantly sensitive to the similarity manipulation; both gave predictions that were as strong across different situations as across similar situations. This was true despite the fact that participants agreed with the experimenters that the different situations were indeed much more different from each other than the similar situations, and despite the fact that *within* each condition, participants' judgments about the similarity of the situations were a good predictor of the strength of their predictions about consistency of behavior—for both American and Chinese participants. In addition, as in the previous study, both American and Chinese participants again gave stronger predictions for low-scope behaviors compared to high-scope behaviors.

## CULTURAL VARIATION IN SENSITIVITY TO THE CONTEXT OF BEHAVIOR

In a follow-up behavioral prediction study, Norenzayan et al. (1998) examined sensitivity to situational constraints, manipulating the degree to which the situation seemed to facilitate or inhibit trait-consistent behavior. Korean and American participants read vignettes of the following type, which is an example of a situation that would seem to inhibit trait-consistent behavior—in this case, helpfulness:

> You just met a new neighbor, Jim. As you and Jim are taking a walk in the neighborhood, a well-dressed man approaches Jim and explains that his car

> is broken down and he needs to call a mechanic. Then with a somewhat embarrassed voice the man asks Jim for a quarter to make the phone call. You find that Jim searches his pocket and after finding a quarter, gives it to the man. On another day Jim is walking toward the bus stop to catch the bus to work. As he is walking, a teenager carrying some books approaches Jim and politely asks him if he can borrow a dollar for a bus ride, explaining that he forgot his wallet at home and needs to get a ride to school. Jim searches his pocket and discovers that he has only one dollar with him. He realizes that if he gives the dollar to the teenager, he will not be able to ride the bus himself and will miss an important business meeting. Do you think Jim will give the dollar to the teenager?

The facilitating condition was identical, except that in the second part participants received facilitating information. Thus, instead of having only one dollar in his pocket, Jim "searches his pocket and discovers that he has several dollars with him, enough money to pay for his bus ride and for the teenager's."

Participants were asked to make predictions, on a one-hundred-point scale, about the likelihood that the actor would perform the target behavior. *Either before or after they did so,* however, they estimated how many people out of one hundred in this situation would perform the target behavior. If East Asians are more sensitive to situational constraints, the difference between their base-rate estimates for the facilitating and the inhibiting scenarios should be greater than those of Americans. Furthermore, if East Asians are more willing than Americans to apply these base rates to the behavior of a single individual, East Asian predictions for the target individual should differ more across situations than American predictions. Indeed, as can be seen in figure 8.1, whether participants gave their base-rate estimates before or after they made their predictions for the target individual, Korean base rates were more extreme than those of Americans—indicating stronger Korean sensitivity to situational constraints. As to the predictions concerning the target individual's behavior (see figure 8.2), when participants had not yet made their base-rate estimates at the time they made their predictions for the single individual, there was no cultural difference in the sensitivity to the facilitation-inhibition manipulation. However, when the base-rate estimates were made *before* the target case predictions, the predictions of Koreans were more extreme (in the direction of the situational information: facilitating versus inhibiting) than those of Americans. In short, if the base rates were made salient—if participants were encouraged to think about the power of the situation in an explicit way before making their predictions—Koreans were more situation-sensitive in their predictions than Americans. For Americans, in contrast, reflect-

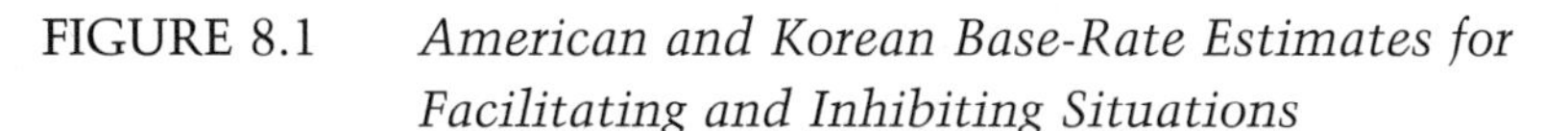

FIGURE 8.1 *American and Korean Base-Rate Estimates for Facilitating and Inhibiting Situations*

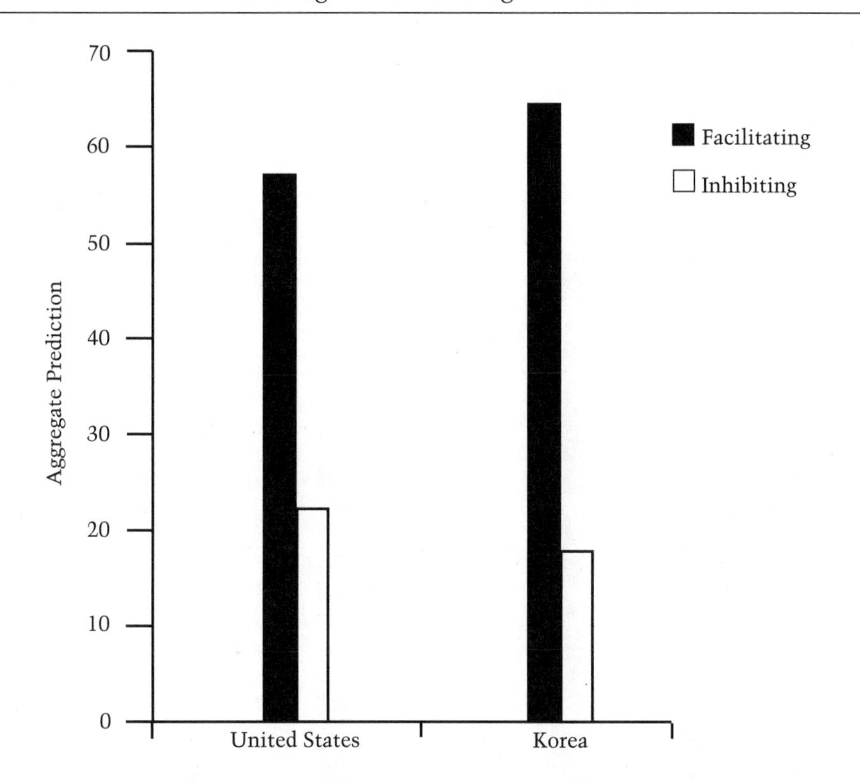


*Notes:* Dependent variable is the estimated number of people out of randomly selected 100 who would engage in the behavior specified in each scenario.

ing about situational power seemed to have no effect on their behavioral predictions for the single individual.

These findings tell us several important things about the lay theories of Americans and East Asians. First, they indicate that East Asians do indeed have dispositional theories and are quite willing to apply them to predictions about actual behavior. Second, they tell us that East Asians, like Americans, can fail to take situational information sufficiently into account, as in the study described earlier in which the similarity of the situations was manipulated. In addition, under some conditions, East Asians can show the same degree of sensitivity to situations that Americans do, such as in the condition of the experiment just de-

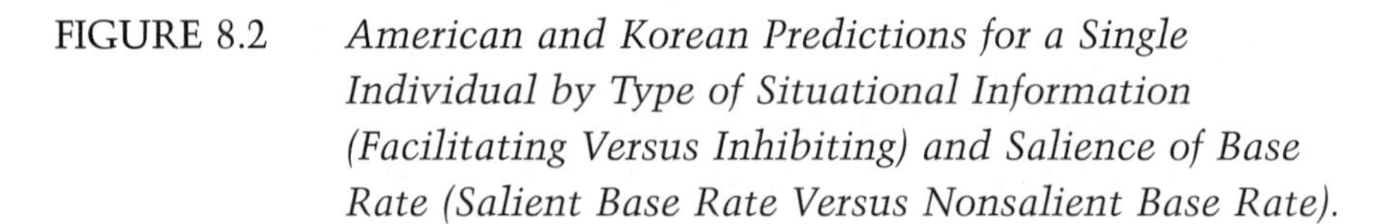

FIGURE 8.2 *American and Korean Predictions for a Single Individual by Type of Situational Information (Facilitating Versus Inhibiting) and Salience of Base Rate (Salient Base Rate Versus Nonsalient Base Rate).*

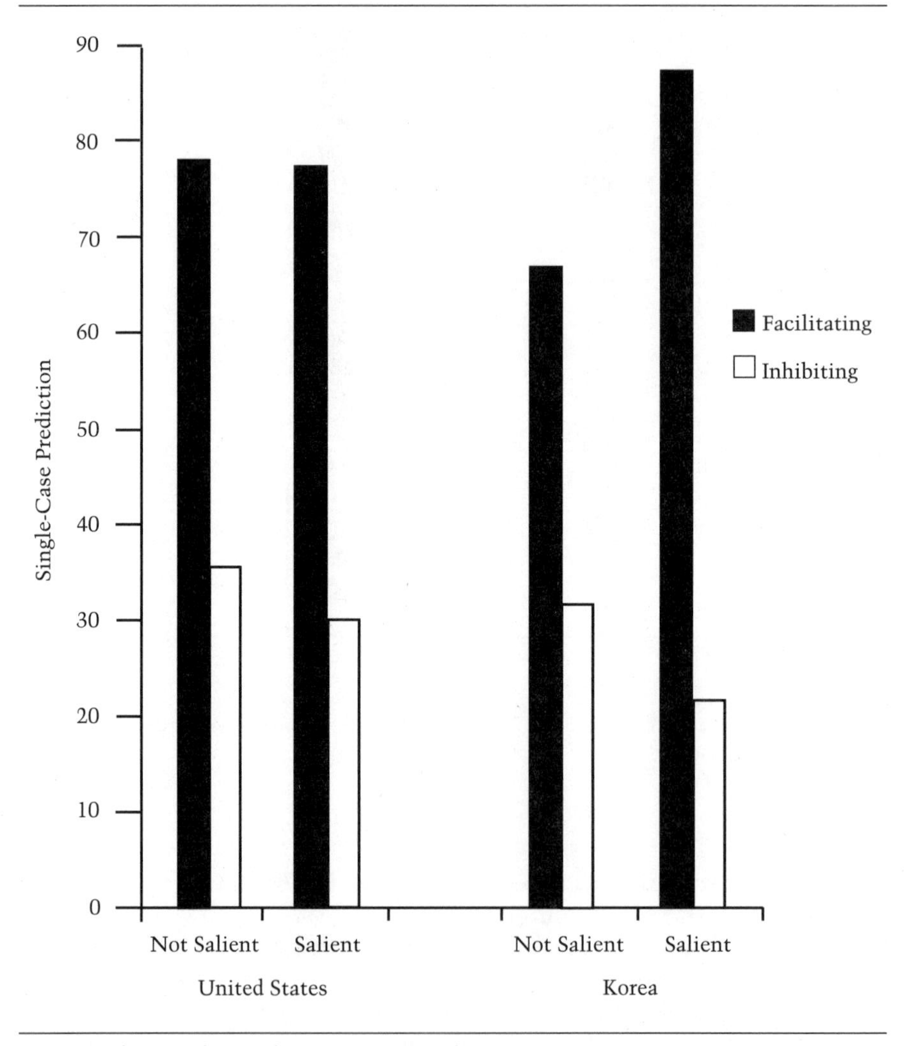


*Notes:* Higher numbers indicate stronger predictons.

scribed, in which the base rates were not made salient before participants made predictions about the target. These observations suggest the possibility that Asians may also show the FAE under some circumstances. Third, these results indicate that East Asians may be more capable of transforming situational information into base-rate information, which then can be used to make more situation-sensitive predictions.

There is some other evidence indicating that East Asians may be more willing to use base-rate information for purposes of causal analysis and prediction. Cha and Nam (1985) have shown that the East Asian understanding of the relevance of the situation is sufficiently great that they are willing to use base-rate or consensus information in the McArthur (1972) paradigm to a much greater degree than American participants. In that paradigm, participants were presented with an item of information about someone's behavior, for example, "While dancing, Ralph tripped over Joan's feet," and then presented with manipulations of three types of information: distinctiveness (Ralph trips over almost everyone else's/hardly anyone else's feet), consistency (in the past Ralph had almost always/hardly ever tripped over Joan's feet), and consensus (almost everyone/hardly anyone trips over Joan's feet). Following the manipulation of information, participants were asked to indicate why Ralph tripped over Joan's feet. Though consensus information would seem to be highly relevant to an explanation, participants' explanations were not much influenced by it. In contrast to McArthur's American participants, Cha and Nam found substantial utilization of consensus information by Korean participants. In fact, Cha and Nam's Korean participants were twice as likely to use consensus information as McArthur's American participants.

Both the findings in the "base-rate salient" condition of the Norenzayan et al. (1998) experiment and the Cha and Nam (1985) results suggest that East Asians are indeed willing to use situational information for social inference where Westerners are not. Work by Choi and Nisbett (1998) and others strengthens this conclusion in another paradigm—that of attitude attribution.

One of the first demonstrations of the FAE was by Jones and Harris (1967), who asked their participants to read an essay, allegedly written by another student, that was either for or against some position on an important social question of the day. When participants were told that the essayist had free choice about which side to take in writing the essay, they inferred, of course, that the actual attitude of the student who wrote the "pro" essay was much more favorable than the actual attitude of the student who wrote the "con" essay. Other participants, however, were told that the target had no choice about which side to take in the essay. For example, they were told that the target was required to write an essay exam taking a particular position. Though logically this information should eliminate participants' inference that the essay reflected the actual attitude of the target, this was far from the case. In fact, the difference between estimated attitudes for pro and con targets was about two-thirds as great for no-choice participants as for choice participants.

A remarkable finding by Jones and Harris (1967), as well as by Snyder and Jones (1974), was that even when participants—prior to estimating the target's opinions—were put through the same no-choice procedure as targets allegedly had been, they continued to persist in their "correspondent inferences." Attributions of attitudes were fully as strong as in the standard no-choice condition! This makes the profundity of the error in the Jones and Harris paradigm particularly clear. It also allows for the possibility of a clear demonstration that Asians can avoid a mistake made by Westerners. Might Asians be open to the situational information to some degree, modifying the extremity of their estimates if they themselves were put through the no-choice procedure?

Choi and Nisbett (1998) duplicated the basic choice and no-choice conditions of the Jones and Harris (1967), study as well as the two extra conditions of the Snyder and Jones (1974) study. In one of these two conditions—the exposure condition— participants were asked to write an essay, just as the target person allegedly had done. Then they read the target person's essay and were asked to judge his or her true attitude. The other condition—the exposure-plus-arguments condition—was the same as the exposure condition, but participants were also shown a list of arguments they might use in their essay and told that the target person was given the same list of arguments. (In fact, the target essay contained all the arguments in the list.) The topic was the advisability of capital punishment. It may be seen in figure 8.3 that Korean participants made a strong and erroneous dispositional inference in the standard no-choice condition. Their inferences were actually somewhat stronger than those of American participants. Just as Snyder and Jones found, Americans in the two conditions in which participants were exposed to the no-choice essay-writing treatment were as likely to make strong correspondent inferences as were participants who were not put through the procedure. Korean participants, in contrast, made less extreme inferences when they were put through the procedure themselves, and even less extreme inferences when they were also shown arguments they could use.

In an effort to gauge any possible actor-observer differences in attribution, participants in the Choi and Nisbett (1998) study were asked two questions. First, they were asked to indicate the degree to which the attitudes expressed in their essay actually reflected their own true attitudes. Second, they rated the degree to which the attitudes expressed in the target person's essay reflected that person's true attitudes. For Korean participants, there was no evidence for an actor-observer effect. Korean attributions for their own attitudes were no different from their

FIGURE 8.3 *Correspondence Bias for Americans and Koreans as the Difference in the Inferred True Attitude Between the Pro-Essay and Anti-Essay No-Choice Conditions*

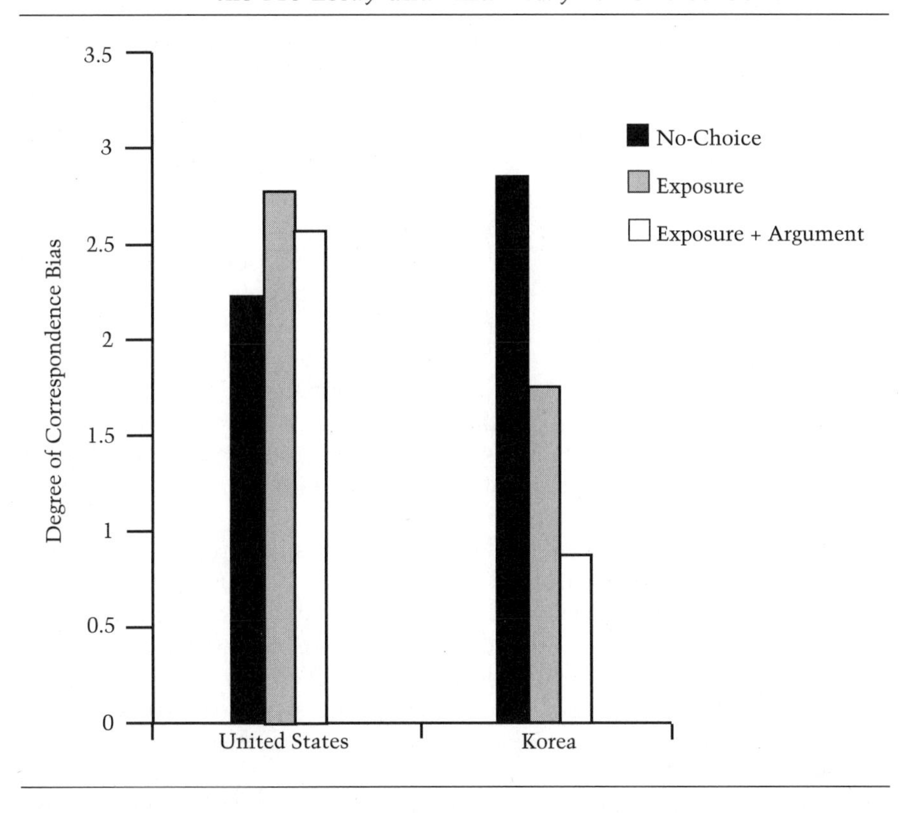


attributions of the target person's attitude. This suggests that Koreans recognized that, just as the attitudes they themselves had expressed had no necessary relation to their actual attitudes, the same was true of the target person. Americans, however, showed the standard actor-observer effect. They thought that the target person's true attitude was closer to the attitude expressed in the essay than was the case for themselves, indicating an inability or unwillingness to see that the situational pressures operating on them were also operating on the target person.

Kitayama and Masuda (1997) and Masuda and Kitayama (1996) also used a paradigm similar to that of Jones and Harris (1967), with Japanese participants. The topic was environmental protection. In the free-choice condition, participants saw a target person either for or against greater protection. In a standard no-choice condition, participants were told that because the experimenter needed a video of one of the two positions, he had asked the target person to read that position rather than the other. Like American participants, and like the Korean participants in the standard no-choice condition of the Choi and Nisbett (1998) study, Japanese participants showed the correspondence bias. (A similar correspondence bias was found with Chinese participants by Krull et al. 1996). The other two conditions in the Masuda and Kitayama study were modeled after a procedure developed by Gilbert and Jones (1986). The study was conducted in pairs. One of the participants assigned to the "observer" condition chose between two identical envelopes that contained essays to be read by the target person. The target person then read the essay chosen by the participant in the "observer" condition in front of a video camera. Here it should be very obvious to the "observer" participant that the target person neither wrote nor chose the essay he read. Even in these conditions, Gilbert and Jones found clear evidence for correspondence bias in American participants. But Masuda and Kitayama found that their Japanese participants in these conditions did not show the correspondence bias. Once the social inducement information was made obvious, the content of the essay had no effect on the attitude inferences of the Japanese participants.

Thus, the evidence reviewed so far indicates that the East-West differences in causal attributions derive primarily from East Asians' relative sensitivity to situational influences on behavior, not from their lack of dispositionist beliefs. More direct evidence for such a conclusion comes from Norenzayan et al. (1998). They developed three arguments about human behavior, each representing dispositionism, situationism, or interactionism. The dispositionist argument emphasized the importance of personality traits in determining behavior, the predictability of behavior from knowledge of personality traits, and the stability of behavior across time and situations. The situationist argument maintained that situations are powerful determinants of behavior, that situational information is more important than personality in predicting and explaining individual behavior, and that people with different personality traits often behave similarly in the same situation. Finally, the interactionist argument presented the view that human behavior is best understood in terms of a complex interaction between personality traits and the situations in which people behave.

As expected, Korean and American participants did not differ in their endorsement of the dispositionist argument (United States = 4.59; Korea = 4.89; $p$ = *ns*). However, Koreans endorsed situationism (United States = 4.68; Korea = 5.23; $p < .005$) and interactionism (United States = 7.32; Korea = 7.99; $p < .001$) more than the Americans did.

This pattern of data, based on the self-report of the participants' lay theory of behavior, converges with that of the various social inference data reviewed earlier.

## THE FAE: ARE EASTERNERS RIGHT WHERE WESTERNERS ARE WRONG?

The cross-cultural studies in social inference raise a very important question: Which culture is more accurate? Two different answers can be proposed. One is that we cannot compare accuracy of causal judgments across cultures because the actual impact of dispositions versus situations on behavior may differ across cultures. For example, it might be the case that situations are indeed a more powerful determinant of behavior in the East than in the West (Argyle, Shimoda, and Little 1978). The second answer is that we can in fact render a normative judgment when participants from different cultures are making judgments about the same social situation and we know the actual contribution of situational and dispositional factors to social behavior in that given situation.

From this second point of view, several studies reviewed earlier allow us to make tentative normative judgments. As we have just discussed in detail, Choi and Nisbett (1998) and Masuda and Kitayama (1996) found that when the situational constraints were made salient by exposing participants to the same constraints as targets, or by making participants impose the constraints on others, Koreans and Japanese, unlike American participants, readily corrected their dispositionist errors to a substantial degree—as everyone should do in such circumstances. Furthermore, when participants were exposed to the same powerful situational constraints as the target person, Koreans, but not Americans, realized that the target person's behavior was no more a true reflection of his attitude than their own behavior was for themselves.

Other evidence supporting the view that East Asians' causal judgments better correspond to normative criteria comes from the prediction study by Norenzayan et al. (1998), which demonstrated that Korean participants utilized base-rate information more than American participants did, and from the finding of more use of consensus information in the McArthur paradigm for Korean participants by Cha and Nam (1985). Both studies indicate that base-rate information or consensus information is incorporated into causal judgments more for Korean participants than for American participants, as it normatively should be. In sum, it appears that East Asian folk psychology, as it relates to causal attribution, better corresponds to the findings and theory of scientific psychology than does American folk psychology.

## WESTERN DISPOSITIONISM AND EASTERN CONTEXTUALISM: SOME PRELIMINARY CONCLUSIONS ABOUT CAUSAL ATTRIBUTION ACROSS CULTURES

So where do we now stand with respect to the continuing saga of the universality of causal attribution processes and the FAE? First, the cross-cultural evidence we have reviewed suggests that dispositional thinking is a widespread mode of thinking across cultures, and that it can be shown to operate in the thinking of East Asians as well.

1. Ethnographic work shows evidence in everyday contexts for dispositional thought in a wide range of cultures in Africa, Asia, the Pacific islands, and the West.
2. Questionnaire studies of personality structure show clear belief in traits among East Asians and considerable convergence with the same lay personality structure used by Westerners. East Asian participants and Americans are equally likely to endorse an explicitly stated lay dispositionist theory of human behavior.
3. East Asians show clear reliance on dispositional theories in predicting behavior; indeed, their predictions show the same degree of such reliance as do the predictions of Americans.
4. Beliefs about the scope of traits, with desirable traits having higher scope than undesirable ones, appear to be the same among East Asians as among Americans. This finding indicates that East Asians and Westerners converge in their implicit beliefs about the dispositional strength of behaviors—that negative behaviors are more dispositionally produced than positive ones.
5. In three different experiments (Choi and Nisbett 1998; Krull et al. 1996; Masuda and Kitayama 1996), East Asians have been shown to display behavior that very closely matches what we call the FAE. It should be stressed, however, that only one basic paradigm—attitude attribution—was used in all three experiments, and other interpretations are possible even for these studies (see Choi and Nisbett 1998).

Second, we can conclude from the cross-cultural evidence that East Asian thinking is more strongly prevaded by situationism than Western thinking.

1. East Asians describe themselves and others more contextually than Westerners do, and they explain the behavior of others more contex-

tually than do Westerners, in controlled experiments as well as in naturalistic settings, such as in newspaper reports of social events. This difference emerges even for relatively "content-free" stimuli, such as when explaining the behavior of cartoon fish pictures on a computer screen.

2. East Asians are more sensitive to behavioral base rates (or consensus information) than Westerners. When encouraged to think about situational power, East Asian predictions of social behavior are more situation-sensitive than Western predictions.
3. When situational constraints are made salient, East Asians readily take into account situational influence and avoid the FAE to a substantial degree (and often completely); under the same conditions, Americans show almost complete insensitivity to situational salience manipulations and show the same degree of the FAE.
4. When asked to evaluate explicitly stated dispositionist, situationist, and interactionist arguments, East Asians endorse situationist and interactionist arguments of human behavior more than Americans do, although the two cultures are equally likely to endorse dispositionism.

Although the diversity of the cross-cultural evidence considered in this chapter allows us to transcend the weaknesses of individual studies and discover emerging general themes, it should be noted that most of the psychological studies reviewed relied on samples derived from college populations, both in the United States and in East Asia. On the one hand, it can be argued that college education across cultures selects people who share a similar set of values and goals, and that it thus has a homogenizing effect on students. That is, higher education around the globe is likely to expose students to a similar set of experiences, values, and knowledge. As a result, it is all the more remarkable that the systematic cultural differences in these studies emerged despite this inherent restriction on cultural variation. On the other hand, the observed cross-cultural convergences, rather than being due to any deep-rooted psychological commonalities across cultures, may be vulnerable to a sampling explanation. However, this alternative possibility seems unlikely for several of the studies discussed earlier. For example, in Choi and Nisbett's (1998) attitude attribution study and in the Norenzayan et al. (1998) study of ratings of lay theories of behavior, both cross-cultural variation and commonality were found within the same sample. In any case, it is obvious that an important task for future research is to extend the sampling range of cross-cultural studies to noncollege populations.

We now consider the central issue of this chapter: if Easterners think as dispositionally as Westerners, how can we explain the cultural difference in causal attribution and prediction? To answer this question, it is important to consider the attribution process in some detail. It consists of at least two qualitatively distinct cognitive operations: an initial dispositional inference and a subsequent situational correction (Gilbert and Malone 1995), or, when people are led initially to focus on the situation, a situational inference followed by dispositional correction (Krull 1993; for a description of the attribution process, see Gilbert and Malone 1995). The evidence we have presented suggests that the primary source of the cultural variation lies in situational inference. Dispositional inference, in contrast, appears to be relatively similar across cultures. This finding helps to explain why some studies discover a cultural difference in attribution and some do not; it also allows us to predict under what conditions we can expect a cultural difference to emerge. When situational cues are unavailable or are far from obvious, East Asians may infer dispositions from behavior as much as Westerners do. However, when strong and salient situational information is present, Easterners more than Westerners will correct their dispositional inferences in response to situational constraints. Thus, we refer to East Asian theories of social behavior as *contextualist* or *interactionist* (rather than situationist), in that behavior is seen as the result of an interaction between the social context and the internal attributes of the actor. Western theories, in contrast, can be characterized as *dispositionist,* because they emphasize the internal attributes of the actor and often slight situational determinants of behavior.

Regardless of whether East Asians can be shown to manifest the FAE—and we suspect that they do (if only because Asian social psychologists of our acquaintance teach the FAE and use examples from daily life in East Asia to support it)—the evidence seems fairly clear that Asians can avoid the error to a very substantial degree under circumstances in which Americans fall prey to it completely. Some of these studies have a clear normative interpretation. Situational constraint information should be taken into account when making predictions, generating causal explanations, or inferring attributes. Personally experiencing the situation confronting the actor should also affect these variables. Furthermore, if East Asians can use situational information significantly more than Westerners, then they have been shown to have not only different theories about the social world but different "epistemologies" that tell them how to make use of information about situations and base rates, resulting in more accurate interpretations of events.

# CONVERGENCE AND DIVERGENCE IN LAY THEORIES OF BEHAVIOR: HOW DID THEY ARISE AND WHAT WILL HAPPEN TO THEM?

## Convergence

A powerful research strategy in cultural psychology's tool kit is its capacity to uncover interesting cross-cultural regularities, parallel to its mission of describing how the cultural context shapes mental processes. It is important, then, to examine the basic similarity between East Asian and Western folk theories of behavior. As we have seen, the two cultures converge—at least when situational information is inconspicuous or unavailable—on the extent to which dispositional information is used to explain and predict the behavior of others. Why should this be the case? There are important theoretical grounds for believing that dispositional thinking is cross-culturally widespread. Social psychologists have long known that a defining characteristic of dispositional thinking is the view that social behavior is the observable manifestation of underlying, invisible, enduring psychological traits—that is, most people believe that traits are not merely superficial summary evaluations of statistical regularities in behavior. This suggests that lay dispositionism is a form of *psychological essentialism,* a cross-culturally widespread mode of thinking by which a hidden essence is attributed to a thing or a category; that essence makes the thing or the category what it is and allows one to make inferences about its observable as well as hidden properties (Atran 1990; Gelman 1992; Gelman, Coley, and Gottfried 1994; Medin and Ortony 1989). Although it is still not known to what extent people in different cultures think in an essentialistic fashion about personality, essentialism in other domains has been reported in a large variety of cultures, from industrial societies to hunter-gatherers, and is believed to play a part in people's folk-biological reasoning, as well as in reasoning about social groups. Gelman, Coley, and Gottfried (1994) describe the striking similarities between biological and dispositional thinking and suggest that dispositionism is essentialism in the domain of folk psychology. Just as the "biological essence" of a zebra causes it to develop a striped coat and eat grass, an individual's personality is her "psychological essence" that causes her to think, feel, and behave in particular ways.

Dispositional thinking could be part of a theory of mind based on "belief-desire" psychology, which consists of understanding the behavior of other people as the product of the joint action of beliefs and desires (Wellman 1990). Although the folk psychological beliefs of cultures differ in fundamental ways (for a review, see Lillard 1998), growing evidence indicates that basic belief-desire psychology is widespread, with data from North America, Europe, East Asia, and at least one hunter-gatherer group in Africa confirming its common occurrence cross-culturally (Avis and Harris 1991; D'Andrade 1987; Flavell et al. 1983; Gardner et al. 1988). On this account, dispositional inference results from the assumption that individuals have beliefs and desires that are consistent across time and place. For example, Mother Theresa was someone who had a chronic desire to assist others and regularly believed that others needed her help. As a result, she acted in a helpful manner all the time. She was a "helpful" person. Thus, dispositions provide inferentially rich frames of regularities within a person that allow us to predict his or her beliefs, desires, preferences, and behaviors—or at least to believe that we can do so.

## Divergence

Although the evidence clearly shows that East Asians engage in dispositional inference, there is a good case to be made that Eastern dispositionism differs from Western dispositionism in an important way. Work by Harold Stevenson and his colleagues (for example, Stevenson and Lee 1996) provides evidence that East Asian dispositional beliefs about achievement behavior are more flexible and sensitive to variation in environmental conditions than those of Americans. East Asians are less likely to attribute achievement behavior to ability and more likely to attribute it to effort. This is because, as we have argued, Easterners' strong belief in the external world as a determinant of human nature influences their personality theory (Munro 1985).

This cultural difference in beliefs about the alterability of personality traits parallels the individual-difference construct as advanced by Carol Dweck and her colleagues (Dweck, Hong, and Chiu 1993) describing differences between an "entity" theory versus an "incremental" theory of personality. Entity theorists readily infer global dispositions from limited behavioral evidence (Chiu, Hong, and Dweck 1997). We propose that entity theory corresponds to Western dispositionism: it consists of a belief that personality traits are relatively fixed. An incremental theory of personality is characterized by a belief that personality traits are malleable, a belief that is also characteristic of Eastern dispositionism. Note that both entity and incremental theorists infer traits from behavior, but incremental theorists make dispositional inferences that are context-specific rather than global, and their trait inferences are more responsive to changes in circumstances (Chiu et al. 1997; Dweck et al. 1993).

Indeed, recently evidence has emerged that East Asians' dispositional beliefs, compared to Americans' beliefs, are closer to those held by incremental theorists. Choi and Markus (1997) found that East Asian dispositional explanations are more context-specific than American ones. More important, Norenzayan et al. (1998) gave to Korean and American college students the scales measuring entity versus incremental theory of personality devised by Erdley and Dweck (1993). Participants were asked to rate how much they agreed with the following four statements, which are known to elicit disagreement from incremental theorists.

1. Someone's personality is something about them that they can't change very much.
2. A person can do things to get people to like them, but they can't change their real personality.
3. Everyone has a certain personality, and it is something that they can't do much about.
4. A person can change the way they act, but they can't change their real personality.

The results showed that Korean students disagreed with each of the four statements more than American students, indicating that Koreans endorse an incremental theory of personality to a greater degree than Americans.

An incremental theory of dispositions in East Asians is consistent with their construal of the self (Markus, Kitayama, and Heiman 1996). Markus and her colleagues argue that people in Eastern cultures use a "tree" as a metaphor for a person, highlighting the endless shaping of internal dispositions by external environment. For instance, in Korea a person is believed to be like a white root that takes on the color of the soil within which it grows. If a white root is planted in red soil, it becomes red. Once the self is likened to a plant, it is evident that the environment is essential for the development, nourishment, and cultivation of the person.

We now consider the more fundamental difference between Eastern and Western folk psychology: the Eastern focus on the field or situation in which behavior occurs, and the Western focus on the object or the actor. How did Eastern and Western cultures become so different? A Chinese philosopher of our acquaintance has said, only half-jokingly, that "it's because the East had Confucius and the West had Aristotle."

Perhaps, but presumably these thinkers did not invent themselves but rather were products of their societies.

It has been suggested by many scholars that the relevant societal differences were economic at base (Gernet 1982 [cited in Lloyd 1990]; Lloyd 1990; Nakamura 1964/1985; Needham 1962). From very early on, East Asians have been agriculturalists, who must cooperate to survive, and their societies, especially if based on irrigation, have been correspondingly complex and interdependent. In such a culture, the social world takes on great importance for the conduct of daily life: attention must be paid to a large number of people and role relations. Europeans, in contrast, were generally nomadic until a much later point and lived by hunting and the keeping of animals. Both hunting and herding encourage individualism: focusing only on oneself and the particular object with which one is engaged rather than simultaneously holding in mind a wide array of obligations and roles.

Witkin and Berry (1975) have argued that modern industrial society requires something like the same focus on the object and the self that hunting and gathering and herding economies do. They argue that, in some respects, hunters, herders, and members of modern industrial society may resemble one another cognitively more than they resemble agriculturalists. Their analysis suggests that, with increasing industrialization of East Asian countries, Easterners may come to resemble Westerners, and there is a bit of evidence to suggest that this may be the case.

Hong, Chiu, and Kung (1996) recently studied the Morris and Peng (1994) "fish paradigm" with a group of Chinese participants who were native to Hong Kong and familiar with Western culture. The responses resembled those shown by Morris and Peng's American or Chinese participants depending on whether the later participants were primed by American or Chinese symbols prior to making attributions for the behavior of the fish. Those participants who were primed by a set of symbols emblematic of American culture (for example, a picture of the American flag or a cowboy) gave more internal attributions, as did Morris and Peng's American participants. Participants who were primed with symbols emblematic of traditional Chinese society (for example, the yin and yang or a Chinese dragon) gave responses more like the external attributions of the Chinese participants in the Morris and Peng study. This suggests that the very rapid and far-reaching Westernization of Hong Kong under British rule, or the long capitalist tradition in Hong Kong, or both, may have created a bicultural population capable of responding quite differently depending on cultural context.

Change in China may be occurring even more rapidly than is suggested by the work of Hong, Chiu, and Kung (1996). Mu, Lee, Stevenson, Liu, and Ge (1997) have shown that expressed desire for individual success has increased enormously among Beijing elementary school children in the last ten years. Shin-Ying Lee and Harold Stevenson (personal communication) report that the mothers of these children, over the same time period, have gone from a primary concern with their children's social development to a concern with their psychological development. Although it is still too early to tell, it begins to seem distinctly possible Westernization, more nearly capitalist economies, or both, are steering East Asians in an individualist direction. On the other hand, there are signs that mainstream European American culture, because of increasing contact with Eastern cultures and practices and non-Western immigrant communities, as well as greater public consciousness of the social condition of marginalized communities, is reexamining its individualistic roots and becoming sensitized to the importance of the social context and the power of the collective in shaping social and psychological practices (see, for example, Betancourt and Lopez 1993; Markus and Kitayama 1994). Hence, East and West may be moving toward one another. As intercultural contact becomes increasingly commonplace, however, the opportunity for cultural misunderstandings also grows. We believe cross-cultural research on causal attribution can shed light on this most important topic.

## CULTURAL MISUNDERSTANDINGS

Early Ionian Greeks living in the eighth century B.C. were the first Westerners who left a written record of their encounters with members of another, culturally different group—the Scythian nomadic tribes on the northern steppes of the Black Sea (Ascherson 1995). Since then, understanding "otherness" or "culture" has emerged as one of the most persistent and fascinating questions in the Western intellectual tradition. Along with cross-cultural encounters have come cultural misunderstandings. Many books have been written about this topic, but research exploring the psychological processes that create and sustain misunderstandings between cultures has begun only recently (for such a recent research program focusing on Latin Americans and Anglo-Americans, see Sanchez-Burks, Nisbett, and Ybarra 1998). Cultural misunderstandings can stem from a variety of psychological differences between cultures (see, for example, Markus and Lin, this volume; Iyengar, Lepper, and Ross, this volume), but what can we learn about them from cross-cultural work on causal attribution? From an attributional point of view, a cultural misunderstanding is likely to occur when two individuals from different cultures attribute an actor's behavior to divergent causes—situational versus dispositional.

We would begin by outlining the conditions under which Easterners and Westerners *converge* in their understanding of each other. The cross-cultural evidence we reviewed suggests that when situational information about the other is entirely absent (or present but inconspicuous), both cultures attribute the behavior of the other to its corresponding disposition; hence, no cultural misunderstanding occurs. Importantly, the evidence amassed by Iyengar, Lepper, and Ross (this volume) also supports this analysis. When thinking about the self or an ingroup member, East Asians and Asian Americans were more situational than European Americans. However, when thinking about an outgroup member, East Asians and Asian Americans were as dispositional and often more dispositional than European Americans. Given that in most intercultural encounters people are likely to categorize the other as an outgroup member, this finding suggests that when situational constraints are not salient, causal attribution as such will not be a likely source of cultural misunderstanding between European Americans and East Asians.

A cultural misunderstanding can occur, however, when salient situational information is available to East Asian and Western observers. Because East Asians take contextual information into account more than Westerners do, they are more likely to attribute the other's behavior to situational constraints, whereas Westerners either continue to attribute the same behavior to disposition or severely underuse the situational information in their judgment of the other. One common example of such a cultural divergence between Westerners and Easterners is in perceptions of dishonesty. Westerners assume that an actor's behavior exclusively reflects his internal dispositions, regardless of the situational constraints on his behavior. As a result, any inconsistency in the actor's behavior is taken as evidence for his dishonesty or inauthenticity—another dispositional inference! East Asians, on the other hand, recognize that people behave differently under different circumstances. As a result, they expect more variability in the actor's behavior than Americans do, and they are more willing to attribute this variability to situational constraints, such as role obligations and social pressure (Fiske et al. 1998).

Evidence for these differences comes from work by Kashima, Siegel, Tanaka, and Kashima (1992), who examined the strength of the belief in consistency between attitudes and behavior and found that this belief was much greater among Australians than among Japanese. The Japanese belief presumably reflects an assumption that situations, not dispositions, are frequently responsible for behavior. Similarly, Iwao (1988) asked Americans and Japanese what they preferred to do when confronted with disagreement between their own and another person's views. Americans reported that they preferred to change the other person's views, whereas Japanese were much more likely to ignore the divergence or to pretend to share the other person's views. Again, this would appear to reflect the Japanese belief that personal relations and situational context must take precedence over "being true to oneself."

Beliefs about the causes of behavior inevitably influence beliefs about what ought to cause behavior. Hampden-Turner and Trompenaars (1993) have written about the conflicts that can result from differing normative assumptions about how contractual relations should be affected by changing situational contexts:

> There have been horrendous misunderstandings between Japanese and Western negotiators about how much the specific terms of a contract matter when the circumstances have radically changed. The most notorious case occurred in 1976–77, in the sugar dispute between Australia and Japan. Japanese refiners agreed to a long-term contract to buy Australian sugar in the autumn of 1974—a time of acute crisis for Japan, since the world price of oil had quadrupled and, with it, the nation's import bills. However, the price of sugar fell precipitously, and Japan found herself contracted to pay $160 per ton above the world price for five years. The Japanese immediately asked for a renegotiation of the terms, on the grounds that mutual benefit to the parties required it. Japanese-Australian relationships were more important than the atomistic price agreed to before world sugar prices slumped. But the Australians took the view that a price was a price. . . . Great bitterness and deep misunderstandings ensued. (123)

To the extent that East and West are converging in their descriptive and normative beliefs about human behavior, misunderstandings like this should become less frequent. In the meantime, cultural psychology has something to contribute to the reduction of such misunderstandings by examining how societies differ in their implicit psychological theories and what role such differences play in intercultural contact.

## REFERENCES

Abimbola, W. (1973). The Yoruba concept of human personality. In *La notion de personne en afrique noire* (pp. 73–89). Paris: Éditions du Centre Nationale de la Recherche Scientifique.

Argyle, Michael, Shimoda, Kimiko., and Little, Brian. (1978). Variance due to persons and situations in England and Japan. *British Journal of Social and Clinical Psychology, 17,* 335–37.

Ascherson, Neal. (1995). *Black sea.* London: Jonathan Cape.

Atran, Scott. (1990). *Cognitive foundations of natural history.* New York: Cambridge University Press.

Avis, Jeremy, and Harris, Paul L. (1991). Belief-desire reasoning among Baka children. *Child Development, 62,* 460–67.

Betancourt, Hector, and Lopez, Steven R. (1993). The study of culture, ethnicity, and race in American psychology. *American Psychologist, 48,* 629–37.

Bond, Michael H., Nakazato, Hiroaki, and Shiraishi, Daisuke. (1975). Univer-

sality and distinctiveness in dimensions of Japanese person perception. *Journal of Cross-cultural Psychology, 6,* 346–57.
Cha, J. H., and Nam, K. D. (1985). A test of Kelley's cube theory of attribution: A cross-cultural replication of McArthur's study. *Korean Social Science Journal, 12,* 151–80.
Cheung, Fanny M., Leung, Kwok, Fan, Ruth M., Song, Wei-Zheng, Zhang, Jian-Xin, and Zhang, Jian-Ping. (in press). Development of the Chinese Personality Assessment Inventory (CPAI). *Journal of Cross-Cultural Psychology.*
Cheung, Fanny M., Leung, Kwok, Law, J. S., and Zhang, Jian-Xin. (1996). Indigenous Chinese personality constructs. Paper presented at the Twentieth-sixth International Congress of Psychology, Montreal (August, 1996).
Chiu, L.-H. (1972). A cross-cultural comparison of cognitive styles in Chinese and American children. *International Journal of Psychology, 8,* 235–42.
Chiu, Chi-Yue, Hong, Ying-Yi. and Dweck, Carol S. (1997). Lay dispositionism and implicit theories of personality. *Journal of Personality and Social Psychology, 73,* 19–30.
Choi, Incheol, and Markus, Hazel R. (1997). Implicit theories and causal attribution East and West. Unpublished paper, University of Michigan.
Choi, Incheol, and Nisbett, Richard E. (1998). Situational salience and cultural differences in the correspondence bias and in the actor-observer bias. *Personality and Social Psychology Bulletin, 28,* 949–60.
Choi, Incheol, Nisbett, Richard E., and Norenzayan, Ara. (1999). Causal attribution across cultures: Variation and universality. *Psychological Bulletin, 125,* 47–63.
Choi, Incheol, Nisbett, Richard E., and Smith, Edward E. (1997). Culture, category salience, and inductive reasoning. *Cognition, 65,* 15–32.
Cousins, S. D. (1989). Culture and self-perception in Japan and the United States. *Journal of Personality and Social Psychology, 56,* 124–31.
D'Andrade, Roy. (1987). A folk model of the mind. In D. Holland and N. Quinn (Eds.), *Cultural models in language and thought* (pp. 112–48). New York: Cambridge University Press.
Digman, John. (1990). Personality structure: Emergence of the five-factor model. *Annual Review of Psychology, 41,* 417–40.
Dumont, Louis. (1985). A modified view of our origins: The Christian beginnings of modern individualism. In M. Carrithers, S. Collins, and S. Lukes (Eds.), *The category of the person: Anthropology, philosophy, history* (pp. 93–122). New York: Cambridge University Press.
Dweck, Carol S., Hong, Y., and Chiu, C. (1993). Implicit theories: Individual differences in the likelihood and meaning of dispositional inference. *Personality and Social Psychology Bulletin, 19,* 644–56.
Elvin, M. (1985). Between the earth and heaven: Conception of the self in China. In M. Carrithers, S. Collins, and S. Lukes (Eds.), *The category of the person: Anthropology, philosophy, history* (pp. 156–89). New York: Cambridge University Press.
Erdley, Cynthia A., and Dweck, Carol S. (1993). Children's implicit personality theories as predictors of their social judgments. *Child Development, 64,* 863–78.
Fiske, Alan P., Kitayama, Shinobu, Markus, Hazel R., and Nisbett, Richard E. (1998). The cultural matrix of social psychology. In Daniel T. Gilbert, Susan T. Fiske, and Gardner Lindzey (Eds.), *Handbook of Social Psychology* (4th ed., pp. 915–81). New York: McGraw-Hill.

Flavell, John H., Zhang, X.-D., Zou, H., Dong, Q., and Qui, S. (1983). A comparison of the appearance-reality distinction in the People's Republic of China and the United States. *Cognitive Psychology, 15,* 459–66.
Gardner, D., Harris, P. L., Ohmoto, M., and Hamazaki, T. (1988). Japanese children's understanding of the distinction between real and apparent emotion. *International Journal of Behavioral Development, 11,* 203–18.
Gelman, Susan A. (1992). Children's conception of personality traits—Commentary. *Human Development, 35,* 280–85.
Gelman, Susan A., Coley, J. D., and Gottfried, G. M. (1994). Essentialist beliefs in children: The acquisition of concepts and theories. In Lawrence A. Hirschfeld and Susan A. Gelman (Eds.), *Mapping the mind: Domain specificity in cognition and culture* (pp. 341–65). New York: Cambridge University Press.
Gidron, David, Koehler, Derek J., and Tversky, Amos. (1993). Implicit quantification of personality traits. *Personality and Social Psychology Bulletin, 19,* 594–604.
Gilbert, Daniel T., and Jones, Edward E. (1986). Perceiver-induced constraint: Interpretations of self-generated reality. *Journal of Personality and Social Psychology, 50,* 269–80.
Gilbert, Daniel T., and Malone, Patrick S. (1995). The correspondence bias. *Psychological Bulletin, 117,* 21–38.
Goldberg, Lewis R. (1990). An alternative "description of personality": The Big Five structure. *Journal of Personality and Social Psychology, 59,* 1216–29.
Guthrie, George M., and Bennet, Alfred B. (1971). Cultural differences in implicit personality theory. *International Journal of Psychology, 6,* 305–12.
Hallahan, Mark, Lee, Fiona, and Herzog, Thaddeus. (in press). It's not just whether you win or lose, it's also where you play the game: A naturalistic, cross-cultural examination of the positivity bias. *Journal of Cross-Cultural Psychology.*
Hallowell, A. (1976). *Contributions to anthropology: Selected papers of A. Irving Hallowell.* Chicago: University of Chicago Press.
Hampden-Turner, Charles, and Trompenaars, Alfons. (1993). *The seven cultures of capitalism: Value systems for creating wealth in the United States, Japan, Germany, France, Britain, Sweden, and the Netherlands.* New York: Doubleday.
Heider, Fritz. (1958). *The psychology of interpersonal relations.* New York: Wiley.
Hirschfeld, Lawrence A. (1995). Anthropology, psychology, and the meanings of social causality. In Dan Sperber, David Premack, and Ann Premack (Eds.), *Causal cognition: A multidisciplinary debate* (pp. 313–50). Oxford: Oxford University Press.
Hong, Y., Chiu, C., and Kung, T. (1996). Bringing culture out in front: Effects of cultural meaning system activation on social cognition. Unpublished paper, University of Hong Kong.
Hsu, Francis L. K. (1953). *American and Chinese: Passage to differences.* Honolulu: University of Hawaii Press.
———. (1981). The self in cross-cultural perspective. In A. J. Marsella, B. De Vos, and F. L. K. Hsu (Eds.), *Culture and self* (pp. 24–55). London: Tavistock.
Ip, G. W. M., and Bond, Michael H. (1995). Culture, values, and the spontaneous self-concept. *Asian Journal of Psychology, 1,* 29–35.
Iwao, S. (1988). Social psychology's model of man: Isn't it time for East to meet

West? Address to the International Congress of Psychology, Sydney, Australia (August).

Jones, Edward E., and Harris, Victor A. (1967). The attribution of attitudes. *Journal of Experimental Social Psychology, 3,* 1–24.

Kashima, Yoshihisha, Siegel, Michael, Tanaka, Kenichiro, and Kashima, Emiko S. (1992). Do people believe behaviors are consistent with attitudes? Toward a cultural psychology of attribution processes. *British Journal of Social Psychology, 31,* 111–24.

Kitayama, Shinobu, and Masuda, Takahiko. (1997). Cultural psychology of social inference: The correspondence bias in Japan. Unpublished paper, Kyoto University.

Krull, Douglas S. (1993). Does the grist change the mill?: The effect of the perceiver's inferential goal on the process of social inference. *Personality and Social Psychology Bulletin, 19,* 340–48.

Krull, Douglas S., Loy, M. H., Lin, J., Wang, C., Chen, S., and Zhao, X. (1996). The fundamental attribution error: Correspondence bias in independent and interdependent cultures. Unpublished paper, University of Missouri at Columbia.

Kunda, Ziva, and Nisbett, Richard E. (1986). The psychometrics of everyday life. *Cognitive Psychology, 18,* 195–224.

La Fontaine, J. S. (1985). Person and individual: Some anthropological reflections. In M. Carrithers, S. Collins, and S. Lukes (Eds.), *The category of the person: Anthropology, philosophy, history* (pp. 123–40). New York: Cambridge University Press.

Lee, Fiona, Hallahan, Mark, and Herzog, Thaddeus. (1996). Explaining real-life events: How culture and domain shape attributions. *Personality and Social Psychology Bulletin, 22,* 732–41.

Leung, Kwong, Cheung, Fanny M., Zhang, Jian-Xin, Song, Wei-heng, and Dong, X. (in press). The five-factor model of personality in China. In Kwok Leung, Y. Kashima, U. Kim, and S. Yamaguchi (Eds.), *Progress in Asian social psychology* (vol. 1). Singapore: Wiley.

Lewin, Kurt. (1935). The conflict between Aristotelian and Galilean modes of thought in contemporary psychology. *Journal of General Psychology, 5,* 141–77.

Lillard, Angeline. (1998). Ethnopsychologies: Cultural variations in theories of mind. *Psychological Bulletin, 1,* 3–32.

Lloyd, G. E. R. (1990). *Demystifying mentalities.* New York: Cambridge University Press.

Lutz, Catherine. (1985). Ethnopsychology compared to what?: Explaining behavior and consciousness among the Ifaluk. In G. M. White and J. Kirkpatrick (Eds.), *Person, self, and experience: Exploring Pacific ethnopsychologies* (pp. 35–79). Berkeley: University of California Press.

Markus, Hazel R., and Kitayama, Shinobu. (1991). Culture and self: Implications for cognition, emotion, and motivation. *Psychological Review, 98,* 224–53.

———. (1994). A collective fear of the collective: Implications for selves and theories of selves. *Personality and Social Psychology, 20,* 568–79.

Markus, Hazel R., Kitayama, Shinobu, and Heiman, Rachel J. (1996). Culture and basic psychological principles. In E. T. Higgins and A. W. Kruglanski (Eds.), *Social psychology: Handbook of basic principles* (pp. 857–913). New York: Guilford.

Markus, Hazel R., Mullaly, P. R., and Kitayama, Shinobu. (1997). Self-ways: Diversity in modes of cultural participation. In U. Neisser and D. Jopling (Eds.), *The conceptual self in context* (pp. 13–61). Cambridge: Cambridge University Press.

Masuda, Takahiko, and Kitayama, Shinobu. (1996). Culture-specificity of the correspondence bias. Paper presented at the meeting of the International Association of Cross-cultural Psychology, Montreal (August, 1996).

McArthur, Leslie Z. (1972). The how and what of why: Some determinants and consequences of causal attribution. *Journal of Personality and Social Psychology, 13,* 733–42.

McCrae, Robert R., Costa, Paul T., and Yik, S. M. (1996). Universal aspects of Chinese personality structure. In M. H. Bond (Ed.), *The handbook of Chinese psychology* (pp. 189–207). New York: Oxford University Press.

Medin, Douglas, and Ortony, Andrew. (1989). Psychological essentialism. In S. Vosniadou and A. Ortony (Eds.), *Similarity and analogical reasoning* (pp. 179–95). New York: Cambridge University Press.

Miller, Joan G. (1984). Culture and the development of everyday social explanation. *Journal of Personality and Social Psychology, 46,* 961–78.

Mischel, Walter. (1968). *Personality and assessment.* New York: Wiley.

Morris, Michael W. (1993). Culture and cause: American and Chinese understandings of physical and social causality. Ph.D. dissertation, University of Michigan.

Morris, Michael W., Nisbett, Richard E., and Peng, Kaiping. (1995). Causal attribution across domains and cultures. In Dan Sperber, David Premack, and Ann J. Premack (Eds.), *Causal cognition* (pp. 577–614). Oxford: Clarendon Press.

Morris, Michael W., and Peng, Kaiping. (1994). Culture and cause: American and Chinese attributions for social and physical events. *Journal of Personality and Social Psychology, 67,* 949–71.

Mu, X., Lee, Shin-Ying, Stevenson, Harold W., Liu, D., and Ge, F. (1997). Growing up in a changing society: Chinese children from 1986 to 1995. Unpublished paper, University of Michigan.

Munro, Donald. (1985). *Individualism and holism: Studies in Confucian and Taoist values.* Ann Arbor: University of Michigan Press.

Nakamura, H. (1985). *Ways of thinking of eastern peoples.* Edited by Philip P. Wiener. Honolulu: University of Hawaii Press. (Originally published in 1964)

Needham, Joseph. (1962). *Science and civilization in China.* New York: Cambridge University Press.

Norenzayan, Ara, Choi, Incheol, and Nisbett, Richard E. (1998). Eastern and Western folk psychology and the prediction of behavior. Manuscript in preparation.

Norenzayan, Ara, Nisbett, Richard E., and Smith, E. E. (1999). Rule-based versus memory-based category learning East and West. Unpublished paper, University of Michigan.

Olivier de Sardan, J. P. (1973). Personalité et structures sociales (à propos des Songhays) [Personality and social structures (regarding the Songhays)]. In *La notion de personne en afrique noire* (pp. 421–45). Paris: Éditions du Centre Nationale de la Recherche Scientifique.

Peng, Kaiping, and Nisbett, Richard E. (in press). Cross-cultural similarities and differences in the understanding of physical causality. In M. Shield (Ed.), *Proceedings of the Seventh Interdisciplinary Conference on Science and Culture.* Frankfort: Kentucky State University Press.

Piedmont, Ralph L., and Chae, Joon-Ho. (1997). Cross-cultural generalizability of the five-factor model of personality: Development and validation of the NEO-PI-R for Koreans. *Journal of Cross-cultural Psychology, 28,* 131–55.

Read, K. E. (1955). Morality and the concept of the person among the Gahuku-Gama. *Oceanea, 25,* 233–82.

Reeder, Glenn D., and Brewer, Marilynn B. (1979). A schematic model of dispositional attribution in interpersonal perception. *Psychological Review, 86,* 61–79.

Rhee, Eun, Uleman, James, Lee, Hoon, and Roman, Robert. (1995). Spontaneous self-descriptions and ethnic identities in individualistic and collectivistic cultures. *Journal of Personality and Social Psychology, 69,* 142–52.

Ross, Lee. (1977). The intuitive psychologist and his shortcomings: Distortions in the attribution process. In L. Berkowitz (Ed.), *Advances in experimental social psychology* (vol. 10, pp. 174–220). New York: Academic Press.

Sanchez-Burks, Jeffrey G., Nisbett, Richard E., and Ybarra, Oscar. (1998). Cultural styles and relational schemas: Implications for intercultural contact. Unpublished paper, University of Michigan.

Shweder, Richard A., and Bourne, Edmund. J. (1982). Does the concept of the person vary cross-culturally? In A. J. Marsella and G. M. White (Eds.), *Cultural conceptions of mental health and therapy* (pp. 130–204). London: Reidel.

———. (1991). Does the concept of the person vary cross-culturally? In Richard A. Shweder (Ed.), *Thinking through cultures: Expeditions in cultural psychology* (pp. 113–55). Cambridge, Mass.: Harvard University Press.

Snyder, Melvin, and Jones, Edward E. (1974). Attitude attribution when behavior is constrained. *Journal of Experimental Social Psychology, 10,* 585–600.

Stevenson, Harold W., and Lee, Shin-Ying. (1996). The academic achievement of Chinese students. In M. H. Bond (Ed.), *The handbook of Chinese psychology* (pp. 124–42). New York: Oxford University Press.

Trafimow, David, Triandis, Harry C., and Goto, Sharon. (1991). Some tests of the distinction between the private and the collective self. *Journal of Personality and Social Psychology, 60,* 649–55.

Triandis, Harry C. (1989). The self and social behavior in differing cultural contexts. *Psychological Review, 96,* 269–89.

———. (1995). *Individualism and collectivism.* Boulder, Colo.: Westview Press.

Triandis, Harry C., McCusker, C., and Hui, C. H. (1990). Multimethod probes of individualism and collectivism. *Journal of Personality and Social Psychology, 59,* 1006–20.

Wellman, Henry M. (1990). *The child's theory of mind.* Cambridge, Mass.: MIT Press.

Whiting, Beatrice B. (1996). The effect of social change on concepts of the good child and good mothering: A study of families in Kenya. *Ethos, 24,* 3–35.

Witkin, Herman A., and Berry, John W. (1975). Psychological differentiation in cross-cultural perspective. *Journal of Cross-cultural Psychology, 6,* 4–87.

Yang, K. S., and Bond, Michael H. (1990). Ethnic affirmation by Chinese bilinguals. *Journal of Cross-cultural Psychology, 11,* 411–25.

9

# INDEPENDENCE FROM WHOM? INTERDEPENDENCE WITH WHOM? CULTURAL PERSPECTIVES ON INGROUPS VERSUS OUTGROUPS

*Sheena S. Iyengar, Mark R. Lepper, and Lee Ross*

to be nobody but yourself—in a world which is doing its best,
night and day, to
make you everybody else, means to fight the hardest battle that
any human being
can fight, and never stop fighting.

—e. e. cummings

WESTERN social theorists have long pondered the relationship between self-perception and social perception, that is, the relationship between the ways we interpret and evaluate our own actions, feelings, and personal characteristics and the ways we interpret and evaluate those of other social actors. Within social psychology, in particular, some theorists have stressed connections or parallels between these two processes (Bem 1967, 1972; Cooley 1902; Mead 1934; Nisbett and Wilson 1977; Schachter 1964), while others have emphasized divergences or differences (Jones 1990; Jones and Nisbett 1971; Storms 1973; Taylor and Fiske 1978). What theorists in both camps have shared, however, is a willingness to speak of an abstract, decontextualized self, and perhaps even more remarkably, of an abstract, undifferentiated other.

The recent flowering of cultural psychology in general (Fiske et al. 1997; Shweder 1991; Stigler, Shweder, and Herdt 1990; Triandis 1995), and the increasing attention to different cultural constructions of the self in particular (Markus and Kitayama 1991; Nisbett and Cohen 1996;

Shweder and Bourne 1982; Triandis 1989), makes it appropriate to reexamine some of the classic theories and generalizations that Western researchers have offered regarding self and other. In doing so, however, we want to introduce into cultural discussions a distinction regarding "others" that seems notably absent in the discussions of self-perception versus social perception introduced in our opening paragraph—namely, the familiar distinction between "ingroup" and "outgroup" members.

The distinction itself, of course, is hardly new. Western investigators have long recognized that social perceivers may stereotype, assume homogeneity in, and show hostility toward outgroup members (Allport 1954; Jones, Wood, and Quattrone 1981; Jones 1972/1997; Sherif 1966; Sherif and Sherif 1953) while displaying favoritism toward ingroup members (Gaertner and Dovidio 1986; Gaertner et al., this volume; McConahay 1986; Moscovici 1984; Tajfel 1970, 1981). Other investigators, notably those working in the social-comparison tradition (Festinger 1954; Taylor 1983; Tesser 1980, 1988) and the reference-group tradition (Crosby 1976; Newcomb 1943; Newcomb et al. 1967), have continually emphasized that self-assessments hinge not only on comparisons with other people in general but also on comparisons of one's attitudes, abilities, wealth, or well-being with those of socially relevant members of one's group.

Nevertheless, deep within the theoretical bedrock of contemporary Western social psychology, one finds seemingly straightforward claims about how individuals respond to the actions of "others," or to the attempts of "others" to influence them, without qualification concerning the *identity* of these "others" or the relevant *relationship* between the parties. In fact, the methodologies adopted by our field in its search for presumably universal laws and generalizations that are somehow independent of social context have led some to describe the heart of experimental social psychology, in the United States at least, as the study of "strangers in strange situations" (Aron and Aron 1986).[1]

Two such general claims regarding self-contained selves versus generalized others provide the empirical and theoretical focus of this chapter. The first claim postulates a "divergence" in attributions and inferences regarding self and other, or "actor" and "observer" (Jones and Nisbett 1971; Nisbett et al. 1973). The second claim proposes that there are differences between the affective and motivational consequences of choices made by the self and those of choices suggested to, or imposed on, the self by others (Cordova and Lepper 1996; deCharms 1968; Deci 1981; Lepper and Greene 1978; Zuckerman et al. 1978).

Recently, we have examined the cultural standing of both of these claims in research that deals explicitly with the ingroup-outgroup distinction and utilizes both Western and non-Western research participants. Before we turn to the details of these research efforts, however, it may be useful to consider, at least briefly, the current status of "culture" in American social psychology more generally.

## CONCEPTUAL AND HISTORICAL BACKGROUND

### Culture, Situationism, and Subjectivism

One of the great lessons of social psychology has been to heighten our appreciation of the impact of social situations. As a discipline, we pride ourselves on our refusal to make hasty or overly broad inferences about the traits or other personal dispositions of social actors, and we eschew explanations for undesirable human behavior that seem to "blame the victim" who responds undesirably to the pressures and constraints of difficult situations. In turn, the goal of understanding the situational determinants of social actions and outcomes has historically obliged us to look beyond the obvious "objective" features of social situations and to focus instead on the subjective representations or construals of the actors involved (Ross and Ward 1996). Indeed, these two lessons have been seen as among the most general and fundamental conclusions from the last half-century of research in social psychology (Ross and Nisbett 1991).

Consequently, it seems more than a little ironic that American social psychologists have, until quite recently, paid so little attention to the topic of culture. Surely there are few factors that can rival the power of cultural differences in determining both the objective situations in which people most often find themselves and the subjective interpretations they are likely to share about the meaning of those situations. As Ross and Nisbett (1991) have suggested:

> Ethnic, racial, religious, regional, and even economic subcultures are in an important sense the distillates of historical situations, as well as powerful contemporary determinants of individuals' behavior. They are, at the same time, important sources of the particular subjective meanings and construals we place upon the social events we observe. (170)

Nonetheless, our collective search for seemingly context-free generalizations, based on "objective" study of interchangeable individual "subjects" who are divorced from their everyday social contexts and networks, seems, with few notable exceptions (McClelland et al. 1953), to have precluded serious attention to culture. Fortunately, within the last few years this situation has begun to change and the study of cultural influences on social behavior has begun to enter the mainstream of social psychology.

## Individualism Versus Collectivism

Perhaps the first major step toward the integration of cultural concerns into Western social psychology derived from pioneering studies by Triandis (1989, 1990, 1995) and others, especially Hofstede (1980, 1991). These authors sought to characterize systematic variations in broad societal goals and values across different cultures, using methods that avoided the simplistic and one-sided comparisons of the ways in which "other" cultures differ from "our own" that so plagued most earlier cross-cultural research efforts.

The most notable contribution of these researchers was the characterization of cultures along a dimension of individualism-collectivism (Hofstede 1980, 1991; Smith and Bond 1993; Triandis 1989, 1990, 1995). However, the theoretical importance of this work lay not only in a general claim that one could observe and measure large and relatively stable cultural differences along this dimension, but also in a contention that Americans (and their close cultural kin, the British, Canadians, and Australians) displayed a level of individualism far above that characteristic of the rest of the world. This finding, in turn, prompted a concern that broad conclusions based solely on research with American subjects might prove far more limited in their relevance to other societies than we had recognized.

## Independent Versus Interdependent Selves

Despite its potential significance, for many years the impact of work on individualism versus collectivism remained relatively limited, and the relevant studies made little effective contact with more mainstream social psychological research of the time. What eventually brought this work to the forefront of social psychology was the effort by Markus and Kitayama (1991) to analyze psychological mechanisms whereby this cultural variable might influence not only the abstract beliefs and presuppositions but also the basic goals and self-concepts of persons growing up in individualistic versus collectivistic cultures. By focusing on the centrality of the self and by tying their analysis explicitly to current paradigms in experimental social psychology, Markus and Kitayama's paper paved the way for a resurgence of interest in issues of culture.

Their basic argument was straightforward: Whereas the distinction between the individual and the group is critical to highly individualistic Americans, the relationship between individuals and their groups may be more fused or more diffuse in collectivist cultures. In America, self-identity emphasizes the distinction between the "independent-self" and others—with heroic individuals endeavoring to stand, as e. e. cummings suggests, as bounded, unique, and autonomous entities, largely uninfluenced by group and environmental pressures (Geertz 1975; Johnson 1985; Sampson 1985, 1988, 1989; Waterman 1981). In Markus and Kitayama's (1991) terms, "the independent-self is a construal of the self in which behavior is organized and made meaningful by reference to one's own internal repertoire of thoughts, feelings, and actions, rather than by reference to those of others" (226). For such persons, preservation of individual integrity is essential to the self.

By contrast, people in more collectivist cultures may have self-systems in which the distinction between the individual and the group is considerably more vague, because within these cultures the relationship between the individual and the social group involves much greater interconnectedness (Kondo 1982). Markus and Kitayama (1991) characterize such individuals as "interdependent-selves" who perceive themselves "as part of an encompassing social relationship" and recognize that their own actions are "determined, contingent on, and to a large extent organized by what the actor perceives to be the thoughts, feelings, and actions of others in the relationship" (227). For such actors, conformity with the group may be seen as personally rewarding as well as socially sanctioned.

In short, the distinction that Markus and Kitayama (1991) draw between individualists and collectivists highlights the relationship between the individual and the group, and the resultant differences in self-concepts or construals. These different types of cultures, they suggest, also differ in the ideals for conduct that they present and the culturally mandated goals for group members implied by these ideals. Whereas members of individualistic cultures may be expected to promote their own goals, to express their own opinions, and to perceive themselves as unique, members of collectivistic cultures may be expected to promote others' goals, to express opinions appropriate to their group and position, and to strive to fit in and belong.

In support of their analysis, Markus and Kitayama (1991) report a number of empirical findings. They suggest, for example, that Americans store more knowledge about themselves than they do about others, and that the Japanese store more knowledge about others than they do about themselves. Other findings suggest that Asians are less likely than Americans to perceive the behaviors of others as stemming from personality traits, implying that they may not perceive others as separate entities to the same degree that Americans do (Bond 1983; Dalal, Sharma, and Bisht 1983; Miller 1984; Shweder and Bourne 1982). Finally, the pervasive individualistic tendency to bolster esteem through self-enhancement (Greenwald 1980) may actually disappear in cultures that promote more interdependent views of the self. Indeed, individuals from collectivist Asian cultures seem, in many social contexts, more inclined to deprecate their own abilities and contributions than to exaggerate them (Kitayama et al. 1997; Markus and Kitayama 1991; Takata 1987).

Subsequent efforts by others have added provocative details to this general picture. In one particularly elegant research program, for example, Morris and Peng (1994) studied the explanations offered by participants from individualistic and collectivistic cultures when they observed animated "interactions" between individuals and groups—for example, when the distance between an individual and a group widened or narrowed. Individualists, they reported, interpreted these abstract representations of interaction patterns in terms of the motives of the individual actor (for example, he or she "caught up with" or "ran away from" the group). Collectivists, by contrast, interpreted these abstract interactions in terms of the motives of the group (he or she was "taken into" or "expelled from" the group).

Other research programs have examined related cultural differences between Anglo-Americans and East Asians by exploring the generalizability or "transportability" of classic Western social psychological phenomena. Many of these studies, thoughtfully reviewed by Norenzayan, Choi, and Nisbett (this volume) and by Kitayama and Masuda (1997), have focused particularly on the conditions and contexts in which dispositionalist personality theories, the correspondence bias, and the failure to utilize base-rate information effectively that characterize our culture seem to apply, or fail to apply, in different societies and/or different cultural subgroups within the larger American society.

Despite their success in illustrating predicted cultural differences, most studies in this tradition retain a degree of ethnocentrism. Almost invariably, it is noteworthy that these studies introduce a classic and well-studied Western experimental paradigm into other cultures, to see whether the same principles or processes will apply there.[2] As a result, "our" paradigms and phenomena retain a position of inherent privilege, making it difficult for us to see the ways in which those paradigms, and the questions they give rise to, reflect basic assumptions of our own cultural heritage. Consequently, we frequently fail to incorporate, even in explicitly cultural research, the sorts of conceptual distinctions, manipulations, measures, and other features of research design that, although generally irrelevant in our own society, might nevertheless be of critical significance in other cultures or in particular subgroups within our own culture.

## NEW RESEARCH: THE INGROUP-OUTGROUP DISTINCTION IN CULTURAL PERSPECTIVE

In our own studies, to which we now turn, we have sought to introduce an important distinction relevant to Markus and Kitayama's (1991) analysis of independent versus interdependent cultures. This distinction, which we believe may be of particular significance to individuals raised in collectivistic or interdependent cultures, centers on the dichotomy between *ingroup* and *outgroup* members.

### Attributions for Self Versus Others

A first instance of experimental ethnocentrism that is of special relevance to our own research efforts is evident in the continuing discussion of actor-observer differences in attribution, and of the perceptual, cognitive, linguistic, and motivational factors underlying such differences (Bem 1972; Jones and Nisbett 1971; Nisbett and Wilson 1977; Ross 1977).

Accounts of cultures less individualistic than our own not only suggest a more interdependent, less autonomous view of the self but also suggest that as the self-other boundary becomes less distinct, the distinction between ingroup and outgroup members assumes greater significance. That is, in linking the self intimately to others with whom one is interdependent (family, friends, and other ingroup members), the self and relevant ingroup members may become psychological entities prone to relatively similar inferential, judgmental, attributional, motivational, and perceptual biases. By the same token, assimilating ingroup members to self may lead individuals to contrast ingroup and outgroup members more sharply, making them relatively more susceptible to different cognitive, perceptual, and motivational biases.

We pursued the implications of this analysis in two attribution theory paradigms, both used initially to explore actor-observer differences (Jones and Nisbett 1971). The first paradigm involved simple trait ascriptions, and the reported tendency for individuals to ascribe traits or dispositions more readily to others than to themselves. The second paradigm concerned the choice of situational versus dispositional explanations for particular actions or outcomes, and the reported tendency for individuals to favor dispositional causes or explanations for others' behaviors but situational causes or explanations for their own.

In both paradigms, we gave research participants of differing cultural backgrounds an opportunity to distinguish, in their attributions, between ingroup and outgroup members. In both paradigms, our working hypothesis was that participants from collectivist backgrounds would make a sharper distinction between ingroup and outgroup. In particular, we hypothesized that participants with Asian and/or Asian American backgrounds would ascribe fewer traits to ingroup members (but not to outgroup members) than would Caucasian Americans. And we predicted that Asian Americans would offer more "charitable" attributions, that is, more situational ones, in explaining actions that could reflect negatively on ingroup members (but not those that could reflect negatively on outgroup members) than would Caucasian Americans.

*Trait Ascriptions for Ingroup Versus Outgroup Members* In a first study, Iyengar and Ross (1996) examined the trait ascription phenomenon first demonstrated by Nisbett, Caputo, Legant, and Maracek (1973). In the context of a larger investigation of the divergent perceptions of actors and observers (Jones and Nisbett 1971), Nisbett and his colleagues (1973) had simply asked people to indicate whether one or the other of various pairs of personality trait descriptors ("kind-unkind," "bold-timid," "extroverted-introverted," and so on) were descriptive of themselves and of various other actors, or whether they "couldn't say" because individual's behavior in that behavioral domain "depends on the situation." With American college students as research participants, the results of this investigation were clear. Whereas the students readily ascribed trait descriptors to family members, friends, and even to public figures like the newscaster Walter Cronkite, they proved relatively reluctant to apply such descriptors to themselves, choosing instead to indicate that their own behavior in the relevant domains "depends on the situation."

Iyengar and Ross (1996) adapted this procedure for the study of potential cultural differences. In particular, three types of respondents—one group of American Stanford University students of Caucasian descent ($n = 92$), a second group of Stanford students of Asian descent ($n = 97$), and a third group of Japanese students at Kyoto University ($n = 57$)—all responded to a version of the trait assessment instrument employed by Nisbett and his colleagues (1973). The instrument, which used English for the Stanford respondents and a Japanese translation for the Kyoto students, included thirteen traits—some clearly positive ("kind," "friendly"), some clearly negative ("disagreeable," "overbearing"), and some more ambiguous or even likely to carry different valences in different cultures ("shy," "assertive"). Each respondent was asked to consider each trait with respect to three separate scales—one pertaining to *self,* one pertaining to his or her *best friend,* and one pertaining to some specific *enemy* of his or her own designation. For each trait, they were simply asked to indicate "yes," "no," or "depends on the situation" with respect to each assessment target.

FIGURE 9.1 *Trait Ascription Study: Rejection of Trait Terms to Describe Self, Friend, and Enemy*

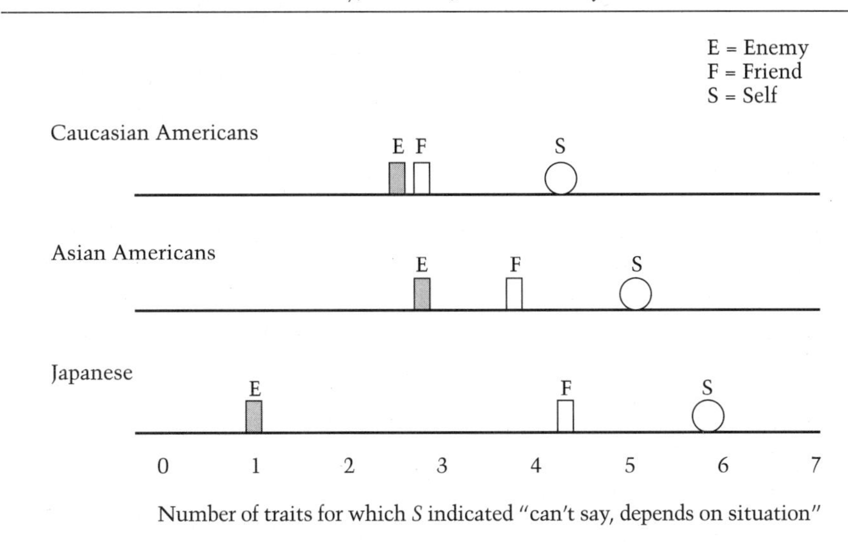


The results of this simple exercise were revealing. Figure 9.1 displays the data. First, the Caucasian Stanford students chose "depends on the situation" significantly more often with respect to self than with respect to others, thereby replicating the basic finding of Nisbett and his colleagues (1973). In addition, these students proved almost as willing to apply simple trait descriptors to their close friend as to their enemy. Japanese students at Kyoto University, however, responded very differently in rating these two types of others. In rating friends, as in rating self, they were relatively more inclined to choose "depends on the situation"—indeed, they selected it significantly more often, in both cases, than did the Caucasian American students (a result consistent with the suggestion offered elsewhere in this volume that people from collectivistic cultures may be particularly sensitive to situational or social constraints). In rating an outgroup member (an enemy), however, they rarely chose "depends on the situation" rather than assigning a trait—in fact, they did so significantly less often than the Caucasian students. In short, the contrast between assessments of friends and of enemies was more dramatic than the contrast between assessments of friends and self—a markedly different pattern of results than that obtained for the Caucasian students.

Interestingly, our sample of Asian Americans and Asian foreign students attending Stanford showed an intermediate pattern of results. Like the Kyoto students, they chose "depends on the situation" more often than the Caucasian students when characterizing themselves, and like the Kyoto sample, they made a clear distinction between friends and enemies in this regard. But unlike the Kyoto students (and like the Caucasian American students), the distinction made between self and friends by these students exposed to both Asian and American views was also quite marked.

Viewed in isolation, the findings for our Caucasian American sample (like the original Nisbett et al. [1973] results) suggest a strong and simple self-other distinction. By contrast, as hypothesized, the findings from the other two samples, featuring students with more collectivistic and less individualistic cultural backgrounds, remind us of the importance, even the centrality, of the ingroup-outgroup distinction in other societies.

*Attributional Charity Regarding Ingroup Versus Outgroup Members* In a second study, Iyengar and Ross (1996) turned their attention to the phenomenon of attributional "charity," that is, the willingness of individuals to take into account situational pressures and constraints, especially in accounting for seemingly negative or antisocial actions (Griffin and Ross 1991). In Western research, of course, the topic of biased attributional assessment, or "attributional charity," has typically focused on the self-serving biases or "ego defensiveness" shown by actors in explaining their own success or failures (see Nisbett and Ross 1980). In this tradition, self-other comparisons are generally introduced to use attributions made by, or about, disinterested others as a relatively "objective" baseline against which to assess the potentially biased attributions that actors make about their own actions and outcomes.

Once again, the unique feature of our present research design was the inclusion of the ingroup-versus-outgroup variable, allowing us to compare the attributional charity afforded to members of these two groups. In particular, students in this study were asked to consider possible explanations for hypothetical negative actions or misdeeds by a resident of their dormitory. Two groups of respondents were employed—one group of Caucasian Americans ($n = 104$) and one group of first-generation Americans of Asian descent ($n = 60$)—all of whom lived in mixed-ethnicity dormitories in which roughly half of the students were of Caucasian ancestry and one-quarter were of Asian ancestry. All students read four vignettes. Two featured negative actions (for example, failure to stop and help a fellow student who had crashed his or her bicycle) by an actor stipulated to be a "friend," and two featured similarly negative actions by an unspecified stranger (that is, someone in the dorm whom the student had not yet met). For each action, students

FIGURE 9.2 *Attributional Charity Study: Strength of Situational Versus Dispositional Attributions for a Negative Behavior by Friend Versus Stranger*

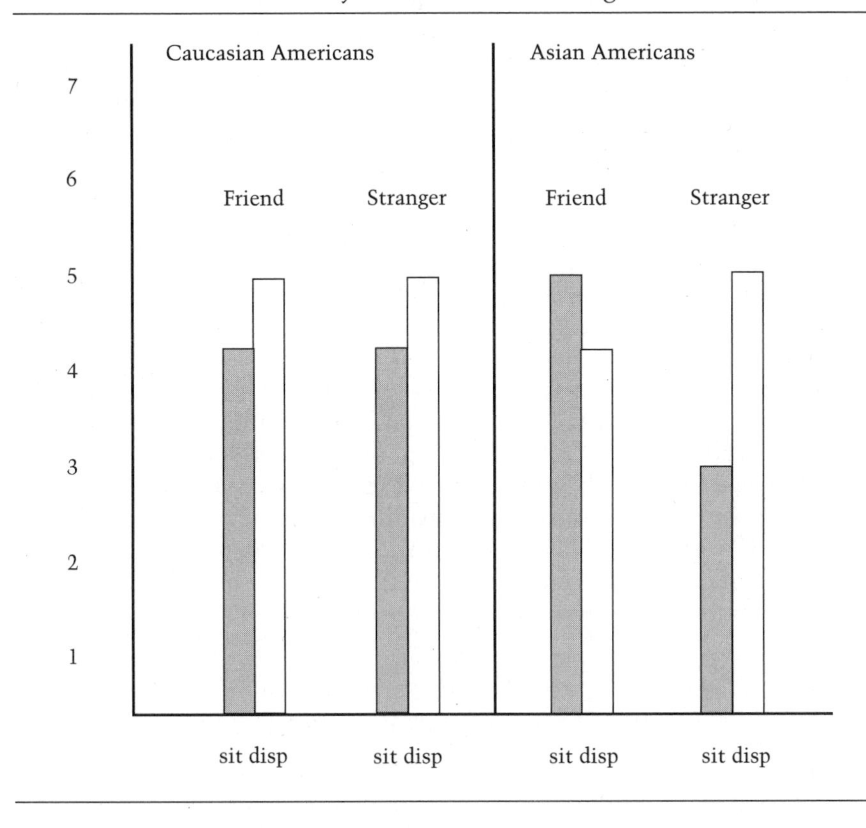


were given a small set of charitable (that is, exculpatory, situational) explanations (for example, the individual failing to render aid was in a hurry and didn't notice the accident) and a small set of dispositional explanations involving negative traits (for example, the individual failing to render aid was an uncaring person). Students were also invited to add explanations of their own if they wished. The aptness or likelihood of each stipulated explanation was assessed using simple seven-point rating scales.

Figure 9.2 shows the results of this study, which once again revealed a clear difference in the two groups' assessments. The Caucasian students showed virtually no tendency to make more charitable attributions for specified friends than for unspecified strangers, displaying in both cases a moderate preference for dispositional explanations over situational ones. By contrast, the Asian Americans showed a clear tendency to make more charitable, less censorious attributions about friends than about strangers; that is, they moderately preferred situational explanations over dispositional ones for friends, but strongly preferred dispositional explanations over situational ones for strangers. In fact, the Asian Americans opted for dispositional explanations in making attributions about strangers more often than did the Caucasian Americans.

Thus, if viewed in isolation, the findings from the Caucasian American sample would lead one to discount the existence of ingroup favoritism in the attribution process—at least for the particular actions and the particular ingroups and outgroups identified in our vignettes. By contrast, if viewed in isolation, the results from the Asian American sample would suggest a strong tendency toward such ingroup favoritism. It is unfortunate that the design of this second Iyengar and Ross (1996) study did not allow us to examine charitableness toward *self* in the attribution process, and equally unfortunate that the study did not include a sample of Asian respondents in their own land.[3] But the data we do have suffice once again to illustrate that generalizations about how individuals make attributions about "others" can become problematic—once we leave the confines of our own culture—unless we make some effort to identify the precise relationship of that "other" to the individual.

## Intrinsic Motivation and the Restriction of Choice by Ingroup Versus Outgroup Members

The second research domain in which the significance of these cultural variables has been explored involves the determinants of intrinsic motivation—in particular, the role that individual choice and personal control may play in motivating individuals from highly individualistic cultures, compared to those from more socially interdependent cultures. Let us turn, then, to this last line of investigation.

Choice is good. What, a typical American might ask, could be more self-evident? Liberty, after all, is enshrined as subordinate only to life itself in our country's Declaration of Independence. Having a choice, obviously, gives individuals the opportunity to select the options that most closely match their personal needs and preferences. In addition, as Markus and Kitayama's (1991) analysis would suggest, choice permits people to express their individuality and display their autonomy.

In fact, the value of personal choice has long seemed obvious to American theorists studying the nature of intrinsic motivation. Indeed, the single most widespread and influential definition of intrinsic motivation, put forward by Deci and his colleagues (Deci 1981; Deci and Ryan 1985), virtually equates the experience of intrinsic motivation with a sense of "self-determination" or personal choice. People want to feel themselves, as another prominent American theorist put it (deCharms 1968), to be "origins" of their own actions, rather than "pawns" of external forces.

In fact, one line of intrinsic motivation research has focused quite directly on the effects of the presence or absence of personal choice. For example, in a prototypic study, Zuckerman, Porac, Lathin, Smith, and Deci (1978) presented undergraduates with a set of interesting manipulative puzzles. In the choice condition, students were told they could choose which puzzles to work with and how long to spend with each; in the no-choice condition, the *experimenter* told students which puzzles to work on and when, yoking the actions of these students to those of the students in the choice condition. At the end of this test period, intrinsic motivation was measured by the amount of unmonitored free-play time that students subsequently chose to spend with the puzzles and by their self-reports of willingness to participate in further tests with such puzzles. The results provided a clear demonstration that students who had been given a choice showed significantly more intrinsic motivation, on both behavioral and self-report measures, than no-choice subjects.[4]

In two related studies, Iyengar and Lepper (1999) added to this basic paradigm of choice versus no-choice one further condition suggested by our theoretical analysis of the potential importance of the identity of the other. In these additional groups, students were assigned particular activities, not by an unfamiliar experimenter, as in traditional no-choice conditions, but by someone who would be expected to be included in the more extended, interdependent concept of self manifested by children of Asian backgrounds. In a first study, this key "ingroup" member making choices for the child was the child's own mother, and the "outgroup" member making such choices remained the experimenter (with whom the child had not previously been acquainted). In a second study, choices in the "ingroup-choice" condition were made by the students' own classmates; choices in the "outgroup-choice" condition were made by children in a lower grade at a rival school across town. To test our hypotheses about the differential relevance of this group membership manipulation for children from individualistic versus collectivistic cultures, these experimental procedures were employed with samples of children from theoretically contrasting cultural backgrounds.

In the first study, third-grade children were asked to do an anagrams task for a specified period of time. In the "personal-choice" condition, these children were asked which of six categories of anagrams (including animals, family, foods) they would like to undertake. In the two imposed-choice conditions, children were assigned categories that had been yoked to those selected by students in the choice condition. Thus, in the outgroup-choice condition, as in previous research, the experimenter simply displayed the choices and asserted that he or she wanted the child to work with the category specified. In the novel ingroup-no-choice condition, by contrast, the experimenter looked through a large set of consent forms and then told the child that his or her own mother had suggested the anagram category. In each of these conditions, of course, half of the children were from Anglo-American backgrounds, and the other half were from Asian American backgrounds.

Two main measures were obtained: initial task performance, as assessed by the number of anagrams children actually completed correctly during the experimental period, and subsequent intrinsic motivation, as assessed by the children's further play with the anagrams after the purported end of the experiment, a time when the children believed themselves to be entirely on their own.

Figures 9.3 and 9.4 display the results, which were highly significant and comparable for both measures. For the Anglo-American children, level of performance and intrinsic motivation were clearly highest in the personal-choice condition and were equally low in the two imposed-choice conditions, regardless of whether a stranger experimenter or their own mother had "usurped" their choices. For the Asian American children, by contrast, performance and motivation were both highest in the ingroup-choice condition (in which their mothers had selected the category of anagrams for them), next highest in the personal-choice condition, and lowest in the outgroup-choice condition.[5]

The second study, examining ingroup versus outgroup choices, involved a rather different context and manipulation. It employed an educational computer activity designed to teach students about arithmetic equations via an instructional game that had been developed in previous research by Cordova and Lepper (1996). Built into this game were half a dozen instructionally irrelevant choices, such as which of four icons would represent one's own "ship" during the game and which icon would represent one's opponent. In this prior study, Cordova and Lepper had shown that the provision of even such apparently trivial choices could produce large educational benefits with Caucasian American pupils. Students who had been given these choices showed significantly enhanced performance at the game, increased liking of the game, higher levels of perceived self-efficacy, and greater subsequent learning from the game than children not given such choice. These effects were apparent not only as the children played the game during the initial experi-

FIGURE 9.3 *Choice Study 1: Performance on Anagrams Task by Condition*

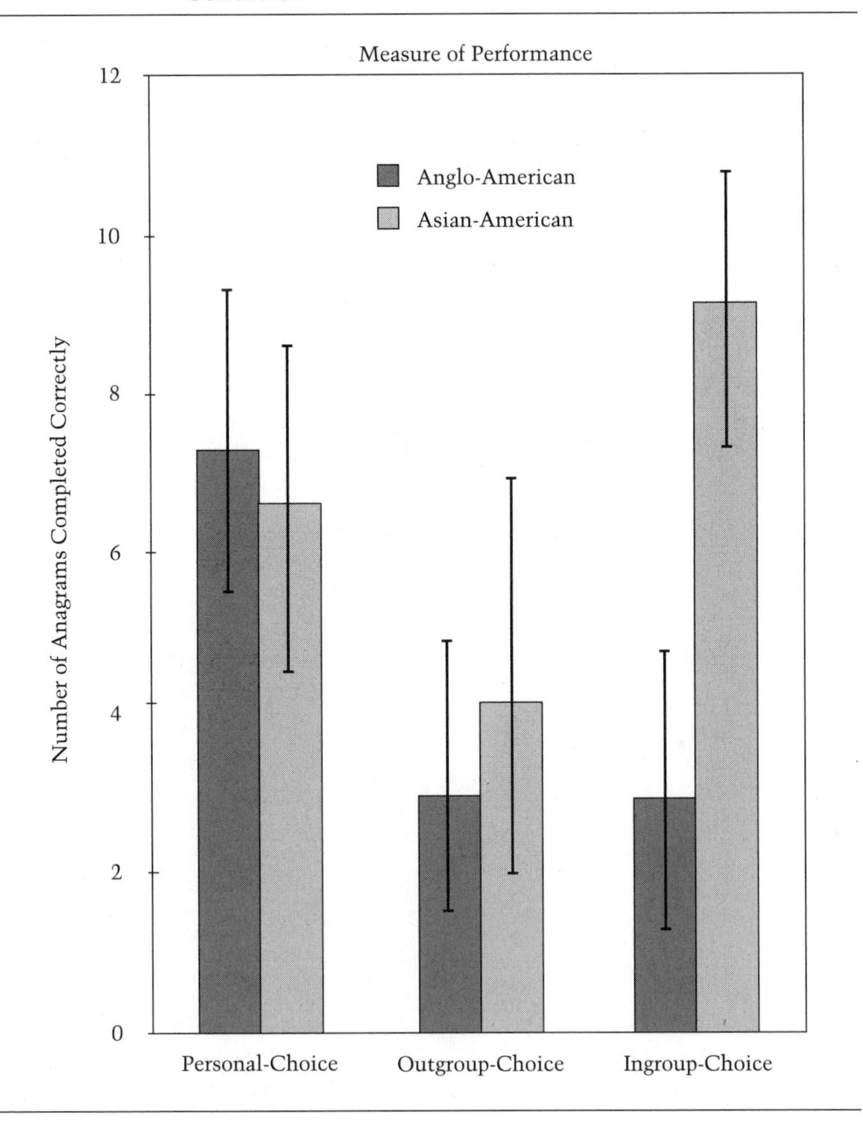


mental session but also in follow-up measures taken outside the computer game context a week later.

In their second study, Iyengar and Lepper (1999) employed the same instructional computer game, but with the modifications necessary to

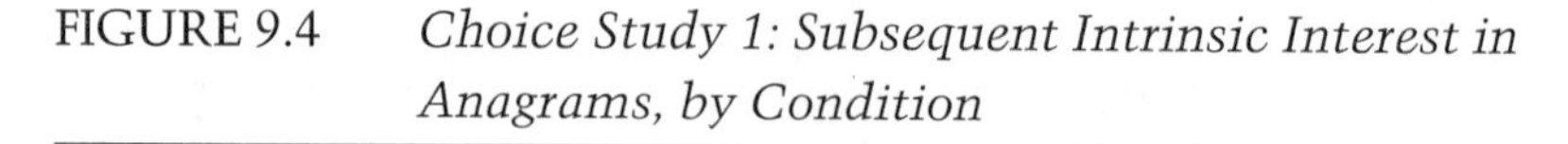
FIGURE 9.4 *Choice Study 1: Subsequent Intrinsic Interest in Anagrams, by Condition*

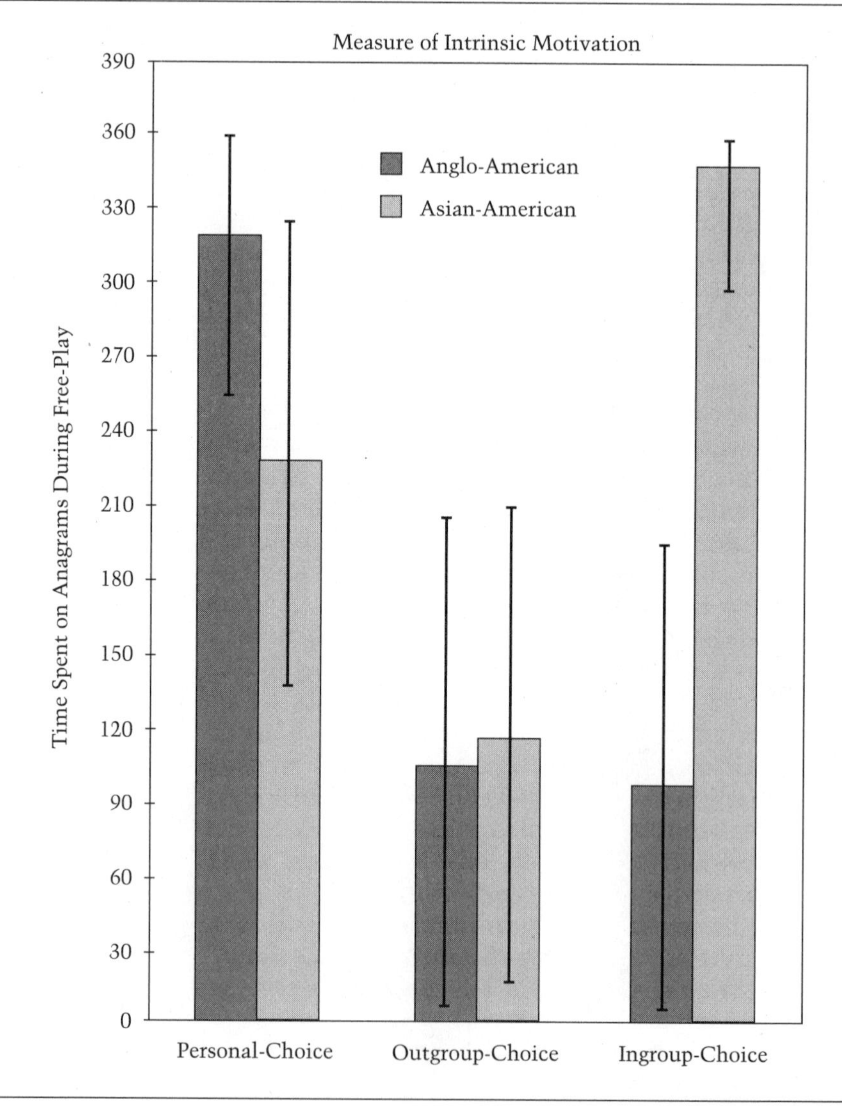


create two contrasting imposed-choice conditions in addition to the standard choice condition. Thus, in the ingroup-choice condition, fifth-grade students were told that the relevant choices had already been made based on ballots previously distributed in their own classrooms. In the outgroup-choice condition, on the other hand, the fifth-graders were told that these same choices had already been made based on a vote by a group of younger outgroup members—that is, third-graders at a rival school. Once again, of course, half of the students were of Anglo-American heritage, and the other half were from Asian American families.

The results from this study were again relatively dramatic. Figures 9.5 and 9.6 display the findings from representative measures of intrinsic motivation and subsequent learning. Once again, for Anglo-American students, the personal-choice condition produced far higher levels of motivation and learning than the imposed-choice conditions, regardless of whether the instructional choices in these latter groups were said to have been based on the preferences of their own classmates or on those of younger children from a rival school. For Asian American students, by contrast, it was the ingroup versus outgroup distinction that proved critical. Motivation and learning were clearly highest in the ingroup-choice condition, where the choices were purportedly those of one's own classmates, intermediate in the personal-choice condition, and lowest in the outgroup-choice condition.[6]

In short, in both of these studies the only crucial distinction for the Anglo-American students seems to have been that between the self and others. For the Asian American students, by contrast, the more important distinction was that between ingroup (including the self) and outgroup. Taken in combination with our prior studies of trait ascriptions and attributional charity, these findings provide substantial support for our analysis of the crucial significance of the ingroup-outgroup distinction in studies of individualistic and independent versus collectivistic and interdependent cultural groups.

## IMPLICATIONS

It is no accident that interest in the topic of culture, especially interest in cultural differences between ourselves and others from the highly collectivistic cultures of East Asia, has surged in the past decade or so. Not only have we seen unprecedented East-West traffic in trade, tourism, immigration, and cultural exchange, but with the end of the cold war and our bilateral rivalry with the Soviet Union, China and Japan have increasingly occupied our attention and have become the target of our doubts and fears, especially as they increasingly assert themselves on the world stage.

Exposure to other cultures, and increasingly to the scholarship of social scientists who live and work in other cultures, offers us a window not only on the limitations of our own "local" psychology but also on the nature of our highly individualistic culture and our way of looking

FIGURE 9.5 *Choice Study 2: Subsequent Intrinsic Interest in Space Quest Game, by Condition*

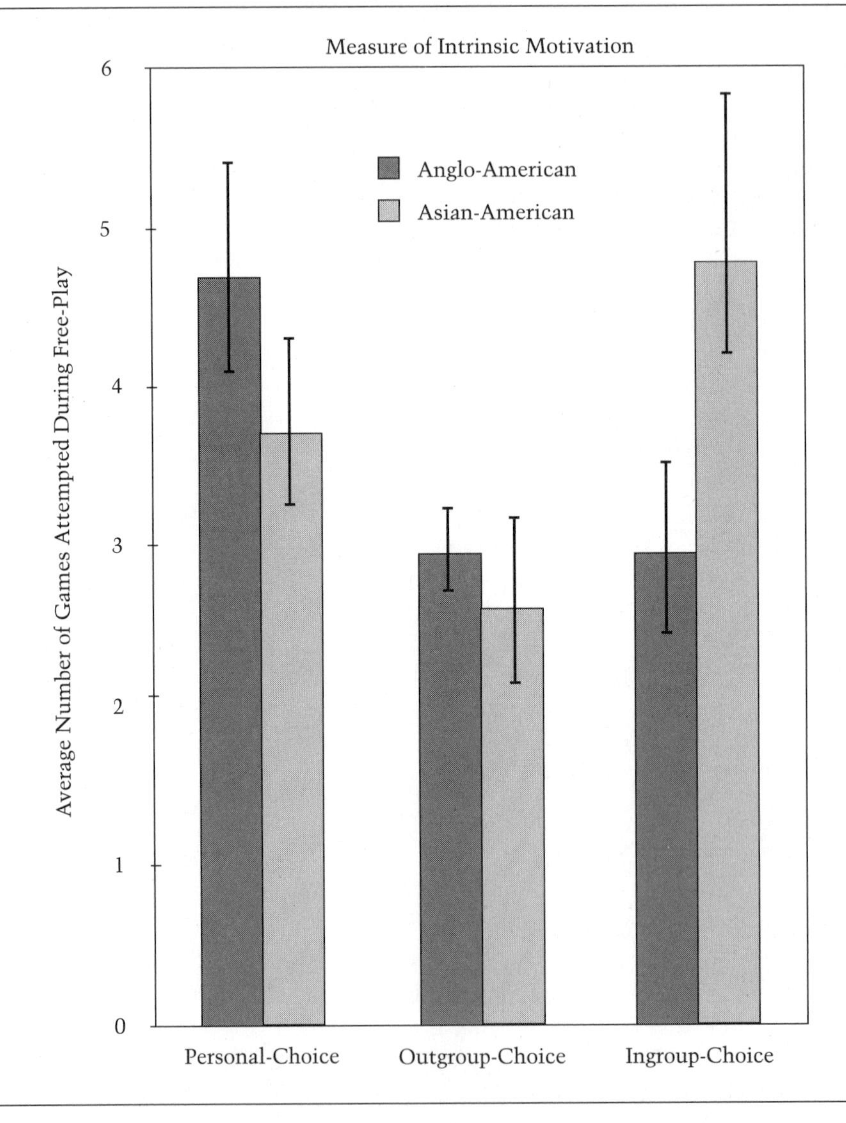


at ourselves and our interpersonal relations. As every seasoned traveler can attest, the time we spend in other lands (and to a lesser extent, the contact we have with travelers from other lands) gives us a sharper, more nuanced appreciation of what we share with other cultures and

FIGURE 9.6 *Choice Study 2: Amount Learned from Space Quest Game, by Condition*

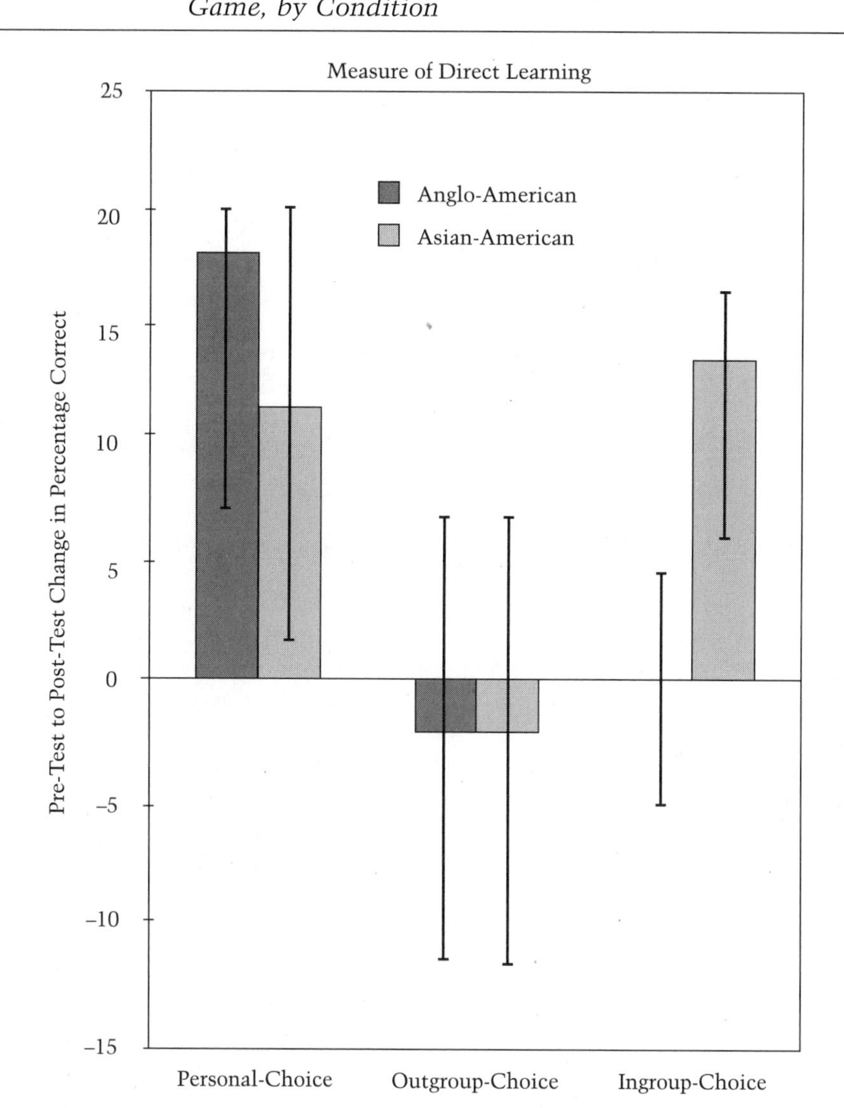


what is distinctive about our own. Although we may misinterpret what we see in other cultures, travel helps us, if we may modify Shweder's (1991) apropos phrase, to "see" culture rather than simply "see through" it. And when we return, although we may feel relief or comfort at being "home," we often feel somewhat alien in that home for a period, experiencing real nostalgia for the different ways of feeling, seeing, relating, or being that we left behind.

## Naive Realism, Conflict, and Misunderstanding

Elsewhere, one of the present authors (Griffin and Ross 1991; Ross and Ward 1996) has discussed the concept of "naive realism." Central to this everyday epistemological stance is the conviction, generally implicit rather than explicit, that our own perceptions and feelings, and our own social and ethical priorities and judgments, are somehow "normal" or "natural" responses to the objective, unmediated reality of events (or to the objective merits of relevant claims and arguments). In turn, these beliefs lead to the further conviction that, to the extent that the perceptions, feelings, or priorities of other individuals or groups *differ* from our own, such responses are *not* normal or natural but must rather be "mediated" by distorting ideology or self-interest. The general relevance of this egocentric stance, coupled with the findings reported in this chapter, is worth exploring with respect to intercultural misunderstanding and conflict.

Consider the practice of nepotism (or similar instances of ingroup favoritism). As individualistic, independent Westerners, we see this practice as corrupt, unfair, and exclusionary, and we see our attempts to regulate such bias as a natural, enlightened, progressive attempt to give individuals the "impartial" and individual consideration to which they justly are entitled. We have similar reactions to the attempts of foreign corporations to maintain exclusive, closed, cooperative links between manufacturers, suppliers, and local markets. That is, we see these traditional practices as an unfair, unwise failure to let the "invisible hand" of the market operate so that individual greed can maximize individual and collective welfare alike.

One strongly suspects that collectivist observers, holding more interdependent views of self, would regard as "natural" attempts to reward loyalty and constancy and to distinguish kinsmen, friends, or others to whom we have ingroup ties from mere acquaintances or even strangers who are interested only in advancing their own immediate economic interests. Collectivists would feel no particular need to explain or justify their cultural practices; instead, they might well feel compelled to search for the peculiar biases that underlie *our* practices and institutions, to explain our seeming fickleness or the almost pathological pursuit of wealth and power "for its own sake" that seems embodied in our "Protestant ethic" (McClelland et al. 1953; Weber 1905/1984). Indeed, they might be particularly hard-pressed to explain the respect we give to driven men and women who seem content, even overjoyed, to run things as disinterested stewards, rather than advancing and protecting the interests of those tied to them by blood or lifelong relationships.

A similar clash of cultures involving issues of impartiality versus favoritism may play itself out in disputes about affirmative action, although here the issue is complicated by the particular historical experiences of America's immigrant groups. On the one hand, the notion of group-based entitlements or sharing of resources and power may be more congenial to Asians, who may also be less offended than Americans of Western European backgrounds by such policies' seeming violation of individualistic notions of fairness or meritocratic "open" competition. On the other hand, Asians, like many historical immigrant groups, may be particular loath (especially in the realm of education) to see the individualist competition (featuring seemingly objective test scores, grade point averages, and other "color-blind" criteria) given less weight when it is precisely that competition that has enabled them to win entrance in the face of hegemonic groups' indifference or even hostility to their aspirations. Certainly, such issues are apt to add new complexities as our increasingly culturally diverse society struggles with historic issues of group inequality.

Situations involving the display of independence or the exercise of choice raise similar possibilities for misunderstanding and even conflict. Relatively independent Westerners may attribute personal reticence, the unwillingness to criticize peers or express strong opinions in group settings (especially settings in which they, as outgroup members, are present), or the reluctance to champion one's own proposals to a lack of confidence, a lack of courage, or even a lack of leadership potential. More interdependent non-Westerners, by contrast, may see displays of Western assertiveness as inappropriately self-serving, overbearing, or lacking in respect for others. Moreover, the members of both cultures are apt to see their own assessments of the others' responses as natural, culture-free, objective, and accurate. And they are apt to see the others' assessments of them as the result of the peculiar cultural lenses that those on "the other side" bring to the task of social perception.

Anecdotal instances of cultural differences in practice, and interpretation, with regard to the exercise of personal choice should similarly be familiar to every traveler. The Western visitor to Japan who finds that her host at a fine restaurant has ordered the same meal for everyone is apt to interpret such behavior as an exercise of social control and a restriction of her own freedom to experiment or to cater to her own idiosyncratic tastes. The same diner, however, may not see anything odd about her own considerable reluctance to order exactly the same combination of appetizer and entrée as the friend ordering before her (much less to choose the same dress or exactly the same landscaping scheme as her neighbor) lest she be seen as a mere "copycat."

In similar fashion, parental involvement with children's schoolwork is likely, in this country, to be rejected by children themselves as oppressive and intrusive interference in their affairs and may often be proscribed by their teachers as ethically inappropriate. In collectivistic societies, in contrast, such involvement may be welcomed by children and teachers alike and is likely to be viewed as a sign of mutual dependence and support (Stevenson and Chen 1989). In addition, individualist and collectivist cultures are likely to display correspondingly divergent beliefs about the empirical consequences of such parental practices for children's eventual learning.

Even the current emphasis in applied psychology on the benefits of self-efficacy and personal responsibility-taking may reflect these same cultural blinders. In America, we herald impressive findings on the educational and health benefits of feeling in control, taking responsibility, or having a positive attributional style wherein failures are attributed to controllable personal factors (Bandura 1997; Seligman 1992). We read books and magazine articles about the need to take charge of our own breast cancer, AIDS, or heart disease, rather than leave it to the sole care of medical professionals. Conversely, we are shocked to discover that in many Asian societies it is considered an affront to one's physician to ask why a particular treatment is being undertaken or exactly how it works. And we are horrified to learn that precise diagnoses and prognoses are generally withheld from terminally ill Asian patients (only their relatives are given the relevant information), because we are convinced that *we* would want to know all and can cite chapter and verse about the benefits to patients of accurate knowledge and an active role in dealing with the management of pain and other symptoms.

In short, we are likely to read relevant experimental and popular literatures with a sense that existential truths, not peculiarities of local culture, are being revealed. And once again, even when we come to appreciate cultural differences and learn to avoid making such overly broad generalizations or characterological assumptions, we may still retain the belief that our preferences and experiences are "natural" and essential, while those of other cultures are to be understood in terms of the specific, distinctive, features of collectivist or Confucian or Asian cultures.

## Concerns and Caveats

While it is important to recognize cultural differences and to shed the egocentrism and ethnocentrism that mar or at least limit much of our work, there are some dangers to be avoided. In emphasizing differences, or even in chiding our colleagues for their unwarranted universalism, we can fall prey to excesses of our own. Recent research in our laboratory shows that pro-choice and pro-life factions, affirmative action opponents and proponents, and even men and women typically *overestimate* their differences both in factual assumptions and in construals of relevant information (Robinson et al. 1995). We suspect that so-called individualists and collectivists may similarly overestimate rather than underestimate their differences and may, as a result, despair unnecessarily about the prospects for finding common ground.

A related danger is that of overestimating the homogeneity, or underestimating the variability, to be found within cultures (especially the "other" culture). Closer examination is likely to reveal that "our" individualism may be more domain-specific (and more restricted to particular subcultures) than we recognize, and closer examination will surely reveal that the labels "collectivist" and "interdependent" are far too broad and undiscriminating to capture the diversity, or fully alert us to the basis, of intercultural differences. We would all be well served, for example, by separating collectivist norms from Confucianist ones (see Dien 1997), and we would do well to recognize that Hindus, Moslems, Japanese, Koreans, and Chinese (to say nothing of the different subcultures within each of these larger groups) are likely to be substantially less impressed than us by their similarities and more attuned than us to their differences.

Finally, in our haste to embrace cultural differences, we run the risk of overlooking similarities that are deep and informative. Despite our much-vaunted "individualism," it is important to recognize the deep communitarian strain that runs through our history and the American penchant for creating philanthropic and voluntary associations to coordinate the joint undertakings of communities (Bellah 1996; Etzioni 1996; de Tocqueville 1848/1969). Americans can also benefit from the nurturance and support of their peers, as suggested by research on the survival of breast cancer patients in support groups (Dunkel-Schetter et al. 1992; Spiegel 1992; Spiegel and Bloom 1983) and the success of group study in aiding minority calculus students (Treisman 1985).

We are confident that further research will reveal domains, practices, and institutions within which collectivists manifest their own strivings for efficacy and channels of self-expression, if not individualism. (Or perhaps we Westerners simply do not understand how karioke, sumo wrestling, and martial arts are expressions of collectivist rather than individualist strivings). We are equally confident that the distinction between ingroups and outgroups will emerge as critical in at least some important attribution and choice domains within the American context. In short, we expect the future of cultural psychology to offer a more nuanced appreciation of the "other," as well as more subtle techniques for avoiding and overcoming potential sources of intercultural conflict.

## NOTES

1. The basis for this characterization seems clear. American social psychologists studying interpersonal processes have consistently excluded from their studies participants in continuing relationships. (Predictably, the main recent exception involves research on *romantic* relationships, although even there the focus is often on initial attraction rather than on the evolving or ongoing features of the relationship itself.) Even when intergroup or intragroup dynamics are the focus of investigation, it is generally previously unacquainted individuals and/or arbitrarily defined groups that are studied. And when such group dynamics are *not* the focus of attention, we invariably study responses to actions by, communications from, or even written information about, strangers—rather than friends, family members, coworkers, or others in long-term relationships. In a sense, relational and social contexts are treated as sources of noise, or even bias, to be eliminated in the search for "basic" underlying processes and functional relationships between variables.
2. The ethnocentricity of American cross-cultural research was even more blatant in previous decades. Most of the time, researchers would directly export specific experimental paradigms, such as those of Asch (1951), Milgram (1963), or Darley and Latané (1968)—even though, as this brief list suggests, many of these paradigms were designed to capture the events or problems of particular points in our social history—for study in a variety of foreign capitals determined more by happenstance or opportunity than by any theoretical analysis of the features of the relevant cultures. But even in the present, more culturally attuned era (and even in the context of challenging universalist assumptions), much research still begins by asking whether "our" self-perception, dissonance reduction, or attribution findings apply in those "other" cultures, with their different social concerns, religious beliefs, epistemologies, or ideologies. Rarely if ever do researchers *start* with other cultures and consider what lessons, specific phenomena, or functional relations observed within them might hold about the nature of human psychology (or rather, the range of possible human psychologies).
3. One additional difference in the methodologies of the first two studies may merit more emphasis and discussion. Whereas students in the first study offered trait attributions about *specific* others (a friend and an enemy of their own designation), students in the second study offered causal attributions about *hypothetical* others (a "friend" and a "stranger" named, but not otherwise described, in the relevant scenario). Thus, it is not clear whether actual misdeeds by specific flesh-and-blood others would have yielded the same lack of ingroup favoritism among our Caucasian American participants, or the same pattern of differences between the Caucasian Americans and Asian Americans. On the other hand, it is noteworthy that even the *generic* designation of "friend" or "stranger" was sufficient to invoke ingroup favoritism among our Asian American students—a hint, perhaps, that such favoritism

may be culturally scripted among our presumably interdependent collectivists but absent (or perhaps dependent on the specific knowledge and relational bonds entailed in an actual friendship) among our presumably independent individualists.

4. A similar set of processes can be seen in earlier, related Western research demonstrating the detrimental effects of superfluous extrinsic rewards on children's intrinsic motivation (Condry 1977; Deci and Ryan 1985; Lepper and Greene 1978; Lepper, Greene, and Nisbett 1973). As these studies show, in our country, inducing children to engage in activities of high initial intrinsic interest in order to obtain some extrinsic reward or to meet some extrinsic constraint typically undermines their intrinsic motivation and task performance.
5. The apparent difference between Asian and Caucasian Americans within the personal-choice conditions, in both this and the next study, proved statistically significant only for the two intrinsic motivation measures (figures 9.3 and 9.5) and not for the two performance/learning measures (figures 9.4 and 9.6), although all four comparisons were clearly in the same direction.
6. There is one comment worth adding to this seemingly straightforward account of methods and results. Both studies present an interesting problem of interpretation, particularly with respect to the Asian children's choices. That is, it is difficult to determine whether it was a matter of *choice* versus *no choice* (or freedom to express one's individuality versus restriction of that freedom) or a matter of *correct* choice versus potentially *incorrect* choice (or appropriate choice versus potentially inappropriate choice). In these studies, as in many others, it can be difficult to determine how much cultural differences are manifested in people's different responses to objectively defined situations or manipulations or in the different ways in which people subjectively construe seemingly constant stimulus situations or manipulations.

## REFERENCES


Allport, Gordon W. (1954). *The nature of prejudice.* Cambridge, Mass.: Addison-Wesley.

Aron, Arthur, and Aron, Elaine N. (1986). *Love as the expansion of self: Understanding attraction and satisfaction.* New York: Hemisphere.

Asch, Solomon E. (1951). Effects of group pressures upon the modification and distortion of judgment. In Harold Guetzkow (Ed.), *Groups, leadership, and men.* Pittsburgh: Carnegie Press.

Bandura, Albert. (1997). *Self-efficacy: The exercise of control.* New York: Freeman.

Bellah, Robert N. (Ed.). (1996). *Habits of the heart: Individualism and commitment in American life.* Berkeley: University of California Press.

Bem, Daryl J. (1967). Self-perception: An alternative interpretation of cognitive dissonance phenomena. *Psychological Review, 74,* 183–200.

———. (1972). Self-perception theory. In Leonard Berkowitz (Ed.), *Advances in experimental social psychology* (vol. 6, pp. 2–62). New York: Academic Press.

Bond, Michael H. (1983). A proposal for cross-cultural studies of attribution processes. In Miles H. Hewstone (Ed.), *Attribution theory: Social and applied extensions* (pp. 144–57). Oxford: Basil Blackwell.

Condry, John. (1977). Enemies of exploration: Self-initiated versus other-initiated learning. *Journal of Personality and Social Psychology, 35,* 459–77.

Cooley, Charles H. (1902). *Human nature and the social order.* New York: Scribner's.

Cordova, Diana I., and Lepper, Mark R. (1996). Intrinsic motivation and the process of learning: Beneficial effects of contextualization, personalization, and choice. *Journal of Educational Psychology, 88,* 715–30.

Crosby, Faye. (1976). A model of egoistical relative deprivation. *Psychological Review, 83,* 85–113.

Dalal, Ajit K., Sharma, Rajeev, and Bisht, Shalini. (1983). Causal attributions of ex-criminal tribal and urban children in India. *Journal of Social Psychology, 119,* 163–71.

Darley, John M., and Latané, Bibb. (1968). Bystander intervention in emergencies: Diffusion of responsibility. *Journal of Personality and Social Psychology, 8,* 377–83.

DeCharms, Richard. (1968). *Personal causation.* New York: Academic Press.

Deci, Edward L. (1981). *The psychology of self-determination.* Lexington, Mass.: Heath.

Deci, Edward L., and Ryan, Richard M. (1985). *Intrinsic motivation and self-determination in human behavior.* New York: Plenum Press.

De Tocqueville, Alexis. (1969). *Democracy in America.* Translated by G. Lawrence. Edited by J. P. Mayer. New York: Harper and Row. (Originally published in 1848)

Dien, Dora S. (1997). Confucianism and cultural psychology: Comparing the Chinese and the Japanese. Unpublished paper, California State University at Hayward.

Dunkel-Schetter, Christine, Feinstein, Lawrence G., Taylor, Shelly E., and Falke, Roberta L. (1992). Patterns of coping with cancer. *Health Psychology, 11,* 79–87.

Etzioni, Amitai. (1996). *The new golden rule: Community and morality in a democratic society.* New York: Basic Books.

Festinger, Leon. (1954). A theory of social comparison processes. *Human Relations, 7,* 117–40.

———. (1957). *A theory of cognitive dissonance.* Stanford, Calif.: Stanford University Press.

Fiske, Alan P., Kitayama, Shinobu, Markus, Hazel R., and Nisbett, Richard E. (1997). The cultural perspective. In Daniel T. Gilbert, Susan T. Fiske, and Gardner Lindzey (Eds.), *The handbook of social psychology* (4th ed., pp. 915–81). New York: McGraw-Hill.

Gaertner, Samuel L., and Dovidio, John F. (1986). The aversive form of racism. In John F. Dovidio and Samuel L. Gaertner (Eds.), *Prejudice, discrimination, and racism* (pp. 61–90). Orlando, Fla.: Academic Press.

Geertz, Clifford. (1975). On the nature of anthropological understanding. *American Scientist, 63,* 47–53.

Greenwald, Anthony G. (1980). The totalitarian ego: Fabrication and revision of personal history. *American Psychologist, 35,* 603–18.

Griffin, Dale W., and Ross, Lee. (1991). Subjective construal, social inference, and human misunderstanding. In Mark P. Zanna (Ed.), *Advances in experimental social psychology* (vol. 24, pp. 319–59). New York: Academic Press.

Hofstede, Geert. (1980). *Culture's consequences.* Beverly Hills, Calif.: Sage.

———. (1991). *Cultures and organizations: Software of the mind.* London: McGraw-Hill.
Iyengar, Sheena S., and Lepper, Mark R. (1999). Rethinking the value of choice: A cultural perspective on intrinsic motivation. *Journal of Personality and Social Psychology, 76,* 349–66.
Iyengar, Sheena S., and Ross, Lee. (1996). *Trait ascription and attributional charity: A cultural perspective.* Unpublished paper, Stanford University.
Johnson, F. (1985). The Western concept of self. In Anthony Marsella, George De Vos, and Francis L. K. Hsu (Eds.), *Culture and self* (pp. 24–55). London: Tavistock.
Jones, Edward E. (1990). *Interpersonal perception.* New York: Freeman.
Jones, Edward E., and Nisbett, Richard E. (1971). The actor and the observer: Divergent perceptions of the causes of behavior. In Edward E. Jones, David E. Kanouse, Harold H. Kelley, Richard E. Nisbett, Stuart Valins, and Bernard Weiner (Eds.), *Attribution: Perceiving the causes of behavior* (pp. 79–94). Morristown, N.J.: General Learning Press.
Jones, Edward E., Wood, George C., and Quattrone, George A. (1981). Perceived variability of personal characteristics in ingroups and outgroups: The role of knowledge and evaluation. *Personality and Social Psychology Bulletin, 7,* 523–28.
Jones, James M. (1997). *Prejudice and racism.* 2nd ed. Reading, Mass.: Addison-Wesley. (Originally published in 1972)
Kitayama, Shinobu, Markus, Hazel R., Matsumoto, Hisaya, and Norasakkunkit, Vinai. (1997). Individual and collective processes in the construction of the self: Self-enhancement in the United States and self-criticism in Japan. *Journal of Personality and Social Psychology, 72,* 1245–67.
Kitayama, Shinobu, and Masuda, Takahito. (1997). Cultural psychology of social inference: The correspondence bias largely vanishes in Japan. Unpublished paper, Kyoto University.
Kondo, Dorinne. (1982). Work, family, and the self: A cultural analysis of Japanese family enterprise. Doctoral dissertation, Harvard University.
Lepper, Mark R., and Greene, David. (Eds.). (1978). *The hidden costs of reward.* Hillsdale, N.J.: Erlbaum.
Lepper, Mark R., Greene, David, and Nisbett, Richard E. (1973). Undermining children's intrinsic interest with extrinsic rewards: A test of the "overjustification" hypothesis. *Journal of Personality and Social Psychology, 28,* 129–37.
Markus, Hazel R., and Kitayama, Shinobu. (1991). Culture and the self: Implications for cognition, emotion, and motivation. *Psychological Review, 98,* 224–53.
McClelland, David C., Atkinson, John W., Clark, Russell A., and Lowell, Edgar L. (1953). *The achievement motive.* New York: Appleton-Century-Crofts.
McConahay, John B. (1986). Modern racism, ambivalence, and the modern racism scale. In John F. Dovidio and Samuel L. Gaertner (Eds.), *Prejudice, discrimination, and racism* (pp. 91–126). Orlando, Fla.: Academic Press.
Mead, George H. (1934). *Mind, self, and society.* Chicago: University of Chicago Press.
Milgram, Stanley. (1963). Behavioral study of obedience. *Journal of Abnormal and Social Psychology, 67,* 371–78.
Miller, Joan G. (1984). Culture and the development of everyday social explanation. *Journal of Personality and Social Psychology, 46,* 961–78.
Morris, Michael W., and Peng, Kaiping. (1994). Culture and cause: American and

Chinese attributions for social and physical events. *Journal of Personality and Social Psychology, 67,* 949–71.
Moscovici, Serge. (1984). The phenomenon of social representations. In Robert M. Farr and Serge Moscovici (Eds.), *Social representations* (pp. 3–69). New York: Cambridge University Press.
Newcomb, Theodore M. (1943). *Personality and social change.* New York: Dryden.
Newcomb, Theodore M., Koenig, Kathryn E., Flacks, Richard, and Warwick, Donald P. (1967). *Persistence and change: Bennington College and its students after twenty-five years.* New York: Wiley.
Nisbett, Richard E., Caputo, Curtis, Legant, Patricia, and Maracek, Jeanne. (1973). Behavior as seen by the actor and as seen by the observer. *Journal of Personality and Social Psychology, 27,* 154–64.
Nisbett, Richard E., and Cohen, Dov. (1996). *Culture of honor: The psychology of violence in the South.* Boulder, Colo.: Westview Press.
Nisbett, Richard E., and Ross, Lee. (1980). *Human inference: Strategies and shortcomings of social judgment.* Englewood Cliffs, N.J.: Prentice-Hall.
Nisbett, Richard E., and Wilson, Timothy D. (1977). Telling more than we can know: Verbal reports on mental processes. *Psychological Review, 84,* 231–59.
Robinson, Robert J., Keltner, Dacher, Ward, Andrew, and Ross, Lee. (1995). Actual versus assumed differences in construal: "Naive realism" in intergroup perception and conflict. *Journal of Personality and Social Psychology, 68,* 404–17.
Ross, Lee. (1977). The intuitive psychologist and his shortcomings. In Leonard Berkowitz (Ed.), *Advances in experimental social psychology* (vol. 10, pp. 173–220). New York: Academic Press.
Ross, Lee, and Nisbett, Richard E. (1991). *The person and the situation: Perspectives of social psychology.* New York: McGraw-Hill.
Ross, Lee, and Ward, Andrew. (1996). Naive realism in everyday life: Implications for social conflict and misunderstanding. In Edward S. Reed, Elliot Turiel, and Terrance Brown (Eds.), *Values and knowledge* (pp. 103–35). Hillsdale, N.J.: Erlbaum.
Sampson, Edward E. (1985). The decentralization of identity: Toward a revised concept of personal and social order. *American Psychologist, 40,* 1203–11.
———. (1988). The debate on individualism: Indigenous psychologies of the individual and their role in personal and societal functioning. *American Psychologist, 43,* 15–22.
———. (1989). The challenge of social change for psychology: Globalization and psychology's theory of the person. *American Psychologist, 44,* 914–21.
Schachter, Stanley. (1964). The interaction of cognitive and physiological determinants of emotional state. In Leonard Berkowitz (Ed.), *Advances in experimental social psychology* (vol. 1, pp. 49–80). New York: Academic Press.
Seligman, Martin E. P. (1992). *Learned optimism: How to change your mind and your life.* New York: Pocket Books.
Sherif, Muzafer. (1966). *In common predicament: Social psychology of intergroup conflict and cooperation.* Boston: Houghton Mifflin.
Sherif, Muzafer, and Sherif, Carolyn W. (1953). *Groups in harmony and tension.* New York: Harper and Row.
Shweder, Richard A. (1991). *Thinking through cultures.* Cambridge, Mass.: Harvard University Press.
Shweder, Richard A., and Bourne, Edmund J. (1982). Does the concept of the

person vary cross-culturally? In Anthony J. Marsella and Geoffrey M. White (Eds.), *Cultural conceptions of mental health and therapy* (pp. 130–204). London: Reidel.

Smith, Peter B., and Bond, Michael H. (1993). *Social psychology across cultures.* London: Harvester Wheatsheaf.

Spiegel, David. (1992). Effects of psychosocial support on patients with metastatic breast cancer. *Journal of Psychosocial Oncology, 10,* 113–20.

Spiegel, David, and Bloom, Joan. (1983). Group therapy and hypnosis reduce metastatic breast carcinoma pain. *Psychosomatic Medicine, 45,* 333–39.

Stevenson, Harold W., and Chen, Chuansheng. (1989). Homework: A cross-cultural examination. *Child Development, 60,* 551–61.

Stigler, James W., Shweder, Richard A., and Herdt, Gilbert (Eds.). (1990). *Cultural psychology: Essays on comparative human development.* New York: Cambridge University Press.

Storms, Michael D. (1973). Videotape and the attribution process: Reversing actors' and observers' points of view. *Journal of Personality and Social Psychology, 27,* 165–75.

Tajfel, Henri. (1970). Experiments in intergroup discrimination. *Scientific American, 223,* 96–102.

———. (1981). *Human groups and social categories: Studies in social psychology.* London: Cambridge University Press.

Takata, Toshitake. (1987). Self-deprecative tendencies in self-evaluation through social comparison. *Japanese Journal of Experimental Social Psychology, 27,* 27–36.

Taylor, Shelley E. (1983). Adjustment to threatening events: A theory of cognitive adaptation. *American Psychologist, 41,* 1161–73.

Taylor, Shelley E., and Fiske, Susan T. (1978). Salience, attention, and attribution: Top of the head phenomena. In Leonard Berkowitz (Ed.), *Advances in experimental social psychology* (vol. 11, pp. 249–88). New York: Academic Press.

Tesser, Abraham. (1980). Self-esteem maintenance in family dynamics. *Journal of Personality and Social Psychology, 39,* 77–91.

———. (1988). Toward a self-evaluation maintenance model of social behavior. In Leonard Berkowitz (Ed.), *Advances in experimental social psychology* (vol. 21, pp. 181–227). New York: Academic Press.

Treisman, Uri. (1985). A study of mathematics performance of black students at the University of California, Berkeley. Unpublished paper, University of California, Berkeley.

Triandis, Harry C. (1989). The self and social behavior in differing cultural contexts. *Psychological Review, 96,* 506–20.

———. (1990). Cross-cultural studies of individualism and collectivism. In John Berman (Ed.), *Nebraska symposium on motivation* (vol. 20, pp. 41–133). Lincoln: University of Nebraska Press.

———. (1995). *Individualism and collectivism.* Boulder, Colo.: Westview Press.

Waterman, Alan S. (1981). Individualism and interdependence. *American Psychologist, 36,* 762–73.

Weber, Max. (1984). *The Protestant ethic and the spirit of capitalism.* London: Unwin. (Originally published in 1905)

Zuckerman, Miron, Porac, Joseph, Lathin, Drew, Smith, Raymond, and Deci, Edward L. (1978). On the importance of self-determination for intrinsically motivated behavior. *Personality and Social Psychology Bulletin, 4,* 443–46.

# 10

# CONFLICTWAYS: CULTURAL DIVERSITY IN THE MEANINGS AND PRACTICES OF CONFLICT

*Hazel Rose Markus and Leah R. Lin*

If everyone pulled in the same direction, the whole world would topple over.

—Yiddish proverb

We have conflict without conflicting. . . . We presuppose that the parties will fundamentally strive to pull together rather than push apart.

—Japanese manager (Pascale and Athos 1981, 48)

WORKPLACES are commonly rife with conflicts—conflicts either already in progress or just one tense interaction away. Many of the ostensible issues seem small, but they often signal powerful fault lines. Who should make the coffee and clean up the kitchen area? Which unit has priority at the photocopying machines? Why does the office manager seem to favor some work groups over others? As American offices increasingly include employees from diverse cultural contexts, the array and scope of these conflicts will surely broaden. The relationship of culture to the content of many of these conflicts may be clear. Should there be Christmas, Hanukkah, and Kwanza decorations in December, or no decorations at all? Should English be the only language spoken in the workplace? However, what may be less clear are the powerful cultural differences in the logic and course of conflict, in the why, when, where, and what of conflict. Many of the patterns and norms of conflict, and of conflict resolution, that are assumed to be universal are in fact specific to European American cultural contexts; they do not yet reflect the variety of divergent perspectives on conflict that are increasingly present in the American workplace.

As highlighted by this chapter's epigraphs, people in different communities and societies can have different understandings and implicit-models of conflict. Some of the questions that distinguish cultural contexts include: Is conflict an inevitable part of social life, or can it be avoided? What are the most likely sources of conflict? What are the goals of conflict (for example, being right, having one's way, or restoring balance between individuals)? What are the expected outcomes? Should conflict be revealed and expressed or kept in the background and underplayed? Can conflict be resolved or only managed? What are the appropriate responses to disagreement—confrontation or silence? Can conflict produce desirable social change? What roles do consensus seeking and compromise play in conflict?

This chapter focuses on what we call *conflictways*—differences in the meanings and practices of conflict. We describe a cultural psychological approach to conflict and review some research analyzing the understandings and practices of conflict observed in four overlapping yet still somewhat different cultural contexts: European American, Asian American, Mexican American, and African American.[1] Approaches to conflict can be found in each of these ethnic cultural contexts that are somewhat distinct from one another. These conflictways reflect particular historically constructed and ethnically patterned arrangements of social life within the American context. The goal here is to begin a description of different models for conflict, not to describe or predict individual behavior. To the extent that individuals now engage or have engaged in only one of these contexts, their conflict-relevant behavior may reflect some of the meanings and practices described here. Yet when individuals engage or have engaged in a variety of cultural contexts, or when the ideas and practices of one context come in contact with the ideas and practices of other contexts, as is very likely to happen in American society, it is difficult to know what to expect for any given individual or group.

Drawing on a still fairly limited set of research findings, our purpose is to point to some differences in the understandings and practices of conflict that may well be implicated in tensions and disputes in multicultural American workplaces. We are still a long way from hypothesizing about the kinds of conflicts that will develop or designing interventions to avoid them. However alternative models of the genesis, course, and outcome of conflict can inform and expand European American perspectives, which have been the foundation for the theoretical and empirical study of conflict in the social sciences and can provide insight into the cultural bases of conflict.

## A CULTURAL PSYCHOLOGICAL APPROACH TO CONFLICT

Central to our discussion is the idea that cultural systems "make each other up" and psychological processes (Shweder 1991). Psychological processes develop as people coordinate their thoughts and actions with the prevalent, historically created and organized systems of cultural meanings and practices (Fiske et al. 1998; Markus, Kitayama, and Heiman 1996). According to this view, cultural systems can be seen as frames within which psychological space is contoured. People's cognitive, emotional, motivational, and behavioral processes are shaped through their engagement in the specific, local, cultural worlds of families, schools, and workplaces. Once shaped, these particular psychological tendencies further facilitate the coordination of the person with a particular cultural world, enabling the person to live flexibly, adaptively, and naturally in a given cultural context. Culturally conditioned people in the course of their everyday lives construct and reconstruct the sociocultural contexts in which they live. Some communities, for example, emphasize the importance of choosing and providing frequent opportunities to make choices. People engaged in these communities often come to desire and require situations that offer personal choice.

People who participate in different worlds, who live within communities and societies that are organized differently from one another, use locally available ideas and practices to guide their interactions, to coordinate their responses, and ultimately to live in culture-specific ways. Szalay (1981), who has developed a model for intercultural communication, says simply that people "develop their own particular interests, perceptions, attitudes, and beliefs, which form a characteristic frame of reference within which they organize and interpret their life experiences. . . . Different cultural experiences produce different interpretations not shown in conventional dictionaries" (27). Those who have been enculturated and socialized in divergent cultural contexts may bring to a dispute different notions of what constitutes a conflict and, very importantly, of how and why to participate or engage in it. They may disagree about which course of action is desirable in a conflict. Even more broadly, they may diverge in their notions of personhood: Who is implicated? Whose business is it? Have I been shamed or dishonored? Have my rights been trampled? They may also disagree about what constitutes meaningful "actions" and "responses" to these transgressions.

A cultural analysis takes into account core cultural ideas and background understandings of conflict, as well as those practices and institutions—from the official and formal to the local and everyday—within which the conflict is manifest. The importance of knowing the backgrounds of the parties in a conflict is hardly a novel suggestion. Deutsch's (1973) classic analysis of the resolution of conflict begins with the observation that whether a conflict has developed between union and management, between nations, or even between husband and wife, it is useful to know about "the characteristics of the parties in conflict (their values and motivations; . . . their beliefs about conflict, including their conceptions of strategy and tactics)," and to know something about "the nature of the social norms and institutional forms for regulating conflict" (6–7).

More specifically, Merry (1986), a legal theorist, maintains that conflict and disputing are cultural behavior,

> informed by participants' moral views about how to fight, the meaning participants attach to going to court, social practices that indicate when and how to escalate disputes to a public forum, and participants' notions of rights and entitlements. . . . The normative framework shapes the way people conceptualize problems, the ways they pursue them, and the kinds of solutions they look for. (2063)

Our contribution to the analysis of conflict is to take the suggestions of Deutsch and Merry seriously and begin to examine culture and conflict systematically. Conflictways vary dramatically among cultural contexts—contexts specified by ethnicity, religion, gender, social class, eductional background, age, or region of the country or world. These variations are not merely differences in how to think about conflict *after* behavior has occurred. Instead, conflictways are fully active in the *constitution* of behavior. Is silence acquiescence or passive aggressiveness? Is a joke a provocation or play? Conflictways are implicated in these responses and are thus an important means by which people engage in and experience their social worlds.

Conflictways include the invisible, tacit, and commonsense understandings that people have about themselves and their worlds, including what is right and wrong, how to proceed, whom to turn to, and what to expect. One of the most important tacit understandings, and one that may be particularly significant for an analysis of conflict, is the view of what it means to be a "good" or "proper" person. In many cultural contexts, the individual is parsed and understood not as a separate or distinct entity, as in the United States, but instead as an interdependent member of a given social unit. Each cultural context's conception of self and its relation to others is an integral part of understanding cultural differences regarding conflict. Two distinct conceptions will be discussed in the following sections.

## Conflict in Individualist Worlds

The empirical and theoretical analysis of conflict has been pursued largely within a Western context, and particularly a mainstream American context. If it is the case that the cultural pervades and cannot be separated from the psychological, then many of social psychology's "basic" understandings of conflict carry Western or European American assumptions about the nature of the individual, the group, and social behavior. Social psychology, the discipline most deeply committed to understanding the social nature of the individual, has been developed within the context of ideological individualism. The central tenet of this ideology is the ontological priority afforded to the separate, essentially nonsocial individual. Subsequently, and secondarily, the individual is believed to enter into social relations or sociality, but on the basis of need and by mutual consent with other similar individuals (Markus et al. 1996; Taylor 1989). The focus in such a view is on the autonomous individual rather than on the social unit of which the individual is a part. The person is cast as an entity who is separated from the external situation and whose behavior is determined by some amalgam of internal attributes. Moreover, the person or the self is believed to be responsible for his or her behavior, and to be the final explanation for that behavior (Landrine and Klonoff 1992; Shweder and Bourne 1984).

The word *individual* derives from the Latin *individuus,* which means indivisible and whole. The way of life based on the individual—individualism—is often analyzed as the critical characteristic of Western society (Baumeister 1987; Carrithers, Collins, and Lukes 1987; Guisinger and Blatt 1994; Sampson 1985). Many argue that it was primarily the Enlightenment that gave birth to the notion of the Kantian individual and to the importance of individual reason and free will. Others suggest that individualism in its current form bears the stamp of late industrial capitalism. Lebra (1992) contends that individualism is a function of a Cartesian categorization system that draws a sharp distinction between self and others and designates thinking and the content of one's thoughts as the critical features of being.

Some scholars hold that understanding individuals as separate from others reflects a much older, probably Greek epistemological preference for breaking objects into their component elements or for placing objects into categories on the basis of necessary and sufficient features for category membership (Nakamura 1964; Needham 1962). The knot of precedents for the individualist construction of the world is still being unraveled, yet whatever its primary sources, clearly individualism is pervasively inscribed and institutionalized in the United States.

Mainstream American society, from the time of the Declaration of Independence, has been built on the notion of the "natural" human rights of individuals (Bellah et al. 1985). Among these rights, the most important is freedom. Freedom has multiple meanings. It refers to the right to express oneself and one's preferences. It also refers to the right to choose what one "wants" and thus to be free from social determination or the influence of others. Freedom implies that one is unshackled or unfettered by others' ideas, opinions, or prescriptions. Reflected in the Yiddish proverb that begins this chapter is the idea that what one thinks or believes is importantly self-definitional and world-making. Knowing and expressing what one thinks, or the ways in which one is "right," is an essential feature of individualist behavior; the operation of the world is believed to depend on it. Expressed differences in opinion are expected, valued, and protected. In the United States, having one's own ideas and the courage of one's convictions, making up one's own mind, and charting one's own course are powerful public meanings inscribed in everyday social practices. In many cultural contexts within the United States, these beliefs are axiomatic to being a person. Notions about the value of compromise and accommodation, while also common and available, are not as widely represented and elaborated in public meanings and institutional practices and policies and thus are not typically the primary or initial considerations in a conflict.

The cultural model of the independent person that prevails in North America and is reflected in the "rational actor" of game theory, the "reasonable person" of the legal system, and the "authentic self" of most psychological theorizing defines certain features as natural, necessary, and good: (1) that the individual is a stable, autonomous, "free" entity; (2) that he or she possesses a set of characteristic, identifying, and self-defining attributes—preferences, motives, goals, attitudes, beliefs, and abilities—that are the primary forces that enable, guide, or constrain behavior; (3) that individuals take action that is oriented toward the expression of their opinions and beliefs, the realization of their rights, and the achievement of their own goals; and (4) that the individual often regards relationships as competing with personal needs and considers the expectations of others and obligations to others as interfering with personal goals (for full discussion of these and other cultural commitments of individualism, see Fiske et al. 1998).

The independence that is believed to characterize individuals cannot, of course, be achieved independently. Rather, independence is a complex of relationships, institutions, and social practices that make people "free and autonomous." Independence provides people with "choices" and creates "opportunities" for achieving, being "in control," and "pursuing success and happiness"; it also affords people the "right" and "responsibility" to assert themselves and confidently stand their ground in a dispute (Fiske et al. 1998). Becoming "independent" in this way and free from the control of others is fostered and made real in many American practices and institutions, including the legal system, the political system, educational systems, and the media (Markus, Mullally, and Kitayama 1997).

The assumptions of individualism have direct consequences for the sources, meanings, and practices of conflict. Within a world organized according to the tenets of individualism and animated by the web of associated understandings and practices, any perceived constraint on individual freedom is likely to pose immediate problems and require a response. Typically the most appropriate response in a conflict situation involves a direct or honest expression of one's ideas. Indeed, it is sometimes the individualist's moral imperative, the sign that one is being a "good" person, to disagree with and remain unmoved by the influence of others. The right to disagree, typically manifested by a direct statement of one's *own* views, can create social difficulties, but it is understood and experienced as a birthright. Further, an individualist perspective, which often tends toward mechanical and determinist understandings of the world, is also likely to assume that there is, in a given conflict situation, a right or a wrong way, that there is one truth—such that A and not-A cannot both be true—and that sufficient debate, argumentation, and application of "reason" will reveal *the* truth (Fiske et al. 1998).

## Conflict in Interdependent Worlds

Regardless of a person's particular set of sociocultural niches within the United States, anyone living in this country is exposed to and lives within institutions—the legal system, the political system, the media—that are founded on and operate within an individualist framework of ideas and practices. Yet individualist notions of personhood are neither the "natural" way nor the only way to think about what it means "to be." In fact, most of the world's diverse cultural systems do not represent the person and the social world in this way at all. And even within the United States, many people also participate in cultural contexts that are not primarily rooted in individualist assumptions.

Interdependent views of personhood not only differ quite dramatically in their particulars but assume that what is obvious and "natural" is that the self is a *relational* entity. The self, from this perspective, is understood as fundamentally interdependent with others. The self cannot be separated from others and the surrounding social context and is typically not seen as "possessing" enduring, trans-situational qualities or attributes of its own in isolation from its relationships and contexts (Fiske et al. 1998; Markus and Kitayama 1991; Morris 1994; Triandis 1989). In fact, understanding other notions of personhood requires dissolving the boundary between self and others or self and society that is such an obvious starting point in many European American and also some North American and European formulations.

In the models of the self that are prevalent in many of the cultures of the world—including China, Japan, Korea, and South Asia as well as those of Africa, much of the Middle East, and Central and South America—the person is inherently and fundamentally connected to others. These cultural models of the person place greater stress than individualist models on social and relational concepts such as empathy, reciprocity, belongingness, kinship, hierarchy, loyalty, honor, respect, politeness, and social obligation. Typically in those cultural contexts, social relationships, roles, norms, and group solidarity are more fundamental to social behavior than self-expression. Although the individual is certainly aware of his or her own desires and interests, he or she is expected to meet others' expectations and work for the good of the dyad, the group, the institution, or the nation. Being a good or respectable person derives from active engagement in the social roles that configure social life and harmonious participation in honorable social relations.

More specifically, the cultural model of the interdependent person defines certain features as natural, necessary and good, including the idea that a person (1) is a flexible, connected entity who is bound to others; (2) participates in a set of relationships, groups, and institutions that are the primary forces that enable, guide, or constrain actions; (3) conforms to relational norms and responds to group goals by seeking consensus and compromise; and (4) often regards personal beliefs and needs as secondary to norms and relationships (for full discussion of the cultural commitments of an interdependent cultural model, see Fiske et al. 1998).

As with individualism, these ideas about relationality and interdependence have multiple sources and are mutually reinforcing. In many East Asian cultures, interdependent views have arisen from several overlapping religious and philosophical traditions. Buddhism, for example, asserts that people and the world must be considered in relative rather than absolute terms. Change is seen as fundamental to reality. Inconsistency and contradiction are to be expected, while the notion of a person as a consistent or unchanging entity is viewed as misleading, if not wrong-headed. Buddhism also encourages empathy and compassion for others with whom we are interdependent. Confucianism and Buddhism both emphasize harmony, selflessness, and subordination of the individual's own interests to the interests of a larger group (Ames, Dissanayake, and Kasulis 1994; Tu 1994). Confucianism also highlights the cultivation of the person into a proper social being, the importance of the social order, and the restoration of harmony through compromise. And Taoism contributes an appreciation of the value in living in the correct way.

From a Confucian perspective, other individuals or groups of other individuals are not separate from individuals; individuals must work through others—families, communities, and nations—to reveal themselves (Tu 1994; Fiske et al. 1998). Confucian society is hierarchical and based on a vertical structure of superiors and subordinates. Ideally, the hierarchy operates not through unidirectional control or through the imposition of the superior's will on the subordinate's will, but instead on reciprocity. Responsibility, wisdom, and benevolence are required of those higher in the hierarchy; obedience, loyalty, and respect are required of those lower in the hierarchy. Bond (1996) notes, for example, that Chinese bosses foster a supportive relationship with their subordinates and secure their loyalties by attending weddings, taking their sections to lunch, visiting sick family members in the hospital, securing mortgages and loans for them, and hiring employees' relatives. Both bosses and employees may then be willing to comply or accede to various demands in order to avoid disturbing this relationship.

With different conceptualizations of the social world come different metaphors and understandings of conflict. According to ethnographic studies in Central and South America (Avruch 1991; White 1994)—regions of the world also characterized by more interdependent models of the person—conflict is often believed to result from tangled interpersonal nets or webs. Lederbach (1991), in his analysis of Costa Rica, for example, finds that people often describe themselves as "trapped inside" a conflict and that the goal is to manage an "exit" through talk or dialogue. The role of a third person, who will connect individuals and maintain the integrity of the interpersonal web in the conflict, is critical. In contemporary Hawaiian culture, conflict is typically described as resulting from "blocked pathways" in the channels of "flowing affect" that connect people to one another. Conflict is represented as entanglements or relationships that "all jam up," and resolution often involves a respected elder who facilitates the disentanglement (Ito 1985; Shook and Kwan 1991). This facilitation includes a number of components, such as confession, apology, forgiveness, and release, that are not commonly invoked in more independent perspectives on conflict.

Some Americans are also likely to have different understandings of and approaches to conflict, such as some Asian Americans, African

Americans, Mexican Americans, southerners, many women—that is, people who are likely to have participated in settings and contexts that treat interdependent, relational ways of being as particularly significant. And it is these largely unrecognized differences that may be one source of tension and difficulty in the increasingly multicultural workplaces of the United States.

Interdependent constructions of the world have powerful consequences for the analysis and practice of conflict. From an interdependent perspective, the underlying goal of social behavior is not the preservation and manifestation of individual rights and attributes, but rather the preservation of relationships. For example, it is better to endure the suffering associated with being wronged than to disrupt harmony by complaining (Wall and Blum 1991). Thus, interdependent conflictways include strategies that emphasize indirectness rather than direct confrontation, the use of mediators or arbitrators, reliance on apology and forgiveness, and avoidance techniques like waiting, withdrawing, and even false promising. In a conflict, one should engage others, persuade them, and draw out their cooperation (Cohen 1996). Often the goal is to avoid hostility or the outbreak of confrontation because of the fear of damaging the relationship or producing lingering animosity (Bond 1996).

Wall and Blum (1991), in a fascinating study of community mediation in the People's Republic of China, report that in contrast to the United States, conflict mediation is a fact of everyday life in China, where there are over one million mediators. Mediators are present in good times and bad, and they make societal harmony their objective. Mediation in China proceeds very differently than it does in the United States, where mediators help the parties hammer out an agreement that protects the individual interests of both parties. First, in China the mediator's knowledge of the disputants is thought to be an asset, unlike the neutrality that is considered essential in the United States. Mediation is regarded as a responsibility to the community rather than to the individual; the community has a right to be safe, educated, employed, and at peace. Mediation is not voluntary, and the mediators, not the disputing parties, initiate the process. Finally, in the United States disputing parties expect personal satisfaction from mediation, while in China the parties may expect only that the dispute will be temporarily managed and some interpersonal harmony restored.

In their analysis of mediation techniques, Wall and Blum (1991) observe that the parties in a dispute are

> educated, persuaded, and advised as to how they should think or act. They are told to consider the feelings of others, to cherish harmony in their families or community, and not to undermine the respect of the neighbors

> or the reputation of the family. The mediator is also quick to argue for concessions that the parties could make, and to present the other side's point of view. (11)

These mediators, who view themselves as society's monitors, often tell the parties how they should think or behave and are less likely to give logical explanations for their recommendations. When an "educated" party capitulates, the mediator asks the relevant party for forgiveness.

From an interdependent perspective, conflict is an inevitable consequence of interdependence and is never resolved but smoothed or blunted for the time being. A quasi-equilibrium can be achieved, but one must be ever-vigilant for the next inevitable disturbance in the shared social space.

## CONFLICT IN FOUR CULTURAL CONTEXTS

Cultural contents constitute a framework within which people attach meanings to conflict and develop practices for approaching conflict. Although these meanings and practices vary dramatically across cultures, the observable diversity is not random variation. Cultural differences in conflictways may be understood in part by examining the view of the individual in cultural context. The following sections attempt to sketch the conception of the self in four cultural contexts within the United States and to demonstrate how these views can be reflected in the meanings and practices that people who live in these contexts commonly associate with conflict. This exploratory analysis is designed to illustrate how cultural interpretations may contribute to social psychology's knowledge of nonmainstream cultural systems and also to examine a set of concepts and phenomena that have remained largely invisible in mainstream research. Since our primary goal is to reveal the usefulness of a cultural psychological approach, we have characterized the models of self and conflict very broadly within each cultural context. It will be important for subsequent analyses to direct more detailed consideration toward considerations such as gender, age, and power within cultural context. Despite these caveats, our initial analysis highlights several tensions that are common to conflict in cultural contexts. Each of the models of conflict examined here reflect somewhat different means of responding to the tensions between the individual and social relationships, between confrontation and indirectness, and between resolution of a conflict and management of it. The expression of these three tensions in each cultural context reveals a multiplicity of conflictways.

## Conflictways in European American Contexts: Individual Rights and Autonomy

The meaning of conflict in many European American contexts, and particularly Anglo-American cultural contexts, reflects a view of the person as an autonomous entity who possesses individual rights and is motivated by a configuration of internal or personal values and goals (Markus and Kitayama 1991; Markus et al. 1996; Markus et al. 1997; Stewart and Bennett 1991; Triandis 1995). In European American cultural contexts, individuals are expected to express their *own* beliefs and pursue their *own* goals; it is their duty to do so because their ideas and attitudes literally define the self. Indeed, behavior is a reflection or expression of individual beliefs and goals. Within this cultural context, people define conflict as perceived incompatibility in individuals' beliefs about an issue, or incompatibility in the accomplishment of their goals (Collier 1988). These lay definitions are consistent with the mainstream social psychological view that conflict arises when incompatible activities occur, and that this incompatibility reflects differences in individuals' ideas, values, and goals (Deutsch 1973).

European American conceptions of conflict are predicated on a notion of the person as an agentic performer of individual actions rather than a responsive being situated in and actively adjusting to a network of relationships. In contrast with the prevalent ideas and practices of Asian American, African American, and Mexican American contexts, conflict in European American contexts is not considered the product of the ongoing process of being in relationship with others. Conflict arises when the activities of two individuals interfere with one another. Thus, conflict emerges from incidental situations rather than as an inevitable consequence of relationality. For people with bounded, individualist selves, conflict with others can be self-defining or identity-promoting. It brings into sharp relief their own desires, preferences, and goals and provides the opportunity to verify or express them.

The paradigmatic expression of the European American perspective on conflict is articulated in Fisher, Ury, and Patton's (1991) best-selling handbook of negotiation strategy, *Getting to YES: Negotiating Agreement Without Giving In.* Even the title of this media sensation suggests that the goal of European Americans in conflict (consistent with the independent view of self) is to arrive at a solution without compromising personal integrity or making concessions. Careful observers of European American conflict, Fisher and his colleagues note that people in this cultural context tend to confront others directly while stridently promulgating a particular position that outlines the actions that they would be willing or unwilling to take. The authors of *Getting to YES* are critical of this positional bargaining strategy because it commits participants to unwise agreements, entails lengthy negotiations, and jeopardizes the long-term relationship between the parties. Nevertheless, the alternative strategy they offer also bears the unique stamp of the European American view of conflict: (1) separate the people from the problem; (2) focus on interests, not positions; (3) generate a variety of possibilities before deciding what to do; and (4) insist that the result be based on some objective standard.

First, by advising negotiators to distinguish the people from the problem, Fisher and his colleagues assume that the content of conflict may be extracted from the relationship between the participants (a peculiar idea in Chinese contexts). Moreover, they assume that this separation facilitates the reconciliation of problematic issues that are inherently extra-relational. They warn that in a positional bargaining situation, "the parties' relationship tends to become entangled with their discussions of substance" (20). A common European American view is that the substance of a conflict lies in the different positions advocated by the participants. Instead, Fisher and his colleagues argue, in their discussion of their second tip, that the substance is the participants' individual interests. Although the authors try to revise the prevailing European American view of conflict, they view "interests" as a manifestation of a set of needs, desires, concerns, and fears that are internal to the person. Again, their suggested revision of European American conflictways is itself a reflection of that cultural view of the person.

In their resolution-oriented strategy, Fisher, Ury, and Patton (1991) also recommend that negotiators generate multiple solutions to the problem. They go so far as to suggest that these solutions be designed to maximize mutual gain. This advice appears to be at odds with the European American preference for single solutions and individual interests. However, ultimately the suggestion is directed toward a particularly European American goal: to identify and decide on a single, binding agreement. Although these authors advise negotiators to brainstorm many possible solutions, all but one of these are to be cast aside once a decision has been made. This decision is considered a primary and enduring outcome of the conflict rather than a transitory agreement that remains open to subsequent negotiation. Furthermore, they recommend that negotiators base their decision on "objective" criteria. "Logical" appeals to principles of fairness, efficiency, or scientific merit, they contend, eliminate competition between individual wills. This view presumes that the relational aspect of a conflict is inevitably a competition between independent agents, and that abstract principles can circumvent this supposedly counterproductive form of relationality to reveal an objectively correct solution.

The meanings attributed to conflict condition when and how conflict develops. Viewed as interference in the accomplishment of an individual's activities, conflict in European American contexts is typically seen as a negative situation to be avoided if possible, or resolved quickly if unavoidable (Nadler, Nadler, and Broome 1985). Larson (1984) observed that European American managers may withhold performance criticism of subordinates in order to avoid the conflict generated by subordinates' negative reactions to the feedback. The tendency to avoid criticism and conflict, in combination with the incidental rather than inevitable view of conflict, contributes to a cultural system in which there are few established, publicly recognized procedures for handling interpersonal conflict.

When conflict cannot be circumscribed, the European American understanding of it as a result of incompatible activities implies the possibility of resolution. If the individuals' activities may be adjusted so that they no longer interfere, the conflict can be effectively concluded. The resolution process ultimately aims to allow the participants to pursue individual activities with minimal delay. Concern for the continuing relationship between the participants is relatively unimportant compared with the concerns for each participant's autonomy.

Since conflict is viewed primarily as a negative event that interrupts individuals' activities, the primary focus in mainstream contexts is typically placed on ending the conflict quickly. Decisions are often made by individuals, but even when groups are involved, majority or split decisions are made with little attempt to build consensus (Kume 1985). These decisions typically permit a single alternative rather than leave open the possibility of other alternatives. Furthermore, these decisions are considered final (Pascale and Athos 1981).

The norms that regulate conflict resolution prescribe rational debate, confrontation with the other, direct expression of opinions, and quick decisiveness (Pascale and Athos 1981; Stewart and Bennett 1991). In the European American conception, rational debate between spokespeople for different positions facilitates an objectively reasonable resolution to a conflict (Kochman 1981). Direct, honest statements of opinion permit the parties to confront the problem. Emotional expression is considered a distraction from the rational debate and an obstacle to conflict resolution.

The desirable mode of behavior during a conflict is detached, cool, quiet, and without affect. Kochman (1981) suggests that because the white middle-class European American mode of discussion or debate is supposed to be dispassionate and impersonal, any display of affect is thought to be dysfunctional, not legitimate, and a sign of weakness. According to Kochman, the idea of rational debate is that the merits of an idea are intrinsic to the idea itself. How much a person cares about the idea and is willing to defend it are irrelevant; it is right or wrong, true or false. In fact, displaying an emotional attachment for one's positions or ideas is believed to be in bad form. The ideas should stand and speak for themselves independent of the people who hold or express them. Rational debate or conflict is thought to proceed best with an air of neutrality or impersonality.

Although the European American approach to conflict is so widely shared and sustained by members of this cultural group that it goes unexamined and uncontested, it can contrast dramatically with the approaches adopted by other groups who engage in mainstream contexts but who also have significant experience in social contexts configured differently. Exploring these differences reveals the particular challenges of intercultural conflict within diverse workplaces in the Unites States.

## Conflictways in Asian American Contexts: Giving Face and Avoiding Confrontation

Although Asian Americans construct ways of life and ethnic identities that distinguish them from Asians who live in Asia, some features of the cultural experience of this group overlap with that of Asians abroad, particularly since most immigration from Asia has occurred in the second half of the twentieth century. Oyserman and Sakamoto (1997) suggest that many contemporary Asian Americans are constructing complex identities that embrace some aspects of American traditions of individualism while still retaining many interdependent meanings and practices. Characterizations of conflict in Asian cultures can then be used to make some initial inferences about Asian American conceptions of conflict, although it is immediately evident that these practices may change in important ways as they come in contact with European American practices.

Analogous to the connection in a European American context between the meaning of conflict and an independent conception of self, the meaning of conflict for Asians reflects an interdependent view of the person. In Asian cultures, the self is defined in relationship to others and is viewed as part of a larger social unit (Markus and Kitayama 1991; Markus et al. 1996; Markus et al. 1997; Triandis 1995). Conflict then is a disturbance or disharmony in the relationship between individuals. This disharmony may arise from disagreement about an issue, or even incompatible activities of the sort that are problematic in European American contexts. However, in Asian cultures conflict is at heart relational rather than activity-oriented. Thus, the Asian conception of relationships influences the meanings that are attached to conflict and the approach that is adopted for dealing with conflict. Among individuals, companies, or nations who live within and through interdependent means and practices, consideration of long-term consequences often prevails. As Cohen (1997) notes, "What price a good result or an 'optimal solution' if the cost is the ruin of the attachment?" (38).

Cultures that foster an interdependent view of self embed individuals in networks of relationships that are expected to endure across a lifetime (Bond 1996; Plath 1980). For conflict, the implications of this social system are threefold. First, the appropriate management of conflict is an important priority because the consequences of conflict are likely to persist over time. Second, the time available for reestablishing relational harmony is extensive because the relationship will continue to exist, even if in disharmony. Third, conflict is an inevitable part of relationships since they endure over such a long time. In the words of one Japanese manager describing conflict with colleagues at work, "We disagree like husbands and wives do in a healthy marriage (or the way close business partners might when they have worked together many, many years)" (Pascale and Athos 1981, 48). From this perspective, once individuals have built a long-term relationship with one another, conflict is an irrepressible, nonpathological, perhaps necessary component of their relationship.

The enduring quality of many relationships in Asian cultures gives rise to the codification and institutionalization of procedures for managing conflicts (Nadler et al. 1985). While people in European American contexts often seek conflict avoidance or resolution, Asian approaches aim for management or control of the conflict. These procedures recognize the differences between the participants and attempt to minimize the negative consequences of the differences prior to confrontation (Cushman and King 1985). As noted by Tu Mu, a Chinese poet of the T'ang dynasty, "He who excels at resolving difficulties does so before they arise" (Tzu 1963, 77).

In Japan conflict management is represented by the metaphor of nemawashi, or root binding (Cushman and King 1985; Kume 1985; Ting-Toomey 1985). Binding the roots of a tree before transplanting it is thought to facilitate its growth following the transition. Analogously, in conflict situations, laying an interpersonal groundwork of discussion and consensus-building activities before taking action that addresses the conflict is thought to help reestablish harmony among the participants and prevent loss of face. Cohen (1997) suggests that informal contact in these contexts allows one to negotiate without negotiating.

Nemawashi is commonly accomplished by the use of three procedures (Cushman and Sanderson-King 1985). First, face-to-face talks among pairs of participants allow them to survey the conflict and persuade others that an appropriate action can be found. Second, in the ringi procedure, the participants circulate a written copy of a proposed action for endorsement. The circulation of the document serves to disseminate information about the action to those involved in the negotiation ahead of time (Stewart 1988) and make participants aware of the emerging consensus. Third, neutral go-betweens may speak to individuals on both sides of a conflict to arrange its management.

The clusters of behaviors associated with nemawashi illustrate the operation of several norms for conflict that uniquely characterize the Asian approach. Indirectness of expression, avoidance of confrontation, and group decision-making are fundamental to nemawashi. Whereas people who live in European American contexts often prefer rational or logical debate, people in East Asian cultures favor indirect communication that uses ambiguity and imprecision to circumvent confrontation and delay commitment to any single proposal (Pascale and Athos 1981; Gudykunst, Ting-Toomey, and Chua 1988; Stewart and Bennett 1991). This conflict management process is time-consuming compared with European American conflict resolution, but it focuses on cultivating flexibility and a willingness to adapt or adjust to a variety of situations. The deliberative pace allows participants to consider multiple alternatives and arrive at a consensual decision that is designed to ensure that none of the participants loses face in overt competition with another (Kume 1985). In European American contexts, once a decision is made it is often viewed as a final resolution of the problem. However, in Asian contexts, even following complicated procedures like those associated with nemawashi, the emerging decision is subject to revision in order to accommodate subsequent changes in events (Pascale and Athos 1981).

Beyond nemawashi strategies of management, Lebra (1984) suggests that the Japanese have developed considerable cultural expertise in enacting strategies that do not allow confrontation to develop, perhaps as a consequence of their interest and focus on sociality and the maintenance of relationships. Besides strategies of anticipatory management (arranging circumstances to avoid situations that typically give rise to conflict), Japanese contexts are characterized by the use of (1) negative communication—when A is angry with B, he does not confront but avoids contact or refuses to respond; (2) situational code switching—parties in a conflict stay away from each other, but behave in a situationally appropriate manner when they do come into contact; (3) triadic management—when a confrontation is threatened between A and B, a third party is asked to mediate the communication; (4) displacement—making a protest in the name of another, revealing frustration to a close other who is not the source of the conflict, or criticizing a less powerful person who is not directly involved; and (5) self-aggression—protesting by exaggerated compliance or obedience, and acceptance instead of rejection of an undesirable plan.

Lebra (1984) stresses that conflict management from the Japanese perspective does not mean conflict *resolution*. In fact, the strategies that she describes may intensify the awareness of conflict. People participating in cultural systems that foster and promote interdependence will interfere with one another frequently, and because of the ever-present possibility of conflict, practices of nonconfrontation and harmony will be well elaborated. Cultural virtuosity with respect to the maintenance and promotion of harmony requires a nuanced understanding of conflict and, Lebra argues, a view of harmony models and conflict models as not mutually exclusive.

All of the well-known strategies for conflict management in Japanese cultural contexts are readily comprehensible from a European American perspective; some, such as triadic management and displacement, are quite common. Yet the idea of managing conflict by trying to prevent it is much less well developed in mainstream settings. From a European American point of view, conflict, although it can be negative in its consequences, is not altogether negative or undesirable. From the interdependent perspective, avoiding conflict, even if doing so entails acceptance or "giving in," is critical and identity-promoting. When selves are defined relationally or through interdependence, disturbing or destroying the relationship threatens self. In interdependent cultural contexts, it is critical to honor the opponent's face or to give face. "Face entails the presentation of a civilized front to another individual within the webs of interconnected relationships in a particular culture. . . . Face is a claimed sense of self-respect in an interactive situation" (Ting-Toomey 1994, 1). Once face has been taken away, it has to be given back by one's opponent; it cannot be restored in other ways. Ting-Toomey and Cole (1990), in delineating problems of intercultural contact, note that while negotiators from interdependent contexts are often particularly concerned with honoring face, negotiators participating in independent worlds are often most adept at threatening face.

A variety of studies and anecdotal reports from European Americans doing business in China also suggest that people in Chinese cultural contexts are likely to be very attuned to the threat or presence of interpersonal conflict. Leung (1987), in a comparison of conflict resolution styles of Hong Kong Chinese students and American students, reports that the modes of conflict resolution preferred by Chinese students were those assumed most likely to reduce animosity. Furthermore, informal procedures like mediation and bargaining were also preferred to explicitly confrontational procedures. In a similar study by Trubisky, Ting-Toomey, and Lin (1991) comparing Taiwanese and American students, the Taiwanese students favored the use of styles identified as "obliging," "avoiding," "integrating," and "compromising." Even in America, Yau and Smetana (1993) found that among Chinese American adolescents, saving parental face was important and respected, and parental expectations were given priority over personal desires in conflict situations. As Asian Americans increasingly engage in Anglo-American contexts, they may be less likely to exhibit traditional Confucian patterns of forbearance and endurance and may seek some compromise between achieving social harmony and satisfying personal goals (Hwang 1988; Yang 1986), but it remains likely that a consideration of the opponent's face will still predominate over confrontation, argumentation, or debate.

According to Bond (1991), in Chinese cultural contexts there are relatively clear rules about when one may disagree, particularly with a superior. He reports that the basic rule is, "Honor the hierarchy first, your vision of the truth second." The subordinate who would try to effect the superior's judgment with strategies like those outlined by Lebra must above all accord the superior face. Moreover, Bond (1991) notes that some agreement must be reached because, "agreeing to disagree" is not an effective strategy in Chinese cultural contexts.

Asian Americans in Asian cultural contexts are likely to avoid a direct expression of their own ideas and may refrain from putting their own positions directly on the table (Cohen 1997). The Asian American's ties to cultural contexts that claim that "the mouth is the source of misfortune" and "heaven moves without a single word" are likely to encourage both a wariness for whatever their opponents are saying on the surface and a search for the meanings behind the words. While European Americans will often assume it is the speaker's responsibility to say specifically what is on his or her mind, Asian Americans may believe they should not communicate their ideas or opinions too explicitly, especially to outgroup members; doing so might be perceived as rude and disruptive. A fifth-century B.C. text of Lao-tzu contends: "A good man does not argue; he who argues is not a good man" (as quoted in Peng and Nisbett, in press). Asian Americans may wait for others to infer what they are thinking or feeling, perhaps based on what has not been said. Such differences in communication practices may well underlie a variety of conflicts in the workplace. Getting directly to the point or refuting another's point may be offensive to Asian Americans. On the other hand, European Americans may understand indirectness as a lack of honesty or weakness in one's convictions rather than as a strategy for conflict management and consensus building.

Moreover, while rational debate and formal argumentation are often considered essential to problem solving and conflict resolution in Euro-American contexts, these practices are not standard in most East Asian cultural contexts, which have historically emphasized harmony and hierarchy (Nakamura 1964). Very recent empirical work comparing European American and Chinese respondents suggests, in fact, that Chinese problem solvers are less likely to pursue a single, "true" resolution but to work to reconcile contradictions or incongruities within an integrated framework. In a series of reasoning studies, Peng and Nisbett (in press) have shown that a compromising approach to contradiction, which is uncommon among Americans, is often observed among Chinese respondents.

European Americans also report difficulties understanding some Chinese practices not only because the Chinese use more indirect methods of communication but also because they appear to hold very different notions of what a contract signifies. For European Americans, a contract represents the end of a negotiation, whereas in many Chinese contexts it is only the beginning (Solomon 1996). For example, Chinese negotiators may ask for special considerations that seem to change the terms of the agreement after the contract has been signed. For the Chinese, the contract establishes a relationship, and a relationship partner can be counted on for extra consideration or special favors. The management of conflict in Asian cultures is an ongoing process in a changing world. In addition to attempting to identify solutions that would restore group harmony, conflict management is itself a harmonizing process that strengthens the social connections between group members as it simultaneously strengthens independent identities, which are rooted in relationships.

## Conflictways in Mexican American Contexts: Respect and Mutual Positive Feelings

Characterizing conflict from Mexican American perspectives is perhaps even more difficult than characterizing it from an Asian American perspective. Conflict in Mexican culture, and in Latin American cultural systems more broadly, has received only meager attention in the social sciences. The work that is available, however, suggests that a variety of values and practices remain important for people who have participated in Mexican cultural contexts even when they are quite fully engaged in American mainstream contexts. Most important, in contexts that are primarily Mexican and Mexican American the individual is viewed within a hierarchical system of relationships. One key quality for being a worthy or honorable person in this system is *simpatia,* or the ability to both respect and share others' feelings (Triandis et al. 1984).

In many Hispanic and Latin American cultural contexts, a person who behaves properly, and thus is esteemed and fulfilled, is one who knows how to judge a social situation and engage in an appropriate level of relatedness, showing the proper courtesy and decorum depending on age, sex, and social status. The capacity to honor others, fulfill one's obligations, and give respect while maintaining respect, or the positive evaluation of others, is critical to a good standing in the community and to survival within that community (Harwood, Miller, and Irizarry 1995). A resolution that ensures an individual's autonomy or guarantees individual rights is often less important in a conflict than resolution that is appropriate to the particular setting and maintains or restores an individual's pride and honor (Cohen 1997).

Compared to many European American contexts, in Mexican American contexts a great emphasis is placed on interpersonal reality and the maintenance of harmony in interpersonal relationships. A recent study (Sanchez-Burke and Nisbett 1998) compared the preferences of Mexican Americans and European Americans for different work situations. Given a choice, Mexican Americans preferred the work situation in which coworkers spend time getting to know each other and establishing relationships with one another before beginning to work. European Americans were more likely to choose the situation in which people cut to the chase and begin working almost immediately, believing that one should not waste time on social trivialities and that results are more important than relationships (Cohen 1997). Such differences in preferences for how to work could well underlie a variety of conflicts in multicultural workplaces.

Although many Mexican American contexts emphasize individuality or the uniqueness of the "spirit" of the individual (Condon 1985), the person is interdependently defined by relationships to others within a familial network (Diaz-Guerrero and Szalay 1991). In Mexican American contexts, the family provides a normatively defined set of relationships that strongly influence what the individual expresses (Delgado-Gaitan 1994). Consistent with notions of interdependence, Collier (1988) found that Mexican Americans defined conflict as a disagreement between individuals. However, reflecting their special attention to the relationship between individuals, Mexican Americans characterized disagreement as a loss of harmony. Thus, the meaning of conflict includes differences in individuals' opinions but represents the disagreement as an interpersonal disturbance.

Greenfield and Suzuki (1997) point out that many Mexican Americans and Latinos are raised to respect elders and accept their opinions without question. The emphasis in institutional settings like schools on the value of logical or rational argumentation may well be at odds with practices of respect. These authors report on a study of conferences between immigrant Latino parents and elementary school teachers (Raeff, Greenfield, and Quiroz, in press) in which the teacher criticized every child for a failure to express his or her views in class. As with schools, workplace settings that require individual assertiveness and the direct expression of one's opinions may be difficult to negotiate for those who have engaged primarily in Mexican contexts. Culturally mandated politeness or respect may be interpreted by supervisors or coworkers, not as deference or respect for authority, but as passivity or apathy.

In Mexican American cultural contexts, the extended family provides a primary social network for self-definition. However, the metaphor of the family may also serve as a model for work relationships. A manager may be treated as the head of a family that includes workers in the position of children (Condon 1985). Both familial and work relationships are regulated by the concept of respeto, a representation of the status differences between individuals. Loosely translated as "respect," respeto refers to the relational status of individuals with differential power (Garcia 1996), based on differences in position, age, or influence (Condon 1985). In Mexican American contexts, the relative status of one individual to another may be an enduring property of a particular relationship rather than a commodity that is subject to change as a result of individual achievement. For example, one Mexican manager explained that an Anglo-American company vice president "tried to 'win' our respect by showing how hard he worked for the company while having only a superficial interest in the rest of us. He had it backwards. Of course we respected him—he was the vice president. But that was about all" (Condon 1985, 22).

Although status differences may shift little over time, respeto requires consistent affirmation in interactions, in which one person is willing to assume the lower status role and the other the higher status role. In Spanish, acknowledgment of the status differences between individuals is communicated partly in the use of the informal (tú) and formal (usted) forms of the pronoun you (Garcia 1996). However, even in English, politeness phrases that are offered by subordinates and expected by their recipients may provide recognition of status differences (Delgado-Gaitan 1994). The notion of respeto and the behaviors attendant to it are means by which people in predominantly Mexican American cultural contexts understand and maintain interpersonal bonds. The primary importance of managing harmonious if unequal relationships in Mexican American cultural contexts is reflected in this approach to conflict.

Conceiving conflict as a disharmony in a relationship (Collier 1988), people living in Mexican American contexts may avoid conflict by using a number of strategies. One is to facilitate cooperation, which may circumscribe many conflict situations. Kagan and Madsden (1972a, 1972b) found that Mexican American children were more likely to cooperate with peers than were European American children, who were more likely to compete than their Mexican American counterparts. Another strategy for avoiding conflict is to control one's negative emotions. McGinn, Harburg, and Ginsburg (1973) found that when European American and Mexican men were presented with hypothetical situations that held potential for conflict with a friend, the Mexican respondents were more likely than the European Americans to report that they would try to avoid negative emotions like anger and irritation. A third strategy for avoiding conflict is to provide information that maintains the relationship between individuals even if the information is misleading about extra-relational realities (McGinn et al. 1973; Condon 1985). For instance, requests may receive responses that are compliant in rhetoric but not in action. The respondent's goal may be to manage the relationship by agreeing to the request rather than risk destabilizing the interaction with a refusal. As Cohen (1997) notes, in some difficult situations "truth is not imperative when a lie avoids unpleasantness." (32)

When these avoidance strategies fail and conflict seems inevitable, confrontational discussions occur in Mexican American contexts (Collier 1988). However, within these confrontations, Mexican American cultural norms may maximize the possibility of reestablishing harmony. For women, this means expressing concern for the relationship and the other person. For men, it means talking to reach a mutual understanding (Collier 1988). The final goal of conflict in Mexican American contexts is often a mutual coordination of feelings rather than a formal agreement or the resolution of an issue. A successful outcome is associated with positive engagement in interpersonal relationships.

## Conflictways in African American Contexts: Advocacy and Confrontation

Analyzing African American conflict meanings and practices is a particularly complex and potentially controversial endeavor. Conceptions of self in African American contexts reflect mainstream models of the autonomous agentic self, but they also reflect interdependent understandings of group identity and belongingness. African American contexts are often described as reflecting a communalism in which group concerns can transcend individual concerns more easily than is the case in primarily European American contexts. Moreover, in many African American settings a clear emphasis is placed on unity, cooperative effort, and collective responsibility. This type of interdependence may be a legacy of African notions of personhood and/or a continuing legacy of involuntary immigration, slavery, discrimination, poverty, and minority status, or some combination of all of these (Morris 1994; Nobles 1972; Oyserman, Gant, and Ager 1995).

Somewhat in contrast to Asian American contexts, in African American contexts, people live within social contexts of friends and extended family but relate to these contexts in terms of separate individuals with unique thoughts and feelings (see Blake 1994). From this perspective, the self is publicly represented by the expression of these thoughts and feelings to others. The self is co-constructed by the individual and the social group as individuals direct their expressions toward relational others and the others respond to these expressions.

Kochman (1981), in one of the few direct comparisons of some European American and African American behavioral styles, observes that in public debate or argument the "black mode," as he calls it, is often animated, interpersonal, emotional, and confrontational. In many African American cultural contexts, being animated or energetic is entirely appropriate in a dispute or conflict. In fact, discussions that are devoid of affect or dynamic opposition are unlikely to be taken seriously or regarded as significant. In an analysis of "black talk," Smitherman (1994) suggests that African American communication often requires a dialogue or a dynamic exchange between A and B, not A lecturing B. Moreover, because it is not universally held that emotion makes an argument less cogent, African Americans sometimes view efforts by European Americans to set aside feelings as unrealistic, illogical, or even politically devious. And indeed, in conflicts between blacks and whites, whites often observe that the level of black affect or anger was inappropriate and thus perceive the argument as illegitimate (Delgado 1995).

In African American cultural contexts, the meaning of conflict may be simultaneously individual and relational. Understood as a lack of agreement between individuals (Collier 1988), African American notions of conflict sometimes imply that individuals have differing points of view but emphasize the discrepancy in participants' positions rather than focusing on the consequences of the discrepancy. In contrast, more European American definitions of conflict often focus largely on consequences, that is, the interference of incompatible beliefs or goals in individual activity.

Although the relational aspect of the African American conceptions of conflict seems similar to Asian concepts of disharmony, the approaches to conflict tied to these meanings are divergent. Unlike people in Asian American contexts, people in African American contexts may confront others about points of disagreement. However, the ensuing discourse is not intended to be a "rational" consideration of the issue with the goal of achieving "objectivity," as argument is constructed in many European American contexts. In African American cultural contexts, the participants in a conflict are often expected to formulate personal positions on an issue and present those positions as advocates. Emotional investment in the position is viewed as a measure of commitment rather than as an impediment to reasoning (Kochman 1981). Combining argumentation, emotion, and metaphor, African American approaches to conflict may be viewed as participation in a joint performance governed by its own cultural logic and rhythm (Abrahams 1964; White 1994). This style of conflict may reflect the cultural value placed on movement, expressive individualism, and affect in many African American contexts (Boykin and Toms 1985).

One goal of conflict in African American contexts is to work toward resolving the problem that initially caused the disagreement by representing personal views in an impassioned confrontation (Collier 1988). However, unlike European American practices, resolution depends on the compelling presentation of arguments rather than attempts to appeal to some objective truth. By forcefully but credibly making a case for their own point of view, people engaged in African American contexts in conflict may persuade others of their position and thereby reestablish interpersonal harmony.

Researchers note that within some African American contexts, there is a distinct concern with expressive individualism and with the cultivation of spontaneity and unique self-expression in ways that can diverge from European American emphases on uniqueness (Nobles 1972). Although believing oneself to be distinct and better than one's peers is also common in many European American cultural contexts (Markus and Kitayama 1991), directly showing off or calling attention to the self is often discouraged. By contrast, according to Kochman (1981), in some African American cultural contexts behavior labeled as "stylin' out," "showboating," or "grandstanding" can be viewed positively.

As is true in many cultural contexts that emphasize interdependence, in many African American cultural contexts it is assumed that people cannot be separated from their positions, and disputes are cast as a contest between individuals rather than between opposing ideas. Once construed as a contest, Kochman (1981) argues, "attention is also paid to performance, for winning the contest requires that one outperform one's opponents: outthink, outtalk, and outstyle them. It means being concerned with art as well as argument" (24). Kochman also notes a difference in ideas about entering a discussion or debate. Observing the differences between white and black gatherings, he notes that in the former the general rule seems to be that people speak in the order in which they are recognized. In black gatherings, he observes, the floor is often given to the person who feels his or her point is most pressing.

Many African American contexts also place great emphasis on the importance of the spoken word—a value that may have particular relevance for styles of argumentation and disputation. Smitherman (1994) argues that the African American oral tradition is powerfully evident in many contemporary African American cultural contexts and is based on a belief in the power of the word. According to the African concept of *nommo,* the word is the life force. Once something is put into words, it is believed to be binding and creative. Highly verbal talkers are respected and valued, as is the "skillful use of rappin', lyin', signifyin', testifyin', playin' the dozens and other verbal rituals" (8). It is not difficult to imagine that important differences between people, in styles of arguing and in the very value of speech, could give rise to powerful misunderstandings and tensions in multicultural workplaces. For example, in European American contexts, arguments with emotion can be viewed as invalid and irrational and may not be taken seriously.

## CONCLUSIONS

Even this cursory analysis of divergent conflictways reveals the potential for powerful differences in the behavior of people who are working side by side in American workplaces. All the meanings and practices of conflict that we have outlined here could be invoked or used by any person or group, yet we have hypothesized that they are differentially distributed across the United States and regions of the world. Moreover, an analysis of this type could easily and productively be extended to include differences in the conflictways of men and women, gays and straights, and working-class and middle-class individuals. Yet most American workplaces still institutionalize and promote only European American conflictways, which tend to focus primarily on the protection and expression of the interests, rights, and ideas of independent individuals who are separate from the positions they advocate. A cultural analysis allows us to see, however, that the notion of the "independent" person is not the only or the natural conceptualization, although within American contexts it is the culturally sanctioned and institutionalized one. Independent persons, like interdependent persons, are social constructions developed within a particular complex of public meanings, practices, and institutions that enable people to become rational, self-interested actors who in conflict situations are primarily concerned with protecting their own beliefs, rights, and interests. Examination of Asian American, Mexican American, and African American cultural contexts reveals an awareness and incorporation of this mainstream emphasis, but also a simultaneous independent concern with many processes of interdependence and relationality.

A cultural analysis could also facilitate a rethinking of some mainstream conceptions of conflict and conflict resolution. What is invisible, taken for granted, or discounted in the analysis of behavior in one cultural context may be focal and objectified in another. In particular, the analysis of conflict in cultural contexts other than those of the European American mainstream reveals the importance of an array of social and relational concepts such as face, honor, respect, sympathy, forgiveness, and interpersonal harmony. These kinds of concepts might be used to reframe the analysis of conflict in more overtly relational terms, which could include a variety of perspectives on conflict; such terms are virtually missing from the social psychological lexicon used in characterizing conflict today. As an example, Ting-Toomey (1994) has outlined a perspective on conflict that would be useful across cultural contexts and developed a theory based on face. Social psychologists have paid little attention to the idea of face, perhaps because face has been considered something "put on" or "acted out" that does not reflect the "real" internal self.

Face, however, may prove a useful concept in considering conflict from a variety of cultural perspectives. Ting-Toomey (1994) suggests that people in all cultures try to maintain and negotiate face in all communication situations and that conflict demands active face-work management. Most people in European American contexts can immediately understand the importance of "maintaining face," but an analysis of other cultural perspectives reveals that an equally important aspect of face-work is "giving face" or acknowledging the legitimacy of the other as a partner in the interaction. Allowing the other person in the conflict to appear sensible, reasonable, appropriate, or to have a sense of self is likely to be important in every cultural system. Giving face would then be a necessary first step in understanding all conflict; it is an attempt to know where the other "is coming from" and thus to learn something about the meanings and practices of the social worlds of others.

As the American workforce becomes increasingly diverse, one challenge will be to illuminate and draw out these alternatives, sometimes quite contradictory approaches to conflict. These differences in approach, as we have tried to illustrate here, are not just superficial style differences; they are tied to significant diversity in social worlds and in what is experienced as good, as moral, and as self. The second challenge will be to examine the consequences of the fact that in most work settings "American ways" are in fact European American ways. Functioning as a diverse society requires workplace practices that produce relatively effective and inclusive environments for people from the variety of cultural contexts that now constitute contemporary America.

## NOTE

1. We use the word cultural context to refer to that loose web of images, ideas, values, and practices that people, who identify themselves with or who are identified by others with these ethnic labels, may have accessible and may engage with, as a consequence of particular ways of life that historically have been associated with these ethnic categorizations. Importantly we do not imagine "European Americans" or "African Americans" as coherent or self-monitoring "groups" whose members recognize each other as members and who co-construct each others lives in the ongoing ways that are often assumed when the word "culture" is applied to a group of people.

## REFERENCES

Abrahams, Roger D. (1964). *Deep down in the jungle.* Hatboro, Penn.: Folklore Associates.

Ames, Roger T., Dissanayake, Wimal, and Kasulis, Thomas P. (1994). *Self as person in Asian theory and practice.* Albany: State University of New York Press.

Avruch, Kevin. (1991). Introduction: Culture and conflict resolution. In Kevin Avruch, Peter W. Black, and Joseph Scimecca (Eds.), *Conflict resolution: Cross-cultural perspectives* (pp. 1–17). New York: Greenwood Press.

Baumeister, Roy F. (1987). How the self became a problem: A psychological review of historical research. *Journal of Personality and Social Psychology, 52,* 163–76.

Bellah, Robert N., Madsen, Richard, Sullivan, William M., Swidler, Ann, and Tipton, Steven M. (1985). *Habits of the heart: Individualism and commitment in American life.* New York: Harper and Row.

Blake, Ira Kincade. (1994). Language development and socialization in young African American children. In Patricia M. Greenfield and Rodney R. Cocking (Eds.), *Cross-cultural roots of minority child development* (pp. 167–98). Hillsdale, N.J.: Erlbaum.

Bond, Michael H., (1991). *Beyond the Chinese face: Insights from psychology.* Hong Kong: Oxford University Press.

———. Ed. (1996). The handbook of Chinese psychology. Hong Kong: Oxford University Press.

Bond, Rod, and Smith, Peter B. (1996). Culture and conformity: A meta-analysis of studies using Asch's line judgement task. *Psychological Bulletin, 119,* 111–37.

Boykin, A. W., and Toms, F. D. (1985). Black child socialization: A conceptual framework. In Harriette Pipes McAdoo and John Lewis McAdoo (Eds.), *Black children: Social, educational, and parental environments* (pp. 33–52). Beverly Hills, Calif.: Sage.

Carrithers, M., Collins, S., and Lukes, S. (1987). *The category of the person: Anthropology, philosophy, history.* Cambridge: Cambridge University Press.

Cohen, J. A. (1996). Chinese mediation on the eve of modernization. *California Law Review, 54,* 1201–26.

Cohen, Raymond. (1997). *Negotiating across cultures.* Washington, D.C.: United States Institute of Peace Press.

Collier, Mary Jane. (1988). Conflict competence within African, Mexican, and Anglo-American friendships. In Young Yun Kim and William Gudykunst (Eds.), *Theories in intercultural communication* (pp. 132–54). Newbury Park, Calif.: Sage.

Condon, John C. (1985). In George W. Renwick (Ed.), *Good neighbors: Communicating with the Mexicans.* Yarmouth, Maine: Intercultural Press.

Cushman, Donald P., and Sanderson-King, S. (1985). National and organizational behavior: Cultures in conflict resolution. In William Gudykunst, Lea P. Stewart, and Stella Ting-Toomey (Eds.), *Communication, culture, and organizational processes* (pp. 114–33). Beverly Hills, Calif.: Sage.

Delgado, Richard. (1995). Legal storytelling: Storytelling for oppositionists and others: A plea for narrative. In Richard Delgado (Ed.), *Critical race theory: The cutting edge* (pp. 64–74). Philadelphia: Temple University Press.

Delgado-Gaitan, Concha. (1994). Socializing young children in Mexican American families: An intergenerational perspective. In Patricia M. Greenfield, Rodney R. Cocking (Eds.), *Cross-cultural roots of minority child development* (pp. 55–86). Hillsdale, N.J.: Erlbaum.

Deutsch, Martin. (1973). *The resolution of conflict: Constructive and destructive processes.* New Haven, Conn.: Yale University Press.

Diaz-Guerrero, Rogelia, and Szalay, Lorand B. (1991). *Understanding Mexicans and Americans.* New York: Plenum Press.

Fisher, Roger, Ury, William, and Patton, Bruce. (1991). *Getting to YES: Negotiating agreement without giving in.* 2nd ed. New York: Penguin.

Fiske, Alan P., Kitayama, Shinobu, Markus, Hazel R., and Nisbett, Richard E. (1998). The cultural matrix of social psychology. In Daniel T. Gilbert, Susan T. Fiske, and Gardner Lindzey (Eds.), *Handbook of social psychology* (pp. 915–81). New York: McGraw-Hill.

Garcia, Wintilo. (1996). *Respeto:* A Mexican base for interpersonal relationships. In Stella Ting-Toomey, William B. Gudykunst, and T. Nishida (Eds.), *Communication in personal relationships across cultures* (pp. 137–55). Thousand Oaks, Calif.: Sage.

Greenfield, Patricia M., and Suzuki, L. K. (1997). Culture and human development: Implications for parenting, education, pediatrics, and mental health. In William Damon, and K. Ann Renninger (Eds.), *Handbook of child psychology* (vol. 4, pp. 1059–1109). New York: Wiley.

Gudykunst, William B., Ting-Toomey, Stella, and Chua, Elizabeth. (1988). *Culture and interpersonal communication.* Beverly Hills, Calif.: Sage.

Guisinger, Shan, and Blatt, Sidney J. (1994). Individuality and relatedness: Evolution of a fundamental dialect. *American Psychologist, 49,* 104–11.

Harwood, Robin L., Miller, Joan G., and Irizarry, Nydia L. (1995). *Culture and attachment: Perceptions of the child in context.* New York: Guilford.

Hwang, Kwang K. (1988). Guanxi and Mientze: Conflict resolution in Chinese society. *Intercultural Communication Studies, 7*(1) 17–42.
Ito, Karen. (1985). Affective bonds: Hawaiian interrelationships of self. In Geoffrey White and John Kirkpatrick (Eds.), *Person, self, and experience: Exploring Pacific ethnopsychologies* (pp. 301–27). Berkeley: University of California Press.
Kagan, Spencer, and Madsden, Millard C. (1972a). Experimental analyses of cooperation and competition of Anglo-American and Mexican children. *Developmental Psychology, 6*(1), 49–59.
———. (1972b). Rivalry in Anglo-American and Mexican children of two ages. *Journal of Personality and Social Psychology, 24*(2), 214–20.
Kochman, Thomas. (1981). Black and white styles in conflict. Chicago: University of Chicago Press.
Kume, Teruyuki. (1985). Managerial attitudes toward decision-making: North America and Japan. In William B. Gudykunst, Lea P. Stewart, and Stella Ting-Toomey (Eds.), *Communication, culture, and organizational processes* (pp. 212–51). Beverly Hills, Calif.: Sage.
Landrine, Hope, and Klonoff, Elizabeth A. (1992). Culture and health-related schemas: A review proposal for interdisciplinary integration. *Health Psychology, 11*, 267–76.
Larson, James R. (1984). The performance feedback process: A preliminary model. *Organizational Behavior and Human Performance, 33*, 42–76.
Lebra, Takie S. (1984). Nonconfrontational strategies for management of interpersonal conflicts. In Ellis S. Krauss, Thomas P. Rohlen, and Patricia G. Stenhoff (Eds.), *Conflict in Japan* (pp. 41–60). Honolulu: University of Hawaii Press.
———. (1992). *Culture, self, and communication.* Ann Arbor: University of Michigan Press.
Lederbach, John Paul. Of nets, nails, and problems: The folk language of conflict resolution in a Central American setting. In Kevin Avruch, Peter W. Black, and Joseph A. Scimecca (Eds.), *Conflict resolution: Cross-cultural perspectives* (pp. 165–86). New York: Greenwood Press.
Leung, Kwok. (1987). Some determinants of reactions to procedural models for conflict resolution: A cross-national study. *Journal of Personality and Social Psychology, 53*, 898–908.
Markus, Hazel, and Kitayama, Shinobu. (1991). Culture and the self: Implications for cognition, emotion, and motivation. *Psychological Review, 98*, 224–53.
Markus, Hazel R., Kitayama, Shinobu, and Heiman, Rachel J. (1996). Culture and "basic" psychological principles. In E. Tory Higgins and Arie W. Kruglanski (Eds.), *Social psychology: Handbook of basic principles* (pp. 857–913). New York: Guilford.
Markus, Hazel R., Mullally, Patricia R., and Kitayama, Shinobu. (1997). Selfways: Diversity in modes of cultural participation. In Ulric Neisser and David Jopling (Eds.), *The conceptual self in context* (pp. 13–61). Cambridge: Cambridge University Press.
McGinn, Noel F., Harburg, Ernest, and Ginsburg, Gerald P. (1973). Individual differences, responses to interpersonal conflict by middle-class males in Guadalajara and Michigan. In Fred E. Jandt (Ed.), *Conflict resolution through communication.* (pp. 105–21). New York: Harper and Row.
Merry, Sally. (1986). Everyday understandings of the law in working-class America. *American Ethnologist, 11*, 253–70.

Morris, Brian. (1994). *Anthropology of the self.* Boulder, Colo.: Pluto Press.
Morris, Michael. W., and Peng, Kaiping. (1994). Culture and cause: American and Chinese attributions for social and physical events. *Journal of Personality and Social Psychology, 67,* 949–71.
Nadler, Lawrence B., Nadler, Marjorie K., and Broome, Benjamin J. (1985). Culture and the management of conflict situations. In William Gudykunst, Lea P. Stewart, and Stella Ting-Toomey (Eds.), *Communication, culture, and organizational processes* (pp. 87–113). Beverly Hills, Calif.: Sage.
Nakamura, Hajime. (1964). Ways of thinking of Eastern peoples: India-China-Tibet-Japan. 4th ed. Honolulu: East-West Center Press.
Needham, Joseph. (1962). Science and civilization in China. *Physics and physical technology* (vol. 4). Cambridge: Cambridge University Press.
Nobles, Wade. (1972). African philosophy: Foundations for black psychology. In R. L. Jones (Ed.), *Black psychology* (pp. 23–26). New York: Harper and Row.
———. (1973). Psychological research and the black self-concept: A critical review. *Journal of Social Issues, 29,* 11–31.
Oyserman, Daphna, Gant, Larry, and Ager, Joel. (1995). A socially contextualized model of African American identity: School persistence and possible selves. *Journal of Personality and Social Psychology, 69,* 1216–32.
Oyserman, Daphne, and Sakamoto, Izumi. (1997). Being Asian American: Identity, cultural constructs, and stereotype perception. *Journal of Applied Behavioral Science, 33*(4), 433–51.
Pascale, Richard T., and Athos, Anthony G. *(1981). The art of Japanese management.* New York: Simon & Schuster.
Peng, Kaiping, and Nisbett, Richard E. (in press). Naive dialecticism and its effects on reasoning and judgment about contradiction. *Psychological Review.*
Plath, David W. (1980). Long engagements: Maturity in modern Japan. Stanford, Calif.: Stanford University Press.
Raeff, Catherine, Greenfield, Patricia M., and Quiroz, B. (in press). Conceptualizing interpersonal relationships in the cultural contexts of individualism and collectivism. In Catherine Raeff and C. Super (Eds.), *The social construction of the child: New directions in child development.* San Francisco: Jossey-Bass.
Sampson, Edward E. (1985). The decentralization of identity: Toward a revised concept of personal and social order. *American Psychologist, 40,* 1203–11.
Sanchez-Burk, Jeffrey, and Richard Nisbett. (1998). The culture of relational schemas and the social cognition of cultural styles. Unpublished manuscript, Stanford University.
Shook, Victoria E., and Kwan, L. K. (1991). *Ho'oponopono:* Straightening family relationships in Hawaii. In Kevin Avruch, Peter W. Black, and Joseph A. Scimecca (Eds.), *Conflict resolution: Cross-cultural perspectives* (pp. 213–29). New York: Greenwood Press.
Shweder, Richard A. (1991). *Thinking through cultures: Expeditions in cultural psychology.* Cambridge: Harvard University Press.
Shweder, Richard A., and Bourne, L. (1984). Does the concept of the person vary cross-culturally? In Richard A. Shweder and R. A. LeVine (Eds.), *Culture theory: Essays on mind, self, and emotion* (pp. 158–99). Cambridge: Cambridge University Press.
Smitherman, Geneva. (1994). Black talk: Words and phrases from the hood to the amen corner. Boston: Houghton Mifflin.
Solomon, C. M. (1996). Turn a blind eye to the world at your own risk. *Global Workforce, 10,* 18–23.

Stewart, Edward C., and Bennett, Milton J. (1991). *American cultural patterns: A cross-cultural perspective.* Yarmouth, Maine: Intercultural Press.
Stewart, L. P. (1988). Japanese and American management: Participative decision making. In Larry A Samovar and Richard E. Porter (Eds.), *Intercultural communication: A reader* (Fifth ed., pp. 182–85). Belmont, Calif.: Wadsworth.
Szalay, Lorand B. (1981). Intercultural communication: A process model. *International Journal of Intercultural Relations, 5,* 133–46.
Taylor, Charles. (1989). *Sources of the self: The making of modern identities.* Cambridge, Mass.: Harvard University Press.
Ting-Toomey, Stella. (1985). Toward a theory of conflict and culture. In William B. Gudykunst, Lea P. Stewart, and Stella Ting-Toomey (Eds.), *Communication, Culture, and organizational processes.* (pp. 71–86). Beverly Hills, Calif.: Sage.
———. (1994). *The challenge of face-work: Cross-cultural and interpersonal issues.* Albany: State University of New York Press.
Ting-Toomey, Stella, and Cole, Mark. (1990). Intergroup diplomatic communication: A face-negotiation perspective. In Felipe Korzennyu and Stella Ting-Toomey (Eds.), *Communicating for peace: Diplomacy and negotiation* (pp. 169–76). Newbury Park, Calif.: Sage.
Triandis, Harry C. (1989). The self and social behavior in differing cultural contexts. *Psychological Review, 93*(3), 506–20.
———. (1995). *Individualism and collectivism.* Boulder, Colo.: Westview Press.
Triandis, Harry C., Marin, Gerardo, Lisansky, Judith, and Betancourt, Hector. (1984). *Simpatia* as a cultural script of Hispanics. *Journal of Personality and Social Psychology, 47,* 1363–75.
Trubisky, Paula, Ting-Toomey, Stella, and Lin, Sung-ling. (1991). The influence of individualism-collectivism and self-monitoring on conflict styles. *International Journal of Intercultural Relations, 15,* 65–84.
Tu, W. (1994). Embodying the universe: A note on Confucian self-realization. In Roger T. Ames, Wimal Dissanayake, and Thomas P. Kasulis (Eds.), *Self as person in Asian theory and practice* (pp. 177–86). Albany: State University of New York Press.
Tzu, Sun. (1963). *The art of war.* Translated by Samuel B. Griffin. New York: Oxford University Press.
Wall, Jr., J. A., and Blum, M. (1991). Community mediation in the People's Republic of China. *Journal of Conflict Resolution, 35,* 3–20.
White, Geoffrey M. (1994). Affecting culture: Emotion and morality in everyday life. In Shinobu Kitayama and Hazel R. Markus (Eds.), *Emotion and culture: Empirical studies of mutual influence* (pp. 219–39). Washington, D.C.: American Psychological Association.
Yang, Kuo-shu. (1986). Chinese personality and its change. In Michael H. Bond (Ed.), *The psychology of the Chinese people* (pp. 106–70). Oxford: Oxford University Press.
Yau, Jenny, and Smetana, Judith G. (1993). Chinese-American adolescents' reasoning about cultural conflicts. *Journal of Adolescent Research, 8,* 419–38.

# Part III

## THE PSYCHOLOGY OF RACE IN THE UNITED STATES

11

# DIVERSITY AND ORGANIZATIONAL IDENTITY: THE PROBLEM OF ENTRÉE AFTER ENTRY

*Marilynn B. Brewer, William von Hippel, and Martin P. Gooden*

AFTER thirty years of antidiscrimination laws and affirmative action policies in the United States, the admission of representative numbers of women and ethnic minorities into most large educational institutions and business organizations has, for the most part, been accomplished. As a consequence, such institutions have moved from the stage of achieving diversity to managing diversity (Thomas 1992). Although the concept of "managing diversity" has multiple meanings in the organizational development literature and practice, for social psychologists it can best be defined as the achievement of full integration of members of minority social categories into the social, structural, and power relationships of an organization or institution. One operational definition of such integration is a lack of conflict for minority individuals between their social identity as members of a particular demographic group and their identification with, commitment to, and achievement in the organization. It is this conceptualization of organizational integration that we use throughout this chapter.

According to the original definition given by Tajfel (1978), social identities are those aspects of one's self-knowledge that derive from membership in social groups, "together with the value and emotional significance attached to that membership" (63). When a particular social identity or category membership is salient, individuals tend to respond to others in terms of their membership in that social category, showing favoritism toward and preferential affiliation with those who share the same social identity (the "ingroup") over those who do not (the "outgroup") (cf. Gaertner et al., this volume). Such category-based preferences appear to arise spontaneously and often without conscious awareness (Dovidio and Gaertner 1993).

Diversity within large organizations brings to the forefront the recognition that individuals have multiple social identities both within and across contexts. Given the social and psychological significance of ingroup-outgroup categorizations, the organizational environment can be greatly affected by which social category distinctions are particularly meaningful or salient within the institutional context. The treatment individuals receive and the quality of their social relationships within the organization are strongly influenced by how they are categorized by themselves and by others. When individuals have dual identities (superordinate and subgroup memberships), social relationships are affected by which identity is "figure" and which is "ground" (Gaertner 1996). The same distinction can be made for the relative importance of demographic/cultural and organizational social category memberships.

When memberships in broad social categories, such as gender and ethnicity, are largely homogeneous within an organizational setting, these social identities tend not to be salient (that is, they are ground rather than figure) and individuals are more likely to be classified and responded to in terms of their organizational group memberships (management position, profession, department, and so on). When members of previously unrepresented minority groups enter the organization, however, the salience of particular social identities is likely to be altered in ways that affect how social relationships within the organizational context are governed. In particular, there may be an asymmetry in the relative salience of types of social identities for members of numerically large majority groups and members of small minorities. The former are likely to be categorized primarily in terms of their position in the organization, whereas minorities are likely to be categorized first in terms of their ethnic or gender identity. Thus, the white engineer is categorized simply as an engineer, while the black engineer is categorized first as an African American and only secondarily as an engineer (Stroessner 1996). Since different social categorizations engage different ingroup-outgroup distinctions and associated biases, such asymmetries at the point of initial categorization may have profound effects on the process of entrée into organizational membership.

## DIVERSITY AND THE SOCIALIZATION OF NEWCOMERS

The processes governing initial entry of minority group members into educational and business organizations involve largely impersonal judgments and decision-making. By contrast, successful integration (entrée) of individuals into the organizational structure engages processes of social interaction, interpersonal relationships, and group dynamics (Jackson, Stone, and Alvarez 1993). One area of social psychological research of potential relevance to the understanding of such integration processes is the literature on socialization of new members into existing social groups (Moreland and Levine 1982, 1989).

According to Moreland and Levine (1989), socialization is the stage of group membership that occurs between the initial entry into the group and the transition to acceptance as a full group member. During this stage, the primary distinction is between "newcomers," individuals who are being admitted into group membership for the first time, and "oldtimers," those who are already full members of the group. It is assumed that the oldtimers have been functioning as a group long enough to have established social ties, norms, and rituals that govern group processes. The socialization process involves some combination of *assimilation* of the characteristics and behaviors of the new member to the ways of the group and *accommodation* by the group to the characteristics of the newcomer. When socialization is successful, the individual and the group reach a stage of mutual commitment that marks the transition to full group membership.

Although the focus of much research on socialization has been on assimilation rather than accommodation, Moreland and Levine (1989) emphasize the importance of recognizing this as a process of mutual adjustment on the part of newcomers and oldtimers. As Jackson and her colleagues (1993) put it, "Socialization encompasses the entire process of mutual adjustment that occurs as newcomers and oldtimers negotiate—both proactively and reactively—the details of a new social order" (59).

According to Moreland and Levine (1989), the criteria for acceptance into full group membership (on the part of both newcomers and oldtimers) are generally higher than the criteria for initial entry. Thus, it takes some time to achieve the transition, which depends on each party's perception of the likelihood that acceptance is possible and their evaluation of how rewarding acceptance will be. Among the factors that facilitate successful socialization are the degree of advance knowledge that the newcomer has about the group (and the group about the newcomer); the extent to which the newcomer is recognized to have abilities and expertise that are important to the group's goals; and the number of personal contacts and amount of interpersonal communication between newcomers and oldtimers.

Within the process of group socialization in general, the effects of demographic and cultural similarity between newcomers and oldtimers become a special issue. When newcomers are visibly identifiable as members of a distinct social category, then category membership and newcomer status are, in effect, superimposed. Such convergent category distinctions tend to make more salient the "us-them" differentiations that engage processes of ingroup bias and intergroup discrimination (Arcuri 1982; Deschamps and Doise 1978)—processes that make the achievement of successful socialization and mutual acceptance more difficult.

## Group Expectancies

The theory of socialization espoused by Moreland and Levine (1982, 1989) holds that both assimilation and accommodation depend in part on the motivation of oldtimers to make efforts to inform newcomers about group values, norms, and procedures and to adjust some aspects of group behavior and norms where needed to accommodate the newcomer in ways that ensure his or her full contribution to the group. This motivation depends, in turn, on oldtimers' expectations that the newcomer is both willing and able to be a valued group member. When newcomers belong to the same social category as oldtimers, ingroup biases operate to create expectancies that the newcomer has the requisite values and abilities to be a full group member. Thus, "outreach" efforts to assimilate and accommodate seem well placed and likely to pay off. That is, the expectation of preexisting similarity may actually work to make accommodation on the part of the group more likely. As a consequence, expectations of similarity and shared values motivate behaviors that make it more likely that the newcomer will indeed become committed to group values.

When newcomers are perceived as outgroup members, the self-fulfilling effects of positive expectancies are not likely to be engendered. Instead, it will be up to the newcomer to "prove" that he or she has the required abilities to be a valued contributor and the willingness to meet the group's goals. Lowered expectancies mean less motivation to assist or accommodate, so the burden of socialization falls on the assimilation efforts expected of the newcomer. Indeed, willingness to change and assimilate may become a test of the newcomer's motivation and suitability for full membership in the organization in ways that are not true for newcomers who are already part of the dominant ingroup.

It should be emphasized that these discriminatory orientations during stages of socialization do not depend on the presence of active prejudice against the newcomer's social category. Merely the absence of the positive expectancies that are accorded to ingroup members can produce large discriminatory effects (Brewer 1997). The presence of negative stereotypes about the minority group exacerbates these expectancy effects, but discriminatory practices cannot be expected to disappear even if stereotypes are changed. In either case, differential orientations toward ingroup and outgroup members contribute to the cycle of attraction-selection-attrition (Schneider 1987) that perpetuates institutional homogeneity. The outgroup newcomer is much more likely to receive the message that there is a lack of "fit" between the group's goals, purposes, and culture and his or her own values and capabilities, a message that leads to higher rates of alienation and attrition (George 1990; Heilman 1983; Jackson et al. 1991).

## Newcomer Expectancies

Much of the analysis of the attraction-selection-attrition cycle focuses on the attitudes of majority group members who represent the dominant culture within the organization. But the expectancies and attributions of the minority newcomers also play a role in socialization processes. In a laboratory study of experimentally created small groups, Moreland (1985) demonstrated that participants who believed that they were newcomers entering a group of oldtimers exhibited strong ingroup-outgroup biases in their perceptions of and behavior toward other group members. Compared to control group participants (who had not actually met previously as a group), subjects who thought they were newcomers had more negative prediscussion expectations about their group participation and displayed more verbal discrimination in their group interactions (directing more positive communications to fellow "newcomers" and more negative communications to other group members). These biases were strongest at the time of the initial group meeting and dissipated over further sessions as the absence of difference between experimental and control subjects became obvious.

The results of Moreland's (1985) experiment demonstrate that self-categorization on the part of newcomers can influence entrée into a group, but also that these effects disappear when there is high similarity between newcomers and oldtimers. For dissimilar newcomers, however, the negative effects of self-categorization can be expected to be reinforced rather than disconfirmed by actual experience.

The perpetuation of negative expectancies is likely to be exacerbated by the natural tendency of newcomers to seek out others in the organization who are similar to themselves. For newcomers who are members of the majority ingroup, this can involve establishing interpersonal relationships with oldtimers who share their group identification as well as bonding with other newcomers. For ingroup members, collaboration among newcomers can facilitate socialization and acceptance by expanding the network of associations between newcomers and oldtimers and creating more pressure for group accommodation to the coalition of newcomers (Moreland and Levine 1989).

Minority newcomers who practice such selective affiliation, however, are less likely to achieve these networking and coalition-building benefits. For minority newcomers, the tendency to affiliate with those most similar to themselves will limit their initial contacts to others who share both their minority and their newcomer status (because there are few minority oldtimers). In this event, selective affiliation is more likely to create enclaves with few network connections to oldtimers, and because the group members are not fully socialized organizational members, subgroup norms that are not convergent with organizational norms and practices may develop. Interpersonal relationships within this subgroup are likely to encourage expression of shared perceptions of discrimination and lack of fit, but in ways that inhibit rather than facilitate the processes of mutual assimilation and accommodation.

## Belonging and Commitment

This discussion of the theory and research on group socialization suggests a number of reasons why the transition from entry to entrée of minority group members into a large organization may not be successful. After the transition is achieved, the sense of belonging to the organization acquired by the new full members inspires organizational commitment and participation (Mathieu and Zajac 1990). According to Gooden (1994), the experience of institutional belonging has two components—the belief that one's own values and abilities are suited to the organization (self-belonging) and the perception that one is valued and accepted by other group members or by the organization itself (other-belonging) (see also Tyler 1989). When socialization fails, both components of institutional belonging are likely to be missing.

Our analysis of the newcomer socialization process suggests that for members of the majority ingroup, socialization into a large organization is facilitated by shared social category membership. Since all ingroup newcomers benefit from the positive expectancies accorded to ingroup members, variations in degree of successful socialization should be related to individual abilities and motivations, independent of their level of ingroup identification. Further, since opportunities for affiliation with other members of the same social category are uniformly high, socialization should be influenced by the quality rather than quantity of ingroup interactions (that is, who one knows is more important than how many one knows). Among members of the majority or dominant social category, then, strength of ingroup identification and preferences for ingroup affiliation should be either positively related or uncorrelated with extent of organizational belonging and commitment. In effect, dual identification with the organization and with ethnic group membership should be nonproblematic for members of the ethnic majority.

By contrast, the dynamics of accommodation and assimilation may create problems of dual identity for members of ethnic minorities. If successful socialization involves greater demands for assimilation from minority newcomers, then social group identity and organizational identity may be experienced as competing or incompatible bases for social identity. Thus, for minorities, ingroup identification and affiliation may come to be negatively related to feelings of organizational belonging and commitment. Note again that this negative relationship can be expected to hold regardless of whether there are actually any cultural differences between the minority and majority groups that would affect the degree of fit between attributes of individual minority group members and organizational norms and procedures. The presence of relevant cultural differences would, of course, exacerbate the negative correlation by increasing the demands for both individual assimilation and organizational accommodation needed for successful integration to occur.

## ETHNIC INTEGRATION IN ACADEMIA: EMPIRICAL EVIDENCE

The diversification of the student bodies of large public universities provides a prototypic setting for examining the relationship between group identification and successful organizational socialization. The cycle of admission and matriculation characteristic of universities ensures that there is a regular process of socialization of newcomers to an organizational structure created by administrators, faculty, and upperclass students. Historically in the United States, the vast majority of the faculty and student bodies of public universities has been white Anglos, and the culture and values of the university are perceived to reflect those of the white-dominated society at large. At least until 1996, aggressive affirmative action policies have increased admissions of previously underrepresented ethnic minorities, such as African Americans, to large state universities at both undergraduate and graduate levels. Yet continued differential dropout rates between Anglo and African American students (and differential achievement among those who stay) attest to the fact that successes at entry are not being matched by successes at retention and achievement in this institutional setting (Brower 1992).

Recent surveys conducted at two U.S. universities provided data on social identification, perceptions of the university environment, patterns of social interaction, and academic achievement of majority and minority students admitted as freshmen. These data enabled us to make a preliminary investigation of the relationship between social identification of ethnic minorities and majorities and organizational commitment in the university context.

For the purposes of this preliminary study, we focused on two potential mediators of the relationship between ethnic identification and organizational commitment and achievement—perceptions of belonging and ingroup affiliation preferences. The research question was whether the pattern of interrelationships between ethnic identification, belonging, affiliation preferences, and academic commitment was different for students of majority versus minority ethnic background. Based on our analysis of socialization processes, we predicted that, compared to whites, minority students would show heightened awareness of ethnic identification as an important aspect of their social identity and would report lower feelings of belonging and commitment to the university and to academic achievement. More important, we predicted an asymmetry in the correlations between strength of own ethnic identity and institutional belonging and academic commitment within the two student groups. Among white students, we expected levels of ethnic identification and ingroup affiliation to be uncorrelated with institutional identification, but for minority students we expected this relationship to be negative.

## Study 1: University of Michigan

The data for our first survey came from a study conducted at the University of Michigan between 1991 and 1993. Over the course of three years, 795 first- and second-year undergraduate students participated in an end-of-the-year questionnaire survey assessing their college experiences up to that point in their careers. The total sample consisted of 215 African American students and 580 Anglo students, recruited from among students who had applied to participate in an academic enrichment program during the preceding year.[1]

The survey questionnaire consisted of an extensive inventory of items designed to assess multiple aspects of the students' college experience. The questions relevant to the present purpose dealt with the extent of the respondent's identification with his or her ethnic group, the respondent's preference for spending time with members of his or her own ethnic group, and the respondent's belief that the university cared about him or her as an individual. This last measure served as our best available proxy for a direct measure of feelings of institutional belonging. It tapped into the "other-belonging" component identified by Gooden (1994) and is supported by research on organizational behavior that indicates that feelings of commitment to an organization depend in part on how committed the organization is perceived to be to the individual (Eisenberger, Fasolo, and Davis-LaMastro 1990; Shore and Wayne 1993).

From the questionnaire data, three composite indices were constructed. The measure of *ethnic identification* consisted of responses to the identification subscale of the Collective Self-Esteem Scale (Luhtanen and Crocker 1991), adapted to refer specifically to ethnic group membership. The measure of *own group preference* consisted of responses to three items assessing the extent to which the respondent preferred to engage in various school-related activities with members of his or her own ethnic group. The measure of *university cares* was composed of four items assessing the extent of the respondent's belief that the university was concerned about him or her. (See appendix 11.1 for items used in each measure.)

In addition to these questionnaire responses, information from the university registrar's office provided data on each student's cumulative grade point average at the end of the academic year in which the survey was completed. This served as a measure of academic commitment and achievement.

*Intergroup Differences* The first step in the analysis was to compare the mean responses of African American and Caucasian students to the three questionnaire measures and their grade point averages. Table 11.1 reports these mean values. African American students overall exhibited stronger levels of group identification, greater preference for spending time with members of their own group, and lower grade point averages than Caucasian students. However, contrary to expectations, no ethnic differences emerged overall on the measure of university caring.

Although the differences between groups were generally as expected, the more important test of our conceptualization comes from analyses of the interrelationships between the composite indices of identification and belonging within each ethnic group. Table 11.2 displays the bivariate correlations among the three composite measures and grade point averages for the white and African American samples. For Anglo students, there was (not surprisingly) a positive correlation between the salience of their ethnic identity and their preference for affiliating with their own group members, but neither of these variables proved to be correlated significantly with perceptions that the university cared about them. However, there was an unexpected direct negative relationship between ethnic identification and academic achievement for Caucasian students that was independent of the other two subjective measures of institutional involvement.

TABLE 11.1 *Mean Composite Scores: University of Michigan Study*

| | Caucasian Subsample | African American Subsample |
|---|---|---|
| Ethnic identification | 3.48<br>(1.28) | 5.08<br>(1.37) |
| Own group preference | 1.96<br>(.67) | 2.83<br>(.74) |
| University cares | 3.63<br>(1.21) | 3.48<br>(1.35) |
| Grade point average | 3.21<br>(.59) | 2.68<br>(.59) |

For African American students, on the other hand, both ingroup identification and, to some extent, preference for the company of members of their own group were negatively associated with perceptions that the university cared about them, indicating that strong ethnic identification was not experienced as compatible with full institutional belonging among minority students. However, strength of ethnic identification did not have a direct correlation with academic achievement as measured by grade point average.

*Direct Versus Indirect Effects of Ethnic Identification* Since the pattern of bivariate correlations was different for Caucasian and African American students, further analyses were conducted within each ethnic group to assess the interrelationships between ingroup identification, institutional belonging, and academic achievement. Specifically, path analyses were conducted separately for African American and Caucasian students to determine whether ethnic identification had any direct or mediated effects on academic outcomes. In these analyses, the identity scale was used to predict students' preferences for being with the ingroup and their beliefs about university caring, and all three of these variables were used to predict grade point average. The results of these path analyses for the two groups are presented in figure 11.1.

For white students, there is no evidence of any negative relationship (direct or indirect) between preferential affiliation with other members of the ethnic ingroup and academic achievement. And salience of ethnic identification was not associated with feelings of alienation from the university. Nonetheless, there was still a small but significant direct relationship between reported self-identification with whites as an ethnic group and lower academic performance.

For African Americans, by contrast, level of ethnic identification

TABLE 11.2 *Intercorrelations: University of Michigan Study*

| | University Cares | Own Group Preference | Grade Point Average |
|---|---|---|---|
| Caucasian Subsample | | | |
| Ethnic Identification | .056 | .225** | −.099* |
| University Cares | — | .032 | .047 |
| Own Group Preference | — | — | −.076 |
| African American Subsample | | | |
| Ethnic Identification | −.229** | .453** | −.029 |
| University Cares | — | −.106 | .070 |
| Own Group Preference | — | — | −.137* |

*$p < .05$, **$p < .01$

was not directly related to academic achievement. Instead, any relationship between ethnic identification and grade point average was indirect, mediated by the effects of preferential affiliation. Strength of ethnic identification was related positively to preferential affiliation, which in turn had a negative relationship to academic performance. Although ethnic identification was also negatively related to perceptions of university caring, this perception had no direct effect on performance.

Overall, then, the results of this initial study provide some support for the idea that the role of ethnic group identity in institutional socialization differs for members of minority and majority ethnic groups. For both African American and Caucasian students, high levels of ethnic identity were associated with preferences for engaging in activities with other members of their own group. However, only for African Americans was preferential affiliation with the ingroup negatively related to academic achievement. Furthermore, for African Americans but not for Caucasians, ethnic identification was associated with negative evaluations of the university as a caring environment, although such evaluations did not prove to have a direct relationship with achievement.

There was also a slight but unexpected direct negative relationship between ethnic identification and academic achievement among the white students in this sample. This result should be evaluated in light of the relatively low level of ethnic identification expressed by Caucasians in general. As indicated in table 11.1, the mean rating for white students on the identification measure was below the midpoint of the seven-point scale. For most Caucasians (as for majorities in general), being white is not a particularly salient or important aspect of their conscious social identity. In this context, those few white students who do score high on the ethnic identity measure may be expressing a form of alienation or disidentification with the university through racial iden-

FIGURE 11.1 *Path Analyses: University of Michigan Study*

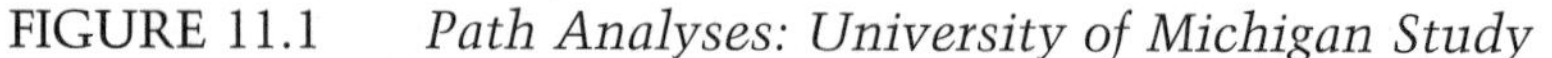

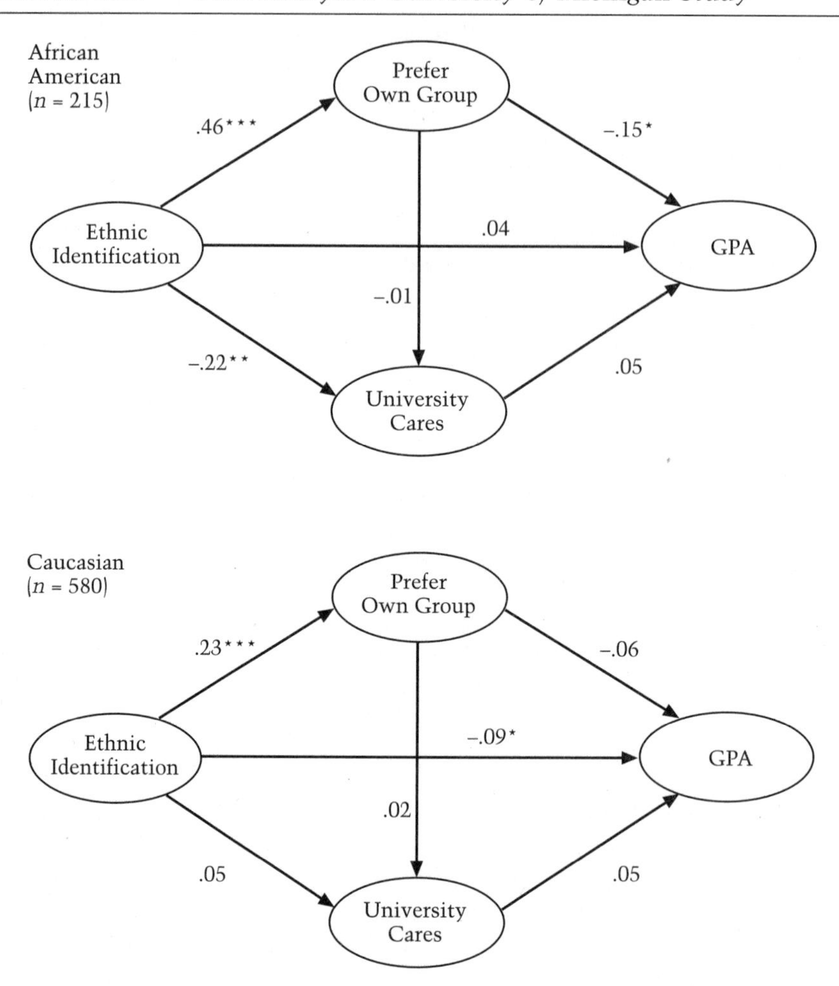


$^{*}p < .05$, $^{**}p < .01$, $^{***}p < .001$

tity. Hence, for white students ethnic identification may be a symptom rather than a cause of disaffection with academic values and performance.

## Ethnic Affiliation Versus Institutional Identification

Results from the Michigan study indicate that subgroup affiliation preferences among African American students were more relevant to academic commitment and achievement than perceptions of the university environment as a whole. This finding is consistent with the conclusion drawn in a recent review of the socialization literature by Moreland and Levine (in press): socialization within a newcomer's immediate work group is more important than organizational socialization as a determinant of organizational commitment. The finding is also consistent with some earlier research indicating that number of white friends is a positive predictor of academic achievement for minority students (Dawkins and Dawkins 1980; Graham, Baker, and Wapner 1984) in college settings. However, it is not ethnic identification itself that is associated with disidentification with the university; ethnic identification and academic achievement are unrelated for minority students except as mediated by patterns of interpersonal relationships and subgroup formation.

This pattern of results contradicts theories that assume that academic achievement for African American students is obtained at the cost of "racelessness," or disidentification with their ethnic heritage (Fordham 1988; Fordham and Ogbu 1986). In the present data, ethnic identification per se is not incompatible with academic achievement. Instead, the pattern of interrelationships between strength of group identification, own-group preference, and grade point average supports the conclusions of Arroyo and Zigler (1995) that it is conflict between affiliative and achievement motives that underlies differences in academic performance. An analysis of data from the National Survey of Black Americans (Demo and Hughes 1990) suggests that the same pattern holds beyond academic settings: economic success among adult African Americans was found to have differential effects on different aspects of black identity. Socioeconomic status was negatively related to separatism and closeness to other members of the ethnic group at the same time that it was positively related to racial self-esteem and evaluation of the ingroup.

In the university context, the conflict between these different aspects of group identification (ethnic pride versus preferential affiliation) may be particularly acute, especially within a large institution such as the University of Michigan, in which there is a single dominant majority and a relatively small minority population.[2] In such a context, members of the majority group are relatively unaware of their ethnic identity and its role in their institutional membership. Their social identity as white Americans and their social identity as university students are essentially interchangeable. For members of the minority category, on the other hand, the two forms of social identity are not so interlinked. Successful socialization and achievement in the organizational setting comes, to some extent, by avoiding preferential association with other members of the ethnic ingroup. Those who are strongly identified with their ethnic group experience the university as a less caring institution, but this leads to lowered academic success only for those who also isolate themselves from contact with majority students.

The nature of the interrelationships between ethnicity, social identity, and academic achievement may differ in a context where the ethnic composition of the student body is distributed more evenly, in multiethnic environments where no one ethnic group is a clear majority. In such a context, the salience of ethnic identity may be heightened for all groups and strength of identification with ethnic ingroups may have direct effects on institutional belonging and academic commitment.

## Study 2: A Replication and Extension at UCLA

By 1992 admissions to the freshman class at the University of California at Los Angeles had achieved a level of ethnic diversity unprecedented in large public institutions of higher education. That year, 33 percent of incoming students were of Asian American or South Pacific origin, 22 percent were Hispanic or Latino, 8 percent were African American, and only 33 percent were Anglo or European Americans. Thus, no single racial/ethnic group constituted a majority of the student body, although the demographic composition of the faculty was still predominantly non-Hispanic Caucasian. Furthermore, in 1992 more than 80 percent of the incoming freshmen lived in residence halls on campus where roommate assignments were made randomly and other policies of ethnic integration were in force. UCLA, then, provided a very different context of ethnic diversity for conducting a conceptual replication of the Michigan study.

Data for the second study came from a questionnaire survey conducted in the freshman dorms at UCLA at the end of the 1992–93 academic year.[3] The floors of three large residence halls were randomly selected for inclusion in the study, and questionnaires were distributed and completed during an evening meeting of residents of the floor. Of the 722 freshman students who participated in the survey, 231 were self-identified as non-Hispanic white, 78 as Hispanic/Latino, and 37 as African American.[4]

The twelve-page survey questionnaire covered a wide range of issues, including evaluations of multiple aspects of university life, self-assessments, and attitudes toward affirmative action and other diversity issues. From this larger context, items were selected for the construction of four measures conceptually similar to those constructed from the Michigan dataset.

For the UCLA survey, the measure of *ethnic identification* consisted of responses to a variety of items tapping the importance of ethnic identity to the individual's self-concept and activities. The UCLA question-

TABLE 11.3 *Mean Composite Scores: UCLA Study*

| | Caucasian Subsample | Latino Subsample | African American Subsample |
|---|---|---|---|
| Ethnic identification | 11.71<br>(3.17) | 15.67<br>(3.21) | 17.13<br>(2.56) |
| Own group preference | 17.14<br>(5.30) | 20.73<br>(6.05) | 24.88<br>(6.99) |
| Institutional belonging | 3.48<br>(.56) | 3.53<br>(.53) | 3.23<br>(.61) |
| Academic commitment | 8.66<br>(1.58) | 8.76<br>(1.44) | 8.94<br>(1.71) |

naire provided a more elaborated measure of *institutional belonging* than had been available from the Michigan survey. Items from the UCLA instrument included ratings of the experienced atmosphere of acceptance at UCLA (other-belonging) and feelings of comfort, fit, and competence within the environment (self-belonging). The total belonging scale was computed as the mean of responses to items tapping both of these constructs. The measure of *own group preference* also consisted of responses to a variety of items tapping affiliative behaviors and preferences for interactions with members of the ethnic ingroup. (See appendix 11.2 for specific items used in each of these scales.)

Since the UCLA survey was conducted in a single session without any personal identification on the questionnaires, we were unable to obtain end-of-year grade point averages for the survey participants. For this study, we relied instead on a self-report measure of *academic commitment,* which consisted of respondents' ratings of the importance of achieving good grades in college and their estimate of the probability that they would complete their academic degree at UCLA (see appendix 11.2).

*Intergroup Differences* Table 11.3 presents the mean scores on the four measures for the three subgroups of students. Although the measure of ethnic identification used in the UCLA study was not directly comparable to the scale used in the Michigan survey, it is of interest to note that the Anglo students at UCLA (unlike those at Michigan) scored above the midpoint on this measure (11.7 on a 20-point scale). This supports our assumption that ethnic identification is more salient for members of all groups in the highly diverse context of UCLA. Nonetheless, the strength of ethnic identification was significantly higher among the Hispanic and African American students than among the whites, even

TABLE 11.4 *Intercorrelations: UCLA Study*

| | Institutional Belonging | Own Group Preference | Academic Commitment |
|---|---|---|---|
| Caucasian Subsample | | | |
| Ethnic Identification | .066 | .415** | .163* |
| Institutional Belonging | — | −.068 | .162* |
| Own Group Preference | — | — | .000 |
| Latino Subsample | | | |
| Ethnic Identification | −.147 | .576** | −.128 |
| Institutional Belonging | — | −.111 | .274** |
| Own Group Preference | — | — | −.296** |
| African American Subsample | | | |
| Ethnic Identification | −.262 | .194 | .005 |
| Institutional Belonging | — | −.563** | .226* |
| Own Group Preference | — | — | −.002 |

*$p < .05$, **$p < .01$

in this context. Blacks and Hispanics were also both significantly higher than whites in reported preference for their own groups. On average, however, the three groups did not differ significantly in institutional belonging or in self-reported academic commitment.

Table 11.4 presents the intercorrelations among the three measures of identification and belonging within each student group at UCLA. Here some interesting differences emerge both between universities and between subgroups at UCLA (though the small size of the UCLA African American sample dictates that findings for this group must be interpreted with caution). Unlike at Michigan, the direct correlation between ethnic identification and academic commitment for white students at UCLA was positive, although there was no relationship between strength of ethnic identification and feelings of institutional belonging (which was also positively correlated with commitment) in this group. For Latinos, the direct correlation between ethnic identification and academic commitment, though negative, was not statistically significant, but the negative relationship between preference for their own group and academic commitment was significant (as for African American students at Michigan). Furthermore, the expanded measure of institutional belonging used in this study was also significantly (positively) correlated with academic commitment for Latino students.

For the African American sample at UCLA, own-group preference and strength of ethnic identification were not significantly positively correlated, as they had been in other samples. This finding may be in part a reflection of unreliability due to small sample size, but it also reflects the exceptionally high levels of self-ratings on these two variables for UCLA blacks compared to other subgroups, particularly on the strength of identification measure (where the average score was greater than 17 on a 20-point scale). Thus, correlations involving the ethnic identification measure may have been depressed by ceiling effects. This subgroup also had the strongest negative correlation between own-group preference and institutional belonging, suggesting that African American students at UCLA constitute more of an alienated ethnic "enclave" than any of our other subsamples.

Path analyses parallel to those computed for the Michigan survey were also computed for the three subsamples at UCLA to summarize the pattern of interrelationships within each ethnic group. The results are depicted in figure 11.2. For whites, the direct relationship between strength of ethnic identification and academic commitment was positive, but unmediated by own-group preference or institutional belonging. As at Michigan, neither own-group preference nor institutional belonging were significant independent predictors of academic commitment for non-Hispanic Caucasian students.

For Latino students, however, both own-group preference and institutional belonging were significant predictors of academic commitment, and as for African Americans at Michigan, there was no direct relationship between strength of ethnic identification and academic commitment, only an indirect relationship through own-group preference. The pattern of interrelationships for African American students at UCLA was somewhat different, with the negative effects of own-group preference mediated by a strong negative relationship with institutional belonging. Again, however, for both minority groups it was not strength of ethnic identification per se that influenced institutional belonging and academic commitment, but only its expression in patterns of interpersonal relationships and subgroup isolation.

At UCLA the degree of asymmetry between majority and minority group members in the correlations between strength of ethnic identification and institutional belonging was stronger than that obtained in the Michigan survey. In both contexts, preferential ingroup affiliation among minority students was negatively correlated with institutional belonging and/or commitment. In the multi-ethnic context of UCLA, however, a strong sense of white identity was not a symptom of institutional disaffection but instead was slightly positively associated with academic commitment.

Because ethnic identification and ethnic affiliation proved to play different roles in predicting the commitment of whites and minorities to academic achievement at UCLA, we took a further look at the determinants of these measures for Caucasian, Latino, and African American students (see table 11.5). When two background characteristics (parental

FIGURE 11.2 *Path Analyses: UCLA Study*

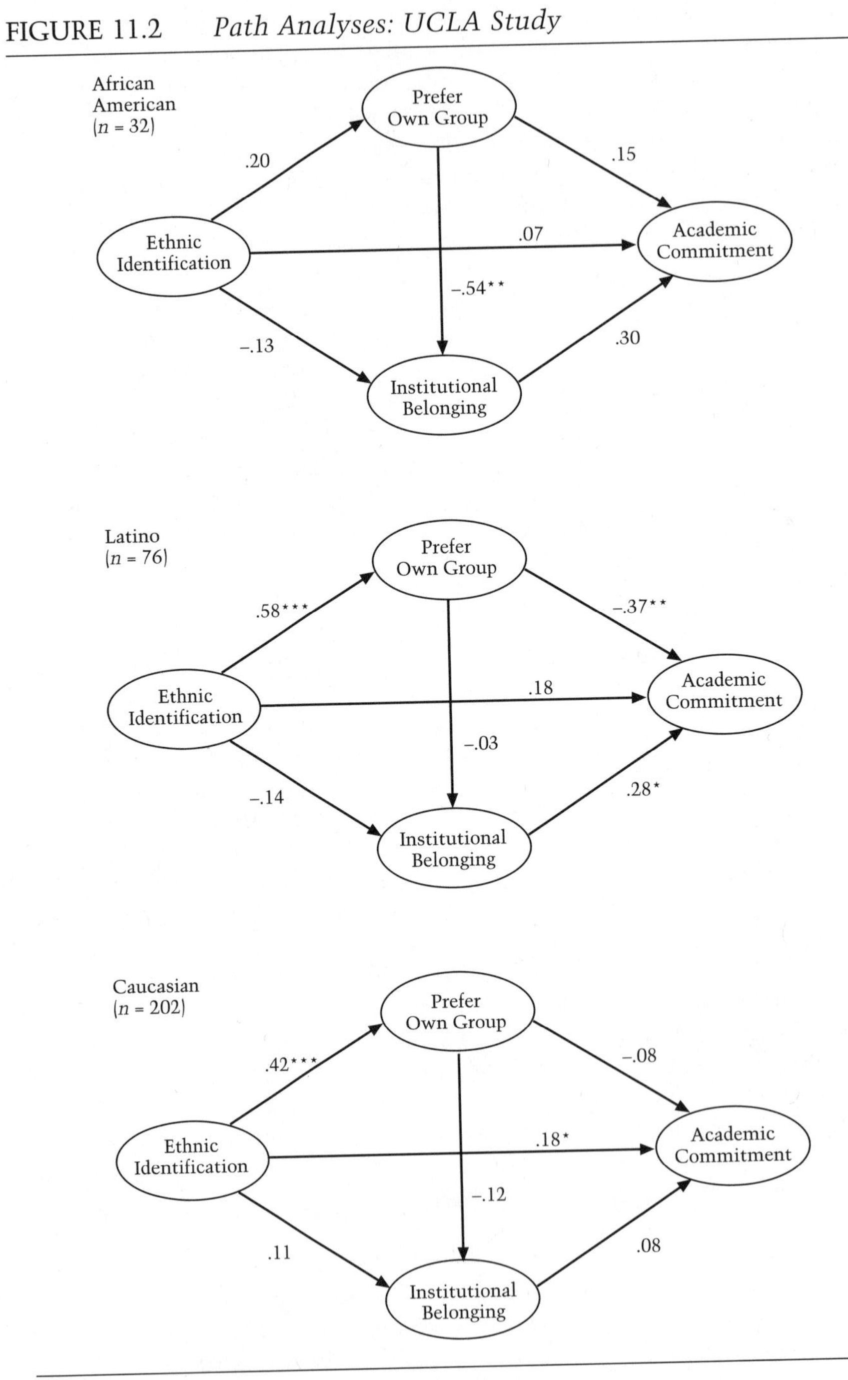


*p < .05, **p < .01, ***p < .001

TABLE 11.5 *Correlations with Background Variables: UCLA Study*

| | Ethnic Identification | Institutional Belonging | Own Group Preference | Academic Commitment |
|---|---|---|---|---|
| Caucasian Subsample | | | | |
| Parental Education | .018 | .068 | .021 | .197** |
| White Background | .111 | .188** | .200** | .199** |
| Latino Subsample | | | | |
| Parental Education | −.207 | −.044 | −.200 | −.037 |
| White Background | −.191 | .068 | −.187 | .113 |
| African American Subsample | | | | |
| Parental Education | −.589** | .299 | −.098 | −.315 |
| White Background | −.241 | −.249 | −.024 | −.237 |

*$p < .05$, **$p < .01$

education and coming from a predominantly white neighborhood and high school) were examined, the degree of ethnic identification and the degree of ethnic affiliation preference of whites were both found to be associated with coming from a predominantly white background, which was also a significant predictor of feelings of belonging at UCLA and academic commitment. Thus, for whites academic commitment was influenced by presocialization in white-dominated academic environments.

For African American and Latino students at UCLA, coming from a predominantly white neighborhood was nonsignificantly negatively related to strength of ethnic identification, but this background factor was unrelated to own-group preference, feelings of belonging, or academic commitment. Ethnic identification for these groups was negatively correlated with parental educational background (a presocialization factor), but the negative relationships between own-group preference and institutional belonging and academic commitment among minority students remained when parental education and neighborhood background factors were statistically controlled. For members of the nondominant ethnic groups, presocialization experiences in white-dominated or multiethnic neighborhoods and high schools apparently had less impact than the socialization experiences they encountered after coming to UCLA.

## GENERALIZATIONS AND IMPLICATIONS

The main point of our analyses has been to demonstrate that the empirical relationship between social identification and organizational commitment/achievement can provide insights about the process of socialization and entrée to the organization for members of different demographic groups. When this relationship is positive (or nonsubstantial) for members of a majority group but negative for minorities in the organization, it can be taken as symptomatic of failure to achieve an organizational environment in which successful entrée is independent of ethnic identification and ingroup ties. Because of the subtle effects of social categorization on socialization and interpersonal relationships, asymmetries can arise even in the absence of overt prejudice or intergroup hostilities.

Results from surveys at both universities converged in identifying ethnic affiliation patterns as the critical mediator between ethnic identification and organizational commitment. For whites, ethnic "enclaving" has little detrimental effect (and in some cases may reinforce institutional belonging), but for minority group members, it appears to be a barrier to socialization into the institution as a whole. In general, enclaves of any kind provide the opportunity for development and reinforcement of "countercultures" that reduce identification with and commitment to the organization as a whole. However, this is not a necessary concomitant of ethnic associations, since there are alternative subculture norms that could reinforce institutional commitment or involvement directed at institutional change. What remains to be determined is what conditions make it possible for some members of ethnic minority groups to maintain a strong sense of ethnic identification *without* limiting interethnic social interactions or reducing organizational participation.

Eliminating any correlation between level of ethnic identification and commitment to the organization is not equivalent to so-called color-blind policies that deny actual or expected differences between organizational members as a function of ethnic identity. We assume that the goal is integration in the sense of mutual accommodation between organization and newcomers of all social categories. Mutual accommodation should be distinguishable from an assimilation model in which minority newcomers must adopt the dominant culture and seek contacts with members of the majority category in order to attain acceptance. Achieving zero correlation between ethnic identification and organizational commitment may require taking ethnicity into account in the process of socialization and attaining organizational fit. It does imply, however, that organizational identity (the roles and abilities that the individual contributes to the organization) takes priority over other social identities in thinking about group members, especially newcomers.

The recommendation that diversity be embedded in organizational functions is based on some assumptions about the basic cognitive-behavioral mechanisms that underlie ingroup-outgroup categorization and its evaluative and behavioral effects. Research on social cognition and stereotyping suggests that overt efforts to suppress or change well-learned category distinctions and their associated stereotypes are rarely successful (Hilton and von Hippel 1996) and may even produce "boomerang" effects (Macrae et al. 1994). There may be an alternative, indirect route to change, however—taking advantage of the fact that individuals can be categorized in multiple ways within any particular situation.

Relatively little experimental work has been devoted to the effects of multiple categorization cues, although there is some evidence that situational or instructional demands can alter the priority with which different categorizations of a target stimulus will be utilized (Macrae et al. 1995; Rudman and Borgida 1995; Smith, Fazio, and Cejka 1996). This suggests that making alternative category systems functionally salient may indirectly alter information processing and eventually the underlying category structure itself. The process of recategorization can be used to alter which ingroup-outgroup category distinctions are most salient (Eberhardt and Fiske 1996).

The relative salience of ethnic categories and organizational roles is inevitably influenced by the distribution and covariation of these categorical distinctions across the organization (Wharton 1992). When ethnic distinctions converge with positions in the organization (functional roles, seniority, and so on), categorical boundaries are reinforced and information processing is facilitated by prior categorization based on ethnicity. If almost all African American college students are social science majors, most women employees are clerical workers, and all black executives are in the human resources department, differentiated representations of members of these minority groups are not going to be formed. In fact, such convergence between category memberships tends to reinforce stereotyping and enhance ingroup-outgroup discrimination (Arcuri 1982).

Embedding diversity requires that organizational roles and ethnic (or other) social identities are cross-cutting within the organizational structure. When the correlation between social category membership and organizational roles is reduced, organizational functioning requires making differentiations within *both* categories. In organizations where role and ethnicity are orthogonal, ethnicity cues must be subordinated to organizational identities in order to function effectively (Brewer 1996). Social psychology experiments on intergroup contact corroborate the effectiveness of cross-cutting category memberships in reducing intergroup discrimination and bias (Hewstone, Islam, and Judd 1993; Marcus-Newhall et al. 1993; Rust 1996). When individuals interact with others who are members of an outgroup on one dimension of social categorization but who are ingroup members on a different dimension that is contextually salient (such as organizational membership or shared organizational roles), judgments and evaluations are less discriminatory. Common identity in one domain apparently mitigates biases based on other categorical distinctions.

When members of minority categories are valued on the basis of the roles that they play in the organizational context, accommodation to demographic and cultural diversity becomes intrinsically linked to work-group effectiveness and organizational success. When ingroup-outgroup categorizations are independent of ethnicity per se, the negative feedback loop between ethnic identification and preferential affiliation and organizational belonging among minority group members can be broken and the value of diversity appreciated.

## APPENDIX 11.1

## MEASURES FOR THE MICHIGAN STUDY

### Ethnic Identification (seven-point scales; Cronbach's $\alpha$ = .83)

- Overall, my (ethnic) group membership has very little to do with how I feel about myself.
- The (ethnic) group that I belong to is an important reflection of who I am.
- The (ethnic) group that I belong to is unimportant to my sense of what kind of person I am.
- In general, belonging to this (ethnic) group is an important part of my self-image.

### Own-Group Preference (four-point scales; Cronbach's $\alpha$ = .82)

- When I study for an exam, I prefer to study with students from my own group.
- If I were seeking advice about my academic career, I would prefer to consult with a counselor or faculty member of my own group.
- I am more comfortable at parties with my own group than at interracial and interethnic parties.

### University Cares (seven-point scales; Cronbach's $\alpha$ = .84)

- How much do you think the university and its staff are concerned about your success?

- How much do you feel the university has made an effort to help you succeed here?
- How much do you think the university cares about you as an individual?
- How responsive is the university to your needs as an individual?

# APPENDIX 11.2

## MEASURES FOR THE UCLA STUDY

### Ethnic Identification (five-point scales; Cronbach's $\alpha$ = .86)

- How frequently do you think of yourself in terms of your ethnic group membership?
- How important is your ethnicity to your identity at UCLA?
- How positive do you feel about your ethnic identity?
- How likely are you to do each of the following on behalf of your ethnic group:

a. Join an ethnic student organization?
b. Vote along ethnic lines?
c. Participate in demonstrations?
d. Sign petitions?
e. Send letters to government officials?
f. Enlist public support?

### Institutional Belonging (five-point scales; Cronbach's $\alpha$ = .79)

- How friendly/hostile is the atmosphere at UCLA?
- How concerned/indifferent is the atmosphere?
- How comfortable/uncomfortable is the atmosphere?
- How cooperative/uncooperative is the atmosphere?
- How often do you experience a sense of belonging at UCLA?
- How often do you experience competence at UCLA?
- How often do you experience exclusion at UCLA?
- How often do you experience respect at UCLA?
- How much do you feel free to say what you want at UCLA?
- How much do you feel you have had to change yourself to fit in at UCLA?

## Own-Group Preference (Cronbach's α = .56)

- Ethnicity of closest friend at home (1 = own group, 0 = otherwise)
- Ethnicity of closest friend at UCLA (1, 0)
- Ethnicity of person most recently dated (1, 0)
- Attitude toward assigning roommates without regard to ethnicity (seven-point scale)
- Attitude toward allowing students to choose roommates based on ethnicity (seven-point scale)
- Attitude toward creating special residence halls reserved for ethnic groups (seven-point scale)
- Feelings of uneasiness in multi-ethnic groups (five-point scale)
- Feelings of competence in interacting in multi-ethnic groups (five-point scale)
- Preference for faculty of same ethnicity (five-point scale)
- Preference for discussing conflicts with members of own ethnic groups versus members of different ethnic groups (five-point scale)

## Academic Commitment (five-point scales)

- How important is it for you to get a high GPA at UCLA?
- How likely is it that you would consider dropping out of UCLA before earning a degree?

# NOTES

1. Funding for the program and the survey was provided by a grant from the Fund for the Improvement of Post-Secondary Education. The nature of the enrichment program (described more fully in Nagda et al. 1998) was to involve students in faculty-student research partnerships. Students who applied were randomly assigned to participation in the program, and approximately half of the students in the sample had participated during the year prior to the survey. Data analyses for the present purposes revealed no relevant differences between participants and nonparticipants, so all analyses reported here collapse across the participation variable. However, this recruitment process ensured that all students in the study had fairly high and comparable levels of motivation for academic involvement and success.
2. African American students constitute approximately 6 percent of the University of Michigan undergraduate student body. Another 11 percent of students are Asian American or Hispanic/Latino, but these two subgroupings constitute very small minorities and thus were not examined in this study.
3. Funding for the survey was provided by a seed grant from the Russell Sage Foundation.

4. The fact that the number of students classified within these specific ethnic categories constitutes less than half of the full survey sample reflects the great diversity of ethnic backgrounds (including many of mixed ethnicity) at UCLA at the time. Students classified as Asian American also constitute a sizable segment of the UCLA student population, but this broad category encompasses a variety of diverse subgroups that individually are relatively small. Therefore, Asian Americans, foreign-born students, and those identified as of "other" ethnic origin were not included in the analyses presented here.

## REFERENCES


Arcuri, Luciano. (1982). Three patterns of social categorization in attribution memory. *European Journal of Social Psychology, 12,* 271–82.

Arroyo, Carmen G., and Zigler, Edward. (1995). Racial identity, academic achievement, and the psychological well-being of economically disadvantaged adolescents. *Journal of Personality and Social Psychology, 69,* 903–14.

Brewer, Marilynn B. (1996). Managing diversity: The role of social identities. In Susan Jackson and Marian Ruderman (Eds.), *Diversity in work teams* (pp. 47–68). Washington, D.C.: American Psychological Association.

———. (1997). Ingroup favoritism: The subtle side of intergroup discrimination. In David Messick and Ann Tenbrunsel (Eds.), *Codes of conduct: Behavioral research and business ethics* (pp. 160–70). New York: Russell Sage Foundation.

Brower, Aaron M. (1992). The "second half" of student integration: The effect of life task predominance on student persistence. *Journal of Higher Education, 63,* 441–62.

Dawkins, Marvin P., and Dawkins, Russell L. (1980). Perceptions and experiences as correlates of academic performance among blacks at a predominantly white university: A research note. *College and University, 55,* 171–80.

Demo, David H., and Hughes, Michael. (1990). Socialization and racial identity among black Americans. *Social Psychology Quarterly, 53,* 364–74.

Deschamps, Jean-Claude, and Doise, Wilhelm. (1978). Crossed category memberships in intergroup relations. In Henri Tajfel (Ed.), *Differentiation between social groups* (pp. 141–58). London: Academic Press.

Dovidio, John P., and Gaertner, Samuel L. (1993). Stereotypes and evaluative intergroup bias. In Diane Mackie and David Hamilton (Eds.), *Affect, cognition, and stereotyping* (pp. 167–93). San Diego: Academic Press.

Eberhardt, Jennifer L., and Fiske, Susan T. (1996). Motivating individuals to change: What is a target to do? In C. Neil Macrae, Charles Stangor, and Miles Hewstone (Eds.), *Stereotypes and stereotyping* (pp. 369–415). New York: Guilford.

Eisenberger, Robert, Fasolo, Peter, and Davis-LaMastro, Valerie. (1990). Perceived organizational support and employee diligence, commitment, and innovation. *Journal of Applied Psychology, 75,* 51–59.

Fordham, Signithia. (1988). Racelessness as a factor in black students' school success: Pragmatic strategy or pyrrhic victory? *Harvard Educational Review, 58,* 54–84.

Fordham, Signithia, and Ogbu, John U. (1986). Black students' school success: Coping with the burden of "acting white." *Urban Review, 18,* 176–206.

Gaertner, Samuel L. (1996). Reducing prejudice by inducing a common group identity. Paper presented at the European Association of Social Psychology Small Group Meeting on Social Identity and Prejudice, Catania, Sicily (September).

George, Jennifer M. (1990). Personality, affect, and behavior in groups. *Journal of Applied Psychology, 75,* 107–16.

Gooden, Martin P. (1994). Belonging as a mediator of academic under-performance among African-American students. Master's thesis, Ohio State University.

Graham, Calvin, Baker, Robert W., and Wapner, Seymour. (1984). Prior interracial experience and black student transition into predominantly white colleges. *Journal of Personality and Social Psychology, 47,* 1146–54.

Heilman, Madeline E. (1983). Sex bias in work settings: The lack of fit model. In Larry Cummings and Barry Staw (Eds.), *Research in organizational behavior* (vol. 5, pp. 269–98). Greenwich, Conn.: JAI Press.

Hewstone, Miles, Islam, Mir Rabiul, and Judd, Charles M. (1993). Models of crossed categorization and intergroup relations. *Journal of Personality and Social Psychology, 64,* 779–93.

Hilton, James L., and von Hippel, William. (1996). Stereotypes. *Annual Review of Psychology, 47,* 237–71.

Jackson, Susan E., Brett, Joan F., Sessa, Valerie I., Cooper, Dawn M., Julin, Johan A., and Peyronnin, Karl. (1991). Some differences make a difference: Individual dissimilarity and group heterogeneity as correlates of recruitment, promotions, and turnover. *Journal of Applied Psychology, 76,* 675–89.

Jackson, Susan E., Stone, Veronica K., and Alvarez, Eden B. (1993). Socialization amidst diversity: The impact of demographics on work team oldtimers and newcomers. In Larry Cummings and Barry Staw (Eds.), *Research in organizational behavior* (vol. 15, pp. 45–109). Greenwich, Conn.: JAI Press.

Luhtanen, Riia, and Crocker, Jennifer. (1991). A collective self-esteem scale: Self-evaluation of one's social identity. *Personality and Social Psychology Bulletin, 18,* 302–18.

Macrae, C. Neil, Bodenhausen, Galen V., and Milne, Alan B. (1995). The dissection of selection in person perception: Inhibitory processes in social stereotyping. *Journal of Personality and Social Psychology, 69,* 397–407.

Macrae, C. Neil, Bodenhausen, Galen V., Milne, Alan B., and Jetten, Jolanda. (1994). Out of mind but back in sight: Stereotypes on the rebound. *Journal of Personality and Social Psychology, 67,* 808–17.

Marcus-Newhall, Amy, Miller, Norman, Holtz, Rolf, and Brewer, Marilynn B. (1993). Cross-cutting category membership with role assignment: A means of reducing intergroup bias. *British Journal of Social Psychology, 32,* 125–46.

Mathieu, John E., and Zajac, Dennis M. (1990). A review and meta-analysis of the antecedents, correlates, and consequences of organizational commitment. *Psychological Bulletin, 108,* 171–94.

Moreland, Richard L. (1985). Social categorization and the assimilation of "new" group members. *Journal of Personality and Social Psychology, 48,* 1173–90.

Moreland, Richard L., and Levine, John M. (1982). Group socialization: Temporal changes in individual-group relations. In Leonard Berkowitz (Ed.), *Advances in experimental social psychology* (vol. 15, pp. 137–92). New York: Academic Press.

———. (1989). Newcomers and oldtimers in small groups. In Paul Paulus (Ed.), *Psychology of group influence* (pp. 143–86). Hillsdale, N.J.: Erlbaum.

———. (in press). Socialization in organizations and work groups. In Marlene

Turner (Ed.), *Groups at work: Advances in theory and research*. Hillsdale, N.J.: Erlbaum.

Nagda, Biren A., Gregerman, Sandra R., Jonides, John, von Hippel, William, and Lerner, Jennifer. (1998). Undergraduate student-faculty research partnerships affect student retention. *Review of Higher Education, 22*, 55–72.

Rudman, Laurie A., and Borgida, Eugene. (1995). The afterglow of construct accessibility: The behavioral consequences of priming men to view women as sexual objects. *Journal of Experimental Social Psychology, 31*, 493–517.

Rust, Mary C. (1996). Social identity and social categorization. Ph.D. dissertation, University of Delaware.

Schneider, Benjamin. (1987). The people make the place. *Personnel Psychology, 40*, 437–53.

Shore, Lynn M., and Wayne, Sandy J. (1993). Commitment and employee behavior: Comparison of affective commitment and continuance commitment with perceived organizational support. *Journal of Applied Psychology, 78*, 774–80.

Smith, Eliot R., Fazio, Russell H., and Cejka, M. A. (1996). Accessible attitudes influence categorization of multiply categorizable objects. *Journal of Personality and Social Psychology, 71*, 888–98.

Stroessner, Steven J. (1996). Social categorization by race or sex: Effects of perceived non-normalcy on response times. *Social Cognition, 14*, 274–76.

Tajfel, Henri. (1978). The psychological structure of intergroup relations. In Henri Tajfel (Ed.), *Differentiation between social groups: Studies in the social psychology of intergroup relations* (pp. 27–60). London: Academic Press.

Thomas, Roosevelt R., Jr. (1992). Managing diversity: A conceptual framework. In Susan Jackson et al. (Eds.), *Working through diversity: Human resources initiatives* (pp. 306–17). New York: Guilford.

Tyler, Tom R. (1989). The psychology of procedural justice: A test of the group value model. *Journal of Personality and Social Psychology, 57*, 830–38.

Wharton, Amy S. (1992). The social construction of gender and race in organizations. *Research in the Sociology of Organizations, 10*, 55–84.

# 12

# SOCIAL STIGMA AND SELF-ESTEEM: THE ROLE OF CONTINGENCIES OF WORTH

*Jennifer Crocker and Jason S. Lawrence*

TO BE STIGMATIZED is to have an attribute or a social identity that calls into question one's full humanity—one is devalued, spoiled, or flawed in the eyes of others (Crocker, Major, and Steele 1998; Goffman 1963; Jones et al. 1984). In nearly all societies, some categories of individuals are stigmatized, and hence devalued (Sidanius and Pratto 1993). In the history of the United States, many racial, ethnic, and cultural groups have been stigmatized and devalued. This devaluation has perhaps been most extreme for African Americans, many of whose ancestors arrived in the United States involuntarily as slaves, and for Native Americans, but many ethnic and cultural groups have experienced similar, if less intense and prolonged, experiences of stigmatization.

In this chapter, our focus is on the consequences of stigma for the self-esteem of those who are devalued. By self-esteem, we mean personal and global feelings of self-worth, self-regard, or self-acceptance. Self-esteem, a central aspect of psychological well-being, colors the affective tone of one's daily experience. High self-esteem individuals report more positive affect (Brockner 1984; Pelham and Swann 1989), more life satisfaction (Diener 1984; Myers and Diener 1995), less anxiety (Brockner 1984; Pyszczynski and Greenberg 1987), less hopelessness (Crocker et al. 1994), and fewer depressive symptoms (Tennen and Herzberger 1987) than individuals who are low in self-esteem. Thus, self-esteem is arguably the most important aspect of the experience of the self. When social stigma results in low self-esteem, it is not only one's social identity in the eyes of others that is spoiled, but also one's experience of the self.

The notion that low self-esteem results from the experience of being stigmatized, devalued, and targeted by prejudice and discrimination has long been a mainstay of social psychological theory. This notion derives from the assumption that the self is socially constructed—it arises out of, and depends greatly on, our interactions with other people and how they view us. According to this view, we cannot understand the self without understanding the social context in which it functions. For example, Cooley (1956) argued that subjectively interpreted feedback from others is a main source of information about the self. We arrive at our self-concepts by a process of "reflected appraisals," that is, imagining how others perceive and evaluate us. These reflected appraisals affect how we perceive and evaluate ourselves, resulting in what Cooley described as the "looking-glass self." Mead (1934) argued that the looking-glass self is a product of, and essential to, social interaction. To interact smoothly and effectively with others, we need to anticipate how they will react to us, and so we need to learn to see ourselves through the eyes of others. Those "others" may be either the specific individual with whom we are interacting or a generalized view of how most people see us, a "generalized other." This representation of how others view us guides our behavior, even when no specific other is present.

The implications of this view of the self-concept for those who are stigmatized are clear. Stigmatized individuals are devalued in the larger social context (that is, by the generalized other) and by many specific individuals with whom they have personal contact. When they are aware of the devaluation of their targeted attribute or their social group, stigmatized individuals imagine that they are, and will be, devalued by others, and they incorporate that devaluation into their self-concept. The result, according to the theory, is low self-esteem among those who are stigmatized.

In this chapter, we consider the evidence for this theoretical prediction, focusing on levels of global self-esteem among members of disadvantaged racial and ethnic groups. We argue that the consequences of stigma for self-esteem are not the same for all devalued individuals and groups. Rather, the consequences depend on the contingencies that determine one's self-worth. We argue that there are both group differences and individual differences in the contingencies on which self-worth is based, and these contingencies determine, in part, the vulnerability of devalued individuals and groups to low self-esteem.

## RACE/ETHNICITY AND SELF-ESTEEM

Empirical research on the consequences of devaluation, prejudice, and negative stereotypes on the self-esteem of members of minority racial and ethnic groups dates to Kenneth and Mamie Clark's (1939) demonstration in the 1930s that African American children preferred white dolls to dolls that had dark skin color. This finding has since been replicated many times (for reviews, see Banks 1976; Brand, Ruiz, and Padilla 1974). The Clarks interpreted their findings as revealing low self-esteem and concluded that the devaluation of African Americans had been internalized by African American children.

For many years the proposition that devaluation, prejudice, and discrimination result in low self-esteem for those who are devalued was taken to be a well-established finding of social science research. For example, Cartwright (1950) argued: "The group to which a person belongs serves as primary determinants of his self-esteem. To a considerable extent, personal feelings of worth depend on the social evaluation of the group with which a person is identified. Self-hatred and feelings of worthlessness tend to arise from membership in underprivileged or outcast groups" (440). Erik Erikson (1956) claimed that "there is ample evidence of inferiority feelings and of morbid self-hate in all minority groups" (155). Gordon Allport (1954/1979) recognized that responses to oppression vary widely, but he suggested that a common consequence was low self-esteem: "Group oppression may destroy the integrity of the ego entirely, and reverse its normal pride, and create a groveling self-image" (152).

These sweeping conclusions about the effects of stigma on self-esteem depended mainly on the evidence of Clark and Clark's (1939) doll studies. However, in these studies self-esteem was not measured directly but inferred from a very indirect measure of preference for white over black dolls. This preference could have resulted from many things other than low personal self-esteem, such as low esteem for one's racial group, or simply a preference for products like those advertised in the mass media (Cross 1991). Thus, the doll preference studies do not provide compelling evidence of low self-esteem in the targets of prejudice. Research that measures self-esteem directly does not support the conclusions drawn from the doll studies. Rather, this research indicates that the self-esteem of African Americans is at least as high as that of European Americans (Crocker and Major 1989; Porter and Washington 1979; Wylie 1979). A meta-analysis of existing studies on the self-esteem of black and white Americans indicates that African Americans have significantly higher self-esteem than do Americans of European descent (Twenge and Crocker 1998). The size of this effect (higher self-esteem among African Americans than European Americans) depends on characteristics of the study and the sample. Interestingly, studies conducted in the 1960s tended to show lower self-esteem in African Americans than in European Americans. Over time, the effect has significantly reversed (Twenge and Crocker 1998). In addition, the effect of higher self-esteem among African Americans is smaller among older samples, and larger in female samples than in male samples. Thus, the finding of higher self-esteem among African Americans has changed over time and is not equally true of all samples. Indeed, Clark and Clark's (1939) interpretation of their results may not have been so wide of the mark at the time they did their research. However, the general pattern of results showing higher self-esteem in African Americans, particularly over the past three decades, clearly challenges the sweeping conclusions of social psychologists that social stigma or devaluation of one's group inevitably, or even usually, results in low self-esteem.

Although the evidence clearly indicates that African Americans do not, on average, suffer from low self-esteem relative to European Americans, this finding raises many questions. What about other racial or ethnic groups that are devalued in U.S. culture? Do they, too, have levels of self-esteem that are as high as, or higher than, that of European Americans? Or are some devalued groups more likely to suffer from low self-esteem? What accounts for the seeming imperviousness of African Americans' self-esteem in the face of pervasive discrimination and devaluation? Are our social psychological theories wrong, or is some other factor at work protecting the self-esteem of African-Americans?

Although the vast majority of research has focused on the self-esteem of African Americans compared to European Americans, some research has examined other racial or ethnic groups. Studies of the self-esteem and well-being of Latin Americans have yielded conflicting results, with some finding increased distress, including low self-esteem, among Latin Americans (Linn, Hunter, and Perry 1979; Roberts 1980) and others not finding such a relationship (Jensen, White, and Galliher 1982; Rogler, Malgady, and Rodriguez 1989). Some Latin American groups (for example, Mexican Americans) appear to be doing well on a variety of psychological and health dimensions, whereas others experiencing similar levels of objective disadvantage have relatively poor outcomes on measures of psychological well-being and general health (for example, Puerto Ricans). Overall, a meta-analysis indicates that Americans of Hispanic descent tend to have lower self-esteem than do Americans of European descent (Twenge and Crocker 1998). Native Americans also tend to be significantly lower in self-esteem than do Americans of European descent (Twenge and Crocker 1998). Of all the ethnic groups in the United States, Americans of Asian descent appear to be most vulnerable to low self-esteem. Studies examining the well-being of Asian Americans typically reveal low levels of self-esteem (Abe and Zane 1990; Kuo 1984; Marsella et al. 1975; Ying 1988). Meta-analysis confirms that Asian Americans' self-esteem is low compared to that of European Americans (Twenge and Crocker 1998).

Interpreting these differences in self-esteem among racial and ethnic groups can be a tricky business. Although the relatively high self-esteem of African Americans clearly flies in the face of social psychological theories predicting that members of devalued social groups will eventually internalize their devaluation, evidence of low self-esteem in Asian Americans does not necessarily provide evidence that supports these theories. First, it is not clear that Asians experience the same level or quality of devaluation as African Americans do. The history of Asian immigration differs in significant ways from that of African immigration, most notably in the degree to which immigration was, and continues to be, voluntary. Asian Americans are the targets of positive, as well as negative, stereotypes, and indeed they have been labeled the "model minority."

Second, Asian Americans may score low on self-esteem inventories for reasons that have little or nothing to do with their experience of prejudice or devaluation. Instead, low self-esteem among Asian Americans may reflect cultural differences in self-presentation styles or in the nature of the self-concept. Indeed, evidence is accumulating that the self-enhancing tendencies so common in the United States are absent in some Asian countries, such as Japan (Heine and Lehman 1997; Markus and Kitayama 1991). Some of this difference may reflect differences in self-presentational styles for completing self-report measures. In the United States, high scores on self-esteem measures may reflect the tendency of many European Americans to present themselves to others in a positive light (Baumeister, Tice, and Hutton 1989). In many Asian cultures, and in Japan particularly, low scores may reflect a norm of modesty in self-presentation (Abe and Zane 1990; Markus and Kitayama 1991; Sue and Sue 1987). In addition to these self-presentation effects, there may be more deep-seated cultural differences in the nature of the self-concept. Whereas most North Americans show a tendency to deflect or avoid self-criticism, Japanese are much more self-critical, focusing on their mistakes and failures (Kitayama 1997). Thus, the low self-esteem of Asian Americans may reflect cultural differences that are unrelated to experiences of prejudice, discrimination, and devaluation. Consistent with this view, research suggests that self-esteem is lower in Asian samples measured in their home culture than among Asian Americans (Twenge and Crocker 1998). Despite these cultural differences that may affect levels of self-esteem observed in Asian Americans, we argue that the experience of devaluation and discrimination contributes to low self-esteem among Asian Americans.

Do Asian Americans believe that they are devalued, disadvantaged, and targeted by prejudice and discrimination? At least among college students at predominantly white universities, the answer to this ques-

TABLE 12.1 *Perceived Disadvantage, Discrimination, and Self-Esteem Among Black, White, and Asian College Students*

| | Whites | Blacks | Asians |
|---|---|---|---|
| Disadvantage | $3.05_a$ (1.00) | $3.96_b$ (1.15) | $3.75_b$ (1.12) |
| Discrimination | $1.61_a$ (1.11) | $4.45_b$ (1.37) | $4.45_b$ (1.29) |
| Self-Esteem | $32.58_a$ (4.63) | $33.70_a$ (4.82) | $29.90_b$ (4.89) |

*Source:* Crocker et al. (1994).
*Notes:* Disadvantage and discrimination are measured on a scale ranging from 1 to 7, with higher numbers indicating more disadvantage and discrimination. Self-esteem is measured on a scale ranging from 10 to 40, with higher numbers indicating higher self-esteem. Standard deviations are in parentheses. Means not sharing a common subscript differ significantly at $p<.05$ or less.

tion appears to be an unequivocal yes. Jennifer Crocker and her colleagues (1994) conducted a study in which they assessed beliefs about disadvantage, discrimination, and psychological well-being in a sample of ninety-six European American, ninety-one African American, and ninety-six Asian American college students at a large, predominantly European American public university. Their measures included *perceived personal disadvantage* across six domains (the extent to which participants thought they were doing worse than others in quality of education, employment [including salaries and wages], recreation, political power and influence, housing, and quality of medical care); *perceived discrimination* (the frequency and extent to which participants personally experienced racial discrimination); and *self-esteem* as measured by the Rosenberg Self-esteem Inventory (Rosenberg 1965), a measure of global, personal self-esteem.

As the means in table 12.1 show, both African American and Asian American students indicated that they were more personally disadvantaged, and experienced more racial discrimination, than did European American students. Asian students indicated that they personally experienced nearly as much disadvantage, and the same amount of racial discrimination, as did African American students. Yet the self-esteem of these two groups differed markedly. Consistent with previous research, African American students' self-esteem was slightly higher than that of European American students, and Asian American students had lower self-esteem than both of these groups.

If the lower self-esteem of Asian American students is related to

TABLE 12.2 *Zero-Order Correlations Between Perceived Disadvantage, Discrimination, and Self-Esteem*

| | Whites | Blacks | Asians |
|---|---|---|---|
| Disadvantage | .02 | −.003 | −.43 |
| | n.s. | n.s. | .001 |
| Discrimination | −.10 | .20 | −.18 |
| | n.s. | .07 | .10 |

*Source:* Crocker et al. (1994).

their experience of devaluation, then we would expect perceived disadvantage and discrimination to be negatively correlated with self-esteem. If, however, Asian students' low self-esteem is a product of culture alone and has nothing to do with their experiences of disadvantage and discrimination, then the association between perceived disadvantage and discrimination and self-esteem should be nonsignificant. As the means in table 12.2 indicate, perceived disadvantage and discrimination are clearly associated with lower self-esteem among Asian American students, although the correlation is not statistically significant for perceived discrimination. This pattern of results stands in stark contrast to the data for African American students. For them, perceived disadvantage was completely unrelated to their level of self-esteem, and perceived discrimination was actually positively related to self-esteem. Although the correlation for perceived discrimination again did not reach statistical significance, it is significantly different from the negative correlation for Asian students.

Before we consider why this is so, it might be useful to consider whether this unexpected pattern of results replicates. Crocker and Coon (1997) conducted a conceptual replication of this study in a different sample of eighty-seven European American, eighty-four African American, and eighty-two Asian American students at a different predominantly white university in the Midwest. In this study, we attempted to query students about perceived disadvantage and discrimination in domains that had greater personal relevance to their lives. Consequently, students were asked to indicate the extent to which they personally felt *disadvantaged* relative to other students, and *discriminated against* in the areas of academic achievement, participation in campus organizations and clubs, participation in social activities, finances and financial opportunities, and treatment from others, including faculty, staff, and other students. Again, we included the Rosenberg (1965) measure of global self-esteem.

As the means in table 12.3 indicate, in this study African American students felt more disadvantaged than did European American or Asian

TABLE 12.3 *Perceived Disadvantage, Discrimination, and Self-Esteem Among Black, White, and Asian College Students*

| | Whites | Blacks | Asians |
|---|---|---|---|
| Disadvantage | $-.66_a$ (.71) | $-.33_b$ (.85) | $-.55_a$ (.76) |
| Discrimination | $0.85_a$ (.74) | $1.56_b$ (1.12) | $1.33_b$ (1.08) |
| Self-esteem | $3.40_a$ (.41) | $3.54_b$ (.36) | $3.12_c$ (.57) |

*Source:* Crocker and Coon (1997).
*Notes:* Disadvantage and discrimination are measured on a 7-point scale. (For disadvantage the scale ranged from −3 to +3; for discrimination the scale ranged from 0 to 6, with higher numbers indicating more disadvantage and discrimination.) Self-esteem is measured on a scale ranging from 1 to 4, with higher numbers indicating higher self-esteem. Standard deviations are in parentheses. Means not sharing a common subscript differ significantly at $p<.05$ or less, except for the disadvantage ratings of blacks versus Asians, $p<.10$.

American students, and the Asian and European American students did not differ from each other. However, Asian students perceived nearly as much discrimination as did African American students, and both groups perceived more discrimination than did European American students. The self-esteem of African American students was significantly higher than that of European American students, who in turn were higher in self-esteem than Asian American students. Given that this study involved a different sample of students, a different university, and a different set of questions about perceived disadvantage and discrimination, these results are remarkably consistent with our previous study. Both studies indicate that Asian students believe that they are discriminated against to nearly the same degree as African American students do. The Asian students have low self-esteem, but the African American students do not.

The correlations between perceived disadvantage, discrimination, and self-esteem, shown in table 12.4, are also similar in some respects to those obtained in our previous study. Again, the results indicate that perceived disadvantage and discrimination are harmful to the self-esteem of Asian students, but not to the self-esteem of African American students. The major difference between the two studies concerns the results for white students. Whereas in our previous study perceived disadvantage and discrimination were not significantly linked to the self-esteem of white students, in this study they were negatively related to self-esteem for white students. This difference for white students may be due to floor effects on perceived disadvantage and discrimination for white students in our first study. Alternatively, affirmative ac-

TABLE 12.4 *Zero-Order Correlations Between Perceived Disadvantage, Discrimination, and Self-Esteem*

| | Whites | Blacks | Asians |
|---|---|---|---|
| Disadvantage | −.27 | −.11 | −.50 |
| | .05 | n.s. | .001 |
| Discrimination | −.40 | −.07 | −.35 |
| | .001 | n.s. | .001 |

*Source:* Crocker and Coon (1997).

tion and the possibility of reverse discrimination are generally more salient issues at this second university. Overall, however, the results for Asian American and African American students are impressively consistent across the two studies. Both Asian and African American students perceived that they were disadvantaged and discriminated against more than European American students, but this perceived disadvantage and discrimination was negatively associated with self-esteem only for the Asian American students. These results provide a strong hint that the apparent imperviousness of African Americans' self-esteem to the experience of devaluation does not extend to Asian Americans.

It appears that the African American students who have participated in our research are somehow inoculated against the negative effects of perceived disadvantage and discrimination on self-esteem, but that the self-esteem of Asian students is vulnerable. We propose that this difference results, in part, from differences in the nature of self-esteem for African American and Asian American students. Specifically, we argue that the self-esteem of African American students is based on different contingencies than that of Asian American students.

## CONTINGENCIES OF SELF-ESTEEM AND VULNERABILITY TO STIGMA: REFLECTED APPRAISALS

The prediction that people who are members of stigmatized or devalued racial or ethnic groups suffer from low self-esteem derives, as noted previously, from the notion of the looking-glass self. In this view, self-esteem depends on a process of reflected appraisals: the individual's self-concept is based on his or her beliefs about the views that others have of the self. From this perspective, self-esteem is not only socially constructed but constructed in the same way for all people. In contrast, we argue that there are differences in the extent to which people derive their self-esteem from reflected appraisals. That is, there are differences in the degree to which people base their self-esteem on the real or imagined approval and regard of others. Only those stigmatized individuals who base their self-esteem on reflected appraisals, or on approval from others, will be vulnerable to low self-esteem.

We have investigated this issue in the context of the stigma associated with being, or feeling, fat (Quinn and Crocker 1998). In our sample of 244 female college students, 129 indicated that they felt fat by rating themselves somewhat or very overweight and indicating that they were more than five pounds overweight; 115 of the women, classified as normal weight, indicated that they did not feel fat by either of these criteria or indicated that they were overweight by less than five pounds. The women completed the Rosenberg Self-esteem Inventory as well as a measure of basing self-esteem on approval from others developed by Wolfe and her colleagues (1998). This measure includes items such as, "I can't respect myself if others don't respect me," and, "Being criticized by others really takes a toll on my self-respect." We conducted a set of regression analyses in which we predicted self-esteem from self-perceived weight and the extent to which the respondents' self-esteem was based on reflected appraisals. The analysis indicated that both feeling fat ($\beta = -.13$, $p < .05$) and basing self-esteem on reflected appraisals ($\beta = -.38$, $p < .0001$) were significantly related to low self-esteem among all women. Adding the interaction between self-perceived weight and reflected appraisals increased the variance explained ($p < .055$).

To examine the nature of this interaction, the relationship between basing self-esteem on reflected appraisals and self-esteem was calculated separately for women who felt thin and those who felt fat. Among women who felt thin, basing self-esteem on reflected appraisals was related to being low in self-esteem ($r = -.28$, $p < .01$), but this relationship was even stronger among women who felt fat ($r = -.46$, $p < .01$). Thus, basing self-esteem on reflected appraisals did appear to be a risk factor for low self-esteem for all of the women in our sample, but especially for those women who felt fat.

This research supports our view that people differ in the degree to which they base their self-esteem on approval from others, and that basing self-esteem on approval from others is a risk factor for low self-esteem among those who are stigmatized. To account for differences in the self-esteem of Asian and African American students, however, we would need to show that there are differences between these two groups in the degree to which they base their self-esteem on others' approval.

## RACE, ETHNICITY, AND BASING SELF-ESTEEM ON OTHERS' APPROVAL

Evidence of differences among ethnic groups in the degree to which they base self-esteem on others' approval was unexpectedly provided by a study of group or collective self-esteem (Crocker et al. 1994).[1] In that study, ninety-six European American, ninety-six Asian American, and ninety-one African American college students at a predominantly white university completed a measure of collective self-esteem developed by Luhtanen and Crocker (1992). Respondents were asked to consider their membership in social groups such as their racial, gender, or religious groups and to answer a series of questions. In some of those questions (the public subscale), respondents were asked to indicate how they thought other people valued their social groups; items on this subscale included ones such as, "In general, others respect the social groups that I am a member of." Other questions (the private subscale) were focused on respondents' private feelings about their social groups; this subscale included items such as, "In general, I'm glad to be a member of the social groups I belong to," and, "I feel good about the social groups I belong to."

The correlations between the private subscale and the public subscale differed enormously across the three groups of participants. For European American students, the correlation was moderate ($r = .43$, $p < .01$); for African Americans, it was essentially zero ($r = -.01$, n.s.), and for Asian students, it was very strong ($r = .68$, $p < .001$). These results suggest that Asian students may base their private views of themselves on how they think others view them, whereas African American students may compartmentalize and disentangle their views of themselves from how they think others view them.

To test this idea more directly, Wolfe and her colleagues (1998) measured the extent to which self-esteem was based on others' approval with a sample of eighty-seven European American, eighty-four African American, and eighty-two Asian American college students. Scores on the measure indicated that European American students were most likely to base their self-esteem on approval from others ($M = 4.78$a), followed by Asian American students ($M = 4.43$b), and African American students were least likely to base their self-esteem on approval from others ($M = 3.83$c, $F[2,250] = 21.04$, $p < .001$). These group differences in the extent to which self-esteem is based on others' approval have since been replicated in a number of college student samples.

This disengagement of self-esteem from the approval of others may be one factor that inoculates the self-esteem of African American students from the negative consequences of devaluation. Asian students, on the other hand, seem to have self-esteem that is more contingent on approval from others—this tendency may increase their vulnerability to low self-esteem. This assumes, of course, that basing self-esteem on others' approval is related to having low self-esteem among individuals who are devalued, disadvantaged, and discriminated against. Consistent with this assumption, basing self-esteem on others' approval was correlated with lower levels of self-esteem for African American ($r = -.41$, $p < .001$) and Asian American ($r = -.41$, $p < .001$) students, but not for European American students ($r = -.04$, n.s.). Thus, self-esteem that is contingent on others' approval appears to be a vulnerability factor for low self-esteem among both African American and Asian American students. The different levels of self-esteem that characterize these two groups is explained, at least in part, by the fact that African American students are less likely to base their self-esteem on what others think of them.

These findings are provocative, but they raise a number of questions to which we do not yet have the answers. One issue is whether African American and Asian American students who base their self-esteem on others' approval are vulnerable to low self-esteem because they are devalued in the context of a predominantly white university or because they are in the numerical minority in that context. At both universities that have served as sites for our research, African American students and Asian American students are very much in the minority. Consequently, these students are much more likely to find themselves in situations (classes, social events, residence halls) in which they are different from most other students. Perhaps this difference is sufficient to lead to low self-esteem in students who base their self-esteem on others' approval. We suspect that difference is not the whole story, however. Rather, we suspect that being different leads to low self-esteem in students who base their self-esteem on others' approval because that approval is not forthcoming. In other words, it is not merely being different, but being different and devalued, that leads to low self-esteem for these students.

Second, we do not know whether the finding that African American students are less likely to base their self-esteem on approval from others generalizes to other African Americans. Although we have replicated this finding many times among college students at predominantly white universities, we have done only one study on a community sample. In that study, 172 women ranging in age from eighteen to ninety-one were paid five dollars to complete a survey about weight and self-concept. Eighty-two of the women were European American, and ninety were African American. The sample was highly diverse in terms of education and income, with the African American women generally of lower socioeconomic status than the European American women. For example, 10 percent of the African American women in our sample, but only 2 percent of the European American women, had not graduated from high school. In this sample, we again found a highly significant difference between African American and European American women in the degree to which they reported basing their self-esteem on others' approval ($p < .0001$). Although more research on other non–college student samples is clearly needed, these data suggest that the tendency for African Americans to base their self-esteem on others' approval to a lesser extent than European Americans do may not be restricted to college students at predominantly white universities.

In addition, the results of this study of a community sample suggested again that among those who are devalued, basing self-esteem on others' approval is a risk factor for poor psychological well-being. All of the women in the sample were asked to classify themselves as overweight or normal weight. Consistent with previous research showing that different cultural standards of beauty and body shape prevail among white and black Americans (Cunningham et al. 1995; Hebl and Heatherton 1998), the African American women who classified themselves as normal weight were heavier than the European American women who classified themselves as normal weight. Controlling for differences in body size (body mass index), feeling fat was significantly related to symptoms of depression among the European American women, but not among the African American women. Furthermore, regression analyses showed that African American women's lower tendency to base their self-esteem on the approval of others accounted for their decreased vulnerability to symptoms of depression when they felt overweight. This research supports our view that disengaging self-esteem from the approval of generalized others protects the self-esteem of individuals who are stigmatized.

## INGROUP OR OUTGROUP REFLECTED APPRAISALS

One obvious question is whether African American students base their self-esteem on what other African Americans think of them, but not on what whites think of them. In other words, it is possible that it is only ingroup members whose approval forms a basis of self-esteem for African Americans. African American students who are aware of white racial prejudice may not consider whites' appraisals of them to be particularly valid. Consequently, they may base their self-esteem not on what whites think of them but on what other African Americans think of them. Attempts to address this issue empirically have provided little support for this view. When students were asked about the extent to which their self-esteem depended on the love of friends and family, African American students again scored significantly lower compared to European Americans (Wolfe et al. 1998, study 2). Furthermore, when a sample of African American students were asked specifically about the extent to which their self-esteem depended on what other members of their own racial group thought of them, scores were similar to those that we have obtained without this ingroup-specific wording. Thus, our findings generalize across the opinions of same-race and different-race others as bases of self-esteem.

## OTHER CONTINGENCIES OF SELF-ESTEEM

Thus far, our research on the link between experiences of being stigmatized or devalued and self-esteem has focused primarily on others' approval as a source of self-esteem. This focus follows quite naturally from social psychological theories arguing that self-esteem is derived from the regard we receive from others. Other research and theory in the literature on self-esteem have suggested that there are many other contingencies on which self-esteem may be based. These other contingencies of self-esteem may also contribute to the different degrees of vulnerability to prejudice and discrimination shown by Asian and African American students. Some of the most frequently mentioned or studied contingencies of worth are considered here.

### Competencies

One view of self-esteem is that it is derived from evaluations of one's specific competencies or abilities (Harter 1986, 1993; Hoge and McCarthy 1984; James 1890; Marsh 1986, 1995; Pelham 1995a, 1995b; Pelham and Swann 1989; Rosenberg 1979; Shavelson, Hubner, and Stanton 1976). A great deal of research has demonstrated that appraisals of one's competencies are related to global feelings of self-worth (Brown 1986; Harter 1986, 1993; Marsh 1986; Pelham 1995a, 1995b; Pelham and Swann 1989; Shavelson et al. 1976).

### Power

Power over oneself, one's environment, and others is a contingency of self-esteem for some individuals (Coopersmith 1967). Power refers to the ability one person has to influence another's ability to reach important goals. Power and competency as contingencies of self-esteem are often related. Being competent may contribute to one's ability to determine one's own outcomes, and having power may provide affordances for competencies. Nonetheless, these two bases of self-esteem are conceptually distinct (Veroff 1982). Power to determine one's own and others' outcomes may derive not only from one's competencies but also from the resources and position one holds (see, for example, Fiske 1993). Individuals may derive a sense of self-worth or self-regard from their ability to control others, determine others' fate, or manipulate others (Coopersmith 1967; Kaufman and Raphael 1991; Maslow 1968; McClelland 1975). Correlational research indicates that high self-esteem is associated with feelings of power and control over oneself and others (see, for example, Heaven 1986).

## Self-Reliance

Like power, the concept of self-reliance is related to competence. However, self-reliance as a source of self-esteem refers specifically to the ability to function independently and to care for oneself. Self-reliance is a widely held value in Western culture (see, for example, Markus and Kitayama 1991). Research suggests that self-reliance is a powerful predictor of self-esteem, even when its association with other, related constructs, such as internal locus of control, are controlled. For example, Mickelson, Crocker, and Kessler (1999) found in a representative sample of more than eight thousand Americans that John Henryism (James, Hartnett, and Kalsbeck 1983)—the belief that the demands of the environment can be met through hard work and determination independently of others' help—was a strong predictor of level of self-esteem even when the effect of ten other personality characteristics, including self-criticism, neuroticism, and internal locus of control, were controlled.

## Love from Family and Friends

Although research indicates that global self-esteem is correlated with how we believe a wide variety of others, even strangers, see us, the affection of close others may be particularly important to self-esteem. Attachment theory, for example, argues that central to views of the self in relationships is the "model of self" or the sense that one is the type of person whom others will love, respond to, and care for (Bowlby 1969). Research suggests that perceived approval or love from family members is related to global feelings of self-worth (Harter 1986). In addition, global self-esteem goes up when people fall in love (Aron, Paris, and Aron 1995)—presumably at least in part because falling in love is usually mutual and hence involves learning that the other loves the self.

## Physical Attractiveness

Ours is a culture in which people in general, and girls and women especially, are evaluated in large part on the basis of their physical appearance (for a review, see Fredrickson and Roberts 1997). One consequence of this objectification is that we learn to evaluate ourselves in terms of our physical appearance. Among adolescents, for example, self-evaluation of one's physical appearance is the strongest predictor of global self-esteem for both boys and girls—stronger than self-evaluations in other domains such as academics, behavioral conduct, athletics, and popularity (Harter 1986). The correlation of self-perceived physical attractiveness with global self-esteem is particularly powerful ($r = .80$) for adolescent girls (Harter 1986). A great deal of research suggests that this is a potentially important contingency of self-esteem across the life span (Pliner, Chaiken, and Flett 1990).

## Virtue

Another potential contingency of self-esteem that has received relatively little attention is one's moral adequacy or virtue (Benson and Lyons 1991; Coopersmith 1967; Steele 1988). As Coopersmith (1967) notes: "Persons who adhere to ethical and religious codes which they have accepted and internalized assume positive self-attitudes by successful fulfillment of these 'higher' goals. Their feelings of esteem may frequently be tinged with sentiments of righteousness, uprightness, and spiritual fulfillment" (41). Adherence to a moral code may lead to the judgment that one is a good, moral, and worthwhile person (Greenberg, Pyszczynski, and Solomon 1986; Solomon, Greenberg, and Pyszczynski 1991).

## God's Love

Religion is a powerful and important force in the lives of many Americans. National surveys of religious attitudes reveal that 90 percent of Americans say they believe in God or a supreme being, and two-thirds say that religion plays an important role in their lives (Gallup and Castelli 1989; Gallup and Bezilla 1992). Religion may have positive effects on self-esteem through the belief that one is loved, valued, and unique in the eyes of God (Benson and Spilka 1973; Spilka, Addison, and Rosensohn 1975; Spilka, Shaver, and Kirkpatrick 1985), especially for black Americans (Blaine and Crocker 1995).

## Social Identity

Social identities may also be a contingency of self-esteem. The importance of social group memberships to self-esteem has been articulated in social identity theory (Tajfel 1982; Tajfel and Turner 1979, 1986; Turner 1982). If one's social groups are valued and compare favorably to other

TABLE 12.5 *Mean Level of Endorsement of Contingencies of Self-Esteem Among White, Black, and Asian College Students*

| | Group | | | | Correlation with | |
|---|---|---|---|---|---|---|
| Contingencies of SE | White | Black | Asian | *F* | Average Level of Self-esteem | Standard Deviation of Self-esteem |
| Others' approval | | | | | −.44*** | .05 |
| Appearance | 4.64a | 3.76b | 4.70a | 9.00*** | −.31*** | .16** |
| God's love | 4.08a | 5.98b | 4.68c | 31.57**** | .12* | −.03 |
| Friends and family | 5.64a | 4.92b | 5.76a | 13.55**** | −.13* | .01 |
| Power | 4.00 | 3.79 | 4.37 | 5.75 | −.11 | .07 |
| Self-reliance | 4.76a | 4.74a | 5.20b | 4.57** | −.23*** | .12* |
| Social identity | 4.00a | 3.85a | 4.51b | 4.94** | −.13* | .05 |
| School competence | 5.72a | 5.22b | 5.72a | 6.03** | −.06 | .14* |
| Virtue | 4.51 | 4.20a | 4.90 | 2.39 | −.06 | .06 |

*Source:* Crocker (1998), unpublished data.
Means not sharing a common subscript differ at $p < .05$.

groups, social identity is positive and global self-esteem is enhanced (see also Rosenberg 1979). Aspects of collective identities, such as having positive regard for one's social groups, believing that others regard those groups favorably, and considering group memberships to be important to one's self-concept, are positively correlated with self-esteem (Luhtanen and Crocker 1992), particularly for individuals who are members of racial or ethnic minorities (Crocker et al. 1994).

We have developed a measure of the extent to which self-esteem is based on each of these contingencies. We hasten to note that the measure is still under development. Some of the scales have high internal consistency (God's love: $\alpha = .93$; appearance $\alpha = .81$). Other scales, however, have lower internal consistency (most alphas in the .60 to .80 range). Hence we consider the measure to be preliminary. Nonetheless, we administered this measure to a sample of 303 college students. The sample included vastly unequal numbers of black ($n = 34$), white ($n = 234$), and Asian ($n = 35$) students; although the study was not designed to assess race differences, analysis of race differences on the factors of the Contingencies of Self-esteem Scale did reveal a number of interesting effects, presented in table 12.5. First, compare African American students' contingencies of self-esteem to those of European American students. African American students were less likely to base self-esteem on appearance, school competence, or love of friends and family, and more likely to base self-esteem on God's love, than were European American students. These effect sizes are quite large—especially for the God's love scale, on which the difference is roughly two standard deviations—and hold for both males and females. However, African Americans students were no less likely to report that their self-esteem was based on power, self-reliance, virtue, or social identity than were European American students. Overall, then, it appears that African American students are not lower in their endorsement of all contingencies of self-esteem. Rather, they appear to have contingencies of self-esteem that are less external and dependent on others than do European American students.

Asian students, on the other hand, appear to have highly contingent self-esteem. Relative to European American students, their self-esteem is more contingent on God's love, self-reliance, social identity, and being virtuous. Asian American students did not differ from European American students in the degree to which their self-esteem is contingent on appearance, love of friends and family, power, or school competence. Most striking are the comparisons between black and Asian students. Asian students' self-esteem is significantly more contingent than that of black students for every contingency except God's love.

The students who completed the Contingencies of Self-esteem Scale also were asked to complete a measure of global feelings of worth each day for a two-week period. From these daily reports of self-esteem, we computed two measures: average level of self-esteem across the two-week period for each participant, and instability of self-esteem. Instability was assessed by calculating the standard deviation of self-esteem scores across the period of the study for each participant, following the research of Kernis, Grannemann, and Barclay (1989). The correlations of average level of self-esteem and instability of self-esteem with the contingencies of self-esteem for the whole sample are presented in table 12.5. Interestingly, God's love, the contingency of self-esteem most strongly endorsed by African American students, is the only contingency of self-esteem that is positively correlated with average level of self-esteem. In other words, the contingencies of self-esteem claimed by black students appear to be more conducive to high self-esteem than the contingencies of self-esteem claimed by white or Asian students. Thus, the tendency of African American students to have less contingent self-esteem, and particularly self-esteem that is less contingent on external and social sources and more contingent on God's love, may explain why African Americans, as a group, do not have lower self-esteem than European Americans, despite their devalued and disadvantaged status (Crocker and Blanton, 1999; Crocker and Quinn 1998). The tendency of Asian students to have highly contingent self-esteem, especially when compared to African American students, may help explain why their self-esteem is more vulnerable in the face of devaluation and discrimination.

Given these differences in contingencies of worth for these students, it is perhaps not surprising that African American students had not only higher self-esteem but more stable self-esteem (average standard deviation = .29a) than did students of European (average standard deviation = .40b) or Asian (average standard deviation = .44b) descent. In light of recent evidence that instability of self-esteem is a risk factor for the onset of depression (Roberts and Gotlib 1997), these differences in contingencies of worth may have implications for the mental health risks of these students.

## ORIGINS OF GROUP DIFFERENCES IN CONTINGENCIES OF SELF-ESTEEM

Why do African Americans, European Americans, and Asian Americans differ in their contingencies of self-esteem? We believe that these differences are related to, and a consequence of, the cultural experiences of these groups—experiences that are fundamentally different. Because their contingencies of self-esteem are dramatically different from the other two groups, we consider first the experience of African Americans.

### African Americans' Cultural Experience and Contingencies of Worth

Since the founding of our nation, African Americans have been devalued and dehumanized. As a group, they have experienced 350 years of slavery, 100 years of legal segregation, and 30 to 40 years of equality under the law (for a discussion, see Sears 1998). Even in the years since the civil rights movement, which transformed the experiences of black Americans in many ways, they continue to be confronted with institutional racism, prejudice, and discrimination (Dovidio and Gaertner 1998; Jones 1998; Sears 1998). Yet, as we have noted, this prolonged experience of devaluation and dehumanization has not resulted in low self-esteem in the majority of African Americans.

It seems likely that the survival and psychological well-being of African Americans have necessitated some degree of adaptation to the circumstances of their life in the United States (see Jones 1998). One aspect of this adaptation, we suspect, involves the contingencies on which self-esteem is based. For example, in a culture in which standards of beauty are based on European American features, particularly the fair coloring and features of northern Europeans, it may be quite adaptive for African Americans not to base their self-esteem on their physical appearance as much as European Americans do. It also seems adaptive for African Americans to disengage their self-esteem from what others in general, and white Americans in particular, think of them. African Americans are well aware of the history of oppression and discrimination against their group. Basing self-esteem on reflected appraisals, as we have argued, is perilous for members of a group that is devalued and dehumanized in American culture. Consequently, cultural values and practices in the African American community may encourage other bases of self-esteem (see, for example, Cross 1971, 1991; Du Bois 1903). Consistent with this view, research suggests that African American parents often teach their children that others are prejudiced against them, and that prejudice should not affect one's self-worth (Phinney and Chavira 1995). Thus, race differences in contingencies of worth may result, in part, from socialization practices that help children cope with prejudice. If this practice reflects a desire to protect children and adults from the consequences of devaluation for self-esteem, it should be particularly true among African Americans who have high levels of group consciousness and hold their group in high regard. Such people are more aware of racism and discrimination (Crocker et al., in press) and are more likely to view the disadvantaged status of black Americans as illegitimate (Gurin and Epps 1975). Some evidence from our research supports this view. Specifically, Wolfe and her colleagues (1998) found that African American students who were higher in private collective self-esteem (that is, who had more regard for their social groups) were less likely to base their self-esteem on reflected appraisals ($r = -.23$, $p < .05$). For whites, private collective self-esteem was unrelated to basing self-esteem on reflected appraisals ($r = .07$, n.s.). In other words, African Americans with a positive group identity were less likely to base their self-esteem on what others thought of them.

A second cultural influence on contingencies of self-esteem for many black Americans is religion and spirituality. African Americans have long been high in intrinsic religiousness (far higher than white Americans), and this emphasis on religion continues into the present (Beeghley, VanVelsor, and Block 1981; Johnson, Matre, and Armbrecht 1991; Taylor et al. 1996). The importance placed on religion by African Americans provides an alternative, and probably more reliable, source of self-worth (Blaine and Crocker 1995). Particularly in religions that emphasize that God loves all people, including those who are despised and rejected by others, faith in God's love may provide an important source of self-esteem. As we have noted, African American college students score nearly two standard deviations higher than white students in basing self-esteem on God's love.

One might suspect that basing self-esteem on God's love is simply another form of basing self-esteem on reflected appraisals—in this case, reflected appraisals from God. If this were true, we would expect to find that God's love and reflected appraisals are positively correlated as bases of self-esteem. Interestingly, among white students, God's love and reflected appraisals are positively correlated ($r = .14$, $p < .05$) bases of self-esteem. Among Asian students, however, this correlation is negative and nonsignificant ($r = -.11$), and among African American students, it is negative and significant ($r = -.33$, $p < .05$). This pattern of results suggests that God's love is similar to other reflected appraisals as a source of self-esteem. Among African Americans, however, God's love may provide an alternative to the approval of others as a source of self-esteem.

## Asian Americans' Cultural Experience and Contingencies of Worth

We suspect that most of the Asian and Asian American students in our sample were not socialized to cope with discrimination by disengaging self-esteem from the approval of others, for two reasons. First, Markus and Kitayama (1991) suggest that there are distinctly different construals and goals with respect to the self among individuals from highly individualistic cultures like the United States and individuals from collectivist cultures such as Japan, China, and many other Asian countries. In the United States, the major goals for the self are to be unique, to stand out, and, if possible, to be superior to others. In collectivist cultures, in which the self is more interdependent with others, the major goals for the self are to fit in and to be harmonious with others. Disengaging self-esteem from the approval of others as a means of coping with devaluation may be more difficult, and more incongruous with the major goals of the self, for individuals from Asian and other collectivist countries. Second, as we noted, disengaging self-esteem from the approval of others as a means of coping with devaluation and discrimination may require group consciousness, or an awareness that one's racial or ethnic group is unfairly disadvantaged and discriminated against. This awareness may be far more developed in African Americans, particularly since the civil rights and black power movements of the 1950s and 1960s, than in Asian and Asian American students.

## ARE SOCIAL PSYCHOLOGICAL THEORIES OF THE SELF WRONG?

Social psychological theory has long assumed that stigmatization and devaluation inevitably take a toll on the self-esteem of those who are devalued. Yet it is now clear that the effects of devaluation and stigmatization on self-esteem are different for different racial and ethnic groups, and for different individuals within those groups. We argue that this is true, in part, because individuals and groups vary in the sources or contingencies of their self-esteem. Although social psychological theory has emphasized the approval and regard of others as a major source of self-esteem, there is wide variation among people in the extent to which others' approval, and especially the approval of unknown, nonspecific, or generalized others, provides a source of self-esteem.

Does this mean that social psychological theories of the self, and particularly the view that self-esteem is based on reflected appraisals, are wrong? Although calling these theories wrong would be too strong, we believe that the reflected appraisals view of the development of the self-concept is more true of some people than of others, and more true of some cultural groups than of others. This view suggests a more complex process by which the self is socially constructed than that suggested by most social psychological theory. The notions that there are many contingencies on which self-esteem may be based, and that people and groups of people differ in the contingencies on which they base their self-esteem as a function of their social context, social position, and social experiences, suggest that a more complex and nuanced concept of the nature of self-esteem is required.

For those who base self-esteem on the approval and regard of generalized others, the experience of devaluation does indeed appear to be linked to low self-esteem. Yet some individuals, and some social groups, particularly African American students at predominantly white universities, seem to have disengaged their self-esteem from the approval of generalized others. All in all, this disengagement may represent an adaptive response to the predicament of being devalued, by enabling stigmatized individuals to maintain a sense of their personal worth in the face of pervasive devaluation. Furthermore, African American students, as a group, seem to have more internal and more stable sources of self-esteem compared with European American students, but especially compared with Asian students. This pattern of more internal and less contingent sources of self-esteem seems closest to the cultural ideal in the United States of self-esteem that is separate and distinct from the approval of others. Yet it may have costs associated with it. Students whose self-esteem is contingent on the approval of their peers, their professors, and others in their environment may be particularly responsive to the socializing experiences of higher education—learning and internalizing the values, norms, and standards of academia. Students whose self-esteem is disengaged from this approval may be less attuned to or may less easily internalize these academic values and norms, and they may pay the price in terms of not becoming an "insider" and suffering from the feeling of not belonging. On the other hand, students whose self-esteem is disengaged from the approval of generalized others may be more willing to question and challenge the ingrained assumptions of their environment and so may be catalysts for changing that environment.

In contrast to the disengagement of self-esteem from others' approval shown by many of the African American students in our research, Asian and Asian American students do not seem to differ from European American students in the degree to which their self-esteem is based on others' approval. The consequence for these students is a vulnerability to low self-esteem in response to the devaluation and discrimination these students experience. Indeed, Asian and Asian American students consistently are more depressed and hopeless, as well as lower in self-esteem, than any other ethnic group we have studied. Although depression is a heavy price to pay, it may have advantages for these students. Those who base their self-esteem on others' approval may more quickly assimilate into the academic scene, and the culture more generally, because they are attuned to the values and norms of the dominant group.

It is important to keep in mind that the group differences we have observed in contingencies of self-esteem do not represent innate or inherent, or necessarily stable, characteristics of these groups. Rather, they represent a blending of cultural beliefs, values, and practices with the particular circumstances of social devaluation, and the meaning that devaluation has for individuals and in the wider social context.

## NOTE

1. The data reported here are based on data reported in Crocker et al. (1994). At the time that article was written, our sample included only thirty-five Asian and Asian American students. Subsequently, we collected data on an additional sixty-one Asian and Asian American students. The means and correlations reported here are identical for the European American and African American students but differ slightly for Asian and Asian American students because of the inclusion of these additional data.

# REFERENCES

Abe, Jennifer S., and Zane, Nolan W. S. (1990). Psychological maladjustment among Asian and white American college students: Controlling for confounds. *Journal of Counseling Psychology, 37,* 437–44.
Allport, Gordon W. (1979). *The nature of prejudice.* New York: Doubleday/Anchor Books. (Originally published in 1954)
Aron, Arthur, Paris, Meg, and Aron, Elaine N. (1995). Falling in love: Prospective studies of self-concept change. *Journal of Personality and Social Psychology, 69,* 1102–12.
Banks, William C. (1976). White preference in blacks: A paradigm in search of a phenomenon. *Psychological Bulletin, 83,* 179–86.
Baumeister, Roy F., Tice, Diane M., and Hutton, Debra G. (1989). Self-presentational motivations and personality differences in self-esteem. *Journal of Personality, 57,* 547–79.
Beeghley, L. Van Velsor, E., and Block, E. W. (1991). The correlates of religiosity among black and white Americans. *Sociological Quarterly, 20,* 49–62.
Benson, Jann, and Lyons, Dan. (1991). *Strutting and fretting: Standards for self-esteem.* Niwot, Colo.: University Press of Colorado.
Benson, Peter, and Spilka, Bernard. (1973). God image as a function of self-esteem and locus of control. *Journal for the Scientific Study of Religion, 12,* 297–310.
Blaine, Bruce, and Crocker, Jennifer. (1995). Religiousness, race, and psychological well-being: Exploring social psychological mediators. *Personality and Social Psychology Bulletin, 21,* 1031–41.
Bowlby, John. (1969). *Attachment and loss,* vol. 1, *Attachment.* New York: Basic Books.
Brand, Elaine S., Ruiz, Rene A., and Padilla, Amado M. (1974). Ethnic identification and preference: A review. *Psychological Bulletin, 81,* 860–90.
Brockner, Joel. (1984). Low self-esteem and behavioral plasticity: Some implications for personality and social psychology. In Ladd Wheeler (Ed.), *Review of personality and social psychology* (vol. 4, pp. 237–71). Beverly Hills, Calif.: Sage.
Brown, Jonathan D. (1986). Evaluations of self and others: Self-enhancement biases in social judgments. *Social Cognition, 4,* 353–76.
Cartwright, Dorwin. (1950). Emotional dimensions of group life. In M. L. Raymert (Ed.), *Feelings and emotions* (pp. 439–47). New York: McGraw-Hill.
Clark, Kenneth B., and Clarke, Mamie P. (1939). The development of consciousness of self and the emergence of racial identification of Negro schoolchildren. *Journal of Social Psychology, 10,* 591–99.
Cooley, Charles H. (1956). *Human nature and the social order.* New York: Schocken.
Coopersmith, Stanley. (1967). *The antecedents of self-esteem.* San Francisco: W. H. Freeman.
Crocker, Jennifer, and Blanton, Hart. (1999). Social inequality and self-esteem: The moderating effects of social comparison, legitimacy, and contingencies of self-esteem. In Tom R. Tyler, Roderick Kramer, and Oliver John (Eds.), *The psychology of social self* (pp. 117–91). Mahwah, N.J.: Lawrence Erlbaum.
Crocker, Jennifer, and Coon, Heather. (1997). Perceived disadvantage, discrimination, and self-esteem among white, black, and Asian college students. Unpublished data, University of Michigan.

Crocker, Jennifer, Luhtanen, Riia K., Blaine, Bruce, and Broadnax, Stephanie. (1994). Collective self-esteem and psychological well-being among black, white, and Asian college students. *Personality and Social Psychology Bulletin, 20,* 503–13.

Crocker, Jennifer, Luhtanen, Riia K., Broadnax, Stephanie, and Blaine, Bruce. (in press). Belief in U.S. government conspiracies against blacks: Powerlessness or system blame? *Personality and Social Psychology Bulletin.*

Crocker, Jennifer, and Major, Brenda. (1989). Social stigma and self-esteem: The self-protective properties of stigma. *Psychological Review, 96,* 608–30.

Crocker, Jennifer, Major, Brenda, and Steele, Claude M. (1998). Social stigma. In Daniel Gilbert, Susan T. Fiske, and Gardner Lindzey (Eds.), *Handbook of social psychology* (4th ed., pp. 504–53). New York: McGraw-Hill.

Crocker, Jennifer, and Quinn, Diane M. (1998). Racism and self-esteem. In Jennifer Eberhart and Susan T. Fiske (Eds.), *Confronting racism: The problem and the response* (pp. 169–87). Thousand Oaks, Cailf.: Sage Publications.

Cross, William E. (1971). *The Negro to black conversion experience.* Brooklyn: The East.

———. (1991). *Shades of black: Diversity in African American identity.* Philadelphia: Temple University Press.

Cunningham, Michael R., Roberts, Alan, Barbee, Anita P., Druen, Perri B., and Wu, Cheng-Huan. (1995). Their ideas of beauty are on the whole the same as ours: Consistency and variability in the cross-cultural perception of female physical attractiveness. *Journal of Personality and Social Psychology, 68,* 261–79.

Diener, Ed. (1984). Subjective well-being. *Psychological Bulletin, 95,* 542–75.

Dovidio, John F., and Gaertner, Samuel. (1998). On the nature of contemporary prejudice: The causes, consequences, and challenges of aversive racism. In Jennifer Eberhart and Susan T. Fiske (Eds.), *Confronting racism: The problem and the response* (pp. 3–32). Thousand Oaks, Calif.: Sage Publications.

Du Bois, William Edward Burghardt. (1903). *The souls of black folk: Essays and sketches.* 3rd ed. Chicago: McClurg and Co.

Erikson, Erik. (1956). The problem of ego-identity. *Journal of the American Psychoanalytic Association,* 4, 56–121.

Fiske, Susan T. (1993). Controlling other people: The impact of power on stereotyping. *American Psychologist, 48,* 621–28.

Fredrickson, Barbara L., and Roberts, Tomi Ann. (1997). Objectification theory: Toward understanding women's lived experiences and mental health risks. *Psychology of Women Quarterly, 21,* 173–206.

Gallup, George H., Jr., and Bezilla, Robert. (1992). *The religious life of young Americans: A compendium of surveys on the spiritual beliefs and practices of teenagers and young adults.* Princeton, N.J.: George H. Gallup International Institute.

Gallup, George H., Jr., and Castelli, Jim. (1989). *The people's religion: American faith in the Nineties.* New York: Macmillan.

Goffman, Erving. (1963). *Stigma: Notes on the management of a spoiled identity.* New York: Simon & Schuster.

Greenberg, Jeff, Pyszczynski, Tom, and Solomon, Sheldon. (1986). The causes and consequences of a need for self-esteem: A terror management theory. In Roy F. Baumeister (Ed.), *Public self and private self* (pp. 189–207). New York: Springer-Verlag.

Gurin, Patricia, and Epps, Edgar (1975). *Black consciousness, identity, and achievement.* New York: Wiley.

Harter, Susan. (1986). Processes underlying the construction, maintenance, and enhancement of the self-concept in children. In Jerry Suls and Anthony G. Greenwald (Eds.), *Psychological perspectives on the self* (vol. 3, pp. 137–81). Hillsdale, N.J.: Erlbaum.

———. (1993). Causes and consequences of low self-esteem in children and adolescents. In Roy G. Baumeister (Ed.), *Self-esteem: The puzzle of low self-regard* (pp. 87–116). New York: Plenum.

Heaven, Patrick C. (1986). Authoritarianism, directiveness, and self-esteem revisited: A cross-cultural analysis. *Personality and Individual Differences, 7,* 225–28.

Hebl, Michelle R., and Heatherton, Todd F. (1998). The stigma of obesity in women: The difference is black and white. *Personality and Social Psychology Bulletin, 24,* 417–26.

Heine, Steven, and Lehman, Darrin. (1997). The cultural construction of self-enhancement: An examination of group-serving biases. *Journal of Personality and Social Psychology, 72,* 1268–83.

Hoge, Dean R., and McCarthy, John D. (1984). Influence of individual and group identity salience in the global self-esteem of youth. *Journal of Personality and Social Psychology, 47,* 403–14.

James, Sherman A., Hartnett, Sue A., and Kalsbeck, William D. (1983). John Henryism and blood pressure differences among black men. *Journal of Behavioral Medicine,* 6, 259–78.

James, William. (1890). *The principles of psychology.* Vol. 1. Cambridge: Harvard University Press.

Jensen, Gary F., White, C. S., and Galliher, James M. (1982). Ethnic status and adolescent self-evaluation: An extension of research on minority self-esteem. *Social Problems, 30,* 226–39.

Johnson, G. D., Matre, M., and Armbrecht, G. (1991). Race and religiosity: An empirical evaluation of a causal model. *Review of Religious Research, 32,* 252–66.

Jones, Edward E., Farina, Amerigo, Hastorf, Al H., Markus, Hazel, Miller, Dale T., and Scott, Robert A. (1984). *Social stigma: The psychology of marked relationships.* New York: Freeman.

Jones, James M. (1998). The essential power of racism. In Jennifer Eberhart and Susan T. Fiske (Eds.), *Racism: The problem and the response* (pp. 280–94). Thousand Oaks, Calif.: Sage Publications.

Kaufman, Gershen, and Raphael, Lev. (1991). *Dynamics of power: Fighting shame and building self-esteem.* Rochester, Vt.: Schenkman.

Kernis, Michael H., Grannemann, Bruce D., and Barclay, Lynda C. (1989). Stability and level of self-esteem as predictors of anger arousal and hostility. *Journal of Personality and Social Psychology, 56,* 1013–23.

Kitayama, Shinobu. (1997). Self-criticism in Japan: Critical self-appraisal or modest self-presentation? Unpublished paper, Kyoto University.

Kuo, Wen H. (1984). Prevalence of depression among Asian Americans. *Journal of Nervous and Mental Disease, 172,* 449–57.

Linn, Margaret W., Hunter, Kathleen, and Perry, Priscilla R. (1979). Differences by sex and ethnicity in the psychosocial adjustment of the elderly. *Journal of Health and Social Behavior, 20,* 273–81.

Luhtanen, Riia K., and Crocker, Jennifer. (1992). A collective self-esteem scale: Self-evaluation of one's social identity. *Personality and Social Psychology Bulletin, 18,* 302–18.

Markus, Hazel R., and Kitayama, Shinobu. (1991). Culture and the self: Implications for cognition, emotion, and motivation. *Psychological Review, 98,* 224–53.
Marsella, Anthony J., Sanborn, K. O., Kameoka, Velma, Shizuru, Lanette S., and Brennan, J. (1975). Cross-validation of self-report measures of depression among normal populations of Japanese, Chinese, and Caucasian ancestry. *Journal of Clinical Psychology, 31,* 281–87.
Marsh, Herbert W. (1986). Global self-esteem: Its relation to specific facets of the self-concept and their importance. *Journal of Personality and Social Psychology, 51,* 1224–36.
———. (1995). A Jamesian model of self-investment and self-esteem: Comment on Pelham. *Journal of Personality and Social Psychology, 69,* 1151–60.
Maslow, Abraham H. (1968). *Motivation and personality.* New York: Harper and Row.
McClelland, David C. (1975). *Power: The inner experience.* New York: Wiley.
Mead, George Herbert. (1934). *Mind, self, and society.* Chicago: University of Chicago Press.
Mickelson, Kristin, Crocker, Jennifer, and Kessler, Ronald. (1999). Personality correlates of self-esteem: Attachment style differences. Unpublished data, University of Michigan.
Myers, David G., and Diener, Ed. (1995). Who is happy? *Psychological Science, 6,* 10–19.
Pelham, Brett W. (1995a). Self-investment and self-esteem: Evidence for a Jamesian model of self-worth. *Journal of Personality and Social Psychology, 69,* 1141–50.
———. (1995b). Further evidence for a Jamesian model of self-worth: Reply to Marsh. *Journal of Personality and Social Psychology, 69,* 1161–65.
Pelham, Brett W., and Swann, Jr., William B. (1989). From self-conceptions to self-worth: On the sources and structure of global self-esteem. *Journal of Personality and Social Psychology, 57,* 672–80.
Phinney, Jean S., and Chavira, Victor. (1995). Parental ethnic socialization and adolescent coping with problems related to ethnicity. *Journal of Research on Adolescents, 5,* 31–53.
Pliner, Patricia, Chaiken, Shelley, and Flett, Gordon L. (1990). Gender differences in concern with body weight and physical appearance over the life span. *Personality and Social Psychology Bulletin, 16,* 263–73.
Porter, Judith R., and Washington, Robert E. (1979). Black identity and self-esteem: A review of studies of black self-concept, 1968–1978. *Annual Review of Sociology, 5,* 53–74.
Pyszczynski, Tom, and Greenberg, Jeff. (1987). Self-regulatory perseveration and the depressive self-focusing style: A self-awareness theory of reactive depression. *Psychological Bulletin, 102,* 122–38.
Quinn, Diane M., and Crocker, Jennifer. (1998). Vulnerability to the affective consequences of the stigma of overweight. In Janet Swim and Charles Stangor (Eds.), *Social stigma: The target's perspective* (pp. 125–43). San Diego: Academic Press.
Roberts, John, and Gotlib, Ian. (1997). Temporal variability in global self-esteem and specific self-evaluation as prospective predictors of emotional distress: Specificity in predictors and outcome. *Journal of Abnormal Psychology, 106,* 521–29.
Roberts, Robert E. (1980). Prevalence of psychological distress among Mexican Americans. *Journal of Health and Social Behavior, 21,* 134–45.

Rogler, Lloyd Henry, Malgady, Robert G., and Rodriguez, Orlando. (1989). *Latin Americans and mental health: A framework for research*. Malabar, Fla.: Drieger.
Rosenberg, Morris. (1965). *Society and the adolescent self-image*. Princeton, N.J.: Princeton University Press.
———. (1979). *Conceiving the self*. New York: Basic Books.
Sears, David O. (1998). Racism and politics in the United States. In Jennifer Eberhart and Susan T. Fiske (Eds.), *Racism: The problem and the response* (pp. 76–100). Thousand Oaks, Calif.: Sage Publications.
Shavelson, Richard J., Hubner, Judith J., and Stanton, George C. (1976). Self-concept: Validation of construct interpretation. *Review of Educational Research, 46,* 407–41.
Sidanius, James, and Pratto, Felicia. (1993). The dynamics of social dominance and the inevitability of oppression. In Paul M. Sniderman and Phillip E. Tetlock (Eds.), *Prejudice, politics, and race in America today* (pp. 173–211). Stanford, Calif.: Stanford University Press.
Solomon, Sheldon, Greenberg, Jeff, and Pyszczynski, Tom. (1991). A terror management theory of social behavior: The psychological functions of self-esteem and cultural worldviews. In Mark P. Zanna (Ed.), *Advances in experimental social psychology* (vol. 24, pp. 91–159). San Diego: Academic Press.
Spilka, Bernard, Addison, J., and Rosensohn, M. (1975). Parents, self, and God: A factor-analytic approach. *Review of Religious Research, 6,* 28–36.
Spilka, Bernard, Shaver, Phillip, and Kirkpatrick, Lee A. (1985). A general attribution theory for the psychology of religion. *Journal for the Scientific Study of Religion, 24,* 1–20.
Steele, Claude M. (1988). The psychology of self-affirmation: Sustaining the integrity of the self. In Leonard Berkowitz (Ed.), *Advances in experimental social psychology* (vol. 21, pp. 261–302). New York: Academic Press.
Sue, David, and Sue, Stanley. (1987). Cultural factors in the clinical assessment of Asian Americans. *Journal of Consulting and Clinical Psychology, 55,* 479–87.
Tajfel, Henri. (1982). Social psychology of intergroup relations. *Annual Review of Psychology,* 33, 1–59.
Tajfel, Henri, and Turner, John C. (1979). An integrative theory of intergroup conflict. In Stephen Worchel and William G. Austin (Eds.), *Psychology of intergroup relations* (1st ed., pp. 33–48). Chicago: Nelson-Hall.
———. (1986). The social identity theory of intergroup behavior. In William G. Austin and Stephen Worchel (Eds.), *The social psychology of intergroup relations* (2nd ed., pp. 7–24). Monterey, Calif.: Brooks/Cole.
Taylor, Robert J., Chatters, Linda M., Jayakody, Rukmali, and Levin, Jeffrey S. (1996). Black and white differences in religious participation: A multisample comparison. *Journal for the Scientific Study of Religion, 35,* 403–10.
Tennen, Howard, and Herzberger, Sharon. (1987). Depression, self-esteem, and the absence of self-protective attributional biases. *Journal of Personality and Social Psychology, 52,* 72–80.
Turner, John C. (1982). Towards a cognitive redefinition of the social group. In Henri Tajfel (Ed.), *Social identity and intergroup relations* (pp. 15–40). Cambridge: Cambridge University Press.
Twenge, Jean, and Crocker, Jennifer. (1998). Race and ethnicity differences in self-esteem: A meta-analysis. Manuscript in preparation, University of Michigan.
Veroff, Joseph. (1982). Assertive motivations: Achievement versus power. In

Abigail Stewart (Ed.), *Motivation and society* (pp. 99–132). San Francisco: Jossey-Bass.

Wolfe, Connie T., Crocker, Jennifer, Coon, Heather, and Luhtanen, Riia. (1998). Basing self-esteem on approval from others: Measurement and data. Manuscript in preparation, University of Michigan.

Wylie, Ruth. (1979). *The self-concept: Theory and research on selected topics.* 2nd ed., vol. 2. Lincoln: University of Nebraska Press.

Ying, Yu-Wen. (1988). Depressive symptomatology among Chinese Americans as measured by the CES-D. *Journal of Clinical Psychology, 44,* 739–46.

# 13

# THE PSYCHOLOGICAL PREDICAMENT OF WOMEN ON WELFARE

*Claude Steele and David A. Sherman*

In reading William Julius Wilson's latest book on urban poverty, *When Work Disappears* (1996), a statement embedded passingly in the introduction captured our attention. In reviewing the contributions of various social sciences to issues of poverty in America, he described social psychology as "a set of factors generally absent from the current debate" (xiv). Wilson (1987, 1996) has long argued that large-scale economic and structural factors, such as the global economy, the drop in industrial jobs, the suburbanization of jobs, and migration patterns, bear most of the responsibility for continuing urban poverty. But he also stresses that other factors are involved, especially cultural and social psychological processes that determine behavioral reactions to the conditions of poverty. It is here, in this last respect, that Wilson feels the absence of modern social psychology. Clearly this level of analysis is relevant. Yet just as clearly, we had to agree with Wilson: social psychology is not much present in this debate.

Our central purpose in this chapter is to take up Wilson's challenge by exploring the social psychology of the welfare experience, in particular the psychological predicament of homeless mothers on welfare, and to describe preliminary research that suggests an analysis of the welfare experience. But we have a secondary purpose as well: to explore the utility of a more context-oriented mode of social psychological analysis—an approach that harks back, of course, to the Lewinian origins of the field (Lewin 1943, 1951).

Central to both of these aims is a concept we call *afforded psychologies.* This term refers to a familiar idea: the "life-space" contexts of people's lives—their socioeconomic position in society, their position in a family, their group identities, the cultures they are immersed in, the status they enjoy, the stigmas they endure, and the opportunities and resources they possess—have a constitutive influence on their psyches that "affords" them some psychologies more than others. That is, one's location in society and in a culture makes a significant contribution to the content, organization, and functioning of one's psychological life.

This may seem to be an obvious point. But in social psychology we have leaned toward explanations of diverse social psychological phenomena in terms of common, generalizable processes (see Shweder 1990). In this pursuit, psychologists have increasingly deemphasized the role of context in mediating social psychological phenomena (Fiske et al. 1998). Although this kind of explanation is an important goal of our science, it may cause us to underemphasize something fundamental about psychological life: because of life context differences between people, not all features of human psychology—particular traits, states, and processes—are equally accessible to all people. For example, when opportunity, support, and encouragement for school are not there for a person, it can be more difficult for that person to sustain a strong academic motivation. Thus, academic identification may not be as accessible to people facing this predicament (Steele 1997). Thinking about human psychology in terms of relatively decontextualized and abstract processes, traits, and states can give the impression that the particular psychological characteristics of people—for example, their attributional styles, their motivations, their cognitive skills, and their emotional tendencies—are equally probable in almost any life context. As something that shapes the development and ongoing transactions of the individual, life context predisposes and enables the development of some psychological characteristics and tendencies more than others; this is what is meant by "afforded psychologies."

However, we are not arguing that the psyche-shaping influence of life context is a rigidly deterministic influence that irrevocably fosters particular characteristics. The term "afforded" was chosen to convey a more indirect influence—one in which life context comprises the conditions of life that must be transacted with, but does not directly determine which psychological characteristics will evolve in those transactions. Life context predisposes, constrains, prompts, punishes, facilitates, frustrates, and scaffolds, but in our reasoning it does not directly determine.

This idea of afforded psychologies helps to clarify several issues related to the psychological predicament of the homeless mothers we have studied. First, it makes it clear that a disadvantaged background does not, of necessity, cause a correspondingly negative internal psyche. In the role of observer, researchers and theorists may too easily assume that negative life outcomes reflect negative internal psychologies—a "poverty personality" of low self-esteem, low self-efficacy, poor future orientation, and so on (see, for example, Mead 1994; Murray 1996). But quite the reverse can be true. In the course of adapting to disadvantages, a person may develop strengths that would not be well afforded by a more advantaged background (Taylor, Wood, and Lichtman 1983). This is not an argument to proliferate disadvantage. It is simply to point out an important reality implied by the afforded psychologies idea: psychological strengths and weaknesses can be afforded by many environments.

Second, it helps to explain how the psychologies of those on welfare can have considerable similarity to the psychologies of people from more advantaged segments of the population—a point developed by Cook and Curtin (1987). Despite profound differences in the socioeconomic and even subcultural aspects of these two life contexts, there are important similarities between them as well. Both the wealthy and the poor in this society share an overarching American culture and history, a national identity, and exposure to many of the same media outlets. This similarity of life context surely affords similarity in psychology.

Third, the concept of afforded psychologies offers at least one definition of the "cultural divide" that is the focus of this book. A cultural divide can be thought of as a boundary in society that separates communities whose socioeconomic structures, opportunities for success, conventions, styles, and norms are so different that they have substantially different psychologies. Another way of saying this is that when groups differ enough in the nature of their sociocultural context as to cause meaningful differences in their psychologies, they are divided by a "cultural divide." Obviously more aspects of a particular context than culture alone could contribute to such a divide. Social structure, race, ethnicity, and religion can have this effect as well. But we endorse the term "cultural divide" as a reasonable, if not completely precise, term for designating a group divide between differentially afforded psychologies.

This conception of a cultural divide is at the center of our analysis. We reason that the predicament faced by women on welfare in contrast to the life context of people in the economically secure middle class constitutes a structural and cultural divide—a difference in life circumstances great enough to spawn some important psychological differences in the people on either side of the divide, their similarities notwithstanding. And we reason that these differences in psychology, while first the product of the divide, can eventually reinforce the divide (Fiske et al. 1998).

Our analysis begins with an assessment of the predicament faced by homeless mothers on welfare. As mentioned earlier, the first point to stress is that their life context has considerable overlap with that of middle-class Americans. (Knowing the great diversity of this group, we nonetheless refer to them as the middle class as an easy way of denoting the more economically secure members of society.) Accordingly, as survey after survey shows (for example, Rainwater 1970; Cantril and Roll 1971; Cook and Curtin 1987), these women share many values, personal goals, and cultural ideals with people in the middle class. But the life contexts of these groups also differ in some profound ways. Compared to the middle class, a fundamental difference of the predicament of homeless mothers is the extreme economic and social uncertainty with which they must contend, and the lack of resources, skills, and support with which they must do so. The people, institutions, and communities in their lives have proven difficult to trust in the sense of being willing or able to foster their progress toward secure employment. Moreover, their lack of skills and resources—typically no health care, no child care, no housing, no family resources, coupled with very little education and few marketable skills—puts their needs so high that no single opportunity is likely to seem as if it could make much of a difference. Unlike the life contexts of the middle class, then, these women face, with children to support, a near-traumatic predicament of life context uncertainty and difficulty.

In transaction with this predicament, we propose that a psychology is afforded that, while by no means characterizing all of these women, may describe a central tendency among them. This "afforded psychological hypothesis" has three parts. The first part is a particularly strong *valuing of self-reliance and independence* in the sense of not being economically dependent on others. In response to a context that is unreliable, we suggest that these women may take a value from the larger society that deemphasizes the importance of having a reliable context for success and reify it into a centerpiece of their worldview. By discounting the importance of the unreliability and threat around them, and increasing the importance of self-reliance and independence, they gain a feeling of personal security.

The second part of this predicament, however, may work against the first part. In response to the unreliability and insufficiency of opportunity in their lives, we argue that homeless mothers on welfare have *difficulty trusting scenarios by which they could gain secure employment* and a better life. They often come from communities that provide very little opportunities for securing middle-class status (Auletta 1982; Bourgois 1996; Dash 1989; Kozol 1988). The opportunities welfare mothers are offered—for example, coursework needed to graduate from high school, minimal training programs in basic vocational skills, and minimum-wage jobs—can seem highly unlikely to lead to success given the constraints they are facing. Moreover, scenarios of advancement are not likely to be well modeled or normatively enforced in the broader communities in which these women live.

Third, the resultant psychology with regard to advancement, then, is likely to be a mix of hopeful commitment to self-sufficiency—they have little other hope—and, in the face of such difficult circumstances, real difficulty in maintaining trust in the available opportunity structure. We hypothesize that they alternate between an effort to be self-sufficient and a loss of persistence in the face of frustration.

It is in this situation, we hypothesize, that people can become susceptible to *short-term decision-making,* which can sometimes worsen their circumstances. This may be the state of mind in which many of the women in our sample allowed themselves to have children at so early an age (Dash 1989; Furstenberg 1976). For a woman from the middle class, having a baby at an early age would interfere with a well-developed scenario of advancement that is broadly supported, if not mandated, in her social world. Such an action would interfere with her graduating from high school, going to college, and with the general development needed to achieve a secure and happy life. For the women in our sample, having a baby early in life was not likely to interfere with such a likely scenario of advancement and in fact may have offered important advantages—a secure relationship in a world of insecure relationships and a mark of passage into adulthood.

Our view, then, is not that these women lack internalized middle-class values and psychological characteristics, but that, from their position in society, it is difficult to trust a representation of how they could deliver themselves to economic security. The lack of such a representation, and a community that reliably supports it, affords them a psychology that is focused more on immediate and short-term needs and opportunities. And this decision-making process, under some conditions, may further mire them in poverty.

Before developing the afforded psychological hypothesis in more detail and presenting preliminary research that supports it, we describe recent developments in welfare policy directed at these women and the alternative psychological models of their experience that predominate in the literature.

## RECENT DEVELOPMENTS IN WELFARE POLICY TOWARD SINGLE MOTHERS

The social safety net for poor families is currently undergoing a radical transformation (Edelman 1997; Pavetti 1997); in our effort to understand the experience of the women who use this system, it is important for our review to understand these changes in welfare policy and their motivation.

Beginning in 1935, the U.S. government provided Aid to Dependent

Children (later renamed Aid to Families with Dependent Children, or AFDC) as an entitlement, meaning a "federally defined guarantee of assistance to families with children who met the statutory definition of need" (Edelman 1997, 4). Welfare, as it came to be known, was almost universally disliked. In his social history of welfare in America, Katz (1986) summarized public attitudes towards welfare:

> Nobody likes welfare. Conservatives worry that it erodes the work ethic, retards productivity, and rewards the lazy. Liberals view the American welfare system as incomplete, inadequate, and punitive. Poor people, who rely on it, find it degrading, demoralizing, and mean. (ix)

In 1996 President Clinton signed into law the Personal Responsibility and Work Opportunity Reconciliation Act (also called the 1996 Welfare Reform Act). This program eliminated AFDC and replaced it with block grants to states to create the program called Temporary Assistance for Needy Families (TANF). TANF differs from AFDC in several ways: (1) it is administered by the states, so there is no federal entitlement or safety net; (2) whereas there was no fixed time limit for AFDC, families are eligible to receive TANF only for sixty months in their lifetime; (3) once TANF recipients have been determined to be work-ready or they have received assistance for twenty-four months, they are required to work; and (4) in order to receive TANF grants from the federal government, states must meet increasing work participation rates and/or decrease the number of people receiving welfare (Pavetti 1997).

These changes were a response to the perceived problem of welfare dependency (Bernstein 1998). At any point in time, people who have been on welfare for eight years or more account for more than half of the people on welfare, giving the impression of a welfare-dependent caseload (Bane and Ellwood 1994). However, this statistic is somewhat misleading, because it is also true that the vast majority of people who start on welfare stay on the rolls less than four years (Bane and Ellwood 1994). That is, although long-term recipients represent only a small fraction of those who have ever received benefits, they tend to accumulate in the system and represent a significant portion of the existing caseloads and welfare expenditures at any given point in time. The 1996 Welfare Reform Act was motivated by the focus of politicians and the media on the long-term recipients, as opposed to the greater number of people who rely on welfare in times of need and move out of the system (Bernstein 1998).

Furthermore, this group of long-term welfare recipients represents a specific, highly identifiable part of the population: young single mothers and their children. More than half of all welfare recipients were teenagers when their first child was born (Harris 1997), and over half of the AFDC budget was spent on welfare for teenage mothers and their resultant families. In today's context—66 percent of American mothers with children now work (Pavetti 1997)—the reliance on welfare for personal support has become less acceptable. Thus, under the current TANF policy, welfare support will be withdrawn after the time limits have been reached, with the assumption that the long-term welfare-reliant women will then support themselves by gaining employment. Reformers assume that this low-skilled group can find employment, but that assumption is seriously contested by some theorists (see Bernstein 1998; Sidel 1996; Wilson 1996).

Two other assumptions about the welfare phenomena—neither of them supported by data—have been used to justify the 1996 Welfare Reform Act (Bassuk, Browne, and Buckner 1996). First, it is assumed that welfare inevitably perpetuates dependency rather than serving as a safety net for people experiencing hard times. Yet as indicated earlier, most poor women use welfare for less than four years (Bane and Ellwood 1994). Second, it is assumed that welfare compromises the "work ethic." Many studies (see, for example, Bassuk et al. 1996; Edin and Lein 1997) have shown that most welfare mothers have worked and that many work while on welfare to supplement the money they receive. Based in large part on these assumptions, which we would argue are based on certain psychological models of the welfare recipients, the provisions of the 1996 Welfare Reform Act have begun to be implemented.

In short, we have reached a curious point in American welfare history: a major policy initiative, the 1996 Welfare Reform Act, has been promulgated in large part as a response to a set of assumptions about the psychology of welfare recipients, especially women who are using welfare to support their families. In the literature on the urban poor and women on welfare in particular, three distinct psychology models have been advanced (Bane and Ellwood 1994; Greenstone 1991): the culture of poverty model, rational choice models, and expectancy or self-efficacy models. We review them in turn.

## Culture of Poverty Models

Research and theorizing on the "culture of poverty" has been extremely influential and has been an important part of the history of welfare theorizing over the past forty years. Oscar Lewis was the first to articulate the culture of poverty thesis. In his book *La Vida: A Puerto Rican Family in the Culture of Poverty* (1966), he described the culture of poverty as an adaptation and reaction of the poor "to their marginal position in a class-stratified, highly individuated, capitalistic society" (xliv). Lewis argued that the culture of poverty could be described in approximately seventy social, economic, and psychological traits. The culture of poverty was most likely to originate under the following conditions: a capitalist economy that features cash, wage labor, and production for profit; a continually high unemployment rate for unskilled labor; low wages; failure to provide social, political, or economic organization for the low-income population; a bilateral kinship system rather than a unilateral kinship system; and a dominant culture that values individual initiative and the accumulation of wealth and explains poverty as the result of personal inadequacy or inferiority.

Lewis (1966) emphasized the intergenerational transmission of the culture of poverty:

> Once [the culture of poverty] comes into existence it tends to perpetuate itself from generation to generation because of its effect on the children. By the time slum children are age six or seven they have usually absorbed the basic values and attitudes of their subculture and are not psychologically geared to take full advantage of changing conditions or increased opportunities which may occur in their lifetime. (xlv)

Thus, the culture of poverty is fixed and likely to be permanent as it is transmitted from one poor generation to the next. Lewis outlined the culture of poverty thesis in an extended introduction to *La Vida* (for a general discussion of Lewis's treatment of the culture of poverty, see Gans 1968; Moynihan 1968). The rest of *La Vida* consists of first-person narratives from the Rios family gathered through questionnaires, interviews, participant observation, biographies, and projective psychological tests.

The evidence for the intergenerational aspect of the culture of poverty comes from the Rios family, in which every major female figure was a prostitute. Because the children were raised by mothers who supported their families through prostitution, the next generation also relied on prostitution as an economic strategy. Despite the problems with Lewis's methodology, including his reliance on anecdotes from such an extreme family, the basic argument of the culture of poverty model—that one learns at one's "mother's knee" adaptive yet harmful values about work, sex, and responsibility—became influential and was adapted to analysis of other poor populations. At the same time Lewis was writing about a Puerto Rican family in the culture of poverty, there were major concerns about black urban poverty in the United States. Michael Harrington wrote *The Other America* (1962) and, in describing the lives of the "other Americans" for mainstream readers, evoked images of a distinctly different culture. In the early 1960s, then, the culture of poverty model prevailed, explaining that the poor make internal adaptations to the external factors of poverty and limited opportunity. The goal of this view was to change the external factors, but in so doing, it easily seemed to be saying that the problem with the poor was their cultural values.

Nowhere is this phenomenon clearer than in Moynihan's report *The Negro Family: The Case for National Action* (1965). Moynihan began by describing how in the wake of the Civil Rights Act of 1964 African Americans would not only want equality of opportunity but equality of group outcome. However, Moynihan argued, equality of group outcome was not likely to happen, for two external reasons. First, racism still existed at all levels in the United States. Second, three centuries of brutal mistreatment had left African Americans in a position where they could not compete, as a group, with other groups that had not been systematically mistreated. While individual blacks might rise to the top, large group differences in outcomes were likely to remain.

Thus, Moynihan began his report by positing that external factors had led to the negative state of the black urban poor. But the focus of his report is on the

> fundamental problem . . . that of family structure. The evidence—not final, but powerfully persuasive—is that the Negro family in the urban ghetto is crumbling. A middle-class group has managed to save itself, but for vast numbers of the unskilled, poorly educated city working class the fabric of conventional social relationships has all but disintegrated. (1965, 1)

In very clear and impassioned language, Moynihan described the "deterioration of the Negro family" as the "fundamental source of the weakness of the Negro community" (5). More specifically, Moynihan argued that the black family was highly unstable, citing as evidence the fact that in 1960 the nonwhite illegitimacy level was eight times greater than the white ratio and that nearly 25 percent of African American births were illegitimate (a number that had gone up to 65 percent in 1997; Harris 1997). This observation led to his conclusion that "the breakdown of the Negro family has led to a startling increase in welfare dependency" (12).

Throughout his report, Moynihan emphasized the legacy of slavery, racism, and unemployment as the causes of the crisis of poverty among urban blacks, yet at the same time he told a deeply cultural story about the internal problems befalling the black family. In the chapter titled "The Tangle of Pathology," he decried the matriarchal structure of the black family: being so out of line with the rest of American society, it "imposes a crushing burden on the Negro male, and in consequence, on a great many Negro women as well" (29). Thus, Moynihan argued, at the psychological level, the black man suffers from being ineffectual and powerless in comparison to his female partner. A vicious circle ensues, as the powerless man leaves the relationship, abandoning his children. Although Moynihan stressed the external factors that had provoked this breakdown in the internal family structure of black Americans, the most salient take-home message of his report was that something was dramatically wrong with the black family. This cultural argument was assumed by conservative critics of welfare who argued that, owing to their deviant behavior and lack of interest in self-improvement, the poor were doomed to destitution (see, for example, Banfield 1970). Social policy initiatives were useless; what the poor needed was cultural rehabilitation. Although liberals were the ones who generated the culture of poverty thesis, they were mostly silent as conservatives espoused cultural or behavioral arguments to explain why the poor remained in poverty (for an extended discussion of the history of the debate on urban poverty, see Wilson 1987).

In contrast to these conservative or behavioral cultural arguments, Wilson (1996) emphasizes that living in a jobless environment may foster a distinct culture where reliance on welfare is more accepted and the obstacles that prevent work prove overwhelming. He argues:

> To act according to one's culture—either through forms of nonverbal action, including engaging in or refraining from certain conduct, or in the verbal expression of opinions or attitudes concerning norms, values, or beliefs—is to follow one's inclinations as they have been developed by influence or learning from other members of the community that one belongs to or identifies with. (66)

In his interviews with African American residents of inner Chicago's ghetto neighborhoods, Wilson found people who supported and reinforced basic American values related to work and individual initiative. Yet given the constraints of the urban environment, especially the limited work opportunities available to black residents, it was often difficult to live up to these values. Ghetto-related behaviors, such as participation in the underground economy or long-term welfare dependence, may not reflect an internalized poverty psychology, as was argued by Mead (1994), but they may be adaptations to the difficult and limited opportunities of the environment.

Although these ghetto-related behaviors, including criminal activity and welfare reliance, may be adaptations to the specifics of the environment, Wilson argues that they are also, in a sense, culturally endorsed. Because these negative behaviors can be observed with greater frequency in ghetto environments than in middle-class environments, they are given a level of acceptance or legitimacy. Thus, although ghetto individuals do not typically express values that deviate from mainstream values, they are more susceptible to acting in the manner consistent with the actions of others in their culture. Low collective self-efficacy is one reason those in the ghetto fail to live up to the mainstream values they espouse (we return to this aspect of Wilson's model in our descriptions of efficacy/expectancy theories of poverty). Low self-efficacy is a psychological adaptation to the jobless ghetto environment and can be thought of as a social psychological variable that exists within the ghetto subculture.

## Rational Choice Models

Rational choice models are the dominant paradigm in economics and policy analysis. According to these models, individuals rationally examine the options they face, evaluate them according to some fixed preferences, and then ultimately select the one that yields the greatest reward or satisfaction. Long-term welfare use, then, is seen as the most reasonable choice of a person considering the possible options. For example, a single mother of two with an absent father and no child support has two means of supporting herself: her own earnings via employment or public assistance from the government. Using 1991 figures, the House Committee on Ways and Means showed that if a woman in this position could earn $10,000 (about $5.00 per hour) instead of receiving welfare benefits, she would be only slightly better off than if she did not work at all. Her disposable income would rise about $2,000, but that would be offset by greater work-related and child care expenses (Bane and Ellwood 1994). Furthermore, she would lose her health care coverage, since she had access to Medicaid while receiving welfare but would be unlikely to have obtained a job with health benefits. Bane and Ellwood (1994) suggest that under the welfare regulations that prevailed in 1991 the rational choice perspective would have seen little gain in working unless "(1) the woman works full-time, (2) she commands wages well above the minimum, (3) day care costs are low, and (4) available welfare benefits are low" (70.)

The rational choice model yields many empirical predictions; some are supported by data, others are not. It predicts that there should be little mixing of welfare and work, as people will choose the option that is most beneficial. Also, welfare recipients should be very sensitive to policy changes, since incentives in the welfare system are the "primary policy lever that might be used to change behavior" (Bane and Ellwood 1994, 74). There is mixed evidence for these predictions. Although Bane and Ellwood support the notion that there should be little mixing of work and welfare by citing a study (U.S. House of Representatives Ways and Means Committee 1992, 676) that claimed only 8 percent of women on welfare from the 1990 census were working at all, other research (Edin and Lein 1997) has documented that women receiving welfare employ multiple work strategies to cover their expenses not covered by welfare. Thus, it is not clear that self-report census data clarify that question completely. In addition, the 1996 Welfare Reform Act has resulted in tremendous reduction of the rolls, showing the effect of incentives on changing behavior.

A dominant spokesperson for the rational choice model is Charles Murray, who in his 1984 book *Losing Ground* evaluated social policy on welfare from 1968 to 1980, starting with Johnson's War on Poverty. Despite the dramatic increase in spending on social programs in this era, the poverty rate remained about the same, around 13 percent. Not only does Murray take the failure to reduce the poverty rate as evidence for the failure of social programs, but he argues that certain social programs made "it profitable for the poor to behave in the short term in ways that were destructive in the long term" (9). More specifically, welfare programs set up an incentive structure that discouraged work and marriage and encouraged dependency and illegitimacy.

> It is not necessary to invoke the Zeitgeist of the 1960s, changes in the work ethic, racial differences, or the complexities of postindustrial economies to explain increasing unemployment among the young, increased dropout from the labor force, or higher rates of illegitimacy and welfare dependency. All these phenomena could have been predicted from the changes that social policy made in the rewards and penalties—the carrots and sticks—that govern human behavior (Murray 1984, 155).

Murray adopts the psychological model that all individuals are rational in making decisions about their lives, calculating probabilities based on the options with which they are presented. The primary difference between the rich and the poor is that poor people "play with fewer chips and cannot wait as long for results" (155). Hence, the poor attempt to maximize short-term gains.

To illustrate his point, he discusses Harold and Phyllis, an unremarkable poor couple, recently graduated from high school, with no plans for college, who must make a decision because Phyllis is pregnant. Murray presents the financial options available to Harold and Phyllis in 1960 and in 1970, before and after the Great Society welfare reforms. In

1960, given the welfare package available, including the man-in-the-house requirement that prohibited unmarried men from living with AFDC recipients, it was clearly favorable for Harold and Phyllis to get married. Harold would have had to take whatever job he could find and support Phyllis because there was no way he could be supported by the welfare package available to her. By 1970, however, the total welfare benefit package, including Medicaid and food stamps, exceeded the purchasing power of what Harold could have made by working. He could also live with Phyllis legally, since the Supreme Court had ruled against the man-in-the-house requirement. In 1970, according to Murray's calculations, getting married would have been irrational: "Harold can get married and work forty hours a week in a hot tiresome job; or he can live with Phyllis and their baby without getting married, not work, and have more disposable income" (160). For Phyllis, in 1970, if they had married and Harold had found a job, she would have lost her AFDC benefits. Yet his minimum-wage job would not have produced any more money than her AFDC benefits, and moreover, he would be in control of the money, not her. Furthermore, as Murray points out, Harold's job would not have been as stable as the welfare system. In 1970 it would have made sense for Phyllis and Harold to not get married, have their child, and receive AFDC (for a critique of Murray's Harold and Phyllis arguments, see Jencks 1992).

Although for the purposes of this review we have separated rational choice models from cultural models of poverty, the 1980s conservative arguments linked the two. The effects of incentives on Harold and Phyllis at the individual level affected the values and attitudes of members of the "underclass" at the cultural level (Auletta 1982). The prevailing argument of the time was that welfare benefits made the poor less self-reliant and promoted joblessness and female-headed households rather than stable, working, two-income family homes. Thus, the poor were victims of welfare benefits; as Murray puts it, "We tried to provide for the poor and produced more poor instead" (9) by sapping the poor of their will to work. Murray's conclusion is that the only way to mend this system is to abolish AFDC and all other forms of welfare.

An extreme version of this rational choice/cultural model is proposed by Gilder (1981), who sees the poor as corrupted by the welfare system, which, in providing for children without fathers in the house, has exempted fathers from responsibility for their children. Akin to Murray (1984), Gilder (1981) writes:

> The most serious fraud is committed not by the members of the welfare culture, but by the creators of it, who conceal from the poor . . . that to live well and escape from poverty they will have to keep their families together at all costs and will have to work harder than the classes above them.(116)

Thus, the poor are acting rationally in accepting benefits instead of working hard; their dependent behavior is a function of the unique economic set of contingencies that the government has created for them. Only cutting welfare benefits and/or requiring work for welfare payments will cure the poor of this culture of dependency.

Most of the evidence taken to support the rational choice model that welfare mothers are weighing the costs and benefits of work and welfare are from large-scale economic surveys (for a review, see Moffitt 1992) or hypothetical models (Murray 1984). Interview studies with welfare-reliant mothers (Edin and Lein 1997) support the notion that women weigh the costs and benefits of work and welfare. However, the issue is not as simple as the economic rational choice models suggest:

> For poor single mothers, the welfare/work choice was not merely a problem of maximizing income or consumption. Rather each woman's choice was set against a backdrop of survival and serious potential material hardship. The mothers with whom we spoke were less concerned with maximizing consumption than [with] minimizing the risk of economic disaster (Edin and Lein 1997, 63).

Edin and Lein interviewed 214 welfare-reliant women and found that most of the women predicated their decisions about work/welfare on previous labor-force experience. Most of the women had work experience, and national data suggest that 60 percent of all current welfare recipients have worked during the previous two years (U.S. House of Representatives 1993). Based on this experience, most of the women knew that returning to low-wage jobs would not make them better off—either financially or psychologically—than they would be on welfare. Furthermore, taking a low-wage job might put them in a worse condition not only because work-related and child care expenses would offset their potential gains but because jobs they were qualified for could end abruptly, leaving them with no choice but to return to welfare, and to suffer in the interim. Women working in low-wage jobs are at least three times more prone to job layoffs than other workers (Blank 1994). In addition, although the welfare experience hurts women's self-esteem, they have a greater fear of what may happen to their children in their potentially dangerous neighborhoods if they are left alone during work hours. Thus, both economic and social psychological factors are relevant to the mothers' choices within this rational choice framework.

## Expectancy/Efficacy Models

The third set of models are the expectancy models (Goodwin 1983; Gurin and Gurin 1970), which are also called the self-efficacy models (Bandura

1997; Wilson 1996). According to expectancy theorists, welfare dependency results when people no longer believe that they can get off welfare. At this point, they no longer take advantage of available opportunities because they are so overwhelmed by their situation. Goodwin (1983) considers expectancies part of one's "psychological orientation," which he measures as part of his analysis of the causes and cures of welfare. Those whose psychological orientation leads them to expect to work and get off welfare are more likely to take the necessary steps to achieve such actions than those who do not have the expectancy of success.

In contrast to the rational choice model, which argues that people evaluate economic options with no regard to the past, expectancy models emphasize what has happened previously to the person and the others who make up the person's reference groups. Successful experiences lead to greater expectations of independence, and failure experiences lead to lesser expectations of independence. Information is also a key component of expectancy models. Dependency may reflect a lack of information: with an imperfect perception of how much they can control their destinies, people develop inappropriately low expectations.

Goodwin's (1983) measure of expectation of economic independence combines two interrelated components: going to work and getting off welfare. These components are operationalized in a 1978–1979 study of AFDC recipients participating in the government's Work Incentive (WIN) program. Participants were asked 250 questions to determine their expectancy level; a typical question was: "At this time next year, how likely is it that you will be: (a) working at a full-time job; (b) receiving welfare; (c) staying home to look after your family" (19).

Goodwin (1983) finds that the strongest predictor of economic independence (working and not receiving welfare) was the expectation of achieving such independence. (However, the total variance explained by expectation variables is quite low.) This expectation was more than just a reflection of the participant's background characteristics. It reflected a feedback loop. His results showed that welfare mothers who had higher expectations in 1978 had higher levels of independence in 1979, and thus had higher levels of expected independence for the following year. The converse occurred for women with low expectations of independence: they did not achieve independence the following year and lowered their expectancies even further. Other factors that contribute to heightened expectations are improved maternal health and increasing age of the children. With improved health and older children, the mother's expectations for work increase, and consequently, she works more and receives fewer welfare benefits.

As noted before, Wilson (1996) makes use of efficacy beliefs to describe the effects of joblessness on the attitudes and behaviors of members of the ghetto poor:

> I would therefore expect lower levels of perceived self-efficacy in ghetto neighborhoods—which feature underemployment, unemployment, and labor-force dropouts, weak marriages, and single-parent households—than in less impoverished neighborhoods. Considering the importance of cultural learning and influence, I would also expect the level of perceived self-efficacy to be higher among those individuals who experience these same difficulties but live in working- and middle-class neighborhoods than among their counterparts in ghetto neighborhoods. (76)

Thus, the perceived environmental restrictions set up by the jobless environment are responsible for problems of efficacy. Growing up in poverty, and seeing the inability of others from their community to maintain jobs that could afford a nonimpoverished existence, has caused individuals in poor urban neighborhoods to doubt their individual ability to survive and succeed independent of government assistance. Wilson bases this efficacy theorizing on interviews conducted with poor men and women in Chicago. He describes the factors leading to this low self-efficacy:

> [The respondents] insisted that despite the opportunities that may be available to many people they are destined to remain in a state of poverty and live in troubled neighborhoods. The respondents argued that inner-city blacks will not be able to progress because inferior education has placed them at a disadvantage. They blame racism and the rising number of immigrants in the United States as major reasons for their inability to improve their position in life. . . . Many of the women feel that they cannot find employment because they have to care for their children. (77–78)

This low self-efficacy is enforced by living in a community where others have similarly negative feelings about their opportunities. The result of this is what Bandura (1997) refers to as low collective efficacy in the inner-city ghetto.

Expectancy or efficacy models and cultural models share the assumption that collective psychological processes determine important behaviors such as dropping out of school, teenage pregnancy, and welfare dependency. However, they differ in their emphasis: cultural theories typically focus on the internalization of these factors and their ability to self-perpetuate over generations, and efficacy theories typically focus on the structural determinants (such as joblessness) that influence the adoption of these beliefs.

## AN EMPIRICAL EXPLORATION: THE BRONX PROJECT

Compared to the culture of poverty model, the rational choice model, and the efficacy/expectancy models, this chapter proposes a more explicitly contextualized view of the psychology afforded homeless mothers on welfare. Our initial research effort, by taking the perspective of the actor, attempts to provide a more useful description of the experience of these homeless mothers on welfare.

In August 1996, we interviewed twenty women at a homeless shelter in the Bronx, New York City.[1] The shelter provides temporary housing and specializes in getting women engaged in education and job-skills activities as a means of meeting their personal goals in life. The shelter is run by Women In Need, Inc., a social service organization.

At introductory meetings held at the shelter, we introduced the project as the "Stanford Interview Project." We told the women that our goal, as social psychologists concerned with welfare policy, was to hear the voices of the women most directly involved. The women signed up for sixty- to ninety-minute interviews that were conducted either in their apartments or in a general meeting room. The women were paid five dollars for the interview and five dollars for child care expenses. Furthermore, they were assured that we were not affiliated with any government agency and that their names would not appear with any quotations.

The twenty women who signed up for the interviews were young, with a mean age of twenty-five (range: seventeen to thirty-eight), and all had children, with a mean number of two (range: one to five children). They were mostly African American (60 percent) or Hispanic (30 percent) and predominantly raised in New York City (85 percent), with an approximately equal number raised by both parents (45 percent) or by their mothers alone (40 percent). All the women were receiving AFDC benefits and were seeking housing subsidies so that they could move out of the shelter and into apartments.

Our goal is to illuminate the psychological predicaments faced by women and the way this predicament affords particular opportunities that shape psychological functioning. In so doing, we examine the particular person-environment transactions that seem crucial in these women's lives. In contrast to the more internally oriented approach obtained from the perspective of the observer, adopting the perspective of the actor highlights the overwhelming contextual factors affecting the decisions and behaviors of these homeless women. To illustrate this analysis, we review two representative interviews from this sample. We briefly describe their background and experience, then explore the same material from the standpoint of the afforded perspective.

## Interview 1

*Background* Our first interview is with a thirty-eight-year-old woman of mixed race, a mother of four children. Several years before the interview, she was quite financially secure, married to a successful man, living in a nice home on Long Island. However, as she described the situation, she eventually had to escape this man's physical and emotional abuse:

> We were married for two years, and he was mentally, physically, emotionally abusive. His son was abusing my son, which led to his son's arrest—he just didn't want me in his household. So I decided that although I had everything, that it wasn't worth my son's and my daughter's and my own well-being. So I left. I didn't have a job or anything. I left everything. I went to live with my sister, but she was evicted from her place. So of course I couldn't pay her rent because it was too much to live in Manhattan. That's where I had nowhere to go, from there.

This woman's story is typical of others we learned about in that she had an emergency situation (abuse) that caused her to first seek assistance from others, her sister. When that assistance was no longer forthcoming, she entered the shelter system. In telling her story, this woman described her difficult history with abusive men. At the age of sixteen, she got pregnant, dropped out of school, and got married. Unfortunately, her husband was extremely abusive: "he beat me through the whole pregnancy." She tried to leave him, but he kept following her and abusing her.

> So I left him—I ran for my life actually, when my son was two months. . . . I keep marrying this type of man, like they are this high authority, but yet I never get an education myself because I meet these men, they just want to tear me down. They do not want me to get an education, they want to keep control. But that's what happened, I ran for my life from him. And . . . after that, he hunt me down, and he beat me and beat me on many occasions.

She eventually escaped this man and his persistently abusive behavior. Eventually she got married again, this time to her current abusive husband.

After fleeing her second husband, and the comforts of her large Long Island home, she entered the shelter system by going to the Emergency Assistance Unit (EAU): "You're not supposed to stay for more than twenty-four hours—I stayed for six days. It was very degrading because you sleep on the floor and you have all these rats running around." (All of the women at the shelter described the EAU as a horrifying, demeaning experience.) From there, she was sent to an assessment center, and then had the opportunity to enter the shelter, where she was receiving help in finding an apartment and getting her high school general equivalency degree (GED).

As a result of being abused as a child and having to deal with racial taunts in high school owing to her mixed heritage, she hated school: "I went to a good high school. I didn't care for school at the time, though, because of the way I was raised. Low level and on. I didn't care for school. Actually, I hated school to tell the truth." This ambivalence toward school can be seen in her feelings about it now. She recognizes that it is important for her to further her education, get her GED, and go to college, but her lifelong difficulties with school and her need for economic self-sufficiency seem to be of primary importance in determining her behavior. "Hmmm. I want to go to college, but it's not as important as having a good job. But I know how to get a good job: you have to get a good education, so I guess that's important, too. But I don't like sitting in a classroom."

At the time of the interview, like most of the women, she was working toward the GED and looking for an apartment.

## *Afforded Perspective*

> I always meet this same type of man, it's unbelievable. Dominating, controlling, abusive. . . . I think it was my responsibility. I just end up in the wrong situations. I don't blame society. Just from my birth . . . it started with my stepfather. He abused me. That's what started my life on the wrong road—he sexually abused me, mentally, physically abused me. And caused me to have a low self-esteem and to meet men like him.

Our analysis of this woman's story would begin by looking at the predicament she was contending with and how it afforded her particular psychological responses. The primary external factor in this woman's life is abuse, beginning with the abuse of her stepfather and continuing with the abuse of her husband and his family against her and her family. In her terms, the abuse of her stepfather caused her to have low self-esteem, which in turn caused her to meet other men like him. Yet, while her experience of abuse may have afforded her low self-esteem, her role as a mother also afforded her great strength and independence. As she described it:

> Being a mother is probably the most important thing in my life. Because I think for each one I went through so much anxiety. . . . I would give my life for any one of them. Because I've had four of them, and for each one there has been some sort of horrible situation. . . . I've had to sacrifice my own well-being for them. So that is the most important role in my life. . . . I could probably live on the streets, I don't care. But because of them, that's the most important thing in my life.

Thus, the afforded perspective has helped to identify the psychological strengths as well as weaknesses that difficult situations have brought out in this woman's life.

Although the woman suggests that low self-esteem led her into abusive relationships, these relationships, on closer examination, may have been the best option open to her in difficult situations. She describes the factors that attracted her to her most recent husband, and how marrying him landed her in trouble—abused, alone, and homeless:

> I liked his lifestyle, kind of, materialistically, but that didn't mean anything. Because I ended up leaving everything anyway. Everything I had I lost, so I didn't gain anything. . . . And I guess when you grow up, and you don't have anything, being abused your whole life, [when you] kind of meet someone who you think can offer everything to you, you kind of overlook certain things. And that's probably what I did.

Not having the resources to secure her independence—family support, an adequate education, financial security—a relationship offering these things became attractive even though she had to "overlook" signs of trouble. Here we see her openness to this relationship not so much as a direct product of an internal trait like low self-esteem but as a transaction between her needs and the opportunities afforded by the relationship. After the abuse developed and threatened her children, a strong motive for independence emerged as she summoned the courage to leave Long Island for the EAU and eventually the shelter. This desire for independence comes through in her future goals:

> To have my own apartment, my own job, my own independence. Not to be dependent on anybody. That's basically it. Not to have anybody control me, my life, my kids. Just to have my own control, to have my own life, not to be dependent on anyone else, nobody. To go and come when I choose to go and come. To do what I choose to do.

Thus, a very different picture emerges: instead of a dependent woman who may perpetuate the cycle of abuse by staying with her husband or leaving for another abusive relationship, here is a woman who identifies independence and control as the key factors in how she wants to transact with her environment. This analysis calls into question the independence/dependence trait dimension as a useful characterization of this woman. In some situations she can be seen as dependent on others, and in other situations as quite independent. Neither internal quality describes her as accurately as examining the psychological qualities afforded by the contingencies of her environment.

## Interview 2

*Background* Our second interview is with a much younger woman, a seventeen-year-old mother of two who had her first child when she was thirteen. She lived with her grandmother, until problems compelled her to leave:

> I grew up with my grandmother all my life, so that you could probably say that since the age of nine I've been on public assistance because she wasn't working so she got on public assistance with me. Last year I got my own budget when I moved out of my grandmother's apartment. I moved out of my grandmother's apartment because my younger son's father, we used to fight a lot, so I went to a battered women's shelter.

From the battered women's shelter, she was referred to the shelter where we interviewed her; she was waiting to move into her own apartment while working at a clothing store during the day. Her two children were in day care while she worked an extremely long day.

When this woman became pregnant at thirteen, she decided to keep the baby:

> In '92, once again, me and my grandmother were going through a lot of problems. I had a boyfriend, and somehow or another I managed to get pregnant. . . . Scared, didn't know what I was going to do. The father told me to get an abortion. We didn't speak at all during my pregnancy. I didn't want to get an abortion because I don't believe in them, and I'm terrified of them. So that's when I had my youngest son.

To what extent did she know about safer sex? "Yeah, I knew about it. I just didn't care. It just didn't bother me. I thought I was invincible, nothing could happen to me." And was caring for a child at this young age difficult? Not particularly. "It was fun. It was like a real live doll. You know how most parents complain that their children get up in the middle of the night, and they can't take it? I never had that with my boys. They came home from the hospital and slept right through the night, so it wasn't that bad."

In contrast to the fun of motherhood was the difficulty of school:

> I was always a terrible student, I can't lie. It wasn't something I could get into. It annoyed me, especially if I couldn't figure something out the first time. It's not for me, I hate it. . . . But then I went back for my GED. Which I failed by six points, but I'm going to take it again, that's no problem. After I get my GED, I'm going to sit down and figure out what it is that I want to do. It happens to be that I'm very confused. I just want to do this and that, it changes everyday.

Her plans are similar to those of many seventeen-year-olds—education, job, stability:

> Getting out of here. Getting myself situated with my apartment. After I get my apartment, I'm going to get my GED. After that I want to go to college. I think for nursing. This might change tomorrow. After that I want to become a nurse. This is what I see myself doing five years from now, being a nurse, being in a different apartment, I might even move down south, I'm not sure.

Her goals are clearly mainstream, in terms of school, work, and family. But to what extent will she be able to achieve these goals?

*Afforded Perspective* Early motherhood had certainly contributed to this woman's present position in a homeless shelter. Why did she have children at such a young age?

> One of my main reasons for having my children is to have somebody to love me, because I felt I didn't get it from my grandmother. If I had these babies, these babies were going to give me the love I needed, that's what I thought at the time.

As a child, she was not provided with love from either her parents (who abandoned her) or her grandmother (who raised her). Her family interactions, then, created a predicament where having children allowed her to fulfill her need for love. While this transaction could be described as a case of behavior driven by "low self-esteem," this characterization would miss the full process she describes by diminishing the interactive, cumulative influence of factors she was facing—neglect, abuse, and an almost complete lack of support and resources with which to function in society.

As she described it, she had been on public assistance since the age of nine. She spoke often of how impossible it would have been to move out on her own had it not been for public assistance. "I had just recently gotten my own budget, which I was very grateful for . . . because if they didn't do that there could have been no way that I could have moved out on my own." She entered the shelter system because she did not want to live in her grandmother's house:

> I'm in a shelter because I want to be in a shelter because I want to be away from my family. I didn't have to move out of my grandmother's house, I chose to. So you can say I'm in a shelter because I want to, not because it was a must and I had nowhere else to go. There are other places I can go, I'm here because I want to be here.

Two opposite interpretations are possible. On the one hand, the woman could be seen as dependent, relying on the government to provide her with housing and financial support. On the other hand, she could be seen as independent, moving away from her grandmother, her only family support, at the age of seventeen with two children. Both of these interpretations emphasize internal qualities. From the afforded perspective, we see a woman trying to survive, be loved, and maintain control of her two children in a context that makes these acts very difficult. The representations of her internal psychology as predisposing dependence or independence are either weakly informative or misleading. The route to understanding her plight seems to lie less in traits than in relationships.

Consider the psychological responses afforded by her relationships. First there is her grandmother. The influence of this relationship can be seen in the reasons she offered earlier for becoming pregnant and for leaving school:

> My grandmother, she was one of those people who says, "I don't care if you go, you do what you want." And if you don't have someone to give you that push, if you know you don't have to do it, you're not going to do it. I didn't go.

With no encouragement, incentive, or modeling from the dominant person in her life, her prospects for school leading to success were not reliable. This relationship, then, as much as any internal state we might ascribe to her, is likely to have been a major contributor to her current situation.

Second, there is the father of her second child, her abusive ex-boyfriend. Again, their relationship can be seen as affording certain behavioral responses. She elaborates on the sequence of events in that relationship:

> I met my second son's father when I was fourteen. I liked him so much, I just thought he was the perfect person. I figured, hey, we got someone we like we should keep him, why not have a baby by him. Big mistake, huge.

> Well, I got pregnant by him, we weren't together for more than three months.

Why did she get pregnant again? The major factors in her life (her family, her community, and her school) did not afford her a "life," a scenario of how she might build an economically secure and happy life that could be trusted in the sense of having sufficient support and resources to achieve it. In contrast to this lack of a "life," having a baby with her boyfriend would provide love for her from both father and child. But it did not work out that way:

> Once again I wanted to have my baby. Everybody tried to convince me not to. I was like, no, I want to have this baby. I got until about my sixth month, and everything just crumbled. He changed. Last September he bust my head open, on the side of my face, I had to get stitches in my head. It was just terrible. The whole side of my face. . . . If I turned like this, you wouldn't know it was me, from this side. We broke up.

The picture of this woman that emerges from her descriptions of her relationships with her grandmother and boyfriend is quite different from that of the immature girl she appears to be. Abandonment (by her parents), neglect (by her grandmother), and abuse (by her boyfriend) are the environmental contingencies that afforded this woman her particular ways of being. The fixed or internal nature of these contingencies may be best understood as a consequence of the constancy of these transactions in her life. To understand the extent to which they are changing, however, as with her new goals for school, it seems best to look at her new situation—enabled by the welfare system—which afforded a change in her opportunities.

## Summary

The afforded perspective, we hope, has helped to reveal how the particular context of these women's lives has afforded them psychological responses that, as the interviews demonstrated, include both strengths and weaknesses. We believe this framework fits into the social psychological context suggested by Wilson (1996): it clearly shows how the lives of poor women are constrained by the pressures under which they live. Our use of the actor's perspective further emphasizes how the agency of these women's lives, like that of the middle class, stems from an interaction between internal psychology, such as their needs for shelter and affection, and the immediate opportunities afforded them by the structure of their lives.

## AFFORDED PSYCHOLOGY HYPOTHESIS

Emerging from the actor's perspective, and the encouragement it received as a framework for understanding our ethnographic interviews, we developed a working theory of the psychology of homeless mothers, especially as it bears on their mobility and economic security. The afforded psychology hypothesis begins with an assumption: the socioeconomic disadvantage, restriction of opportunity, lack of reliable family support, and social isolation of homeless women on welfare places them in life-space contexts that, compared to those of the middle class, are severely unreliable, economically and socially. They have few of the requirements of a secure life—health care, child care, housing, reliable employment, or family support. And they have little education and few marketable skills with which to cope with this context. This predicament, we reason, affords a psychology with several components.

The first is a strong valuing of self-reliance and independence: they do not want to be dependent on others to meet their needs. In a life context that does not reliably meet their needs or support their development, they may come to value self-reliance almost as a faith, as the only reasonably plausible means of optimism about the future. Among the things these women have to count on, the self may be the most reliable. Of course, this argument involves an irony: women seen by the outside world as dependent in fact hold very strongly to a faith in independence.

The second component of the afforded psychology hypothesis is that the uncertainty of the context of these women's lives makes it difficult for them to trust a scenario for upward mobility. In their life context, they are less likely to be exposed to information about mobility and achievement or to be exposed to other people who have overcome the kind of disadvantage they encounter. And even when such a scenario is envisioned, these women may find it difficult to trust in it, considering the uncertainty of their environment and the probable lack of social and resource support.

The third component of the theory follows from the first and second: Without a developed scenario of upward mobility, it is difficult for these women to implement—with concrete instrumental actions—their commitment to self-reliance and independence. This is not to say that their motivations for independence are not important. But rather, we would stress that for their motivations to influence economic outcomes, the women must have a viable opportunity structure.

Finally, we reason that the lack of a well-developed scenario of upward mobility is likely to also make the self-regulation and decision-making of these women more susceptible to the immediacies of their lives. With no compelling representation of their long-term future to bear in mind, these women may focus more on their immediate needs, pressures, and desires and less on long-term strategies that might help move them toward economic security. As noted earlier, it may be precisely this psychological state of affairs—the absence of a trusted path to a better future—that allowed some of these women to have children at an early age in the first place. For them, having children so young interfered less with believable and supported futures, compared to more enfranchised middle-class women, and answered a more urgent need for affection and social connection.

## Comparing the Afforded Psychology Hypothesis to Other Models

To further clarify the reasoning of this model and to distinguish some of its implications, we briefly contrast it with each of the three models reviewed earlier.

*Culture of Poverty Models* There are several important differences between the afforded psychology hypothesis and culture of poverty models. Of first importance, we do not assume that a bounded cultural community of poor people is necessary or even sufficient to sustain the poor economic outcomes of women on welfare. Rather, the more fundamental cause of these outcomes is the inadequacy of the opportunity structure in the lives of these women, and the corresponding underdevelopment of upward mobility plans. To experience these difficulties, one need not live in a low-income community, though living in such a community would probably enhance these difficulties. But just as important, the afforded psychology hypothesis assumes that the environments of homeless mothers have much in common with the environments of people who are better off in society. In this respect, we follow the lead of Wilson (1996), who argues that the culture of the inner-city ghetto includes ghetto-related elements, such as greater tolerance of teenage pregnancy and welfare reliance, but also includes a predominance of mainstream elements. Wilson's surveys, like our interviews, found a great deal of overlap in values and attitudes between the poor and the working classes.

Another difference has to do with the role of dependency-tolerant values in mediating the poor outcomes of these women. Some culture of poverty models (for example, Lewis 1968; Mead 1994) argue that poverty is caused, in significant part, by poor people's internalization of a dependency value framework that eschews work in preference to public assistance. These views are persistently countered by evidence that people in low-income communities report valuing work as much or more than people in middle-class communities (see, for example, Wilson 1996;

Cook and Curtin 1987). But some of these theorists (for example, Mead 1994) would seem to take these self-reports as inflated by self-presentational needs. Other theorists who incorporate a cultural perspective make greater use of the economic contexts in explaining the poor outcomes of welfare mothers and others in low-income communities (for example, House 1981; Wilson 1996). They grant the women their strongly pro-work values and argue that the environments of these women do not allow them consistent means to fulfill them.

The proposed analysis is in greater sympathy with this latter view. It takes at face value the women's endorsement of pro-work values and explains their poor economic outcomes, like the latter set of theorists, as due to a lack of means, in both their backgrounds and ongoing conditions. What we add to this approach, based on our research, is the proposal that what is most limiting about their life context is its persistent inability to provide and support reliable opportunities to secure employment. It is this aspect of the women's life context that exposes them to chronic and threatening unreliability and fosters the psychological adaptations we described earlier.

Our argument, then, does not deny the role of culture. We acknowledge, for example, that in areas where many people lack the means of fulfilling their preferred values, not doing so can become more normative—at least in the sense of allowing greater tolerance of unfulfilled values than in other communities (see, for example, Wilson 1996). Such an influence is a cultural influence—a greater tolerance of less preferred behaviors affords, at least some of the time, a greater incidence of such behaviors. But, we see this "cultural" adaptation as rooted in social structure, a life context of such unreliable means of upward mobility as to undermine the development of viable scenarios for such mobility. Were this aspect of the life context to change, the hopeful implication of our analysis is that the development of such scenarios would change, too.

*Rational Choice Models* The rational choice model, as it is applied to the welfare experience, has an important commonality with our model: it takes the actor's perspective, as we have called it, the perspective of the women confronting the situations of their lives. And it also views the resultant behavior of the women as the product of person-situation transactions rather than the direct consequence of internalized traits. But the part of the women's life context best represented in this model's depiction of the welfare experience are the contingencies of welfare policy itself (see, for example, Moffitt 1992). The "rational choices" the women must make are those made available by the contingencies of welfare policy. These policies do have enormous importance in the lives of these women. But so do other relevant contingencies. And this is where the afforded psychology hypothesis, we suggest, extends the concept of rational choice as it pertains to these women. It tries to describe the broader contextual contingencies under which their important life choices are made—the persistent economic uncertainty, the unreliability of their relationships, the alternative economic opportunities available to them (see, for example, Edin and Lein 1996), and the lack of well-envisioned or supported plans for future economic security. By including these contingencies in our model, we want to retain the assumption that women on welfare are rational actors but deepen our understanding of the full range of contingencies that shape their experience and decision-making.

*Expectancy Models* As described earlier, the expectancy models—for example, self-efficacy theory (Bandura 1997), learned helplessness theory (Seligman 1975), and the study of expectancies among the unemployed poor (Goodwin 1983)—share a certain logic with regard to homeless mothers and the psychology of poverty more generally: by undermining people's expectation of success and self-efficacy, disadvantaged circumstances can also undermine their motivation and effort to attain secure employment and a better life. Moreover, when one's social world is comprised of people in similarly difficult positions, low expectations and low self-efficacy can even be conveyed as community norms (Wilson 1996; see also Sampson, Raudenbush, and Earls 1997).

Our analysis, while similar in some aspects, is different in emphasis. The afforded psychology hypothesis argues that the most fundamental mediator of economic outcomes for homeless mothers is the environmental context of their lives, and that the economic expectations and self-efficacy that they express are less important than the opportunities they are afforded. Because the unreliability of these women's lives undermines their representation of upward mobility, the expectations they express are not likely to be tied to specific plans and strategies. Rather, their efficacy beliefs are more likely to reflect their hopes for a better future. And for this reason, their expressed expectations may be relatively unpredictive of their behavior. This is supported by the tendency we observed in our interviews for the women to be optimistic about their control of important outcomes (essentially positive self-efficacy) and yet be relatively unmotivated to pursue upward mobility behaviors (such as going to college).

Thus, the lack of life context supports and scaffolding for the kind of development that enables a secure relationship to the labor market is more important in mediating the outcomes of homeless mothers on welfare than a particular level of employment expectation and self-efficacy. If poor women on welfare were exposed to reliable opportunities for skill development, then their individual level of expectation and self-efficacy with regard to those opportunities might be more predictive of their behavior. But in the absence of a clear opportunity structure, self-reported expectations and efficacy may have less meaning. We do not dismiss the importance of individual expectations and self-efficacy. But we do stress that for these constructs to have predictive value, there must be viable structures for their implementation.

## Initial Evidence for the Afforded Psychology Hypothesis

In this section, we describe some of the evidence for the assumptions of the afforded psychology hypothesis that comes from our interviews in a Bronx homeless shelter. Clearly this evidence constitutes no definitive test of the model. But it does illustrate the psychological predicament facing these women as well as the processes and assumptions inherent in our reasoning.

*Did These Women Sense That Their Environments and Relationships Were Unreliable?* What was striking in the women's accounts was the frequency with which they described a lack of reliability in their social worlds, in particular being betrayed by many of the important people in their lives. The list of "betrayers" included their parents ("I really had no mother figure, so I figured, let me do what I want to do." "When I was ten, my father tried to rape me. And I told my mother, and my mother wouldn't believe me. From that day on, my life changed, because my mother started hating me"), their teachers ("And the teachers, too, can be a real problem, there're a lot of racist teachers"), often their peers ("I met up with the wrong crowd of people. . . . When you don't have any money, you have to go to a public school, and . . . all you see is drugs, violence, people beating up on people"), and their boyfriends ("There was just a black-eye too many, and I woke up and that was it"). They also reported being betrayed by the larger institutions in which they had transacted, such as schools ("This was the name of the GED school, 'Street Academy.' That says it all"), the shelter system ("Hell! I was at the emergency assistance unit for four days. It was bad. There is people there that use drugs, there's people that have AIDS. We were sleeping on the floor"), and the larger society ("I felt that being homeless, or being on welfare, it's like making a cake and you give the good pieces of the cake to the people who can afford it, and you give the crumbs to whoever is last, and I am not a crumb. I don't want to be considered a crumb"). All of these potential sources of support were unreliable or failed to provide them with the guidance, approval, or material assistance they had so badly needed. Their mistrust, in short, was a rational reflection of, and response to, the unreliability of their life experiences.

These representative quotes all make the point that the relations and institutions in these women's lives have either not provided them with reliable support or mistreated them. They describe environmental contexts that range from the terrorizing to the neglectful but are all difficult to trust.

*Does The Sense of Environmental Unreliability Spawn a Strong Expressed Valuation of Independence and Self-Reliance?* From their phenomenological perspective and self-descriptions, the women at the shelter put a high importance on independence (Sherman 1998). Although some of their actions could be interpreted as acts of dependence, they described them as acts of independence. We asked the women how they came to be on public assistance and in the shelter system. Many women linked their reasons for being in the shelter to their desire for independence. As one twenty-three-year-old mother of one put it: "I just want to live on my own, be very independent. That's basically it. And from here [the shelter], that's where I'm trying to start from."

Many of the women described problematic situations with their parents that had caused them to want to move into the shelter system as a way of seeking independence. As one twenty-two-year-old mother of one put it, "It was my choice. I didn't want to go home and live with my parents, which I could've, but I didn't want to. I wanted some type of independence. . . . I thought, I'm not going to mooch off my mother. That's what stimulated me to do this." This desire for independence may seem quite extreme—it is not uncommon for twenty-two-year-olds to be supported by their parents—but it reflects the unreliability of her parental support.

The link between lack of social trust and independence is clear in these quotations. Given the situations of abuse and other violations of social trust these women described, it was of primary importance for them to assert their independence from these negative situations and to take control of themselves and their families. They did this by entering the shelter system, an important step toward personal autonomy.

*What Representations of Upward Mobility Do These Women Have?* The women varied in their plans for the future. Some had clearly articulated plans, including education. A typical plan was to first get a GED and then to move on to college, as one nineteen-year-old mother of one intended to do:

> The first thing I have to do is get my GED, I have to get that. I am going to take the test in January. Right now, I'm just studying, and I'll take the test in January. I've already applied for college, I just have to fill out my financial aid papers, and from there when I get my grades from the GED I'll see what college will accept my scores, which I hope is a good score then I could get into a good college, then I'll start studying from there.

However, other women, while planning on improving their education, seemed less confident that education would lead to economic success. One woman echoed the sentiment that education is important, yet she didn't seem to trust that education would truly lead to self-sufficiency. First, when asked what her plan was, she reported that it was "to go to school. To further my education. To see what the excuse will be once I have my education." When asked to elaborate on this last point, whether she saw education as a viable option, she responded:

> Not really. But they do, the system does. The system feels that if you're educated then none of this will happen to you. Who am I to argue with them, so okay, fine, I'll get my education, but I know that that's not so because I was taking care of myself before, and I didn't have a college education. But I guess they feel if you go to college then something happens. That's what I have to comply with, so I have to go school.

The women often expressed ambivalence about their role as students, although this ambivalence took many forms. Some, like this woman, described education as important to reaching some goal, not because she personally believed that education would lead her to success, but because that was what she had been told by the system. As she noted:

> People say you be educated and you go to college, well, I know a lot of people who go to college, and they have degrees, bachelor's, and they're working in McDonald's. I don't think that because I lack education that I put myself in a predicament where I can't pay my rent. That's not so, it can happen to anybody, whether you have a college degree or not.

Thus, there is no representation that college could lead to economic success. If the expectation is that college could just as easily lead to a job at McDonald's, then it makes sense that this aspiration would not regulate the women's behavior in this context.

*Is There Evidence of a Preference in These Women for Behaviors Instrumental to More Immediate Needs and Desires over Behaviors Instrumental to Less Immediate Upward Mobility?* The decisions to have children and leave school clearly demonstrate a preference for behaviors that fulfill immediate needs. The women often described a family context that did not support their continued pursuit of long-term goals like education. The following woman, a nineteen-year-old mother of one, seemed to have academic success within her grasp, but aspects of her family environment did not afford her the emotional support needed to make the commitment to education:

> I was an A student. I was a vocal major. I was class president. But I did it because I wanted my mother to be proud of me. But she never, never said, "Good job." My report card would stay where I put it. She didn't care. When I met my daughter's father, I started cutting school to be with him. That was about eleventh grade, and I winded up dropping out of high school completely. I passed eleventh, and I got to twelfth, but I never went back because I got pregnant.

Thus, this woman, like many of her peers, became pregnant and left school. However, it is crucial to see this behavior in terms of the immediate needs for support and affection that it fulfilled. Pursuing a long-term plan did not meet the emotional needs of this woman because it wasn't scaffolded by her environment, but pursuing the relationship with her daughter's father did provide her with what she needed.

## CONCLUSION

The quotes from our interviews are, of course, merely illustrative of the psychological predicaments facing women on welfare. But they do display the perspectives that deterred us from trying to describe these women in terms of internal traits and states. Such constructs would deemphasize the shaky relationship these women have always had with the environmental scaffolding of mainstream success, thus obscuring the role of their environment in affording them the psychology they have. Such constructs would also convey a different implication for how to improve these women's lives. Most likely, they would focus policy on the psyche of these women—for example, building their self-esteem or trying to encourage their internalization of middle-class values (values that they persistently report having)—rather than on their relationship to mainstream society and on developing the soundness and reliability of their opportunity structure.

In fact, our reasoning suggests that the influence of internal traits such as skill level, self-efficacy, and self-reliant values cannot be manifest when social trust is weak. Lack of social trust preempts the influence on behavior of otherwise facilitating internal characteristics. In fact, we saw no large deficits in such characteristics; the women in our study seemed high in self-esteem and reasonably confident in their ability to do the things that a reasonable level of success would require. But we did see apprehension over whether they had an opportunity structure that they could count on. And we suggest that this worry, as a reflection of the real context in which they have lived their lives, may be more important in determining their futures than the measured strength of their internal traits.

Thus, we conclude with an emphasis on whether the environment affords an opportunity structure that can be trusted or is weak against the difficult odds that women on welfare face. This approach is relational. It characterizes the psychology of the women in terms of their relationship to their context. This approach is also hopeful. It may be easier to build a trustable opportunity structure for these women than to somehow alter their psyches.

In a recent newspaper column, Molly Ivins (1997) made the point that what teenage single mothers need are not more lectures about values: "These girls don't need lectures on abstinence. And they don't need lectures on birth control. What they need is a life." And this "life"—some promising future that they can believe in—will itself come to regulate their behavior. We concur, and propose that if women on welfare are afforded an opportunity of a "life" then their behaviors and outcomes will come to reflect the values and aspirations that they already possess.

---

We would like to thank Heejung Kim, Hazel Rose Markus, Lee Ross, and the members of Steele Lab for their comments throughout this project and Joni Bohnam, Lisa Hellrich, and Elizabeth Spence for their assistance in preparation of the manuscript. This project was funded by the Russell Sage Foundation.

## NOTE

1. Interviews were conducted by David Sherman, Craig Santerre, and Claude Steele. We extend our gratitude to the women of the shelter for talking with us, as well as the many people who made this project possible including Karen Commeret, Linda Glickman, Anthony Mallon, Lynn Millheiser, Sylvia Ridlen, Ophelia Smith, and Rita Zimmer.

## REFERENCES

Auletta, Ken. (1982). *The underclass.* New York: Random House.
Bandura, Albert. (1986). *Social foundations of thought and action: A social cognitive theory.* Englewood Cliffs, N.J.: Prentice-Hall.
———. (1997). *Self-efficacy: The exercise of control.* New York: Freeman.
Bane, Mary J., and Ellwood, David T. (1994). *Welfare realities: From rhetoric to reform.* Cambridge, Mass.: Harvard University Press.
Banfield, Edward C. (1970). *The unheavenly city: The nature and future of our urban crisis.* Boston: Little, Brown.
Bassuk, Ellen L., Browne, Angela, and Buckner, John C. (1996). Single mothers and welfare. *Scientific American,* 60–67.
Bernstein, Jared. (1998). *Reformulating welfare reform.* Report for Hunter College School of Social Work. New York: Economic Policy Institute.
Blank, Rebecca M. (1994). The employment strategy: Public policies to increase work and earnings. In S. H. Danziger, G. D. Sandefur, and Daniel H. Weinberg (Eds.), *Confronting poverty: Prescriptions for change* (pp. 168–204). New York: Russell Sage Foundation.
Bourgois, Philippe. (1996). *In search of respect: Selling crack in el barrio.* New York: Cambridge University Press.
Cantril, Albert H., and Roll, Charles W. (1971). *Hopes and fears of the American people.* New York: Universe.
Cook, Thomas D., and Curtin, Thomas R. (1987). The mainstream and the underclass: Why are the differences so salient and the similarities so unobtrusive? In John C. Masters and William P. Smith (Eds.), *Social comparison, social justice, and relative deprivation: Theoretical, empirical, and policy perspectives* (pp. 217–64). Hillsdale, N.J.: Erlbaum.
Dash, Leon. (1989). *When children want children: The urban crisis of teenage childbearing.* New York: Morrow.
Edelman, Peter. (1997). The worst thing Bill Clinton has done. *Atlantic Monthly, 279* (March), 43–58.
Edin, Katheryn, and Lein, Laura. (1997). *Making ends meet: How single mothers survive welfare and low-wage work.* New York: Russell Sage Foundation.
Fiske, Alan P., Kitayama, Shinobu, Markus, Hazel R., and Nisbett, Richard E. (1998). The cultural matrix of social psychology. In Daniel T. Gilbert, Susan T. Fiske, and Gardner Lindzey (Eds.), *The handbook of social psychology* (4th ed., pp. 915–81). New York: McGraw-Hill.
Furstenberg, Frank F. (1976). *Unplanned pregnancy: The social consequences of teenage pregnancy.* New York: Free Press.
Gans, Herbert J. (1968). Culture and class in the study of poverty: An approach to anti-poverty research. In Daniel Patrick Moynihan (Ed.), *On understanding poverty: Perspectives from the social sciences.* New York: Basic Books.
Gilder, George F. (1981). *Wealth and poverty.* New York: Basic Books.
Goodwin, Leonard. (1983). *Causes and cures for welfare.* Lexington, Mass.: Lexington Books.
Greenstone, J. David. (1991). Culture, rationality, and the underclass. In Christopher Jencks and Paul E. Peterson (Eds.) *The Urban Underclass.* Washington: The Brookings Institution.
Gurin, Gerald, and Gurin, Patricia. (1970). Expectancy theory in the study of poverty. *Journal of Social Policy, 26,* 83–104.
Harrington, Michael. (1962). *The other America.* New York: Macmillan.

Harris, Kathleen M. (1997). *Teen mothers and the revolving welfare door.* Philadelphia: Temple University Press.
House, James S. (1981). Social structure and personality. In Morris Rosenberg and Ralph H. Turner (Eds.), *Social psychology: Sociological perspectives* (pp. 206–42). New York: Basic Books.
Ivins, Molly. (1997). Abstinance, birth control and caring. *The Fort Worth Star Telegram* (Texas), September 11,1997, p. 9.
Jencks, Christopher. (1992). *Rethinking social policy: Race, poverty, and the underclass.* Cambridge, Mass.: Harvard University Press.
Katz, Michael B. (1986). *In the shadow of the poorhouse: A social history of welfare in America.* New York: Basic Books.
Kozol, Jonathan. (1988). *Rachel and her children: Homeless families in America.* New York: Crown.
Lewin, Kurt. (1943). Defining the "field at a given time." *Psychological Review, 50,* 292–310.
———. (1951). Problems of research in social psychology. In Dorwin Cartwright (Ed.), *Field theory in social science* (pp. 155–69). New York: Harper and Row.
Lewis, Oscar. (1966). *La Vida: A Puerto Rican family in the culture of poverty.* New York: Random House.
———. (1968). The culture of poverty. In Daniel Patrick Moynihan (Ed.), *On understanding poverty: Perspectives from the social sciences* (pp. 187–220). New York: Basic Books.
Mead, Lawrence M. (1994). Poverty: How little we know. *Social Service Review, 3,* 22–50.
Moffitt, Robert. (1992). Incentive effects of the U.S. welfare system: A review. *Journal of Economic Literature, 30,* 1–61.
Moynihan, Daniel Patrick. (1965). *The Negro family: The case for national action.* Washington, D.C.: Office of Policy Planning and Research, U.S. Department of Labor.
———. (Ed.). (1968). *On understanding poverty: Perspectives from the social sciences.* New York: Basic Books.
Murray, Charles. (1984). *Losing ground: American social policy, 1950–1980.* New York: Basic Books.
———. (1996). Keeping priorities straight on welfare reform. *Society, 33,* 10–12.
Pavetti, Ladonna (1997). *How much more can they work?: Setting realistic expectations for welfare mothers.* Report to the Annie E. Casey Foundation. New York: Urban Institute.
Rainwater, Lee. (1970). *Behind ghetto walls: Black families in a federal slum.* Chicago: Aldine.
Sampson, Robert J., Raudenbush, Stephen W., and Earls, Felton (1997). Neighborhoods and violent crime: A multilevel study of collective efficacy. *Science, 277,* 918–24.
Seligman, Martin E. P. (1975). *Helplessness: On depression, development, and death.* San Francisco: Freeman.
Sherman, David A. (1998). Welfare mothers and the culture of poverty: Dependence or independence? Paper presented at the Culture Mini Conference, Stanford University (August 1998).
Shweder, Richard A. (1990). Cultural psychology: What is it? In James W. Stigler, Richard A. Shweder, and Gilbert Herdt (Eds.), *Cultural psychology: Essays on comparative human development* (pp. 1–46). Cambridge: Cambridge University Press.

Sidel, R. (1996). *Keeping women and children last: America's war against the poor.* New York: Penguin Books.

Steele, Claude M. (1988). The psychology of self-affirmation: Sustaining the integrity of the self. In Leonard Berkowitz (Ed.), *Advances in experimental social psychology* (vol. 21, pp. 262–302). New York: Academic Press.

———. (1997). A threat in the air: How stereotypes shape intellectual identity and performance. *American Psychologist, 52,* 613–29.

Taylor, Shelly E., Wood, Joanne V., and Lichtman, Rosemary R. (1983). It could be worse: Selective evaluation as a response to victimization. *Journal of Social Issues, 39,* 19–40.

U.S. House of Representatives. Committee on Ways and Means. (1992). 1992 *Green Book: Background material and data on programs within the juristiction of the Committee on Ways and Means.* Washington: U.S. Government Printing Office.

———. Committee on Ways and Means. (1993). 1992 *Green Book: Background material and data on programs within the juristiction of the Committee on Ways and Means.* Washington: U.S. Government Printing Office.

Wilson, William Julius. (1987). *The truly disadvantaged.* Chicago: University of Chicago Press.

———. (1996). *When work disappears: The world of the new urban poor.* New York: Knopf.

# 14

# THE DISTINCTIVE POLITICAL VIEWS OF HATE-CRIME PERPETRATORS AND WHITE SUPREMACISTS

*Donald P. Green, Robert P. Abelson, and Margaret Garnett*

DIVERSITY—cultural, racial, linguistic, religious, sexual—is resented and resisted by many. This resistance may take many forms, ranging from subtle forms of discrimination and exclusion to ethnic war and genocide. While many of the essays in this volume focus on the manifestations of intercultural abrasion in schools, workplaces, and public discourse, we have chosen to focus our attention on hate crime, or criminal conduct motivated by animus toward a victim's race, religion, ethnicity, or sexual orientation.

Our understanding of hate crime draws on a variety of theoretical perspectives, for clearly one cannot explain hate crime without reference to simmering historical conflicts, economic resentments, political events, the character of the criminal justice system, the mass media, and so forth. In this essay, however, we wish to emphasize the role of social psychological causes. In contrast to many recent studies of ethnic conflict, which tilt in the direction of economic explanations and examine aggregate rates of intergroup violence (Olzak 1992; Tolnay and Beck 1995), we focus here on the mindset of individuals associated with hate-crime or white supremacist activity. Based on a survey of suspected hate-crime perpetrators and white supremacists, we find that discomfort with social change, not heightened feelings of economic resentment, set these individuals apart from the general public. These findings, we believe, offer important insight into the genesis of hate and hate crime.

## THE CRIMINOLOGY OF HATE CRIME

The surge of white supremacist activity during the early 1980s and growing public outcry over bigoted violence brought into existence new efforts to monitor hate-crime and right-wing activity. Public interest organizations such as Klanwatch, the Anti-Violence Project, and the Anti-Defamation League devoted enormous resources to information gathering. With the passage of hate-crime laws in dozens of states and at the federal level, these data collection efforts were augmented by law enforcement agencies. Although statistical information concerning hate-crime and white supremacist activity remains far from perfect, scholars are beginning to sift through clues to the nature and causes of intolerant behavior.

The evidence gathered to date points to two important causative factors. The first, suggested by Green, Strolovitch, and Wong's (1998) cross-sectional analysis of racial/ethnic hate crime in the community districts of New York City, suggests the importance of minority influx into predominantly white neighborhoods. The number of anti-minority attacks occurring from 1987 to 1995 was largest in neighborhoods in which whites had long been the dominant racial group and where non-whites had begun to move in. Second, Green and Rich's (1998) study of anti-black hate crime in North Carolina counties from 1987 to 1993 found evidence linking cross-burnings to both white supremacist demonstrations and rates of black-white intermarriage. In addition to minority influx, then, the crossing of formerly forbidden racial boundaries and white supremacist organizing activities predict a surge in racially motivated crime.

Ecological studies of hate crime also suggest the limited role played by economic conditions. Green, Glaser, and Rich's (1998) time-series analysis of historical rates of anti-black lynching in the South and contemporary rates of hate crime in New York City found little or no connection between hate crime and deteriorating economic circumstances. Similarly, cross-sectional analyses find equivocal (Green and Rich 1998) or nonexistent (Green, Strolovitch, and Wong 1998; Karapin 1996; Krueger and Pischke 1997) relationships between unemployment rates and hate crime.

The results of these studies suggest that xenophobic reactions follow as established groups confront outsiders whose growing numbers and social practices challenge the preexisting hierarchy in which they occupied a favorable position. Plausible though this interpretation may be, the ecological information on which it rests is inherently limited in what it can tell us about the social psychology underlying hate crime and hate-group activity. At a minimum, we need more insight into the beliefs and attitudes of those who engage in these forms of conduct.[1] In what ways are the political, economic, or social views of white supremacists and hate-crime perpetrators distinctive?

It is by no means a foregone conclusion that the opinions of white supremacists and hate criminals differ from those of the general public. Some white supremacists may harbor a visceral sense of hatred and contempt for racial minorities; others merely feel a sense of disdain for peoples they perceive to be less civilized; still others insist that the pride they take in being white implies no ill will toward other races. Consider, for example, these postings on right-wing Internet sites:

> All you stupid fucking NIGGERS should still be slaves. You are worthless pieces of shit and the scum of the earth. I hope all you motherfuckers die. (whoever@144.26.12.109, March 25, 1996, http://www.thetasys.com/oldwos/wall-mar96.html)

> Recently, here in Halifax, Blacks were complaining that high school courses are geared specifically toward White students. . . . They seem to think that schools should lower requirements for them . . . just as we already lower job requirements so that minorities can better qualify for them. Maybe if these students paid more attention in class instead of acting up . . . they might get better marks. But that's a mighty big "might." (B3K, undated, http://www.io.com/~wlp/aryan-page/cpn/upfront19.html)

> No genuine White Nationalist would engage in gratuitous cruelty against other races. No genuine White Nationalist is interested in oppressing other races. We are fighting for the right to our own nation free of outside interference, just as other races should have the same right. (editor's comment, June 25, 1995, http://www2.stormfront.org/letters2.html)

Although harder to document with illustrations culled from the Internet, some hate-crime perpetrators genuinely despise the groups from which their victims are drawn, while others seem to engage in this form of activity because their friends put them up to it (Comstock 1991; Levin and McDevitt 1993). Moreover, as we move from racially charged issues to political attributes, such as media consumption, political interest, party affiliation, and the like, it becomes more difficult to anticipate the degree of contrast between these special populations and the general public.

This study represents the first effort to compare systematically the views of hate-crime perpetrators, white supremacists, and the general public. In this respect, it builds on previous ethnographic research, such as Hamm's (1993) study of the neo-Nazi skinhead subculture, depth interviews with white supremacists reported by Langer (1990) and Ezekiel (1995), and Pinderhughes's (1993) group discussions with white hate-crime perpetrators in New York City. Conversations with white supremacists, particularly those occupying a leadership role in right-wing organizations, suggest that they hold distinctive attitudes on topics having to do with the desirability of interracial contact and the need for whites to exhibit racial pride. Hate-crime perpetrators, on the other hand, seem to lack an overarching racial ideology. They defend their neighborhood turf against outsiders, these studies suggest, as a way of venting frustration with their dim economic prospects (see also Willems 1995).

Although there is much to commend in these ethnographic works, they suffer from certain drawbacks. First, they do not attempt a systematic comparison between the general public and the special subpopulation under study. This gap leaves open the question of how much of the public harbors views that overlap with those of these fringe groups. Second, the interviews were conducted in a context that may have influenced how respondents answered the questions put to them. The person who, in the guise of white supremacist or hate-crime perpetrator, is approached for an interview may be predisposed to answer questions in character (Goffman 1959). What happens when these people are approached in the context of an ordinary opinion survey, where it is assumed that the interviewer knows nothing of their group affiliations or criminal background?[2] Absent pressures to conform to putative social roles, do these respondents express distinctive political and social views?

## OVERVIEW OF STUDY DESIGN

### Questionnaire Design

The survey instrument contains sixty-two questions, running approximately fifteen minutes in length. The instrument contains four broad categories of questions. *Convergent items* comprise issues, such as environmental protection or behaviors such as media attention, on which there is no reason to suppose that the special and general populations differ. *Divergent items* attempt to capture the putative differences between special and general populations. Conducted between 1993 and 1995 by the University of North Carolina at Chapel Hill's Institute for Research in Social Science, questions were pretested on Carolina Polls. Based on the results, we devised survey questions designed to tap discomfort with social-cultural change, exclusionary sentiments directed at blacks and gays, and a propensity to endorse extreme statements in defense of white interests or the "traditional way of life." The next category, *economic evaluations,* comprises respondents' assessments of their job security and descriptions of their own personal finances (both prospective and retrospective), as well as those of their community (again, prospective and retrospective). This category also includes measures that tap the respondents' general level of economic resentment toward "newcomers" and sense of frustration with the financial condition of "ordinary people." Finally, *demographic measures* allow comparison across broad sociological groupings. These measures, as we note later, also facilitate the proper identification of respondents drawn from the special population.

## Sample

The perpetrator/supremacist sample was derived from an initial pool of suspected hate-crime perpetrators and participants in hate-group activity in North Carolina between 1986 and 1995. This initial pool of names was compiled from the archives of North Carolinians Against Racial and Religious Violence (NCARRV), an advocacy group whose data consist of newspaper clippings from both major metropolitan and community papers in North Carolina, primary source material from hate groups (newsletters, flyers, meeting reports), and victim reports to NCARRV and affiliated monitoring groups. The compilation of names was done by members of our research team, who were given access to NCARRV's data.

Using the names and other identifying information from NCARRV's archives, a phone list of 301 potential respondents with 165 distinct names was compiled using the 1995 edition of Pro-Phone CD-ROM. Since we did not wish to alert respondents to the purposes of our study, care was taken to delete from the list leaders of white supremacist groups, who, on being approached for an interview, might forewarn other members of their group. After some of the initial 301 phone numbers proved inaccurate, a second search, using the 1996 edition of Pro-Phone CD-ROM, yielded an auxiliary phone list of 75 potential respondents. In the final perpetrator sample, 46 respondents emerged from the initial list of 301 (plus 12 additional respondents who refused initially but decided to participate after being offered $20), and 24 emerged from the corrected second list of 75.

In the interest of comparability, the sample of the general population was drawn from a pool of listed phone numbers. Using listed numbers enables interviewers to ask for a specific respondent when calling a household, making the general population survey parallel to that of the special population and obviating the need to enumerate adult residents, as would be necessary using random digit dialing. A sample of listed phone numbers was drawn at random by Survey Sampling, Inc., for the purpose of obtaining seven hundred completed interviews. In turn, the survey organization that conducted the interviews selected respondents at random from this list. As we point out later, this sampling frame netted a disproportionate number of male respondents; from our standpoint, this sampling bias is an advantage, since the perpetrators and supremacists are preponderantly male.

## Supremacist Population

In the first half of the 1980s, Glenn Miller's White Patriot Party (WPP) symbolized white supremacist activity in North Carolina, both because of the high visibility of its activities (rallies, newsletters, paramilitary training sessions) and because of its charismatic and publicity-seeking leader. With an ideology that fused Confederate nostalgia, Christian Identity theology, and Germanic Nazi imagery, the White Patriot Party was well organized and had a recruiting and support network that extended beyond North Carolina borders. The party was officially disbanded in 1987 following the indictment and conviction of its leadership on federal charges. However, it continued to seize headlines when, in November 1987, two party members were indicted by a grand jury on sixteen criminal counts (including three counts of first-degree murder) relating to the January "commando-style" attack on an adult bookstore, during which five men were shot in the head at close range. In that same year, three WPP members were arrested in Fayetteville on their way to rob a Pizza Hut to raise money to organize the murder of anti-WPP attorneys, including Morris Dees of the Southern Poverty Law Center and federal prosecutors. The high-profile nature of the White Patriot Party's criminal activities provided much of the impetus behind the formation of the Governor's Task Force on Racial, Religious, and Ethnic Violence and Intimidation, whose work would eventually result in the passage of North Carolina's ethnic intimidation statute in 1990.

While the White Patriot Party was occupying the headlines, other, older white supremacist groups were occupying the streets. Between 1987 and 1995, the Christian Knights of the Ku Klux Klan (CKKKK), under the leadership of Virgil Griffin, staged marches nearly every weekend in towns all over the state. Occasionally covering two towns in one day, the marches featured members in full Klan regalia, speeches, and anti-Klan protesters. Sometimes marches were followed up by a rally, potluck, and cross-burning on a member's private property. Several years of frequent marches have made the Christian Knights the most visible white supremacist group in the state.

Following a dispute over a perceived lack of militancy in the CKKKK, former Grand Dragon Terry Boyce split from Griffin's group in 1989 to form the Confederate Knights of America. Boyce led his followers at demonstrations and inter-Klan rallies, maintaining a phone line whose weekly messages frequently advocated lynching. The Confederate Knights quickly developed ties to skinhead groups and focused most of its recruiting efforts on young people. Another variant of the Ku Klux Klan, known as the Invisible Empire of the KKK, was also active in North Carolina during this period. Leaving the marching to the Christian Knights, the Invisible Empire focused most of its public efforts on holding rallies and distributing literature. The Invisible Empire was the most secretive and militaristic of the Klan organizations operating in North Carolina and maintained ties to groups along the East Coast. In 1992 the Invisible Empire lost a major court battle with the Southern Poverty Law Center, losing $37,000 as well as its office equipment, monthly newspaper, and membership list. The group apparently has operated underground since that loss.

Two former White Patriot Party leaders, Gordon Ipock and Cecil Cox, formed the Southern National Front (SNF) in the wake of the official disbanding of the WPP. The Southern National Front was quite active in 1987, staging ten marches that year, but in early 1988 Ipock announced that he had founded a North Carolina chapter of the Maryland-based National Democratic Front (NDF). The NDF appeared to absorb the SNF, taking over much of its leadership and customary activities. Chief among these was an annual rally at the state capitol building to protest the state holiday honoring Martin Luther King's birthday. Unable to recover from infighting at the national level, the NDF faded from public view after 1989.

White supremacist groups have occasionally channeled their efforts into groups that are oriented, at least on the surface, toward electoral activity. The most prominent of these was the Populist Party, described by NCARRV (1991, 11–12) as a group of Klansmen and neo-Nazis surrounded by more mainstream conservatives. Populist Party members held regular meetings, often inviting speakers from white supremacist or far-right groups. Not officially affiliated with any other white supremacist group, the Populist Party eschewed the marches and literature distributions favored by the Klan groups and instead used public-access cable television to air neo-Nazi videos and announcements about party meetings and speakers. Monitoring groups describe the Populist Party as a vehicle for mainstreaming white supremacist political action—teaching racists to "put away the sheets and put on the business suits." Although openly racist, anti-Semitic, and homophobic commentary is commonplace at Populist Party meetings, members and candidates are urged to moderate their tone in public and to employ the code words and phrases that worked well for David Duke, the party's 1988 presidential candidate.

White supremacy also surfaces in certain religious groups. Christian Identity churches are a visible presence on the white supremacist landscape in North Carolina, particularly in the Piedmont area. The most active of these was Ben Klassen's Church of the Creator; its monthly newspaper, *Racial Loyalty,* became popular among skinhead groups outside North Carolina. Klassen deplored what he called the "rotten Jewish core" of Christianity and advocated a religion of "Creativity"—basically a primitive race-as-religion theology. Klassen and his followers, as well as other Identity groups, distributed literature and organized protests with specific targets (such as the Persian Gulf War and interracial congregations), in contrast to the regular, generalized marches and rallies of Klan groups. Klassen committed suicide in 1993.

Although there are many ideological differences between the various white supremacist groups operating in North Carolina, their literature and public speeches reveal common political ideas that go beyond the expected appeals to racial separation. Many espouse a quasi-populist ideology that is anti–big business and highly distrustful of the federal government. Their rhetoric is often characterized by nostalgia not only for a racially based social order but for a "simpler" time when rural life and family farming dominated the North Carolina economy. Rural life is viewed as inherently virtuous, and farming one's own land as a morally superior occupation. Cities, and urban life in general, are decried as places that allow race-mixing, encourage new gender roles, and discourage self-reliance. It is important to note, however, that not all facets of supremacist ideology coincide with small-government conservatism. These groups call for government intervention in areas that help make traditional rural lifestyles viable in a postindustrial world; for example, they endorse higher farm subsidies and demand additional rural health clinics. As we will see later, the policy inclinations of adherents to racist groups are leavened with a strain of populist liberalism.

## Hate-Crime Perpetrators

During the period 1987 to 1993, NCARRV documented 390 incidents of cross-burning, violence, vandalism, graffiti, and criminal threats thought to be motivated by prejudice against the victim's race, religion, ethnicity, or sexual orientation. More than three-quarters of these incidents were directed against two groups, blacks and homosexuals. Approximately one-third involved violence against a person; about half featured destruction of property or criminal mischief; the remainder consisted of criminal threats.

Our data collection methods cause the perpetrators in our sample to be drawn from the two ends of the spectrum of violence in hate crimes. Those perpetrators who commit physical assaults, burn crosses, or, at the opposite extreme, repeatedly send harassing letters or phone calls are much more likely to become known to police or monitoring agencies. The perpetrators who account for the majority of hate crimes—

shouted epithets, property damage, graffiti, threatening behavior that stops short of assault—are unlikely to become known, because victims are seldom able to identify those responsible. Thus, for example, one of our perpetrator respondents was arrested after using his pickup truck to terrorize a black woman and her two children, repeatedly chasing them up and down the street, causing severe injuries to the woman.

At the harassment end of the spectrum, another respondent was reported to an advocacy group after making death threats to the pastor of a gay and lesbian church and harassing church members during services. Cross-burnings that are not specifically tied to any hate-group activity are also represented in our perpetrator sample. Because of this "incident bias," our sample is probably older than the general perpetrator population. Additional factors limiting the numbers of young perpetrators in our sample include protections in the criminal justice system for youthful offenders, the reluctance (or legal inability) of newspapers to print the names of minors associated with possible criminal activity, and the tendency on the part of communities, law enforcement, and even victims to dismiss hate crimes committed by young people as pranks.

## Ostensible Premise of the Study

Respondents drawn from both general and special populations were read the following introduction at the start of the interview:

> Hello, my name is [first name]. I'm calling from the [survey firm] in Greensboro, and we're conducting the North Carolina Public Opinion Survey. We are calling to hear your opinions about crime, gun control, and other political issues in North Carolina. The interview will take approximately fifteen minutes.

Those who sought more information about the aims of the survey were told:

> The purpose of this study is to collect the views of North Carolina residents on important legislative issues. We are interested in gathering the opinions of people from all over the state of North Carolina and from all walks of life. Our aim is to find out how people really think about the important issues facing our state and nation today. Our poll draws its names from phonebooks all over the state in order to get the views of many different kinds of people, some of whom might not ordinarily have an opportunity to participate in a survey. Your participation means a lot to us. We'd be glad to have you verify that this is a legitimate study. You can call 1-800-[number] between nine and five o'clock Eastern Standard Time, and someone will return your call.

FIGURE 14.1 *Response Rates of Special Population*

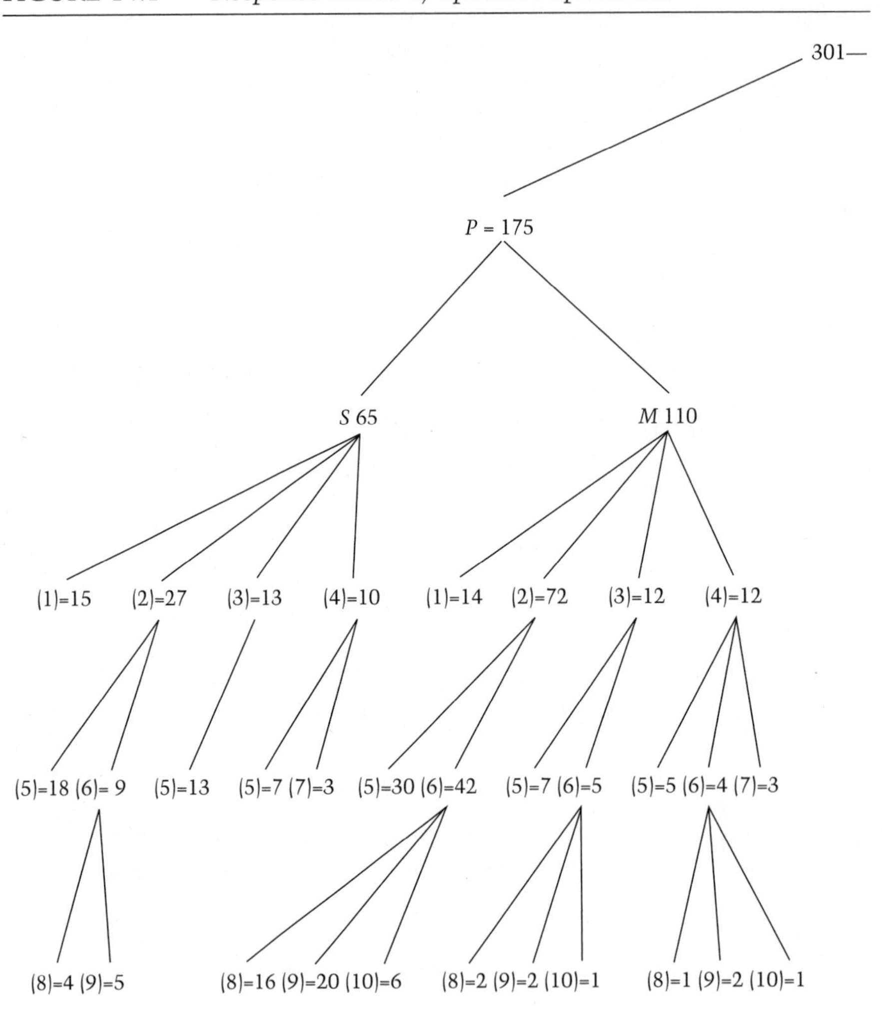


Line 1: Total sample of names = 301
Line 2: Divided into perpetrators and supermacists
Line 3: Divided into single-option and multiple-options
Line 4: What occurred in phase 1 of survey?: (1) = interviewed successfully; (2) = problem number; (3) = no answer; (4) = refusals
Line 5: (5) = no alternative found in subsequent search of Pro-Phone; (6) = alternative found in sample of 75; (7) = refusals paid to convert
Line 6: What occurred in phase 2 of survey?: (8) = interviewed successfully; (9) = unsuccessful because of number; (10) = refusals

FIGURE 14.1: *Continued*

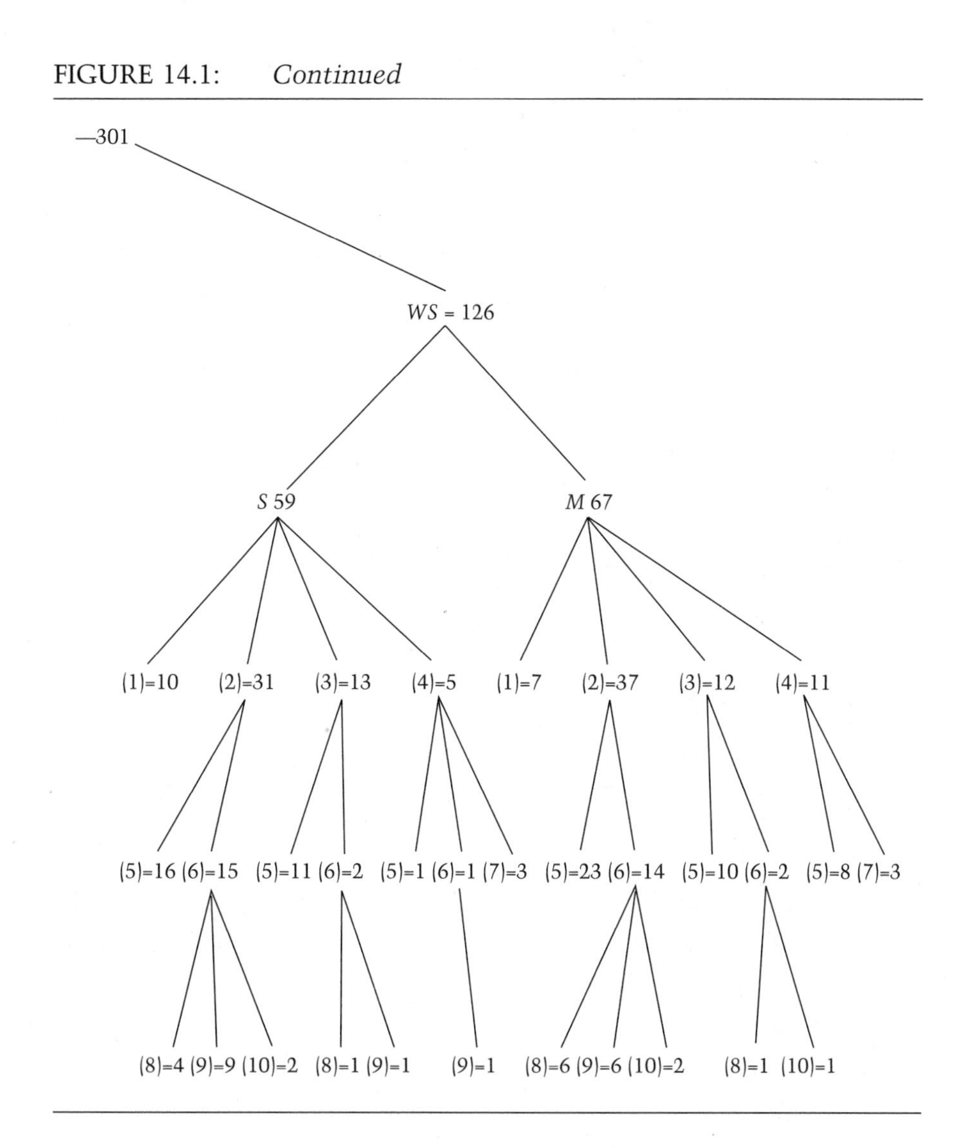


We took pains to craft this statement in such a way as to avoid falsehood. We assumed, and human subjects committees at Yale University and the University of North Carolina at Chapel Hill concurred, that a more forthright depiction of the survey's aims would have seriously undermined the response rate among those in the special population. Every effort was made to guarantee the confidentiality of responses, particularly those of the hate-crime perpetrators and white supremacists.

FIGURE 14.2 *Response Rates of General Population*

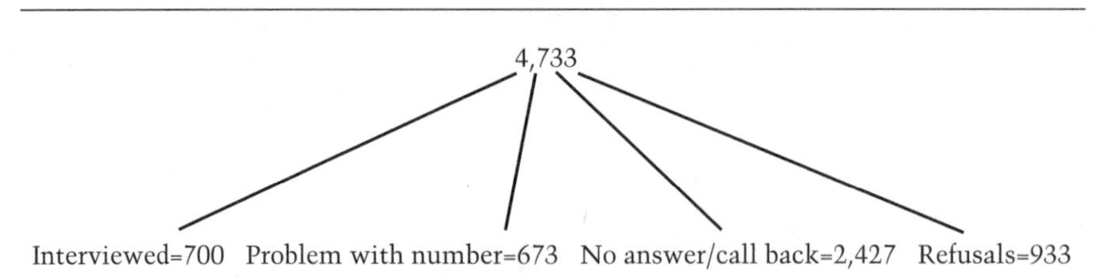


Since the survey firm that performed the interviews and coded the data is a nonacademic organization, it was felt that confidentiality was more likely to be protected if those working on the survey knew nothing of its aims or the nature of the special population. Interviewers and administrators in the survey firm were told merely that the special population encompassed names that had been "in the news" in North Carolina. This firm and its employees have not to date been debriefed, as we plan to reinterview these respondents in the future.

## Method of Administration

Surveys were conducted by an experienced professional interviewing staff using computer-assisted telephone interviewing. Phone interviewing offered certain important advantages. In addition to being less expensive and allowing for tighter quality control, phone interviewing eliminated any risk of personal injury to the interviewers. To safeguard interviewers further, they were instructed to identify themselves to respondents by their first names only. As it turns out, interviewers reported no incidents of abusive or threatening reactions from respondents drawn from the special population pool, and indeed, postinterview ratings of respondent cooperativeness and suspiciousness show that the perpetrators and supremacists who agreed to be interviewed were slightly less problematic than respondents drawn from the general population. Ironically, the few irate respondents who lodged complaints turned out to be people whose liberal inclinations caused them to be outraged at what they perceived to be a racist or inflammatory questionnaire.

## Response Rates

Figures 14.1 and 14.2 illustrate the disposition of the special population pool of 301 numbers (figure 14.1), and the general population pool of 4,733 randomly generated phone listings. While the disposition possibilities for our special population are more complex, the figures show essentially similar rates of response. For both pools, the percentage of successful interviews completed from the initial pool is approximately 15 percent (15.3 percent for our special population, 14.8 percent for the random pool). Refusal rates are also comparable, although the general public appears slightly less cooperative—19.7 percent refused to participate, as compared to 12.6 percent of our special population.[3] Willingness to participate in surveys, as well as the difficulty of finding a specific individual from phone records, does not differ substantially between the two populations.

### Criteria for Verifying Identities of Special Population Respondents

As indicated by the ratio of the initial pool of names to the final list of identified perpetrator respondents, identifying the specific individual for whom we were looking was often difficult. This difficulty arose at multiple points in the process of deriving the sample. NCARRV's archives date back to the mid-1980s, so the information (address, occupation, and so on) on some members of our initial pool was more than ten years old. Additionally, some portions of the archival files contain only names of perpetrators or hate-group activists, with no additional identifying information. While Pro-Phone CD-ROM can be searched using a variety of different combinations, we had no way of knowing with certainty whether, for example, a hypothetical perpetrator we knew as Bob Johnson would be listed in the phone records as Bob Johnson, Robert Johnson, R. Johnson, or B. Johnson. However, the additional demographic information supplied by the respondents during the survey interview (age, occupation, length of residence at current address) made it possible to identify thirty-seven respondents with a high degree of certainty.

## COMPARISON WITH BENCHMARK SURVEYS

### Demographic Comparison to General North Carolina Population

Judging from North Carolina census data, our survey of the general public yields a sample that is significantly older and disproportionately male. As noted earlier, this difference stems from the sampling technique of drawing from the population of listed phone numbers, which is likely to produce a respondent pool dominated by heads of household. However, for the purposes of comparing our general survey population with our special population, these demographic differences increase the

TABLE 14.1 *Demographic Characteristics*

| | North Carolina Population[a] | Survey Population |
|---|---|---|
| Sex | | |
| Male | 3,211,425 | 497 |
| | 48.4% | 70% |
| Female | 3,417,212 | 203 |
| | 51.6% | 29% |
| Age | | |
| Eighteen to twenty-four | 766,650 | 17 |
| | 15.3% | 2% |
| Twenty-five to thirty-four | 1,152,229 | 108 |
| | 23.0% | 15% |
| Thirty-five to forty-four | 1,008,277 | 139 |
| | 20.1% | 20% |
| Forty-five to fifty-four | 705,099 | 160 |
| | 14.0% | 23% |
| Fifty-five to sixty-four | 585,832 | 115 |
| | 11.7% | 16% |
| Over sixty-five | 802,057 | 154 |
| | 16.0% | 22% |
| Race | | |
| White | 5,011,248 | 594 |
| | 75.6% | 84.9% |
| Black | 1,455,340 | 79 |
| | 21.96% | 11.3% |
| Native American | 82,606 | 10 |
| | 1.25% | 1.4% |
| Asian/Pac. Isl. | 50,395 | 1 |
| | .76% | .1% |
| Other | 29,048 | 8 |
| | .44% | 1.1% |
| | $n$ = 6,628,637 | $n$ = 700 |

[a]Figures on North Carolina population are taken from U.S. census data.

likelihood that the attitudinal differences observed in our survey are independent of age and gender effects. Our general survey population contains a higher percentage of whites than the North Carolina population at large, but a comparison with the Spring 1996 Carolina Poll (table 14.1) indicates that this racial breakdown is similar to other randomly sampled populations in the state.

## Survey of the General North Carolina Population

Viewed in conjunction with other statewide survey populations, our general respondent population is more conservative, both politically and socially. These comparisons are laid out in detail in table 14A.1. For example, our respondent population tends to be more supportive of Jesse Helms (Q3) and more in favor of the death penalty for convicted murderers (Q8). Socially, our general population sample is markedly more conservative than respondents in comparable surveys. They are significantly more likely to agree that employers should be able to fire homosexual employees (Q6), to approve of traditional gender roles (Q29), to describe themselves as uncomfortable with changes in the traditional way of life in the state (Q35), and to be regular church attenders (Q49). The differences with other surveys on racial issues are generally smaller than the gap on sexual orientation or "tradition" issues. Our general population sample reports a higher level of media exposure, both television and print, the gap in print exposure being somewhat larger (Q24 and Q25). Both the age distribution and the number of retirees indicate that our sample is somewhat older than that of the Carolina Poll, which accounts for many of the differences noted here.

## COMPARING SUPREMACISTS, PERPETRATORS, AND THE GENERAL PUBLIC

Having established the close correspondence between our survey of the general public and other surveys using different sampling methodology, we now proceed to the central substantive issues concerning the distinctiveness of the perpetrator and supremacist respondents. To minimize the confounding influence of variables such as race and age, we restrict the analysis to white respondents under the age of forty-five.[4] This winnows the sample down to 14 hate-crime perpetrators, 9 white supremacists, and 217 respondents from the general public. Lest this seem an unworkably small number, we should mention at the outset that the results one obtains using whites of all ages (and hence more observations) are similar to what we report here.

### Political Attitudes

Table 14.2 compares the opinion distributions of the general public, hate-crime perpetrators, members of white supremacist organizations, and respondents whose names coincided with those of perpetrators/supremacists but whose identifying characteristics showed that they were not the persons we sought to interview. One would expect the views of the mistaken identity sample, therefore, to resemble those held by the general public. The five items listed in table 14.2 illustrate the general pattern of results one finds among the full range of survey questions

TABLE 14.2 *Views of Public, Perpetrator, and Supremacist Whites, Age Eighteen to Forty-Five, on Selected Issues*

| | General Public (percent) | Perpetrators (percent) | Supremacists (percent) | Mistaken Perpetrator/ Supremacists (percent) |
|---|---|---|---|---|
| Government's role in health care: | | | | |
| Government should provide | 61 | 71 | 67 | 58 |
| Individuals should provide | 31 | 29 | 22 | 26 |
| Neither/both (volunteered) | 4 | 0 | 11 | 15 |
| Don't know/refused | 3 | 0 | 0 | 0 |
| Level of immigration should be | | | | |
| Increased | 1 | 0 | 0 | 5 |
| Kept at current levels | 36 | 7 | 22 | 32 |
| Decreased | 59 | 93 | 78 | 58 |
| Don't know | 3 | 0 | 0 | 0 |
| Refused | 1 | 0 | 0 | 0 |
| Should there be a law against interracial marriage? | | | | |
| Yes | 9 | 50 | 44 | 11 |
| No | 86 | 43 | 56 | 84 |
| Don't know | 3 | 0 | 0 | 0 |
| Refused | 1 | 7 | 0 | 5 |
| "Whites need to organize themselves." | | | | |
| Agree | 35 | 50 | 78 | 47 |
| Disagree | 60 | 50 | 22 | 47 |
| Don't Know/Other | 4 | 0 | 0 | 0 |
| Refused | 1 | 0 | 0 | 5 |
| Uncomfortable with those who seek to ban the Confederate flag? | | | | |
| Very uncomfortable | 23 | 36 | 89 | 21 |
| Somewhat uncomfortable | 31 | 29 | 0 | 37 |
| Not at all uncomfortable | 44 | 36 | 11 | 37 |
| Don't know/refused | 1 | 0 | 0 | 5 |
| Number of cases | 217 | 14 | 9 | 19 |

asked. Questions tapping broad orientations toward government intervention in areas such as health care or social services reveal small differences between the four groups. With respect to health care, for example, perpetrators and supremacists take a slightly more liberal position than the general public about the desirable level of government intervention. However, when the issue shifts to admitting immigrants into the United States or banning marriages between blacks and whites, perpetrators and white supremacists differ sharply from the general public. Contrasts such as these emerge on a variety of items having to do with the exclusion of outgroups (for example, whether blacks or gays should not move into neighborhoods where they are not wanted, or whether employers should have the right to fire gay employees).

Items that tap directly into white supremacist ideology are where we find differences of opinion both between the general public and the special population *and* between perpetrators and white supremacists. Just 35 percent of young whites in the general public agreed with the statement "White people need to organize themselves in order to fight reverse discrimination." This figure rises to 50 percent among hate-crime perpetrators and to 78 percent among white supremacists. Even more striking are the contrasting reactions to "people who want to ban the display of the Confederate flag." Among the general public, fewer than one in four are made "very uncomfortable" by such people. A somewhat higher proportion (36 percent) is found among the hate-crime perpetrators. By contrast, 89 percent of the white supremacists are made very uncomfortable by those who seek to ban the Stars and Bars.

Several of the items not shown in table 14.2 yield similar contrasts between supremacists and perpetrators. The statement "The traditional American way of life is disappearing so fast that we need to use force to save it" is endorsed by 30 percent of the public and 57 percent of perpetrators (some of whom have in fact used force in an apparent effort to save it). This jingoistic appeal wins agreement from 67 percent of the supremacists. One final indication of how the ideological slant of a question can highlight intergroup differences may be found in answers to a pair of questions about residential segregation. The first "agree"/ "disagree" item, "Whites and blacks are both happier when they live in separate neighborhoods," is designed to call to mind the long-standing white supremacist argument that race-mixing is inimical to the interests of both blacks and whites. The second, "Blacks shouldn't push themselves into neighborhoods where they're not wanted," gets at the same exclusionary sentiment but does not call to mind supremacist ideological themes. Interestingly, the contrast between the opinions of supremacists and perpetrators is marked in the former case (78 percent versus 50 percent) and muted in the latter (56 percent versus 64 percent).

The emergent pattern of results suggests that perpetrators and supremacists hold distinctive political and social views. Their exclusionary impulses—as manifest in views toward immigration, interracial marriage, and the rights of gay men—differentiate them from the general public. At the same time, supremacists differ from perpetrators. Members of supremacist groups are much more likely to see a need for white activism and to condone the use of force to protect tradition. The distinctive orientation toward collective action extends also to symbols of white solidarity. The issue of banning the Confederate flag elicits a distinctive response from the supremacist, but not from the hate-crime perpetrator. In sum, the supremacist harbors a more elaborately structured set of ideological views. Although one cannot tell from our data whether these views follow from or cause membership in hate groups, they appear to be the kinds of genuine convictions that are offered to strangers outside the milieu of the hate groups themselves.

## Economic Evaluations

In order to assess the link between extreme political behavior and economic conditions, we asked respondents a variety of questions concerning their personal finances, the economic health of their community, and the economic well-being of "ordinary" people and "longtime residents." Following the wording used in the General Social Surveys and National Election Studies, queries concerning personal financial circumstances were framed both retrospectively ("Would you say that you are better off or worse off financially than you were a year ago?") and prospectively ("Now looking ahead, do you think that a year from now you will be better off financially, or worse off, or just about the same as now?"). Also included was a measure of personal economic vulnerability: "If you lost your job for any reason, how easy or difficult do you think it would be for you to find a job that would be acceptable to you? Would it be very easy, fairly easy, fairly difficult, or very difficult?"

Questions concerning the economic status of the community parallel the first two questions concerning personal finances: "Would you say that your community's economy has gotten better, stayed about the same, or gotten worse?" "Do you expect local economic conditions to get better, stay about the same, or get worse in the next year?"

The third set of items were designed to have a more jingoistic tone, tapping economic resentment and frustration. Respondents were asked whether they mostly agreed or disagreed with statements such as: "In recent years, longtime residents of this state have been losing ground economically, while newcomers have been gaining," and, "The economic prospects for ordinary people have been improving in recent years."

Responses to each question are broken down by general and special populations in table 14.3. The pattern of responses to questions concerning personal financial circumstances is weak and inconsistent. The general public gives a more upbeat assessment of its financial progress over the past year, but its economic expectations for the future are no different from those held by perpetrators or supremacists. In terms of employment, perpetrators appear to be a bit more vulnerable, but the differences between them and the general public are slight and not statistically significant.

Consistent with their retrospective evaluations of their personal finances, perpetrators and white supremacists offer a more negative assessment of their community's economic condition over the past year. A very similar pattern obtains when respondents are asked whether the economic prospects of "ordinary people" have improved in recent years. Half of the general public says that they have, in comparison to one-fourth of the special sample. A similar contrast emerges when the economic circumstances of long-term residents are compared with those of "newcomers" or when respondents predict the economic future of their community. Overall, the general public expresses more favorable economic evaluations, but the gap between it and the special population is small to moderate in size. Because many of the perpetrators and supremacists we interviewed were last associated with hate-crime or hate-group activity several years before our survey took place, one cannot rule out the possibility that the passage of time had eroded the link between economic frustration and extreme political conduct. Our results at least suggest that chronic economic frustration does little to account for differences between the general and special populations.

## DISCRIMINANT ANALYSIS

Discriminant analysis offers a more systematic way to identify the distinctive characteristics of supremacists, perpetrators, and the general public. Using all of the items in the survey, two discriminant functions are estimated, and white respondents under forty-five are assigned a probability of membership in each of the three categories.[5] If it were the case that no distinguishing traits marked the three groups, each group's discriminant functions would have the same mean value. On the other hand, if the survey items were highly discriminating, those in the perpetrator sample would be classified as perpetrators, supremacists would be classified as supremacists, and members of the general public would seldom be classified as perpetrators or supremacists.

The two discriminant functions correctly assign 83 percent of the

TABLE 14.3 *Economic Assessments of Public, Perpetrator, and Supremacist Whites, Age Eighteen to Forty-Five*

| | General Public (percent) | Perpetrators (percent) | Supremacists (percent) | Mistaken Perpetrators/ Supremacists (percent) |
|---|---|---|---|---|
| Personal finances versus last year: | | | | |
| Better off | 65.4 | 57.1 | 44.4 | 73.7 |
| Same | 15.7 | 14.3 | 22.2 | 15.8 |
| Worse off | 18.4 | 28.6 | 33.3 | 10.5 |
| Don't know | .5 | 0 | 0 | 0 |
| Personal finances this time next year: | | | | |
| Better off | 48.4 | 57.1 | 44.4 | 42.1 |
| Same | 46.1 | 42.9 | 55.6 | 47.4 |
| Worse off | 4.6 | 0 | 0 | 0 |
| Don't know | .9 | 0 | 0 | 10.5 |
| How easy would it be to find another job? | | | | |
| Very easy | 16.6 | 15.4 | 12.5 | 31.6 |
| Fairly easy | 51.8 | 38.5 | 50.0 | 47.4 |
| Fairly difficult | 23.3 | 23.1 | 25.0 | 15.8 |
| Very difficult | 7.8 | 23.1 | 12.5 | 5.3 |
| Don't know | .5 | 0 | 0 | 0 |
| Community finances versus last year: | | | | |
| Have gotten better | 42.4 | 28.6 | 22.2 | 42.1 |
| Have stayed about the same | 44.2 | 50.0 | 55.6 | 47.4 |
| Have gotten worse | 12.9 | 21.4 | 22.2 | 10.5 |
| Don't know | .5 | 0 | 0 | 0 |
| Community finances this time next year: | | | | |
| Will get better | 34.1 | 21.4 | 55.6 | 47.4 |
| Will stay about the same | 43.8 | 50.0 | 11.1 | 36.8 |
| Will get worse | 18.9 | 28.6 | 33.3 | 15.8 |
| Don't know | 3.2 | 0 | 0 | 0 |
| "Longtime residents are losing ground" | | | | |
| Agree | 59.0 | 78.6 | 66.7 | 52.6 |
| Disagree | 31.3 | 14.3 | 33.3 | 36.8 |
| Neither/both | 1.8 | 0 | 0 | 0 |
| Don't know | 7.8 | 7.1 | 0 | 10.5 |

TABLE 14.3: *Continued*

| | General Public (percent) | Perpetrators (percent) | Supremacists (percent) | Mistaken Perpetrator/ Supremacists (percent) |
|---|---|---|---|---|
| "Economic prospects of ordinary people are rising." | | | | |
| Agree | 49.3 | 28.6 | 22.2 | 63.2 |
| Disagree | 48.4 | 71.4 | 77.8 | 36.8 |
| Neither/both | .5 | 0 | 0 | 0 |
| Don't know | 1.4 | 0 | 0 | 0 |
| Refused | .5 | 0 | 0 | 0 |
| Number of cases | 217 | 14 | 9 | 19 |

respondents to their appropriate group (see table 14.4). The first function in effect distinguishes the general public (mean = −.21) from perpetrators (mean = 1.91) and supremacists (mean = 2.08). The strongest (standardized) predictors in this first equation are views concerning interracial marriage, Jesse Helms, whether employers should have the right to fire homosexuals, whether immigration should be restricted, and whether "a husband's job is to earn money, and the wife's job is to look after the home and family."[6] Questions concerning personal or community financial performance or outlook, while not inconsequential, contribute relatively little to this level of predictive accuracy. Omitting the seven economic assessments from the analysis lowers the overall level of assignment accuracy to 79 percent.

The second function further differentiates perpetrators (mean = −1.14) from supremacists (mean = 1.64). Here the items that best distinguish supremacists are preference for Pat Buchanan over Bill Clinton in a ballot test, discomfort with "northerners moving into the state, spreading liberal ideas," and discomfort with "people who want to ban the display of the Confederate flag." Following close behind is the one economic evaluation item that is framed in terms of resentment against outsiders: "Longtime residents of this state have been losing ground economically, while newcomers have been gaining." None of the other economic items contributed appreciably to the discriminant function.

It is interesting to note that just two of fourteen perpetrators in our sample are classified as white supremacists, and just one of nine white supremacists fits the profile of a hate-crime perpetrator. While one cannot say a priori how many hate crimes any given perpetrator might commit or what fraction of all incidents are committed by white suprema-

TABLE 14.4 *Discriminant Analysis (White Respondents Under Age Forty-Five)*

| | General Public (percent) | Perpetrators (percent) | Supremacists (percent) | Mistaken Perpetrators/ Supremacists (percent) |
|---|---|---|---|---|
| Predicted group | | | | |
| General public | 84 | 14 | 11 | 79 |
| Perpetrators | 10 | 71 | 11 | 11 |
| Supremacists | 6 | 14 | 78 | 11 |
| Number of cases | 215 | 14 | 9 | 19 |

*Note:* "Mistaken perpetrators and supremacists" denotes respondents whose names coincide with the names of actual perpetrators or supremacists but whose age, race, occupation, and other personal characteristics (other than political or social attitudes) ruled them out. This group was not included in the estimation of the discriminant functions. They are included here to gauge the predictive accuracy of the estimates obtained from the discriminant model.

cists, this pattern of results is consistent with the fact that hate-crime perpetrators are seldom linked to white supremacist organizations.

In sum, the discriminant analysis lends support to the notion that reactionary views typify both perpetrators and supremacists. Both groups are distinctive in their endorsement of traditional sex roles and discomfort with homosexuals or interracial mixing. Setting apart North Carolina supremacists is their concern with challenges to symbols of southern pride and their antipathy to those who would disrupt traditional southern ways of life, concerns that in the spring of 1996 were embodied in the candidacy of Pat Buchanan, particularly given media reports suggesting that Buchanan campaign activists had attended right-wing political functions.

One useful feature of discriminant analysis is that it enables us to assess the accuracy with which we have identified the actual perpetrators or supremacists among the respondents interviewed in our special sample. Recall that respondents were classified on the basis of extrinsic criteria (race, age, occupation, and so on), not the political opinions they expressed. Among the nineteen respondents under the age of forty-five who seemed not to match the profiles of actual perpetrators/supremacists, fifteen (79 percent) are classified as members of the general public. This proportion is statistically indistinguishable from the 84 percent rate at which respondents from the general population are assigned to this category by our analysis. This result offers some assurance that our method of linking respondents to available background information is fairly accurate.

## DISCUSSION

Understanding the motives of white supremacists and hate-crime perpetrators requires an understanding of how their political and social outlook differs from that of the general public. This study augments previous research findings in several ways. Our investigation assessed the political attitudes of rank-and-file white supremacist group members, not leaders, and did so in an impersonal context where interviewees were free from social pressures to hew to the group's ideological doctrine. Perpetrators, by the same token, were interviewed in the guise of ordinary citizens; the interviewers themselves had no knowledge of the respondents' special background. Finally, the respondents were selected using reproducible, if flawed, sampling techniques and were interviewed using a standardized interview schedule.

At the same time, our study is not without important limitations. Respondents were drawn from one state and, despite our best efforts, were not interviewed in great numbers. This study, therefore, is properly regarded as only one step toward a more comprehensive and variegated depiction of these groups.

One conclusion to be drawn from our results is that white supremacists and hate-crime perpetrators are not notably more frustrated economically or more pessimistic about the financial future of their communities than the general public. This finding contradicts the argument that economic downturns engender frustration or competition for scarce resources, in turn producing hate crime (Hovland and Sears 1940; Tolnay and Beck 1995; see also Green, Glaser, and Rich 1998). It is significant in this regard that hate crimes are often characterized by the absence of pecuniary motives: synagogues are vandalized but not looted; gay men are assaulted but not robbed; minorities receive threatening messages that make no mention of extortion.

Of greater explanatory value than economic concerns are the distinctive exclusionary sentiments of hate-crime perpetrators and white supremacists. The specter of race-mixing, immigration, and the blurring of gender roles looms much larger in the minds of these respondents than it does for corresponding members of the general public. Supremacists in our sample are further distinguished by their concern over threats to southern identity and their sense that whites must organize to defend themselves.

While perhaps not surprising, these conclusions attest to both the staying power of political orientations and the capacity of conventional survey methods to gauge them. The respondents in our sample were last observed in connection with hate-crime or hate-group activity years before the surveys took place. Nevertheless, the perpetrator and supremacist respondents remain distinctive in their political and social views. Just three of twenty-three respondents in our perpetrator and supremacist samples offered survey responses that caused our classification analysis to dub them members of the general population. Conversely, 16 percent of the whites under forty-five in the general population matched the characteristics associated with perpetrators or white supremacists.

What of this 16 percent, of which roughly one-third are putative white supremacists? No matter how generously one chooses to estimate the ranks of white supremacist groups (compare, Hamm 1993), their numbers do not begin to approach this fraction of the young white public. Much the same point can be made about the number of hate-crime perpetrators in the population. But just as there are more people highly sympathetic to environmental protection than there are members of environmental organizations or active participants in efforts to clean up the environment, hate-crime perpetrators and white supremacists are drawn from a much larger pool of like-minded individuals.

For this reason, no psychological explanation can make sense of hate crime without considering the mechanisms by which individuals are spurred to action, be it hate crime or right-wing activism. A great many social psychological forces come readily to mind: pressures to go along with, or prove oneself among, a group of bigots looking for action; the blandishments of a charismatic leader; community norms concerning attacks against minorities; to name but a few. Here, we wish to call attention to a psychological mechanism that has been termed "entitativity," or the perception that an outgroup is an internally cohesive actor poised to take action on behalf of its interests (Abelson, Dasgupta, and Banaji 1998).

In the prejudice literature, there is the striking nonfinding concerning whites who have contacts with a few blacks in an equal-status atmosphere at school, at work, or in the neighborhood. They come to feel more favorable toward the blacks with whom they interact, but this change toward more positive regard rarely generalizes to produce a positive (or less negative) regard for blacks in general (Rothbart and John 1985). The standard explanation that psychologists give for this puzzle is that the blacks in the interaction are categorized as essentially different from blacks in general—they are "subtyped," that is, categorized as well-educated blacks, or as friendly, nice individuals, and so on. A more important factor, we hypothesize, is that conceptions of individuals and of groups are fundamentally different (Abelson et al. 1998).

The perception that such groups have begun to invade the neighborhood or threaten the primacy of the formerly dominant group creates a heightened sense of anxiety. This invasion may have a physical dimension, as when newcomers move into a community or join its workforce. The encroachment may also be cultural. By culture, we mean a well-defined corpus of rituals (sacred or profane), activities, appearances, territory, possessions, and beliefs that are shared by an entitive group of individuals. Group culture can be viewed as a kind of Lewinian "life space," containing all the things that group members consider intrinsic to their self-definition as members. We assume that a sense of encroachment arises when an outgroup acts, or threatens to act, in a way that restricts the scope of the group's life space or makes the exercise of options within it difficult.

The most obvious examples of perceived encroachment involve both physical invasion of turf and challenges to cultural practices, as when minorities play "their" kinds of music, speak "their" languages, or display "their" kinds of dress in places regarded by whites as white neighborhoods. (Indeed, some of the most bitter antagonisms between groups have sometimes exploded over such small but symbolic acts.) We have seen here that supremacists and perpetrators are especially *opposed* to such encroachment. We speculate that they are also particularly *agitated* by it (Green, Strolovitch, and Wong 1998). The social changes they see around them foreshadow ever-increasing threats to the preexisting hierarchy. They see themselves locked in a Manichean struggle between themselves and insurgent groups, one that is causing them gradually to lose control over their territory and familiar ways of life. The inexorable march toward mongrelization dominates white supremacist doctrine, which concludes that only through white supremacy can Aryans prevent their ways of life from being overwhelmed by sinister forces. The views of hate-crime perpetrators are doubtless less systematic, but we suspect that for them the prospect of group encroachment is as ominous and salient. Some repair to all-white enclaves, while others stand and fight.

# APPENDIX

TABLE 14A.1 *Comparison of Benchmark Surveys*

| Question Text | Answer Choices | Verified Perpetrators and Supremacists | General Population | Comparable Population[o] | |
|---|---|---|---|---|---|
| Q3. How would you rate Jesse Helms as senator? | Excellent | 16.2 | 18.6 | 13.0[g] | |
| | Pretty good | 35.1 | 31.3 | 23.2 | |
| | Only fair | 24.3 | 21.3 | 26.8 | |
| | Poor | 21.6 | 23.9 | 29.1 | |
| | Don't know | 2.7 | 4.6 | 7.8 | (and refusals) |
| | Refused | — | .4 | — | |
| | | 100.0% | 100.0% | 99.9% | |
| | | (*n* = 37) | (*n* = 700) | (*n* = 620) | |
| Q6. Do you think that employers should or should not be able to fire people who announce that they are homosexual? | Should be able to | 51.4 | 27.6 | 14.4[c] | |
| | Should not be able to | 37.8 | 57.9 | 68.6 | |
| | Don't know | 10.8 | 13.1 | 4.8 | |
| | Refused | | 1.4 | 1.8[j] | |
| | | 100.0% | 100.0% | 89.6% | |
| | | (*n* = 37) | (*n* = 700) | (*n* = 598) | |
| Q8. Do you favor or oppose the death penalty for persons convicted of murder? | Favor | 91.9 | 77.6 | 72.5[e] | |
| | Oppose | 5.4 | 15.4 | 16.6 | |
| | Don't know | 2.7 | 6.7 | 10.9 | (and refusals) |
| | Refused | | .3 | | |
| | | 100.0% | 100.0% | 100.0% | |
| | | (*n* = 37) | (*n* = 700) | (*n* = 636) | |
| Q10. Do you think that spending on national defense should be increased, decreased, or kept about the same? | Increased | 24.3 | 20.0 | 20.8[a] | |
| | Decreased | 32.4 | 23.0 | 37.5 | |
| | Kept the same | 43.2 | 52.3 | 41.7 | |
| | Don't know | | 4.6 | | |
| | Refused | | .1 | | |
| | | 100.0% | 100.0% | 100.0% | |
| | | (*n* = 37) | (*n* = 700) | (*n* = 26) | |
| Q11. Do you think the number of | Increased | 5.4 | 3.0 | 00.0[a] | |

| | | | | |
|---|---|---|---|---|
| immigrants permitted to enter this country should be increased, decreased, or kept at current levels? | Decreased | 73.0 | 61.4 | 70.8 |
| | Kept at current levels | 21.6 | 32.0 | 29.2[i] |
| | Don't know | | 3.3 | |
| | Refused | | .3 | |
| | | 100.0% | 100.0% | 100.0% |
| | | ($n$ = 37) | ($n$ = 700) | ($n$ = 26) |
| Work status: Last week were you . . . | Working full-time | 73.0 | 57.0 | 61.1[h] |
| | Working part-time | 5.4 | 4.1 | 7.7 |
| | Going to school | 0.0 | 1.0 | 4.6 |
| | Keeping house | 0.0 | 4.3 | 7.8 |
| | Retired | 10.8 | 23.0 | 13.3 |
| | Unemployed | 2.7 | 3.1 | 2.5 |
| | On disability | 2.7 | 5.7 | |
| | Other | 5.4 | 1.4 | 2.5 |
| | Don't know | .0 | .0 | .0 |
| | Refused | .0 | .3 | .5 |
| | | 100.0% | 100.0% | 99.9% |
| | | ($n$ = 37) | ($n$ = 700) | ($n$ = 662) |
| Q24. How many days out of the last seven did you watch either the local or national news on television? | 0 | 5.4 | 5.6 | 5.2[h] |
| | 1 | 10.8 | 2.0 | 3.5 |
| | 2 | 0.0 | 5.4 | 6.7 |
| | 3 | 10.8 | 8.0 | 8.0 |
| | 4 | 2.7 | 6.9 | 11.1 |
| | 5 | 10.8 | 12.1 | 12.2 |
| | 6 | 5.4 | 5.6 | 6.3 |
| | 7 | 51.4 | 53.6 | 46.4 |
| | Don't know | 2.7 | .9 | |
| | Refused | | | .5 |
| | | 100.0% | 100.0% | 99.9% |
| | | ($n$ = 37) | ($n$ = 700) | ($n$ = 662) |
| Q25. How many days out of the last seven did you read a daily newspaper? | 0 | 21.6 | 17.0 | 18.1[h] |
| | 1 | 5.4 | 9.4 | 9.9 |
| | 2 | 2.7 | 9.1 | 13.3 |

(*Table continues on page 456.*)

TABLE 14A.1: *Continued*

| Question Text | Answer Choices | Verified Perpetrators and Supremacists | General Population | Comparable Population[o] | |
|---|---|---|---|---|---|
| | 3 | 5.4 | 5.7 | 10.4 | |
| | 4 | 13.5 | 4.7 | 5.1 | |
| | 5 | 13.5 | 7.9 | 8.1 | |
| | 6 | 2.7 | 4.1 | 5.7 | |
| | 7 | 35.1 | 41.7 | 28.7 | |
| | Don't know | | .3 | | |
| | Refused | | | .6 | |
| | | 100.0% | 100.0% | 99.9% | |
| | | ($n$ = 37) | ($n$ = 700) | ($n$ = 662) | |
| Q27. Now I'd like to ask a few questions on some different topics. There's been a lot of discussion about the way morals are changing in this country. If a man and a woman have sexual relations before marriage, do you thinks it's . . . | Not wrong at all | 29.7<br>($n$ = 37) | 24.3<br>($n$ = 700) | 26.9[f,k]<br>($n$ = 619) | |
| Q28. What about sexual relations between two adults of the same sex—do you think it is always wrong, wrong only sometimes, or not wrong at all? | Not wrong at all | 5.4<br>($n$ = 37) | 11.0<br>($n$ = 700) | 11.4[b,k]<br>($n$ = 621) | |
| Q29. Do you agree or disagree with this statement: "A husband's job is to earn money, and the wife's job is to look after the home and the family." | Agree | 37.8 | 32.0 | 27.9[f] | |
| | Disagree | 54.1 | 60.9 | 67.5 | |
| | Neither/both | 8.1 | 4.1 | | |
| | Don't know | | 1.9 | 4.6 | (and refusals) |
| | Refused | | 1.1 | | |
| | | 100.0% | 100.0% | 100.0% | |
| | | ($n$ = 37) | ($n$ = 700) | ($n$ = 619) | |
| Q30. Do you think there should be laws against marriages | Yes | 37.8 | 19.4 | 11.7[g] | |
| | No | 56.8 | 75.1 | 83.7 | |

| | | | | | |
|---|---|---|---|---|---|
| between blacks and whites? | Don't know | 2.7 | 4.1 | 4.7 | (and refusals) |
| | Refused | 2.7 | 1.3 | | |
| | | 100.0% | 100.0% | 100.1% | |
| | | ($n$ = 37) | ($n$ = 700) | ($n$ = 620) | |
| Q30B. do you think that abortion should be . . . | Legal under any circumstances | 8.1 | 15.9 | 21.4[e] | |
| | Legal under certain circumstances | 67.6 | 66.1 | 57.6 | |
| | Illegal at all times | 21.6 | 15.1 | 17.0 | |
| | Don't know | | 1.9 | 3.9 | (and refusals) |
| | Refused | 2.7 | 1.0 | | |
| | | 100.0% | 100.0% | 99.9% | |
| | | ($n$ = 37) | ($n$ = 700) | ($n$ = 636) | |
| Q31. Suppose a black couple living in your community were harassed and threatened at their home by people who singled them out because of their race. What do you think most people in your community would say? Would they express sympathy for the black couple, or would they just let it go? | Express sympathy | 67.6 | 68.3 | 68.3[c] | |
| | Let it go | 27.0 | 20.6 | 21.0 | |
| | Other | 2.7 | 1.6 | 4.9 | |
| | Don't know | 2.7 | 9.0 | 5.9 | (and refusals) |
| | Refused | | .6 | | |
| | | 100.0% | 100.0% | 100.1% | |
| | | ($n$ = 37) | ($n$ = 700) | ($n$ = 598) | |
| Q32. How about yourself, would you express sympathy for the black couple, or would you just let it go? | Express sympathy | 70.3 | 83.7 | 86.0[C] | |
| | Let it go | 21.6 | 7.7 | 6.2 | |
| | Other | 2.7 | 4.6 | 5.7 | |
| | Don't know | 2.7 | 3.3 | 2.1 | (and refusals) |
| | Refused | 2.7 | .7 | | |
| | | 100.0% | 100.0% | 100.0% | |
| | | ($n$ = 37) | ($n$ = 700) | ($n$ = 598) | |
| Q33. Tell me whether you agree or disagree with this statement: "Blacks shouldn't push themselves into neighborhoods where they're not wanted." | Strongly agree | 21.6 | 10.1 | 9.8[g] | |
| | Agree | 37.8 | 31.3 | 25.5 | |
| | Disagree | 18.9 | 34.6 | 37.8 | |
| | Strongly disagree | 18.9 | 15.0 | 20.9 | |
| | Don't know | | 7.0 | 6.0 | (and refusals) |
| | Refused | 2.7 | 2.0 | | |
| | | 100.0% | 100.0% | 100.0% | |
| | | ($n$ = 37) | ($n$ = 700) | ($n$ = 620) | |

(*Table continues on page 458.*)

TABLE 14A.1: *Continued*

| Question Text | Answer Choices | Verified Perpetrators and Supermacists | General Population | Comparable Population° | |
|---|---|---|---|---|---|
| Q34. How about this statement: "Gay men and lesbians should not push themselves into neighborhoods where they're not wanted." | Strongly agree | 35.1 | 21.7 | 12.6[g] | |
| | Agree | 24.3 | 30.7 | 31.5 | |
| | Disagree | 32.4 | 27.6 | 33.3 | |
| | Strongly disagree | 5.4 | 10.6 | 15.4 | |
| | Don't know | | 7.4 | 7.1 | (and refusals) |
| | Refused | 2.7 | 2.0 | | |
| | | 100.0% | 100.0% | 99.9% | |
| | | ($n$ = 37) | ($n$ = 700) | ($n$ = 620) | |
| Q35. In recent years, there have been a lot of changes in North Carolina, with new lifestyles, and new people moving in who have different ways. Some people feel that these changes don't fit into the traditional way of life in the state. Other people welcome these changes. How do you feel about the changes in the way of life here? All in all, are you comfortable with these changes, uncomfortable with these changes, or haven't you paid much attention to them? | Comfortable with changes | 24.3 | 35.6 | 41.6[g] | |
| | Uncomfortable with changes | 32.4 | 24.7 | 18.3 | |
| | Haven't paid much attention | 43.2 | 34.6 | 30.4 | |
| | Depends | | 3.3 | 5.1 | |
| | Don't know | | 1.1 | 4.6 | (and refusals) |
| | Refused | | .7 | | |
| | | 100.0% | 100.0% | 100.0% | |
| | | ($n$ = 37) | ($n$ = 700) | ($n$ = 620) | |
| Q36. Let me give you some particular examples of things that might make some people uncomfortable. For each one, tell me whether it makes you feel very uncomfortable, or not at all uncomfortable: Immigrants speaking languages other than | Very uncomfortable | 37.8 | 20.0 | 17.4[h] | |
| | Somewhat uncomfortable | 29.7 | 33.3 | 37.6 | |
| | Not at all uncomfortable | 32.4 | 45.4 | 40.9 | |
| | Don't know | | .9 | 4.0 | (and refusals) |
| | Refused | | .4 | | |
| | | 100.0% | 100.0% | 99.9% | |
| | | ($n$ = 37) | ($n$ = 700) | ($n$ = 662) | English. |

|  |  | | | | |
|---|---|---|---|---|---|
| Q37. . . . Northerners moving into the state, spreading liberal ideas. | Very uncomfortable | 29.7 | 14.9 | 11.0[g] | |
| | Somewhat uncomfortable | 32.4 | 25.9 | 21.0 | |
| | Not at all uncomfortable | 37.8 | 53.9 | 61.9 | |
| | Don't know | | 4.0 | 6.1 | (and refusals) |
| | Refused | | 1.4 | | |
| | | 100.0% | 100.0% | 100.0% | |
| | | ($n$ = 37) | ($n$ = 700) | ($n$ = 620) | |
| Q38. . . . Rap music. | Very uncomfortable | 48.6 | 38.6 | 28.6[g] | |
| | Somewhat uncomfortable | 24.3 | 24.6 | 30.8 | |
| | Not at all uncomfortable | 16.2 | 32.9 | 36.4 | |
| | Don't know | 10.8 | 3.3 | 4.3 | (and refusals) |
| | Refused | | .7 | | |
| | | 100.0% | 100.0% | 100.1% | |
| | | ($n$ = 37) | ($n$ = 700) | ($n$ = 620) | |
| Q39. . . . People who want to ban the display of the Confederate flag. | Very uncomfortable | 62.2 | 27.7 | 27.6[g] | |
| | Somewhat uncomfortable | 16.2 | 25.7 | 26.9 | |
| | Not at all uncomfortable | 21.6 | 41.4 | 36.2 | |
| | Don't know | | 3.9 | 9.3 | (and refusals) |
| | Refused | | 1.3 | | |
| | | 100.0% | 100.0% | 100.0% | |
| | | ($n$ = 37) | ($n$ = 700) | ($n$ = 620) | |
| Q40C. Here are two statements that people sometimes make when discussing the environment and economic growth. Which of these statements comes closer to your own point of view? | "Protection of the environment should be given priority." | 70.3 | 60.7 | 64.4[d] | |
| | "Economic growth should be given priority." | 16.2 | 26.0 | 26.3 | |
| | Both | 8.1 | 4.3 | | |
| | Don't know | 5.4 | 8.0 | 9.3 | (and refusals) |
| | Refused | | 1.0 | | |
| | | 100.0% | 100.0% | 100.0% | |
| | | ($n$ = 37) | ($n$ = 700) | ($n$ = 604) | |

(*Table continues on page 460.*)

TABLE 14A.1: *Continued*

| Question Text | Answer Choices | Verified Perpetrators and Supermacists | General Population | Comparable Population[o] | |
|---|---|---|---|---|---|
| Q41. Some people think of themselves as southerners; other do not. How about you? Do you generally think of yourself as a southerner? | Yes | 78.4 | 70.1 | 72.8[h] | |
| | No | 18.9 | 27.3 | 23.0 | |
| | Don't know | 2.7 | 2.0 | 4.1 | (and refusals) |
| | Refused | | .6 | | |
| | | 100.0% | 100.0% | 99.9% | |
| | | ($n$ = 37) | ($n$ = 700) | ($n$ = 662) | |
| Q42. In general, when it comes to politics, do you think of yourself as a . . . | Democrat | 24.3 | 31.3 | 34.2[h] | |
| | Republican | 27.0 | 32.1 | 35.5 | |
| | Independent | 37.8 | 31.7 | 20.0 | |
| | Other | 8.1 | 1.3 | 4.4 | |
| | Don't know | 2.7 | 1.9 | 5.9 | (and refusals)[m] |
| | Refused | | 1.7 | | |
| | | 100.0% | 100.0% | 100.0% | |
| | | ($n$=37) | ($n$=700) | ($n$=662) | |
| Q43. Are you currently registered to vote? | Yes | 86.5 | 87.6 | 82.1[h] | |
| | No | 13.5 | 11.4 | 17.5 | |
| | Don't know | | .7 | .4 | (and refusals) |
| | Refused | | .3 | | |
| | | 100.0% | 100.0% | 100.0% | |
| | | ($n$ = 37) | ($n$ = 700) | ($n$ = 662) | |
| Q45. How many years of school have you completed? | Eight or less | 2.7 | 6.4 | 2.9[h] | |
| | Nine to eleven | 21.6 | 12.1 | 9.2 | |
| | Twelve | 27.0 | 27.3 | 31.1 | |
| | Thirteen to sixteen | 37.8 | 39.8 | 45.3 | |
| | More than sixteen | 10.8 | 13.5 | 10.5 | |
| | Refused | | .9 | 1.0 | |
| | | 100.0% | 100.0% | 100.0% | |
| | | ($n$ = 37) | ($n$ = 700) | ($n$ = 662) | |

|  |  | | | | |
|---|---|---|---|---|---|
| Q49. How often do you attend religious services? | Never | 10.8 | 8.0 | 10.4[h] | |
| | Once a year or less | 2.7 | 7.1 | 9.9 | |
| | Several times a year | 16.2 | 12.4 | 14.5 | |
| | About once a month | 10.8 | 8.6 | 9.8 | |
| | Two to three times a month | 21.6 | 12.6 | 10.9 | |
| | Every week | 21.6 | 33.6 | 30.8 | |
| | More than once a week | 16.2 | 16.1 | 12.8 | |
| | Don't know | | .9 | .9 | (and refusals) |
| | Refused | | .7 | | |
| | | 100.0% | 100.0% | 100.0% | |
| | | $(n = 37)$ | $(n = 700)$ | $(n = 662)$ | |
| Q50. What is your religious preference? | Catholic | 8.1 | 7.1 | 6.7[h] | |
| | Baptist | 62.2 | 42.4 | 47.7 | |
| | Methodist/United Brethren | 5.4 | 12.9 | 12.2 | |
| | Presbyterian | 5.4 | 5.6 | 5.2 | |
| | Other | 18.9 | 32.0 | 25.7 | |
| | Don't know | | | 2.5 | (and refusals)[n] |
| | Refused | | | | |
| | | 100.0% | 100.0% | 100.0% | |
| | | $(n = 37)$ | $(n = 700)$ | $(n = 622)$ | |
| Q52. How long have you lived at your present address? | Less than six months | | 2.3 | 19.2[a] | |
| | One year | 5.4 | 4.3 | 3.8 | |
| | Two years | 2.7 | 8.4 | 19.2 | |
| | Three to five years | 13.5 | 17.6 | 23.0 | |
| | Six to ten years | 33.4 | 18.8 | 23.0 | |
| | Eleven to fifteen years | 13.5 | 10.4 | 0.0 | |
| | Sixteen to twenty years | 8.1 | 10.9 | 7.6 | |
| | More than twenty years | 8.1 | 26.4 | 3.8 | |
| | | 100.0% | 100.0% | 100.0% | |
| | | $(n = 37)$ | $(n = 700)$ | $(n = 26)$ | |
| RACE. What race do you consider yourself? | White or Caucasian | 100.0 | 84.9 | 80.8[h] | |
| | Aryan (vol. only) | | | | |
| | Black or African-Amer. | | 11.3 | 14.5 | |

(*Table continues on page 462.*)

TABLE 14A.1: *Continued*

| Question Text | Answer Choices | Verified Perpetrators and Supermacists | General Population | Comparable Population[o] |
|---|---|---|---|---|
| | Native American | | 1.4 | 2.2 |
| | Asian or Pac. Isl. | | .1 | |
| | Other | | 1.1 | 1.5 |
| | Don't know | | .3 | |
| | Refused | | .9 | 1.0 |
| | | 100.0% | 100.0% | 100.0% |
| | | ($n$ = 37) | ($n$ = 700) | ($n$ = 651) |
| AGE. What is your age? | 18–24 yrs. | 5.4 | 2.0 | 12.0[h] |
| | 25–44 yrs. | 56.8 | 35.0 | 44.7 |
| | 45–64 yrs. | 27.0 | 37.0 | 33.0 |
| | 65+ yrs. | 8.1 | 22.0 | 10.3 |
| | Refused | 2.7 | 1.0 | |
| | | 100.0% | 100.0% | 100.0% |
| | | ($n$ = 37) | ($n$ = 700) | ($n$ = 651) |

[a]1994 American National Election Study (ANES)
[b]Spring 1992 Carolina Poll
[c]Spring 1993 Carolina Poll
[d]Fall 1993 Carolina Poll
[e]Spring 1994 Carolina Poll
[f]Spring 1995 Carolina Poll
[g]Fall 1995 Carolina Poll
[h]Spring 1996 Carolina Poll
[i]ANES wording adds "from foreign countries" after "immigrants"; answer choices are "increased a lot," "increased a little," "kept the same," "decreased a little," "decreased a lot"—"increased" and "decreased" items have been combined for comparison.
[j]Carolina Poll included a "depends" answer choice; it was chosen by 10.4 percent of respondents.
[k]Carolina Poll included an answer choice "almost always wrong"; because of the difficulty of assigning these respondents to our categories, we've included only the categorical "not wrong" for comparison.
[l]Carolina Poll included an answer choice "other"; 1.3 percent of respondents fit this category.
[m]Carolina Poll wording omits the prase "when it comes to politics."
[n]Other named response categories, on both our survey and the Carolina Poll, have been collapsed into the category of "other."
[o]Numbers in this column may not add to 100 percent due to rounding.

---

This paper was funded by grants from the Harry Frank Guggenheim Foundation, the National Science Foundation, and the Institution for Social and Policy Studies at Yale, none of which bear any responsibility for the content of this report. The authors are grateful to Jay Dixit, Jack Glaser, Andrew Rich, Dara Strolovitch, and Janelle Wong for their help collecting data.

## NOTES

1. Questions such as these are easily multiplied. What small-group contexts contribute to hate crime? What is the contribution of the nature and activities of the police force? What is the link between aggregate public opinion and the occurrence of hate crime?
2. A related concern has to do with the haphazard process by which respondents were sampled. Langer (1990) and Ezekiel (1995) conducted in-depth interviews with small convenience samples, while Hamm (1993) and Pinderhughes (1993) interviewed clusters of people within formal or informal groups. Since populations of white supremacists and hate-crime perpetrators are by their very nature difficult to identify, let alone sample, informal sampling may be the only workable way to proceed. In our study, we made an effort to follow a set of sampling procedures so as to enhance the replicability of our findings (see also Franklin 1996).
3. This figure may seem unusually low, but it is comparable to rates typically achieved by commercial polling organizations. The response rate such organizations usually report omits from the denominator those phone numbers that resulted in neither a completion nor a refusal.
4. The general population survey contains nonwhites, whereas the perpetrator or supremacist sample consists only of whites. Respondents from the general population are also much older on average; since age is correlated with racial conservatism, this characteristic of the general population potentially masks some of the contrast in opinions. Once the samples are restricted to those under forty-five, the mean age in the supremacist, perpetrator, and general public samples differ by less than one year. We have also experimented with other controls to correct for the fact that the general population survey contains a higher percentage of women (just two of the twenty-three perpetrators and supremacists analyzed below are women) and that approximately half of the general population respondents were interviewed by black interviewers, whereas the special population respondents were interviewed only by whites. Controlling for the sex and race of the interviewer, however, does not alter the substantive conclusions reported here.
5. To avoid discarding observations on account of missing data, several of the variables were recoded into dichotomies or trichotomies, with "don't know" responses placed into a seemingly appropriate category (often the middle).
6. The fact that the Helms evaluation should be a significant predictor may seem surprising, given the results in table 14A.1 showing that the special and general populations view Helms similarly. The contrast emerges, however, when age differences between the two groups are controlled.

# REFERENCES


Abelson, Robert P., Dasgupta, Nilanjana, and Banaji, Mahzarin R. (1998). Perceptions of the collective other. *Personality and Social Psychology Review, 2,* 243–50.

Comstock, Gary D. (1991). *Violence against lesbians and gay men.* New York: Columbia University Press.

Ezekiel, Raphael S. (1995). *The racist mind: Portraits of American neo-Nazis and Klansmen.* New York: Viking.

Franklin, Karen. (1996). Hate crime or rite of passage?: Assailant motivations in anti-gay violence. Doctoral dissertation, California School of Professional Psychology, Alameda.

Goffman, Erving. (1959). *The presentation of self in everyday life.* New York: Doubleday.

Green, Donald P., Glaser, Jack, and Rich, Andrew. (1998). From lynching to gay-bashing: The elusive connection between economic conditions and hate crime. *Journal of Personality and Social Psychology, 75,* 82–92.

Green, Donald P., and Rich, Andrew. (1998). White supremacist activity and cross-burnings in North Carolina. *Journal of Quantitative Criminology, 14,* 263–82.

Green, Donald P., Strolovitch, Dare Z., and Wong, Janelle S. (1998). Defended neighborhoods, integration, and racially motivated crime. *American Journal of Sociology, 104,* 372–403.

Hamm, Mark S. (1993). *American skinheads: The criminology and control of hate crime.* New York: Praeger.

Hovland, Carl I., and Sears, Robert R. (1940). Minor studies of aggression: IV. Correlation of lynchings with economic indices. *Journal of Psychology, 9,* 301–10.

Karapin, Roger. (1996). Explaining the surge in right-wing violence by German youth. Unpublished paper, Hunter College.

Krueger, Alan B., and Pischke, Jorn-Steffen. (1997). A statistical analysis of crime against foreigners in unified Germany. *Journal of Human Resources, 32,* 182–209.

Langer, Elinor. (1990). The American neo-Nazi movement today. *The Nation, 251* (July 16), 82–105.

Levin, Jack, and McDevitt, Jack. (1993). *Hate crimes: The rising tide of bigotry and bloodshed.* New York: Plenum.

North Carolinians Against Racist and Religious Violence (NCARRV). (1991). 1991 Report: Bigoted violence and hate groups in North Carolina. Report by North Carolinians Against Racist and Religious Violence, Durham, N.C.

Olzak, Susan. (1992). *The dynamics of ethnic competition and conflict.* Stanford, Calif.: Stanford University Press.

Pinderhughes, Howard. (1993). The anatomy of racially motivated violence in New York City: A case study of youth in southern Brooklyn. *Social Problems, 40,* 478–93.

Rothbart, Myron, and John, Oliver P. (1985). Social categorization and behavioral episodes: A cognitive analysis of the effects of intergroup contact. *Journal of Social Issues, 41,* 81–104.

Tolnay, Stuart E., and Beck, E. M. (1995). *A festival of violence: An analysis of southern lynchings, 1882–1930.* Urbana: University of Illinois Press.

Willems, Helmut. (1995). Development, patterns, and causes of violence against foreigners in Germany: Social and biographical characteristics of perpetrators and the process of escalation. *Terrorism and Political Violence, 7,* 162–81.

# 15

# CULTURAL RACISM: THE INTERSECTION OF RACE AND CULTURE IN INTERGROUP CONFLICT

*James M. Jones*

"RACE" HAS been a persistently troubling issue in American society from its inception. The idea of race evolved in a peculiar and defining way in Western Europe and was elaborated with profoundly contradictory fervor in the American experiment in democracy. For roughly half a millennium, the subject of race has stood for differences that define who "we" are, who "they" are, and how those differences rationalize divergent lots in life. Race has driven a wedge between people and been at the core of human conflict.

It is my view that one of the barriers to understanding contemporary race relations in the United States is that the biological and cultural meanings of race are confounded. Beliefs about the biological and cultural inferiority of Africa-descended people, and the cultural inferiority of American Indians, are amply documented in our social histories (see, for example, Banton 1977; Jones 1997). But because "race" emerged in nineteenth-century North America as a biological concept, the "race problem" has historically been framed in biological terms. Races are hierarchically arrayed and differences explained by differential biology (Jefferson 1787/1955). The modern era of race relations began with a commitment to racial equality based on the assumption that, except for the trivial distinctions associated with skin color, there are no important biological distinctions to be made. This view was well expressed three decades ago by a panel of scientists reporting to the American Association for the Advancement of Science:

> From a biological viewpoint the term race has become so encumbered with superfluous and contradictory meanings, erroneous concepts, and emotional reactions that it has almost completely lost its utility. The term

> should be replaced with the concept of population. It is hoped that the understanding of the biological nature of populations will eventually lead to the abandonment of the term race. (Mead et al. 1968, 59)

Thus, by the end of the 1960s, we had scientifically rejected biological differences in race and politically and socially moved toward the principle of biological parity, a key element of race-neutral public policy. In this new climate, deficient individual character, or an absence of values and beliefs that enable one to represent the dominant cultural mores, replaced biology as the best explanation for persistent racial differences. This non-biology-based racism has been labeled "enlightened racism" (Jhally and Lewis 1992) and the "new racism" (Barker 1981). Rejecting the biology of race, or even accepting the idea that race is "socially constructed," does not eliminate the foundation and influence of racism. If anything, it makes it harder to detect and ameliorate.

Our history and normative beliefs in the cultural inferiority of Africans and their descendants were characteristic of our popular culture (Jones 1997). Africans were thought to be "primitive," to be lacking in culture, defined as attainments and accomplishment (Jenks 1993). I have argued that racism based on culture is as significant as racism based on biology (Jones 1972, 1997). Cultural racism is based on two ideas: (1) a belief in the inferiority of the cultural products, values, methods, and structures of a people who are assigned to a racial category; and (2) the cultural consequences of race-based discrimination and inferiority/superiority assumptions. The belief in racial inferiority that underlies modern racism rests simultaneously on biological and cultural grounds. As a society, we have more or less rejected the biological basis for racial differences, but we have neither acknowledged nor addressed in a meaningful way the cultural basis of racial inferiority that I contend is at the heart of cultural racism.

Thus, our contemporary understanding of race relations is compromised by our failure to appreciate the intersection of race and culture in accounting for "race effects." Our understandings of and beliefs about race effects form the basis not only of public policy remedies but of our understanding of the causes of further antipathies. It is therefore important to acknowledge this confusion and to consider the differential consequences of biological and cultural bases of racism.

In this chapter, I address in turn: (1) cultural racism and some consequences of employing this approach for our understanding of contemporary racial conflict, including the culture-biology interaction; (2) cultural sources of racial conflict, which derive in part from racism and in part from cultural differences; (3) culture-based mechanisms, labeled TRIOS (Time, Rhythm, Improvisation, Oral expression, and Spirituality), that locate the sources of racial conflict in culture and its psychological consequences; and (4) psychological principles that may be derived from this account of African American culture and how the psychological consequences may exacerbate racial disharmony.

## CULTURAL RACISM

There are many accounts of the ways in which "race" evolved as a concept in Anglo-American thought and political practice (see, for example, Banton 1977; Smedley 1993). Race distinguished people by virtue of both their "cultural" attributes—where they were from, how they dressed, their tastes, behavioral propensities, values, and temperaments—and their putatively biological attributes—height, build, hair and eye color, skin color, and so forth. Over time "cultural" attributes fused with biological ones, so that people who could be readily defined by how they looked were also characterized by what they did, preferred, believed, and so forth. This fusion can be called *racialism,* defined as "a cognitive structure that organizes perceptions of people around racial categories and connects these perceptions of phenotypic qualities to beliefs about essential internal qualities that describe the racial category" (Jones 1997, 357). The tendency to ascribe internal attributes to things that can be classified by their external features is the very general human tendency toward "psychological essentialism" (Medin 1989). The essential qualities that give meaning to human categories can be both physical (such as skin color) and psychological (ideas like locus of control, self-esteem, or delay of gratification). Culture and its individual-level correlate, personality, join biology as a basis for human racial categorization.

Although by this reasoning race implies culture, there has been a persistent tendency to think about race in biological terms. For example, a person of Hispanic origin (ethnic label) may be either black or white (a racial label). The tendency to treat race and culture (in this case, ethnicity) independently allows one to propose race-based neutrality (a color-blind society) that can and should ignore ethnic and cultural variation. This notion is reflected in the viewpoint of former Secretary of Education William Bennett, who, in a speech to young black children in Atlanta on the occasion of the birthday of Martin Luther King, made the following claim: "I think the best means to achieve the ends of a color-blind society is to proceed as if we were a color-blind society. . . . I think the best way to treat people is as if their race did not make any difference" (Sawyer 1986, A8).

The problem alluded to by Bennett is that the only just society is a color-blind one because when we take color (read race) into account, we tend to discriminate. By implication, when we ignore race, we don't. Abundant social psychological research shows convincingly that we do discriminate on the basis of race, even when we are unaware either that race is relevant or that we have been influenced by it in our judgments or behavior.

We also believe that psychological attributes define racial categories, and that the pattern of thoughts, feelings, and behaviors that make them up define cultural differences that coincide with race. Thus, one may still hold to racial judgments even if the biological basis of race is rejected. Since the cultural basis of race has been characterized along the same inferiority/superiority dimension as the biological distinctions, cultural racism remains as a residue of expunged biological racism. The relative imperviousness to change of racial categories that are hierarchically arranged is aided and abetted by the processes of psychological essentialism. This is true whether the essentialism is based on biological, personality, or cultural attributes.

Thus, to understand the persistent effects of racism in our society we must recognize the significant influence of culture in racial judgments. One well-used definition of culture comes from Kroeber and Kluckhohn (1952), who define culture as "patterned ways of thinking, feeling and reacting, acquired and transmitted mainly by symbols . . . [that may,] on the one hand, be considered as products of action, [and] on the other, [as] conditioning elements of future actions" (181). Three aspects of this definition are important: (1) patterns of thought, feeling, and action are transmitted across generations and over time; (2) cultural systems are the results of behavior or experience (dependent variable); and (3) cultural systems condition future behaviors (independent variable).

The first point attests to the continuity of culture over time and its continuing influence across generations. To understand contemporary thoughts and feelings about race we must recognize the role that historical events and conceptions have played in the unfolding of American culture. Figure 15.1 offers a graphic connection between cultural, institutional, and individual levels of "race effects." What we believe about race, in part, fits the cultural template handed down across generations, a template of racial difference and inferiority. Institutions embody these cultural beliefs and implement them as a matter of practice. Individuals are consequently socialized into a cultural context in which cultural norms and beliefs about race become the implicit or explicit socialization agenda.

This top-down approach is balanced by a bottom-up approach by which individuals assume socialization roles in institutional contexts and, through their individual internalization of racial socialization and

FIGURE 15.1 *A Schematic Representation of the Dynamic Interplay of Culture and Race*

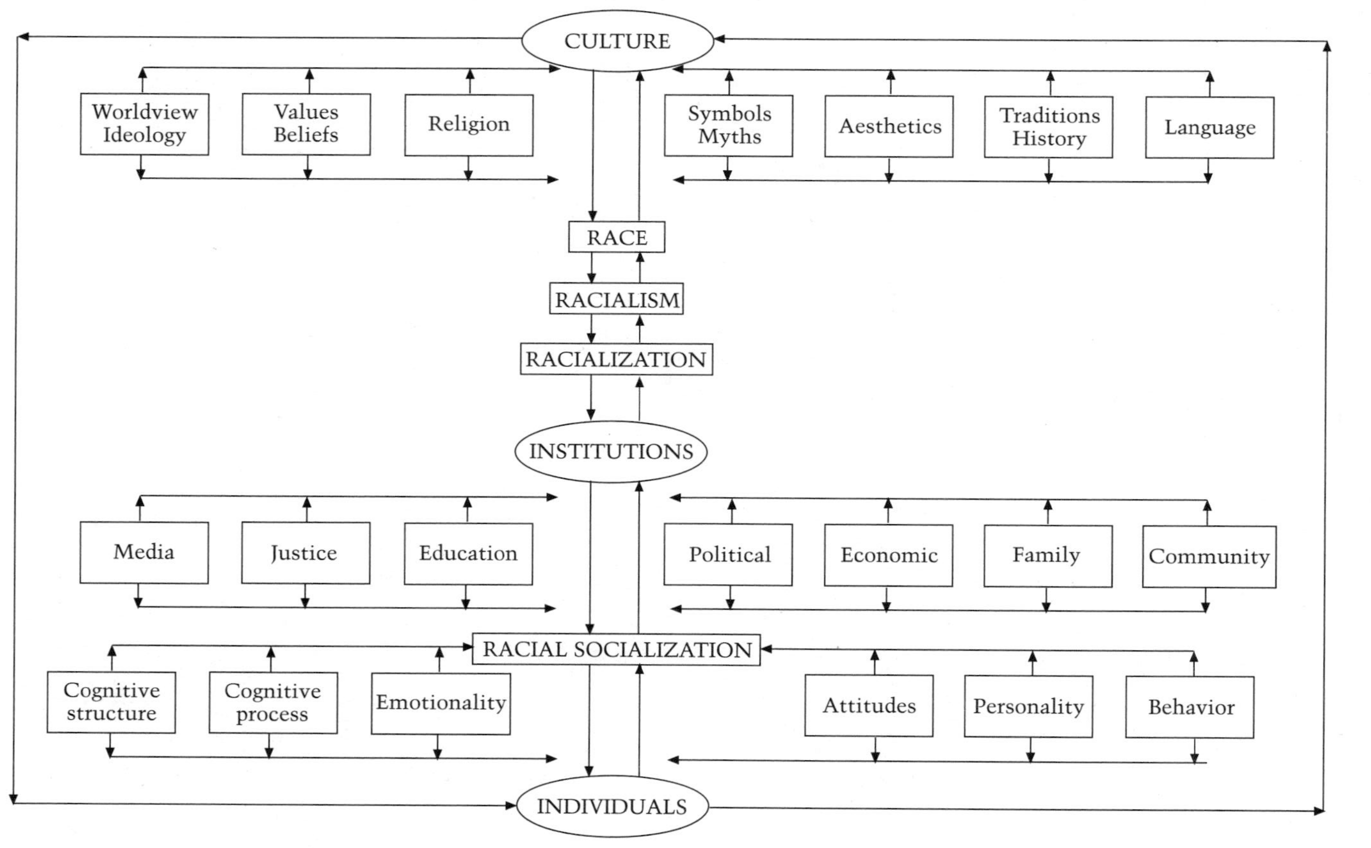

epochal context effects, may modify institutional practices and thus modify the cultural context of race. Subsequent generations are then exposed to an altered cultural view of race. To illustrate, the defining stereotype of blacks in the 1930s characterized them as musical, happy-go-lucky, superstitious, ignorant figures (Katz and Braly 1933). In contemporary stereotyping, the "ignorant" label remains (now cast as "unintelligent"), but "hostile/aggressive" has become the dominant characteristic (Devine and Baker 1991). Generations of young people socialized to this normative belief about race will acquire cognitive structures and emotional attachments that vary from those acquired in the 1930s. As a result, the nature of the problem of interracial interactions is now different.

It is also the case that the racial identities of African Americans have undergone fundamental change, from a universalistic, deracinated, stigma-avoiding identity to one that embraced the stigma of skin color and asserted its value and humanity. The slogan "black is beautiful" captured this fundamental psychological change and perhaps, to some extent, contributed to the changing stereotype of African Americans.

The last two points suggest that culture determines behavior and results from it. Cultural differences result, then, from two types of sources: *evolutionary*—the characteristic beliefs, symbols, language, values, and mores of the originating culture; and *reactionary*—the experiences that members of a racial group have on the basis of their racial group membership. Each socially significant racial group originated in a cultural context that informed its adaptation and ways of coping in the United States. Language, a sense of community, family and interpersonal relations, values, and beliefs gave shape and character to their mode of being in this country. Although there may be differences of opinion as to what the specific elements of cultural character are, it is reasonable to expect that defining cultural characteristics can be shown to influence the adaptation and behavior of cultural groups that are racially defined (Sowell 1992).

But in the United States, blacks were enslaved. That experience diverged from the experience of all other racial groups and established a unique context of adaptation and coping. The cumulative consequence of adapting to and coping with this cultural status is a major element of contemporary African America culture. By virtue of divergent experiences defined by race, African Americans are inclined to see the world differently, expect people to behave differently, and interpret their own experience differently. Thus, differential cultural systems are part of the cultural divide that offers different interpretations of history and expectations of the future. For instance, racial differences in judgments about the O. J. Simpson criminal verdict and his guilt or innocence did not *create* a racial divide, they *expressed* it.

The fact of cultural differences linked to race is natural and, of itself, not problematic. However, races differ dramatically in their access to and ability to maintain power. Racism is founded on beliefs in racial inferiority, but it is realized in the exercise of power to make those racial beliefs effective. I call this aspect of the race equation *racialization*—the institutional ways in which race is taken into account. We can "racialize" our society directly, as we did with slavery or with Jim Crow, under which "race" was defined largely by biology and approximated by skin color. But we can also racialize indirectly by culture, since race and culture are intertwined. This indirect racialization comes in many forms, including what former Senator Bill Bradley called "white skin privilege" (West 1997), socioeconomic class (Wilson 1987), or geographical segregation (Massey and Denton 1993). Our society is racialized to such a degree that claiming to "ignore race" is simply not an option.

Racialism provides the psychological significance of race, and racialization is its institutional implementation. The cultural values and beliefs about racial differences and value-based racial hierarchy enable the perpetuation of racism over time. Racism confounds our basic sense of fairness, equality, and opportunity. The American self-concept of freedom and dignity is compromised by racism, resulting in the "American Dilemma" (Myrdal 1944):

> The "American Dilemma" is the ever-raging conflict between, on the one hand, the valuations preserved on the general plane which we shall call the "American Creed," where the American thinks, talks and acts under the influence of high national and Christian precepts, and on the other hand, the valuations on specific planes of individual and group living, where personal and local interests; economic, social, and sexual jealousies; considerations of community prestige and conformity; group prejudice against particular persons or types of people; and all sorts of miscellaneous wants, impulses, and habits dominate his outlook. (lxxi)

The "old" American dilemma drew stark contrasts between the virtue of the American creed and the vice of racial bigotry—right was compromised by wrong. But in the "modern era," we have a new American dilemma (Jones 1998) in which race-neutral, individual-level opportunity and merit (right) conflicts directly with the need to ameliorate continuing race-based discrimination and cumulative racial disadvantage by taking account of race (another right). This new American dilemma describes opposing viewpoints about the heart and soul of America as a fair, open, and socially just society. The biological basis of race need not be invoked to implicate the cultural divide that engulfs contemporary discussions of race.

## Culture-Biology Interaction: The Culturgen

Although we have rejected biological bases of race, it is clear that culture and biology are not completely independent. For example, accounting for cognitive processes and personality structures, Plomin (1990) argues that 35 percent of the variations among siblings within families can be explained by genetic factors, but 65 percent by environmental factors. Lumsden and Wilson (1981) argue that the intersection of culture and biology is a coevolutionary process. In this view, culture is a mixed-level process whereby individual behavior is genetically driven, but macrocultural forces (social norms, expectancies, and so forth) shape its expression. Epigenetic rules guide the linkage of genes and culture through learning processes. Gene-induced responses (fear, joy, anger) are shaped and molded by epigenetic rules that govern their expression. Secondary epigenetic rules might include: smiling signals friendliness, anxiety arises in the company of strangers, incest is taboo. Gene-controlled behaviors (such as sex, facial expression, and physiological arousal) thus become expressed in ways that are acceptable or expected in a cultural context. The unit of translation between genes and culture is the "culturgen." Culturgens represent those gene-culture translations that are most favored in a given culture, and hence they summarize both biology and cultural patterns.

This coevolutionary process allows us to speculate that cultural differences may produce biological differences, and vice versa. Racial differences are both biological and cultural and derive simultaneously from features of cultural expression that diverge on the basis of race. In a societal context that emphasizes cultural homogeneity, these divergent, race-based effects add a profound complication to the racism story.

## Summary

Cultural racism rests on the ideology of racial hierarchy and its sustaining practices. The confounding of the cultural and biological bases of race, and the tendency to equate the biological aspect with racism, make arguments for a "color-blind" or "race-neutral" approach seem plausible and meritorious. However, the egregious excesses of racism have been handed down over generations and are woven into the symbolic and ideological structure of our society, the practices of our basic institutions, and the psyches of our citizens. Contemporary racial conflict must be understood as a resultant of these cultural dynamics, and amelioration of racial conflict must pay attention to, not ignore, these foundations of racism.

## CULTURAL SOURCES OF RACIAL CONFLICT

I have argued that race and culture are intertwined in our society and our psyches. Racism based on beliefs in the inferiority of others and the superiority of the self has been understood in terms of biology, and hence the problem is symbolized by skin color. Redemption from racism comes in the form of disregarding the stigmata of skin color. But racial inferiority/superiority rests as much or more on an evaluation of culture. Antiracist activities have by and large focused on eliminating racial differences, defined biologically. This approach sees skin color as the *only* difference, one that does not signify any meaningful human capacity. But what about the cultural dimension?

Cultural racism assigns fundamental human inferiority to people who act, think, and feel in ways that diverge from a self-defined, preferred cultural norm. Africans were thought to be inferior not only biologically but also in their cultural accomplishments. To the extent that biological inferiority was responsible for cultural inferiority, removing the biological explanation meant that Africa-descended people "could" achieve advanced levels of culture—Western culture. Thus, racial progress became linked to cultural changes in racial identity. Racial biology, in this enlightened view, does not preclude achieving "white" cultural capacity.

As a result of this cultural assumption, the problem of dealing with racism became more complex than simply a matter of asserting racial equality; it set the parameters in cultural terms. The greater one's capacity to adopt and master the essential cultural attributes of whites, the more legitimate were one's claims to equality. One's race was a limiting condition on one's humanity. However, one could transcend that limit simply by mastering the cultural markers of white society. The conflict across race became, therefore, both more subtle and more insidious.

Cultural racism simultaneously asserts the superiority of Anglo-American culture and the inferiority of African culture. Attempts to counteract the premise and consequence of biologically based racism were quite different from the antidote to cultural racism. One such antidote, Africentrism, takes two theoretically derived forms: retrieval of value in an African past, and reduction of value in the European past. I believe, therefore, that racial conflict is fueled and perpetuated by the fact that cultural racism has not been acknowledged for its implications for the psychological well-being of targets of racism.

Affirming one's race in a society that holds racelessness as the model on which equality rests forces one either to abandon racial consciousness or psychologically to distance oneself from cultural norms that are experienced as dehumanizing (Steele 1997; Steele and Aronson 1995). Protective disidentification allows one to retreat from the stigmatizing world of racism, but at a cost to opportunity-enhancing performance (Steele and Aronson 1995). Arroyo and Zigler (1995) provided empirical evidence for this psychological tension when they showed that although African American adolescents who scored high on a measure of racelessness had better academic performance, they also were at risk for poor mental health outcomes (such as depression).

This conflict over culture is a byproduct of cultural racism. It is one reason racial conflict has to some extent been rekindled in the last decade and a half. The premise that race was biologically meaningful led to an idea about racism and its consequences that was flawed. If there are no meaningful biological differences, then treating people as if their race makes no difference is the right thing to do. But the cultural superiority assumption is not considered in this equation. Thus, for targets of racism, this "remedy" is dehumanizing at worst, or challenges one to make bifurcating choices at best.[1]

The confusion about race and culture has psychological consequences for targets of racism. In a society that cherishes individual liberty and judges people according to a cultural definition of merit, cultural racism challenges one's sense of self. Since judgments of superiority bear an obverse relationship to judgments of inferiority, celebrating America often has a subtext implication of denigrating America's racial minorities. Conversely, celebrating diversity seems too often to imply denigrating America and its traditions. The linkage of race and culture in cultural racism sets the stage for a zero-sum consideration of race in which racial conflict can be ignited both in ignoring and in paying attention to race (in other words, the "new American dilemma"). In the next section, I speculate on specific ways in which cultural variations may exacerbate racial conflict.

## TRIOS: THE FOUNDATION OF AFRICAN AMERICAN CULTURE

Africans differ from Europeans in physical appearance and in culture and its psychological consequences for individuals (Jones 1972; Jordan

1969). Skin color has stood as a proxy for a complex worldview about humanness, value, and virtue. Racism, broadly conceived, establishes a hierarchical array of human groups and legitimates the beliefs, institutional arrangements, practices, policies, and the ensuing race-based hierarchy. Africans are dark people, and Africa was termed the "Dark Continent." Darkness meant incapacity and deficiency; whether it was explained by genes or culture or both, this view stripped persons of African descent of inherent value in the Western world.

In this value-based construal of race, it is very difficult to assimilate such differences to goodness. Early in the civil rights decade of the 1960s, the British historian Hugh Trevor-Roper (1963) argued that there is no African history from which we can learn anything. History is studied for the purpose of uncovering where we have come from and how we got where we are. But according to Trevor-Roper, African history has nothing to teach us because the world is dominated by "European techniques, European examples, European ideas . . . there is only the history of Europeans in Africa. The rest is darkness" (871). Against this backdrop of cultural racism, it is difficult to think about Africa-descended people in America, and racial equality, without denigrating the cultural origins of these people. One way to avoid this denigrating viewpoint is to consider the psychological manifestations of African American culture as a fusion of evolutionary and reactionary processes. TRIOS is conceived as one way to do that.

TRIOS is an acronym for five dimensions of human experience—Time, Rhythm, Improvisation, Oral expression, and Spirituality. I argue that these dimensions of psychosocial experience are universal, but subject to the cultural conditioning that gives them distinctive patterns and expression (Kroeber and Kluckhohn 1952). I further argue that this cultural conditioning constitutes the framework through which basic processes of perception, cognition, and emotion are filtered. Thus, "experience-near" (Shweder and Sullivan 1992) phenomena are the resultant of the filtering and conditioning that TRIOS concepts make possible. They are the cultural elements that can be juxtaposed with the experience-near elements of European culture.

For simplicity, we may take as exemplars of that conditioning the attributes cited by William McDougall (1921), which distinguished the "races of Europe" (Nordic, Alpine, and Mediterranean, in descending hierarchical order). These elements include "Providence," which McDougall characterized as "hoarding" and which we more recently label delay of gratification; "introversion," which is contrasted with extraversion, (characterized by gregariousness and ultimately submission); "curiosity," which provides an abstraction of self that makes suicide possible and homicide less likely; "will," which permits domination of others;

and "intelligence" or intellect, a cognitive capacity that can be measured (IQ tests for McDougall are referenced as "mental anthropology").

TRIOS, then, represents an alternative way of conceiving the experience-near mechanisms that make up mind *and* culture. Cultural racism ignores or denigrates those attributes that appear to be at odds with or in opposition to the Europe-derived and valued psychosocial tendencies. In the following pages, I briefly describe the origins and nature of the TRIOS elements.

## Time

Time is the substrate of life and consciousness (Ornstein 1977). More important, perceptions of time take on values, which dictate behavior and the valuations of human affairs. The valuing of time has been referred to as "temponomics" (McGrath and Kelly 1986). In temponomic societies, time may be saved, wasted, or invested, much like any other valued resource. When time is not of value in its own right, none of these attributes pertain. Thus, time is not simply a reference for the unfolding of behavior but constitutes a fundamental value that organizes and dictates societal structures, perceptions, and beliefs. This expanded meaning of time is aptly described by the historian of the South Mechal Sobel (1987).

> In the complex of values, the perception of time is the most significant one. A culture's sense of time is the key to its nature, and for an individual a particular and developed sense of time is an essential parameter of personality. When the perception of time changes, all other values are affected; conflicts in worldviews are likely to center on conflicts in perceptions of time. (21)

There is an expression in Trinidad, West Indies, that "any time is Trinidad time" (Jones 1986). What this means is that time has no independent status and value with the capacity to dictate behavior and choice. Rather, time is a dependent variable responsive largely to the feelings, desires, and behaviors of individuals. Time is controlling in a temponomic society, but not in a nontemponomic one. Once one escapes the control of time, feelings and preferences become more accessible and more likely to be acted on (Zimbardo, Marshall, and Maslach 1971). In a temponomic society, delaying gratification is considered an ability (Mischel 1961) and punctuality a duty to time's value. But in nontemponomic cultures, for example, Brazil, punctuality is not a virtue (Levine, West, and Reis 1984).

The psychological story is about preparation for the future (what we may call future orientation) by conserving capital and not squandering it (what McDougall [1921] called Providence). This attitude presumes two things: a causal connection between present behavior and future outcomes, and the inherent value of distal goals (Jones 1986). Orienting toward the future requires psychological restraint, denial of preferences, and emotional suppression. One of the most conspicuous losses of freedom impelled by slavery was the loss of temporal freedom, and the disconnection of soul and behavior. The psychological liberation from slavery is the liberation from control in all of its aspects. TRIOS offers specific mechanisms for regaining personal control in a society where external control is difficult to come by. Controlling time is, in its essence, psychological liberation. The other elements of TRIOS may also be understood in terms of psychological control.

## Rhythm

Rhythm defines a recurring pattern of behavior within specified time frames. Time is necessarily implicated in rhythms. Behavioral enactments occur within temporal units. The regularity of the behaviors and the values of the temporal units (an adagio has broad time values and an allegro narrow ones) create the rhythmic experience. A waltz, minuet, jitterbug, or twist represents a dance whose form and style depend on the rhythmic contours of the music. One may gain control over rhythms by changing the temporal units and adjusting the behavior accordingly. One can cut time in half to slow it down, or double time to speed it up. Or, as Eubie Blake described the early days of ragtime, you can create irregularity in rhythms by practicing anarchy against the metronomic regularity of the time-beat relationship (personal comunication, May 15, 1972). Instead of apportioning eight beats evenly between two measures, four beats each, one can apportion them unevenly, with one measure getting three and a half beats and the other four and a half, thus *squeezing* or *stretching* notes to fit one's rhythmic sensibilities or desires.

Again, with rhythms we find that the capacity to alter them fits psychological needs for freedom. Rhythms dictate behavior in time. Freedom is gained by adjusting behavior and/or time to fit the psychological freedom one desires. We have acknowledged the need for rhythmic freedom by instituting things like flextime at work. Rhythm links the external and the internal, or what is called entrainment (McGrath and Kelly 1986). When the match is made, synchrony occurs and the maximum productivity ensues. When the match is not made, disharmony or asynchrony occurs, efforts are inefficient, and mental or physical dysfunction may occur.

Racism often introduces asynchronies or disharmonious connections between internal and external states. Pierce (1970) calls these race-based insults or ambiguous occurrences "microaggressions." Lazarus (1981) calls them "daily hassles" and shows that physical well-being is affected more by an accumulation of daily hassles than by major life events. The TRIOS model suggests that rhythm may serve as a proxy for the cumulative effects of microaggressions and daily hassles, and that gaining behavioral control over the environment may require that one adapt rhythmic control through either accommodation (adjusting the internal aspects) or assimilation (adjusting the external aspects). At its core, rhythm is an ecological variable conceived in a transactional framework with psychological properties and consequences. Following on the Gibsonian model of perception (Gibson 1979; McArthur and Baron 1983), environmental affordances merge with psychological attunements to create the rhythmic behavioral act. These acts are significantly affected by the cultural context in which they occur and by the personality characteristics of the acting parties.

## Improvisation

Improvisation is "a combination of *expressiveness* and *invention,* or *creativity,* which occurs *under time pressure*" (Jones 1997, 488). Again, we find freedom at the core. Improvisation is inherently free by virtue of its spontaneity. But it is not random, and it is not haphazard. Improvisation is inherently "problem-focused." That is, we are inventing or creating toward a purpose. Two of the most conspicuous forms of improvisation are music and sports.[2] Improvisation takes an underlying foundation—say, grammar or musical structure—and then, under the constraints of time (a rhythmic order), configures a text or specific scale to make some coherent statement that expresses a point. Because the improvisation is done "on-line," it is unique and bears the signature of the author. Improvisation is necessarily a fusion of the author and the performer in one person. Characteristic patterns of time-based problem-solving may rise to the level of a "self-signature" that we call style.

Watching basketball in the 1940s and 1950s was to see a game designed to create a specific outcome in a specific way with as little left to chance as possible. In contrast, Julius "Dr. J" Erving described his style as a leap into the air to look for spaces that would afford the kind of shot he could take and make. Improvisation, again, is liberating. It is an important skill to have when faced with an unanticipated situation. Improvisation bends external situations or contexts to one's personal goals, needs, or desires. The cap worn backward, the single glove, the pants leg rolled up, all are examples of an improvisational style that is expressive, psychologically liberating, and self-defining.

## Oral Expression

Oral expression can be thought of as the expression of one's true self through oral means. The sum total of the oral tradition, in Asante's (1987) phrase, is "Orature" (vocality, drumming, storytelling, praise singing, and naming). Orature captures human creation and life itself. In Bantu, nommo means "word" and gives meaning to the physical body (Jahn 1961; Asante 1987). It is through the spoken word that the most enduring verities are revealed and preserved. A newborn child is not fully human until he or she has been named, and that name has been officially pronounced. The *word* embellishes and completes creation. Senghor (1956) describes how Orature accompanies the work of a goldsmith: the prayer recited by the goldsmith, the hymn of praise sung by the sorcerer, and the dance that accompanies the completion, all contribute to the work and signal its completion and its beauty. Orature confers meaning on events, reveals truths of existence, and binds people together in common understanding and purpose.

The crucial aspect of Orature is its immediacy: all meaningful behavior, values, and beliefs are defined by context. It becomes important, then, to share in experience in order to understand it. Experience cannot be abstracted, out of context, in a meaningful way. Morality, even value, is bound up in context. Cole, Gay, Glick, and Sharp (1971) found that the Kpelle of Liberia were reliably poorer than Americans at memorizing lists of words. This was true even when the researchers tried to encourage categorization as a mnemonic device. However, when the twenty items to be recalled were embedded in a folk story, the Kpelle subjects not only remembered them all, but in the order in which they appeared in the story. Context gave the words meaning that they did not have independently. This raises the possibility that standardized tests may not adequately measure the ability of anyone who lives in a predominantly oral culture, because the cultural context that gives meaning to knowledge or belief is absent in the testing situation. Allen and Boykin (1991) have shown that when African American children are allowed to learn material in a physical movement context, they learn it better and recall it with greater accuracy.

Another consequence of the context-rich nature of Orature is the creative freedom it allows in the expression and decoding of the meaning of things. In Trinidad, the practice of picong (ritualized insult) is widespread and serves to democratize the society. No one is above being brought down by a barbed insult or twist of meaning. When I was visiting Trinidad in 1973, a U.S. basketball team came down for an exhibition. They were tall, fast, and high-jumping and proceeded during warmups to dunk one after another in increasingly flamboyant ways.

The audience was not impressed. "Eh nuh, wat allyuh wanna do break de rim or wat?" They would laugh at the idea that these dramatic dunks had the purpose of demonstrating outstanding ability and creativity, rather than simply breaking the rim. A corollary to picong is mamaguy. Whereas picong seeks to insult, mamaguy seeks to praise, but not really. It is damning by false praise ("You speak with an excellent Trinidadian accent" [*"not!"*]), and thus another way of verbally controlling the interaction and conveying meaning that may be privileged to the ingroup or, if shared with the ingroup, used as a leveler like picong.

In African American culture, language is also used as an avenue of control through privileged meanings and neologisms. "Bad" becomes "good," "cool" defines an essence of spirit and self, and "dope" becomes "bad," which we know is good. "Stupid" is not dumb but smart. The use of language in slavery times required neologisms and privileged uses to hide collective action from slave owners and overseers. Over centuries it has become one of the most stable means of asserting self-control in a potentially hostile or at best indifferent context. Rap is a contemporary extension of this evolutionary process. Rap is more than a style of singing and rhyming; it is an expression of reality and assertion of self that is not filtered through powerbrokers of the mainstream (George 1998). It creates its own authenticity for those who are "down with it." These mechanisms of self-control and personal freedom can bond individuals together in a concerted reality, and they can also be used to distance oneself and one's group from others who are potentially harmful. The story of intergroup conflict becomes one of divergence of experience and psychosocial mechanisms of control.

## Spirituality

Finally, spirituality can be defined as the belief in nonmaterial causation in human affairs (Jones 1986). That is, what happens to us is determined, in some measure, by forces or energies beyond our control. Those forces are not haphazard but part of a system of meaning and energy that determines human events. According to Jahn (1961), the basic force, Ntu, influences human beings (muntu), all things (kintu), all places and all time (hantu), and all modalities of existence (kuntu). A person who is spiritual shares cause-effect agency with ntu and does not claim it all for himself or herself.

In our society, control is a defining property of well-being. As articulated by McDougall (1921), "will" and "introversion" are positive properties and "extraversion" and "gregariousness" are negative. Self-actualization implies that the pinnacle of selfhood can be achieved through personal agency. Those who fail to accomplish this actualized state may be thought of as "pawns" rather than "origins" (DuCharms 1966), as external as opposed to internal in their locus of control (Rotter 1966), or as field-dependent rather than field-independent (Witkin et al. 1962). Moreover, research shows that having control can confer better physical health among nursing home patients (Langer and Rodin 1976), and that the illusion of control can cause people to overvalue things over which such control is exerted, such as bingo cards (Langer 1983).

Whereas each of the first four TRIOS elements provides a form of personal control, spirituality seems to be a way of divesting oneself of control. If we are sharing the responsibility for human affairs, then no one is fully responsible for his or her own behavior. If one looks at the public opinion polls about major events, the black-white gap almost always reflects to some degree a belief in a lower level of personal responsibility for any given outcome, whether it's O. J. Simpson's culpability, President Clinton's, or that of the average poor person or person of color. A major divide in America is between those who believe that responsibility is always shared and those who label individuals in terms of outcomes that their behavior or character presumably caused. We have done many cross-cultural studies of the Fundamental Attribution Error (FAE) and find that it is not so easily replicated in interdependent cultures like Japan. This analysis suggests that it should be more difficult to replicate among African Americans as well—not, however, because of the general effects of interdependence so much as the consequences of the spiritual worldview that extrahuman forces play a role in human affairs.

Thus, looked at in a slightly different way, spirituality liberates one from the expectation of personal responsibility in a world that denies the full range of options and opportunities. Spirituality can also be considered one of the mechanisms that liberate one from the dominance of cultural expectations and constraints. Whether this shared responsibility is seen as a kind of self-handicapping or a legitimate cultural belief, it is one of the important elements of the psychological evolution of persons of African descent.

## Summary

TRIOS describes psychological processes and tendencies that provide an experience-near template of cultural difference. The mechanisms of TRIOS provide psychological control and affirm the self as well as the collective in a societal context that devalues them both. The challenge of racism for its targets is to create and preserve a positive self and an instrumental identity. The historical evolution of African American culture has resulted in large part from the coping-adaptation sequences that derive both from African origins (evolutionary) and from the challenges of racism in the American context (reactionary). As a result, the psychology of African Americans is heavily context-dependent. The psychological manifestations of TRIOS also serve to strengthen the bond within the group and to protect group members from assaults. Racial conflict, by this account, results from the divergence in cultural forms and their meanings that are signified by TRIOS and its adaptations to the varieties of racism. The next section describes three psychological principles that can be derived from the TRIOS account.

## PSYCHOLOGICAL PRINCIPLES OF AFRICAN AMERICAN CULTURE

At its core, the psychological mechanisms that sustain and define African American culture derive from African origins, as summarized by TRIOS, and their adaptations in reactions to the ecological challenges of racism. It is appropriate to ask how TRIOS mechanisms serve to sustain and support psychological well-being for targets of racism. I offer three possibilities.

### Individuality Affirms the Collective Rather Than the Self

It is common now to juxtapose individualist and collectivist orientations as cultural syndromes with specific psychological consequences (Markus and Kitayama 1991; Triandis 1997). We tend to think of non-Western cultures as more commonly collectivist, and African cultural orientations fit this conception. Nobles (1991) has offered the collectivist version of the Cartesian cogito as "I am because we are, and because we are, therefore I am." However, we are faced with what may appear to be a conflict between collectivist principles and an overt form of individualism in the case of African Americans. As described earlier, rhythm, improvisation, and style are all strong expressions of internal states and sensibilities that carry unique individual signatures. How might we place this TRIOS-based individualism in a context of collectivism?

Figure 15.2 suggests a principle by which this can be accomplished. This figure suggests two ways in which an individualistic orientation may be fostered. One is a reaction to race-based stigma. This mechanism may lead one to distance oneself psychologically from the racial collective, thereby deemphasizing its role in the individual case. This mechanism has been identified in a variety of ways in the psychological literature. For example, Claude Steele (1992, 1997) describes disidentification as a process by which one rejects psychological domains that

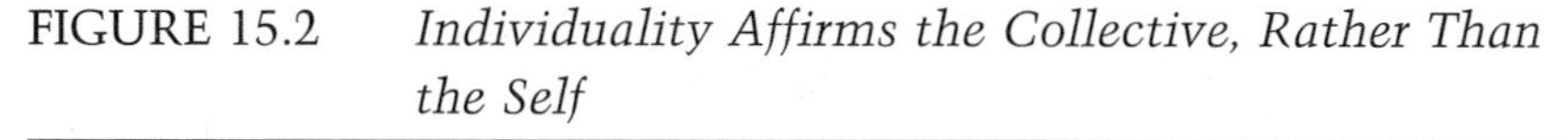

FIGURE 15.2 *Individuality Affirms the Collective, Rather Than the Self*

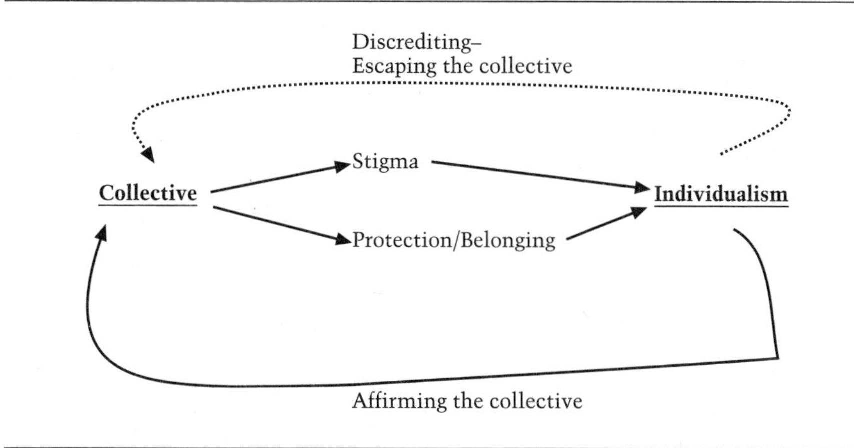


may be stigmatizing in favor of ones that are more hospitable to the self. For example, when faced with stereotype threat contexts, African Americans have been shown to reduce their interest in race-stereotypical activities (jazz, sports, and so on). Cross (1991) describes the early stages (pre-encounter) of racial identity in terms of a "de-racinated" self, one in which racial identification carries stigma and retreating from it becomes a means of reducing its adverse psychological effects. The net effect of retreat from a collective identity is to forge an individualistic identity that may have benefits in a society in which a color-blind approach is held out as the avenue to opportunity.

This view of individualism suggests a negative role for race and does not necessarily comport with the TRIOS account. Another way in which individualism can reflect the TRIOS account is in the *affirmation* of the collective through individualism. If the self-expression and self-signature described by TRIOS are cultural values, then the degree to which one exemplifies these values will affirm them, thus providing support for the collective. In this regard, affirmation requires a reinforcing community that bears witness to the affirming behavior. If, as I suggest, improvisation, Orature, spirituality, and rhythmic complexity are values, then individuals who express them in unique ways affirm them.

Figure 15.2 suggests two competing ways in which the collective can influence the individual. That both forces can be present at the same time is a source of the "double-consciousness" described nearly a century ago by Du Bois (1903). On the one hand, the collective can be a source of protection and promote and thus support individual needs for belonging. Evidence is clear that racial assimilation can prove psychologically harmful when one is marginalized or rejected in the newly assimilated environment (LaFromboise et al. 1993). When the collective is a source of protection and belonging, then adhering to and exemplifying the cultural ethos becomes self-validating.[3]

## Self-Actualization and Collective Affirmation Through Psychological Freedom and Control

Racism can be construed as a physical and psychological assault on its targets. The U.S. history of slavery and Jim Crow racism, at worst, were dehumanizing, culturally validated instruments of such assaults. At its least pernicious, racism has kept its targets in the margins of participation in citizenship rights and opportunity structures. The critical question is: How does a member of a targeted group claim his or her authentic humanity and worth in such a dehumanized or marginalized context?

I argue that human authenticity arises from psychological freedom and control, both of which are severely challenged by slavery and the ongoing legacy of cultural racism. TRIOS offers a way to understand the psychological mechanisms of freedom and control. The cornerstone of TRIOS is context—those proximal parameters of experience that give meaning to events, behavior, feelings, and language. Context may be controlled directly, by choosing locations where choice is possible, or indirectly by utilizing contextual cues to determine the meaning of things.

Self-actualization is bound up in collective affirmation, as noted earlier. The psychological freedom of the individual is limited by the perceived psychological freedom of the group. Some find freedom by distancing themselves from the group, while others find it by affirming the group. In the former case, freedom is found in shedding the limitations of race. In the latter case, freedom is found by shedding the power of others to define one's humanity and that of one's group. The former approach may narrow, and the later widen, the racial divide.

TRIOS provides the psychological mechanisms of freedom and control when behavior and psychological well-being are context-dependent. Improvisation and Orature allow one to control the meaning of things in language and behavior. In language, words denote control, peace, satisfaction, ability, and character. The control comes by imposing meaning that challenges or reverses the conventional mainstream lexicon. In this dynamic, meaning and value are often reversed. Bad is good, transparent is powerful ("cool pose" [Majors and Billson 1992]), and black is beautiful. The transparent self is inaccessible to those who would harm it. (If the eyes are the window to the soul, wear shades!) But the demagogic self (the overt, hot pose that threatens convention and asserts demands that, if not met, will have undesirable repercussions) is frightening to those who are restrained by social mores and convention. The transparent and demagogic selves work in tandem to retreat and attack, keeping the "enemy" off guard, maintaining control of one's inner self.

Time is a source of constraint and control. Doing what I want when I want to is the ultimate source of control. Living in the present is one way to exert personal control, particularly when others (in specific or general) are perceived as manipulative. Reality is the present, the moment, and "keeping it real" is a way to maintain control over value and meaning. My reality is authentic on its own terms. My humanity is real if I remain true to my perceptions and understandings and feelings. The TRIOS legacy provides the mechanism for maintaining these psychological strategies of control liberation from cultural racism.

## Rejection of Linearity and Absolutism in Human Affairs

Finally, there is an inherent relativism that results from the TRIOS-based dependence on context. In the spirituality of TRIOS, force is in all things, and nature is not opposed to but shared with humans. Time is not linear, proceeding from the past to the future just as an arrow flies by necessity in accordance with the laws of gravity. Rather, time is cyclical, turning back on itself so that the future is unreal, receding as a mirage into the past. Swahili does not even recognize the future but finds meaning only in the present (sasa) and the past (zamani) (Mbiti 1970).

Another principle that emerges from TRIOS is diunitality (Dixon 1976), by which opposites are joined. Good is not opposed to evil but helps to make it up. Diunitality is implicated in the principle of cultural psychology, which asks the question: How do mind and culture make each other up? (Shweder and Sullivan 1992). This is not to make an empty theoretical philosophical claim, but to account for the dramatic divide in social perception and political attitudes across racial divides. It could be said of the racial divergence in opinions that one group sees material-based absolutism as a fundamental principle of meaning and value, and another group sees spirit and relativism as the foundation. The human calculuses that derive from these perspectives are dramatically different and not only reflect but perpetuate the racial divide.

Another consequence of the TRIOS model is that, as noted earlier, causality is not a uniquely human affair. Therefore, because human agency is shared with spirit, there arises a degree of cause-effect uncertainty. The FAE may be understood as a bias toward reducing cause-effect uncertainty. That it is important is also suggested by Hofstede's (1984) "uncertainty avoidance" cultural dimension. We may distinguish cultures in terms of their desire to avoid uncertainty. Again we find a cultural divergence that rests on the racial divide.

Finally, one broad implication of the nonlinearity of cultural perspective is that narratives, not abstractions of value and morality, provide the foundation for being and living. Narratives are the stories of life that hold lessons for living and revealed truths. Narratives embed symbols and their meanings in a living account of collective experience. These symbols and the narratives in which they are embedded acquire psychological force and form an interpretative schema for one's experiences. Thus, the context-rich nature of African American psychological experience is driven and sustained by a sociohistorical narrative of race and culture. This narrative provides continuity with the past and makes it available and accessible in the present.

## CONCLUSION

Race has been a source of intergroup conflict throughout our cultural history. Debates about whether and how we should take race into account often founder on unacknowledged linkages between the biological and cultural aspects of race. It was believed that the elimination of race from social judgment would ameliorate, if not solve, the "race problem." But the race problem is much too complex to be solved by ignoring it.

The complexity of race is suggested by a cultural analysis that links the past and the present in individual psychologies, institutional structures and practices, and overall cultural standards, beliefs, symbols, and attitudes. Moreover, this analysis instantiates racism that is culturally based on beliefs about the inferiority of African culture relative to European culture. The implication of cultural racism is the diminished humanity of Africa-descended people. The psychological consequence of cultural racism for its targets is the development of psychological mechanisms that affirm the self and the collective in ways that draw on the evolutionary cultural capacities I describe as TRIOS.

The race-neutral or color-blind approach to social policy suppresses differences or sees them only as impediments to social justice. It is my belief that we could learn about human adaptation and coping from the psychological mechanisms of African American culture. We could develop a more sophisticated understanding of intergroup conflict by examining the mechanisms of adaptation that widen the distance between groups, even when interactions are not based on negative or hostile intentions. We could also learn about mechanisms for developing ingroup solidarity that join individualist and collectivist tendencies. This knowledge could help us bridge the gap between the dichotomous view of dependent and interdependent bases of culture. The TRIOS mechanisms could also provide a better understanding of the dynamic influence of context on human behavior and of how human beings can maintain their spirit in the face of persistent and recurring assaults on their humanity.

---

I am grateful to two anonymous reviewers and to members of the Social Psychology of Cultural Contact Working Group, whose suggestions helped considerably to make this a better chapter.

## NOTES

1. The tendency to pit a racial identity against an "American" identity was illustrated in an interview with Jesse Jackson when he ran for the presidency in 1984. Marvin Kalb, host of *Meet the Press,* asked Jackson, "Are you a black man who happens to be an American running for the presidency, or are you an American who happens to be a black man running for the presidency?" (Jones 1997, 264). I call this tendency to separate one's racial identity from mainstream identity the "bifurcation of self."
2. This example is meant to illuminate the basic processes and consequences of improvisation and is not limited to sports and entertainment, which are domains in which racial stereotypes abound.
3. This mechanism works somewhat like terror management (Greenberg et al. 1992), by which one, under threat of death, reaffirms the values and mores of the collective. I would suggest that threats of racism may have the same psychological consequence as contemplating one's own death. Exemplifying the values of the collective may have the effect of conferring protection and immortality.

## REFERENCES

Allen, Brenda, and Boykin, A. Wade. (1991). The influence of contextual factors on Afro-American and Euro-American children's performance: Effects of movement opportunity and music. *International Journal of Psychology, 26(3),* 373–87.

Arroyo, Carmen, and Zigler, Edward. (1995). Racial identity, academic achievement, and the psychological well-being of economically disadvantaged adolescents. *Journal of Personality and Social Psychology, 69,* 903–14.

Asante, Molefi. (1987). *The Africentric idea.* Philadelphia: Temple University Press.

Banton, Michael. (1977). *The idea of race.* Boulder, Colo.: Westview Press.

Barker, Martin (1981). *The new racism: Conservatives and the ideology of the tribe.* Frederick, Md.: Aletheia Books/University Publications of America.
Cole, Michael, Gay, John, Glick Joseph, and Sharp, Donald. (1971). *The cultural context of learning and thinking.* New York: Basic Books.
Cross, William E. (1991). *Shades of black: Diversity in African American identity.* Philadelphia: Temple University Press.
Devine, Patricia G., and Baker, Sara M. (1991). Measurement of racial stereotype subtyping. *Personality and Social Psychology Bulletin, 17,* 44–50.
Dixon, Vernon J. (1976). Worldviews and research methodology. In Lewis M. King, Vernon J. Dixon, and Wade W. Nobles (Eds.), *African philosophy: Assumptions and paradigms for research on black persons* (pp. 51–102). Los Angeles: Fanon Center Publication/Charles R. Drew Postgraduate Medical School.
Du Bois, William E. B. (1903). *The souls of black folk.* Chicago: A. C. McClurg and Co.
DuCharms, Richard. (1966). *Personal causation.* New York: Wiley.
George, Nelson. (1998). *Hip hop America.* New York: Viking Press.
Gibson, James J. (1979). *The ecological approach to visual perception.* Boston: Houghton Mifflin.
Greenberg, Jeff, Simon, Linda, Pyszcynski, Tom, Solomon, Sheldon, and Chatel, Dan. (1992). Terror management and tolerance: Does mortality salience always intensify negative reactions to others who threaten one's worldview? *Journal of Personality and Social Psychology, 63,* 212–20.
Hofstede, Geert. (1984). *Culture's consequences: International differences in work-related values.* Beverly Hills, Calif.: Sage.
Jahn, Janheinz. (1961). *Muntu: An outline of the new African culture.* New York: Grove Press.
Jefferson, Thomas. (1955). *Notes on the state of Virginia.* Edited by W. Peden. Chapel Hill: University of North Carolina Press. (Originally published in 1787)
Jenks, Chris. (1993). *Culture: Key ideas.* New York: Routledge.
Jhally, Sut, and Lewis, Justin. (1992). *Enlightened racism:* The Cosby Show, *audiences, and the myth of the American dream.* Boulder, Colo.: Westview Press.
Jones, James M. (1972). *Prejudice and racism.* Reading, Mass.: Addison-Wesley.
———. (1986). Racism: A cultural analysis of the problem. In John F. Dovidio and Samuel L. Gaertner (Eds.), *Prejudice, discrimination, and racism* (pp. 279–314). Orlando, Fla.: Academic Press.
———. (1997). *Prejudice and racism.* 2nd ed. New York: McGraw-Hill.
———. (1998). Psychological knowledge and the new American dilemma of race. *Journal of Social Issues, 54,* 641–62.
Jordan, Winthrop. (1969) *White over black: American attitudes toward the Negro, 1550–1812.* Baltimore: Penguin Books.
Katz, Daniel, and Braly, Kenneth. (1933). Racial stereotypes of one hundred college students. *Journal of Abnormal Psychology, 28,* 280–90.
Kroeber, Alfred L., and Kluckhohn, Clyde. (1952). *Culture: A critical review of concepts and definitions.* New York: Random House.
LaFromboise, Teresa, Coleman, Hardin, and Gerton, Jennifer. (1993). Psychological impact of biculturalism: Evidence and theory. *Psychological Bulletin, 114,* 395–412.
Langer, Ellen (1983). *The psychology of control.* Beverly Hills, Calif.: Sage Publications.

Langer, Ellen, and Rodin, Judith. (1976). The effects of choice enhanced personal reponsibility for the aged: A field experiment in an institutional setting. *Journal of Personality and Social Psychology, 34,* 191–98.

Lazarus, Richard. (1981). Little hassles can be hazardous to health. *Psychology Today* (July), 58–62.

Levine, Robert, West, Laurie, and Reis, Harry. (1984). Perceptions of time and punctuality in the United States and Brazil. *Journal of Personality and Social Psychology, 38,* 541–50.

Lumsden, Charles J., and Wilson, Edward O. (1981). *Genes, mind, and culture: The coevolutionary process.* Cambridge, Mass.: Harvard University Press.

Majors, Richard, and Billson, Janet M. (1992). *Cool pose: The dilemmas of black manhood in America.* Boulder, Colo. Westview Press.

Markus, Hazel R., and Kityama, Shinobu. (1991). Culture and the self: Implications for cognition, emotion, and motivation. *Psychological Review, 98,* 224–53.

Massey, Douglass S., and Denton, Nancy A. (1993). *American apartheid: Segregation and the making of the underclass.* Cambridge, Mass.: Harvard University Press.

Mbiti, J. S. (1970). *African religions and philosophy.* Garden City, N.Y.: Anchor/Doubleday.

McArthur, Leslie Z., and Baron, Reuben. (1983). Toward an ecological theory of social perception. *Psychological Review, 90,* 215–38.

McDougall, William. (1921). *Is America safe for democracy?* New York: Scribner's.

McGrath Joseph, and Kelly, Janice. (1986). *Time and human interaction: Toward a social psychology of time.* New York: Guilford.

Mead, Margaret, Dobzhansky, Theodosius, Tobach, Ethel, and Light, Richard. (Eds.). (1968). *Science and the concept of race.* New York: Columbia University Press.

Medin, Douglass. (1989). Concepts and conceptual structure. *American Psychologist, 44,* 1469–81.

Mischel, Walter. (1961). Delay of gratification, need for achievement, and acquiescence in another culture. *Journal of Abnormal and Social Psychology, 62,* 543–52.

Myrdal, Gunnar. (1944). *An American dilemma: The Negro problem and modern democracy.* New York: Harper.

Nobles, Wade W. (1991). African philosophy: Foundations of black psychology. In R. Jones (Ed.), *Black psychology* (3rd ed., pp. 47–64). Hampton, Va.: Cobb and Henry.

Ornstein, Robert (1977). *The psychology of consciousness.* New York: Harcourt, Brace and Jovanovich.

Pierce, Chester M. (1970). Offensive mechanisms. In F. Barbour (Ed.), *The black seventies.* Boston: Porter Sargent.

Plomin, Robert (1990). *Nature and nurture: An introduction to human behavioral genetics.* Belmont, Calif.: Brooks/Cole.

Rotter, Julian. (1966). Generalized experiences for internal and external control of reinforcement. *Psychological Monographs, 80* (whole no. 609).

Sawyer, Karen. (1986). King scholars steal Bennett's lines. *Washington Post,* January 15, A8.

Senghor, Leopold. (1956). L'esprit de la civilisation ou les lois de la culture négro-africaine. *Presence Africaine* [Paris, France].

Shweder, Richard, and Sullivan, Maria A. (1992). Cultural psychology: Who needs it? *Annual Review of Psychology, 44,* 497–523.
Smedley, Audrey. (1993). *Race in North America: Origin and evolution of a worldview.* Boulder, Colo.: Westview Press.
Sobel, Mechal. (1987). *The world they made together: Black and white values in eighteenth-century Virginia.* Princeton, N.J.: Princeton University Press.
Sowell, Thomas. (1992). *Race and culture.* New York: Basic Books.
Steele, Claude M. (1992). Minds wasted, minds saved: Crisis and hope in the schooling of black Americans. *Atlantic Monthly, 269,* c41, 68–78.
———. (1997). A threat in the air: How stereotypes shape the intellectual identities of African Americans and women. *American Psychologist, 52,* 613–29.
Steele, Claude M., and Aronson, Joshua. (1995). Stereotype threat and the intellectual test performance of African Americans. *Journal of Personality and Social Psychology, 69,* 797–811.
Trevor-Roper, Hugh. (1963). The rise of Christian Europe. *The Listener,* November 28, 871–75.
Triandis, Harry C. (1997). *Individualism and collectivism.* Boulder, Colo.: Westview Press.
West, Cornel. (1997). *Restoring hope.* Boston: Beacon Press.
Wilson, William Julius. (1987). *The truly disadvantaged: The inner city, the underclass, and public policy.* Chicago: University of Chicago Press.
Witkin, Herman A., Dyk, R. B., Paterson, H. F., Goodenough, D. R., and Karp, S. A. (1962). *Psychological differentiation.* New York: John Wiley.
Zimbardo, Philip G., Marshall, Gary, and Maslach, Christine. (1971). Liberating behavior from the time-bound control: Expanding the present through hypnosis. *Journal of Applied Social Psychology, 1,* 305–23.

# Index

Numbers in **boldface** refer to tables and figures.